ETERNAL
TROUBADOUR
the IMPROBABLE LIFE of
TINY TIM

Justin Martell with
Alanna Wray McDonald

JAW
BONE

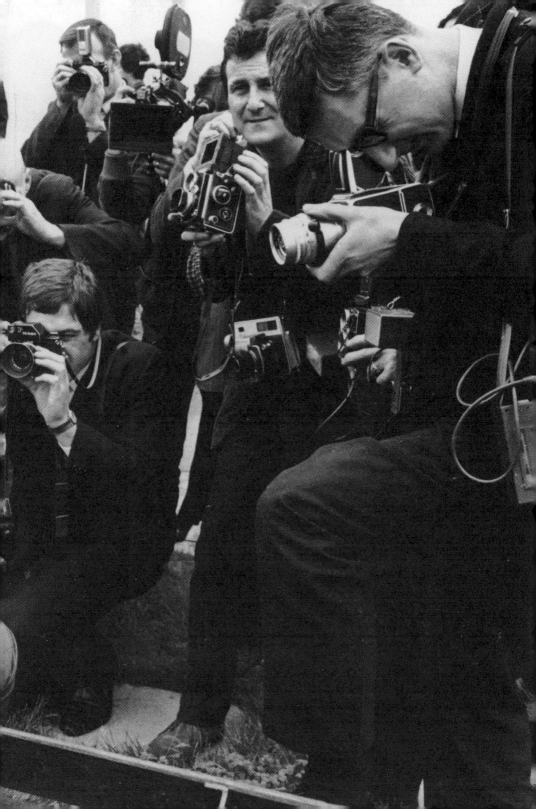

This book is dedicated to my mother, Michelle Audette O'Donnell, and also to two of Tiny's biggest advocates and my friends, the late Martin Sharp and the late Ernie Clark. JUSTIN MARTELL

For my strong mom, who gave me books. ALANNA WRAY McDONALD

ETERNAL TROUBADOUR
The Improbable Life Of Tiny Tim
Justin Martell with
Alanna Wray McDonald

A Jawbone book
First edition 2016
Published in the UK and the USA by
Jawbone Press
3.1D Union Court,
20–22 Union Road,
London SW4 6JP,
England
www.jawbonepress.com

ISBN 978-1-908279-87-3

EDITOR Tom Seabrook
JACKET DESIGN Mark Case

Printed by Everbest Printing Co Ltd, China

1 2 3 4 5 20 19 18 17 16

CONTENTS

'I feel that I've done my best to keep romantic crooning alive. It's not really that hard. I would say it's just a matter of closing your eyes and dreaming. People may that now is not the time for crooning, but I think that if a song is good, it's good for all time. There have been thousands and thousands of hit songs on record and sheet music—songs that deserve to be remembered forever. After all, just as much happened yesterday as is going to happen tomorrow. That's why words like then and now don't mean anything to me. It's true the great crooners have faded away, but that doesn't mean that the beauty and romance and peace they worked so hard to create has faded with them. It can still be with us—it's alive and real—in fact, I heard it just this morning.'

TINY TIM, 'THE GREAT CROONERS,' *PLAYBOY*, DECEMBER 1969

'The Tiny Tim image is not one that people rejoice over. It is an image that [is] the Master of Confusion. What is he? What is he saying? Is he a geek? Is he a queer? They can't relate and they're ashamed to say they even remember me. … If I say I'm putting you on, they'd say, I told you so. If I said I'm not, they'd still say the same thing. The difference between me and Rudy Vallee, Frank Sinatra, Elvis Presley, is with them, people said, Aaahh! With me they said, Uugghh! The emotion of negativity was so, so emotional that they had to be there. I was the one they loved to hate.'

TINY TIM TO THE *PHOENIX NEW TIMES*, NOVEMBER 3 1994

INTRODUCTION
BY HARRY STEIN,
AUTHOR OF *TINY TIM: AN UNAUTHORIZED BIOGRAPHY*

When Tiny Tim burst on the scene in the late 60s, like most everyone else I assumed that if not precisely a fraud, he was surely a put-on. How could he not be? From that otherworldly falsetto to his stringy hair and pancake makeup, from the ukulele in the shopping bag to the absurd formality with which he addressed even children, to his bizarro answers to questions about women and sex, no one was that weird by accident. Not even in the 60s. Indeed, smirking away with friends in my girlfriend's dorm room the night in 1970 he married Miss Vicki on *The Tonight Show*, we had no doubt this was America's new low in anything-for-ratings cynicism.

It was only about four-and-a-half years later—November 12 1974, to be precise, as the vastly entertaining and scrupulously researched book in your hands confirmed—that I began to understand how wrong we'd been. Unable to sleep that late evening, I snapped on the TV, and there was Tiny Tim, back on Johnny Carson's guest couch after a long hiatus. I would soon learn that this is what was known as a 'charity booking,' for in the interim, both Tiny's career and his personal life had taken a steep nosedive. Talking to Carson, he was almost somber, seeming to have no interest in playing to the audience. When Carson expressed his regret over the collapse of his marriage, Tiny waxed philosophical: 'Well, Mr. Carson, we're still married in the eyes of the Lord. My door is always open to her. All I ask is that she get a VD test.'

As the audience erupted in astonished laughter, Carson bounced his pencil on the desk and gave his patented blank stare. Yet, watching, it couldn't be clearer the guy meant it. I walked into my editor's office the next morning and announced: 'I want to write about Tiny Tim.'

All of this was of course well before Justin Martell was born, yet when he embarked on *Eternal Troubadour*, it was with eyes far more open than mine had been. As a longtime student of Tiny and his oeuvre, he already knew what I was only now about to find out: that far from merely a freakish flash-in-the-pan, the performer known as Tiny Tim (*né* Herbert Khaury, and with a dozen or so names in between) was seriously gifted. Indeed, his talent went beyond merely recording the long-forgotten music of another era, for he uncannily reproduced vocal stylings of the original recording artists. In this way, almost singlehandedly, he was responsible for bringing back from oblivion an entire and quite wonderful musical genre.

I got my first glimpse of this the very first day we met. As we talked in an unkempt motel room in Decatur, Illinois, he fell to reminiscing about his early days in the business and his friendship with Bob Dylan. He recalled telling Dylan that in key ways he was reminiscent of the flapper-era crooner Rudy Vallee—adding that to show that he pulled out his uke and sang Dylan his own 'Like A Rolling Stone,' except in Vallee's voice, then followed it by singing Vallee's classic 'My Time Is Your Time' in Dylan's voice; at which point, he reproduced the entire performance there for me. Both renditions—of Vallee's reedy tenor and Dylan's gritty whine—were spot-on, pitch-perfect, incredible.

That evening, in the seedy club in downtown Decatur where Tiny and his little troupe were appearing, I saw the same magic. The crowd started out a bit unruly—they had obviously come to have a few laughs at the expense of the oddball they used to see on TV—but by the end of Tiny's set they were totally hooked. The guy was just a terrific performer.

True enough, he also was weirder than anyone I'd ever met—and ever more so, the better I got to know him. You simply never knew what would come out of the guy's mouth, all of it delivered with the utter sincerity of a choirboy. Moreover, over the years, navigating the gutters of show biz, he'd attracted other characters almost as strange as he was, in a couple of cases even more so.

While as an outsider I found it endlessly fascinating, it also became clear that for those with whom he worked, the guy could be a total nightmare. Tiny was thoroughly self-absorbed, a narcissist intent on doing everything on his own terms and in his own way—from showering every time 'nature calls' to splurging on cosmetics and hockey sticks—and, when challenged, he wouldn't hesitate to invoke the Lord in self-defense. Little wonder that he ran through so many managers and agents or that he was constantly being sued for having broken contracts signed without a moment's forethought.

Eternal Troubadour captures all that, and a great deal more. Martell's research is nothing short of prodigious; he seems to have tracked down almost every interview Tiny gave over the years, and almost every recorded performance. Indeed, what I like about it most—and have no doubt Tiny would also—is the focus it puts on the music. In that regard, this book could not be more aptly titled. Strange as he was, infuriating as he could often be, Tiny Tim left the world a genuine and important legacy. With *Eternal Troubadour*, Justin Martell passes it on to a new generation.

NEIGHBORHOOD CHILDREN

What has become of the neighborhood children?
I used to know.
'NEIGHBORHOOD CHILDREN,' FROM *TINY TIM'S SECOND ALBUM*, 1968

It began in 1877, with a patent filed by Thomas Alva Edison. The phonograph: the first machine capable of reproducing recorded music and simultaneously enabling individuals to possess music in a new way, to collect it, and to enjoy the voices of the stage from the comfort of their homes. As the Gutenberg Bible transformed renaissance Europe's relationship to the written word, so the phonograph brought with it a new and intimate relationship between listeners and music. Concert halls and traveling performance, which were previously responsible for the comparatively sluggish popularization of song across the United States, lost their cultural impact as the phonograph, with the continued assistance of inexpensive sheet music, allowed the public to consume music at an accelerated rate.

New York City, America's financial and artistic capital, led the country in the turn-of-the-century composition of songs and music publishing, the center of which was Tin Pan Alley. Named for its cacophonous collection of songwriters and 'song pluggers' banging away on cheap pianos—like so many tin pans banging in an alley—the phrase Tin Pan Alley came to represent not just a physical location but the music industry of the United States in general. It was home to a diverse assemblage of musicians and some of the greatest twentieth-century popular music composers in America: George and Ira Gershwin, Irving Berlin, Hoagy Carmichael, Cole Porter. The popularization of the phonograph during its acoustic era introduced the sonorous voices of Henry Burr, Billy Murray, Al Jolson, and Irving Kaufman. Finally, the adoption in 1925 of the microphone and electrical amplification allowed for a softer and warmer vocal delivery, and yet another class of celebrity arose: crooners. Rudy Vallee, Bing Crosby, Russ Columbo, and others sang emotional, romantic, nostalgic, and patriotic songs—songs increasingly influenced by a black population shifting north, songs written by a new generation of immigrants, songs which coalesced into a new American identity.

It was to this exciting and volatile environment that twenty-year-old Toiba Staff; her four sisters, Leah, Bella, Mary, and Yetta; and their mother, Shifra, sailed from Brest-Litovsk, Belarus, on the SS Kroonland, arriving at Ellis Island on January 2 1913. With just a few belongings, the family headed north, getting only so far as Washington Heights, Manhattan. Like millions before, Toiba assumed an Americanized name, 'Tillie,' and as her family settled into their new life, America headed into World War I.

Tillie was of Polish descent and spoke only Yiddish, having been raised in an Orthodox Jewish family. She found it difficult to adjust to the English language and American customs, but she managed to find work sewing women's blouses in the sweatshops of New York City's garment district, several blocks away from the musical chaos of Tin Pan Alley, unaware then of its life-changing significance to her. She would remain employed there for the next several decades.

In the late 1920s, Tillie, who was interested in the ideals of Marxism and Communism, met Butros Hanna Khaury at a lecture. Khaury was a Maronite Catholic from Zabbūghā, Lebanon, who at the age of twenty-three had departed from the port of Le Havre, France, on the *SS Chicago* and arrived in New York City on March 14 1913. He also worked in the garment district as a repairman for knitting machines. He asked Tillie on a date, and though she stood a head taller than he, the two became a couple.

Tillie's audacious decision to date a Christian man of Middle Eastern descent made her something of a pariah among her relatives. Furthermore, Tillie and Butros were both nearly thirty years old, and Tillie's sisters had all settled down in a timely manner, leaving Tillie alone and unmarried. Even more distressing to her family was the fact that she and Butros did not marry after dating for an extended period of time. As Marxists, Tillie and Butros saw it as a contradiction of their beliefs to marry. 'They were Commies,' Tillie's niece, Roslyn Rabin, explains. 'They believed in free love.'

Tillie's family was in for another shock when, in the late summer of 1931, she announced her pregnancy. On April 12 1932, she went into labor prematurely and was rushed to East Park Hospital, where doctors performed a Cesarean section.* The procedure—a dangerous one in 1932—almost killed both of them, and the child suffered a temporary loss of oxygen.

Fortunately, they both survived, and baby Herbert was brought home to 609 West 173rd Street in northern Manhattan. However miraculous his birth, Herbert's initial loss of oxygen had notable effects on this physical and mental development. His widow, Miss Sue, speculates that the process left him both mildly autistic and palsied. 'The Cesarean undoubtedly saved his life, and his mother's life, too … but if the doctors had waited just a few more minutes, he might have been profoundly disabled.' When interviewed for the documentary *Street Of Dreams*, Tillie had nothing but fond, albeit vague, memories of her son's infancy. 'He was a wonderful baby. He never cried.'

Even as a toddler, Herbert was in tune with one of his lifelong obsessions: the opposite sex. 'Jascha Heifetz was born with the creative ability to play the violin; other people are born with the other natural gifts,' he later told *Playboy* magazine, in an interview in 1970. 'I honestly contend that I was born with a natural gift for young ladies.'

At the age of four, Herbert experienced what he considered to be his first crush. While sitting on the steps of a church on Wadsworth Avenue, he was approached by two teenage girls who began 'giggling and playing' with him. The encounter left a lasting impression on him.

When Herbert was five years old, Butros moved the family to a two-bedroom apartment on the third floor of a tenement apartment building in Hamilton Heights, at 142nd and Amsterdam Avenue. Here, too, young Herbert grew preoccupied with watching young girls from the apartment window. Each morning, he rose early to receive a wave from a pretty Spanish girl who passed the building on her way to school.

This preoccupation with girls may have been influenced by the liberal nature of his parents, who did not have a bedroom door. His cousin Bernie Stein was fond of saying, 'Tiny's parents were like the first hippies—they did everything their own way.' As an adult, he would emphasize this childhood fact frequently. 'He would describe the whole set up of the apartment in great detail,' Miss Sue recalls. 'Here was the living room. Here was the hallway.

---

* After adopting the Tiny Tim persona, Herbert Khaury often gave vague, evasive answers when asked about his age. Accordingly, some sources have listed him as being born as early as 1923. However, both his birth certificate and passport, as renewed on February 24 1988, confirm that he was born in 1932.

Here was the bedroom and here was the kitchen and here was [my parent's] bedroom. And, he would repeat, *there was no door* on the bedroom. It kind of goes along with that whole hippie thing: nudity, free love, let it all hang out.' Herbert would mention the lack of door on his parent's bedroom 'with an expression of embarrassment, terror and dread … [and] I think it was very traumatic for him.'

Herbert's appreciation of female beauty manifested itself in his childhood fantasies as well. He was fond of fairy tales that featured beautiful princesses. He became enamored with the idea of an Eternal Princess: a young girl who embodied his dream qualities, waiting to be discovered. 'I really, always dreamed of finding the fairy princess,' he reveals on his album *Songs Of An Impotent Troubadour.* 'Of going into the fairy tales of *The Wizard Of Oz* and those things and finding an enchanted land with a princess like Snow White where we never got old.' Inspired by this idea, Herbert convinced a friend to go in search of her in a forest in New Jersey. To their disappointment, she was not there, and Butros had to go find the boys and bring them home.

* * *

Both Tille and Butros were music lovers in thier own ways. Tillie enjoyed operas and attended them whenever she could afford to. Butros, during his bachelor years, filled his apartment with canaries in birdcages. When asked why he kept all the birds, he replied that he 'just loved to hear them sing.' It was not long before their son joined them in their love of music. 'Herbie always sang,' Tillie told *TV Mirror* in 1968. 'While doing my housework, I would sing and my son would listen and memorize the lyrics and melody.'

'Even in a baby carriage, he was singing,' Butros told the same publication. 'One day I said to my wife, He's going to be a great singer when he grows up.'

When Herbert was five years old, his father brought home a vintage wind-up gramophone and an old Columbia 78rpm record featuring Henry Burr's haunting rendition of 'Beautiful Ohio.' In those days, Herbert was not strong enough to wind up the machine, so his mother often helped him. He was entranced by it. He would sit for hours, ear to the horn, eyes closed.

One afternoon, the Khaurys were visited by a gentleman from the Wurlitzer Music School, selling music lessons door to door. Tillie, who had taken notice of her son's musical abilities, offered him lessons on an instrument of his choosing. He chose the violin, and Tillie shelled out $50 for weekly lessons. Herbert's interest in the violin was short-lived, however.

His teacher, a Russian immigrant named Mr. Witek, smacked the hands of his students when they made mistakes. Before long, Herbert informed his mother that he no longer wished to play. But the violin did offer him his first stage performance: a school play, during which he emerged from a jack-in-the-box playing one.

At the age of six, Herbert asked for and received a guitar from his parents. His mother offered to sign him up for lessons, but he decided to teach himself instead. 'He taught himself everything,' Tillie later told *TV Mirror*. 'He started writing music and lyrics for the guitar when he was six. I used to worry because he would lie on his bed all day long and write and sing to his guitar. I would say, Why don't you go out on the street and play? But no, he wanted only to stay with his music. I told him I would take him to … a good vocal coach. He wouldn't hear of it. No. He didn't want to study anything with anyone.'

In 1942, the Khaurys moved to another apartment in Washington Heights at 601 West 163rd Street, where the family would remain for close to forty years. 'The apartment looked like those in the *New Yorker* cartoons,' Miss Sue later wrote, in an article entitled 'Memories Of My Husband.' 'Two old people sitting in an almost bare room illuminated by a single light bulb hanging from a chain, and big cracks in the walls. It was devoid of any sign of comfort or aesthetic appeal.

Members of Tillie's family also lived in the same apartment building and would visit often. Butros generally made himself scarce on these occasions, and had a strained relationship with Tillie's family. Their initial disapproval of his ethnicity, religion, and failure to marry their sister and legitimize his offspring was compounded by his frequent unemployment; Tillie often acted as the main provider for the family, while they also found themselves at the mercy of welfare on occasion.

The majority of Tillie's relatives were financially stable, and they did not hold back from open criticism of Butros. When they visited, Tillie's sisters often berated 'Khaury' in Yiddish while Tillie nodded in agreement.

The contention that Butros was negligent in his duties as a father and husband is not entirely accurate, according to Miss Sue, who believes he was a victim of the Depression Era. The idea that Butros was a slacker or failure, she says, 'was a bit unfair of [Tillie], since Butros was a repairman for knitting machines, which was a skilled trade. Under normal economic conditions he probably could have supported the family. However, [Tillie's] bitterness may have grown as she had to work very hard in the sweat shops while he was looking for a regular job, or was underemployed.'

It was during a regular visit with her sisters that Herbert overheard Tillie telling his aunts about her excruciating experience giving birth to him, and how she was glad she had not had more children. A child can easily misunderstand such talk, and Herbert often wondered if his mother regretted having him. Many times after that he opted to spend time during family gatherings with his grandmother, a widow whose husband had been a Talmudic student back in Belarus. She would read to Herbert from the scriptures in Hebrew. Though his mother was often critical, his grandmother treated him gently and stressed the importance of staying 'close to God.' When the decision was made that she move to a nursing home, Herbert was devastated. He vowed to never send his own parents away.

As the years progressed, the contrast in his parents' personalities became increasingly apparent. It was Butros's passive demeanor—often shown by his unwillingness to respond to criticism—that was passed on to his sheepish son.

'[Herbert's] mother especially disliked his good-natured personality,' says Miss Sue. 'It reminded her of her husband's easygoing, passive nature, which she had come to disdain, and she often said so. She seemed to have come to agree with her family's opinion of her husband as an incompetent, due to his inability to support the family. Her extended family … further undermined her marriage and made negative comments about Tiny as well.'

Miss Sue's understanding of Tillie is not, however, that she was a villain. 'I think his mother was a brilliant woman, too, with a scintillating personality at times,' she explains. 'He said she had an apparently unintentional humor, and that is where he got his ability to make people laugh. She reminded him of Lucille Ball, of all people. Because she was so magnetic and interesting, she may have become bored with Butros eventually, or she may have tired of their bickering.'

Another source of contention for young Herbert was a constant comparison between himself and his high-achieving cousin, Harold 'Hal' Stein. As babies, Herbert had been the slower to walk and talk. In school, Herbert had mediocre grades, did not do well in sports, carried himself clumsily, was unkempt, and preferred to be left to his fantasies. Harold excelled in school and sports, was clean cut, and was very sociable. The family agreed that Harold was destined for great things.

'My cousin could study for literally eight hours a day, but I couldn't even bear it for an hour. My mind was always in some other place. I guess I was more interested in romance than education,' Herbert later told *Playboy*.*

Herbert's 'ragamuffin' appearance was another cause of concern for Tillie. His hair was unruly, his clothes wrinkled, and his shoes often untied. She took him to get braces—an expensive procedure at the time—and encouraged him to have an operation to minimize his nose. Afraid of operations, he refused.

Herbert's first and only physical altercation occurred with Hal, largely fueled by the rivalry unfairly imposed upon them by their parents. Hal punched Herbert in his nose, causing him to collapse and ending the tiff abruptly. Afterward, keen to avoid roughhousing of any sort, Herbert became known as a 'sissy.' He joined the Boy Scouts but found he was not a fan of the outdoors and quit shortly thereafter.

Herbert's atypical personhood was intensified by his gradual adoption of effeminate mannerisms, which would later play a large part of his public persona. The first instances of Herbert's gender-bending personality came from his love of Shirley Temple movies. After watching a few of the child star's films, he began to impersonate some of her mannerisms. In time, his gentle nature seemed to endear him to many of the boys and girls in his own neighborhood. They would tease him in jest, but would not allow other children from outside the neighborhood to pick on him maliciously.

Nevertheless, on occasion he found himself without friends to back him up. One afternoon, while he was playing on his own in the park, several young boys began to berate him and throw clumps of dirt at him. Tillie came to his rescue and began to chastise her son's tormentors, but Herbert, tugging at his mother's arm, told her not to yell at the boys, because it was 'just their nature.'

For Miss Sue, Herbert's 'passive tendencies' with regard to other children 'came in part from his dislike of his parent's loud disagreements. He seemed determined to be courteous to a fault. Even when severely taunted, he never retaliated physically with other children. He may have taken pride in sweetness and excessive politeness as a way of turning his lack of ability to defend himself into a virtue. He had a way of turning all his deficits to his advantage.'

---

* Even when her son was an adult, Tillie still reminded him about how she felt. In footage filmed in 1979 for *Street Of Dreams*, Herbert is seen holding up a picture of him and his Cousin Hal from when they graduated junior high school. After he mentions that Hal ended up working as the promotional director at Nassau Broadcasting, Tillie looks at the picture for a second and says, 'He took a better position than you.'

True to her character, Tillie did not see the virtue in turning the other cheek. 'She continued to urge him to stand up to other people when they argued with him or persecuted him,' Miss Sue explains. 'She wanted him, and virtually ordered him, to defend himself verbally, if not physically.'

Butros, on the other hand, advised his son to look the other way and ignore his detractors. 'Sonny,' he would say, 'pay no attention to what the boys say, because one day they will hear about you.'

* * *

As Herbert grew older, his parents' relationship continued to deteriorate. Frustrated by Butros's passivity and her awkward son, and fueled by her sisters' negativity, Tillie began to go on tirades, berating her husband and son. Part of her frustration stemmed from her own exhausting employment. At the sewing factory—which was owned by her sister and brother-in-law, Mary and Hyman Berliner—Tillie was pierced through the hand twice by sewing needles, had part of a roof collapse on her, and once collapsed herself from fatigue. The small-town nature of their neighborhood and the close proximity of her family also made it difficult for Tillie to escape judgment from her family and neighbors.

Unable to find steady work, Butros moved from job to job and provided little regular support for his family. By Herbert's teenage years, Butros had left the garment district entirely. He briefly owned an antique shop, which Herbert showed no interest in helping him run, before settling on repairing and selling watches on a street corner. In time, Butros became increasingly bitter and remote, and Herbert found that his father was not as supportive of him as he once was.

A significant turning point occurred when, one day, Butros brought Herbert to work with him. The curious young boy wandered over to a nearby newsstand and surveyed the selection of comic books on offer. His father had given him a penny to spend, but he could not find anything to buy with it. So, instead, he decided to perform a social experiment. He walked over to a store entrance, tossed the penny inside, and giggled as he watched the customers react to the sound of it bouncing across the floor. His amusement was short-lived, however, as soon Butros appeared and beat him in front of a small crowd of onlookers.

Physical violence became a frequent occurrence in the Khaury household, and Herbert began taking solace in his locked bedroom. Years later, he recalled, 'I had a fantasy, even back when I was three or four years old, of going to a fairyland where there would be no strife.'

'My father was ready to leave,' he told Lowell Tarling in 1992, 'and leave me with my mother, because he couldn't take it no more. He was a quiet man, she was a hard-working woman, and when she talked she never stopped. And with the accent, it was very irritating. But she was working hard. And I saw her cry, and I said to my father, Please don't leave. And he kept his promise of that day, he never left again.'

Though his parents did not split, their tumultuous relationship left a profound impression on him. Years later, in an article for *Esquire* magazine called 'The Perfect Mother,' he advised readers not to fight in front of their children. 'The home life is what a child will remember,' he wrote. 'I definitely don't believe in arguments. ... Divisions in the home are terrible.'

In the summertime, the Khaury family, along with Tillie's relatives, vacationed at Livingston Manor in the Catskills. Herbert, disinterested in outdoor activities, developed crushes. One evening, he sat on the porch listening to a show hosted by WMCA in New York City called *Jerry Baker Sings*. At its onset, he looked down and noticed Marlene Barnett, a girl his age who had caught his eye earlier that day, sitting on a porch below. He decided to sing along to the show to get her attention, and it worked. After a few songs, the young girl introduced herself, and the two became friends.

Though he had received no formal vocal training, Herbert had been studying several do-it-yourself books on the subject. From one book, *How To Sing For Money*, he took a suggestion that he retained throughout his career: 'When you sing into a microphone, make believe it's the ear of your lover.' Utilizing this technique and others, Herbert made Livingston Manner the site of some of his earliest performances. In the evenings, he would sometimes sing a cappella renditions of '(I Got Spurs That) Jingle, Jangle, Jingle' and 'Oh Playmate, Come Out And Play With Me' for the resort's guests. His audience was largely made up of his younger relatives and their friends. The younger kids, including Hal's younger brother, Bernie Stein, followed Herbert around 'like he was the pied piper.' They sat transfixed as he sang encore after encore of 'Ghost Riders In The Sky' around a campfire.

Herbert loved the attention and loved to entertain. Once he took a BB from his BB gun and pretended to write a tiny message on the bullet. When the kids asked him what he was doing, he responded, 'writing a message to God.' He then transcribed the messages of each child onto the BB, and dramatically shot it into the night sky, surrounded by a young crowd of awed onlookers.

Back in the neighborhood, Herbert became friends with a boy named Artie Wachter, the captain of the neighborhood curb ball, stickball, and football teams.* Wachter, who lived on the opposite end of the block, formed a soft spot for Herbert and always selected him to play on his team.

'Yeah, he was goofy, let's face it,' says Wachter, who still recalls Herbert fondly, some seventy years after their ball games. 'He would show up to play ball and they would just laugh at him, but he didn't let anything bother him. His personality was more or less the same [as it was later on]. A lot of people thought he was acting, but he wasn't. He was such a truthful guy and an honest person and a person that would do anything for you, but he was abused by the kids growing up at that time. They laughed at him and made fun of him. I don't know what it was, but I kind of took to him. I always stuck him on my team because nobody wanted him. I never met a person in my life before or since that was so warm and so truthful and honest—I can cry just thinking about him.'

Herbert also became a member of Wachter's gang, the Flashes. 'We were an athletic gang,' Wachter explains, 'but we had to fight at times because people thought we were a bunch of sissies because we wanted to play ball. Needless to say, Herbie was not a fighter, which was fine—we tried to mainly play ball. We had a clubhouse in the basement of the apartment building where Herbie lived. The super let us have it. We had a couple of chairs and whatnot. We also had a record player—in those days it was 78s … you could just listen to Herbie sing forever.'

Wachter remembers Herbert's indomitable spirit on the street turned athletic field. 'He wasn't very good, but he loved playing the sports. I guess that's why I always chose him, because he just had so much heart, and he wanted to play, and he'd hold his own sometimes. He wasn't afraid. I don't think he ever changed, really. He was one in a million as far as I'm concerned.'

A creative problem-solver, Herbert developed techniques to help make up for his lack of athletic prowess. Because he was a slow runner, he trained himself to bat left-handed, which enabled him to start a step closer to the base.

Another of Herbert's hobbies was collecting comic books, despite his

---

* Curb ball and stickball were modified versions of baseball, created to compensate for the lack of actual sporting equipment. Similarly, for the neighborhood football games, the children clumped newspaper into the shape of a football and secured it using rubber bands.

father's belief that they were 'spoiling' his mind. In 1941, he acquired first editions of *Cisco Kid*, *Daredevil*, and his particular favorite, *Captain America*. 'We were attracted to each other immediately,' he later said of a *Captain America* comic book. 'Bucky,' Captain America's sidekick, inspired Herbert to tell others that his middle initial stood for Buckingham, instead of Butros. Later, he would sometimes have mail delivered to the house under the name 'Count Herberto Buckingham Khaury.'

By 1942, Herbert's *Captain America* collection was up to date and in mint condition. Unlike other children who shared or traded their comics, Herbert preferred to read them alone. However, his collection was compromised by his first 'full-time crush.' Audrey Dash was the superintendent's daughter, and she bore a striking resemblance to the actress Gene Tierney, whom Herbert had admired since seeing first seeing her in the film *Belle Star* in 1940. When she asked to borrow issue 8 of *Captain America*, Herbert could not say no. Later, Audrey's father, looking for something with which to smack Audrey for misbehaving, grabbed the comic book and beat her with it. Issue 8 of *Captain America* was never returned, and the idea of having an incomplete collection was too much for Herbert to bear. Shortly thereafter, he destroyed his collection.

In 1943, Herbert was hospitalized with appendicitis. Though it was a common, albeit serious, condition, the eleven-year-old believed he had put too much strain on his body and was now being struck down for being greedy. As he later told Harry Stein for the 1976 book *Tiny Tim: An Unauthorized Biography*, which chronicled Herbert's life and career up until that time, 'I'd foolishly tried to carry a case of Coke five blocks because a guy on the street offered me a quarter.'

Fearing additional injuries, following his appendicitis Herbert decided that he would no longer exert himself physically. Since he would no longer play curb ball, he began to follow the Brooklyn Dodgers, and would listen avidly to their games on the family's cathedral-shaped GE radio from the confines of his room. He made scrapbooks that covered the day-to-day activities of his new favorite team. A few years later, he sent a theme song he'd written for the team to the Dodgers' President and General Manager Branch Rickey. To his amazement, he received a reply: 'The Dodgers only make music with a ball and bat.'

Looking for a sport to follow during baseball's off-season, Herbert settled on hockey. 'Basketball and football didn't click with me,' he later told the

Albertan Weekend Magazine. 'Then I saw an ad for Madison Square Garden. It was love at first sight. I picked the Toronto Maple Leafs because the name was so close to nature. I'll stick with them all the way.'

Because of the self-imposed limitations on physical activity, Herbert spent more and more time in his room, daydreaming and listening to records and the radio. His favorite radio programs included *Our Gal Sunday*, *The Romance Of Helen Trent*, and *Aunt Jenny's Real Life Stories*. His other two favorites, *Your Hit Parade* and *Manhattan Merry-Go-Round*, featured hit songs, and when Herbert heard a new song he liked he purchased the record. 'I'd developed this tremendous passion for records,' he later told *Playboy*. 'I used to buy four or five new releases a week. I even loved the smell of shellac.'

As part of the ritual, he began to memorize the details of the recordings—the years recorded, label recorded on, performers, even the matrix numbers—and kept a notebook to write down his weekly predictions for the radio's top ten records. 'I used to pride myself on my ability to pick a hit before it actually made it,' he said. When he got one wrong, his parents would hear the muffled sounds of jumping and cursing behind his door.

When not listening to radio programs, Herbert began creating his own. He would sing the songs he had heard and act out the entire program in his mind on what he later described as his own personal radio station. The first of these self-created programs featured a character named Red Richard, who, along with his brother, The Atom, would spy on villains and criminals.

His next creation was entitled The Needle. The main character was an 'ordinary mortal' named O'Neill who had fallen into a deep hole, wherein he had an encounter with 'creatures who live deep inside the earth.' They kindly gave O'Neill a magic amulet, which turned him into a sewing needle of any size when rubbed. As a microscopic needle, O'Neill could spy on enemies undetected and, on a whim, turn himself into a giant needle and impale evildoers. His nemesis was The Thimble.

Years later, he remained most proud of a 'show' he created he called *The Tom Berry Show*. It combined several elements from actual shows with 'The Wish That I Wish Tonight,' from the 1945 Peter Godfrey film *Christmas In Connecticut*, as its theme song. After singing the show's theme, Herbert would speak, as Tom Berry, and sing other popular songs. *The Tom Berry Show* was the longest running of all the programs he created. It wasn't until 1948, when he turned sixteen, that he took it off the airwaves of his internal radio station.

While Herbert was aware of and interested in the popular songs of his childhood, it was songs from the turn of the century and the thirty years that followed that resonated with him most strongly. He began to idolize crooners like Rudy Vallee, Bing Crosby, and Russ Columbo, as well as earlier pioneers of the acoustic recording industry like Billy Murray, Henry Burr, and Irving Kaufman. He connected to the music so intensely that he would later report feeling 'like a vampire sucking blood from the past' as he absorbed the spirits of the singers and the mood of the era. Utilizing the gramophone like 'a space machine to the past' when listening to Rudy Vallee's version of the 'The Stein Song,' he worked himself up into such a fever that he felt like Vallee singing the song through his megaphone in 1929.

The music of the turn of the century appealed to him because he felt it represented a time that was hopeful, lighthearted, and free. 'After 1935,' he later wrote, in an article for *Playboy* magazine entitled 'The Great Crooners,' 'romance was dying in the world as Hitler was tearing up Europe and by the end of World War II it seemed that cynicism and despair had taken hold of the public. But not me—not with the spirit of Rudy Vallee living inside me.'

No doubt some of Herbert's nostalgia for that era was inspired by his parents. 'Some of those times he remembered, and some were so long before his time that he only captured the flavor of them by watching his much older parents, principally his mother, singing along to the radio as she cooked supper or ironed the family's clothes,' says Miss Sue. 'Lots of the music he loved was popular in her youth, and some was from eras that would have been remote even to her parents. He knew of those times only from books, and conjecture.'

Herbert spent much of his free time at the New York Public Library, reading about the early years of the phonograph industry and its popular recording artists. Immersing himself in the music of the past did not seem unusual to him because, the way he saw it, all popular music through the decades was linked. 'There's all branches of music from jazz to classical to reggae,' he later told *Goldmine* magazine. 'But popular music will always be the main root. All the rest are the branches of the tree. Why is that? It's very simple. John will always tell Mary, I'll remember you by that song.'

After school, Herbert would shut himself in his room and enter his private world. 'I never really had people over the house, and my parents were away most of the time, working,' he later said. 'Frankly, I was alone so much of the time that when my dear parents would finally come home, I'd wish that I was alone again.' When his parents were home, he recalled, they 'would not dare' interrupt what he was doing when his door was closed.

'I used to get a thrill just watching the shellac records spinning around on the turntable,' he wrote, in *Playboy*. 'I'd press my nose to the label, and it was like magic to me. I actually felt I was living in the grooves. … Maybe I'm a living ghost of the past, but it's more than just singing to me. I go into a trance and usually end up sitting there in my room with my head lodged inside the horn for hours.'

As he allowed himself to drift mentally further and further from his small bedroom and dingy tenement building, he could see himself in New York City, ten, twenty, and thirty years prior. Listening to old songs, he continued, was 'like being inside a time machine. I start imagining that I can step out into the street and still see horse-drawn trolleys rolling down Broadway, Model A Fords chugging along Central Park West, actors dressed as doughboys in jodhpurs and puttees recruiting men to fight the Kaiser, angry drunks pounding on the doors of the speakeasies, and Charleston contests and Wall Street suicides and mobs of screaming women lining the streets, hoping to catch a glimpse of Rudy Vallee outside the Brooklyn Paramount Theater.'

Many of the old 78s he listened to featured patriotic songs from World War I, like 'Over There,' 'It's A Long Way To Tipperary,' and 'How I Hate To Get Up In The Morning.' His appreciation for these songs, as well as his developing patriotism, was compounded by his exposure to radio broadcasts, films, and posters, promoting the military and heroes of World War II. Seeing the parades of soldiers retuning from Germany and Japan affected him deeply. Inspired by the soldiers fighting overseas, Herbert made his first record, an a cappella version of 'Say A Little Prayer For Our Boys Over There,' for 25 cents via a Voice-O-Graph machine in an arcade.*

He also became enamored, fittingly, with classic motion pictures from the golden age of Hollywood. He obsessed over female stars like Gene Tierney, Grace Kelly, June Haver, Terry Moore, and Gloria Jean, and pinned pictures of them all over his room. After watching Jane Powell in the 1945 film *Song Of The Open Road*, he was so intoxicated by her beauty that he sent a letter to United Artists, requesting a visit from the actress at his home. A few weeks later, he received a signed 8x10 photo of Powell and a note reading, 'Though we appreciate your interest in Miss Powell, our stars don't make a policy of visiting the homes of fans.'

Herbert dreamt of meeting the glitterati of Hollywood. 'You see,

---

* Using the Voice-O-Graph machine, he also recorded a version of 'I Had A Little Talk With The Lord' around this time.

Hollywood was the closest thing to a fairyland I could think of,' he told *Playboy* in 1970. 'Everything seemed so mystical and, most important, there were so many beautiful girls there.'

For Herbert, none compared to Elizabeth Taylor. After starring in her first motion picture, *There's One Born Every Minute*, Taylor became a familiar face in movies, on television, and in magazines. In 1946, at the age of fourteen, she published a clever little book, *Nibbles And Me*, about her adventures with her pet squirrel, Nibbles. Herbert, who was the same age as Taylor, bought the book and read it over and over again. He also began keeping a scrapbook about Taylor that featured virtually every article and photograph published of her. In school, he annoyed his classmates by talking about his obsession with Taylor. He also penned a poem about his celebrity crush:

You came like a star that shines in the blue,
You're like the roses sprinkled with dew,
Eyes that gleam like glitter and gold,
And a heart that's neither harsh nor bold.

In August 1947, Taylor's film *Cynthia* was released.* Herbert saw it six times in the theater. Years later, in 1969, he admitted to television host Jack Linkletter that he cried while watching it, 'because [Taylor] was so pretty.' When asked if he had cried all six times, he clarified that he cried during only two of the viewings, adding that he had been in a state of 'dreaming and ecstasy' for the other four.

Shortly after *Cynthia*'s release, fifteen-year-old Herbert Khaury came face-to-face with the girl he had spent the past few years dreaming about. On September 17 1947, in the late afternoon, Elizabeth Taylor and her mother returned to their room in the St. Regis Hotel in New York City to change clothes between appearances. Herbert had told the concierge that he was the president of Taylor's fan club and was allowed to proceed past the front desk and into the elevator. When he arrived on Taylor's floor, he

---

* The film also starred George Murphy. In the 1960s, Murphy took a break from show business and entered the world of politics as a Republican. After being elected to the US Senate, Murphy appeared with Tiny Tim on an episode of *The Tonight Show*. During the show, Tiny remarked that he enjoyed Murphy's performance in the film. 'Oh my goodness,' said Murphy, stunned that someone remembered the movie, as it was considered obscure compared to some of his other films, like *For Me And My Gal*.

ran headlong into her mother, who was less convinced by the poorly crafted fan-club story. Eyeing him skeptically, she noticed that Herbert was holding a scrapbook. 'Leave your scrapbook with me,' she instructed him. 'I'll have Elizabeth sign it.' As he was handing over the scrapbook, Elizabeth's door opened, and the young starlet poked her head out, locking eyes with Herbert momentarily.

Herbert quickly ran downstairs to the throng of people waiting in the lobby for a glimpse of the rising young star. Asked if he had seen Taylor, Herbert replied, 'Yes ... but I don't think she likes me, because when she saw me her eyes popped out.' Shortly after, Taylor emerged from the elevator, passed through the crowed lobby, and stepped outside for her taxi. But before getting in she turned, looked directly at Herbert, and blew him a kiss.

The incident left a profound impression on him. 'It inspired me,' he later told Alexander Laurence of *CUPS* magazine. 'I wanted to make it to her level.'

Herbert's fondness for Hollywood beauties did not detract from his school crushes. In January of 1949, a girl in Herbert's homeroom named Carmen Quintera caught his eye. Every morning before switching classes, Herbert spent time admiring her from across the classroom. 'She was fifteen at the time—long black hair, a roundish face and luscious heavy lips—and when our eyes met for the first time, I can't begin to describe how I felt,' he told *Playboy*. 'I got so excited that I had to go and hide.'

Just as he memorized the details of his favorite records, he also endeavored to discover specifics about the life of whichever girl sustained his current obsession. His first objective was to learn their addresses. One day, after school, he traveled a few blocks from his apartment to Quintera's building to write down her address. Before he had the chance, she approached him and asked why he'd been staring at her in class, and why he was standing in front of her building. Without a word, Herbert took off running. When he arrived home he picked up the telephone and dialed her number. 'I'm sorry I ran away,' he huffed. 'But you understand.'

Shortly thereafter, Herbert worked up the nerve to ask Quintera out on a date. Before the girl had a chance to answer, however, Herbert rescinded his offer. 'Dating would have brought us too close together,' he later noted. 'It would have spoiled the fantasy. As long as you keep that distance between you and your dreams, then the mystery remains pure.'

Even when pursued by girls he liked, Herbert remained distant and non-committal. Years earlier, in 1944, during one of the family's stays in the

Catskills, he had noticed an eleven-year-old girl named Lila Cordian. After two weeks, he worked up the nerve to speak with her and duly 'fell even more in love.' One day, Lila lured Herbert down to the swimming pool and swam out to the deep end, beckoning him to join her. But Herbert froze up, too afraid to attempt the arduous swim to the deep end.

The next day, Lila was upset and not speaking to him. Herbert resolved to get her attention with theatrics and pretended to fall and injure his leg. To his pleasure, she ran over to check if he was OK. When he revealed that he had feigned his injury, she stormed off under a nearby tree. 'If you really want to make it up to me,' she said, 'come over to this tree.' Once again, Herbert froze. 'She wants to kiss you,' someone whispered to him. He remained rooted to the spot, thus ending their short flirtation.

Retrospectively, he maintained that it was not physical satisfaction that he was seeking. 'Even in those fantasies, I never thought of anything lewd,' he said. 'I never even thought of kissing. Just to have these girls in my dreams, to know that they were mine, that they were saving their best smiles for me, was a pure spiritual bliss. It was a fantastic state of rapture.'

In 1948, the introduction of Dial Soap to the consumer market sparked Herbert's connoisseur-like sampling and knowledge of consumer products, particularly products related to personal hygiene. In fact, he would go on to contend that the safety pin and perforated toilet paper were man's best inventions.

The creators of Dial sent sample bars to many American households. When the little package arrived at the Khaurys' apartment, Herbert tried it out eagerly. He was so impressed that he 'literally told everyone … how great the soap was.' Such was his interest in these products that he even began to read consumer reports at the library.

'The fact that Herbie grew up in such dire poverty undoubtedly contributed to his fixation … with consumer items that most people find unworthy of conversation,' Miss Sue contends. 'He was part of that Depression generation that popularized game shows where the grand prizes were major appliances and life-time supplies of detergent.'

* * *

As the 1940s drew to a close, things were coming to a head at George Washington High School. Instead of focusing on his work, Herbert spent his time under the school stairwells, singing to girls, and was held back twice. The faculty considered him odd, and he annoyed his teachers, one of whom called him the 'smiling idiot.'

During a typing and filing class, which Herbert took because of the overwhelming ratio of women to men, his teacher asked him to adjust a window. After watching Herbert struggle with what seemed to be an easy task, the teacher decided he was playing the fool. She threatened to send him to the principal's office. 'I don't care,' Herbert sassed. 'He's just an old man.'

Tillie met with the principal and was able to convince him not to kick Herbert out of school. However, he continued to annoy the school administration. Shortly thereafter, he was in trouble again for listening to baseball games under the staircase with a portable radio instead of going to physical education class. 'So that was the end of that,' he later told Lowell Tarling, 'and they told me to leave.'

The year was 1950, and Herbert's formal education was officially over.

Herbert's behavior was the subject of many loud fights with his parents back home. 'Look at your cousin [Hal],' Butros told him. 'He's going to college and you haven't graduated high school.'

'What kind of son is this? What kind of boy is this?' Tillie asked, turning to her husband and pointing at him. 'It came from you!'

Tillie had for years been embarrassed by her husband's shortcomings, in light of her sisters' families' successes. Her nephews had college plans and were destined to become lawyers, hold high-paying business jobs, and start families of their own. Herbert, meanwhile, was a dropout with no prospects.

After a grace period, Tillie demanded that Herbert find work and support himself. He visited the Lawrence Employment Agency, which gave him a list of businesses that were hiring. Initially, they all rejected him because of his lack of a diploma. Since no one would hire him, he was forced to bend the truth. When asked if he had finished high school, he began answering in the affirmative. As far as he was concerned, he *was* finished with school. If an employer looked up his high-school transcript and found that he had only attended school for three years, he would reply, 'Well, I never said I graduated.'

Eventually, Herbert was hired in the same neighborhood where his parents had worked: the garment district. His job was to deliver beads. 'I thought it was going to be light work,' he said, 'but the beads turned out to be very heavy.' On his first day, he managed, by the skin of his teeth, to deliver almost every order; however, while trying to deliver his final order, he lost control of his pushcart and it tipped over in the street, spilling thousands of beads. The

Lawrence Employment Agency secured him a few more jobs in the garment district, but after learning that he'd been dismissed from those, too, the agency stopped offering him work.

Next, he lost a job delivering telephone books, because he was too weak to carry them and was afraid of being bitten by dogs in the unfamiliar neighborhoods on his route. After that a job replacing the bobbins on sewing machines in a factory. Then, it was a job with the US Postal Service, from which he was fired for dragging a mail sack on the ground behind him, because, like the telephone books, it was too heavy for him to carry. Finally, he abandoned the sack in the hallway of an apartment building after he heard a dog barking. He assumed that he would be fired, and stopped showing up for work. Later, he joked that it took several weeks to for the post office to send him his notice of termination.

In his spare time, Herbert noticed a few ads featured in a newspaper called *Show Business*. He responded to an ad headlined 'Big Break,' placed by a talent promoter who would send amateur singers to auditions at nightclubs. If the singer did well, the promoter would have him or her sign a contact.

Herbert's first audition, at Mom Grant's Riviera on 43rd Street, was not a success. 'I bombed out,' he told *Playboy*, 'but this was the first time I performed with a microphone, and I knew that I wasn't singing very well with it.'

That same year, Herbert became a regular viewer of entertainer and ukulele player Arthur Godfrey's television show *Arthur Godfrey And His Friends*. The show, which had a prime-time spot on CBS, featured a variety of regular guests sandwiched between Godfrey's own musical performances. 'Arthur Godfrey brought back the ukulele,' Herbert told the Ukulele Hall of Fame in 1995. 'By 1951, the ukulele was flowing.' In his view, Godfrey restored the instrument back to the popular heights of the 1920s and Cliff 'Ukulele' Ike.

Godfrey played and promoted a white plastic Maccaferri Islander ukulele. Taking notice of his son's interest in Godfrey, Butros purchased him an Islander ukulele of his own. 'Mr. Godfrey was adamant, every product he sold—even plastic—had to be good,' Herbert later recalled. 'That Islander was made to perfection … it could compare to a lot of better ones.'

Along with the Islander ukulele, Godfrey used an accessory that attached to the neck of the instrument that allowed him to play chords easily by pressing buttons. Herbert did not like the attachment, however, because it 'pulled the strings,' and he 'wanted to learn the hard way.' He struggled until purchasing the book *You Can Play The Ukulele* by Arthur Godfrey and Don Ball, which help immensely. He also began to audition regularly for Broadway shows such as *South Pacific* and *My Fair Lady*. The ukulele proved to be more convenient during auditions than bringing sheet music for the piano player. 'Usually, when you audition for shows … there's a pianist there who plays four bars of the song, you give them the sheet music, and the auditioner says, Thank you, next! Or, if they say, Step over to the side—that's a hot sentence. I never heard that. I wanted something to accompany me without a piano player so … if I never made it I wouldn't have to hang my head in shame and ask for my sheet music back, I could get right out.'

Herbert's parents, meanwhile, had not forgotten their main priority for their son and harangued him to find and hold a job. After applying six times, he was hired as a messenger for Loew's, Inc. on March 1 1951. 'I had always loved old movies, and it was a real thrill to work in the head office of that theater chain,' he said. Loew's Theaters was a part of MGM Studios and facilitated the distribution of films the studio produced in Hollywood. Though he was only making $35 a week, he was working out of the Loew's State Theater at 1540 Broadway, which housed the Loew's MGM headquarters in an adjoining building. The company gave him a movie pass, which allowed him to see pictures for free, and he often viewed up to four movies in one afternoon. Working at Loew's also put him in direct contact with many of the stars of the era, and he began an extensive autograph collection: Debbie Reynolds, Arlene Dahl, Charles Boyer, June Allyson, and Claudette Colbert. Years later, biographer Harry Stein, who had a chance to examine this autograph scroll, noticed that Perry Como's included the comment, 'Sing up, Herb.'

Emboldened by these celebrity encounters, Herbert asked if he could sing for the guests at the Loew's Christmas party. His boss agreed and gave Herbert a few minutes to perform a number. The party attendees, including Nicholas Schenk, the president of the company, gathered around to watch his a cappella performance. 'I sang a song called "Never,"' he later told *CUPS* magazine. 'I was uptight and bombed out. Right after Christmas, something had to change.'

After singing at a few at parties, he was disappointed to find out that most listeners, especially the women, were not impressed. 'The girls there weren't moved by my singing the way they were by Frank Sinatra's. Lord knows how I feel about women, so you can imagine how disturbing this was to me,' he said. He prayed for a change in his singing style.

***

'I must watch my spending,' Herbert frequently chastised himself in his journal. 'I'm spending my money very foolishly.' But no matter how much he vowed to start saving his money, he regularly spent most of his meager paycheck on records and sheet music. One periodical, *Record Changer*, sold old 78s. Readers would send in bids, and at the end of the month the highest bidder would receive the record listed. Not wanting to miss out on records he wanted, Herbert would bid up to five or six dollars. He also noticed an ad placed by Jacob Schneider, a music store proprietor near the Coliseum in New York (now the Time Warner Building on Columbus Circle). Here, Herbert found what he described as the 'most fantastic music store in the world.'

Herbert discovered a kindred spirit in Schneider, who 'had any record you could possibly want and could tell you when it was recorded, on what label and how many copies he had in stock.' Still, Schneider, sensing Herbert's enthusiasm, frequently gouged him for old and unvalued records, sometimes charging an exorbitant five dollars. Not wanting to be cut off from his vintage music fix, Herbert paid what Schneider asked. 'He was a very nice man,' he later wrote, 'but if you asked him to sell you a record for less, he'd kick you right out of the store.'

Herbert also frequented the Merit Music Shop, and on one occasion he came up with a stack of records worth $175. The store's owner, Mr. Meltzer, said, 'Kid, I know you're making $40 a week, so just give me $20 a week until you pay it off.' Desperate to pay off the bill, Herbert went to the racetrack and bet his other $20. 'I must not be much of a gambler,' he wrote, 'because for the next nine weeks, I was giving Mr. Melzer half my pay.'

In the evenings, Herbert traveled to Greenwich Village to try out new material at whatever dive would put him on the bill. His father sometimes humored him by listening to his songs, while his mother usually shrugged him off, saying, 'Oh, don't bother me now. I have no time.' They both remained adamant that Herbert should remain focused on his job at Loew's, which was quickly losing its intrigue.

CHAPTER TWO
THE HUMAN CANARY

I might have never made it, but I never would have quit.
TINY TIM TO JOHNNY PINEAPPLE, NOVEMBER 11 1994

Despite being battered by discouragement and rejection, Herbert continued auditioning in amateur singing contests around New York City and New Jersey. 'Today I went to two Broadway agents for singing,' he wrote in his diary. 'One said I should give it up. I say never.' Propping himself up with positive aphorisms, he doggedly repeated an Alexander Graham Bell quote: 'When one door closes, another opens.'

Eventually, a door of sorts opened in the form of Bud Friar, a fifty-five-year-old talent representative who worked out of a bathroom sized office, drank only 7 Up, and suffered from a persistent lack of success. Friar's roster was an eclectic hodgepodge of artists like Piccolo Pete, an eighty-year-old piccolo player. They would perform at amateur talent shows at clubs like the Lighthouse Cafe, the Blue Room, and the Old Alliance Club. First place received five dollars, second was three dollars, and third was one dollar. Bud Friar entitled himself to half of every award. Of the ten or twelve acts at each amateur show, ordered from least to most impressive, Herbert generally performed first or second. He sang songs, both old and new, in his natural tenor voice and accompanied himself on either guitar or ukulele. He would usually rank in fifth place, on rare occasions climbing as high as third. 'I didn't go over too well but I'll keep on,' he wrote after one performance.

'The audience understood that we were just amateurs,' Herbert told *Playboy*, 'but I remember one time that someone in the crowd turned on a siren during my number to drown me out. I was persistent and made it a point to finish the song. However, I was beginning to realize that there would have to be a change in what I was doing.'

His diary entries from 1952 reflect a private uncertainty as to whether or not his aspirations would be realized. 'All in all it was just another day—of thinking,' he wrote on January 2. 'Will I be a success in singing? What is my future?' As his twentieth birthday approached, he was growing depressed and bored with his surroundings. Most of his friends had grown up and moved away. 'Brody has a nice looking girl, Lynch has a nice looking Chevrolet, Casey is living in the Bronx with his wife,' he wrote bitterly.

Herbert found himself in the company of a younger gang of boys, aged twelve to nineteen, who called themselves the New Pros: Gigolo, Gerald, Skippy, Bo, and Gabby. The new crew teased him, once inviting him to their clubhouse only to spray him with water. Another time they put flour in his hair. He often referred to the gang as 'bastards,' and ignored them when they spoke to him on the street. He missed his old friends and was nostalgic for ball games with the old gang. 'I went in the street at about 4:30 and found no guys were around,' he wrote. 'It's different now. At one time, this block was living with ball playing. Now it's dead. I shall never forget those days.'

Not only was he bored with his neighborhood, but the initial excitement of his job at Loew's had long since dissipated. 'Today, except for a few periods of joy, I was mad at everyone,' he wrote. 'I was sad, disgusted and blue. I don't know why, but I guess that messenger job at Loew's is the cause of it. It's been ten months already, and I am still a messenger. My varicose veins can't hold out any longer. But I'll stick to Loew's until my break comes.'

His dissatisfaction with his position fueled a growing disdain for his coworkers, especially his boss, Miss Elinor, whom he began to refer to only as 'the bitch.' His coworkers, too, were often the subjects of profane and sometimes racist rants in his diary. One was a 'lousy fag,' another a 'cross-eyed bitch of a woman,' and one of his bosses, Mr. Marcus, a 'fucking kikey Jew bastard.' Distressed by these negative thoughts, he assured himself that he really did not believe in his own vitriol. 'I really have no racial prejudice on anyone,' he wrote. 'I just get mad.'

Maliciousness was not an emotion that Herbert was comfortable with. Seeking a way to eliminate these negative thoughts, he began a relationship that would, in time, govern his every thought and action—a relationship with Jesus Christ. 'I always taught him to obey the Ten Commandments. That is the rule of life,' Butros later told *TV Mirror*. 'I would tell him, "You have to obey. If you do harm to other people you do harm to yourself. It always comes back to you." Not that I had to teach him this, you understand?

I explained the Bible to him as best I could. He would ask me questions, and we would talk.'

'We never pushed our religious faiths on him,' Tillie told *TV Mirror*. 'We let him decide for himself. He would go to [the] synagogue with me one day and the Catholic church the next day with his father.'

Herbert's earliest memory of praying was as a young boy. In his building one afternoon, he was stopped in the hallway by a drunk woman. Pulling him into her apartment, she accused him of theft and threatened to have her brutish boyfriend beat him up if he did not return the item or tell her who had. Terrified, Herbert lied and blamed another boy in the building, Billy Foody. She locked Herbert in her bedroom and set off to verify his story. He snuck out through her fire escape and returned home. Then, full of remorse and guilt for having lied, he got on his knees and prayed for forgiveness.

Up to 1952, aside from assorted instances of fervent prayer in crisis, Herbert had done little to observe seriously either his father's Christianity or his mother's Judaism. That year, a young member of the neighborhood invited him to a prayer meeting hosted by the founder of World of Life Fellowship, Inc., John Von Casper 'Jack' Wyrtzen. Wyrtzen's proselytizing organization was specifically aimed at converting young people to Christianity. Herbert, lonely and with a predisposition for idolatry, rapture, piety, and passion, was an easy sell.

'There I was, living in a tenement on a block crowded with thousands of people, and my heart was filled with cursing and sin,' he later told *Playboy*. 'It was like a miraculous gift when I discovered Christ; I had someone I could talk to personally.'

Herbert's adjustment to living according to Christian values was not instantaneous. On April 28 1952, he wrote, 'I swore to Him that I must suffer and endure all hardships and pains. I must do it. I have faith he'll guide me.' The following day, he added, 'I must admit I cannot keep what I said yesterday. I feel it is bad, but I must be myself.'

It was during this time that Herbert developed his holy trifecta of priorities, which remained consistent throughout his life, and was repeated often: 'Jesus Christ comes first, romance comes second, and show business comes later.' He began peppering his speech with phrases like 'thank God-to-Christ' and integrating religious hand motions into his mannerisms, kissing his hands as though there were holding rosary beads. On the wall above his bed, he twice scribbled in black marker the slogan 'Jesus Christ Is My Lord.' He also began addressing all of his diary entries to the Lord.

While religion may have helped him from execrating his employers and coworkers in his diary, Herbert was still restless at Loew's and becoming increasingly lackadaisical in his work. Despite receiving a raise in May 1952, he began to goof off, just as he had in high school. 'Miss Elinor said she'd fire me if I didn't stop my fooling,' he wrote, three days after getting the raise. 'As if I care.' When he was passed over for a promotion the following month, he became even more incensed. 'How long will I be a sucker for Loew's?'

On August 29 1952, against the wishes of his parents, Herbert quit his job at Loew's. Working for the theater had only intensified the twenty-year-old's desire to perform. Nevertheless, Tillie and Butros, now both in their mid-sixties and approaching retirement, demanded that he keep working, and Herbert, in partial compliance, began failing at a slew of odd jobs. He took an aptitude test for the unemployment board, and it was determined that he was best suited for entry-level work, like elevator operation or dishwashing.

Herbert accepted menial jobs of this nature but often quit after a day or sometimes just a few hours. He spent one day as a messenger at an airport terminal, one day as a mailroom clerk at American Express, one day at United Artists, four hours at Reuben Donnelly, one day at the New York Public Library, another at Macy's, and one hour in a jewelry store. He called them 'famous one day jobs' and made excuses at the unemployment office that they were too difficult for him, due to his varicose veins. He even began to reject jobs offered to him by his unemployment agency, justifying it to himself on the basis that show business was 'lingering inside.'

With a war raging on the Korean peninsula, Herbert, still an ardent patriot, decided he would serve his country and join the military. Asked which branch of the military he wished to join, he thought for a moment and answered, 'The Air Force.'

'Why is that, son?'

As he was a huge fan of the *Buck Rogers* comic, the answer seemed obvious. 'Because I want to go to the moon,' he replied.*

Although he maintained that he had been earnest in expressing his desire to go to the moon, he did admit that it had been a means of ensuring he would

---

* After US astronauts successfully landed on the moon in 1969, Herbert returned to the same recruiting station to confront them. 'They would not admit their mistake,' he said.

not be drafted. 'I knew my act of playing dumb worked, But I was serious [about] my intentions of going to the moon,' he wrote in his diary. He also tried to join the US Marines and the navy. 'I passed the [navy's] census, but they'll call me when they need me.' In 1955, he watched as his cousin Harold was accepted into the army and rose quickly to the rank of corporal. Harold's brother Bernie followed him two years later.

Beyond his failure to hold work, Herbert further aggravated his parents by spending his meager and inconsistent income on his musical pipe dream. On one occasion, he spent $30 of his $35 unemployment check on records, and on another he 'got hell' from his folks after spending his entire tax return on musical instruments. Beginning in 1953, and lasting well into the next decade, his diaries are filled with references to domestic unrest, such as 'big noise between my parents and I' on one occasion and a 'violent clash with my mother' on another. During one argument, his parents punished him by breaking some of his records and his mandolin.

Though his diaries detail a consistently volatile relationship with his parents, Herbert later romanticized their struggles in an interview with *Playboy*. 'I kept buying records and sheet music, looking for a new hit or an old treasure among the dust,' he said. 'My poor parents were struggling, but I always had a melody in my heart.'

Instead of intensifying the job search, Herbert began spending more time in his room, listening to records and singing songs.* As a connoisseur of pop culture, particularly the music of Tin Pan Alley, he noticed that his favorite singers all had unique but definitive vocal styles. He noted that the early singers of the acoustic era, like Burr, Murray, and Kaufman, had powerful, bombastic voices, which suited the recording equipment of the time, while singers post-1925—crooners like Vallee, Crosby, and Columbo—had softer voices better suited to the electric microphone.

'Rudy Vallee seemed to be singing so easily on his records while I was straining my voice,' he noted, 'singing very loud and never really going over with audiences.' It was each singer's individual style, he realized, that had resonated with radio listeners and the record buying public. How then could he stand out in the throngs of aspiring entertainers?

For several months, Herbert prayed to God to help him find a unique vocal quality. One evening, whether by accident or divine inspiration, he

---

* His collection of 78s would grow so vast that some sources later reported that it numbered somewhere near 4,000 records.

remembered a night back in 1949 when he had recreated a male-female duet from *Manhattan Merry-Go-Round* by singing both the high and low parts.

'It came about as I was lying in bed and producing the shows again in my own mind,' he later said. 'And then I said, oh, my goodness—this was in '49—I was singing "The Old Ferris Wheel," which they had done at that time and I said, Gee, it's strange, but I can go up high as well and I started looking into it.'

Herbert decided to experiment again with this high voice. How would it sound if he sang a whole song in that high voice, as opposed to just the female parts in a duet? He tried it with Tony Bennett's 'Because Of You,' and he knew immediately that he was on to something. 'Like the snap of a finger, the idea came to me to try singing in a higher voice,' he told *Playboy*. 'And not only was it easier on my throat but I found that I was thrilling myself as well. I was being moved by my own sound; and I figured that if I could move myself like Mr. Vallee moved me, then something must be in the wind.'

Herbert sang a few songs for his parents in his new style. 'You sound like a sissy,' Butros told him. His mother did not offer much in the way of encouragement either, remarking, 'He lives in dreams.' Herbert was not deterred. In fact, he saw it as a positive sign that his father was not a fan of his new voice, given his father's musical tastes. 'I must sing the "sissy" way,' he wrote in his diary.

'[My father] didn't like Rudy Vallee,' he later recalled, in an interview with Johnny Pineapple. 'He didn't like hardly any singer that women swooned for. He liked the straight, legitimate voices. The minute he rejected it—Good Lord, forgive me—I knew I had something, so I continued.'

Next, Herbert shared his falsetto voice with some of the younger children in the neighborhood.

'What happened to your other voice?' they asked.

'I lost it,' said Herbert.

'Can you get it back?'

Herbert ran into Joe Lynch of the new gang on the block and performed a falsetto rendition of 'High Noon' for Lynch and his girlfriend. 'For the first time, I sang this song in that key,' he recalled. 'Joe Lynch was a macho man for 1953, and his girlfriend was staring at me when I did that song. Her eyes opened wide, and she couldn't get her eyes off the sound, and he was saying, I can't believe it. That was a turning point.'

At parties, Herbert began to sing love songs to girls in his high voice. The girls giggled but did not mock him. He recalled a passage from Rudy Vallee's autobiography: 'If you can walk into a bar and you have something different and the crowd stops and listens, you've got something.'

'So I practiced,' he recalled. 'It came by the whole spirit—not by might, nor by power, but by my spirit, sayeth the Lord! I started experimenting with all the songs of the day.'

Soon after, Herbert landed a small guest spot on ABC's *All-Night Show*, hosted by DJ and future *Eddie Fisher Show* regular Fred Robbins. It was his first television appearance. Elated, he sent a letter to his friends at the Loew's Theater, notifying them of the appearance, which they enthusiastically hung on the office bulletin board. After waiting for almost four hours, and with only fifteen minutes left on the program, Herbert got his debut. He broke into a falsetto version of 'You Belong To Me' and Robbins, perhaps startled, suddenly signed off, cuing the show's credits, which ran as Herbert performed. He was not invited back.

As Herbert modified his act, he also decided it was time for a more serious instrument. Arthur Godfrey had recommended the Islander Ukulele for beginners, but also promoted a $25 ukulele made by Favilla for more experienced players. When he had saved enough money, Herbert purchased a Favilla for himself and was impressed by its sound. 'I swear it was just as good as a Martin,' he later told the Ukulele Hall of Fame. The Favilla ukulele would become his main instrument for the next thirteen years.[*]

Until now, Herbert had played guitar and ukulele right-handed, but he had begun to experience severe headaches on the right side of his head, and came to the conclusion that the headaches were caused by straining the right side of his brain. Just as he had taught himself to bat with his left hand for curb ball, he taught himself to write and play instruments with his left hand.[†] Shortly thereafter, his headaches subsided, which convinced him that this theory was correct.

As Herbert evolved his style, he came to the conclusion that 'Herbert Khaury' did not the fit the romantic image he was attempting to cultivate. Rudy Vallee and Bing Crosby had names that were 'short and easy to remember,' and the early crooners never balked at name changes—in fact, few of Herbert's idols performed under their given names, and many had multiple aliases.

Herbert's first alias was Vernon Castle, but he dropped it after discovering that a popular dancer used the same name. Next came Larry Love, which

* He can be seen playing it in the 1967 pilot episode of *Ironsides*.
† He began to write left-handed diary entries in March 1954.

brought forth even more giggles from the girls.* He also adopted the habit of blowing kisses to his audiences, a mannerism he borrowed in part from Shirley Temple but also in honor of the kiss Elizabeth Taylor had blown to him in 1947. When advised by his father's attorney that he could legally perform under an alias 'anytime, as long as it was not for fraud,' he began to use the name 'Larry Love' onstage.

Headaches cured, new uke, new name, new voice, Herbert returned to the Old Alliance Club and entered the same amateur contest in which he had participated several times before. This time, however, the reception was much different. When it was his turn to perform, he took a deep breath and stepped up to the microphone. Strumming his ukulele softly, he sang 'You Are My Sunshine' in falsetto. To his surprise, he was applauded. He won second place and was awarded three dollars.

The next day, Herbert was invited back to the Old Alliance Club—not as a contestant, but as a performer. 'I sang "Please Don't Talk About Me When I'm Gone" and "A Shanty In Old Shanty Town" as the audience cried, More, more, more, we want Larry,' he wrote. 'I was there until 2:30am. I sang at tables and did imitations.'

'It happened,' he wrote after another victory. 'I tried my style I do at home and praise the blessed Lord Jesus they screamed and I did at least two more in that way, six songs in the whole evening ... I've more joy over this happening than on past winnings.' He continued to split his first place prize—$5—with Bud Friar.†

A few days later, he performed in his 'new style' at the Lighthouse Cafe and came in first place out of ten. More wins were forthcoming, but some were not entirely legitimate. The man tasked with finding the talent at the Lion's Club had seen Herbert perform previously and said, 'Look, kid. When it comes time for the audience to pick the winners, I'm going to hold my hand over your head a little longer to get more applause for you, and then we'll split the money.' 'I didn't think it was fair,' Herbert later told *Playboy*, 'but I liked to win, so I let him do it.'

Though he felt that his 'high voice' was romantic, Herbert learned in

---

* Herbert later confided to an interviewer for the *Toronto Star* that he would have preferred to have made it under the name Larry Love.

† Though Friar was content to take half of his client's meager earnings, Herbert once overheard even the man who was supposed to be guiding him on his way to the top telling someone, 'He's got something, but he'll never make it.'

short order that his new style had a polarizing effect on his audience. If half the crowd liked him, the other half hated him. However, considering his previous style had been by and large ignored, he was happy that audiences were at least paying attention. He wrote of one incident, 'I went to sing in an amateur show at the Dyckman Theatre … I had to be taken out by two cops and a fireman who put me in a car and I was driven safely to the subway. The crowd was mobbed at the front and later came to the side. An egg was thrown at me onstage.' He caused such a furor that the theater owner invited him back the next day to perform as Larry The Weird One.

There were more short-lived stage names: Emmitt Swink, Texarcana Tex, Varlee Roth, Rollie Dell, Alexander Hemmingway, Judas K. Foxglove, Darry Dover, Capo Cashmerey. Most aliases and their accompanying personas lasted only a few weeks and afforded Herbert with the opportunity to depart from his 'romantic' Larry Love. Emmitt Swink, for instance, wore a black cape and used a cane, while Texarcana Tex played a guitar and sang country songs. He believed that changing his character increased his chances of discovering an act that resonated with an audience. If one persona failed, he simply wiped the slate and tried again.

As Herbert's act morphed, so did his personal appearance and presentation. He began speaking in an exaggeratedly high voice and developed affected mannerisms of antiquated gentility, such as calling all women 'Miss' and all men 'Mister.'

'Now to explain my voice,' he wrote in his diary. 'First of all when I talk I speak very high and sometimes in a "sweet friendly way," this would seem very "queer" to lots of people and cause them to wonder about me. Yet despite this, I find it a way to bring cheerfulness and laughter into a heart despite the burden and comments on this way of talking lots of time. … Yet, despite all criticisms of me I know Christ knows why I mean to talk this way. To make others happy in His grace and the tone of voice.'

Years later, *Playboy* interviewer Harold Reimis asked Herbert what his parents had made of all the changes in his voice and evolving affectations. 'There were things other than my voice that disturbed them,' he replied.

Tillie and Butros had little opportunity to adjust to Herbert's rising pitch before he introduced another drastic change. 'I decided I was not good looking, and I didn't want to cut this nose because I was afraid of operations,' he later told Laurence Alexander of *CUPS*. 'So I took a challenge to try to make it with this long nose.'

Herbert began fashioning his look after an old painting he discovered on a piece of sheet music featuring 1920s actor/icon Rudolph Valentino. In the painting, Valentino appears in white makeup with rouged cheeks, his hair slicked back, parted on one side and creeping over his ears. Inspired, Herbert parted his hair on the side and let it grow decidedly longer than Valentino's. He also purchased white face power, which he applied heavily.*

Butros watched his son exit the bathroom wearing makeup for the first time with raised eyebrows. 'Now he's a *sissy*!' he announced.

In the face of overwhelming derision, Herbert comforted himself by clarifying his intentions in his diary. On March 8 1955, he wrote, 'Some may think I'm a sissy with my hairdo and complexion but it's all for the girls.'

'I felt very romantic,' Herbert later told *Playboy*, 'and began to feel like my old spiritual self with women. That's when I started to wear white face powder—as white as a sheet. I don't suppose my parents could understand why I was walking around the streets that way, but I felt it fulfilled something that had been growing in me since the age of five.'

For Herbert, the makeup was also connected to an obsession with cleanliness and purity. 'Well, to me, this was a way to keep in touch with purity,' he continued. 'A beautiful woman from the age of eleven to the age of twenty-five can be the essence of life and youth if she can keep herself morally, spiritually, and cosmetically clean. So, to me, this white powder was not a stage effect to help my career; it was the symbol of purity and youth and of my personal twenty-four-hour-a-day involvement with romance.'

As his hair crept down, it became a source of contention with his parents. When they demanded he go for a haircut, he went to the barber and returned home having had only a few locks cut off. There are abundant references to conflicts over his hair in his diaries. 'My mother and father got mad—woke up and almost hit me,' he wrote on one occasion. 'My folks want me to cut my hair short—I don't. I should.'

In moments of reflection and introspection, Herbert considered his joblessness, appearance, and overtaxed parents. On August 9 1956, he wrote, 'If it were not for the everlasting mercy of Jesus, I would have been long gone. For no one has been as lazy, loving idleness, without a job at twenty-four, a funny hairdo—criticisms of people, two old folks still working because of me.'

---

* He also experimented with tan makeup but found that it made him 'feel too heavy' in his soul.

* * *

Beginning in his teenage years, Herbert kept an increasingly stringent shower schedule. Its impetus was an accusation by a neighbor kid that he smelled bad. By the time he had transformed himself into Larry Love, Herbert was showering several times a day and washing his face up to eight times daily with Pawns & Landers cream. Another of his favorite products, Lady Esther Natural Estrogenic Hormone Cream, claimed to revive aging skin with the slogan 'Stay Lovely … Stay Loved … with Lady Esther.' These products, marketed to middle-aged women, appealed to Herbert's multi-layered, hard-to-follow desires for purity, youth, women, and show business. 'The common denominator was glamor,' Miss Sue says, 'the magical element that Herbert thought was missing from his own, supposedly defective appearance, and his gritty, impoverished life.'

During a 1996 interview for NPR's *Fresh Air*, host Terry Gross asked, 'Excuse this cheap bit of psycho-analysis: what you're saying is that you felt unattractive, you felt like a freak, and to transcend that you kind of turned yourself into a freak?'

'I was a very ugly person when it came to looks,' Herbert replied. 'They looked at it as a freak, you know, with the white makeup, the world looked at it that way, the world looked at the hair like that—especially in the fifties, the middle fifties—but inside one's heart, I felt that I was [a freak]—especially wearing white makeup, not dark makeup because … I've always looked at the princesses I adored in my dreams to be equal with white light [and] beautiful springtime. I wanted to feel within me, with the songs and everything, that I had a sensuality with the women I liked.'*

Although he occasionally vacillated in his reasoning for his eccentric look, Herbert was always quick to credit himself with originality. He had long hair before The Beatles popularized the 'mop-top' and wore makeup twenty years before artists like Alice Cooper and KISS and thirty years before Boy George. 'Whatever [Al] Jolson did to black face, it happened here with white face and long hair,' he told Terry Gross.

Though female reactions were almost exclusively negative, he enjoyed the fact that women were now paying attention. 'Naturally, some of them laughed at me and called me an idiot or cursed me,' he continued. 'One girl called me a "witch" right there in the street.'

---

* Herbert carried his makeup, lotions, creams, and other cosmetics around with him everywhere in a large shopping bag with his ukulele sticking out of the top.

Neighbors and audience members were equally cruel. Some just called him 'nose' or 'beak.' Some would laugh or take photographs. One man who lived near Herbert would not speak to him if anyone was around, but if the two ran into one another alone, the man would harass him. 'If I had a son like that, I'd shoot him!' he said. Another man stopped him on the street and said, 'You make me want to throw up my breakfast!' And he was occasionally threatened with violence. 'If you don't get out of here right now, I am going to break your neck with my bare hands!' came one greeting from a Brooklyn bartender.

Most of the reactions Herbert received were borne of genuine confusion. Once, while purchasing subway tokens, the man in the booth looked at him and asked, 'What is this? Charles Dickens?' Around the neighborhood, people were heard asking each other, in Yiddish accents, 'Vat is 'appening to 'erbie?'

Sometimes the confrontations were harmless. 'The fellas kidded me about my sissyish appearance but the girls looked at me,' he wrote one day. A few days later, however, it was different. 'Today I met a group of fellows … they were under the impression that I am effeminate because of my singing and voice … I received a blow on the mouth from one of the fellows, who had been drinking, but the Lord's strength was so much on me that I hardly felt it.'

'Keep walking and keep smiling,' he told himself. Although some of the reactions were truly threatening, Herbert largely found the constant influx of negative comments amusing. 'It used to give me some kind of pleasure when people got angry,' he told *Playboy*. 'It was thrilling to me to expose the underpinnings of their hearts.'

In time, he became immune to nearly every insult hurled his way. Only God's opinion mattered. 'They don't know me,' he later said. 'God knows me, and that's a comfort.'

'He had a deep need to be the center of attention, to get a rise out of people,' Miss Sue explains. 'Luckily he was born with the perfect face, voice, and personality to accomplish this. Just to be noticed was an affirmation of sorts, to his way of thinking. This reinforced his sense of being someone—that his existence mattered. He would make [people] sit up and take notice, and once he had achieved that, he used his militantly positive attitude, charm, and humor to "woo" them into liking him, which obviously a great many people did, perhaps ambivalently, and in spite of their initial reactions. When he talked about his mother's reaction to his long hair, makeup, and exaggerated falsetto voice, there was an unmistakable twinkle of amusement and what appeared to be defiance thinly disguised as innocent wonderment.'

Herbert's parents began to search for an answer to their only child's bizarre transformation. They combed their families' histories for a precedent for his behavior but found nothing. 'Darlings, don't even try,' he told them.

Perhaps to his delight, Herbert's appearance now made him ineligible for any sort of 'regular' job. During this period, he worked briefly as a delivery boy for a clothing store on Madison Avenue. Every day, at noon, he would freshen up his makeup and apply lotion to his hands in a bathroom stall. It happened that his manager, Mr. Armstrong, once caught Herbert exiting the stall.

'Something smells sweet,' Armstrong announced as he sniffed the air. Herbert was fired later that afternoon under the auspices of two employees returning from Korea and wanting their jobs back.

By this time, Herbert was in his early twenties and still living with his parents, who had grown particularly displeased with his habit of returning from nightclubs at sunrise. 'Sleeping all day, coming home at five in the morning, is this how a nice boy acts?' Tillie asked.

'My parents were deeply shocked by what I was doing,' Herbert later explained. 'And, besides that, they were both sick: my father had diabetes and my mother had high blood pressure. In fact, not a day went by that I didn't expect them to suddenly drop dead.' Herbert's parents believed profoundly in his failure as a performer, and sometimes Tillie would hide his ukulele in an attempt to prevent him from going out.

Herbert continued to turn to the Bible for guidance, as he explained to *Playboy* in 1970. 'I prayed to Jesus Christ, knowing that he could see the loneliness in my heart. I told him that as long as he thought it was right for me to be in this business, I would never stop trying. I figured that even if my parents died before I made the grade, at least their spirits would know.'

The comfort Herbert found in the Bible did nothing to quell the frequent fights he had with his parents. He would tell them he was going to be a great star of the 60s, 70s, 80s, and 90s: 'Don't you dare try to discourage me. Someday you'll see my name in lights on Broadway, because even though you think I'm a bum now, I have Jesus Christ with me, and if he helps me play the game right, then I'm going to make it!'

'He's sick,' Tillie replied.

Often, when Herbert argued with his parents, they would kick him out of the house. On April 27 1956, he wrote, 'Today I really gave my folks a bad time. I was thrown out of the house and stood in the cold rain for $2\frac{1}{2}$ hours.'

Later that year, the confrontations between Herbert and his parents turned violent, as documented in Herbert's diaries. 'I really got it when I came home—my folks were angry. My ma threw things at me, threatened to kill me.' Late one night, when Herbert got home, Butros grabbed his guitar and whacked him in the back, cracking the instrument. Another time, as Herbert was on his way out, Butros grabbed his son's genitals, yelling, 'You have about as much class as this!'

Herbert became so agitated that he grew violent himself. 'I got in a fight with my dad, putting my hand to his eye … dad got a cop,' he wrote. 'Dad said I must obey. My ma was crying and I committed a mortal sin.' Herbert went to confession after the incident. The priest recommended he see a psychiatrist if he could not follow the Catholic way, but the fights lingered oppressively, even more so than his failures in show business. Herbert lamented the incident for days to come. A week later, he told himself, 'I must not hurt my folks, I must be 100 percent perfect in thy way.'

Finally, Tillie and Butros decided to have their son psychologically evaluated. At first, Herbert argued obstinately that Jesus Christ was his doctor. On September 10 1955, he wrote, 'I argued once more about my father's plans for psychiatric lack of faith in thinking I was in a sick condition while pretending to be OK. Only Jesus is my doctor.' He relented a short while later and agreed to allow a psychiatrist to visit him at home. The doctor recommended that Herbert be medicated. He refused.

The argument over Herbert's refusal to be medicated carried on for a year. On July 29 1956, he wrote, '[My father] talked of my taking pills doctor recommended—my weak will, seeing a psychiatrist, getting a job (the hardness of it), etc.' He complied only after his father offered him money to take medication. 'I should not have done it—I lost faith,' Herbert wrote. The next day, however, he began to hide the pills under his tongue; the day after that, he stopped playing along completely, and threw the pills away. 'It is wrong to do, but I can not compromise with the devil.'

Earlier that year, while retrieving the mail, Herbert had met a fourteen-year-old neighbor, Bobby Gonzalez. Despite his years of pining over women, both local and famous, Herbert became visibly aroused. Embarrassed by the incident, he began wearing a long, black raincoat—and, later, an 'athletic supporter'—to hide the fact that he became aroused whenever he saw the boy. Despite this, the two became friends and began spending a great deal of time together.

Herbert wrote about his escapades with Bobby in great detail in his diaries.

On February 9 1956, he noted, 'I saw [Bobby] and once more Satan was defeated as he tried to make my mind obey evil sexual thoughts.' Bobby liked to roughhouse, which had a remarkable effect on his lonesome and libidinous friend. He pulled Herbert's collar, pushed him over in his chair, slapped him with his belt, made Herbert give him piggy back rides, used him as a human punching bag, and displayed his incredible strength by picking Herbert up over his head and spinning him around. 'He's only fourteen. I'm twenty-four. He's that strong,' Herbert remarked in his diary.

Bobby's boyish roughhousing left Herbert in a constant battle with his 'sexual risings' and 'erupting seed.' As they spent more time together, he wrote one self-recriminating diary entry after another. 'Worst day ever in not doing enough grace for Jesus in fighting evil,' he wrote, on December 24 1956. '[Bobby] used me as a punching bag, but all the time I had an erection bulging out of loose pants … not a word of it was mentioned, but he saw. Thru Christ this devil will be defeated.'

Over time, it seems, Bobby too became 'excitable' around Herbert. 'I must not talk of sex to Bobby,' Herbert wrote. 'He gets erupted.'

Herbert appeared to have romantic feelings for Bobby, but he blamed his sexual desires on Satan and declared that the love he felt for the young boy was simply emblematic of how he should feel for all men. He devoted numerous pages of his diaries with long, rambling essays on the subject. In one, dated December 15 1956, he pondered whether the kinds of things he and Bobby were doing together were 'wrong':

At first I was disturbed by having eruptions … [but] it is not impossible for two people of the same sex to have a sense of love (spiritual love not sexual let me state that here and now) toward each other. … Did Bobby also have the same spiritual love as I had for him? I don't know. All I do know is that the cause of my eruptions especially at the touch of his hand, was (1) because of a job in accepting a temptation, and overcoming it for Christ, and (2) because of a spiritual love. …

Does not any person do it? Do we not see piggyback rides in the streets? Exercising in gyms? Of course we do. But in this case, tho' my aim is to do whatever I can in Christ's grace, to make Bobby or others happy, I have to say it's wrong. … What guarantee is it that the Devil is not working in Bobby at the same time? What guarantee is it that, like a magnet, Bobby too has the same feelings and temptations? Therefore in order to defeat the Devil in Christ's grace I must … call a halt to any touching, no matter how little, until eruptions die out, and a touch from Bobby comes down to be like a touch from anyone else. … Remember, it is not wrong to be tempted. It is wrong to heed to temptation, or to cause it to linger by doing right things at wrong times.

Despite the temptations Herbert experienced, he did try to pursue a normal friendship with Bobby. They traded fashion tips and recorded songs together, and Herbert even gave Bobby a ukulele. He listened to the boy's stories of his father's use of corporal punishment on Bobby and his two sisters, and let him take refuge in the apartment anytime his father came home in a rage and began smashing dishes. As a token of good will, he gave his rosary beads and a Bible to Bobby, encouraging him to find Jesus. And though he still did not have a job of his own, he went job searching for Bobby.

Additionally, Herbert was determined that Bobby stay in high school and began to spend long hours at the library, writing Bobby's research papers and doing school projects for him. When Bobby graduated from middle school in 1957, Herbert made him a fake newspaper with a congratulatory headline. He was very encouraging of the younger boy and wrote excitedly of Bobby's acceptance by Manhattan Aviation High School. 'I pray [that Bobby] will have a great future and, at twenty-five, never be like me.'

It was not long before Herbert's parents became aware of the sexual overtones in the two boys' relationship. 'My ma saw [Bobby] sprawled on the bed and got mad,' Herbert wrote in his diary. Tillie began to refer to Bobby as Herbert's 'sweetheart,' and while she was vehemently opposed to his show-business aspirations, she became upset when Herbert canceled a performance to spend more time with the boy.

When his parents began to treat Bobby coldly, Herbert again threatened violence. On Christmas Day 1957, he wrote, 'Today I sinned severely in the morning. I had an argument with my folks over the treatment of Bobby Gonzalez yesterday. I even said I'd kill my mother if she said anything to him in the wrong way. All this dear Lord on Thy birthday.'

One night, Bobby snuck into Herbert's room, and the two laid in bed together, whispering in each other's ears. When it was time for him to leave, they decided that he would exit through the front door but leave it partially open to avoid making a noise. But as Bobby left Herbert's room, the door squeaked, and Butros awoke. Herbert distracted his father as Bobby made his exit, but when Butros heard a whistle from the courtyard below, he ran to the window and spotted the boy hiding in the shadows. Butros put two and two together and flew into a rage, hurling a string of insults at Herbert. 'Sneak! Liar! Good-for-nothing!'

The drama escalated. On February 22 1957, Herbert wrote, 'I hit my father and mother—I didn't mean to. But I got in an 'acting' mood and they threatened to stop Bobby from coming here, and also threw things around. I was trying to scare them I instead got carried away!'

A few days later, on March 4, after his parents agreed that Bobby would be allowed over until 11pm and would be treated cordially, Herbert acquiesced to their demand that he be examined by three psychiatrists. He detailed the experience in his diary.

Today … I saw three psychiatrists at medical center who suggest I go to Bellevue hospital. Tho' they did not say, if I went it would have meant I would have stayed there. But for the good Lord's grace I did not go. I told them all about how I believed in Christ, His sweet blessed mother, His church, my instruction in Catholicism, my beliefs in not kissing or dancing with girls till marriage for Jesus' sake, that is, I believe it to be an occasion to sin, my poetry writing to girls, wrestling in my younger age with sperm falling, my diet, that is my food eating, hair style, cleansings etc. All of which my folks find 'funny.' … Perhaps, I need, or am more mentally sick than all of Bellevue's cases, but if finding perfect peace, peace that the world can never know less they come unconditionally to Christ and His church, if finding perfect peace, in Christ and his Church as I unworthy as I am, have, in sharing his blessedness of having him, the sound of all Love in the many ways he's acknowledged to me all things, then I am crazy if he should ever (God forbid!) renounce them, to live man's way. … True, I do things that the world sees as wrong. (1) My giving last four dollars to Bill whose aunt died (2) my mixing with younger folks (3) my eating habits, etc., my perhaps low or high way of talking, but … rather let men call me crazy, than lose His grace. I must live for Christ, even if it means forsaking my sweet folks.

Herbert later revealed to Miss Sue that his mother wanted him institutionalized, but his father would not allow it. As he later told biographer Harry Stein, 'It didn't really surprise me that my dear mother would let me be committed, because she'd never had any confidence in me. She was a wonderful mother—a saint!—but she just never had any confidence in me.'

As Bobby grew older, he began to smoke, drink, skip school, and get into fights. He would often show up to Herbert's house, drunk and bloody, and brag of cruising around town in stolen cars. He also began associating with a gang, the Jesters. When Bobby was kicked out of Manhattan Aviation and sent down to Chelsea Vocational High School, Herbert wrote, 'I am concerned very seriously with his school work … I pray to stick with Bob through thick and thin.'

Bobby threatened to end his visits unless Herbert cut his hair and stop talking about God. Herbert responded by informing Bobby's father about his truancy. For a time, Bobby avoided Herbert completely, and Herbert became so distraught that he sought advice from a priest. With tears in his eyes, he finally confronted the teenager on the street; Herbert apologized, and they reconciled. Shortly thereafter, Herbert gave Bobby a key to his house. Bobby repaid him by visiting with a group of ruffians, raiding the refrigerator, smashing valuables, and cutting open a down pillow and scattering the feathers around the house while Herbert and his parents were out. Unable to leave Bobby to the mercy of his parents, he covered for him, concocting a story that the damage had been done by another group of boys who had gained access through the unsecured kitchen window. 'Have I let [Bobby] become an idol?' Herbert asked himself, in a moment of lucidity. 'I pray never. I'm doing it for love.'

As their relationship grew increasingly tumultuous, the more overtly homosexual it became. By the end of 1958, Herbert wrote of frequent 'massage sessions' that would often lead to 'rumbles' on his bed. 'I felt Satan delighted in this,' he wrote, on November 19. 'No evil was done, but I knew with my erection there was a sensual delight.' The next day, Herbert informed Bobby that massaging was 'out.' Bobby responded by punching Herbert repeatedly in the arm. 'Massaging was restored' the next day, and 'seed was split when in jest Bob slapped my rear end across his knee.'

One night, Bobby fell asleep in Herbert's room while Herbert was massaging his back. They were soon discovered. 'Dad came in my room put the light on and almost blew a fuse when he saw Bob, who was still asleep. He paced the floor. I tried to assure him. But finally Ma came in the room, saw Bob, and BOOM!! THAT WAS IT! Out he went—and I got hit—yelling, etc.'

Herbert's relationship with Bobby Gonzalez ended with Bobby's marriage in 1960. The two would occasionally get together for 'massages' when Bobby came back to visit the neighborhood, but the era of Bobby was effectively over.

Many years later, in 1994, Herbert revisited the relationship during an interview with Joan d'Arc and Mark Westion for *Newspeak KataZzzine*, though he fibbed about the age difference. 'Now, I don't really like guys, but I'm sensual, or at least I was,' he explained. 'One time I had, not a homosexual affair, but I massaged this guy, he was sixteen and I was about twenty-two. There was a great attraction. I tried to get out of it for a long time. I can't explain it to this day ... there was a strange sensuality there ... you know, in this life you can be as straight as an arrow, but you never know who you are going to meet, man or woman, who is going to knock you off your feet! It can't be explained. So many things just can't be explained.'

'His whole life was a rebuttal to his mother's negative prognostications,' Miss Sue notes, 'and his mannerisms and persona were almost certainly designed purposely to drive her crazy. How can you obey a person who constantly tells you to stand up for yourself, when doing so would be to capitulate to the very person urging you not to do so? Also, how do you rebel against someone who tells you to "be a man"?'

'For years there was a bitter feeling about me in the house,' Herbert later wrote, in an article for *McCall's* entitled 'My Mother, Right Or Wrong.' 'I must have robbed my parents of twenty years.'

In general, Herbert's entire extended family was discouraging of him. In additional to his mother's chronic comments—'What kind of a man is this?'—Herbert was asked by his Godmother, 'What are you? A fairy?' The sole exception was his aunt Leah, whose own son was also a musician. She offered words of encouragement, telling the rest of the family, 'Someday he'll be something, because he has nerve.'

Eventually, Herbert became uncomfortable attending family functions at all. In 1955, he skipped his grandmother's funeral, despite the fact that they had been close when he was a child. The following year, he skipped his cousin's bar mitzvah, writing in his diary that his parents 'were mighty embarrassed and disgraced and deeply hurt I was not there. So was I ... they are ashamed of my hair—and actions.' His cousin Bernie stopped by later and asked why he had not attended. Herbert explained that his parents were ashamed of him. Butros, who overheard the conversation, was furious. 'He hit me,' Herbert wrote.

When Herbert's cousin Harold married in 1958, Harold's in-laws forbade him from inviting his strange cousin to the wedding, and Harold did not protest. Butros and Tillie attended, but Herbert was considered 'too much.' 'I only pray his marriage will be a happy one,' Herbert wrote in his diary. Miss Sue confirms that the incident was the source of a 'life-long hurt.'

* * *

On the show-business front, Herbert had been managing his own career since December 1957, following Bud Friar's retirement due to illness. In 1959, Herbert finally landed his first steady job at Hubert's Museum & Flea Circus. Hubert's was, by and large, a freak show. As the *New York* Times once observed, it 'rang the death knell for respectable entertainment on 42nd Street.' First opened in 1925 by one Hubert Miller, by the late 1930s it had been taken over by Bill Schork and Max Schaefer, who moved the museum into the basement and opened an arcade in the top two floors. If the scene inside had been bizarre when it was on the street level, the move underground made the experience unspeakably surreal.

Schork and Schaefer gave the museum its own entrance, separate from the arcade. Patrons could enter directly from the street, immediately below the marquee. When entering the museum, one passed through a turnstile and walked down an angled flight of stairs into a hallway with linoleum floors. The walls were lined with imposing posters of the show's star attractions: Martha, The Armless Wonder; Cliko, The Dancing Bushman; Dewise Purdin, The Handless Sharpshooter. In 1959, a poster featuring Larry Love, The Human Canary, was added to the line-up.

Herbert rejected the idea that those who performed at Hubert's were 'freaks,' noting that he preferred the term 'oddities of nature.' Six days a week, eight times a day, he performed on one of Hubert's subterranean stages for $50 a week, on the bill between a woman with elephants' feet and a sailor who played 'Anchor's Away' on ten empty bottles. A barker would announce Herbert's performance: 'And now we come to the next one: he looks like a man, but sings like a bird!'

The curtains opened, revealing Herbert, dressed in a ratty tuxedo with scraggly hair, caked white makeup, warbling songs like 'Tears On My Pillow,' accompanying himself on his ukulele.

'Oh, terrible,' one woman said in disgust after witnessing his act. 'Sick.'

Patrons apparently found Herbert so odd-looking that he was almost fired on his first day after the current manager of Hubert's, ex-fire-eater R.C. Lucas, received several complaints. Over time, however, Herbert began to develop a following. One afternoon, he was visited by a friend from the neighborhood who, to Herbert's dismay, told Lucas about Herbert's lower singing voice. Lucas badgered Herbert to demonstrate the lower tone, and Herbert eventually consented. Lucas then enthusiastically pushed to change

Herbert's billing from 'The Human Canary' to the slightly more dignified 'High And Low.' He offered to keep Herbert on the bill for an additional twenty weeks. Such an idea was unacceptable to Herbert, however, as he was committed to using his high voice exclusively.

In 1960, Herbert left Hubert's and changed his name from Larry Love to Darry Dover. 'When I didn't make it by the end of the 50s, I got scared,' he told *Playboy*. 'I started to feel like time was passing me by. So as we inched into the 60s, I changed my name ... and started using both the high and low voice for variety.'

The 1950s had not been kind to Herbert Khaury. His career aspirations were regularly discouraged, either earnestly or cruelly, both by strangers and by those he loved. His personal appearance was considered loathsome. His dogged optimism was dismissed as delusion and self-deception. He fit few labels apart from 'freak.' A rising tide of social and cultural change was beginning to take hold in America, bringing a climate that would celebrate originality and have room for numerous variations on the human theme. For Herbert, however, these developments were still distant.

CHAPTER THREE

AMERICA'S ANSWER TO THE BEATLES

When The Beatles first came out, there was a lot of advertisements that they were coming before we heard them. It was excellently done. When they first came out, I called up Variety *and I said, 'Hey, I had this long hair going back to '54. Someone took my style.' So the woman said, 'Look, did you ever hear of The Three Stooges? Well, they had hair like that, too.' So that was the end of that.*

TINY TIM TO *THE LOST LENNON TAPES*, 1988

As Vietnam began to simmer, America slipped nervously into the 60s. Herbert was acutely aware of the shift—or at least, of his fledgling career's insistence to remain as such on into another decade. 'If I made it on the high voice alone in the 50s,' he later told *Playboy*, 'I could've been as big as Elvis Presley. You see, when an artist makes it with a bang, he can usually stay in that mystical fairyland of success for only two or three years before the public gets used to him. Then he has to start working harder, I figured … I could switch to the lower one when the novelty wore off.'

Herbert likened his potential for success to the Dodgers' redress of their 1951 defeat at the hands of the Yankees by winning the World Series in 1955. He continued making the rounds of nightclubs, publishing companies, auditions, and talent promoters. He received a few bites from music publishers, but was mostly rejected. 'You just threw away a million bucks,' he would retort, as he left one office and entered another across the hall.

Around this time, Herbert was introduced to George King, a nefarious forty-five-year-old agent who wore a beret, sported an Errol Flynn mustache and a cigarette holder, and carried a flask containing Seagram's 7 and orange juice in his back pocket. While King did have some legitimate contacts at clubs in the city, he was also involved in various sordid schemes to con aspiring artists. He placed ads in *Show Business* magazine and charged responders $25 to appear in a 'test film.' He would shoot a short reel featuring the actor and promise to shop it to talent scouts but then disappear.

It did not seem to bother Herbert that King was a scam artist. In fact, he would later call King 'a genius in his own right.' King listened to Herbert's varied repertoire, told him, 'Kid, you've got something,' and agreed to manage him—or, rather, Darry Dover.

In October 1960, they took a trip to Greenwich Village. King scoped out a popular coffeehouse and struck up a conversation with the manager. King, whom Herbert would describe as having 'nerve galore,' gestured for Herbert to come and join the conversation. 'Grab your ukulele and give him a song,' he instructed.

The owner chuckled as Herbert performed a duet with himself. He then followed with 'Tip-Toe Thru' The Tulips With Me,' a Nick Lucas tune featured in the 1929 film *Gold Diggers Of Broadway* that had done well in clubs since Herbert added it to his repertoire in 1958.[*] Amused, the manager agreed to add Herbert to the night's bill for exposure, but without pay. King agreed.[†]

In March 1962, Herbert was offered a regular gig at the recently opened Cafe Bizarre. The narrow club was lined with tables, sawdust covered the floor, and the menu featured items like 'Witches Brew' and 'Schizophrenic Sundays.' It was a hotspot for beatniks, folkies, and political radicals, and would later become home to personalities like Andy Warhol and The Velvet Underground. Herbert performed two nights a week for ten dollars a night. George King took a 50 percent cut. He deserved it, Herbert later said, 'because, you know, he was wandering, too.'

While working at the Cafe Bizarre, he became enamored with a waitress named Ellie Halsey. Five feet seven with long brown hair, Herbert called her 'a gem' and a 'classic's classic.' He soon learned her father was the owner of a major New York City newspaper, and that she, like many other young women, had left the security of her wealthy family's home to rough it in

---

[*] Though the song would later become his de facto theme song, Herbert was unsure where exactly he had first heard it. 'I can't remember the exact source,' he later said, but it would have been either while watching *Gold Diggers Of Broadway* or from the recording issued by Brunswick Records.

[†] George King is one of many questionable manager-types with whom Herbert was associated during this era. According to Miss Sue, another one of these 'gentlemen' posed as a Catholic priest and collected 'donations' door to door.

the village. When Ellie invited him up to her apartment for yogurt, he was floored, but she was fired before he had the chance to take her up on the offer. Rick Allman, owner of the Cafe Bizarre, threatened to fire Herbert too if he went.

Not wanting to disappoint George King, Tiny decided not to challenge Allman. Hoping to see Ellie again, Herbert made a habit of hanging around on her block, but he never ran into her. Though it broke his heart 'not to see her one more time,' as he later put it, he resigned himself to the fact that she was gone and penned a song in her honor.

> *Hello, Ellie Halsey,*
> *Hello Ellie, Dear,*
> *How have you been feeling,*
> *Since I saw you yesteryear?*
> *Was it last December,*
> *Or was it in May?*
> *Still you look as lovely,*
> *As when I saw you yesterday.*

Perhaps he should have taken the risk, as after working at the Cafe Bizarre for only a month, King pulled Herbert from the bill after a disagreement with Allman, who accused King of taking an exorbitant percentage of Herbert's earnings. King moved Herbert to the Cafe Wha? around the corner, but after two weeks he was let go again following a rendition of 'Nature Boy' in which he 'felt the song so strongly' that he began to rip off his clothes, beat the floor with his fists, and bite his hand. 'They thought it looked like an epileptic fit, so they threw me out,' he later told *Playboy*.

During his brief stint at the Cafe Wha?, Herbert had his first encounter with an up-and-coming singer-songwriter who called himself Bob Dylan. As mutually destitute artists, they often shared plates of fries, cheeseburgers, or pork and beans. Herbert made enough of an impression on young Dylan that Dylan would later write about meeting him there in his 2004 autobiography *Chronicles: Volume One*. The two would remain friendly acquaintances.

After a few stints at the Playhouse Cafe and the Third Side, Herbert was approached about recording a full-length album, and he agreed. The album, given the clever title *Darry Dover & The White Cliffs*, was recorded in a studio with a full band. Herbert sang grossly off-key on the tracks, mutilating a collection of twelve standards including 'Be My Love,' 'You Make Me Feel So Young,' and 'Indian Love Call.'*

Herbert offered differing explanations as to why he sabotaged the album. In 1976, as reported by Harry Stein in *Tiny Tim*, he said, 'It may be the worst record ever produced. In those days, I'd sometimes sing off-key on spite.' However, in a 1982 interview with Wes Bailey on a cable access show in Omaha, Nebraska, he offered a longer and more detailed explanation.

'That was done in 1962,' he recalled. 'At that time, I was walking the streets of New York and anyone who wanted to record me, it was a thrill. So at the time they had a sixty, seventy-year-old gentleman called Max The Butcher who sang completely off-key and he thought that he was great. Basically, he spent all his money to invest in his career; he wanted to be a star. So these people came along and took his money and they all had a laugh. Ironically, his record started hitting the charts and he dropped dead, he couldn't take success. So when that happened, this was about '61, they saw me coming down the street and they said, He can be the successor of Max The Butcher. So we went into the studio, and I had to play the role of Max The Butcher and sing off-key.'

As there is no information available on Max The Butcher, Herbert's justification seems circumspect; however, his feverish desire for fame makes an image-ruining stunt seem plausible. Bizarrely, Atlantic Records expressed interest but dropped the album after a falling out between producers during negotiations. The tapes were shelved, and Herbert returned to live performance.†

* * *

As 1962 turned into 1963, George King facilitated yet another name change for Herbert. Perhaps attempting to cash in on the rising popularity of British musical acts, King started billing Herbert as Sir Timothy Tims, later whittling it down to Tiny Tim. 'I decided to put him in a top hat, a cutaway, and spats and have him do a British accent,' King told Harry Stein. 'The trouble was, he couldn't pull off the British accent, so I had to come up with a new name. That's where Tiny Tim came from. The name had nothing to do with

---

* The other nine cuts were 'Oh, How I Miss You Tonight,' 'Let Me Call You Sweetheart,' 'On The Good Ship Lollipop,' 'Secret Love,' 'Animal Crackers,' 'Don't Take Your Love From Me,' 'If I Didn't Care,' 'I Got A Pain In My Sawdust,' and 'Toot Toot Tootsie (Goodbye).'
† According to Miss Sue, Tiny would often sing off-key on purpose in certain situations. 'If there were the slightest hint of mockery,' she says, 'he would go into defensive mode and sing badly.' The reason being, if people were going to laugh, he was determined to find a way to make them laugh harder.

Dickens or any of that·shit. It just happened to be close to Sir Timothy Tims. It made him easier to book.'

According to Tiny, the name change was part of a clever deception engineered by King. The name 'caused an optical illusion,' he told Johnny Pineapple. 'When I went into clubs, they were looking for a midget. That's what happened there.'

Since he had garnered a modest following as Darry Dover, the switch to Tiny Tim was gradual, and during early 1963, Herbert bounced back and forth between the two names. Two 78 demos he recorded during the transition bear the name 'Tiny Tim' on the label, with 'Darry Dover' scribbled underneath and in parentheses.[*]

Herbert was first billed as Tiny Tim at a club called the Surfside. He was not paid a salary but sang for donations. He split the few dollars he collected in the donation basket with George King nightly. Ultimately, the Surfside's owner felt that Tiny's act was not appropriate for his clientele, and advised him to perform in bars frequented by drag queens. Tiny was not offended. 'I was beginning to get hot,' Tiny told *Playboy*, 'and the law of averages was working for me, and [then] I got the best job I ever had at the Fat Black Pussycat.'

Word of Tiny Tim's act began to spread more seriously during his tenure at the Fat Black Pussycat, where the patrons were not limited to the underground scene. 'The man who hired me, Mr. Tom Zeigler, really had faith in me and never fired me. In the six months I worked there I really built up a name.' Other artists who performed there at this time include Bill Cosby, David Frye, and Richie Havens.

A live recording made at the club on February 24 1963 emphasizes the tonal shift in reaction to Tiny's material. 'We have a different kind of music for you right now—a different kind of personality,' says the gentleman introducing Tiny Tim, presumably Tom Zeigler. 'This gentleman is also very, very serious about his talent, and about his music, and his art, and he's very, very quickly picking up a following, and wherever he goes people come, and they listen, and they appreciate. Let's have a great big, hand for Tiny Tim.'

Tiny Tim's set is short, lasting only about seventeen minutes, but it's clear he left an impression on the audience. 'I hope you'll approve of this song, my dear friends,' says Tiny as he steps up to the microphone, 'because if

---

[*] The demo tracks were Tiny's original compositions 'Whispering Voices' and 'My True Love.' The demo version of 'My True Love' was made available on the 2011 vinyl-only release *Tiny Tim: Lost & Found Volume 1 (Rare and Unreleased 1963–1974)*.

you don't, I'm sorry, but this is one of those numbers that touches me at this time of night. It's a very serious number, comes from a show.' Strumming his ukulele, he performs a falsetto rendition of 'I Enjoy Being A Girl,' dropping suddenly, at the end of the song, into his low voice for shock value. He follows it up with a duet with himself on 'We Could Make Believe,' laughing at points for effect, and stomps his foot during Rudy Vallee's 'My Time Is Your Time.' After Bing Crosby's 'Million Dollar Baby' and Russ Columbo's 'You Called It Madness (But I Called It Love),' he has the audience eating out of the palm of his hand. It was clear that he had developed his winning formula.

In March 1963, Tiny Tim auditioned and got a gig at the Page Three, a West Village club he later described as 'the Copacabana of the village for those who never quite made the grade.' For a period of time, Tiny Tim performed at both the Fat Black Pussycat and the Page Three, but he soon moved his act exclusively to The Page Three. From 10pm to 4am, six nights a week, Tiny Tim performed for forty-one dollars total.

The Page Three attracted a more affluent audience, and most of the clientele were members of the gay and lesbian community. 'The only straight people in the club were the owners, the bartenders, the entertainers, and a few of the clientele,' Tiny told *Playboy*. 'In fact, some of the men who worked there would use the word she when they were talking about other men, but we all kind of got used to that.'

Due to his effeminate mannerisms and the club's overt sexual leanings, Tiny was frequently assumed to be homosexual, when in fact he had by now come to identify himself as 'ultra-conservative.'* 'If I had a label I would call myself the Master of Confusion,' he told David Tibet, in a 1995 interview for *Ptolemaic Terrascope* magazine. 'My ideas were so different from them. I was just there like an invisible mannequin. I had to exist in such a molded character, not trying to offend anybody, and at the same time not trying to hide what I thought was truthful to Jesus Christ.'

Tiny's religious beliefs later motivated *Playboy* interviewer Harold Ramis to ask how he felt about the environment at the Page Three and whether he personally 'condoned homosexuality among consenting adults.' Tiny replied, 'The scriptures say that the effeminate shall not enter the kingdom of heaven and neither shall the homosexual. But the scriptures also say that judgment is

---

* Tiny's father also identified as a conservative. Tillie, on the other hand, was quite liberal. Surprisingly, in the 1960 presidential election, she was able to persuade her son to vote for the democrat candidate, John F. Kennedy.

for the Lord alone. … If a man has a personal communion with Christ, then the Lord is the only one who can judge him. It's not up to the preacher to decide who is going to be saved and who isn't. If I didn't believe that, I'd have never made it in show business.'

Though Tiny may have fundamentally disagreed with the lifestyles of the Page Three's patrons, he didn't mind the attention. 'Even though the girls liked each other there, I loved having so many beautiful girls around,' he said.

The MC at the Page Three was an elderly eccentric micro-manager of a man named Kiki Hall. He ran the club's performance schedule meticulously and included himself on the regular line-up. Hall's already bizarre persona was exacerbated by his abnormally large cranium. He suffered from hydrocephalus, a build-up of fluid in the deep cavities of the brain. Jazz pianist Dave Frishberg, another protégé of the Page Three, would later describe him as a 'pain in the ass.'

Tiny did not mind Hall, though. Even though Hall would dock $5 from Tiny's pay if he were a minute late for work, he made Tiny feel 'accepted.' Frishberg recalled, 'In the context of the Page Three staff, entertainers, and clientele, Tiny Tim didn't seem all that bizarre.'

Tiny Tim's set at the Page Three usually consisted of four songs: three in falsetto and one duet with himself. If the audience cheered for an encore, Tiny would look to Kiki Hall. If Hall nodded in approval, he was allowed to perform a fifth song. His falsetto renditions of 'I Enjoy Being A Girl' and 'I Feel Pretty!' were real crowd-pleasers.

* * *

While he was accepted within the confines of the Page Three and other places in Greenwich Village, many people still reacted violently to Tiny Tim's appearance. An avid fan of baseball and hockey, Tiny attended sports games frequently, and in doing so he found sports fans to be a less accepting crowd than his Greenwich Village compatriots. During a home game for the New York Rangers against Tiny's beloved Toronto Maple Leafs, Tiny, wearing an oversized Maple Leafs pin, cheered so enthusiastically that he drew a great deal of attention from Rangers fans. One group of rough teenage boys began throwing beer cans and yelling 'Get the witch!' They chased him out of the rink and down into the subway. He attempted to escape onto a train car, but the boys boarded just after and surrounded him.

'Shame on you,' said an old woman who observed the incident from her seat. 'Leave the poor thing alone.' The boys backed off and left. Tiny sat in the seat next to the old woman. She promptly got up and moved.

One night at the Page Three, Tiny was introduced to entertainer and activist Hugh Romney, who would later become Wavy Gravy. Romney, like Tiny, was a little older than the rest of the Greenwich Village crowd, and the two clicked instantly. Romney was the poetry director at the Gaslight Cafe on MacDougal Street and began bringing Tiny there to perform in the evenings when the microphone was open.

Romney had become a self-described 'traveling monologist' and would often give humorous lectures while opening for acts like John Coltrane, Thelonious Monk, and Ian & Sylvia. In the summer of 1963, Romney had the idea to put together a show, comprised of three acts, called *The Phantom Cabaret*. On the bill were Romney, Tiny Tim, and Moondog, the blind Viking who chanted his poetry at the corner of 45th Street and 6th Avenue while accompanying himself on homemade percussion instruments.

In late July, Tiny returned to the Fat Black Pussycat for the debut of *The Phantom Cabaret*. The show was well attended, and, according to Romney, very well received. The July 1963 issue of the *Village Voice* featured a group photograph of Romney, Moondog, and Tiny Tim. Accompanying the photo was a review by J.R. Goddard entitled 'Ghouls At The Fat Black Pussycat.' It was Tiny's first significant review.

First comes Tiny Tim. His image has little to do with Christmas goose, though the facade of Dickens' little crippled innocent is there. Out he prances, a slight, flowing-haired creature with a hook nose that would have made him a fortune in vaudeville comedy, blowing kisses and repeatedly squeaking 'Thank you—how sweet you are.' On this level he's a real camp as he glides through nostalgic favorites like 'Pardon Me Pretty Baby,' or 'Little Man You've Had A Busy Day' in a fantastic falsetto accompanied by a toy banjo. Then he jolts you by abruptly switching into a deep crooner's voice for 'Avalon' or a militantly manly 'California Here I Come ...'

But 'TT' does more than evoke the 20s and 30s. Patriotic songs become particularly ridiculous when he sings them. And whether intentional or not, his crooner-queenly ballads get double-edged as they satirize those sentimental times too. If you were to hear him only (preferably on one of those old Brunswick radios that looked like liquor cabinets), you'd take him as a highly successful imitator. But watch that marvelous clown's face, the ridiculous banjo, the constant swaying of his body, and the reaction is far different. Hysterically funny, yet funny on so many levels. Tim is a surrealist who can leave your senses jangled and your belief in popular Americana badly cracked …

Despite the positive response, *The Phantom Cabaret*'s engagement at the Fat Black Pussycat was to last only one night. The next morning, the doors were chained as a result of the considerable back taxes owed on the property. 'The phone kept ringing and ringing and ringing because we were a hit,' says Romney, 'but nobody could catch the show. It drove people crazy.'

In an attempt to salvage the show, Romney spoke with Julian Beck and Judith Malina, the curators of the Living Theatre. They volunteered to host *The Phantom Cabaret* at midnight, after their productions. '[The Living Theatre] was the most avant-garde theatre in America, if not the world,' he recalls.

At this time, the Living Theatre was presenting its now-famous production *The Brig*. Because *The Brig* is set in a military prison, The Living Theatre's stage was completely encased in barbed wire and chain link, which added yet another element of the bizarre to *The Phantom Cabaret*. After performances of *The Brig*, most of the audience and cast would stay for the after-show. 'At approximately midnight we would make a huddle and go *BONG … BONG … BONG*,' says Romney. 'Then Tiny would come out with his little shopping bag and his ukulele behind the barbed wired of *The Brig*, and it was spectacular. Then I would go on after Tiny and then Moondog would close the show.'

The Phantom Cabaret's new home at the Living Theatre caught the attention of the *New York Times*. In an article titled 'Old Music Taking On New Color,' dated August 17 1963, journalist Robert Shelton gave a brief description of the show, describing Tiny as 'a scraggly-haired satirist who devastates the sentimental pop songs of yesteryear in a hilarious falsetto.'

As the show gained more notoriety, Moondog quit because of his discomfort with Romney's disparaging statements about the president and the government, and also because he thought Tiny Tim was a 'sissy.' 'Well fuck 'em and feed 'em fruit loops, as Kinky Friedman so aptly put it,' says Romney. 'We got Sandy Bull to take Moondog's place and nobody seemed to mind.'

Tiny's staunchly conservative views stood in stark contrast with those of virtually everyone who now surrounded him. He did not express his views outwardly, however, and it was assumed by Hugh Romney and his associates that Tiny shared their anti-establishment beliefs. The fact that Tiny incorporated the World War I protest song 'I Didn't Raise My Boy To Be A Soldier' into his act must have further endeared him to them.

As for Tiny's eccentricities, Romney seemed to understand and appreciate him as a genuine talent. He was amused when Tiny came off the stage trembling, saying, 'Oh, Mr. Vallee came inside and he wouldn't leave … now I've lost my Crosby power!' According to Romney, 'People either got Tiny and what he really was, or otherwise it would be a geek show—like somebody biting the head off a chicken.'

Through the Living Theater, Tiny also became friendly with prolific experimental filmmaker Jonas Mekas, who directed the film adaption of *The Brig*. Tiny would often attend poetry readings and film screenings hosted by Mekas at the theater during the afternoons. 'Our projector would sometimes break down, and Tiny would stand up in the audience and sing for everyone while we fixed it,' Mekas recalls. 'Everyone enjoyed him.' Mekas also saw the appeal of Tiny Tim on film and captured with his trademark 16mm Bolex some of the earliest known footage of Tiny. In one reel, abstract angles and dramatic lighting accentuate Tiny's bizarre countenance, as he performs in an abandoned loft. Another features Tiny walking in front of the Polish Day Parade, wearing an oversized pair of sunglasses. These shots later appeared in his 1976 compilation of his own rare footage, *Lost, Lost, Lost*. Mekas also recorded several hours of audio of Tiny singing, which has yet to be released.

That same year, Tiny made an appearance in Jack Smith's feature-length psychedelic montage *Normal Love*. Smith, an underground filmmaker, had gained some notoriety earlier in 1963 with his film *Flaming Creatures*, a cinematic assault featuring nudity, transvestism, and homosexual activity. *Normal Love* featured many notable personalities associated with New York City's underground arts scene.*

---

* Tiny supposedly appears toward the conclusion, plucking a plastic ukulele while a huge cake is wheeled out behind him, but his scenes are not included in the versions of the film that circulate among collectors today. Outtakes from Tiny's sequence in *Normal Love* are said to have ended up in two other Jack Smith films: 1964's *The Yellow Sequence* (aka *Normal Love Addendum*) and 1983's *Respectable Creatures*. Ron Rice, who worked on the props for *Normal Love*, filmed a project of his own during breaks in the shooting. His *Chumlum* contains around fourteen seconds of Tiny sitting in a broken down car, with yellow feathers sticking out of his hair, wearing an exorbitant amount of makeup, and sniffing a bouquet of flowers.

* * *

Back at the Page Three, Tiny retained his regular engagement, with a large poster outside billing him as 'America's Answer To The Beatles.' He treated audiences to falsetto versions of 'I Saw Her Standing There' and 'I Want To Hold Your Hand.' One night, a man came into the bar, saw Tiny, and exclaimed, '*This* is the answer to The Beatles!? … Well, how much are they paying you here?'

'Forty-one dollars a week,' Tiny replied.

'Stop!' the club's owner, Mr. Domico, interjected. 'He don't know what he's saying. He's making 100 bucks a week here.'

After the man left, Domico scolded Tiny. 'Don't say that. How can I have my star work here for $41? Tell them you're making $100.'

The atmosphere at the Page Three made up for his low salary. Not only was he able to rub shoulders with Nipsey Russell, Sarah Vaughn, Shelly Winters, and Tennessee Williams, but he came to call the Page Three 'the palace of beauty,' as it provided an ideal vantage point from which to admire a host of ladies. However, since the majority of the women at the Page Three were not interested in men, Tiny Tim was able to admire their beauty without the risk of religious transgressions. 'I loved all of them,' he told Richard Barone in 1976, 'because they live in a wonderful, strange world. They are magnificent beauties, a lot of them, and they have a very fantastic power, and I was so thrilled to be with their company … I would thank the good Lord for their beauty. I was one of the few men that they allowed to their parties.'

Tiny would carry bags for some 'beauties,' and for others he went so far as to clean their houses just to be near to them. He also began hording mementos—things that the girls would touch or use, such as lipstick or plastic stirrers. Though he generally maintained that his intentions were innocent, he later told *Scram* magazine about a girl he met named Miss Roberta. 'She was lovely. She had the body of Raquel Welch and she used to hug and touch me. You can say what you want, but I wished she dominated me. I wanted to be dominated by her in the worst way. She was quiet, gentle but firm. But pure thoughts aside, I wanted her to chain me to her bed and make love to me all night long!'

Looking for a way to demonstrate his admiration for the women at the Page Three, Tiny Tim began his tradition of handing out trophies to 'classics.' The first girl to receive one such award was eighteen-year-old Miss Snooky.

Tiny noticed Miss Snooky, who reminded him of Greta Garbo, when she entered the Page Three on St. Patrick's Day 1963 wearing a long trench coat. 'She had long black hair,' he would recall. 'She even had part of a tooth missing, but she was still beautiful. She was some tough girl, I shook when I looked at her, but she was nice to me.' Snooky would often use a cigarette to fill the gap from her missing tooth.

In December of the same year, Tiny Tim decided that Miss Snooky was 'a classic' and worthy of a trophy. He first delivered to her a letter informing her that she had been selected as the most beautiful girl he had seen all year. In the first week of 1964, he returned with a $25 trophy with an engraving that read:

To Miss Snooky
*The Queen of Them All**

To accompany his trophies, Tiny would pen songs for the girls and record them at a small 42nd street studio called Sanders Recording Studio. The owner, Mr. Sanders, would shave the grooves off old 78s and record new tracks on the smooth surface. For six dollars, Tiny could record a two-sided disc; the first side would feature a spoken dedication to the 'classic,' and the other a song he had composed specially for her. After cutting a record at Sanders, he would go to a photo booth at the train station, take four photos for a quarter, cut out the best one, and tape it over the label.

In the case of Miss Snooky, the spoken side of the disc featured Tiny Tim speaking in a comically high pitch. 'Hello, Miss Snooky. This is Tiny Tim saying, it was so wonderful meeting you at The Page Three on March 17 1963. You really touched my heart, and believe me, I mean every word I say. My heart is trembling even when I think of you; when I saw you there, with your black hair. I just had to write this song for you. To you, beautiful, Miss Snooky.'

The flip side featured a song he wrote for her, 'The Spaceship Song.'[†]

If I could drive a spaceship, dear,
I'd take you to the stars,
And you would be alone with me,
As we'd fly next to Venus and Mars.

Miss Snooky was later arrested on prostitution charges.

---

* Miss Snooky lost the trophy in August 1964; Tiny Tim had a replacement made for her.
† Tiny also wrote another song for her called 'You Are Heaven Here On Earth (To Me).'

* * *

Tiny sent some of the songs he wrote for the 'angels that touched' his heart to different songwriting contests and even responded to 'song-poem' ads taken out by song sharks. These songs included 'When I'm Feeling Sad,' which he wrote for Miss Geraldine; 'Jane,' which he wrote for a Miss Jane; and 'Our Little Secret,' penned for fifteen-year-old Miss Lorna. He also wrote a few songs that were not inspired by any particular girl. They ran the gambit from the rock'n'roll song 'Pretty Baby' to country & western–style numbers like 'Don't Call Me Anymore.'

While he admired the girls he knew at the Page Three, Tiny Tim's fascination with young, female celebrities never waned. He had admired Tuesday Weld since 1959, just as he had admired Elizabeth Taylor. 'I was always crazy about Tuesday Weld,' he told Richard Barone, 'but I just could never get near her.' With dozens of pictures from movie magazines pasted above his bed, he gazed at her before he went to sleep at night and when he woke up in the morning. In 1960, Tiny Tim had written a song for Weld called 'Dear Tuesday,' and in 1961 he paid a few dollars to record it in hopes of giving her the record.

The most important message,
This letter has to say,
I've had to write it over,
In my own special way,
I'd like to say, I love you,
Love you, darling, dear Tuesday.

Finally, in 1964, Tiny caught up with Weld as she was leaving the upscale nightclub the Basin Street East with a group of friends. He approached her and gave her the record he had made a few years prior, along with an 8x10 he had taken of himself in a photo booth for his 1963 Christmas card. It featured Tiny Tim making a grotesque face, looking, in his words, 'like a wild maniac … with wild hair.'

'Who's your friend, Tuesday?' a member of her entourage chuckled.

Tuesday Weld accepted Tiny Tim's gifts with a smile. 'She probably threw the record away,' Tiny later mused.

By early 1964, George King was becoming increasingly annoyed with what he saw as flaky behavior from his client. King had secured Tiny a job at the Ratfink Room, which, according to King, paid $250 a week. However, because of Tiny's loyalty to the Page Three, he was late on several occasions and was let go. King believed that Tiny Tim was becoming 'too independent and was no longer worth the aggravation.' Even though Tiny's contract wasn't due to expire until 1973, the two decided to go their separate ways.

With King out of the picture, the Page Three's Kiki Hall and up-and-coming manager Ronnie Lyons took over Tiny's management. Lyons worked with acts like comedian Lenny Bruce, Jay & The Americans, and Hugh 'Wavy Gravy' Romney; he persuaded the protective Kiki Hall to allow him to explore other opportunities for Tiny. '[Kiki Hall] was nice, but tough,' Lyons recalls. 'He came on tough. He knew I had Tiny's best wishes at heart ... I put [Tiny] together with Lenny Bruce. Lenny never saw Tiny Tim before.'

At the insistence of Ronnie Lyons and Hugh Romney, Lenny Bruce went to the Page Three to see Tiny perform. He was immediately enamored with Tiny, and was thrilled when Hugh Romney gave him a record featuring Tiny's song for Miss Snooky, 'The Spaceship Song.' According to Romney, Bruce played the record to everybody he met. 'He'd say, You have to listen to this!' In fact, Bruce played the record so much that he completely wore out the grooves.

When Bruce visited the Page Three to meet Tiny, the two got along instantly. 'He told me he thought I was far out, and I told him I thought he was far out,' Tiny told *Goblin Magazine* in 1996. Bruce found Tiny Tim's anecdotes about life amusing, especially those about the young women he admired, and would often record Tiny singing songs and talking about different subjects, including sex. The two became close and made quite a pair.

In April 1964, Tiny Tim opened for Bruce in Greenwich Village at the Cafe Au Go Go. The duo performed at the cafe twice, and both times undercover police officers in the audience arrested Bruce on obscenity charges after the show. Despite his ongoing legal battles and the possibility of a prison sentence, Bruce scheduled another show with Tiny at the Fillmore East for November 25. Bruce took out full-page ads in *New York Journal American* and the *Village Voice*:

LENNY BRUCE
SPEAKS FOR PROFIT
TINY TIM SINGS FOR LOVE

However, because of Bruce's tendency to detail his experiences with the judicial system during his shows, the authorities were scrutinizing his every utterance, and Tiny arrived at the venue to find Lenny Bruce arrested and their show canceled.

Aside from a gig he secured for Tiny as the opening act for Jay & The Americans at a one-off show at Parrot Club in Seaside Heights, New Jersey, Ronnie Lyons soon found out that he had his work cut out for him. For one reason or another he could not get anyone with mainstream connections to take a chance on Tiny Tim. 'I took [Tiny] to Phil Spector,' Lyons says. 'Phil Spector turned him down. How did it go? They thought he was nuts! I took him up to [talk show host] Les Crane … when he went to sing for Les Crane he couldn't sing, he was so nervous. His voice just cracked up. He was terrible. So they didn't book him.'

Tiny's idolizing of the many young women at the Page Three made him great sidekick material, and they invited Tiny to accompany them to parties, almost as an eccentric accessory. This may have offered more exposure than Lyons's efforts, as Tiny was continually Trojan-horsed into parties to which he might not otherwise have been invited. At these events, Tiny was introduced to celebrities and entertainment insiders such as pop singer Dion, composer Lionel Bart, songwriter Hamilton Camp, and actor Al Lewis.* At one party, Les Paul backed Tiny on guitar for a version of 'Ain't She Sweet,' and at another, he met The Rolling Stones just as their first hit single, 'Time Is On My Side,' was hitting the US *Billboard* chart. Mick Jagger, intrigued by the strange figure he saw in the room, approached Tiny Tim and asked him to play a song. Tiny Tim picked up his ukulele and went into a falsetto rendition of 'Time Is On My Side,' complete with his tongue-clucking, clock-ticking sound effects. 'He just looked at me with his eyes wide open,' Tiny later told *Scram* magazine. Jagger later attended one of his shows at the Page Three.

Although Tiny did not use obscenities, and generally steered clear of any lewdness, he did exhibit attention-getting behavior outside of his stage show. A fan of Erle Stanley Gardner's *Perry Mason* novels, with a propensity for role-

---

* One night, Tiny was approached by Lewis, who was then popular as one of the stars of *The Munsters*. 'I want to make you a star,' said Lewis. Tiny spent the evening with the actor, following him across town to another bar where Lewis introduced him to his friends. After that night, however, Tiny Tim never heard from him again. Tiny later ran into Lewis in 1968 at a party at Phil Spector's house when 'Tip-Toe Thru' The Tulips' was on the charts. '[Al Lewis] couldn't face me because he knew he was guilty,' Tiny Tim told Jim Foley in 1994. 'He let me go and here I was, a big star.'

playing games, the thirty-two year old would sometimes work himself up into such a mood that he actually 'felt like a detective.' Leroy Becker, a friend of his, suggested the name 'Judas K. Foxglove' for Tiny Tim's detective alias. As a follower of current events, his attention was caught by the murder of two young women on the Upper East Side of Manhattan in November of 1963, known as the Wylie-Hoffert Career Girl Murders. In April and early May of 1964, while the police were celebrating the arrest of a James Whitemore Jr., who was later found to be innocent, Tiny Tim was formulating his own conclusions.

When Tiny entered the New York Police Department, wearing a black trench coat and claiming to have information about the murders, the police were alarmed. 'They sat me down and grilled me, and I told them I had a theory about the murder,' he told *Scram* magazine. 'I told them that I thought their uncle committed the murder. They told me to stick to singing, and they would solve the murder and that was the end of that. … I felt that my theory on the Wylie case would be welcomed by the police.'

Shaken by the treatment he had received at the police station, Tiny quickly dropped his new alias. 'I thought to myself, What have I gotten myself into?' he told the *Ackley World Journal* years later. 'I never used that name again anywhere.'

Knowing that he could not rely exclusively on the exposure he received from the Greenwich Village club circuit, Tiny continued to haunt publishing houses, including the famous Brill Building. 'I started on the tenth floor and worked my way down to the first,' he later told *Goldmine*. 'At each office I'd say, Hel-looooo my friends, in my hand is a number one hit, which I wrote. Is anyone listening?'

In the summer of 1964, Milton Glaser was listening. A graphic artist famous for his 'I Heart NY' design who was then the head of Push Pin Studios,* Glaser caught Tiny's act and immediately informed his friends, freelance journalists David Newman and Robert Benton, of his plans to record Tiny at a studio on 5th Avenue. When Newman and Benton inquired as to what exactly *is* a Tiny Tim, Glaser grabbed an envelope and scribbled a caricature with wild, curly hair, a large, beak-like nose, and a wide, toothy grin. Since Glaser was a graphic artist, Newman and Benton believed that the drawing was a fictional character Glaser had designed for an advertising campaign.

---

* Glaser would go on to co-found *New York Magazine*.

After some explaining, Glaser was able to convince his two incredulous friends that Tiny Tim was indeed a real person, and that they could see him if they came to the recording session he had scheduled.

When Newman and Benton arrived at the studio, the session had already begun. The two later wrote about what they had seen on the other side of the glass in their article 'Why The Truth About Tiny Tim Has Never Been Told On These Pages,' which was published in *New York Magazine* four years later, on June 10 1968.

> In the studio proper, approaching the microphone, was a vision. It was, indeed, Tiny Tim. Six feet tall—and there the resemblance to other men ends ...
>
> The sound that issued from the loudspeaker was uncannily like that heard on old, thick records one played on a windup Victrola. Except for the greater clarity, it was truly the sound of thirty or forty years ago. It was incredibly good. Tim sang both the man and the woman, imbuing each with strong characteristics. It was a virtuoso performance, beyond all doubt. Or something.

Tiny performed 'On The Old Front Porch,' 'Ever Since You Told Me That You Love Me (I'm A Nut),' 'We'll Make A Peach Of A Pair,' Button Up Your Overcoat,' 'If I Had A Talking Picture Of You,' 'Ten Little Fingers And Ten Little Toes,' and 'This Is The Missis,' treating the entire studio session as a live concert, replete with blowing kisses and addressing the audience.* The resulting recording was pressed onto a flexi-disc that was included in issue #45 of Push Pin Studios' newsletter, *Push Pin Graphic*.

In the meantime, Newman and Benton completed their article about the bizarre experience, but their editor, Clay Felker, did not share their excitement. 'This isn't the sort of thing people want to read over their Sunday breakfast when they open the *Herald Tribune*, you guys,' he said. A few months later, Newman and Benton submitted the Tiny Tim article to a British magazine called *Town*, the editors of which accused them of 'putting on England.' Tiny, on the other hand, was tickled just to have been paid to make the recording.

Though the details are vague, Tiny was subsequently introduced by Jay & The Americans member Kenny Vance to fledgling record producer Richard

---

* The versions of 'On The Old Front Porch' and 'Ever Since You Told Me That You Love Me (I'm a Nut)' predate the versions on *God Bless Tiny Tim* by four years.

Perry. Instead of throwing Tiny out, like many of his peers had done, Perry invited Tiny into his office and asked him to perform. True to form, Tiny obliged Perry's request, and, as Perry would later tell it, 'pulled out his ukulele and started to sing, and I lunged for the tape recorder.' The two quickly became friends, and Perry was enamored with Tiny's versatility.

'I liked the many different spirits that lived within him,' Perry told Lowell Tarling, in a 2002 interview. 'I'm a great admirer of variety and nobody incorporated variety in their vocal style abilities better than Tiny ... plus I also loved his theatrical potential. I was very much into making theatrical records, and he was a perfect artist to do that with.' Perry began to brainstorm ideas for potential recording projects he could produce for Tiny. Their meeting would turn out to be very fortuitous.

In July of 1965, the NYPD sent an undercover officer, posing as a customer, into the Page Three. The officer indicated that he would pay for a girl and asked a waitress if she could bring him one. When the waitress fulfilled his request, arrests were made, and the Page Three lost its liquor license. Though the owners attempted to reopen the place as a coffeehouse, things were not the same, and Tiny knew his longest and best-paid engagement was coming to an end. 'Dear Lord, never since Jan 1963 have I been so down and out,' he wrote on July 27. 'Page Three is almost ended. Hall going away. No employment insurance, Ronnie [Lyons] calls tonight's performance awful ... also no prospects—But thanks for you Blessed Jesus, I will come back ... this is only the beginning. I am going to hit the big time and be a star Lord willing.'

Tiny's engagement at the Page Three ended shortly thereafter. 'So there I was,' he later told *Playboy*. 'Out of a job and stuck with a reputation for working in perverted places.'

CHAPTER FOUR
YOU ARE WHAT YOU EAT

The king is sleeping, said Tiny Tim, but your secrets are safe with me.

OPENING LINE FROM BOB DYLAN'S LOST SONG 'DUNCAN AND JIMMY,' C. 1967

When the Page Three's doors closed, Tiny felt lost. He had severed most of his ties with other clubs in favor of the Page Three. Performing with *The Phantom Cabaret* was no longer an option. The Living Theater had been shut down by the IRS, and Hugh Romney had relocated to the West Coast.

As the winter approached, Tiny fell into a state of despair. 'Thanks for a nice day at home,' he wrote in his diary, 'yet the fact remains that the pressure gets hotter. Almost everyone has left—Mr. Hall doesn't call. Ronnie is busy. There is no job—no money, my folks come closer to death every second. … Poverty wants me more each second. Yet tho I am at the lowest point I've ever been so far—I believe I will be a star, Lord willing, I believe this slump will break any second and that my enemies, my folks' enemies will weep—not laugh.'

Tiny changed his name to Rollie Dell and waited for something to happen. He was still living at home, and the pressure from his parents had not slackened.

Tiny later related Tillie's taunts to biographer Harry Stein. 'What are you going to do now?' she would say. 'You're only a village performer, known as someone sick. The only ones who like you are people as odd as you.'

'You'll never get anywhere singing in that sissy voice,' Butros said.

'I'm sorry to say, in all fairness, you'll never be anything,' Tillie added.

'I went to my room,' Tiny later told *Rolling Stone*, 'and I got down on my knees and said, "Oh blessed Lord Jesus, you've seen the situation here with my parents. You've heard the applause and you've seen the celebrities that have come up to me. Am I to cut my hair now, am I to go back to being a messenger boy again?" … I got off my knees and tried show business again. I was not given a sign I should quit.'

On December 6 1965, Tiny was leafing through a copy of *Show Business* magazine when he spotted an ad for an amateur talent contest at the Champagne Room on MacDougal Street in Greenwich Village. He entered as Rollie Dell—and won. The victory gave him the chutzpah to try his luck at a hip new club called Steve Paul's The Scene. Paul had been a successful publicist for the Peppermint Lounge during its heyday and decided to open his own venue in 1964. Initially, the club featured only an in-house piano player, but Paul was ambitious and began to book some of the industry's hottest up-and-comers: Janis Joplin, Jimi Hendrix, The Turtles, and Spanky & Our Gang. The acts attracted mostly college students: those who were too square for the Village but still wanting a taste of counter-culture. Tiny described the venue as 'being for rich kids that wanted to act like Village hippies.'

Tiny traveled to 301 West 46th street, the theater district just west of Times Square. Clutching a shopping bag holding his ukulele, he approached the entrance of the club. The cold winter air chipped away at his motivation, but he remained positive. 'You gotta do it,' he told himself over and over. He walked under a black canopy with psychedelic lettering and descended a flight of stairs into a labyrinthine basement and surveyed the Scene. The walls and floor were painted black, and sparsely placed red lights illuminated the dark room. On the other side of a jungle of tables and chairs, which were also black, was a small, low stage.

'Yeah, what do you want?' asked a bouncer.

'Oh, dear,' Tiny stammered. 'I was wondering if I could do a set?'

'Not here, kid,' said the bouncer as he pointed to the door.

Just as Tiny was about to leave, a man that he would later describe only as a 'wonderful colored chap' remembered him from the Village.

'Hey, that's Tiny Tim!' the man exclaimed. Steve Paul noticed the commotion and instantly recognized Tiny Tim from *The Phantom Cabaret*. He intervened and granted Tiny a set. It was near closing time, but Paul stepped onto the stage and made an announcement. 'Don't go yet, folks,' he said. 'You've got to hear this guy.'

'To me, it was like the last of the ninth with a three-and-two count outs,' Tiny later told *Playboy*, 'and I was never in better voice; the spirit of the Lord was never as strong in me as it was then, and I really knocked the place down. I was flabbergasted.'

Paul requested that he come back the next night, and Tiny began the 117-block walk home, dumb with excitement. He noted in his diary that he 'went over swell at Steve Paul's The Scene—where the "in-crowd" goes.'

Lost in a reverie, Tiny was rudely awoken when he arrived home. His family's apartment building was on fire. Neither the Khaurys nor their apartment was harmed, but Tiny wondered if the fire was a harbinger of misfortune, clouding his future at the Scene.

The following day, feeling unsure as to whether Steve Paul actually wanted him to return, Tiny drafted a letter thanking Paul for allowing him to perform and included his address and telephone number, should Paul wish to contact him. Tiny mailed the letter, and a month of silence followed.

'This is a sign that it's time to give it up,' said Butros.

'It can't be a sign just because you want it to be,' Tiny retorted.

During this time, Tiny endured increasingly alarming harassment by a young man in his neighborhood. 'It's a shame what you're doing to your parents,' he told Tiny. 'If you don't cut your hair by Lincoln's birthday, my friend and I are going to do it for you.'

Not knowing what to do, Tiny did what he did in any time of turmoil—he prayed. The next day, the phone rang and Steve Paul was on the line, inviting him to move his act exclusively to the Scene. Though it was unpaid at the outset, Tiny accepted the gig gladly. The Scene was regularly booking the hottest talents in the music business, as well as attracting a never-ending supply of females to watch them. 'With all the beautiful girls there, it was like heaven to me.'

Before and after his sets, Tiny talked extensively with the young women who came to the club. Unlike the counter culture's prevailing message of rebellion, non-conformity, and insubordination, Tiny encouraged good behavior. He would sing Irving Kaufman's 'Stay Home Little Girl Stay Home' and tell many of the girls caught up in the momentum of the 60s to return to their mothers.

Don't go, you'll be left all alone,
Stay home, little girl, stay home.

Tiny quickly became a favorite at the Scene, and the club's publicist, Wally Cedar, landed him a spot on *The Merv Griffin Show*. Though Tiny had appeared on local programs, this was his national television debut. His first, practically non-existent feature on Fred Robbin's *All-Night Show* had been augmented, in 1965, with a brief feature on *The Joe Franklin Show*.

'[Franklin] called me and told me to smile at the camera and not say a word,' Tiny later told *Scram Magazine*. Griffin, likewise, was a little taken aback by Tiny's image, and a few days before the filming, he attempted to cut Tiny from his show. Furious, Wally Cedar demanded that Griffin put him on, and Griffin finally gave in. During his March 7 appearance, Butros sat in the audience and watched as Tiny accompanied himself on his ukulele and sang 'Livin' In The Sunlight, Lovin' In The Moonlight' and 'People Will Think We're In Love' as a duet with himself. 'Mr. Griffin was very nice,' Tiny told Harry Stein, 'though I could tell he didn't know how to approach me. He kept hesitating and stuttering.'

Tiny's performance received mixed reviews. Comedian Professor Irwin Corey appeared alongside Tiny, and in an attempt to sway comedic leverage, asked, 'Who is this thing here walking around with the ukulele and long hair? … A disgrace!' Happily, Corey's disparaging remarks fell on deaf ears. Arthur Treacher, Griffin's co-host, enjoyed the performance. 'How would you like to see [Tiny Tim] back?' he asked the audience. They erupted in applause. Tiny's impression was that he 'was a success,' and though Griffin might have been unnerved by Tiny, he booked him for six more appearances.

Around this time, Tiny received a call from Hugh Romney. Since relocating to California, Romney had re-formed *The Phantom Cabaret* at a venue called the Little Theater near the Hollywood Ranch Market. He offered to cover airfare, pay ten dollars a night, and provide lodging, if Tiny would come to the West Coast and perform along with him, Del Close, and Severn Darden, in *The Phantom Cabaret Strikes Again!*

When Tiny accepted the invitation, Kiki Hall was chagrined. 'You're going to blow your career, the only chance you have.'

'I'm sorry, but I have an obligation to Hugh Romney,' Tiny replied.

Earlier in 1966, Romney had organized a concert for Tiny at a popular venue, the Coffee Gallery in San Francisco, and the venue's owner had erected a special stage for the event. Romney was to pick him up at the Oakland Train Station in a Rolls-Royce filled with daffodils. Shortly before Tiny's arrival time, however, Romney received a telegram:

I CAN'T COME. MY MOTHER WON'T LET ME.
—TINY TIM

This incident still grinds Romney's gears. 'You can imagine my reaction!' he exclaimed. 'I had a Rolls-Royce filled with daffodils!'

After careful negotiations with Kiki Hall, a compromise was reached that Tiny could go but would have to return to New York in five in weeks for the taping of his next appearance on *The Merv Griffin Show*. He departed for Los Angeles on March 9. It was not the prospect of missing his next television appearance that worried him; it was his absence from the current object of his obsession, Barbara Williams.

Williams, a nineteen-year-old African-American girl from Amityville, Long Island, was different to the other girls of Tiny's infatuations in that she reciprocated his affection. The two met in July 1965, and she had been the recipient of his 1965 trophy. At first, Williams visited Tiny at his parents' apartment and performed for him with her guitar. 'Never have I had such fun so steadily with a girl as I have had with Miss Barbara Williams,' Tiny wrote in his diary. 'Let me say however most humbly thanks as such a beautiful girl sees anything like she sees in me.' Though flattered by her advances, Tiny became evasive about calling her his girlfriend, citing his lifestyle and appearance. Eventually, he gave in, and they began to go steady.

'We also took in mind the many pressures we'd be going through from society, and the world,' he wrote in his diary. 'She being colored, and me with my long hair and powdered face. But knowing the odds would be against us especially between our folks we decided to go through with this with the Lord guiding us.'

Tillie would often bemoan Williams' visits. 'His parents were very disapproving of [Barbara Williams],' Miss Sue explains, 'but I think he was able to relate with a women that was very, very different than his mother.' Williams mailed love letters to Tiny while he was in California, and, undeterred by Tillie, spent hours sitting by the telephone at Tiny's parents' apartment, waiting for him to call.

* * *

In LA, Hugh Romney had undergone a transformation. He was dating Bonnie Beecher, the girl who allegedly inspired Bob Dylan to write 'The Girl From The North Country.' 'When I met him in '62 he was ... straight as an arrow, and he wore a suit and tie,' Tiny later told *Goblin Magazine*. 'When I met Mr. Romney at the airport [in 1966] he [now called himself] Wavy Gravy, he was beating a piece of meat with a stick and was totally different.* I'm not sure what brought

---

* Tiny's timeline is a few years off. It wasn't until 1969 that Romney would assume the Wavy Gravy alias after it was given to him by B.B. King at the Texas Pop Festival.

on the change but it may have been acid … something called out within his soul to change.'

Tiny was given the back bedroom on the ground floor of Romney's house in Sunland, on the outskirts of Los Angeles. '[He] was very unusual as a house guest,' Romney recalls. 'He took four or five baths a day … we used to take him … to the Hollywood Ranch Market.* This was the ultimate late night scene in Los Angeles and Tiny would go there … and get about twelve cans of Popeye's Spinach and that's it. He would take that to his room and consume it.'

One rainy morning, Romney woke to discover the arrival of *Further*, the psychedelic school bus used by Ken Kesey, the Merry Pranksters (Kesey's drug-fueled entourage), and members of the Grateful Dead, to travel the county throwing Acid Test Parties. Downstairs, he found Tiny Tim, in a bathrobe, his face covered with a thick layer of cold cream, watching the entire company cooking eggs in Romney's kitchen.

Neal Cassady, legendary Beat Generation character and *Further*'s driver, had woken Tiny. 'Ohh, Mr. Neal Cassady knocked on my door,' Tiny told Romney, 'and he wanted some grass … but he had just been standing on a whole lawn-full!'

At the Little Theater, for the first time in his career, Tiny was given creative control of his show. He used the opportunity to showcase his serious numbers, and temporarily shelved a few of his kitschy songs. Many influential personalities came to see Tiny's act, including Barry McGuire and Donovan. Donovan had remembered seeing Tiny a year earlier, when Allen Ginsberg had taken him to the Scene. 'I had never seen anything like him,' Donovan later wrote in his autobiography, *The Hurdy Gurdy Man*, 'and marveled at his arrival onto the scene.'

Bob Dylan, whose song 'Rainy Day Women #12 & 35' was on the charts, also made it out to see his friend from the East Coast. Tiny noticed Dylan was in the audience. 'Ladies and Gentlemen,' he said, 'I have a great star in the audience. I don't want to embarrass him, but it is the famous Bob Dylan. I want to thank Mr. Dylan for coming to the show.'

Tiny pulled sheet music for Dylan's 'Positively 4th Street' out of his pocket and proceeded to give the song an Al Jolson–style treatment. At the song's conclusion, he kneeled and belted, 'It's not tenth street, ninth street, eighth street, seventh street, sixth street, fifth street, but positively fffooouuurrrttthhh

---

* The owners of the Hollywood Ranch Market took a liking to Tiny Tim and one night had him perform 'Old Shep' and 'I Didn't Raise My Boy To Be A Soldier' over the intercom.

sssttttrrreeettt!' It brought down the house, and Dylan autographed Tiny's 'Positively 4th Street' sheet music. The following night, they attended the same party and chatted for some time.

Tiny was also spotted at the Little Theater by Lenny Bruce's mother, comedienne Sally Marr, who reconnected Tiny and her son. Bruce had certainly not forgotten Tiny. During their long break in communication, Bruce would often listen to the recordings he had made of Tiny back in New York. Bruce invited Tiny to stay for two nights at his house. Visitors to the Bruce house gawked at Tiny, finding him lounging in a large, wicker chair in Bruce's garden. While many New Yorkers, hip to the outsider music scene in the city, may have been at least peripherally aware of Tiny Tim, he was completely unheard of on the West Coast.

Bankrupt, ill with pleurisy, and worn down from his legal battles, Bruce would often request songs from Tiny, like Billy Murray's 'Let Me Join The Army,' Arthur Field's 'I Don't Want To Get Well (I'm In Love With A Beautiful Nurse),' and his favorite, which he would ask for up to four times a day, Irving Kaufman's 'When Will The Sun Shine For Me?'*

During his stay, Tiny was introduced to Bruce's ten-year-old daughter, Kitty. A house favorite, she sometimes performed for houseguests. During Tiny's stay, a guest teased her, and she retreated in tears. Tiny followed and found her in the arms of her grandmother. 'Look here,' he said, taking the young girl aside. 'Do you want to sing in public? Or do you want to sing in your room? Because if you don't want to sing in public, never again come out in front of the audience. If you want to sing in public, you're going to have to know how to take the negatives.' He decided to give her what he later called 'army training.' He had Kitty sing, and during her performance Tiny, dropping into his natural New York accent, heckled her with phrases like, 'Come on!' and 'Get her off the stage!' renewing her determination and confidence.

Before leaving California, Tiny played a successful show at the Committee in San Francisco. Upon returning to New York, however, his good vibrations took a nosedive. His appearance on *The Merv Griffin Show* had caused quite an uproar. While Tiny was away, hundreds of letters from irate viewers poured in from across the country asking, '*What* did you have on?' Griffin received phone calls at his home from angry viewers demanding he explain the 'thing'

---

* Bruce passed away three months later, on August 3, of a morphine overdose. Tiny would later tell his friend and record producer Martin Sharp that Bruce was the 'finest person' he had met in show business.

that called itself Tiny Tim. The negative blowback made the executives at Westinghouse-CBS nervous, and they canceled Tiny's additional appearances on the program. A few episodes later, Arthur Treacher turned to Merv Griffin and asked, 'What happened to Tiny Tim?'

'Who?' Griffin replied.

However, with Tiny's return to New York, things began to heat up with Barbara Williams. Almost immediately upon his return, Williams proposed to him while they strolled together on Riverside Drive. They agreed to be 'spiritually engaged,' and a week later, they put their hands on a Bible and were 'spiritually wed.' Tiny even began referring to her as his 'spiritual wife.'

In a long-winded addendum scrawled over the unused accounting ledger in the back of his 1966 diary, Tiny explained that they had decided on a 'spiritual' marriage rather than an actual one as he wanted to become famous first before getting married so that he could provide for his wife, and she wanted to finish school. 'This was a completely new experience for me,' he wrote. 'Never have I gone steady before. Yet here I was engaged.' Not only that, but the more time he spent with her, the more he was tempted to cast aside his principles. 'I tried to keep her away from me,' he later said, in an interview with John Elder, 'but we got into a passionate affair. The Devil tried to tempt me. He said, "Give up. Give up. Everybody's doing it. Do the same." Thankfully the Lord rescued me.'

Before the Lord rescued him, however, Tiny did allow himself to succumb to his first kiss and some heavy petting, which led to what he described as 'forty-four days of sin.' 'I sinned—I became a slave of sin,' he wrote ashamedly. 'I found myself putting my lips in places I shouldn't have, and having her do the same. I found myself showing her my body completely uninhibited by clothing.'

Tiny was surprised to find himself speaking with a deeper intonation while with Williams, and that he was possessive of his spiritual wife. Though he 'loved her 200 percent,' the relationship became strained when Williams tried to assert control over Tiny's use of cosmetics. Williams was becoming like the others who had scrutinized his habits, and Tiny grew defiant. 'She must realize I will not let a woman dominate me,' he wrote.

Tiny pretended for a period of time that he had stopped using hand creams, but he was quickly found out. 'You're lying to me,' Williams said. 'You're still using hand creams.'

'Yes, I am,' Tiny replied tersely. 'I'll do what ever I want.'

'Get out of here!'

To prove his masculinity, Tiny again succumbed to temptation and kissed her. 'Next thing, at her house, sensualities happened,' he later recalled. However, these 'sensualities' did not prevent Williams from ending their 'two months of fighting and turbulence' on June 30 1966.

'You'll never make the big time,' she said. 'You'll always live with your mother, you can't help yourself.' It was just as well. For the time being, Tiny was freed from sexual temptations, and he could resume his role of spiritual advisor to the young females at the Scene without feeling like a hypocrite.

* * *

That summer, despite financial setbacks and declining business, Steve Paul began paying Tiny $50 a week. Even with exposure to established acts such as The Shangri-Las, Mitch Ryder, The Mothers Of Invention, Muddy Waters, Sam The Sham, and José Feliciano, Tiny nevertheless felt his spirits deflating. 'I found that the gloom began to set in again,' he later told *Playboy*. 'I felt I'd been [at the Scene] long enough … the crowds were getting used to me. The novelty was wearing off.'

Tiny and his small cadres of supporters continued to explore other means of exposure. Ronnie Lyons was able to secure him regular appearances on radio host Bob Fass's free-form radio show, *Radio Unnameable*, on WBAI. In addition to covering a wide variety of political topics, Fass featured, and is credited with giving early exposure to, a great number of counterculture figures of the era, including Bob Dylan, Arlo Guthrie, The Fugs, Melanie, and Cat Mother & The All Night Newsboys.

A unique and unusual personality himself, even Fass was taken aback when he met Tiny Tim. 'I was startled by him,' Fass recalled. 'He looked like a tattered bird … He would hang out at the station. I first saw him at the Commons. It seemed pretty odd to me, but also interesting because of the old songs he was singing.'

Lyons also approached the comedy team of Bob Booker and George Foster about making an album with Tiny. The pair had co-written and produced Vaughn Meader's record-selling album *The First Family*, and the Grammy-nominated album *You Don't Have To Be Jewish*. Lyons had Richard Perry brought in to produce, and the prolific arranger Artie Butler was also brought on board. Butler's résumé included arranging 'Sally Go 'Round The Roses' for The Jaynettes and, a year later, would include 'What A Wonderful World' by Louis Armstrong. Booker and Foster sought to recreate the ambiance of the types of clubs where Tiny performed by bringing in a live audience, along with tables and chairs, an approach Perry felt was wrong. '[Richard] wanted to do it one way,' said Lyons. '[Booker and Foster] brought in a live audience to sit there, for Tiny Tim to sing before them. It was the completely wrong way to do it, but our options at that time were so limited.'

The session took place on August 17 at a Capitol Records studio, where Tiny was backed by a forty-piece band conducted by Artie Butler. The song selection included 30s and 40s staples such as 'Hi Neighbor,' 'Wing And A Prayer,' 'Hooray For Hollywood,' 'Chickoree Chick,' and 'Pistol Packin' Mama.' The audience of seventy included Jay & The Americans, along with *Village Voice* journalist Fred McDarrah.

'[Tiny Tim] stood up there ready to be molded into an idol of our times,' McDarrah wrote in a subsequent article, 'looking very much like a hawk-nose Bette Davis in spats. Tall and gaunt and wearing a suit that Adolphe Menjou made famous in the 30s, big knot cravat, pearl stickpin, white carnation, blowing kisses to the audience with his hands that flutter like delicate birds.'

A post-session party took place where Tiny's forthcoming merge with mainstream show business was celebrated. 'Even though he avidly follows the Dodgers and the Toronto Maple Leafs,' McDarrah continued, 'it is hard to get away from the impression that Tiny Tim sleeps in an ancient gramophone and makes love to old movie posters. Is this pop music's new direction?'

Tiny did not share McDarrah's optimism. 'The result, in my opinion—a complete flop,' he wrote. Inexplicably, the album was never released. According to Lyons, Booker and Foster simply 'couldn't sell' the recordings.

Presumably dissatisfied with the Booker and Foster session, Richard Perry decided to bring Tiny into the studio and do things his way. He had been mulling over Tiny's repertoire and potential project ideas for over a year. So, for the first and only time in his career, Perry borrowed $600 from his father-in-law, record producer George Goldner, and scheduled studio time. The sessions ultimately yielded four demo tracks: two different versions of the staple 'April Showers,' the Leadbelly classic 'Little Girl (In The Pines)'— both of which Barbara Williams had shown to Tiny before their split—and Tom Paxton's 'I Can't Help But Wonder (Where I'm Bound).' Due to the minuscule budget, Perry played every instrument for the recording.

Perry recognized Tiny's talent as both a serious musician and a whimsical entertainer. He recorded a lighthearted, falsetto version of 'April Showers' and a darkly baritone version of 'Little Girl (In The Pines),' two pieces that complemented one another in their disparities. Though Perry had an offer from Buddah Records—as is confirmed by the existence of a sole Buddah acetate featuring an alternate version of 'April Showers,' with horn overdubs, and 'I Can't Help But Wonder (Where I'm Bound)'—he refused it, feeling that the label would not treat Tiny with 'dignity and respect.'

'[I wanted a] whole big commercial thing, like here's the next thing, not just a creep-out,' Perry told Lowell Tarling. 'I didn't want to take the chance of Tiny having a legitimate bomb on his hands, because a company didn't merchandise and promote the product properly.' Perry ultimately released two of the tracks, 'April Showers' and 'Little Girl,' on Blue Cat Records, a subsidiary label of Red Bird Records, owned by Goldner. The label put Tiny in his own category: 'Camp Rock.'

Though it would appear that Blue Cat did little to promote the release, both white label promos and stock copies of the 45 were pressed as Blue Cat 127. The single did not chart, and copies of this 45 are nearly impossible to find. Perry did not release any additional tracks from the session, perhaps due to the stagnant outcome of the release.

In November, Tiny returned to Los Angeles for an appearance in the upcoming made-for-TV-movie *Ironside*, which preceded the successful TV series. He performs a falsetto rendition of Rudy Vallee's 'Whistling In The Dark' while a skeptical Robert T. Ironside, played by Raymond T. Burr, looks on. The scene was shot at the Universal Pictures lot, in a set recreation of an underground nightclub, similar to Tiny's usual venues. Tiny landed the role after being tracked down by a casting agent who remembered him from *The Merv Griffin Show*. He was paid $300 for the appearance, and performed for personnel on set. 'I made a hit with the set singing,' he wrote in his diary.*

In December 1966, appearances by The Young Rascals and The Blues Project revived interest and business at the Scene. Regardless, Tiny Tim felt a disconnect with his audience, and with 1967 just around the corner, he thought it might be time to move on. Steve Paul, who had peppered the Scene's promotional materials with advertisements like 'Tiny Tim … Tonight through infinity' and 'The INCREDIBLE TINY TIM … 365 NIGHTS A YEAR,' was staunchly opposed.

---

* In his diary, Tiny also mentions making a recording for Epic Records, which ultimately went unreleased, while in California. An undated acetate from Gold Star Studios, featuring the songs 'Groovy Go-Go Girls' and 'I Want To Be Your Chauffeur,' may very well be the recording in question.

'Tiny, I'll keep you here no matter what happens,' he said.

'Thanks as Mr. Steve says he has faith in how I sing despite the silence and sometimes boos,' Tiny wrote in his diary.

Though Paul vowed to keep Tiny on the bill at the Scene, did the club's promotional items advertising that Tiny would be on the bill 'through infinity' mean that Paul believed the darling of his posh discotheque was not capable of achieving anything greater? As 1966 elapsed, Tiny, accompanied by The Blues Project, led the Scene's audience in a New Years Eve sing-along.

Though Tiny was prepared to stay the course at the Scene, he did make a significant change to his personal life when he ended once and for all his long-time secret fling with Bobby Gonzalez. Gonzalez visited the old neighborhood in early January and went to see Tiny at his home. When Gonzalez made an advance, Tiny turned him down. 'Refused to indulge,' he wrote in his diary. 'Fooling with men is not my life—Jesus be praised.'

* * *

By January 1967, Peter Yarrow (of Peter Paul & Mary) was a regular at the Scene and had begun working with photographer and cinematographer Barry Feinstein, who was then married to Mary Travers (Mary), on an experimental film about the counterculture entitled *You Are What You Eat*. According to Yarrow, the aim of the film was to show 'images that personified the kind of nuttiness and craziness of what was being explored at the time.'

To Yarrow, Tiny Tim exemplified that particular quintessence. Yarrow wanted to feature Tiny both in the film and on its soundtrack, which was to be released by Columbia Records. 'He was sincere, and he was caring, and he was loving, and he was not like other people,' Yarrow recalls. 'The fact of his acceptance and embrace was different among certain kinds of people … many just saw him as weirder than weird and that was that, but there were many others that found him delightful. In a way, his acceptance was part of opening the door to a general acceptance of people who were not like other people—they didn't have to be marginalized.'

Barry Feinstein was less philosophical in his approach. 'I was just going for an introduction to Tiny Tim. I wanted people to see who he really was … he was a nut! He was very nice … he was fun to work with.'

Yarrow's approach as musical director was as loose as Feinstein's directorial approach. '[Feinstein] wasn't shooting it with synced sound,' Yarrow says, 'so we just put music to it and looked at it and saw what worked and then I wrote songs for it. John Simon did, too.* That kind of intuitive logic or intuitive methodology was characteristic of the time and still is the way in which people create. They look for a language the resonates and go for it.'

Yarrow approached Tiny about working on the film and, hungry for exposure, Tiny naturally agreed. John Simon paired Tiny with a curious quintet known as The Hawks. The Hawks had gained notoriety while touring with Bob Dylan during a tumultuous and amphetamine-fueled period from September 1965 through May 1966. Simon later produced their first solo album, 1968's *Music From Big Pink*, and the group rapidly rose to prominence, not as The Hawks, but as an Americana staple: The Band.

The Band's organ player, Garth Hudson, recalls that The Band quickly took a liking to Tiny, who he says was 'pleasant, easy to work with, and [we] found his repertoire intriguing. We knew he was a dedicated artist, and also I think everybody in The Band knew about that era that he loved.'

After rehearsals on February 3 and 4, and a session canceled due to a blizzard on February 7, Tiny's tracks and scenes with The Band were recorded live on February 9 at the Balloon Farm, a club in the East Village owned by Dylan and Yarrow's manager, the ubiquitous Albert Grossman. Yarrow explains his approach. 'We set up microphones and the sound system and just recorded it live to the master. ... It's very unusual to go right to tape and that's it, but, in that era ... it never went through a mixing process, it was just The Band and Tiny.'

Eleanor Barooshian, who appears and sings with Tiny in the 'I Got You, Babe' segment of the film, later told Ernie Clark, 'We did it in the freezing cold in the East Village in NYC! He was a fun person! It was my idea to sing "I Got You, Babe" at the Scene with him and Peter Yarrow saw us do it and asked us to do it in the film.'

Barooshian came upon the idea of performing the song with Tiny after her all-girl trio The Cake had performed on a triple bill at the Scene with Tiny and The Chambers Brothers. Barbara Morillo, another member of The Cake, recalled that when she and her bandmates would arrive at the Scene, Tiny would excitedly greet them and kiss their hands. 'He was a fixture,' Morillo recalls. 'I guess it was a time where there was so much love in the air, you know, for life, that everybody just accepted everybody ... I'm on the audio part singing background [on Tiny's songs with The Band] ...

---

* John Simon was at that time a producer at Columbia records, responsible for the 1966 hit 'Red Rubber Ball' as recorded by The Cyrkle, among others.

They didn't even show The Band or us singing background [in the film].'

Yarrow agreed to put Eleanor Barooshian in the film as he was intrigued by Tiny's relationships with the young women who hung around the Scene and wanted them to be portrayed onscreen. 'One of the things that was wonderful and startling was the degree to which the young, female flower children and teeny-boppers just loved him,' he explains. 'They all kind of mothered him and thought he was just a hoot and a darling.'

The session itself, which spanned over twelve hours, was complicated by the types of idiosyncrasies that were typical of Tiny Tim. Accustomed to performing as a solo act, Tiny had difficulty adjusting to The Band's accompaniment and the process was tedious. Tiny was also unwilling to suspend his compulsive aversion to public restrooms during the recording. 'Nothing seemed to go quickly or smoothly,' Morillo recalls. 'We had to stop the whole production, because he had to go to the bathroom. He went home. We were all just standing around waiting. I don't know how long it took ... over an hour.'

When Tiny returned, Morillo asked why he did not use the bathroom at the club. 'Oh, no,' Tiny replied, while applying a fresh layer of Elizabeth Arden powder to his face. 'I must cleanse the area.'

'That's the same brand my mother uses,' Morillo observed, eyeing the powder.

'Ohh, I always say, in any garden, it's Elizabeth Arden!' Tiny giggled.

According to Yarrow, Tiny needed very little direction. Barry Feinstein just set up his camera and rolled. 'He just did his thing,' says Yarrow. 'He didn't need any direction ... there was a certain kind of authority in the way we were doing things at the time where we just believed in ourselves in a way that was not filled with the cautious concern about whether we were breaking new ground or not ... in terms of creating art. Nobody analyzed why this was the way to do it, we just knew it was meaningful.'

They recorded versions of 'Be My Baby,' 'Memphis,' and 'I Got You, Babe.' One final session, held a week later, on February 16, yielded an inspired version of Al Jolson's signature song, 'Sonny Boy.' Today, 'Sonny Boy' remains the most memorable performance of the session for Garth Hudson, whose distinctive keyboard stylings are featured prominently on the track.

Yarrow was very pleased with the material he had created with Tiny. 'I think [the tracks] are really fine pieces of work and stand on their own for what they are,' he says. '[Tiny] was kind of a Dadaistic statement of performance art that reshaped our point of view of what a singer could be, what a man could be. He was totally an individual in these ways ... there's no question that he was wonderfully talented.'

At the culmination of the filming, Tiny returned to the Scene, while Yarrow began to edit the several hours of footage they had captured in New York, Hollywood, and San Francisco for an unspecified date of release.

* * *

It was working with The Band that brought Tiny back onto Bob Dylan's radar. The day after his session with The Band, Tiny learned that Dylan wanted him to visit his home in Woodstock and to appear in a film project. Five days later, on February 13, Tiny wrote an entry in his diary from Dylan's home.

> *Dear Lord, There are no words big enough to say but thank you o Lord for the thrill and ecstasy to be one of the privileged few who stayed at Mr. Bob Dylan's house— as well as having a chance to be playing his upcoming television spectacular in April, Lord willing ... to be a close friend of the world's greatest entertainer today, to stay and sleep in his house, to be a part of his television show, well, this was too much—and to top it all he is paying me for it.*

'I'll say one thing,' Tiny later revealed, in an interview with Ernie Clark, 'the meeting with Bob Dylan was another classic moment. I'll never, ever forget it.' Tiny, who had brought his customary shopping bag of cosmetics, was given a 'big, gigantic suite,' where he freshened up before his meeting with Dylan. They met at midnight, Tiny recalled, and initially made small talk about the Toronto Maple Leafs, before Tiny told Dylan he was 'to folk music [today] what Rudy Vallee was to romantic music in the early days of radio.' Tiny then proceeded to sing Dylan's 'Like A Rolling Stone' in the style of Vallee, and Vallee's 'My Time Is Your Time' in the style of Dylan. In return, Dylan picked up his guitar and sang a version of 'Cool Water.'

For the next two days, Tiny filmed scenes for Dylan's film, appearing alongside Paul Stookey (of Peter Paul & Mary), Richard Manuel, and Dylan himself. 'What a thrill it was to go with them as they shot scenes from location to location,' he wrote. 'Thank you as Mr. Dylan praised my acting—but thank you—O Lord for the gifts you O Lord have given me ... [Dylan] is not only greatly gifted but has a fantastic mind—an interesting type of humility as well.'

In between takes, Tiny performed for Dylan's children and his wife, Sara, whom Tiny described as 'beautiful as well as wise.' Upon leaving Woodstock, on February 15, he added, 'I pray to keep [Dylan's] friendship to remember his delicateness.'

Dylan was apparently so pleased with Tiny's performance that he had him return for two more days of filming on March 1 and 2. By then, Tiny was completely spellbound, praising Dylan in his diary as 'the greatest single entertainer in the world today.' The unlikely duo also sang together, and Dylan even let Tiny play his guitar. One session was recorded in the 'Red Room' in Dylan's house. Tiny was paid $88 for his appearance in the film, although, as he later told Ernie Clark, 'I would have done it for free!'

Exactly what Dylan had been filming at the time remains something of a mystery. D.A. Pennebaker, who directed the acclaimed documentary of Dylan's 1965 tour of the UK, *Dont Look Back*, later told biographer Howard Sounes that Dylan had borrowed a camera from him and had been shooting 'a circus film.' According to Bob Spitz, the celebrated journalist known for *Beatles: The Biography*, Dylan had Tiny 'play the part of Philip Granger, a down-and-out drifter.'*

Tiny's spirits were boosted further when the TV movie *Ironside* aired on March 28, but he was disappointed to learn in early April that Dylan's 'circus film' was not going to be released. 'The Bob Dylan thing is out,' he wrote. 'Once more I am down but I will come back strong.'

Bob Dylan never sought Tiny out again; according to Ronnie Lyons, Dylan, while intrigued by Tiny, did not envision him as a mainstream success. 'Dylan thought he was great, you know?' said Lyons. 'Not marketable, but unique enough to put in the movie, you know?'

Around this time, Lyons, who was by then working for Albert Grossman and managing The Electric Flag and The Paupers, found that Tiny was becoming too much of a nuisance. 'I was really not too involved with Tiny Tim at the time [he filmed with Dylan]. I was too turned off, honestly. It was too hard. Too much conflict. Too many managers. Nothing positive. Tiny was very flaky.' Lyons, too, faded out of the picture.

* * *

* The footage would go unseen for over forty years until a few seconds of Tiny with Dylan and Richard Manuel were included in the 2015 short documentary *Bob Dylan & The Band—The Basement Tapes—The Legendary Tales*.

Among the other celebrities with whom Tiny rubbed shoulders during his tenure at the Scene was Tommy James of Tommy James & The Shondells. James had attended the Scene one evening in the spring of 1967 and caught Tiny's act. 'He'd been around for a long time, under various names,' James recalls. 'When I first saw him, I thought he was a comedian and, you know, we're all cracking up, laughing, thinking he was trying to be funny, and a third of the way through the first song we realized he wasn't kidding. So, we just shut up and listened.'

After Tiny's set, James rose from his seat to try and speak to Tiny and tell him how much had enjoyed his performance. However, Tiny quickly slipped out of the club with barely a word to anyone. According to Steve Paul, 'He will walk back to his apartment to go to the bathroom and then come back to the club and play the next set.' When Tiny returned, he and James had a short conversation. 'I said, I love the old tunes,' James recalls. 'I patted him on the back, and then it was time for his next set.'

Tommy James and Tiny Tim never again crossed paths, but James always had a fondness for Tiny. 'He was one of the most interesting people that I ever saw in show business,' he says. 'You could not help but love him. There's probably many lessons that can be learned from Tiny Tim about show business and what we call celebrity status and all that kind of stuff … he was a good soul, and he was exactly offstage what he was onstage. He was just *him*. He was such a strange combination of things that you really had to look at a guy like that with … a kind of reverence because of the way he was and having to deal with people poking fun and stuff like that and, yet, he had the strength to go up on stage and be a star. Most people would run from that.

'Obviously, there were things about Tim that were probably a little disturbing. There was obviously something … not 100 percent about him, but he had this incredible ability, once you got past … people poking fun in the audience; once he got to be on stage for a while, people kind of got to like what he was doing.'

It was around this time, too, that Charlie Barrett of *Billboard* magazine caught Tiny's act at the Scene. 'It was such an offbeat act to be performing a 1920s song,' he wrote. 'People were titillated and amused … [his performance was] quite good and very professional.' Barrett also noted that members of Jefferson Airplane had been in the audience that night to see Tiny's act.

Though Tiny had found relative acceptance in familiar and intimate settings, his performance in Montreal at Expo '67 was an unfortunate deviation. The audience in Montreal was not prepared to accept him as a representative of American culture. On the first day of the Expo, April 27, Tiny was scheduled to perform at what was then the largest exhibition and hotel complex in the world, the newly constructed Place Bonaventure, on a bill with The Blues Project and Suzanne Verdal.* He was warned not to go on because the crowd, which numbered around 8,000 people, was 'ugly,' but he was undeterred. 'Nothing bothers me, my dear friends,' he told those accompanying him. 'One night they threw hamburgers at me.'

Tiny opened his set with 'Hello, Hello,' and the audience began to boo. Already agitated, they quickly turned hostile, lobbing beer cans in Tiny's direction. After being hit with a few, Tiny postured himself in a batting stance—'just like [Maple Leafs goaltender] Terry Sawchuk'—and began to bat flying cans with the backside of his ukulele. He still managed to finish his three-song set before the police came to his rescue and escorted him offstage. Backstage, his supporters were shaken up by what happened, so Tiny began to cheer them up with an impromptu performance. 'There's your headline,' he said. 'Backstage Hit. Frontstage Flop.' The bewildered press said of Tiny, 'Whoever he was, he had courage.'

The spring of 1967 gave way to the infamous Summer of Love, and in June Steve Paul decided to crash the Monterrey Pop Festival, with Tiny in tow, hoping to get him on the bill. It seemed like a good idea, considering the three-day festival boasted the first major American performances of both Jimi Hendrix and Janis Joplin, both of whom had played at the Scene prior to achieving major stardom. The festival attracted some 200,000 attendees and was considered a showcase for the cutting edge of the expanding counterculture. Paul and Tiny arrived in California within hours of the festival opening. The two managed to find a hotel room, and Paul even finagled a slot for Tiny on the bill. However, Paul had done the negotiating without Tiny present. When he brought Tiny to the Monterey County Fairgrounds for his performance, the concert organizer got a good look at him and declared, 'No way.'

Instead of performing in the festival, Tiny set up camp in the Hunt Club, which served as the festival's green room. It wasn't long before he had attracted an audience. Illuminated by the light from a cigarette lighter, Tiny performed a series of songs that even included Bob Dylan's 'Rainy Day Women #12 & 35.' Later, he performed a few songs that he usually reserved for private

---

* Suzanne Verdal was the wife of sculptor Armand Vaillancourt. She is alleged to have inspired the popular Leonard Cohen song, 'Suzanne.'

moments with young girls from the Scene: 'Stay Home Little Girl Stay Home,' 'King For A Day,' 'Laugh Clown Laugh,' and 'My, What A Funny Little World This Is!'*

Just to have been in the mix with Jimi Hendrix was enough to make the trip worthwhile for Tiny. When he was later asked what Hendrix thought of him, however, Tiny was unsure. 'Well, I don't think he heard much of [my music],' he said, 'you know, but he was his own individual person. He was definitely a complete original. I can tell you, he didn't have time to think of my music. He had too many women around him. I tell you, he was really great.'

Upon returning from the Monterey Pop Festival and resuming work at the Scene, Tiny served as the opening act for a rambunctious band, whose sound, like Tiny's, was uncharacteristic of the times: The Doors. 'Jim Morrison I knew very well at that time,' Tiny said in 1979. 'He was so good looking—he had a following before he was famous. … He offered me a song called "People Are Strange," which he wanted me to do, but the next week "Light My Fire" was in the Top 10, and that was it. I only saw him again once after that. He was on his way to the top.'

As with most things involving Jim Morrison, the engagement was not without some controversy. *Happening Magazine* reported that when Doors co-manager Asher Dann attempted to subdue Morrison after he narrowly missed Tiny Tim's head while swinging a microphone out into the audience, they ended up in a 'bloody fist fight onstage.' 'Tiny Tim is scared stiff,' a concert promoter chuckled, turning to another onlooker. 'Morrison just missed his head.'

* * *

As the new year approached, it was time for Tiny to present another woman with one of his priceless trophies. However, 1967 was a controversial year for trophies. The first went to the uncontested Miss Cleo Odzer, a seventeen-year-old beautiful blond who wrote a column about new talent in the area called 'Cleo's Pop Sounds' for the Greenwich Village–based newspaper the *Downtown*. She was also a frequent visitor to the Scene and was dating Keith Emerson, the keyboard player for The Nice. Tiny referred to her in his diary as 'Queen Cleo' and described her as 'an angel—one to whom I could dream and could live in dreams with forever.'

---

* The performance also included versions of 'Stay Down Here Where You Belong,' 'Hello, Hello,' and 'Don't Bite The Hand That's Feeding You' that predate the versions he later recorded for Reprise Records.

The second trophy was given to another beauty named Miss Corrine 'Corky' Dukker. '[Another] girl who inspires me and puts a temperature in what songs I do is Miss Corky Dukker,' Tiny revealed. 'Oh, there are no words big enough to describe how beautiful she is. I consider Miss Dukker to be the new Miss Greta Garbo. She is only eighteen yet her face is so beautiful like a painting by Rembrandt. When I feel her beautiful presence near me, my heart skips a beat at a speed faster than lightning.'

The trophy had not originally been intended for Corky, but for Miss Jane Cole, a pretty nineteen-year-old sophomore at Queens College who had become friends with Corky and Corky's friend Alan. Together, the three of them frequented the Scene.

Tiny became very animated at the sight of the two girls. '*Oh! Miss Jane, Miss Corky! I'm so happy!*' Miss Jane says today, imitating Tiny's enthusiasm. 'He'd get all excited, and he would take out some songs from the 20s and 30s—the sheet music. He would tell us what songs he was going to do that night, and we'd wait for his show and cheer him on like crazy.'

Tiny's diary confirms Jane's story. 'Thanks for every second near beautiful Miss Jane from Queens College,' he wrote, on July 27. 'She was so beautiful. I could not hold those moments long enough—what a girl. Every second with her was divine.'

One snowy night, the three went to see Tiny play at the Scene, only to be told by Steve Paul that he was performing across town at the Scene East. 'We have to go and support Tiny,' Alan insisted. They drove across Manhattan to the Scene East, where they found there were only four people in the audience. Jane and Corky lifted Tiny's spirits immensely. 'Well let's just have a good time,' Tiny said. 'We'll do the show and maybe you and Miss Corky would like to get up and do something.' Jane and Corky decided that they would sing an impromptu 'Bye Bye Birdie.'

'Ladies and gentlemen,' Tiny improvised. 'Here are … The Birdie Sisters!'

As the months went by, Tiny grew very close to the two girls. 'We were amazed; we thought he was so funny. He was like a total freak to me. I had no idea [if] he was able to even get it on with a girl because he was so excitable.' In a show of affection, Tiny once got drunk at the Scene and raised his glass to Miss Corky each time he took a sip. Corky began to work at the club around this time but was fired after being accused of stealing some records from the venue. Tiny refused to perform again until Paul allowed her back into the club as a patron.

Later, it came to Jane's attention that, though she had been in the running for one of Tiny's trophies, Corky and Alan had knocked her out of the box. The two had grown jealous when Jane began to spend more time with her boyfriend in the Bronx than with them at the Scene. 'I got cut off from Tiny Tim … [Alan] decided to tell Tiny that I was a *bad* girl,' says Jane. 'Tiny believed him that I was a bad girl. I saw him after, but I didn't get the greeting that I used to get and I didn't get the trophy that Corky got!'*

* * *

In the meantime, Tiny Tim was increasingly worried about the future of his career and was beginning to grow desperate. Virtually penniless, and often without money for the subway, he had a lot of time to think things over on his long walks home. 'What would I do if the Scene closed?' he asked himself. Again, Tiny prayed and briefly looked for another physical change he could make to spice up his act. He began painting one half of his face white and the other brown. He called the style 'split personality for the 70s.'

'I actually tried it three or four times,' he later told *Playboy*. 'I was made up that way one day in the subway and, with my long hair, it must have looked pretty surprising. Anyone who saw me from one side would think I was brown-skinned, but then when they passed me, they saw I was half white. They did some quick double takes.'

When his 'split personality' proved a dud, Tiny reverted to his old style, but he began thinking about cutting his hair at the end of the year if he didn't make it. His depression was further fueled by his parents, who still offered nothing in the way of emotional support. In fact, Tillie did not like to be seen in public with her son. In the rare instance that the two of them would go out together, Tillie would leave first and then Tiny would follow a minute or so later. 'I know how ashamed you are to be seen with me.'

Tillie also did not understand her son's eating habits. By 1967, Tiny had reverted to a strict vegetarian diet consisting of onions, bananas, sunflower seeds, and honey. Tiny's cousin Roslyn Rabin visited the Khaury apartment and witnessed a bizarre scenario involving Tillie and Tiny. 'His mother prepared a fantastic salad for his lunch and it was late, and he was very hungry,' she recalls. 'He finally sat down for lunch and was about to eat the salad when his mother approached him saying, Herbie you like it? Herbie said, It's good,

---

* Miss Corky and her friend Alan later appeared as background dancers on Rowan and Martin's *Laugh-In*.

I love it! Tillie snatched it away saying, No, it's not good for you, I'll make you something else! I still remember the look on his face.'

Tiny was an outcast to his entire extended family. 'Until he was famous as Tiny Tim, he was Herbie, the weird cousin,' says Eddie Rabin, Roslyn's son. Eddie had heard stories about 'Crazy Cousin Herbie' but had never met him. One afternoon, while riding the subway, Eddie looked into the car behind his and caught his first glimpse of his crazy cousin. 'I saw this older guy, with long hair, reading a comic book, and I knew it was Tiny Tim,' Eddie recalls. 'He looked so weird, I didn't go into the car and introduce myself, even though I knew he was my cousin.'

While the hip audience at the Scene may have been tickled by Tiny's kooky act, he was still the subject of ridicule in public. He attended a Dodgers rally at Connie Mack Stadium in Philadelphia and became so excited that he whipped out his ukulele and began to sing 'Livin' In The Sunlight, Lovin' In The Moonlight' in his falsetto. He was consequently ejected from the event. Anther time, Tiny was the victim of an attempted mugging. When he pulled out his empty pockets, the thieves purportedly felt so badly that they offered *him* money.

One rainy night in July, Tiny arrived at the Scene, descended the stairs as he had hundreds of times before, and felt his heart sink as he perused the meager audience. He was tired, but he performed as planned. After opening with 'Let A Smile Be Your Umbrella,' he told himself, 'Look, even though there are very few people in here, you've got to keep hustling.'

Mid-performance, he noticed a well-dressed man in the audience who was laughing audibly and thoroughly enjoying himself. After the performance, the man approached Tiny. He introduced himself as Mo Ostin, the General Manager of Warner Bros Records, and expressed interest in signing Tiny to Frank Sinatra's subsidiary label, Reprise. Ostin, a shrewd businessman armed with a battalion of lawyers, was not phased by Tiny's legal baggage or eccentricities. 'I signed unusual people all the time, whether it was The Fugs or the Sex Pistols or Captain Beefheart,' Ostin told *Rolling Stone* in 1995. 'Tim was so unusual, he was so freaky, it just appealed to that perverse side of me.'

Tiny was floored. Within days, Ostin was negotiating with Tiny's lawyer, Mr. Seidel. A week later, on August 8, Tiny signed a contract with Reprise. In the meantime, he remained at the Scene. When Tiny learned on Wednesday, November 15, that Reprise wanted him in Los Angeles by the following

Monday, Steve Paul protested that he wanted Tiny at the Scene for another week. As he had no official contract with Tiny, Paul may have become nervous that Tiny might cut him out of his management.

Paul was not alone. In total, Tiny was about to leave behind six managers and a few unfulfilled contracts. 'Thanks O Lord for thy patience with me,' he had written in his journal in 1966, 'and although there may be hassles with my past signings when I make it big (Lord willing) thanks for the moment.'

On Sunday, November 26, Tiny performed in New York City for the last time as an unknown at the Village Theater. During the performance, a shoe was thrown from the audience and smacked him in the side of the head. He was undeterred. 'Never was the voice so-oo bad in front of so-oo many,' he wrote, as he sat on the train on the way to California. 'I believe however (Lord willing) this is the start of a GREAT SUCCESS. I will one day knock the house down with Miss Cleo there.'

CHAPTER FIVE
WELCOME TO
MY DREAM

If I fell down today I could always say that at one time in my life, for a moment,
I stunned them all.

TINY TIM TO *TV GUIDE*, OCTOBER 12 1968

Tiny arrived in California on November 29 1967. He took up residence at
the Hollywood Hawaiian Hotel and was promptly reunited with his old friend
from New York, Richard Perry. Perry had recently been hired by Warner Bros
as a producer, had already produced Captain Beefheart's acclaimed album
Safe As Milk, and was hungry for a new project. He had included the singles
produced with Tiny on Blue Cat Records in 1966 among his demos during his
interviews with Warner Bros. 'Oh, we just signed him,' someone remarked,
upon seeing the Tiny Tim cuts.

'Oh, Yarrow must be the producer,' Perry said, thinking it would make
sense for Peter Yarrow to get the job, given that Peter Paul & Mary were
signed to Warner Bros and Yarrow had recently collaborated with Tiny.

'No, we're looking for a producer for him.'

'So that's when I knew that fate brought us together again,' Perry recalled,
'and I think—if I'm not mistaken—we may have called him on the phone
right then and there.' Tiny and Perry began to plan Tiny's first major label
release, *God Bless Tiny Tim*. With the backing of a major studio, and a $25,000
budget, the two launched into the project.

God Bless Tiny Tim 'was the realization of a dream that Tiny and I both
had,' Perry told journalist Chris Campion in 2006. 'The high falsetto voice is
all that most people remember. That was the least interesting aspect to me. I
immediately saw in him the ability to be a true showman. There was nothing
that he wasn't capable of doing.'

'When it came time,' Perry told *Rolling Stone*, 'we just got together, Tiny with his ukulele and me on the piano, and we worked things out.' Perry aimed to recreate the juxtaposition of sound and style he used on the 'April Showers'/'Little Girl' single. Though Tiny was skeptical about performing contemporary material, he agreed to Perry's suggestion that the album be split between Tiny's older repertoire and Perry's modern numbers, primarily written by obscure up-and-comers.

One of those songwriters was Paul Williams, who would later achieve huge successes with hits for Barbra Streisand and The Carpenters. In 1968, however, Williams was relatively unknown. Richard Perry was also producing an album by Williams's group, The Holy Mackerel, and Williams was thrilled when Perry selected a song he had co-written with fellow singer-songwriter Biff Rose, 'Fill Your Heart.'

'Tiny Tim was truly one of a kind,' Williams recalls. 'He would never address me as anything but Mr. Williams—an honor I was unaccustomed to. I was a relatively unknown songwriter at the time, and yet Tiny treated me as if I was Irving Berlin. And it wasn't shallow flattery. He was genuine in his respect for almost everyone I saw him communicate with. Needless to say, the world was capable of cruel responses. I never saw him react in any way but mild shock, usually accompanied by his famous, fluttery *ooooooh*. If his character was a put-on, he was a brilliant actor. I believe he was the man he presented himself to be.'

Williams remembers Tiny as somewhat difficult yet endearing during the recording session. 'He kept Richard Perry jumping, and I think might have been a bit of a handful for whoever worked with him,' he says. 'But he had a sweetness, and in a world where cookie cutter conformity makes for an easier softer way Tiny had the courage to be himself.'

Despite his gratitude to Perry and Tiny for giving him a chance, the inclusion of 'Fill Your Heart' on *God Bless Tiny Tim* did make Paul Williams question his career choices. 'I had two songs I wrote,' he told Broadwayworld.com in a July 2010 interview. 'One was … called "Fill Your Heart" and Tiny Tim recorded it … And the same day, I had a song called "It's Hard To Say Goodbye" by Claudine Longet. I thought, Claudine Longet and Tiny Tim … what kind of a songwriter am I?'

For the arrangements, Perry selected Artie Butler, who had already worked with Tiny on the unreleased Booker and Foster session at Capital Records. 'I remember those sessions vividly,' he recalled. 'I think I was perfect [to arrange] for Tiny and understood him. … I have to tell you, I know he was a strange act—we know he was talented, there's no question about it, but he was one of the nicest and one of the most intelligent … he was just a nice man. He was a gentle soul. I always thought that he knew something we didn't know. We thought he was strange; I think he was right and we're strange. He was like a happy soul. He was just on a plane that we didn't have a clue about.'*

Butler shared Perry's vision that the album would not succeed if they surrendered to campiness. 'I loath gimmicks,' Perry told *Rolling Stone* in 1969. 'I guess my mind does go in the direction of the unexpected, because I like things that hit with tremendous impact … and *make it* besides. It's like Tiny's laughter on the first cut of the second side of his first album. Maybe he's laughing at people who laughed at him. Maybe it's something else. But it fits.'

Some of LA's most distinguished session players were assembled for the recording, including members of the notorious Wrecking Crew: guitarists Tommy Tedesco and Howard Roberts, bass player Charles Berghofer, pianists Mike Melvoin and Larry Knechtel, trumpeter Anthony Terran, trombone player Lew McCreary, saxophone player Gene Cipriano, and percussionist Gary Coleman. Tiny must have known he was in good hands. 'I will make Reprise Records a star,' he remarked confidently in his diary.

After a week of rehearsals, sessions for *God Bless Tiny Tim* began on December 11 1967, at TTG Studios in Los Angeles. Richard Perry gave Tiny a pep talk before they entered the studio. He reminded him of the chance he had taken on him on the 'April Showers'/'Little Girl' single and revealed that though his father had discouraged him from working with Tiny, he had always had faith in him. They began with Tiny's selections, Maurice Chevalier's 'Livin' In The Sunlight, Lovin' In The Moonlight' and the Billy Murray/Ada Jones duet 'On The Old Front Porch,' and Paul Williams and Biff Rose's 'Fill Your Heart.' Regarding 'Livin' In The Sunlight, Lovin' In The Moonlight,' Tiny recalled Maurice Chevalier's displeasure with his version. 'He would shake his head listening to mine. If he heard the nice words I said about him, he might have kept quiet! Still, I was very happy with the way I sounded on that.' Tiny also remained fond of 'Fill Your Heart,' later telling Ernie Clark, 'Mr. Perry liked the song, and I agreed with him. It was a strange song for me to sing.'

On December 12, work continued with 'On The Old Front Porch,' and

---

* On learning of this, Miss Sue notes that it is the first time she has heard anyone else express something she felt as soon as she met Tiny: 'He began to seem like the *only* normal person I knew … the rest of the world began to seem aberrant.'

then moved on to Tiny's selection, George M. Cohen's 1902 composition 'Then I'd Be Satisfied With Life.' It was one of the 'rare, rare' songs in repertoire, and Tiny added some personal touches to the lyrics. 'If Hettie Green would only be my wife' became 'If Tuesday Weld would only be my wife.'* 'All I want is partridge for my breakfast' became 'All I want is wheat germ for my breakfast.' 'If I only stood in with the steel-trust rake off' became 'If I could only stay sixteen forever.' 'Pierpont Morgan waiting on the table' became 'Rockefeller waiting on the table.' And 'Sousa's band playing while I eat' became 'Lombardo's band playing while I eat.'

A female voice, moaning 'Oh, Tiny!' in response to 'If Tuesday Weld would only be my wife,' was delivered by Andy Warhol superstar and Velvet Underground singer Nico. Perry rearranged the song to have a western style and encouraged Tiny to add a southern twang to his delivery. 'It always fascinated me how [Tiny] came to know that music because it wasn't something he would have readily been exposed to sitting in his apartment in New York,' Perry later told Lowell Tarling. 'They didn't make that many country records, like the old 78s weren't nearly as plentiful as the Rudy Vallee, Bing Crosby, Russ Columbo type of music.'

They also worked on 'The Other Side,' a song sung from the perspective of a fish witnessing the end of the world as a result of melting polar ice caps. Written by up and coming songwriter Bill Dorsey, the song is by some distance the furthest removed from anything else in Tiny's repertoire.†

The following day, December 13, they tackled two more of Tiny's selections: Irving Berlin's forgotten gem from 1914, 'Stay Down Here Where You Belong,' and the infectious 1913 Eddie Morton ditty 'Ever Since You Told Me That You Love Me (I'm A Nut).' The former is perhaps the best example of Richard Perry and Tiny Tim's mutually beneficial collaboration. Tiny's versatility served as a vehicle by which Perry could experiment with different production styles, and Perry's prowess allowed Tiny to prove that pop music of any era, is timeless. The song is sung from the perspective of the Devil, who warns his son not to go up to earth, as there is 'more heat up there than there is down below.'

---

* Hettie Green was the richest woman in America when the song was written in 1902.

† Dorsey would later pen several songs for The Monkees' NBC TV special, *33 1/3 Revolutions Per Monkee*. No official soundtrack of the program has ever been released, but some unofficial versions have surfaced featuring a demo version of 'The Other Side,' thought to be performed by Dorsey.

Perry's modern arrangement included a psychedelic organ, fire crackling sound effects, and vocals drenched in reverb. Some of his genius was lost on Tiny, however. 'Stay Down Here Where You Belong' made him 'particularly unhappy,' he told Harry Stein, during an interview for *Tiny Tim: An Unauthorized Biography*. 'Even though most people liked it, I thought it was awful. It didn't have the quality of the old sound.'

Irving Berlin, who had written the song when Americans were largely opposed to the United States entering World War I, and who most likely was happy to have it eclipsed by his patriotic songs like 'God Bless America,' was baffled by its resurrection. 'Let me tell you the story here,' Tiny later told Ernie Clark. 'Irving Berlin, when he heard in '68 that I had sung this song, actually called up Warner Bros and wanted to know where I got it. I said that I got it from Henry Burr [who sang it in 1915], and he couldn't believe that somebody knew it!'*

'Ever Since You Told Me That You Love Me (I'm A Nut)' was typical Tiny Tim fare, sung in his patented shrill falsetto against a driving bass line and folksy fiddle interludes. Tiny regarded it as 'another great song' and thought that it might have made a suitable second single.[†]

On December 15, they worked on two of Perry's selections, 'Strawberry Tea' and 'The Coming Home Party.' 'Strawberry Tea,' written by Gordon Alexander, is a foray into baroque psychedelia. Featuring harpsichord and breezy orchestral arrangement, with lyrical references to 'sherbet moons,' 'rainbow pools,' and 'silver angels drift through timeless, never-ending June.'[‡] Tiny remained fond of the track, stating that it was one of Perry's selections that he 'really liked.'

'The Coming Home Party' was one of the only selections Perry brought in that had been written by established songwriters. Composed by Diane Hildebrand and Jack Keller, it details the experience of a man visiting home and trying to keep his cool at a party thrown for him by the company he once kept—and Tiny hated it.

'[It's] the worst song [on the album]!' Tiny told Ernie Clark. 'This is a

---

* Comedian Groucho Marx, who had a personal relationship with Berlin, would often sing the song publicly in order to embarrass Berlin, who once offered him $100 not to perform the song again.

† The song was actually used instead of 'Fill Your Heart' as the B-side of 'Tip-Toe' in some foreign territories such as France and Spain.

‡ Gordon Alexander released his own album, *Gordon's Buster*, on Columbia records shortly after.

song I never would have recorded, but Mr. Perry wanted to have this on the album. ... No offense to the writers, but I don't like story songs. My opinion is always give the public ten top hits on an album. Never try to experiment with your talents on the audience's dollar.'

After a three-day break, Tiny and Perry were back to the studio on December 19, tackling Tiny's choice, 'Tip-Toe Thru' The Tulips With Me,' and Perry's choices, 'Daddy, Daddy What Is Heaven Like?' and 'This is All I Ask.' 'Tip-Toe' would become the album's only single, and would thereafter be synonymous with Tiny Tim, and Tiny Tim with the ukulele. It may come as a revelation to some, then, that Tiny did not play ukulele on the track. It did, however, take some years for him to admit this fact.

'I didn't play the ukulele part on "Tip-Toe,"' he told Johnny Pineapple in 1994. "A professional musician [played it] ... it's amazing.' He did however play small ukulele parts on 'Never Hit Your Grandma With A Shovel' and the introductions to 'Then I'd Be Satisfied With Life' and 'I Got You, Babe.'

'Daddy, Daddy, What Is Heaven Like?' by writer/producer Artie Wayne is a conversation between a young boy and his father after the death of the boy's mother. 'I liked the melody of that.' Tiny told Ernie Clark. '[It] could have had a chance for the Top 10.' Perry suggested Tiny record the father's character in a bombastic, Southern baritone reminiscent of Johnny Cash.

'This Is All I Ask,' the album's sweeping orchestral closer, was written by Gordon Jenkins. A crooner classic, it has been recorded by everyone from Frank Sinatra to Andy Williams. Tiny's earnest delivery epitomizes Perry and Butler's approach to making the record a 'combination of the serious and [Tiny's] child-like approach.' Gordon reportedly thought Tiny's version was 'one of the tops.'

'I treated Tiny like he was a crooner,' Artie Butler recalled of the session. 'I wrote the arrangements as if I was writing for a regular crooner like Sinatra or Jack Jones.'

After a break for the holidays, Perry and Tiny returned to the studio in January to wrap up work on 'On The Old Front Porch,' 'Stay Down Here Where You Belong,' and 'The Other Side.' They also recorded the album's introduction, 'Welcome To My Dream,' a forgotten number from the 1946 film *Road To Utopia* starring Bing Crosby. Though it came from Tiny's repertoire, Perry believed the song was perfect to open the album. 'It opens up with [that song],' he later explained, 'because this is someone who was thrown out of every office in the record business.'

These sessions also yielded a cover of Sonny & Cher's 'I Got You, Babe,' recorded as a duet between Tiny and himself, and 'The Viper.' The latter stands out as perhaps the oddest track on the album, a classic campfire tale of a 'viper' (Tiny) who calls a terrified apartment tenant (also Tiny), to announce his imminent arrival, culminating in the punch line, 'I'm the Viper, I've come to vipe your vindows.' Tiny later said that he included it as a tribute to songwriter Norman Blagman, who briefly managed him, and who wrote 'Put The Blame On Me' and 'Give Me The Right' for Elvis. '[Blagman] was a great songwriter and should have been a big star,' Tiny told Ernie Clark. 'I told him once that if I ever made it I would not forget him, so I used "The Viper."'

While 'Tip-Toe Thru' The Tulips With Me' would be forever linked to Tiny Tim's legacy, the entire album is considered a masterpiece not only by Tiny Tim enthusiasts but also by numerous critics. 'No one, in a million years, would have ever thought that Tiny Tim would be able to make, not only an album,' Perry later told *E!*, 'but, an album that, I am very proud to say, was revered by the rock intelligentsia, by the public, everyone.'

Warner Bros/Reprise shared Perry's enthusiasm and 'really flipped' when Perry made a presentation of the album for the whole company. Tiny, however, became much more critical of the album in subsequent years, conceding that Perry 'did a good production' but complaining bitterly that, for him, something was amiss. 'Even though the first album [was successful],' he told Harry Stein, 'I was far from satisfied with it. With the exception of a few cuts … I'm not proud of that album. Something was missing. You can fool the public, but you can't fool yourself.'

* * *

Aside from recording, Tiny had been busy enjoying a highly active social life in Los Angeles. He had taken a liking to Miss Pam, a secretary at TTG recording studio, and, unable to wait until the end of the year, awarded her with one of his trophies. He had also been spending a lot of his time with a new friend, the twenty-year-old blonde-haired, blue-eyed Miss Robin, whose nearness, Tiny said, made his songs 'take on a vibrato different than at normal times.'

Aside from inviting Robin to his recording sessions, Tiny managed to convince Richard Perry, at least momentarily, to agree to let her sing with him on his next album. He had her photographed alongside him during the album cover photo shoot with acclaimed art director and photographer Ed Thrasher, and dropped her name—alongside those of Miss Cleo and Miss Corky—into a spoken-word portion of 'Then I'd Be Satisfied With Life.' Robin also accompanied him to an early screening of Peter Yarrow's *You Are What You Eat*. There, they mingled with Mama Cass Elliot and Papa John Phillips of The Mamas & The Papas as well as Beatles press officer Derek Taylor.

On January 22, with *God Bless Tiny Tim* in the can, Richard Perry threw a party for Tiny at his house. That same evening, Tiny's first appearance on *Rowan & Martin's Laugh-In* aired on prime time. Tiny's introduction to Dick Martin and Dan Rowan had taken place when Richard Perry brought Tiny to meet them during a break in recording *God Bless Tiny Tim*. Following a well-received pilot episode, which aired in September 1967, the first episode was scheduled to air on January 22 1968. The show's creators were working feverishly on the new season, and had formed an ensemble cast of young comedians, including Henry Gibson and an as-yet-undiscovered Goldie Hawn.

Laugh-In producer George Schlatter was heavily engaged in a writing session when he was interrupted by a request from Digby Wolfe, another of the show's writers, to introduce a special guest. At first, George denied the request, but he begrudgingly conceded after Wolfe's insistence. In walked Richard Perry, followed by Tiny Tim.

'What do you do?' George asked skeptically. Tiny proceeded to pull his ukulele from a paper shopping bag and launch into a falsetto rendition of a nonsensical British novelty song from 1943, 'Mairzy Doates.' As Tiny performed, Richard Perry eyed the other men in the room, who gradually lost themselves to hysterics. 'I'd never seen a room with grown men crying,' Perry later told *E!* 'I mean, everybody was laughing so hard there were tears coming out, and I had seen him perform a countless number of times, I started crying as well. It was really amazing.'

'We wanted some acts that were extremely unusual and bizarre,' Dan Rowan later told *Pageant* magazine. 'We knew we had a winner when Tiny Tim walked through the door and pulled that ukulele out of his shopping bag. We cut two shows with him.'

Tiny later described the meeting as 'the only audition I ever made.' In fact, in order to secure a spot for Tiny on the show, *Laugh-In's* producers had told skeptical NBC executives that Tiny was a celebrity in disguise. Additionally, Schlatter saw to it that co-host Dick Martin did not meet Tiny before the taping, nor have any knowledge of his appearance. Co-host Dan Rowan turned to Martin during the show and said, 'I've got a surprise for you.'

'You're kidding.' said Martin with a grin. 'You've got a surprise for me so early in the evening?'

'Wait till you see this, pal,' Rowan said, turning to the camera. 'Straight from Greenwich Village, and his first appearance anywhere, Tiny Tim!'

Out stepped Tiny Tim wearing his patented white makeup and a wrinkled sports coat, toting his ukulele in a large shopping bag. Dan Rowan left the stage, leaving Tiny and Dick Martin standing next to one another. After blowing a few kisses to the audience, Tiny reaching into his shopping bag, pulled out his ukulele, and began a medley of 'A Tisket A Tasket' and 'On The Good Ship Lollipop.'

After a moment of genuine shock, Dick Martin regained his composure and began to ham it up, making exaggerated expressions and reacting to Tiny's high notes and hand gestures, giving license to the stunned audience to laugh at Tiny's bizarre performance. When Tiny finished, the *Laugh-In* band played an outro as Tiny gathered his things and, blowing kisses to Martin and the audience, left the stage. Rowan joined Martin.

'A real surprise for you?'

'You searched high and low for that one, didn't you?'

'It kept him out of the service.'

'I bet the army burned his draft card!'

The studio audience ate it up, and Tiny predicted in his diary that the appearance 'will be the big one.'

Tiny Tim's segment was sandwiched between stars like Pam Austin, Flip Wilson, Barbara Feldon, and The Strawberry Alarm Clock. But it was Tiny Tim who struck a nerve. The NBC publicity department was flooded with letters, 98 percent of which, according to Tiny, were not positive. 'The reaction to his first appearance was immediate and fantastic,' Dan Rowan told *Pageant*. 'Letters and phone calls poured in. *What is he? Who is he? What kind of put-on is this?* And Dick and I had to answer, He's for real.'

As Tiny recalled in a 1979 interview, one letter contained a caricature of him that said he had 'underarm odor,' while another called him 'a disgrace to TV.' 'This was half of the country,' he added. 'Oh, how horrible … yet, they were all viewing it when I was on. … Whether they liked me or not, I don't know, but there was something to draw them, you see? Whether it's good or bad, if you have that drawing charisma for TV, they have to look at you. It puts that dial on.'

A few days after *Laugh-In* aired, Tiny returned to New York City by train.

He was still living with his parents, and the pressure was still affecting him. 'Had a nice day with my folks at home—but I was mean and bad to them,' he wrote in his diary. 'Thanks as they're still alive—after what I've done.'

He had been down this road before—a major studio recording and a network television appearance—but last time the recordings went unreleased and the network, intimidated by bad press, decided not to have him back. Back in New York, Tiny began spending time with his East Coast friends while staying in touch with Richard Perry by telephone. He located Miss Corky and Miss Cleo, who had tied for most beautiful girls of 1967, and gave them the trophies he had been unable to present before leaving for California.

* * *

On February 5, *Laugh-In* aired its second segment with Tiny. Once again, Dan Rowan brought Tiny Tim onstage to sing for a skeptical Dick Martin.

'I've got another surprise for you,' Rowan told Martin.

'Oh! For a minute I thought you were going to bring back Tiny Tim!' Martin laughed.

With that, a voice rang out from backstage—'You called? Leader?'—and out walked Tiny Tim. The audience cheered. Before leaving Martin alone with Tiny, Rowan turned to him and said, 'Wait until you see this, Dick. Tiny has added a bit of choreography to his usual presentation.'

'And there is nothing usual about Tiny Tim's presentation!'

As Tiny pulled out his ukulele, a hush fell over the audience. Tiny sang 'Tip-Toe Thru' The Tulips With Me'—the first time he had played the song on national television. After the song, Tiny again blew kisses to Martin and the audience before disappearing backstage. Rowan then joined Martin on the stage again and said, 'He's like a fine wine! He just improves with age!'

'I think his cork slips, too!' quipped Martin.

In New York, some of Tiny's former associates caught wind of his new trajectory. A Mr. Schacter, with whom Tiny had apparently signed a contract in September 1966, sent a letter to Warner Bros, threatening suit should *God Bless Tiny Tim* be released. Kiki Hall from the Page Three, who had retained some control as one of Tiny's handlers, called Tiny's apartment and cursed at Butros, forcing Tiny to sever all ties with him. Soon, Hall, too, would launch a lawsuit of his own, about which Tiny vowed emphatically, 'Most sincerely I say that I will be singing in the streets before he gets a cent.'

Contrary to Perry's warning, Tiny visited Steve Paul at the Scene, where

Paul urged Tiny to sign a contract with him. Tiny declined but promised to visit again soon. Afterward, a frantic Paul sent Tiny a telegram at his house, stating, 'Perhaps I will understand in the future.' Despite all Paul had done, Tiny no longer needed him or the Scene, and he had arguably paid his dues by performing for close to two years, nightly, for little pay. 'I believe fighting times as well as successful times are on the horizon for me,' Tiny wrote in his journal.

Toward the end of February, Tiny appeared on the cover of *Billboard* magazine and was pleased when a couple of young girls recognized him in the library. As the weather warmed, so did Tiny's career, and on March 4 1968, Tiny, along with his parents, heard himself on the radio for the first time. Bob Fass played cuts from *God Bless Tiny Tim* on *Radio Unnameable* on WBAI in New York City. The next day, WNEW DJ William B. Williams also began playing the record, and Tiny appeared on Fass's program in person. Before leaving New York, Tiny visited the Scene one more time, where Steve Paul made a last ditch effort to officially sign Tiny as his client. Tiny did not budge. On March 16, he returned to Los Angeles.

With the album recorded and its release scheduled for the following month, Warner Bros' next order of business was finding Tiny a management film to handle engagements substantial enough to garner publicly for the upcoming release. The label approached the brand-new management firm Campbell Silver Cosby, Inc., founded by movie producer Bruce Campbell and Roy Silver, the manager of popular comedian and the third partner in the company, Bill Cosby.

The corporation, located in Beverly Hills, had close to one hundred employees, many of whom were eager to be talent managers themselves. Tiny had been on Roy Silver's radar since 1962. He had been working at the time for Albert Grossman, who threatened to fire Silver if he signed Tiny. Now, with the power to sign whomever he pleased, Silver approached an enthusiastic young upstart, Ron DeBlasio, about Tiny.

'I got to tell you,' said Silver, 'this is something here that I don't know I can do, but if you want to do it, you can do it … but this guy is a wacko.'

'Well they're all wackos,' DeBlasio replied.

'No, no, no, you don't understand,' said Silver. 'This guy is a *major* wacko.'

'Really?'

'Oh, yeah.'

'Well, get me a copy of the album.'

Silver provided DeBlasio with a copy of the album, and, upon listening to it, DeBlasio was floored.

'What are you talking about?' DeBlasio demanded. 'This is great!'

'Wait until you see him,' Silver replied with a grin.

Shortly thereafter, Mo Ostin brought Tiny Tim to DeBlasio's office. 'He came in. He had on the same outfit he was wearing on the cover of the album,' DeBlasio recalls. 'He had his ukulele, and white makeup, and hair that looked like he didn't wash. He had very sincere eyes and was really reaching out. That's the thing that really impressed me. He was odd, but he wasn't dumb. He was probably unaware and naive, but he definitely had a lot of spark and asked the right questions, I thought.'

Ostin explained that he had invested a lot of time and effort into Tiny Tim and needed the best management possible. 'He needed things other than the traditional way of promoting an album,' says DeBlasio, who was intrigued but not yet ready to make a decision. 'I thought he was … odd. I told him I would get back to him, and it wasn't about fifteen minutes after leaving the building, Tiny was already on my phone talking to me like I was his manager!'

Knowing now that he would soon have to make a decision, DeBlasio told Tiny he would call him back and spoke to Roy Silver, who gave him one more chance to back out, asking, 'Are you sure you want to commit to this thing? It's up to you.'

'This guy's already on the phone!' exclaimed DeBlasio.

'So what do you think?' asked Silver.

'You know,' DeBlasio replied, 'there isn't a template for him, because he does not fit in any of the categories of the present music business right now, but it's adventurous enough and risky. There's no other career like this, and it's a hell of a challenge. Yeah, I think I'd like to take on this challenge. It could be pretty provocative, it also could be mind bending, and it also could be a major pain in the ass, and it probably could be all three of these.'

'It probably will be all three of those,' said Silver.

'Well, all right,' said DeBlasio, sealing the deal. He would later relate that the next few years 'seemed like a lifetime.'

It became clear almost immediately that managing Tiny would entail a great deal more than securing concert and television appearances, when Tiny asked Silver's permission to go out to the Whisky A Go-Go with Miss Catherine, the girl who had abruptly replaced Miss Robin as the apple of his eye. As Tiny fretted over this Miss Catherine, whom he believed might marry him, his management was busy making moves to secure him a more prominent spot on an upcoming episode of *Laugh-In*—this time for a song and an interview.

After Rowan's introduction, the entire cast filed out, one by one, between two billboard-sized pictures of Tiny Tim, and sang a tribute song to him. Upon the final note, Tiny shuffled onto the stage between the large photos, with Goldie Hawn trailing behind him, throwing flower petals into the air. He was dressed in his usual wrinkled sports jacket, but this time had a large black cape—a curious costume piece evidently given to him by Roy Silver—draped over his shoulders. Standing between Rowan and Martin, Tiny Tim, for the first time, answered a few questions.

First, Rowan asked his age. 'Oh! I feel so young!' Tiny replied, speaking just like he sang—in falsetto. 'I really feel nineteen again!' This would be Tiny Tim's standard answer to this question for some time to give him the appearance of timelessness. (In reality, he was nearing his thirty-sixth birthday.) After discussing his upcoming album and role in *You Are What You Eat*, the conversation turned to Tiny's voice.

'When did your voice change?' Martin asked.

'Oh, it was always like this!'

The audience was in stitches, and Tiny was really hamming it up. He reached into his shopping bag, took out a ukulele case, and gently extracted his ukulele with trembling hands. 'Oh, there it is again!' Martin commented, 'look at it just slide out of there!' 'Tip-Toe' was the album's single, and the obvious choice to perform again. This time he accompanied himself on the ukulele, with support from the *Laugh-In* band, who played an arrangement similar to the album's. Strumming, blowing kisses, and warbling away with his eyes looking up at the studio ceiling, Tiny Tim finished the song amidst laughter and thunderous applause. At the end of the tune, Hawn handed him a bouquet of flowers and pulled him offstage as he furiously blew kisses to the audience before disappearing from sight.

The *Laugh-In* appearances did a tremendous amount to generate publicity. The single 'Tip-Toe Thru' The Tulips With Me' was strategically released on April 3, the day before Tiny was scheduled to make his first appearance on *The Tonight Show* with Johnny Carson. Tiny had been booked on the show by a man named Craig Tennis, who had done so on a tip from a friend who had seen Tiny on *Laugh-In*. Tennis knew he was taking a risk that might impact his own career. Nevertheless, after a pre-show interview with Tiny and Ron DeBlasio, he prepared a briefing and a series of potential questions for Carson to ask during the interview. He later related to biographer Harry Stein that his briefing included the following warning:

TINY TIM IS OUTSPOKEN, AND WHEN HE GETS WRAPPED UP IN A SUBJECT WILL CONTINUE WITH IT FOREVER. HE WILL, AND CAN, TALK ON VIRTUALLY ANY SUBJECT, INCLUDING IMPURITIES IN SOAP. HE IS FOR REAL, BUT WHAT HE REALLY IS, IS THE REAL QUESTION.

On the afternoon of April 4, Dr. Martin Luther King Jr. was assassinated. Craig Tennis weighed in on the scenario during an interview for the Tiny Tim episode of *E! True Hollywood Story*, stating, 'It was rather distressing to have this frivolous, although highly entertaining, spot [with Tiny Tim] on the air while the other networks were simultaneously airing retrospectives on Dr. King.'

Tennis also told Harry Stein that other members of the staff and crew at *The Tonight Show* kept their distance from him when he showed up with Tiny at the studio. Johnny Carson, too, would later admit that he was never 'more startled' than he had been on the night of Tiny Tim's first appearance on the show. 'The first time I heard that name you all think of Tiny Tim, Dickens' *Christmas Carol*, but somebody said, No this is a fella who calls himself Tiny Tim and he is *different*. Which was the understatement of two decades!'

'This album, right here,' Carson announced to the audience, holding up a copy of *God Bless Tiny Tim*, 'I understand was the biggest advanced seller at the recent record convention in Miami Beach ... and people like Bob Dylan, Peter Paul & Mary, predicted that this next gentleman is gonna be the biggest record seller, I guess, of this coming year. ... [He's] very sincere. He *is* different [*audience laughter*]. No, no really! Like a flower child or something like that.'

'This is not the day and age of ordinary or run of the mill,' added sidekick Ed McMahon, 'and he is certainly not ordinary or run of the mill.'

'That's right. Would you welcome, please, Tiny Tim ... '

Doc Severinsen's band played a brief arrangement from *God Bless*, and Tiny entered the stage. He performed 'Tip-Toe' and 'Livin' In The Sunlight, Lovin' In The Moonlight,' which were met with enthusiastic applause. Blowing kisses and bowing, he wandered over to the guest chair. Johnny Carson, famously quick on his feet, was at a loss for words.

'That, uh, heh. That's the damndest act I've ever seen,' he finally said. Armed with Craig Tennis's questions—which urged him to ask about Tiny's age, hygienic habits, and feelings about girls—Carson dug in, opening by praising Tiny's performance of 'Livin' In The Sunlight' but appearing increasingly thrown by each of Tiny's answers. With Carson clearly rattled, Ed McMahon attempted to get off the stage to prepare for a commercial, declaring, 'I'll be backstage if you need me!'

Eventually, Carson was able to take command of the interview, touching on all of the major topics upon which the media would thereafter focus incessantly. When asked about his influences, Tiny detailed his affinity for Henry Burr, Irving Kaufman, Billy Murray, and Arthur Fields, prompting Carson to ask Tiny his age, eliciting a giggle from Tiny, thus inciting laughter and applause from the audience, with Tiny answering, 'Ageless.'

From there, after Carson remarked that Tiny looked 'to be in good shape,' Tiny explained his unique diet. 'I have a lot of wonderful health foods,' he said. 'See, the inside of the body must have as much care as the outside. I have a concoction of sunflower seeds, wheat germ, and pumpkin seeds, all in one glass, and I put honey on top of that and I eat it with a spoon, and it's so nutritious that it seems to vibrate my whole body and after that, you know, honey is really the basis of life, and I eat a lot of honey. Also, I have lots of raw vegetables. Grapefruits, raw grapefruits.'

Having opened the flood gate to Tiny's views on personal health, Carson asked Tiny to explain why he had been described as a 'shower nut.'

'Well, it's just I love to keep my body clean,' he replied. 'It's not just that the body alone has to be clean, the soul has to be clean first and if the soul is clean then the body can be always clean. I love to keep my body clean afterward so I can be, uh, real pleasant in public. … For instance, sometimes a girl and a boy may go on a date, and she may say to him, Darling, I just remembered I have to go home, but she may be thinking, Why doesn't he use so and so's soap? So basically I always love to keep clean.'

This gave Carson a chance to subtly ask if Tiny preferred women. 'Are you, um … I'll think of something. Are you married?' Carson asked. Tiny giggled loudly in response, prompting Carson to reach for a pen and paper and ask whether he should 'put that down as a no.'

'Marriage is such a wonderful thing,' Tiny replied, 'but I couldn't get married for a long time, because I love all those beautiful girls, just to look at them, of course, and to write songs and poetry to them and to give them advice about romance.'

'Do you date often?' Carson asked.

'No, I don't go out too often on dates, because I love to follow the Dodgers in baseball and the Leafs in hockey, and the thing is, I get so romantically involved in hockey when the Leafs play in the wintertime and the Dodgers play baseball in the spring … I can't do anything else when the Dodgers and Leafs play, especially when they're involved in the Pennant Race and the Stanley Cup Playoff.'

'In other words,' Carson asked, 'if a game's on, between the Maple Leafs and a girl, you'd take the Maple Leafs?'

'Oh-ho-ho-hoooo!' Tiny giggled.

To close the segment, Tiny performed a version of 'Ever Since You Told Me That You Love Me (I'm A Nut).' The song's lyrics, particularly 'there's something wrong with me' and 'it feels so queer,' sent the audience into hysterics. Upon finishing, Tiny stood up from the guest couch and left the set through the stage curtains, but not before becoming tangled up in them. Carson helped Tiny untangle himself, looked back at the audience, and pronounced, 'Well, uh, there's no business like show business, that's like no business I know! We'll be right back, folks!'

The reception to Tiny's appearance on the show was tremendous, and Tiny knew he had struck a nerve, writing in his diary that he had gone 'over very good on the Johnny Carson show and really almost brought the house down.' *Laugh-In* had given Tiny his national debut, but the nature of the show left audiences wondering whether or not this androgynous creature with bedraggled hair, a battered ukulele, falsetto voice, and a repertoire of vintage songs was for real. Tiny's appearance on *The Tonight Show* made it clear that Tiny Tim was not just a character for *Laugh-In*, and revealed some stranger truths about this man who had until recently lived with his parents, subsisted on a diet of honey, wheat germ, and pumpkin seeds, harbored an obsessive affinity for cleanliness, and who would rather watch the Dodgers or Maple Leafs rather than go on a date with a girl. And now they wanted more.

CHAPTER SIX
THE HOLY FREAK

In May [1968], the whole world said what my neighbors and relatives were saying: 'What's wrong with this guy?'

TINY TIM TO KENT THOMPSON OF THE *IOWA FALLS TIMES*, MAY 1 1993

As the spotlight of fame turned its unforgiving gaze upon Tiny, every part of his personhood came under scrutiny. The fact that he had been so unabashed about his bizarre lifestyle both exhilarated and disappointed the media. Eager to dredge up inconsistencies in his innocent demeanor, they continued to question his authenticity. 'If Tiny Tim weren't for real, he would have been demolished by Johnny Carson,' a critic for United Press International argued on Tiny's behalf. 'Instead, Tiny Tim was completely untouched by the wisecracks, left himself wholly and innocently vulnerable—thereby becoming indestructible—and transformed Carson into a straight man, winning away the audience and even the show.'

Though Tiny Tim's eccentricities and his music would become inexorably linked, *God Bless Tiny Tim* was standing its ground as a viable musical product. As the album arrived at number 125 on the *Cashbox* charts in April, Tiny wrote in his journal, 'I believe it will be #1 by July 15.' Indeed, the record was on the move, and Tiny's management, along with Reprise Records, were doing their part in making sure it continued. Though many who saw Tiny on TV found his persona and music perplexing, many of the reviewers who sat down to actually listen to *God Bless Tiny Tim* were astounded by what they heard.

In his review for the *New York Times* dated April 28 1968, Albert Goldman declared, 'Tiny Tim has never sounded better than he does on his recent album. Richard Perry, the record producer, did a remarkable job of contextualizing the artist's essence within the ambiance of psychedelically inspired rock music. The album is a dream theater that echoes beguilingly with all the voices of

Tiny Tim … to say that these are the most perfect impersonations of old singers ever heard would hardly do justice to the art that has re-embodied these entertainers in electronic avatars, summoning them up out of the past to caper again before a strobe-lit oleo.'

For Rick Du Brow of UPI, the album was 'a masterpiece, an instant collector's piece that reveals [Tiny Tim's] timeless feel for music both old and new, and radiates a shining innocence throughout the uproarious humor, touching ballads, and new world musical commentary. It is not merely a record, but a show, a major production that transmits the magic of theater.'

In June, *LIFE* magazine's Al Aronowitz called *God Bless Tiny Tim* 'one of the most dazzling albums of programmed entertainment to come along since The Beatles introduced the new genre of pop with *Sgt Pepper's Lonely Hearts Club Band*. If *Sgt Pepper* was a wide-screen epic, Tiny's album is a full-length animated cartoon, with Tiny doing all the voices.' A year later, Alexander Ross of *Maclean's* echoed these sentiments, hailing the album as 'probably the most interesting musical effort since The Beatles' *Sgt. Pepper* album.'

Of course, there were the inevitable bad reviews, such as one from Chick Ober of the *St. Petersburg Times*, published on June 15 1968. 'The accompaniment is frequently so loud that Tiny Tim's reedlike tones are obliterated,' he wrote, 'and that could be a blessing … The program includes ["Tip-Toe"], which has become the Tiny Tim trademark. If you've never heard it, congratulations. … Perhaps he should make another album and forget the falsetto. But then it must have taken guts and a strong stomach to make even one Tiny Tim album.'

Nonetheless, the album sold 100,000 copies within a week of its release, and Tiny began to pick up some good press. The *New York Times* had all but ignored Tiny Tim until *God Bless* broke; now it ran Albert Goldman's glowing article, 'And He Keeps His Ukulele In A Shopping Bag.' In the article, Goldman came out swinging in defense of Tiny Tim and seemed bent on making sure that the newspaper made up for the fact that it had been asleep at the switch regarding one of New York City's most interesting acts.

'Tiny Tim is a holy freak,' Goldman wrote. 'How splendid that today the word should be a term of endearment and unabashed admiration. He reduced Johnny Carson to his straight man with a few child-like answers; Carson, his radar scanning the house, realized immediately that Tiny Tim's obvious vulnerability made him untouchable.

'Tiny Tim belongs not to an age but to an ancient tradition … what lifts

[him] miles above nostalgia, the rickey-tick, the pop archaeology of even the finest rock groups, The Beatles, the Stones, The Lovin' Spoonful, is that where they are doing an "impression" of something they hardly know, he is directly in touch with a musical and theatrical past that speaks from his mouth with the frightening authority of a dybbuk.'

Tiny called Goldman's piece 'the greatest article anyone had ever written about me' and was most pleased that Goldman had mentioned the names of the artists he emulated, Irving Kaufman and Arthur Fields. As much as Tiny loved the article, however, some of the *Times'* readers disagreed with Goldman's exhalations, resulting in a slew of letters to the editor. On May 19 1968, the paper ran three letters from readers who had a hard time grasping the article.

The first, from Eleanor Van Zandt of New York City, began, 'Albert Goldman is correct in saying "Only today could Tiny Tim have become a famous entertainer." Ours is the only age to embrace the spurious and glorify the sick. Otherwise, Mr. Goldman seems rather confused. Tiny Tim is not the Moulin Rouge by Toulouse-Lautrec, but the Charenton by P.T. Barnum; not St. Theresa in drag but Medusa in the Emperor's New Clothes. Let's give this poor "lost lithograph" a shampoo and see that he gets lost again. Come, come, Mr. Goldman, you *can't* be serious.'

Next came a much shorter response from a Robert LaBarbe, also of New York City: 'Tiny Tim? Yich!'

The third letter, from a Leif P. Wilson of Fort Walton Beach, Florida, carried several questions for Goldman. 'Are you, or are you not putting us on with that article? If you are expressing your evaluation of his talents in a straightforward and honest manner, about all I can say is that you are entitled your own opinion even though it may deviate a little from the norm. But, sir, if you are being satirical I would have to say that your article was the most fantastic display of wisdom insight I have ever read. In a word, to your way of thinking—veracity or absurdity?'

Goldman's points were not lost on all of his readers, however. A few weeks later, the *Times* ran a response from a Robert J. Cahn of New York City in defense of Tiny Tim and Goldman.

I am distressed by the sick, hate-filled reactions of the three readers whose letters you published to Tiny Tim and to Albert Goldman's story about him. If the public personality of this uniquely gifted comic artist were phony, fraudulent, a put-on, their comments *might* be justified. But, as Mr. Goldman's story made clear, he is exactly the same person privately that he is while performing: his wonderful eccentricities and enthusiasms are *real*; his perpetual optimism is *exactly* that and he is the only genuinely and completely innocent adult I have ever met, or am ever likely to meet.

As shocked and confused as Goldman's readers were, the vitriol espoused in their letters did nothing to hinder Tiny as *God Bless Tiny Tim* entered the *Billboard* album charts at number 167 on May 4, a few days after Tiny made his second appearance on *The Tonight Show* on April 30.

'He's a very gentle,' Carson began, only to be interrupted by the audience's laughter. 'He is! He's a very gentle, humble guy. What can I tell you about him? … And he is back. Is he gonna sing for us? Would you welcome Tiny Tim.'

With an oversized button reading 'Charge Dodgers' pinned to his suit jacket, Tiny appeared onstage with his ukulele in hand and treated the audience to a falsetto version of the 1936 hit 'At The Codfish Ball,' prompting the audience to clap along to the beat. When Tiny sat down in the guest chair afterward, with the audience still cheering, Carson said, 'I'll tell you, you absolutely break it up here. You break it up.'

'Thank you, Mr. Carson,' Tiny replied, 'for what you've done and for what everyone has done.'

'How have things been going since you were last here?' asked Carson.

'Mr. Carson, you don't know what being on this show has done,' said Tiny, drifting into a sort of stream of consciousness. 'I'm not trying to say it to make you feel good—it's the truth. The fact is that I've been getting calls, uh, from Alabama and friends have come up to me in the street and they say, oh, we saw you on Mr. Carson's show and I said, well, everyone was so nice to me and they seem to say to me, and they say to me was it easy for you to talk with him? Did he make you feel at ease? I said, not only did he make me feel at ease, but he's so healthy.'

The audience exploded with laughter at the homoerotic tenor Tiny's compliment seemed to take. Nevertheless, Carson accepted the compliment.

'Ha ha,' he replied, 'that's the first time anyone's told me that … I appreciate the compliment. A clean body is a clean mind.' Tiny then revealed that, inspired by Carson, he had started a new workout routine, which involved six sit-ups, six push-ups, and clapping his hands above his head ten times. This, too, was met with laughter from the befuddled audience.

At one point in the conversation, sensing that perhaps the audience doubted his sincerity, Tiny remarked, 'People think I'm putting them on. They can think whatever they want, but they can do what [politician] Al Smith said and "take a look at the record."'*

'You like the old songs, don't you?' Carson asked, steering the conversation back to music.

'I love rock'n'roll now,' Tiny explained. 'Not only that, but I'm crazy about rock'n'roll: great songs like "Mother In Law," "Let The Little Girl Dance," and "You Got What It Takes." These are beautiful, melodic tunes ... I believe that melody makes the song ... I love rock'n'roll.' Then, in a complete contrast to his endorsement of rock'n'roll, he picked up his ukulele and treated the studio to a falsetto version of 'Animal Crackers.'

After that, Tiny pulled ingredients from his shopping bag and mixed up his concoction of wheat germ, sunflower seeds, pumpkin seeds, and honey, right on the show while the incredulous Carson and the audience watched. At Tiny's insistence, Carson tried a spoonful, causing the audience to erupt with laughter at his facial expressions while chewing.

'I'll tell you, it's very good,' he conceded, after swallowing.

At the close of the segment, Tiny treated the audience to another surprise. *The Tonight Show* band, outfitted with a string section, broke into 'This Is All I Ask', and Tiny dropped into his tenor. It was the first time he had performed in his natural voice on television. Carson was impressed. The audience watched in stunned silence.

Returning to the guest chair, Tiny found Carson nodding with approval. 'I'll tell you, well, you broke it up again, Tiny. That's kind of a Russ Columbo style on that one?'

'Mixed with Mr. Crosby,' said Tiny, clearly pleased.

'There's more there than meets the eye,' said Carson, as the audience began to laugh again. 'No, I meant that as a compliment! I meant that as a compliment!'

Unbeknown to audiences, Roy Silver and Ron DeBlasio had refused to let Tiny appear unless he performed 'a serious song.'

* * *

'Dear Lord, Thanks for the most fantastic happenings,' Tiny wrote on May

---

* Al Smith was the deceased former governor of New York, and a Democrat nominee for president in 1928.

2. 'People stop me wherever I go on the streets and I sign autographs ... although I've hardly rested, and have a hoarse throat due to a cold, it is wild.'

On May 9, Tiny opened a bill featuring H.P. Lovecraft, Crome Syrcus, and The Loading Zone at the Fillmore West Auditorium. He was backed by The Holy Mackerel and a few of the musicians who played on *God Bless Tiny Tim*. 'To paraphrase the back of his album,' said the man introducing Tiny to the San Francisco crowd, 'the world is wide with many things within, but few so rare as him, God bless Tiny Tim.' The introduction was met with a huge round of applause, and Tiny shuffled out onto the stage to a prerecorded version of the 'The Stripper.'

Tiny opened the show with 'Livin' In The Sunlight, Lovin' In The Moonlight,' during which he halted the song's intro several times to thank the crowd for their applause, followed by 'Animal Crackers' and then 'On The Old Front Porch.' From there, he performed a live version of 'The Viper,' which served as an introduction to 'Stay Down Here Where You Belong.' Then, and perhaps playing up to his audience, he displayed a 'little pipe' given to him by a Miss Anne, who 'made it herself.' The crowd cheered enthusiastically.

'My dear friends, it's such a thrill to be here in San Francisco, and I can't thank you for your wonderfulness ... [and] at this time we're going to try something different,' he said, before delivering a version of Lavern Baker's 1954 hit 'Tweedlee Dee' in an Elvis-style baritone. He then concluded the show with 'Tip-Toe,' 'I Got You, Babe,' and, after calls for more, an encore of 'Earth Angel,' during which Tiny narrowly missed his cue to sing due to his profuse thanking of the audience. *Time* later reported that the hip audience were 'rapt, incredulous, amused—everything but indifferent' as they listened to Tiny's 'vibrato voice quivering like a hummingbird's wings.'

It seemed that 'Tip-Toe''s trajectory meant breaking onto the *Billboard* singles chart was only a matter of time. It did so on May 18, while Tiny was being photographed for the cover of *Esquire*, entering at number 83. To complement Tiny's unconventional style, the single broke unconventionally, too, as Tiny explained in a 1979 interview. 'Normally when a record breaks, it breaks from California back to New York,' he said. This time, however, things were different. 'California would not play the record ... it was way out ... too extreme ... so Seattle broke it, but nothing happened. Finally, one out of ten million shots, Rick Sklar, the [program director of WABC] in New York, decided to go on it a month later and he broke the record from New York, which is usually where records wind up. So good old New York didn't let me down … it went back to California a hit already. Some disc jockey, I think it was Birmingham, Alabama, went on strike. He said he refused to play the record. That's how much pandemonium that record received.' In fact, many radio stations played the song as a gimmick, sometimes playing only a few bars to lead in to ad breaks.

On May 14, in a paradoxical turn of events, Tiny was invited to enjoy a Dodgers game from the home team's dugout. In contrast to the jeers and threats he had received the year prior, this time the police were on hand to control rabid fans leaning over the dugout roof for Tiny's autograph. Broadcaster Vin Skully even announced on the air that Tiny was in attendance. When the Dodgers lost 3–1 to the Houston Astros, an Astros player called out to Tiny, 'Let's see you tiptoe now!'

Tiny continued watching games from the dugout for some time. 'It's so vitally important to me to be as close as I can get to my Dodgers!' he told the *Los Angeles Herald-Examiner*. 'I just want to reach out from the dugout and touch the grass.'

With Tiny's new celebrity came an unofficial invite into Hollywood's upper echelon. Dean Stockwell sent him a gift and invited him to his home. Cynthia McAdams visited him at his hotel. He visited Zsa Zsa Gabor at her house. He attended parties with Warren Beatty, Julie Christie, Elsa Lancaster, Candice Bergen, Leslie Cannon, Tommy Boyce, Bobby Hart, and Oliver. He rubbed shoulders with Jack Lemmon, Jackie Cooper, and Phil Spector at LA's nightclubs. He was so busy and in demand that his schedule would not permit him to attend the roast of Tom Jones or sing the national anthem for the Dodgers. At one party, Beatty introduced Tiny to his old obsession, Tuesday Weld, and the entire party paused to watch as Tiny serenaded her with 'Dear Tuesday.'* In the wake of Robert Kennedy's assassination, Shelly Winters invited Tiny to her house and explained that she was responsible for President Kennedy's death, as she had not acted on a premonition that he would be killed. 'When did you have this premonition that the president would die?' he asked her. 'Did you see the date, did you see who would do it, did you see the time and place?' She had not and, after Tiny left, she never spoke to him again.

Tiny also began to receive attention from performers past who hoped his fame would help them, as well as performers present who wanted to help him

---

* Asked about the encounter during a 1994 interview, Tiny admitted, 'She didn't look as good as I thought she would. That's why I've learned to expect less when you're looking at a picture until you see the person.'

succeed. He was visited by Nick Lucas, who was thrilled Tiny had mentioned him on *The Tonight Show* and wanted to tell audiences he was 'still around.' Lucas would later call Tiny Tim the 'best press agent I ever had' and told Johnny Carson he was 'happy that a wonderful guy like Tiny Tim inherited ["Tip-Toe"].' He and Tiny also made plans to do a little tiptoeing through the tulips together at a future concert appearance. Tiny also received a visit from Harry Tobias, the songwriter behind 'Take Me To My Alabam'' and 'Sweet And Lovely.'

Tiny went to meet Irving Kaufman at his home in Encino, Los Angeles. The two sat at a piano Kaufman had in his parlor and sang songs that Kaufman had helped popularize. 'We sang together, Irving Kaufman and I— just imagine, so many years later, here I am—with my idol, far, far away from New York—both of us—singing songs around a piano in Irving Kaufman's house,' Tiny later told the *Chicago Tribune*. 'And you know, he said he really liked the way I sang not only his songs, but all the others. Can you imagine— Irving Kaufman saying that to me—now—in the 1960s. Or me meeting Mr. Kaufman at all?' At the close of the meeting, Kaufman was apparently moved to tears when Tiny performed for him, in Kaufman's style, a song Kaufman had popularized, 'Stay Home Little Girl, Stay Home.'

Tiny also visited Rudy Vallee at his home. Though the meeting began awkwardly—Tiny star-struck and Vallee unsure how to approach him—the ice was broken when Tiny produced a Rudy 78 from his shopping bag. Vallee took Tiny on a tour of his illustrious house, showing him all of the memorabilia he had collected from his own career. At the close of the visit, Tiny revealed that his birth name was Herbert, and Vallee revealed that his was Hubert. He signed a note for Tiny, 'To Hubert to Herbert.' 'It was a miracle's miracle,' Tiny later said of the meeting.

Although Tiny was likely more excited by recognition from Lucas, Kaufman, and Vallee, he also received a telegram from George Harrison, which read, simply, 'You're a gas.' If that was not enough, John Lennon had contacted Tiny's management about having Tiny perform at the Royal Albert Hall.

Tiny was receiving an ever-increasing amount of attention from the female sex—a fact that simultaneously tempted and terrified him. 'I tell you everywhere I've went I've seen beautiful girls,' he told Johnny Carson. 'Just like Will Rogers said, I never met a man I didn't like. I say, I've never met a girl I didn't like.' Indeed.

If his intention was to control his libido, he started strong. For instance, he threatened to 'push the door down' when Richard Perry encouraged Miss Catherine to kiss Tiny. However, his chaste morals were being pressured. On May 19, while a Miss Coran applied makeup to his face, he ejaculated in his pants. Afterward, he applied baby oil to her back and massaged her. Upon her departure, he purchased ten bottles of beer and began to drink them. Later that night, he was joined in his hotel room by the GTOs, a notorious band of groupies and aspiring girl singers who were closely associated with Frank Zappa. Initially, he was so frightened by their arrival en masse that he began shaking violently. After excusing himself to take a shower, he returned to the room, by which time only two members of the group remained. According to his diary, he embraced one of them, Miss Cynderella, for 'twenty to seventy seconds.' But things did not stop there. The next day, Miss Cynderella and Miss Mercey returned, bringing with them fellow GTO Miss Christine. Soon, Tiny and Miss Cynderella were 'kissing and rolling on the floor.'

'Oh Lord what is happening?' Tiny wrote in his diary. '[I am] forgetting thy grace oh Lord save me from sin in Jesus' name I pray.' Tiny was in such a state that his management had to cancel a radio appearance with KRLA, while Ron DeBlasio and Richard Perry made arrangements to move Tiny immediately from the Hollywood Hawaiian to the Sunset Marquis Hotel.

On a trip back to New York, Tiny continued to experience the 'effects of sin' and had several run-ins with Miss Beverly, a receptionist for Warner Bros. The two drank wine together, kissed, and, somewhere along the line, Tiny again orgasmed in his pants. On May 28, a man named Gary Greene was officially placed on Tiny Tim's payroll at $100 a week with the exclusive job of deterring Tiny Tim from sinning. 'God Bess Mr. Green,' Tiny wrote. 'I pray for the hard job he has.'

On May 25, *God Bless Tiny Tim* entered the *Billboard* Top 100, jumping from number 150 to number 79, while 'Tip-Toe' had moved up to number 69. Meanwhile, Tiny was inundated by fan mail from admirers ranging from eight-years-old to the elderly, many of them showering him with gifts. He vowed that he would answer every piece of fan mail by hand, even if it took twenty years, 'because that's what [fans] would love, and I'd love to do it, too.'

As Snoopy admired a framed photo of Tiny Tim in a *Peanuts* comic strip, the debate raged as to whether or not Tiny's 'character' was 'put-on.' When asked about his voice, he replied, 'That voice is all happiness and sunshine … a field of flowers and beauty in the face of a young girl.' When asked about his age, he replied, 'I really believe I'm nineteen, and I try to stay that way.' Quizzed about the details of his obsessive bathing, he readily admitted that he brushed his teeth six times a day, took one big shower a day, and 'little showers after nature calls.' When asked why he bathed so often, he explained, 'I love to keep continually clean, because when I'm with girls, they are always the essence of purity.' When asked how he viewed himself, he replied, 'Just plain lucky.'*

Record Mirror editor David Griffiths sought to cut to the chase and spoke with Roy Silver directly. 'He believes what he's doing completely,' Silver told Griffiths. 'He's always like that—if it's an act it's the greatest I've ever seen.' Interviewed by *Pageant*, the publication responsible for dubbing Tiny '1968's answer to John Wayne,' Silver insisted Tiny's personality was genuine. '[Tiny is] a personality who has the virtue of being so kind and harmless,' he said. 'He generates a wonderful, indefinable warmth.'

Meanwhile, Jon Gordon, one of Tiny's growing number of publicists, told *Maclean's*, 'I believe that Tiny, number one, is sort of like a mirror. And if a guy comes in and he's uptight, he's going to see in Tiny whatever he's uptight about. ... When you meet him, don't go in with any preconceived things. That's number one. No preconceived innocence; no preconceived anything. Just meet him and form your own impressions. And then what you should do is try to believe what you see. Because that's where Tiny *is*. He's not fooling anybody. He *couldn't*. You'll see. He's just ... real.' *Time*, too, quoted an unidentified friend of Tiny's who asserted that his 'total absorption in his role ... [is the] purity of his madness.'

Still, many were unable to believe that an act seemingly 'ready-made for today's bizarre music scene' had been created organically, rather than as a gimmick by some clever marketing agency. Exasperated in its attempts to 'ferret out the secrets of Tiny's bizarre origin,' *Photoplay* described the process as a 'journey through *Alice's* looking-glass where nothing is as it seems.' *Newsweek*, too, was unable to come up with very much, conceding that his background was 'shrouded in mystery.' Nevertheless, virtually every outlet, small and large, had an opinion.

For *Time*, Tiny's success had 'helped place him in a cultish tradition that goes back through Shakespeare's clowns all the way to the Roman circus—

---

* Tiny himself contributed to some of the misinformation, particularly about his age. Though he was thirty-six at the time, some sources listed him as being as old as forty-eight. He later admitted to Howard Stern that this was because he had told the World Almanac that he was born in 1923 instead of 1932, later citing it as the 'only lie' he had ever told.

that of the holy fool … But holy papaya powder, who is fooling whom?' *Newsweek* called him 'the last innocent … the laughing stopped when this mystical musical medium summoned his voices, a pleasing tenor and a Jeanette McDonald–esque soprano, in renditions of classic crooner ballads that rivaled in authenticity the old crank-handled gramophone itself.' As far as *Rolling Stone*'s Jerry Hopkins was concerned, 'Tiny Tim is real, that is, in a sense a peculiar butterfly … like nothing you've ever experienced before, quite odd, but above all, gentle and beautiful.'

Silver Screen's Aphra Bren called Tiny 'the kind of beauty that borders on the grotesque—so different that it must be accepted as a whole new thing—a one of a kind face and personality.' In *Photoplay*, Harriman Jamis asked, 'Is Tiny Tim sincere or just this year's novelty act? Is he sweet and innocent or just plain weird? Is he dedicated or decadent? A saint or nutty as a fruitcake? A philosopher or a phony? What do you think?'

For Paul Harvey of the *North Carolina Dispatch*, 'Tiny Tim, the antithesis of everything "cool," is what his contemporaries would themselves truly prefer to be.' The *Albertan* called him 'a modern Tiresias who has seen the curse of his civilization. And he's telling it like it was when things were a whole lot better.' *Ramparts* described Tiny as 'a haunted house … inhabited by ghostly song-and-dance men,' while UPI's Rick Du Brow declared, 'I believe him. I absolutely believe him. Absolutely.'

While some journalists were intrigued by Tiny's mysterious background and willing to concede that he possessed 'real, if weird, vocal and ukulele talent,' others were more critical, odiously comparing his perceived lack of talent to that of Elva Miller, the fifty-nine-year-old California housewife who had enjoyed a brief moment in the spotlight with her off-key hit version of 'Downtown' a few years earlier.

Lloyd Shearer of *Parade* was intrigued by 'several hundred letters about a thirty-two-year-old-boy soprano who calls himself Tiny Tim.' The letters, which came in from all across the country asked questions like, 'Isn't Tiny Tim really Margaret Truman making her comeback in show biz?' and 'Is this strange creature, Tiny Tim, male, female, or in between?'

Having read up on Tiny's background, Shearer deduced, albeit correctly, that 'no boy raised on the streets of upper Manhattan, no veteran of amateur nights, endless auditions, saloon concerts, song tryouts, and Greenwich Village night clubs emerges the naive, gullible ninny that [he] likes to affect.' Upon meeting Tiny face to face, Shearer imposed on him a word association test.

'Black.'
'White.'
'Freud.'
'Terrible.'
'Psycopathia sexualis.'
'*Ooh*, Mr. Shearer!'

'I perceived then that much of Tiny Tim's act was a put-on,' Shearer concluded, 'that he is not entirely the strange, bizarre, oddball he so innocently plays. He is in fact a rather sophisticated, well-read young man who knows something about Freud, Krafft-Ebing, D.H. Lawrence, and the sleazy slices of life … the public is buying what he has for sale—laughs.'

Tiny let a bit of his image slip when he admitted to *TV Mirror* that he did not always exclusively eat his concoction of honey, wheat germ, sunflower, and pumpkin seeds. 'Well, sometimes I cheat,' he said. 'You know, I believe the good Lord put all foods on earth to be good but the thing is, if I can, I'd love to stay away from meat. But sometimes I do drink beer. But only in California. There's a special beer there with Rocky Mountain spring water. I do hope some of the beers in New York take an example from that—because who knows what kind of water they're putting into it.'

In addition to interviews with Tiny and his management, many journalists based their articles about Tiny on a fanzine entitled *The True Fantastic Story Of Tiny Tim*. Though it suffered from chronic inaccuracies, it adhered strictly to the 'flower image' of Tiny that his managers were attempting to construct. The teenybopper rag was chock full of pictures of Tiny and included a three-and-a-half-foot foldout poster. The magazine contained articles like 'Tiny's Own Personal Story,' 'His Secret Love,' 'Why He Had To Happen,' and lists of his Loves (which included hotdogs, flowers, and the philosophy of Christ) and Hates (war, cigarettes, songs about drugs). The magazine also featured a fictitious series of interviews at Colony Records in New York, supposedly conducted with people purchasing *God Bless Tiny Tim*, called 'Just Why Do People Love Tiny,' with answers ranging from 'Nostalgia, I guess' to 'Tiny Tim blows my mind.'

The magazine skirted around Tiny's support of Vietnam, writing only that he 'never talks about politics, although that embodies something that is very important to him, and that is peace… if Tiny could have one single wish realized, it would be for peace in the world.' It did delve more deeply, albeit still vaguely, into his religious beliefs. 'Tiny is a very devout Christian, even though he is the product of a mixed marriage, and the Prince of Peace is his ideal. He is constantly quoting from the Bible.' There was no mention, however, of his belief in abstinence before marriage, his conservative beliefs, or any of the other unpopular aspects of his moral code.*

Although Tiny had told several outlets that he would never get married, the magazine devoted three pages to his 'Secret Love,' the girl of his dreams. The section was adorned with dreamy looking photos of a doe-eyed Tiny, looking off longingly into the middle distance, dreaming of a girl who would have an 'agelessness and a timelessness ... that makes the Mona Lisa as beautiful today as she was the day she was first painted ... here is the face that Tiny Tim sees when he closes his eyes, as he sings.' She would be aged between fifteen and twenty-five and 'perfectly shaped, oval face ... flowing hair ... eyes are wide and deep ... the lips full and sensual ... [and] a look of serenity, and tranquil peacefulness.' As for whether meeting a woman would change Tiny, the article asserted it would not: 'She is so much a part of him already, and Tiny is such a happy individual, that finding the woman of his dreams could only make him that much groovier.'

Among the more puzzling aspects of the magazine are its listing of Tiny's first name as 'Herberto' and the introduction of a made-up middle name, Buckingham. One section, 'Why He Had To Happen,' gives the principal reason for Tiny's success as 'the need for novelty.' It concludes with yet another commentary on the times: 'Out of pandora/Tiny Tim's shopping bag, comes not hope (there is no hope left for the H-bomb age), no, not hype, but nostalgia, the final saving grace of a graceless age. Novelty first, nostalgia following. Vide, Tiny Tim.'

Given the efforts and production Warner Bros and Richard Perry had put forth to give *God Bless Tiny Tim* dimension, it seems strange that his management would allow him to be pigeonholed as a novelty. Nevertheless, a plethora of other publications took their cues from *The True Fantastic Story Of Tiny Tim*, with articles popping up in the *Saturday Evening Post* and *Inside TV*, along with gossip and pop-culture magazines aimed at female readers. *Tiger Beat, Teen Life, TeenSet, FAVE, Movie Mirror, Silver Screen, TV Radio Mirror,* and *Photoplay* all ran pieces on him, making sure to include information about his ambiguous love life, and Tiny was also quoted as saying, 'God Bless You Tiger

---

* It is rumored that Tiny often discussed religion on *The Tonight Show*, only for such talk to be edited out before the episode aired.

Beat Readers!' The headlines frothed with fluff: 'The Secret Sadness of Tiny Tim,' '45 and Never Been Kissed—the pure and simple saga of a pure and simple soul,' 'Tiny Tim, You've Got To Love Him, Too,' 'The Naked Truth About Tiny Tim's Weird Weird World.' All the teen magazines carried Tiny Tim fact sheets ('Rock'n'roll music excites him,' 'Birds in flight make his heart beat faster,' 'The scent of flowers change his mood'). One even declared that 'his look is becoming so popular that Tiny Tim clothes are going to be put on the fashion market.' The same man who had previously made some women ill at the sight of him was now marketed as a heartthrob.

One fan, Donna G. from Kirkland, Washington, mailed an acrostic name poem she had written for Tiny to a fan magazine.

Terrific	**T**ender
Irresistible	**I**ntriguing
Neat	**M**agnificent
Yummy	

Tiny was parodied and caricatured endlessly in comic strips like *Family Circus* and *Archie*, and in parody magazines such as *Mad*, *Cracked*, and *Sick*. *Laugh-In* was quick to satirize Tiny's heartthrob portrayal by featuring a snapshot of Tiny's impressive nose and announcing a 'new contest' from *Tiger Beat*: 'To all those unable to guess the exact number of blackheads on Tiny Tim's nose, goes a beautiful 8x10 glossy of Dick Clark sucking on a tube of Clearasil.' Other publications joined in, with *Reading Eagle* publishing a fake fan letter to Tiny: 'Dear Tiny, I love all your records. You are the most. I'm sorry I have to write this letter in crayon. Where I am, they won't allow me to use anything sharp.'

Tiny Tim merchandise began to hit the shelves, too. Sheet music featuring Tiny's image was issued for 'Tip-Toe,' 'Livin' In The Sunlight, Lovin' In The Moonlight,' and 'Then I'd Be Satisfied With Life.'* Warner Bros also issued a *God Bless Tiny Tim Songbook*, which included 'Tip-Toe' and 'I Got You, Babe,' as well as standards such as 'By The Light Of The Silvery Moon.' 'God Bless Tiny Tim' stickers, pins and postcards, a mock campaign button endorsing him for 'President and First Lady,' a bootleg Tiny Tim–style Troll doll, and a Tiny Tim shopping bag featuring a caricature drawn by *Realist*

---

* Sheet music was also later released for 'Bring Back Those Rockabye Baby Days.'

cartoonist Richard Guindon all became available. A Tiny Tim brand ukulele and instruction book were conceptualized, but not produced, because Tiny's management felt they would hurt his image. 'We figured in six weeks every kid in the country would have one. Then Tiny would get known as a novelty,' Ron DeBlasio told *Eye* magazine.

Tiny Tim tribute records surfaced as well. Sunny Records issued a single by Tiny's Little Friends featuring a chorus of children singing 'God Bless You Tiny Tim' and 'We Want Him (Tiny Tim),' as produced by the enigmatic and mysterious Milan. Epic Records issued its own tribute to Tiny Tim, 'We All Love Tiny Tim' by Peter Pan & Wendy, a product of Phil Wainman, who would later produce The Sweet and Bay City Rollers. Imitating the Artful Dodger, future Sweet founder Steve Priest contributed vocals to the track.

We all love Tiny Tim,
And we're very fond of 'im,
'Cause he's sucha lovely fella,
A real lovely fella,
And we're very fond of 'im!

With *God Bless Tiny Tim* at number 66 on the US charts and 'Tip-Toe' at number 46, Tiny's gigs became increasingly involved. On June 28, he performed a significant engagement at the Santa Monica Civic Auditorium. In an attempt to cash in on Tiny mania, two leading Los Angeles pop radios stations, KLRA and KHJ, went head to head in a strange rivalry to promote the concert. Officially, KLRA was hosting the event, which it advertised using Tiny voice-overs and station promos, and offered 100 tickets on air. Meanwhile, KHJ, determined to catch the wave, purchased the remaining 3,400 tickets to give away on air and announced a celebrity-stocked VIP party on the stage after the show.[*]

Campbell Silver Cosby hired stage designer Joe Gannon to design an elaborate stage show involving chandeliers, Grecian columns topped with nude female statuettes against a sky blue cyclorama, and live birds fluttering around a park bench. Tiny entered the complicated scene through an illusion of clouds.

---

[*] Much of this information is from an essay written by former KHJ DJ Ron Jacobs. Jacobs recalled also that he was able to get out of a speeding ticket when he was driving Tiny in exchange for an autograph for the officer's young daughter. Tiny obliged on the condition that the officer shake his hand.

'I made Richard [Perry] come out of the pit with a full orchestra, and he wasn't seen,' Gannon recalls. 'In other words, when the show started, it wasn't seen, and the whole orchestra comes up on that huge riser in front of the stage. I had done a whole bunch of things onstage: eight, twelve feet tall Grecian columns put up there and had lit them in two different directions and Tiny comes out on stage with a lot of smoke and carrying his bag ... we also had flying doves. He couldn't take them so he shooed them away. He thought they were gonna get hurt or something, so it didn't work out too well. They were all over, and he's waving his arms around. If I remember correctly, they were trained birds and were supposed to fly out from stage right to land on the bench where he was sitting and singing, and he was afraid of the birds ... he shooed them away [during the show]. It was an [event]. I don't remember it too much, because I was pretty wacked ... I was a little stoned.'*

'It was a hippie happening!' Ron DeBlasio recalls enthusiastically. 'But it also was a showcase for our company, Campbell Silver Crosby, and we had some of our other artists on there performing, but the real attraction was Tiny. It was an extravaganza, we had a full orchestra, with lights and sound and staging and for a young company it was a real hallmark. Not only did we have people like Mama Cass and other celebrities there, but there were a lot of industry people that wanted to know what [Tiny] was all about. [Joe Gannon was a] really strong stage arranger to put it together, and it was really wild. The Santa Monica Civic had a faint aroma of grass ... the expression those days was a "happening," and this was a happening.'

Richard Perry conducted the orchestra through an overture medley of *God Bless Tiny Tim*, and Tiny followed with an a cappella rendition of 'Welcome To My Dream.' Together, they recreated most of *God Bless Tiny Tim* and added a few songs from Tiny's repertoire, including 'Save Your Sorrows For Tomorrow,' 'As Time Goes By,' 'I Hold Your Hand In Mine, Dear,' and 'Earth Angel.'

FAVE magazine reported that Tiny 'knocked 'em dead,' while *National Insider*'s Frank Nathalio raved, 'Viewing him in Santa Monica, all of a sudden I could see what moved his fans—falsetto, kisses, giggles, ugliness, and beautiful. Tiny Tim, I realized, is for real; a true freakage confluence of the ridiculous

---

* As a token of his appreciation, Tiny went to Gannon's house for his daughter Cassy's tenth birthday party. *Motion Picture* magazine later carried a multiple-page photo spread of Tiny performing at the party. Unable to resist a chance to knock America's favorite oddball, the headline asked, 'Would <u>YOU</u> want Tiny Tim at your child's party?'

and the sublime.' Roy Silver, too, would later tell biographer Harry Stein that following the concert he felt 'tremendous hope.'

'Everyone was so nice to me,' Tiny later told Johnny Carson. 'It was such an exciting concert. For the first time I sang in an auditorium so well equipped with thirty wonderful musicians and, of course, Mr. Gannon, who did the staging with the clouds coming out of the ground and everything and, also, Mr. DeBlasio and Mr. Perry, who did the direction, they were all so wonderful to me. It was so wonderful to come out of the clouds and into this wonderful group of people in Santa Monica. I can't forget that wonderful night.'

The star-studded after-party was attended by Sally Field, pop trio Dino Desi & Billy, Sajid Kahn, Phyllis Nesmith, Mama Cass Elliott, Papa Denny Doherty, *Star Trek*'s Walter Koenig and George Takai, Beach Boys Mike Love and Carl Wilson, actor Andy Prine, actress Brenda Scott, songwriter Jimmy Webb, and Monkees member Peter Tork. As KHJ reported, Jimmy Webb 'thought [he] was marvelous.' The Monkees' Mickey Dolenz called him 'the most important artist we've had in a decade of music, and that's legit.' For Joni Mitchell, Tiny was 'a true troubadour, singing to people of those things that have always concerned them,' while for Nancy Sinatra he was 'one of *the* groovy people, no question. … he's ready to come out and play for any audience, for any good cause.' As far as Mary Travers was concerned, 'Tiny's songs and his unique way of delivering them gives his work the quality of folklore, almost. Singlehandedly, he has resurrected a whole body of work that might have been completely forgotten and lost to us. This is an important contribution and I have a great deal of admiration for this individuality of Tiny Tim's.'

The Beatles, too, gave Tiny their official endorsement during an appearance on *The Kenny Everett Show*. 'Play Tiny Tim,' said John excitedly. 'He's the greatest ever, man! You see if I ain't right!'

'He's real,' Paul added.

'He's real, man. We saw him.'

'It's like—it's a funny joke at first. But it's not, really. It's real and it's true.'

'He's great,' John concluded, before breaking into song. 'Tiny Tim for President / Oh, Tiny Tim for Queen!'

CHAPTER SEVEN

MY COMMUNITY

At this moment I am the biggest star in the country. I have gone from here in California to the tip of New York. I am invited to parties with all the great stars of Hollywood with beautiful girls. I am the toast of the city here in Hollywood, as well as in New York, people ask me for autographs, kiddies from five years old adore me to teenagers as well as adults and college groups.
DIARY ENTRY, JULY 27 1968

Tiny was not delusional. By July 1968, Tiny-mania had reached a fever pitch. On June 29, the day after his performance at the Santa Monica Civic Auditorium, *God Bless Tiny Tim* moved up to number 16 on the *Billboard* charts, while 'Tip-Toe Thru' The Tulips' peaked at number 17. Though Tiny had in mind a number 1 single, breaching the Top 20 was a massive accomplishment.

As the album spread across the continent, Tiny began touring the US, performing everywhere from Phoenix, Arizona, to Hampton Beach, New Hampshire. In Detroit, he was mobbed by teenage girls during a performance at the Edgewater Amusement Park. Delighted, he ripped off his tie and threw it into the crowd, which excited them further. Caught up in the moment, he began ripping the buttons off his vest and threw those, along with some love beads, into the crowd. The crowd responded by throwing beads back at him.

On July 20, with *God Bless Tiny Tim* was enjoying its second week at its peak spot of number 7 on the *Billboard* chart, Tiny performed two shows at the Miami Beach club the Image. Four thousand people squeezed into the venue, causing the *Miami News* to comment that the 'air conditioning was not powerful enough the handle the extra large audience.' Tiny, however, netted a cool $5,000 for the engagement, about which the *Miami News* noted, 'Not bad for two forty-five-minute shows and about twenty minutes of rehearsal to adjust the sound.'

As *God Bless* and 'Tip-Toe' slowly descended from their peak positions, Warner Bros decided it was time to issue a second single. Instead of issuing another single from Tiny's first album, the label issued a recording of a 1924 number originally recorded in the blackface/mammy style, 'Bring Back Those Rockabye Baby Days.' The choice was a bizarre one—probably Tiny's, since he later recalled showing 'them' the song. Furthermore, Reprise had produced ten-inch acetates of a planned 'Then I'd Be Satisfied With Life'/'Strawberry Tea' single.

One reviewer later called 'Bring Back Those Rockabye Baby Days' a 'paranoid retreat into baritone.' Perhaps its release was an attempt to save Tiny from being pigeonholed as a falsetto singer. The finished product—even with 'This is All I Ask' as the B-side—just did not pack the punch of 'Tip-Toe.' Something was missing, and Tiny knew it. He later blamed his disappointment with the single on the lack of 'an engineer who understands the different eras,' and on himself, for not being in great voice, likening his vocals to 'an orange half squeezed.' He once even called the song 'simply horrible.' Nevertheless, he was obliged to promote the record before its July 17 release.

The audience had responded well to the song when Tiny debuted it during an appearance on *The Tonight Show* in early July, a week before its release, though they did not clap as enthusiastically as they had for his opening song which, coincidentally, was 'Then I'd Be Satisfied With Life.'*

'They like it,' Carson observed, referring to his audience. 'That's your new single record, huh?'

'Yes, Mr. Carson, it'll be out next week.'

'That's an old song, isn't it?'

'Yes, it was done in 1924 by the late, great Miss Lee Morse and she was wonderful ... I'm so thrilled that for the first time on the 17th of next week it'll be released and once more the public will be able to hear this great number which was written by Mr. Silver.'

'What was the question I asked?'

If Tiny was disappointed with how the single sounded, he must have been doubly disappointed by its performance; entering the *Billboard* chart at number 96, 'Bring Back Those Rockabye Baby Days' moved up one place the following week and then dropped completely from sight in August. There was little time to dwell on that, however, as Tiny was to open at Caesar's

---

* Tiny also performed a version of the 1923 classic 'Dinah,' complete with scatting and sound effects of 'Dinah-might' and ocean liners.

Palace in Las Vegas on August 15. Tiny announced the impending 'Vegas situation' on his July appearance on *The Tonight Show*, commenting, 'Gee, it seems interesting.' When asked about his fans, Tiny detailed all of the recent attention he had been receiving during live appearances. 'You know, if you wear a $10,000 coat and if [the fans] want it and you happen to be a celebrity,' he said, 'I say give it to them because they made you.'

'I don't say that at all,' Carson interjected. 'They ain't gonna get no $10,000 coat of mine!' The discussion then led inevitably to the other aspects of Tiny's success, with Tiny revealing some details about his finances, which would later become the source of speculation and controversy. Asked whether the success and money had changed him, Tiny replied, 'Not really. I know it sounds crazy, but I haven't got a cent because all my management takes and they put it aside for me or for them.'

'What do you mean, for them?' Carson asked.

'For their commission. Whatever they want. But they're so wonderful to me ...'

'You don't care about money?'

'No ... I'm just so happy, thank-God-to-Christ, that I just made this grade, though it was such a big challenge.'

'Don't ever change, Tiny Tim. Just stay plain, simple—just as you are,' Carson said endearingly during the interview. However, Tiny's 'plain, simple' nature was a source of worry for many who knew him well. One telling anecdote comes from Tiny's childhood friend Artie Wachter. Tiny and Wachter had fallen out of touch after Wachter joined the United States Air Force. By 1968, Wachter was living in Denver, Colorado, and one night was called to 'check this guy out!' on the television. Wachter halted when he recognized his childhood friend. 'I don't believe it! It's Herbie!'

The next day, Wachter was able to put in a call to Tiny's management and got through to Tiny. 'Hey, Herbie,' he declared, when Tiny answered. 'This is a voice from the past!'

'I haven't heard your voice in so many years!' Tiny exclaimed. 'We've got to get together!'

Shortly thereafter, Wachter visited Tiny at the Sunset Marquis Hotel. Despite Tiny's busy schedule, the two found a few minutes to relive the old days and played an improvised game of hockey with a puck and stick Tiny had in his room, using a coffee can for a goal.

Wachter observed how Tiny now had very little freedom. 'The managers kept him under lock and key,' he recalls. 'I never got to spend very much time with him because he was on a schedule and was like a dog on a leash. He didn't know how to say no.' He also began to wonder about Tiny's control over his finances. Noticing a check next to Tiny's bed, he asked, 'Hey, you got a check on the nightstand here. Why do you have it laying out here?'

'That's my pay,' Tiny replied.

'What do you mean?'

'My agent gives me $100 every week, and I can do with it what I want.'

Wachter did not press the issue.

The truth was, whether his earnings were small or large, Tiny was always kept in the dark about the financial aspects of his own career. A few years earlier, he had allowed the likes of Bud Friar and George King to take exorbitant shares of his meager earnings in order to keep playing the small clubs and dive bars. Now, with more on the line, a docile Tiny dared not shake the boat. He later claimed that the first time his management spoke to him of his finances was only to tell him that they would not disclose his earnings from the Santa Monica Civic Auditorium as it would 'shock' him. Furthermore, he claimed later that he only learned of his $50,000 income from the week-long engagement at Caesar's Palace in the trade papers.

'So those were great years,' he told Johnny Pineapple. 'Things were rolling. I never saw any of this cash. I just got about $100 a week. They put me in a nice hotel ... in West Hollywood ... and they put their hands [over the statements, which said how much he was making] and said, "We'll hide your salary, because you'll tell the press. You can trust us." Well, whether I did or didn't, I wanted to make it big and a name meant more than money. My poor father—may he rest in peace—and so many others didn't agree.'

In subsequent years, Tiny was forthright in his belief that his management took more than their fair share of his earnings during his profitable years. They denied it vehemently. Truly, Tiny simply had no idea how much he made, offering conservative estimates of 'over half a million dollars' and high estimations of 'two to four million' when asked in later years. The truth likely lies somewhere in the middle.

From the start of his mainstream career, Tiny was giving away pieces of himself. His 1968 journal reveals that by February 1968, his lawyer, Mr. Seidel, was entitled to 7.5 percent of his earnings. Other lawyers also commanding fees were currently embroiled in settling with Tiny's gaggle of one-time agents and managers. 'And contracts!' Roy Silver exclaimed, when discussing the issue with

Harry Stein in 1975. 'Every two seconds there was another guy springing out of the woodwork claiming to own 29 percent of him, or 14 percent, or 21 percent. It was mind-boggling how many contracts he'd signed over the years. We spent thousands of dollars—not his money, either!—on lawyers.'

Mark Hammerman, a friend of Silver's who worked for Campbell Silver Cosby and served for some time as Tiny's road manager, was able to get an inside look into Tiny's finances as he checked him in and out of hotels, arranged his travel, and collected money from concerts and appearances. From what he saw, much of the money Tiny earned was swallowed up by the greater enterprise that was Tiny Tim.

'The Silver management took 20 percent of his earnings,' he explains. 'The booking agency took 10 percent. Lawyer took 5 percent. Business manager took 5 percent. He started to complain that he made so much money but had nothing. He would conveniently forget how much he spent at the hotel and [on] his staff. I don't know what he was thinking at the time—the orchestra, the backup singers—management doesn't pay for that, the artist does. Anything he wanted, he got, and didn't stop to think where it came from.'

Indeed, Tiny had mismanaged his money since his job at Loew's, and while he now received only $100 in cash per week, his management often caved to his demands for additional purchases. He even detailed his excessive spending in interviews. 'He bought himself $1,200 worth of musical instruments—a banjo and two guitars,' the *Victoria Advocate* revealed, after an interview with Tiny. 'And he was able to indulge his strange passions. He is passionate about pills. He takes some forty a day now that he can afford them. There are pills with every vitamin known to science, pills with such ingredients as rose hips, bovine organs and wheat germs. He washes them down with mineral water or organic apple juice.' In his own journal, Tiny wrote about binging on 'fifteen lettuce-and-tomato sandwiches' and wrote of 'how foolish' he had been with his spending.

'I never even handled his money,' Roy Silver told Harry Stein. 'All of his finances were under the control of a business manager, who had absolutely nothing to do with us. ... He seems to have delusions of grandeur about what his financial situation was, but the truth is he never made all that much money. Sure, he made $50,000 for the Vegas show, but it cost $50,000 to put the thing on.'

Set designer Joe Gannon supports Silver's contention that Tiny never considered the production costs of his shows. 'What you read about him making that kind of money is not what he made,' Gannon says. 'I have a good idea what he was getting in Las Vegas for the week or whatever, considering what it costs to go do one of those shows out there. With me not spending too much money, but still with birds flying and magicians, all that sort of thing happening, that production up there would cost some money, as it does today.'

* * *

In August, after an appearance at the 1968 Newport Pop Festival which placed Tiny—with second billing only to Jefferson Airplane—alongside such contemporaries as The Animals, The Byrds, the Grateful Dead, The Chambers Brothers, Iron Butterfly, Steppenwolf, and Canned Heat, he and his entourage convened in Vegas to rehearse for the August 15 opening at Caesar's Palace. 'I hope [the casino doesn't] insist [Tiny wear a tuxedo], it would destroy his image,' Ron DeBlasio told the press.

Tuxedo or no tuxedo, Tiny's management had assembled quite an impressive show, once again under the direction of stage designer Joe Gannon. The show performed twice nightly in the 980-seat Circus Maximus room, with magician Harry Blackstone Jr. as the opening act. 'I've created some simple illusions for you tonight,' he would announce, 'but now there are grander illusions I'm going to create.' *SNAP!* Blackstone snapped his fingers and a curtain parted, revealing a six-piece jazz ensemble, frozen underneath a spotlight. 'Do you remember this?' *SNAP!* The group started to play. 'And do you remember this?' *SNAP!* Dean Martin's female dance troupe, The Golddiggers, emerged on the stage, tap-dancing in unison. *SNAP!* A full-orchestra appeared. *SNAP!* A plume of smoke and Tiny appeared onstage, singing 'Welcome To My Dream.' The show would close, of course, with 'Tip-Toe,' tulip petals raining from the ceiling.

'We were out to impress people,' Silver later explained. 'They were paying us seventy five thousand a week, and for that kind of money he wasn't just gonna stand there with his ukulele. Besides, we wanted to ease the pressure on him by surrounding him with a strong show.'

'We had a lot of faux pas trying to keep things out of Tiny's way,' Joe Gannon recalls, 'including the flying birds and him tiptoeing through the tulips as it were. Those days were a little crazy for me, I was having such a good time … My thing was is that I had total control of the lighting, which is my forte. We kept the show moving pretty good.'

On opening night, plastic tulips and oversized 'GOD BLESS TINY TIM—Caesar's Palace' buttons were placed on each chair. After the encore,

Tiny received a standing ovation from the 'standing room only' audience. At a party after the show, Tiny was photographed with Dean Martin's daughters, Deana and Claudia.* Over the next few nights, he was visited by such other notable figures as George Hearst (son of Mr. William Randolph Hearst), Hollywood journalist Dorothy Manners, attorney-turned-manager Nat Weiss, and Caesar's Palace owner Jay Sarno. Rudy Vallee also sent a telegram, wishing 'a happy and successful engagement to a very fine and real person.'[†] Elvis Presley, too, sent Tiny a telegram to wish him luck.

'The opening was unreal,' Ron DeBlasio recalled. 'The idea was to present him Vegas-style, so we took the show we already did and added a lot more to it … a lot more. … The audience didn't quite know what to do with it. Some people were laughing, some people booed, but not very loud. The atmosphere of the Vegas show room, which was very slick at that time, sort of felt odd.' About three-quarters of the way through the show, Tiny felt that he was losing the audience, so he began to improvise, pulling his ukulele out of its shopping bag and singing a duet with himself. 'It really looked like something from outer space, but also out of spirit. It succeeded in getting the audience back. Some of them laughed but others saw it … as performance art, which it was, and it worked … it set the tone, and people started talking about it.'

Roy Silver later reported that the show was critically successful but had a disappointing turnout. In any event, Caesar's Palace extended the engagement by an extra three days, to August 24, at $7,500 a night. Even so, Tiny would later cite the engagement at Caesar's Palace as a big miscalculation on the part of his management.

'I regret doing Vegas too quick,' he said in 1979. 'I was offered to do a part with Rowan and Martin for $550 [a week, touring during the summer of 1968] … and my manager wanted me to open up in Vegas where, naturally, it was $50,000 a week … I said I'd rather go with Rowan and Martin and break in more slowly, but he didn't want that, and I regret not doing that.'

Richard Perry was along for the ride, too, but he later told Harry Stein that the idea of putting Tiny in huge theaters seemed counter-productive. He also believed that Tiny was typically received better in more intimate settings, and was critical of Tiny himself for not trying harder to protect his

---

* Dean Martin himself made some jokes at Tiny's expense on his own show, once stating, 'I haven't felt as good since I sat on a Tiny Tim record.'
† Tiny then saw Vallee shortly thereafter. When he thanked Vallee for his telegram, Vallee pointed at Tiny and replied earnestly, 'Tiny, I really mean that.'

own interests. 'It was like taking a wild animal out of the jungle and sticking him in a cage,' he told Stein. 'Tiny is a troubadour in the truest sense of the word. Obviously there was much more money to be made the other way. And Tiny was so grateful for any kind of fortune that he allowed himself to be merchandised as a clown. He never had the balls to stand up to anyone.'*

Perry recounted taking Tiny to the Hog Farm, a hippie commune founded by Wavy Gravy in Tujunga, California, earlier that year. While he was there, Tiny performed for an hour, perched on a canyon cliff, as an audience consisting of peace activists, a then-unknown Charles Manson, and some Hell's Angels listened with reverence, heads bowed to the ground. 'That magic he had over those people was never understood by a mass audience,' said Perry.

Tiny might have come to the conclusion in hindsight that Vegas was a poor career move, but he had no problem enjoying the spoils of these prestigious venues during the course of the engagements. One evening, in his Caesar's Palace suite, Tiny called room service and ordered everything on the menu. When it arrived, he arranged it in a pattern on the floor and bed and sat in the middle. He also began to leave exorbitant tips, giving one waiter $80 for delivering a few cups of coffee. 'Why not?' he later mused. 'I was in a position to be generous and still be well off.'

His management was less than pleased. 'Ron DeBlasio was crazy with the whole thing,' Joe Gannon recalls. '[Tiny] started out with all the ice creams, because he liked ice cream. Next thing I know, I heard … that he ordered everything. Finally, they had to go and stop him and say, no, that's not the way it is.' Eventually, his management began advising the kitchens at the hotels to bring him a cheeseburger, fries, and a coke, regardless of his order.

Another troublesome aspect of Tiny's stay in Vegas concerned women. Tiny's 'sexual bodyguard,' Gary Greene, was seemingly not invited to Vegas, and, in fact, may have been out of the picture completely by that point. As Tiny noted in his diary on June 18, 'Situation with Mr. Greene—uneasy and confused.' On the evening of August 22, Tiny gave a teenage fan, Miss Candy, the key to his hotel room at Caesar's Palace. Later, having second thoughts, Tiny had Ron DeBlasio and his wife, actress Sharon Farrell, search the room

* Tiny also received an offer to appear in a film with Bob Hope. His management requested a script change that Hope would not agree to. 'I said, Look, you don't tell Bob Hope what to do,' Tiny later told *Playboy*. 'But they insisted that they were handling my career and that they knew what was best for me.'

for the girl. When she did not turn up, they assumed that she too had had second thoughts and not gone to the room. After the DeBlasios left, however, Tiny found her hiding in the shower. 'Sin was high,' he wrote of their night. She and Tiny showered together. Afterward, he spread honey and peanut butter all over her body. It's not difficult to imagine what happened next, but Tiny described it in his journal as 'ten hours of sin.'

The next afternoon, Miss Candy's mother showed up at Tiny's hotel, looking for her daughter. Miss Candy's age was not disclosed, but her mother's presence indicated that Candy may have been a minor. Tiny disclosed the incident to Ron DeBlasio, who must have been thoroughly relieved when Miss Candy kept the evening's events to herself. The media, hungry for a scandal, had been unable to prove that the somewhat androgynous Tiny Tim was a homosexual, but would have jumped at a story about perversion or pedophilia. Tiny, however, was more concerned with the impact the events had on his mortal soul than their career-sinking potential.

'Miss Candy did not tell her mother,' he wrote. 'Even though I escaped a rough situation, I still committed a deep sin. I let you down O Lord as well as my manager. I made Thy word a mockery O' blessed Jesus. I pray for the strength to keep Thy laws. Don't let me stray from thee. You are everything to me and thy ways are the best ways.'

* * *

On August 24, Tiny bid farewell to Miss Candy and her mother and returned to Los Angeles, only to run straight into the arms of another set of problems. *Billboard* carried an advertisement for Tiny's new single, 'Be My Love,' from a forthcoming album entitled *Concert In Fairyland*. Unfortunately, Warner Bros had not commissioned this unanticipated release. It was a product of the hitherto unknown Bouquet Records.

Concert In Fairyland turned out to be a repackaged version of the album Tiny had recorded in 1962 under the name Darry Dover & The White Cliffs, upon which he had purposely yet mysteriously sung out of key. The producers had sped up Tiny's vocals and added grating, canned audience noise over the entire album. To add insult to injury, one of the people behind the release was Perry's father-in-law, record executive George Goldner. Insultingly, the album's producers asked Warner Bros for $25,000 in exchange for not releasing the album. Prior to this, another producer with tracks from 1966 had already been paid $5,000 to stifle his recordings. This time, Warner Bros refused to pay, presuming that a small label would not release an album by an artist with whom a conglomerate like Warner Bros had an exclusive contract. Unfortunately, Bouquet Records called Warners' bluff and released it.

'Tip-Toe''s failure to break into the Top 10, and the subsequent failure of 'Bring Back Those Rockabye Baby Days,' meant that Warner Bros, Tiny's management, and Richard Perry were banking on a strong second album. Sessions for the legitimate second album had not yet begun, however, and *Concert In Fairyland* was selling well in the wake of *God Bless Tiny Tim*. Furthermore, Sammy Cahn and Nicholas Brodzsky, the writers of 'Be My Love,' were threatening a lawsuit for 'killing' the song. Tiny later admitted that he did not blame them. 'If you are familiar with the album then you know there were twelve standards which were butchered,' he told Ernie Clark. 'This has to be the worst album ever created in the history of mankind.'

Despite the damage that the bootleg record did to his career, Tiny interpreted the entire debacle as cosmic retribution for his management's rush to book big-money engagements rather than first establish him as a recording artist. 'I'll never forget the looks on the faces of Roy Silver, Richard Perry, and Ron DeBlasio when they saw the ad for the fake album,' he later told Harry Stein. 'That almost made it worth it for me. I thought it served them right for delaying the second album.'

When Harry Stein told Roy Silver about Tiny's belief that his management was in some ways responsible for *Concert In Fairyland*, Roy was incensed. 'It's astounding to me that he can blame us,' he told Stein. 'I mean, it was he who'd recorded the damn phony album, not us. As a matter of fact, he'd recorded all over the place, under a million different names. He'd recorded enough material for a hundred pirate albums.'

Action was taken, lawyers were called, and as they got to work, Tiny was rushed into the studio on August 17 to record a brand-new single: a cover of the 1966 Sopwith Camel hit 'Hello, Hello.' When it was time to cut the track—this time, a paranoid retreat back to falsetto—Tiny claimed that the 'high voice was not there at that time.' To try to compensate, he lathered his neck with Vick's VapoRub, but he remained hesitant about the song selection. 'It needs more words, it's too new,' he protested. 'Can I change it around?'

DeBlasio rushed in to counter Tiny's argument. 'It's so you, Tiny,' he said. 'It fits you like a suit.' Tiny let out a loud '*UMMMFFF*,' and twenty takes later, 'Hello, Hello' was finished. Despite Tiny's weak vocal performance, Richard

Perry thought the track was 'great anyway,' and it was released as a single, coupled with 'The Other Side,' on August 28 1968, peaking briefly at number 122 before disappearing in early September.

'To top a bad album off, I killed "Hello, Hello," too!' Tiny later mused.

* * *

Interest in Tiny as a personality continued unabated, and on August 30, the Federal Bureau of Investigation office in London, wondering about the outlandish phenomenon, sent a message to FBI director J. Edgar Hoover, requesting 'all background data known concerning the subject as expeditiously as possible in order to [CENSORED].' The subject in question was 'Herbert Khauri, [sic] AKA Tiny Tim.'

On September 9, Hoover's office sent a message to the Special Agents in Charge in Chicago, Los Angeles, and New York. Other than confirming that Tiny was a 'popular TV and nightclub entertainer,' FBI headquarters could not provide its SACs with much more information, relying on a May 17 article in *Time* for the few details it could share. The SACs, via their local contacts, were supposed to 'determine subject's association with Frank Sinatra [CENSORED] and hoodlum elements.'

SACs in Chicago interviewed four contacts 'familiar with hoodlum activities' regarding Tiny Tim but came up dry. In New York, the SAC only produced Tiny's home address, lawyer's name, management information, and current residence. In Los Angeles, three contacts were interviewed. One contact found it 'unusual for a relatively new star to appear for one week at Caesar's Palace in Las Vegas,' but otherwise, no substantive information surfaced. Having yielded no results, the FBI inquiry ended on September 23.

Had the FBI asked Tiny if he thought himself a criminal, he may have answered to the affirmative. Despite enlisting the aid of Linda Lawrence, wife of Rolling Stone Brian Jones, and Ron DeBlasio, Tiny 'sinned again' with a Miss Judy, who joined him for a shower and allowed him to lick honey off of her body, and a Miss Monica, on whom he sprayed whip cream and licked it off. During his rendezvous with Miss Monica, Tiny's sputtering conscience kicked in and he suddenly 'acted crazy to make her leave.' 'Get under the blankets. Quick!' he yelled, running around the room. 'They're bombing England!' It worked. Miss Monica picked up her shoes, patted Tiny on the head, and said, 'Take it easy.' He never saw her again.

In an act of desperation, Tiny began shooing away all interested females, even those who made no sexual advances, and even those who shared (or perhaps humored) his Christian views. Days after his rendezvous with Miss Monica, Tiny met Miss Joan Stephens. Though they refrained from physicality, Tiny frightened himself when he 'told her everything' about himself. Not wanting her to 'get the first move and hurt me by rejecting me,' he sent her a telegram:

DEAR MISS STEPHENS, I CANNOT SEE YOU TONIGHT TOMORROW OR EVER AGAIN IN THIS WORLD GOOD LUCK.

'You told me many times that Jesus Christ works in many ways,' Miss Joan responded. 'I guess this is one of them. I was starting to have deep feelings for you, and I guess he thought it should not be, so he sent his message through you.'

In September, Tiny Tim's face, along with those of singer Arlo Guthrie and actor Michael Pollard, graced the cover of *Esquire*, beneath the sarcastic headline 'The Beautiful People: Campus Heroes for 68/69.' The men were 'beautiful,' *Esquire* explained, 'because they have succeeded in doing their thing. They have defied the Establishment and won. That makes them campus heroes.'

The same day, Tiny admitted in his diary that 'Hello, Hello' had failed but vowed, 'I will get a number one single.' With sessions for a legitimate and aptly titled *Tiny Tim's Second Album* beginning in a few days, Tiny reported that he had 'spoken with Mr. DeBlasio about recording myself the right way.'

This seemingly spontaneous change to defensiveness set the tone for a rocky working relationship with Richard Perry during the second album's recording. Though he had been somewhat malleable during their first recording session, Tiny was in battle stance from the get-go.

Once again, Warner Bros had allocated a sizable budget and considerable manpower for what the label must have anticipated to be a surefire success. Once again, the album was to be collection of songs by new writers, selected by Perry, and vintage songs from Tiny's repertoire. Similarly, the album was to include a varied collection of musical styles with full orchestration. This time, Perry enlisted a different assortment of arrangers, including Gene Page, Perry Botkin Jr., and Darnell Pershing. Despite their impressive resumes (Page had arranged 'You've Lost That Lovin' Feelin',' Botkin worked on 'Feelin' Groovy,' and Pershing was a future Johnny Mathis arranger), Tiny was unenthused. 'I pray for Mr. [Artie] Butler, who … should be arranging this,' he wrote.

In the end, Perry's selections included a song he co-wrote with Tommy Kaye of 'One Man Band' fame, 'Have You Seen My Little Sue?,' Tom Paxton's 'Can't Help But Wonder Where I'm Bound,' 'Neighborhood Children' by Pasquele Zompa and Bernard DeCaesar, 'It's Alright Now' by Hoyt Axton, 'Christopher Brady's Old Lady' by Anders and Poncia, and 'My Community' by Roger Atkins and Carl D'Errico, who had written the Animals hit 'It's My Life' and 'Great Balls Of Fire.' Meanwhile, Tiny retained the greater number of choices, selecting 'Come To The Ball,' 'My Dreams Are Getting Better All The Time,' 'We Love It,' 'As I Walk With You,' 'She's Just Laughing At Me,' 'Down Virginia Way,' 'I'm Glad I'm A Boy,' 'My Hero,' and 'As Time Goes By.'

Straightaway, Tiny and Perry clashed over two of Tiny's choices. 'As I Walk With You' was written by George King, and Tiny wanted to make King 'smile when he heard it,' while 'Down Virginia Way' had been penned by Irving Kaufman and Arthur Fields. Kaufman had given the song to Tiny during their meeting over the summer. Perry was miffed at Tiny's stubbornness. 'I didn't like him coming on like a star,' he later told Harry Stein. 'Where did he come off demanding that we include crappy songs on that album?'

Nevertheless, Tiny got his way by complaining to Roy Silver, who, in turn, strong-armed Perry. As Tiny later explained to Ernie Clark, Perry knew Kaufman meant a lot to him but felt that 'Down Virginia Way' did not fit with the rest of the album and suggested they save it for a future project. 'He may drop dead by the third album,' Tiny replied. 'I want to do it while he's alive.' After Silver's intervention, Tiny ended up recording the song against Perry's wishes. 'I was very satisfied with the recording,' Tiny told Clark, 'and I was very glad, praise the Lord, Mr. Kaufman lived to see that.'

Perry also conceded to recording 'As I Walk With You,' but Tiny was indignant at Perry's decision to use an accordion-driven arrangement, which he believed was intended to deliberately sabotage the song. Ron DeBlasio witnessed problems in the studio, remembering Tiny's stubborn insistence that they record a song that had been sent to him by a fan from Florida. The song was recorded, but ultimately left off the album.[*] Whatever else occurred in the studio during the latter half of September 1969, Perry and Tiny were fed up with each other. 'Mr. Perry and I were at complete odds,' Tiny remarked, while Perry later stated that they had 'spent too much time together at that point.'

---

[*] Of the outtakes from *Tiny Tim's Second Album*, the only ones to ever see the light of day are covers of Cab Calloway's 'Frisco Flo' and The Doors' 'People Are Strange,' both of which are on Rhino's 2006 compilation *God Bless Tiny Tim: The Complete Reprise Records*.

One highlight of the turbulent recording session was a visit by Frank Sinatra, who had heard Tiny was recording in the same studio and stopped by to meet him. 'And *he* came over to meet *me*, you know?' Tiny told the *Chicago Tribune*. 'Mr. Sinatra said he had been looking forward to meeting me and was glad he did, you know?' Tiny told Sinatra about a time in December 1943 when he had seen him exit a side door of a theater in Manhattan straight into a cab surrounded by a mob of girls. Sinatra grinned and replied, 'Tiny, those were the days.' Their meeting was captured in a photo which Sinatra featured prominently on the back of his Christmas 1968 release *Cycles*.

* * *

With the new album in the can, Richard Perry busied himself mixing the project, and Tiny took off for Vancouver, British Columbia, for a show at the 15,000-seat Pacific Coliseum, where he headlined a triple bill featuring local acts The Collectors and Country Joe & The Fish. It was Tiny's first appearance in western Canada, and it was up to Warner Bros' Western Canadian Promotions Manager Bruce Bissell to make sure Tiny's records were in the local stores, and the arena filled up.

Bissell had been 'amazed' by *God Bless Tiny Tim* but was still unsure how to promote the appearance. 'I thought, man, what am I gonna do with this guy?' he recalls. 'I had no idea what he was like, what kind of a person I was gonna meet, or how I was gonna promote it to sell tickets.' Bissell tipped off the press as to Tiny's arrival time, and a crowd of several thousand converged on the airport for his arrival on September 20. In front of a photo-snapping press, Bissell presented Tiny with a custom-made Maple Leafs hockey sweater and a new ukulele and brought him to have his hair trimmed. Tiny also attended a Little Richard performance, and the two met each other backstage after Richard's show.

Bissell was immediately impressed with Tiny's gentle personality, and quickly felt protective of him. 'I remember getting into customs out at the Vancouver International Airport; the customs people just made him stand around and wait and stand there and he never complained. He just said, Oh, Mr. Bruce, they're just doing their job. He was so patient with everybody and really had a wonderful heart.'

The show in Vancouver featured much of Tiny's regular repertoire, with Al Jolson's 'I Gave Her That,' 'Bring Back Those Rockabye Baby Days,' Nick Lucas's 'High In The Hills,' and Billy Murray's 'I Love Me' all thrown into the mix. As with Tiny's other shows, Bissell knew that many had come to gawk, and, like Richard Perry, he felt that putting Tiny in a large arena was inappropriate for his performance style. 'The atmosphere was really mixed,' he recalls. 'It was very tough [for him to] project [to such a large] audience. There was no comparison when he was in an intimate atmosphere … a lot of people came because they were curious. They weren't big fans or anything. They wanted to see this person and just see what all the yelling was all about. It was a really split audience.'

On September 25, *You Are What You Eat* opened at the Carnegie Hall Cinema in New York City. With Tiny Tim now arguably the most famous— or at least most recognizable—person in the film, his likeness was featured on all of the promotional and publicity materials, which advertised 'a psychedelic montage of a nation in the throes of its first revolution.' This was an apt description, as the film was a collage of young people, associated with various arms of the counterculture, carousing, dancing, smoking marijuana, wearing crazy clothes, in bed together, protesting, or as one reviewer put it, 'Children, hung up on sensation, thumbing their noses at the world, accepting anything that will outrage conventional straight folks.'

Despite the impressive array of artists and personalities who appeared in the film and/or on its soundtrack—The Electric Flag, Frank Zappa, Peter Yarrow, Paul Butterfield, Super Spade, David Crosby, Hamsa El Din, and Barry McGuire—and the creative cinematography by Feinstein, the film lacked direction. Yarrow himself would concede that 'from the time it was made to the time it was released, there was a shift and the texture and feel of what was going on had changed. It no longer captured the cutting edge of now.' In what was perhaps an omen, the film's star, Super Spade, a charismatic, drug dealer from San Francisco's Haight-Ashbury scene, was murdered prior to its release, allegedly by the mob.

Supporting Yarrow's intuition that the film no longer 'captured the cutting edge' was Reneta Adler and Vincent Canby's review in the *New York Times*. 'The film is incredibly inept and ugly at times,' they wrote. 'None of the musicians, including Tiny Tim, who makes some complicated but winning appearances, are at their best in the movie.' Other reviewers followed suit, with one calling the film 'an impressionistic record of things as they were, a psychedelic tintype now chiefly of interest to historians.' Despite some veiled praise, and a review from prolific critic Judith Crist who told viewers to 'go with it,' the film disappeared after screenings in New York and California. Nevertheless,

Columbia Records issued a soundtrack album, which includes a pair of unique mixes of Tiny's 'Be My Baby' and 'I Got You, Babe.' Two other songs he performed with The Band in the film, 'Sonny Boy' and 'Memphis Tennessee,' are absent. 'We only had so much time on the album,' Yarrow explains. 'I guess we wanted a representation on the album of what the film was about. I think that probably was the reason [why those tracks were left off].'

On the day of the opening, Tiny was already in New York for a meeting with his attorney, Charles Moerdler, about the outstanding issues surrounding *Concert In Fairyland*. He spent the afternoon handing over his journals for 1960 through 1963 to provide a window into the circumstances surrounding the creation of the Darry Dover & The White Cliffs tapes.

Previously, on September 5, the *New York Times* had reported that Tiny had successfully obtained a show-cause order in the New York State Supreme Court to prohibit Bouquet Records from using his likeness or name in advertising. The *Times* also reported that Tiny was suing for a million dollars in damages. Five days later, the paper followed up with a report that Tiny had successfully obtained an injunction prohibiting the sale of *Concert In Fairyland* and its single, 'Be My Love,' which was deemed 'latent piracy.' It was reported that, in addition to damages, Tiny was also seeking the destruction of the records.

The following day, Tiny and Moerdler met with Goerge Goldner's attorneys. It is unclear, however, whether the case made it to court or was settled outside of court. Moerdler, aside from noting that Tiny 'looked at life through much rosier glasses than most of us do' and recalling that, after their meeting, Tiny visited his house to sing 'Happy Birthday' to his two-year-old daughter, was not able to provide any additional information. 'I cannot tell you [the outcome of the suit] for two reasons,' he explained. 'One, I believe there was a confidentiality agreement on resolution. Second, I don't remember the resolution, which makes me believe there was confidentiality, because I would not remember things where I have agreed to confidentiality.' One wonders if the resolution was kept confidential from Tiny himself, just as his earnings at Santa Monica and Caesar's Palace had been censored.

Shortly thereafter, on October 4, Tiny traveled down to Miami to appear on *The Jackie Gleason Show*. Rehearsals ran for three days, during which time Gleason invited Tiny to his house to watch part of the World Series. The two posed together for a photographer from the Associated Press, Gleason strumming Tiny's uke and Tiny brandishing one of Gleason's golf clubs.

Unlike *The Tonight Show*, Tiny's segment on Gleason's show was scripted.

When asked for his impressions of Miami Beach, Tiny called it 'absolutely marvelous.' He found the ocean so 'breathtaking,' in fact, that he had written a little poem about it: 'I looked upon the ocean / And it beckoned me out there / But I couldn't go in the water / For it would ruin my hair.'

'That was just beautiful,' Gleason exclaimed. Tiny then performed 'Save Your Sorrows,' 'Tip-Toe,' 'Fill Your Heart,' and a parody version of 'Livin' In The Sunlight, Lovin' In The Moonlight,' to which the notoriously luscious Gleason added the line, 'Like a shot of brandy, you've been fine and dandy, we've had a wonderful time!'

Gleason went off script at the close of the episode. 'We've had a lot of fun tonight, but I've had the pleasure of working with one of the nicest, one of the most sincere and one of the most religious guys I've ever met, Tiny Tim.'

The next day, Tiny flew to New York to rehearse for the following day's appearance on *The Ed Sullivan Show*. 'No performer has ever created such a furor in show business as New York City's own Tiny Tim,' said Sullivan in his introduction. 'Ladies and gentlemen, here is a fine, real nice person,' he continued, to chuckles from the audience. 'No! Wonderful! I will say, he is the first—the real love child, Tiny Tim!'

Tiny appeared with neatly combed hair, in the same outfit he had worn for the cover of his new album: a stylish sky-blue suit jacket, a matching blue tie patterned with white flowers, and pair of mod, green-plaid pants. He belted out 'I Gave Her That' in a deep, Jolson-style baritone. After taking out his ukulele and using his falsetto for the comical 'I Wonder How I Look While I'm Asleep' and 'I Got You, Babe,' Tiny closed out the segment with 'A Little Smile Will Go A Long, Long Way,' sung in the tenor style of Irving Kaufman. Sullivan had Tiny's parents stand up and take a bow, and then addressed Tiny, who skipped the falsetto and used his regular speaking voice to thank his 'dear fans.'

It seems Tiny, or someone pulling the strings, was making an attempt to shift his public persona from the androgynous derelict that had first appeared on *The Tonight Show* to a polished, fashion-forward act. While at the Ed Sullivan Theater, Tiny was photographed with Tillie and Butros for the cover of the forthcoming second album. 'Dear Lord,' he later wrote, 'Years ago I told my father that he would be in the front row when I did *The Ed Sullivan Show*. No one believed it then. But thanks to you O blessed Jesus it happened today. … Thanks as it was a success … Blessed be God.'

The excitement did not end there. After returning briefly to Los Angeles to fulfill a prestigious engagement for the Robert Kennedy Foundation (on a bill with Boyce & Hart, The Moody Blues, Joe Tex, and The Rascals), Tiny took his act across the Atlantic, arriving in England on October 25. Tiny had revealed to Carson that he would be traveling to England in the fall, and Carson had cheered him enthusiastically, 'You'll kill 'em! You'll kill 'em over there. I bet you'll be a bigger hit in England and get more newspaper space than you've gotten here so far.'

With England's curiosity already piqued, Tiny began to make the rounds on Britain's top programs, including *The Dave Allen Show*, *The Mike & Bernie Show*, and *Tonight* with Kenneth Allsop. Despite the upward trajectory, however, relations between Tiny and Ron DeBlasio were becoming strained. Originally, Tiny had agreed to DeBlasio's managerial demands, such as the signaling system DeBlasio had created for interviews, wherein he would itch his nose or tug on his ear if he did not want Tiny to answer a specific question. Tiny's journal entries from this period contain daily mentions of 'rough ordeals' or 'near-disaster blow-ups.' They fought over the songs Tiny selected for his appearances on TV and radio, and even whether or not Tiny should comb his hair (which he was reluctant to do, according to Miss Sue, because he feared it might cause it to fall out). Things became so tense that Tiny even considered 'throwing' one of his TV performances out of spite. Luckily, Richard Perry was on hand to talk him down.

As Tiny made the rounds in London, he blew up *Record Mirror*'s printed assertion that he had a 'false image.' The paper eventually admitted that Tiny 'turned out to be genuine,' much to the dismay of the press, but was relieved that, at the very least, 'he was interesting.' Indeed, after interviewing Tiny for the *Sunday Times*, journalist Allen Brien confirmed that the press had resigned itself to the fact that Tiny was indeed real. 'Is he a freak? No. His falsetto might be more convincing if he were. Is he a genius? Not unless Donald Peers is. Is he a fake? No more than most modern entertainers. He is friendly, cheerful, relaxed, almost wholesome. He is not fooling us, but we may be making a fool out of him. Still, so long as we pay the price, who is he to complain?'

Meanwhile, *Weekend & Today* assured its readers that Tiny must be 'functionally sane,' given that he could 'sing and strum a ukulele, go to a baseball game, dress himself, and shop for old gramophone records.' It also confirmed that Tiny was 'not a homosexual … transvestite, [or a] double-sexed creature of dark, queer passions.'

Tiny caused quite a stir when he arrived on Carnaby Street in a convertible Rolls-Royce to shop for cosmetics, stopping to throw bouquets of flowers and blowing kisses to the crowd. 'Was it Charles Atlas? Was it Mighty Mouse?' asked *Record Mirror*. 'No, but nearly as big, it was the great American phenomenon Tiny Tim ... Tiny Tim is real and in full colour!' Later, Tiny was photographed by Antony Charles Robert Armstrong-Jones, first Earl of Snowdon and husband to Princess Margaret. Snowdon then drove Tiny back to his hotel in his Austin Healy convertible, with onlookers gawking at the sight of him riding in an open car with an English Lord. 'Give my regards to the Queen!' Tiny said, as he bid Snowdon farewell. Snowdon's photographs appeared alongside many of the news stories about Tiny's visit, while as a sort of icing on a strange cake, *Playboy* Bunnies were photographed putting up billboards of Tiny's profile from the back of *God Bless Tiny Tim* to advertise his debut at the Royal Albert Hall. 'It was pretty wild,' DeBlasio recalled.

On October 30, Tiny performed at the prestigious venue, 'presented by Keystone in aid of the National Association of Boys' Clubs' and backed by the forty-four-piece National Concert Orchestra, conducted by Richard Perry who wore a coat and tails. The opening acts were Peter Sarstedt (known for 'I'm A Cathedral'), Joe Cocker, and The Bonzo Dog Doo-Dah Band. In addition to a message from Tiny, exclaiming, in all capital letters, 'I'M REALLY SO VERY VERY HAPPY TO BE HERE IN BRITAIN TO SING FOR ALL YOU LOVELY BEAUTIFUL PEOPLE. GOD BLESS YOU ALL,' the program for the evening contained a series of best wishes from Bill Cosby and the directors/executives at Campbell Silver Cosby, as well as a reprinted version of a telegram Tiny had received from Deep Purple wishing him luck. Tickets were £37 (around $88 at the time).

The *Sunday Times'* Allen Brien described the theater's atmosphere as a 'pressure cooker' and wrote that the stage was piled high 'with more flowers than would grace a gangster's funeral,' and all for Tiny, 'the ostrich who tried to pass as a canary.' He also noted the division in the crowd that night: 'The usual charity-show supporters in their box-shouldered dinner jackets ... and the reputation makers, trend-setters, hippies and hoppies ... dressed like fugitives from an old Sunday-night TV movie.' The audience contained members of The Beatles and The Rolling Stones, Marianne Faithfull, Harry Nilsson, and several of the Royal Family.

Before leaving for England, Tiny had told *TV Guide* magazine, 'I am not a sissy. The gentle me is only half the picture. Clark Kent, after all, can turn into

Superman.' Aware that England was wondering if he was a freak or hoax, Tiny seemed keen to surprise them all by putting on his best Clark Kent and leveling with the audience that night. Dropping the giggles and high speaking voice, he addressed the crowd as an artist who was very serious about his music, though the hint of extra vibrato in his singing voice indicated that he was probably a bit nervous.

Tiny was allowed considerable room to improvise and experiment, strumming a guitar for 'Love Is No Excuse,' and after acknowledging that he had the 'great pleasure of hearing' that The Beatles and the Stones were in the audience, pulling out his ukulele for falsetto versions of 'Nowhere Man' and '(I Can't Get No) Satisfaction.' He also performed Bob Dylan's 'Like A Rolling Stone' as Rudy Vallee and Vallee's 'My Time Is Your Time' as Dylan, after relating the story of his visit with Bob. Though the audience was almost silent at the onset of the concert, by the third song they were enthralled. During the course of the show, the applause and laughter steadily increased, as if to say, 'Now we're getting it.' When the show ended, the audience called for Tiny to return to the stage for a full fifteen minutes.

Tiny knew he had gone over well. 'The poor English … didn't know what to expect,' he later told the *Chicago Tribune*, 'I've been in that situation before. I just went right into my first two numbers fast and tried to win them over … you know, they liked it. They really liked it, you could tell.'

Even British pop star turned ukulele-champion Ian Whitcomb, initially irked by the suggestion that he had taken up the ukulele because of Tiny Tim, was impressed by the show. 'I was moved by his sincerity and genuine love of the old songs and singers,' he later said.

Australian artist and *Oz* magazine founder Martin Sharp had attended the show that night too, at the behest of his roommate Eric Clapton, and it blew his mind. As the show unfolded, he recalled, 'I was just amazed at his brilliance and his humor and his passion for singing these songs. Tiny seemed to travel through time using the vehicle of song … most singers seem to belong within their own niche, they belong to their era and their period, but he seemed to belong to all periods.'

Sharp confirmed that the whole audience was completely entranced by Tiny's performance. 'People were amazed,' he said. 'It was a black tie event. It was packed, and they went wild for him. Sometimes they laughed at him … so, there was a curiosity about Tiny, but the audience went wild.'

'Everything was gorgeous,' Ron DeBlasio recalled of the exciting moment.

'We had lots of luminaries there from the music business … it was fantastic. We got lots of kudos.'

Allen Brien of the *Sunday Times* was impressed, too, even if he was disappointed by the realization that Tiny was, in fact, simply eccentric. 'Even when he took the female parts, sometimes in duet with himself, there was nothing distasteful, or even particularly weird in his mimicry,' he wrote. 'He is no more peculiar and unearthly than, say, Jimmy Savile or Barry Fantoni … [but] he can sing, sincerely and melodiously in a natural tenor, campily and mockingly in a forced soprano.'

While Tiny would have most likely been more than happy to return to the stage and give the audience at the Royal Albert Hall the encore they called out for, he was quickly whisked away to a party at the Playboy Club. Tiny was speeched and honored and gave interviews to the press. The Rolling Stones' Brian Jones, drink in hand, even posed next to a cardboard stand-up of Tiny for a photograph. Later, Mary Hopkin visited him in his hotel room. Perhaps in another attempt to show that he was not going to be a stooge for his management, he debated with Hopkin over America's role in Vietnam.

On November 3, Tiny and his entourage left England for Paris. For the next several days, his face appeared frequently on the covers of the London tabloids. The following day, 'Hello, Hello' was released in France, replete with a psychedelic picture sleeve. In Paris, Tiny continued to clash with DeBlasio, going so far as to inform him that he no longer wanted him as his manager. While there, Tiny attempted to purchase a $100 bottle of French perfume, and he binged so heavily on food and wine that he threw up.

After a series of photo shoots and appearances on French TV, Tiny continued on to Germany on November 7. In Hamburg, he was ushered into a packed press conference, right as, in the United States, Nixon was declared the winner of the 1968 presidential election. Then it was on to Bremen, for a TV appearance and a visit to the home of Apple Corps press officer Derek Taylor, where Tiny, Perry, and Taylor listened to a dub of *Tiny Tim's Second Album*, which Perry had brought along. Tiny wrote of a 'little dispute' with Perry following the listening session, but nothing substantive. Summing up the trip, Tiny wrote, 'My popularity [is] beginning to take shape in England after quote a rough first visit.' His 'Great Balls Of Fire' charted at number 45 in England shortly after his departure.

Returning to his old neighborhood in New York, Tiny had transformed from outcast to prodigal son. His first girlfriend, Barbara Williams, who had broken up with him for his refusal to cease wearing makeup, mailed him a letter: 'I walk the streets wondering why did I ever break up with you.' Tillie, who had once been embarrassed to be seen on the street with her son, had begun to mention him in conversations with her friends. Mrs. Semmelweiss, a friend of Tillie's for twenty years, was stunned when one day Tillie revealed that Tiny was her son. 'Herbert?' she asked, confused. 'The one who used to sing to the children on the street corner? I never knew he was your boy!'

'WELCOME HOME TINY TIM' was scribbled in chalk on the side of Tiny and his parents' building. Amid this fervor, Tillie and Butros finally agreed to play ball with the media. Sitting in their living room, the two granted their first interview, for a squeaky clean article entitled 'Tiny Tim's Parents Tell: Why God Has Blessed Our Son.'

'He was a very gentle boy and the children seemed to understand him,' said Tillie. 'As he grew older, I didn't like some of the friends he brought home because they would try to make him bad and I would tell him so. He would say, Mother, there is no bad *and* good. There is *only good*. He didn't learn anything from them, but they learned plenty from him! I'm not a braggart, but even his teachers at school would tell me, I've never seen such a child. Everybody loved him. … He was very bright, very unusual.'

Butros chimed in with his own historical revision, claiming that he had been 'proud of [Tiny] since the day he was born.' Tillie also provided some fantastic information about Tiny's strange eating habits, noting that Tiny had been born a 'pure soul' and that he was 'born a vegetarian … I couldn't trick him into eating any kind of baby food that had meat mixed in it.'

Tillie, whom the reporter observed 'seemed tense, nervous, and quite bewildered by her son's sudden international fame,' could not completely shake her natural cynicism. 'So much money he is making! Who gives such a prize? Who are these people? … I don't understand, but I am very honored that people should love him.' Something else puzzled her, too: 'Why did it take everybody so many years before they decided my son had talent?'

'*Our* son,' Butros added.

Despite glossing over many of the details of Tiny's strained childhood and school life, and fabricating stories of their unwavering parental support, Tillie and Butros could not hide their complete incredulity at his success. 'I can't understand, I tell you the truth,' Tillie said, 'but he has something by nature. It just took us a long time to realize.'

* * *

When Tiny arrived back in the States, he did, indeed, finish off the year 'in fine style.' On December 1, he made his second appearance on *The Ed Sullivan Show*, performing 'Great Balls Of Fire' and the medley of 'I'm Glad I'm A Boy' / 'Girl' / 'My Hero' from the forthcoming *Second Album*, along with a one-off rendition of 'School Days.'* Sullivan called him 'fabulous and unbelievable.'

The same month would also see Tiny introduced to a couple of musical superstars. First, as Tiny later related it, George Harrison caught wind that Tiny was in New York City at the same time and sent an invite for Tiny to visit him at his apartment. 'What a thrill just to be invited there!' Tiny said later, when interviewed for *The Lost Lennon Tapes*. 'I was very happy meeting this great giant, but I had no idea what would happen when I actually saw him face to face.'

On his arrival at Harrison's apartment, Tiny was escorted in and was surprised when a closet door swung open and four people came stumbling out. Though he thought at first that it was all four Beatles, it was actually Harrison, Jane Asher, Nat Weiss, and another he did not know. 'All of the sudden I got tongue-tied.' Tiny recalled. 'Seeing Mr. Harrison face to face, I realized I was with the biggest seller of records—him and The Beatles—in the history of recorded music ... all of the sudden a mountain came down, and I didn't know what to say. I didn't want to spend five or ten minutes looking at the ceiling!'

Tiny told Harrison about Miss Jill, a girl he had met in California in 1966, to whom he had first performed his falsetto version of 'Nowhere Man.' He politely asked Harrison if he could 'do a few bars,' and Harrison encouraged him. Tiny pulled out his ukulele and managed only a few bars before Harrison cut him off, and then, grabbing his tape recorder, instructed him to start over and do a brief Christmas introduction.

---

* 'School Days' was performed in the style of Byron G. Harlan. Harlan was quite a bit older than contemporaries such as Billy Murray and Irving Kaufman, and his old age was most certainly audible in his performances. With most probably unaware of who Byron G. Harlan was, most viewers must have just thought that Tiny's rendition of the song as 'an old man recalling his youth,' was just an avant-garde performance choice rather than an homage, as Tiny sucked his lips back over his teeth and sang the song as if he were a toothless old man. As Tiny explained, performing it in such a way was essential to tapping into Harlan's spirit. 'I didn't really start to feel the spirit of Mr. Harlan until I started singing his songs as if I had no teeth,' he wrote in *Playboy* in 1969, 'but once I did that, I was able to bring him to life within me.'

'Oh, hello to you nice Beatles,' he began. 'Uh, it's so wonderful, what a thrill it is talking here in Mr. Harrison's presence, Mr. Weiss's presence, and all his nice, wonderful friends. And the thing is, I just want to say Merry Christmas to you all, ha ha, and, uh, a Happy New Year, ha ha.' The results were included on *The Beatles' 1968 Christmas Record*.

Next, Tiny was scheduled to appear on the TV show *The Hollywood Palace* with Bing Crosby, which he described in his diary as 'the greatest show I have ever done.' Before the taping, however, Tiny came down with a 'cough and chest condition.' Determined to meet his lifelong idol, he ordered a flu shot and medicated himself with a concoction of cold pills, Vick's VapoRub, and Halls peppermints. Coincidentally, a fire at the studio postponed the taping and bought Tiny another day's recovery.

Bing's introduction, though scripted, was quite warm. 'We're very proud to have on our show tonight a young fella who represents one of the most phenomenal stories in show business,' he began. 'Here for the first time on *The Hollywood Palace*, the man who made tulips the national flower, Tiny Tim!' Tiny performed a few songs from the *Second Album*—'Come To The Ball,' 'My Dreams Are Getting Better All The Time,' 'Great Balls Of Fire'—and sat down with Bing for a short conversation.

'You have quite a style there,' Crosby told him. 'I don't know how to categorize it. Well, it's spirited!'

'Thank you, Mr. Crosby. Gee, Mr. Crosby, I really mean every word I'm saying—'

'Call me Bing, not Mr. Crosby. You'd make me a senior citizen. Would you call me Bing? I called you TT, you can call me Bing. But you've followed my career for a while?'*

'Uh—er, yes, Mr. Bing,' Tiny replied, to much laughter and applause from the audience.

Having become acquainted with Tiny during rehearsals, Crosby was reportedly very impressed with Tiny's knowledge of his early career. 'Bing Crosby was very understanding and looked at [Tiny] as a serious artist,' said Ron DeBlasio, who was on hand for the rehearsal and taping. 'When Tiny started talking to Crosby about all those old recordings, he was pretty impressed.'

---

* Johnny Carson, who was watching, was amused by this exchange. When Tiny made his next appearance on *The Tonight show*, Carson greeted him with, 'Good to see you, TT. That's what Bing Crosby called you on *The Hollywood Palace*. He said, well, TT.'

'Without trying to boast,' Tiny told Bing, 'I've collected almost all your records, seen almost all your movies—why, I might know some things about your career you might have forgotten.'

'You know what I'd like to do, TT?' Bing replied. 'I'd like to put you to a little test. We'll have a little game here. I'll sing a bit of a song and you tell me what picture it was from and then you have to sing another song from the same picture.'

First, Bing sang 'Down The Old Ox Road,' and Tiny knew the details: *College Humor*, 1933. Tiny then sang a snippet of 'Learn To Croon,' to which Crosby replied, 'You could throw a Labrador through that vibrato of yours.' Talking to Martin Sharp years later, Tiny recalled a deep sense of communion while reminiscing with Bing. 'Now, looking at his face when I did one song from his early years,' Tiny told Sharp, 'when he heard that, [Crosby] looked and said, Give that guy a box of Snickers. Nobody laughed. Nobody in that studio laughed. Then he did another song and I did this one [and] I looked at his face and I know he didn't understand ... then he said for the second time, give that boy another box of Snickers. And no one laughed. ... I personally think he was so surprised and couldn't believe that from this long-haired thing he couldn't understand, it was one thing to see this, but to hear, in a sense, his own youth. This was a great thrill!'

Tiny and Bing—perhaps Crosby's oddest screen pairing until his 1977 collaboration with David Bowie—were clearly enjoying each other as they wrapped up the segment. 'I got you now!' Bing exclaimed as he sang 'Please,' to which Tiny responded correctly by singing 'Where The Blue Of The Night Meets The Gold Of The Day.' When Tiny countered Bing's rendition of 'Love Is Just Around The Corner' with 'June In January,' Bing mimicked Tiny's delivery of the final words of the verse, 'with you,' a moment that amused Tiny for years to come. Finally, they were joined onstage by Bobbie Gentry, and the three closed out the segment by singing 'In The Cool, Cool, Cool Of The Evening' together, with Bing and Bobbie singing the low parts and Tiny the high. 'You O Lord know the joy and outcome of this day with Mr. Crosby. Thanks again O Blessed Jesus,' Tiny wrote in his journal that night.

From there, Tiny flew to New York for a December 17 appearance on *The Tonight Show* alongside James Mason and Sheldon Leonard. Then it was on to Miami for the highest paying gig of his career: $65,000 for a ten-day engagement at the Fontainebleau Hotel. After a few days of rehearsals, during which time he attended the premiere of Jackie Gleason's *Skidoo*, Tiny opened at the Fontainebleau on December 20, performing two shows a night with support from Spanky & Our Gang.

Occurring concurrently with Tiny's engagement at the Fontainebleau was the Miami Pop Festival. Tiny had not been invited to perform, but he was probably banking more than many of the acts at the festival combined. He was, however, invited to the post-festival wedding between Spanky McFarland (of Spanky & Our Gang) and Medicine Charlie of The Turtles, photos from which were circulated to the press. The wedding did yield an awkward moment, which Tiny detailed in his diary, when Tiny locked eyes with Steve Paul, who was also an attendee. The two just smiled at one another. In between shows, Tiny performed for kids at a local children's hospital, hobnobbed with *Bonanza* star Lorne Green and Connie Francis at parties, and talked religion with Jackie Gleason.

Despite receiving good reviews for the show, Tiny continued to clash with Ron DeBlasio. Rudy Vallee had called Tiny and announced, 'I want to be on *your* bill next year.' Tiny was ecstatic. 'Oh, what a thrill,' he later said. 'Here's a man who I listened to who was so dominant in romance with the songs he sang. I closed the lights when I heard his early—'28, '29, '30—records, here was someone who wanted to be on my bill … it was a thrill.'

Tiny promised Vallee he would speak with Roy Silver. When he shared the news with Ron DeBlasio, however, DeBlasio was nonplussed. 'Tiny, you don't need him on the bill,' DeBlasio said. 'He's [old]. His voice is gone. He tells blue jokes. It's no good for your image, but we'll handle him. We'll take the blows. We'll know what to tell him.' Tiny would later learn that Roy Silver had, in fact, called Rudy Vallee at his office, requesting that Vallee bring his scrapbook. 'Look, we'll call you, but we don't think you're the right image for Tiny Tim's show,' Silver told him. Tiny was outraged. 'As if he had to bring a scrapbook!' he later scoffed. 'That was a shocker to me.'

As the fights with Ron DeBlasio intensified, DeBlasio threatened to fire Tiny as a client. Tiny responded by throwing him out of his room. The next day, on Christmas Eve, an exasperated DeBlasio left Miami and flew back to California, leaving Jeff Wald in his stead. Tiny spent the next day on the phone with Richard Perry, Mo Ostin, publicist Sandy Gallin, and Roy Silver, informing them all of his disagreements with DeBlasio. He also clashed with Wald over his spending.

John Rodby, who served as Tiny's conductor for the Fontainebleau engagement, remembers a fight on New Year's Eve. 'Jeff went through great pains to try to see to it that Tim would at least save some money out of the thing,' Rodby recalls, 'and I suppose, by extension, see to it that he didn't spend the management's portion of the fee as well. But Tim, who was also an excellent mimic, got to the point where he could mimic Jeff Wald's voice.'

That night, while Wald was at dinner, Rodby and the rest of the musicians making up Tiny's orchestra watched as Tiny phoned room service and, in Jeff Wald's voice, ordered thirty-one bottles of expensive champagne to be sent to the room. When Wald returned from dinner, there was a knock on the door. Wald opened the door to find a gentleman from room service with the thirty-one bottles of champagne and a bill in excess of $1,000. Flying into a rage, Wald stormed into Tiny's room and slammed him up against the wall.

'Why would you do a thing like that?' he demanded. 'You know I'm trying to save your money! You know I'm trying to see to it that you come out of this thing with something!'

'It's all right, Mr. Wald,' Tiny replied. 'I bought a bottle for you, too!'

As 1968 drew to a close, Tiny was crowned 'Novelty of the Year' by the Associated Press in a recap of the pop music developments of the year. He also raked in several awards from *Eye* magazine's first (and last) annual rock poll: 'Hope of the Year,' '1968's Public Nuisance,' 'Bad Trip Album of the Year,' 'Beautiful Person of the Year,' and '1968's Private Delight.'

LIFE magazine issued a retrospective for the 'incredible year '68.' In the 'Winners and Losers' section, Tiny was pictured among the likes of Simon & Garfunkel, Rowan & Martin, illustrator Peter Max, Nobel Peace Prize recipient René Cassin, the first African-American congresswoman, Shirley Chisholm, Andy Warhol, the first man to reach the North Pole, Ralph Plaisted, and Janis Joplin, about whom *LIFE* remarked, 'When the male voice was Tiny Tim's, what was left to choose for the female sound but the raspy songs of Janis Joplin.' Of Tiny, however, *LIFE* concluded that the 'former Larry Love, the singing canary of a Broadway freak show, would naturally become our leading male vocalist. We truly found a loser in Tiny Tim.'

On December 31, Tiny wrote in his diary, 'Dear Lord, thanks for greatest year I've ever had. It was the year of fulfillment. All my past diaries will reveal what this year has achieved. If not for you, O blessed Jesus, it could have never been. ... I pray for others who have ambitions and dreams to come true if it is right with you O Lord. ... Blessed be God for all, I pray now rest.'

CHAPTER EIGHT
BEAUTIFUL THOUGHTS

We used to try to work to go through the airports and sneak into the VIP room or even the security offices to wait to board the plane, but certain airports, there's no way to get there without going through the concourse, and we were mobbed. We were mobbed, and [Tiny] would slow down and look around and smile and everyone's going, Come on! Come on! Come on! It was howling and it was that day, every day, whenever we appeared anywhere.

ROAD MANAGER MARK HAMMERMAN

God Bless Tiny Tim finally faded from the charts during the week of December 7 1968, after seven months on *Billboard*. *Tiny Tim's Second Album* and its strong single, 'Great Balls Of Fire' b/w 'As Time Goes By,' released on December 24, aimed to correct the setbacks caused by the failed singles and the damage done by *Concert In Fairyland*, which sold 100,000 copies before it could be pulled from the shelves.

Billboard predicted that *Second Album* would prove a 'steady seller' for Reprise and described Tiny's rendition of 'Great Balls Of Fire' as a 'knockout treatment.' *Rolling Stone*, too, raved that it was 'worth paying the price of the album to hear' its single: 'His insanely versatile voice soars beyond the boundaries of style and gender. No song is safe from his fire falsetto. ... When Frank Zappa satirizes a song or an era, he rips it to shreds. Tiny Tim loves it to death and is (perhaps) equally effective.'

In fact, everyone was impressed with the new single. 'It was very good,' Ron DeBlasio said, while Tiny called it 'my best recording for Reprise.' And when Jerry Lee Lewis—The Killer himself—listened to the cut at the behest of Tiny's West Canadian A&R man Bruce Bissell, he said, 'I don't know who that cat is, but he sure can do it.'

Tiny's first move of 1969 was a return to Los Angeles to tape a few segments for *Laugh-In*. This time, the show's writers found something more interesting than torturing Dick Martin with Tiny's eccentricities. In the segment, Rowan and Martin discuss the end of the 60s and wonder which of the prior decades constitutes the 'good old days'. Then Tiny sings a song representing each decade from the 20s to the 60s. For the 20s it's Gene Austin's 'When My Sugar Walks Down The Street,' with Tiny in a yellow raincoat; the 30s is Bing Crosby's 'Out Of Nowhere' as a duet with Goldie Hawn; three women imitate The Andrews Sisters singing 'I Left My Heart At The Stage Door Canteen' and Don't Sit Under The Apple Tree' with Tiny joining in dressed as a sailor for the 40s; for the 50s, Tiny in a blue-sequin suit channels Elvis for 'Hound Dog'; and, finally, Tiny's 'Tip-Toe' represents the 60s.

In another segment, Tiny performs 'Ragtime Gal' with Goldie Hawn, who finishes the piece by sitting on his knee and rubbing noses with him. Predictably, Tiny became enamored with the budding actress. 'Miss Goldie, one of the stars of the show and who I sing to still haunts me,' he wrote in his diary. '[I have] thoughts of Miss Goldie's costume. She is real pretty. I believe she "feels" the pressure. God bless her.'*

Tiny's early performances on *Laugh-In* were integral to his initial popular recognition. He believed that the exposure had been entirely positive, and years later, when television personality Morton Downey Jr. asked Tiny if *Laugh-In* had 'helped or hurt' his career, he replied that it 'helped immensely.' However, some argue that these and later appearances on *Laugh-In* contributed to an over-simplification of Tiny's character and performance, and ultimately hindered his career. In his memoir of his friendship with Tiny, Lowell Tarling writes that a 'five minute segment on [*Laugh-In*] was not an ideal medium for such a complex performer,' and that while it gave Tiny tremendous exposure, it did so 'at a big cost to his artistry … was he a singer or a comedian?'

While in LA, Tiny awarded Miss Joan Stephens his trophy for 1968, even though he had cut off communication in September. He then abruptly sent her a telegram telling her that he was going to die of a mysterious illness in six months, in order to curb any feelings that the trophy might have resurrected in her.

---

* Phyllis Diller and Vincent Price were also guest stars on the episode. While taping one segment, Tiny was supposed to hold a sword up to Price's neck. According to a later interview with Wes Bailey, when Tiny refused, Price jokingly urged him to stop holding the thing up, yelling, 'Come on, you ninny!'

Tiny was in California only briefly before he and his newly hired road manager Mark Hammerman flew to Chicago to promote the *Second Album*. Flanked by two promotions men from Reprise, and soon after by DeBlasio and Wald, the Tiny team set out to repair the damage caused by *Concert In Fairyland*. They gave in-person appearances at record stores and parties for disc jockeys, as well as dozens of radio and television interviews, including *The Irv Kupcinet Show* in Chicago.

The time Tiny spent in Chicago also led to the creation of a semi-official Tiny Tim Fan Club. Rita McConnachie, a twenty-two-year-old Chicago native, had been intrigued when she saw Tiny on his first *Laugh-In* segment. The following day, she heard an incredulous radio DJ announce that his station had been inundated with phone calls asking about Tiny Tim. Fascinated, Rita purchased *God Bless Tiny Tim* and loved it. That Christmas, she made Tiny a three-foot-tall Christmas card, to which he replied with a telegram, calling the card the 'best and most unusual' he had ever seen.

When Rita heard that Tiny was coming to Chicago in January 1969, she attended one of his events, where, unaware of their prior correspondence, Tiny picked her from a crowd. 'Somehow, he looked at me and asked me to come onstage,' she recalls, 'and then he said he'll talk to me in a little bit so they put me backstage.' She accompanied Tiny to his appearance with TV host Irv Kupcinet, and, later, Tiny introduced her to fellow fan Sharon Fox at a promotional party. After the party, Tiny and the girls stayed up all night chatting. Tiny moved on to Detroit, but Rita and Sharon began working on the first of three issues of their newsletter, the *Tiny-Gram*. Their intent was to inform fans of upcoming shows, television appearances, and album releases.

When the press began to rely on the *Tiny-Gram* for information, Tiny's management sanctioned its activities. 'We got so much publicity for him,' McConnachie recalls. 'All the columnists were mentioning him and us and the managers thought this was great. They really did. We didn't realize what we were doing. We thought it was more of a fan thing [but] it ended up being more for press.' The two girls also served as a link between Tiny and his fans, forwarding fan mail to Tiny, and kept extensive scrapbooks on his career.

In Detroit, Tiny received a plaque from the mayor of Hazel Park. He then traveled on to Boston and Philadelphia, where 'crowds came in overflowing masses' at two different Sears locations. The tour moved on to Atlanta, finally ending in Dallas, on January 23, where 10,000 people arrived at a record store to see him. So many people came, in fact, that the event turned into a near-riot. 'People were pushing and pushing to try and get in the door,' Hammerman recalls. 'They ended up busting the whole glass window of the store … we went out through the stock room and out the back door and got in the car, and we had a police escort to get back to the hotel.'

Despite the massive crowds, Hammerman was frustrated by the prevailing attitude that Tiny was a gimmick, a lark. 'That was the most frustrating thing for me,' he says. 'I would talk to reporters and [invite them] to see him perform, and they'd be like, Yeah, really? What else does he do after he sings "Tip-Toe"? … The credibility factor was missing.'

Hammerman's frustration was reflected, too, in *Second Album*'s failure to rival *God Bless Tiny Tim*'s success. Despite the positive reception to the single, and its promotion on *The Ed Sullivan Show* and *The Hollywood Palace*, 'Great Balls Of Fire' spent only two weeks on the charts, peaking at number 86. Tiny attributed the failure of 'Great Balls Of Fire' to the same 'credibility factor' that frustrated Hammerman. 'It almost broke out. In fact, it broke out in Phoenix, Arizona, but all of a sudden it dropped,' he later said. 'It almost made it because they couldn't believe it was not Jerry Lee Lewis.'

Tiny maintained for the rest of his life that *Concert In Fairyland* was directly responsible for *The Second Album*'s commercial failure. By the time it had been pulled from stores, he told Wes Bailey in 1982, 'the damage had been done. … Naturally, when the real second album came out … it didn't move anymore, and I didn't have a good reputation in the business.'

* * *

Tiny returned to California on January 24 for a brief respite. While there, he attended a sermon by Reverend Jack Wyrtzen, the charismatic preacher who had converted Tiny to Christianity in the 50s. Wyrtzen, eager to reconnect with the now famous Tiny, made a point of scheduling a private meeting.

Tiny was soon back on the road. On February 1, he appeared at Ontario's University of Waterloo, performing to an audience of nearly 2,000. The *Hamilton Spectator*'s Stewart Brown noted that rousing sets by local rock groups Penelope Road and The Marc Tymes 'failed to raise the reverberation roused by one south-paw kiss, blown from the crest-scrubbed teeth of the madman-of-the-moment.' *Toronto Globe & Mail* critic Melinda McCracken reported that the crowd 'loved [Tiny], and cheered him on with great whoops of glee,' while Brown added that Arthur Godfrey might 'consider recalling *You Too Can Play The Ukulele*. … Forget [Tiny's] music, he's a funny entertainer.'

Reprise ads for *Tiny Tim's Second Album* proclaimed 'THE LEGEND ENLARGES,' and it was not lost on the media that Tiny's figure, too, had enlarged. 'Now he has the soft plump figure of a sixty-year-old professor,' McCracken observed, 'the result of successes in Las Vegas and the Fontainebleau Hotel in Miami, and lots of crunchy peanut butter and raw honey.' Indeed, at a post-show press conference, Tiny expounded upon the virtues of chunky peanut butter: 'There's no point in eating peanut butter unless you can really feel the chunks.'

From Ontario, Tiny traveled to New Jersey for a two-week engagement at the Latin Casino in Cherry. He played a tight show, which once again featured The Golddiggers, but the turnout was disappointing. 'Unfortunately, the public attention that he got in the papers and in the news and all that was much greater than the attendance he got at his performances,' Hammerman says. 'He played to a lot of empty rooms, because nobody really believed it. Everybody thought it was a gimmick.'

On the surface, Tiny was undeterred by the poor turnout at his concerts. 'He loved to perform, loved to perform, whether it was for one or one-hundred,' Ron DeBlasio recalled. 'He'd say, Mr. DeBlasio, don't worry, I always performed for the empty chairs ... I don't care how many people are there as long as someone is there.'

While he had not let on to DeBlasio and Hammerman that he was worried, Tiny later claimed that he knew his popularity was beginning to wane when he saw the low turn-out at the Latin Casino. 'I'll tell you when the popularity slipped,' he said in 1979. 'Well, started to slip. I'd say about February of 1969 when I was at the Latin Casino in Jersey, and I'll tell you the honest truth that I saw there was not full houses and that was the time I played big arenas ... I said to myself, Tiny Tim, you have to start all over again.'

From New Jersey it was on to New York City for an appearance on *The Tonight Show* on February 19, for which Tiny opted to sing the 1918 hit 'Have A Smile For Everyone You Meet And Everyone Will Have A Smile For You' along with Irving Kaufman's 'Stay Home Little Girl Stay Home'—strange choices, considering neither appeared on the *Second Album*. Tiny then pressed on for an appearance in Cleveland, where he hung out with Boyce & Hart, finally returning to California on February 28. Upon arriving in Los Angeles, he wrote of 'clouds of decision ... in the wind' regarding his management. What followed was a short stagnant period in March, which offered some much-needed downtime.

When he wasn't in his hotel room listening to his 1909 gramophone or taking piano lessons as part of a flight of fancy about the 'dawn of a new career' which he believed would 'be as big if not more as my uke tradition,' Tiny was spending a lot of time with his latest crush: high-school-age Miss Tricia Porch, whom he described as 'temptation no. 1.' Tiny attended her senior prom, and the young girl began visiting him in his room frequently. Tiny eventually 'succumbed to sin,' as he put it, when he ejaculated in his pants while cleansing her face. After that, he banned the temptress from his room.

Aside from an appearance at the N.A.R.M Record Convention and an interview on *The Jack Linkletter Show*, Tiny's biggest appearance that month was a Maple Leafs game in Oakland, California. The Leafs rolled out the red carpet, and Tiny was invited into their locker room. He gave interviews and was photographed wearing his Leafs hockey sweater, while defenseman Tim Horton even gave Tiny his stick.

On March 30, Tiny performed in Lockhart Park as part of the First Annual Fort Lauderdale Easter Rock Festival, hosted by WSRF Surf Radio, sharing the bill with Canned Heat, Strawberry Alarm Clock, Steve Miller Blues Band, The Grass Roots, Three Dog Night, Chuck Berry, Sweetwater, Morning Glory, The New Buffalo Springfield, and Creedence Clearwater Revival.

Upon returning to California, Tiny and Richard Perry began to put down ideas for a new album and single. Despite the bad blood from the *Second Album* recording, Perry seemed willing to continue collaborating with Tiny. However, Tiny was even more determined to dictate the course of his third album. 'Around this time, too, I started worrying about the way I was being handled in the recording studio,' he later told Harry Stein. 'I was very grateful to Mo Ostin for giving me my break, but I'm ultrasensitive about the way I sound on records. This is not an ego trip. I just know for a fact that I am the only one who knows how to record myself.'

In a diary entry dated April 10, Tiny described having to 'put my foot down' over his belief that 'It's A Long Way To Tipperary' could be a hit. Perry's objection, though not recorded, was presumably that he felt the World War I song was antiquated in light of prevailing pacifist beliefs of the youth of 1969. When his first choice was rejected, Tiny began pushing for the 1917 World War I classic 'America, I Love You.' When he was soundly informed that his next single would be 'On The Good Ship Lollipop,' he countered by insisting that 'America, I Love You' be the single's B-side.

When Perry buckled, Tiny requested that Roy Silver step in. In his diary,

Tiny noted that 'Mr. Perry did not like the idea of my coming to Mr. Silver first,' but remained firm in his belief that 'America, I Love You' would 'go all the way to number one.' He finally got his wish to record the song on April 21, the day before he left for a week of shows in Hawaii.

Meanwhile, Warner Bros/Reprise's market research indicated that the majority of Tiny's album purchases were being made by and for children. So, naturally, the label wanted Tiny to deliver a children's album in addition to the singles recorded for a third album. Tiny and Perry went into the studio together on April 11 for an epic demo session during which they taped some fifty song ideas. The majority of the songs were penned by Irving Caesar, the famed songwriter responsible for 'Swanee' and 'Tea For Two,' whom Tiny had recently befriended. They were predominately about animals ('Bill The Buffalo,' 'Lina The Laughing Hyena') or being a good Samaritan ('Tommy Tax' and Let's Make The World Of Tomorrow Today').

Tiny arrived back in Los Angeles on April 28, and work continued on the new album on May 1. It was then that Tiny discovered that Richard Perry had delegated the responsibility of producing him to his engineer Gene Shiveley. Tiny's confusion is noted in his diary, in which he referred to Shiveley as 'my new producer (?) (under Mr. Perry)' and 'my producer by proxy.' After spending six days in the studio with Shiveley, Tiny began to feel slightly more at ease with the switch, writing of a 'great night recording' with Shiveley.

In the midst of the disagreements and stop-start recording sessions, Tiny made an appearance, alongside Don Rickles, at the eleventh annual Grammy Awards, announcing Simon & Garfunkel's nomination for Best Contemporary Pop Performance (Vocal, Duo or Group) for 'Mrs. Robinson.' The show was overseen by *Laugh-In* producer George Schlatter, and Tiny's appearance was likely thanks to him. By enlisting Gary Owens as the show's announcer and adding the likes of Dan Rowan, Dick Martin, and Flip Wilson to the line-up of presenters, the 1969 Grammys played like a special edition of *Laugh-In*.

The humor of Tiny's bit with Rickles was mostly at Tiny's expense. Tiny wore a cape and called Rickles his 'all-time favorite crooner.' The seemingly peeved Rickles took a few digs at Tiny, asking, 'Isn't Halloween over?' and 'How did you get past the guards?' Tiny continued to praise Rickles, calling him 'too marvelous for words,' but when Rickles demurred, Tiny cautioned, 'I don't like you like that, Mr. Don. Take my advice and stay vicious.'

'Don't tell me what to do, you ding-a-ling, long-haired noo-noo.'

'Oh, I love it! I love it!' Tiny exclaimed.

Though the first half of 1969 saw Tiny spending a lot of time in his room at the Sunset Marquis, his concert and appearance schedule was beginning to pick up again. He even listed Woodstock in a list of potential shows in his diary. On May 8, he arrived in Houston for two nights, then went on to New York for a May 12 appearance on *The Tonight Show*, for which he played a game of hockey on the stage and scored a goal against Rickles. On May 13, he opened at the College Inn restaurant in the Sherman House Hotel in Chicago with the Golddiggers serving as both his opening act and as part of the main show. He received a standing ovation on the opening night.

In Chicago, Tiny met with Ulysses 'Jim' Walsh, an American record collector, columnist, and radio broadcaster who had written a 'Favorite Pioneer Recording Artists' column for *Hobbies* magazine since 1942, exhaustively chronicling the careers of all artists 'making records before electric recording was introduced in 1925.' Tiny was an enthusiastic reader of Walsh's column, and had gained much of his knowledge of turn-of-the-century recording artists from Walsh's writings. The two were photographed together with a wind-up gramophone, alongside Stephanie Muller, queen of the Chicago Antiques Exposition and Collector's Fair, an event sponsored by *Hobbies* magazine that Tiny also attended while in town. Walsh attended one of Tiny's performances at the College Inn, and was introduced to the audience. He later reported that he felt Tiny was 'one of the most sincere, courteous, and thoroughly nice persons he [had] ever met and completely deserving of his success.'

Tiny spent most of his downtime over the next two weeks with a young fan named Carol Chase. After only a few days together, Miss Carol informed Tiny that she wished to marry him. Tiny agreed, but then proceeded to cancel the plans several times, only to reinstate them after some persuading from Miss Carol. Tiny involved everyone in the drama. He phoned Tricia Porch and 1966 trophy recipient Marylin Rosenbery to solicit their opinions. He consulted with Ron DeBlasio, who advised him against the marriage. At a party, he even asked Hugh Hefner, who wisely told Tiny that he might be 'rushing.'

De facto fan-club presidents Rita McConnachie and Sharon Fox were also on hand to give Tiny advice. '[Miss Carol was] a very good looking girl,' McConnachie recalls. 'She was a stewardess. He made us stay up all night with him to talk him out of this wedding, and we did. He really just felt like if she kept pressuring him, he'd probably have to give in. ... She was definitely after him for whatever reason, and it wasn't anything to do with love. I think it was because he was a top celebrity and he had money and all this stuff.'

Tiny also called Reverend Wyrtzen for advice. On May 25, the last day of Tiny's Chicago engagement, Wyrtzen dispatched two members of the Word of Life Fellowship to Chicago to meet Miss Carol and discuss the marriage with Tiny. Shortly after this visit, Tiny sent a telegram to Carol informing her that the marriage was off. It is not clear on what grounds Wyrtzen's agents objected to the marriage, but Tiny wrote in his diary, 'It must be you first O' Jesus, never any mixed marriages.'

The following day, Tiny returned to LA. He was relieved that Miss Carol did not accompany him, as they had originally planned, although he found himself getting sentimental about her. He spent the next three days filming a small role for Robert Mitchum's *The Good Guys & The Bad Guys* and recorded his own version of the film's theme, 'The Ballad Of Marshall Flagg.'* 'Thoughts, memories, and melancholy moments of Miss Carol linger as I played sentimental songs and thought of her,' he wrote in his diary, while anxiously waiting by the phone for a phone call from her.

* * *

In June, Doubleday published *Beautiful Thoughts*, a forty-four-page collection of Tiny's philosophies on life, such as 'Romance is the main objective in life' and 'If your name isn't working for you, change it,' with accompanying psychedelic illustrations by Hal Frazier and Paul Hauge. Given his busy tour schedule, Tiny, of course, did not sit down and write the book; rather, it was compiled by an editor at Doubleday after 'extensive conversations' with Tiny. The small book sold 40,000 copies almost instantly, and competed for attention at the 1969 American Booksellers Association convention with Kurt Vonnegut Jr.'s *Slaughterhouse-Five* and Lillian Gish's *The Movies, Mr. Griffith, And Me*.

The book also features tributes to people Tiny admired and adored, including the poem he wrote for Elizabeth Taylor in 1947. Another section features a collage of Tiny's 'memories,' with images of Rudy Vallee, Bing Crosby, and even an illustration of an Elizabeth Arden jar with 'Miss Corky's Cookie' inside of it. Tiny would later sit down with television host David Frost and explain some of the more ambiguous passages of the book.

'I've been reading your book, *Beautiful Thoughts*, to try and get your

---

* It remains unclear why Tiny's scenes were ultimately cut from the film and his version of the theme scrapped.

message,' said Frost. 'I'm fascinated by some of the things in here. There's an interesting thing. Can you explain that one: *Don't investigate dark passages?*'

'It really means, don't press your luck,' Tiny explained. 'If things are going good, why go against them?'

Frost ran through a few more Tinyisms, including 'If you're playing a part, be perfect' ('in other words, be the part you play'), 'Dreaming is better than parties' ('the thoughts of dreaming [are] better than the reality that usually happens'), and perhaps the oddest of the lot, 'I'd rather be a lobster than a wise-guy.'

'The lobster gets the peaches when they fall,' Tiny replied. 'This is also a part of a song title in 1912 that Billy Murray did,' he added, before breaking into song:

I'd rather be a lobster than a wise-guy
I'd rather be a good thing than a sport
The lob may be a joke but still he's never broke
The wise-guy is the one who's always short.'

On June 1 1969, Tiny arrived in Washington State to kick off a month-long book tour, which would be one of the most influential periods of Tiny's life, cementing him firmly into the annuals of popular culture.

CHAPTER NINE

MISS VICKI

There's something about Miss Vicki I can't describe, but I found it impossible to resist. It's a strange spiritual uplift that moved me every moment we were together … she is so beautiful that this thing has grown and grown, from a mustard seed into a vine. It's true that I told people I could never get married, but I believe that there are things a man wants for himself and things the Lord wants for him. … Believe me, the four or five months we were engaged seemed like two years because of the mental and spiritual pressures I felt.

TINY TIM TO *PLAYBOY*, 1970

On June 3 1969, Victoria Budinger awoke to her mother's voice. 'Wake up! Come on! We're going to Wanamaker's today!' The seventeen-year-old groggily obliged. The Budingers were a middle-class family living in Haddonfield, New Jersey: Vicki's father, Alan, was a traveling art-supply salesman and sometimes artist whose work had required the family to relocate frequently, and Vicki, the second youngest of five sisters, had recently dropped out of school due to complications brought on by the family's repeated moves and had taken a job as an usherette. Her three older sisters had already moved out of the house; her younger sister was still in elementary school.

Vicki and her mother took the train to the Wanamaker's in Philadelphia. By noon, they had made their way to the fifth floor, where they inadvertently walked into a Tiny Tim *Beautiful Thoughts* book signing. Vicki had first seen Tiny on television the previous year. Though her parents usually watched *Bonanza*, one evening they caught Tiny's segment on *Laugh-In*. Vicki was intrigued. 'I thought he was really interesting and different,' she later recalled. 'There was something about him that made me want to hear and see more.' She bought a copy of *God Bless Tiny Tim* and watched his subsequent TV appearances.

Knowing her daughter was a fan, Mrs. Budinger purchased a copy of

Beautiful Thoughts, and the two got in line for an autograph. Soon Tiny Tim emerged to address the crowd. A few hecklers shouted 'sissy' and 'queer'; Tiny ignored them and instead looked out into the crowd, making eye contact with Vicki. Unsure if he was actually looking at her, she waved to him shyly. Tiny momentarily lost his bearings, and, glancing back in her direction several times, muttered to himself, 'Get away from me, Satan, in Jesus's precious name.'

After singing 'Tip-Toe,' Tiny sat down for the autograph session. Vicki made her way along the line, and when she arrived, he looked at her for a long moment. Tall and slender in a silver-gray dress, with shoulder-length brown, wavy hair, clear brown eyes, and an innocent, unassuming disposition, she must have stood out to her thirty-seven-year-old admirer. She handed Tiny two books to sign: one for her and one for her mother.

'What's your name?' Tiny asked, pen in hand.

'Vicki,' she replied, softly.

Tiny put his pen to the front cover and wrote, 'To Miss Vicki, God bless you always—Tiny Tim.'

Vicki noticed a Band-Aid on Tiny's hand and asked about it. 'It's for removing warts,' Tiny blurted out. Despite his cringe-worthy response—about which *Motion Picture* magazine would later sardonically comment, 'You just don't hardly find these romantic moments anymore'—Vicki then came back along the line again with a second copy of *Beautiful Thoughts*. Again Tiny signed her book, but he failed to give her an address or phone number.

Tiny's friend Pat Barreat was on hand that day and witnessed Tiny's reaction to meeting Miss Vicki. 'He was totally transfixed,' she recalls. I remember him sending his manager to find her and find out who she was. He just went completely crazy. He just had a look. Then he talked about her the whole rest of the day. He had to know all about her. He just loved her at first sight … he said she was the most beautiful girl he ever saw.'

After the book signing, Wanamaker's hosted a dinner for Tiny, his management, executives from Doubleday Publishing, and a few members of the press. When it came time for Tiny to give a brief talk about his book, he could speak only of 'Miss Vicki.'

'Ladies and gentlemen,' he told the guests, who included John Wanamaker himself, 'I know I'm here for a book tour, but I can't talk about that. I just met a beautiful girl and I didn't ask for her address, and I was afraid to give her mine. All I know is her name was Miss Vicki, because she bought two books.'

One local reporter promised that he would print a story about Tiny's search for Vicki. As was later reported by the press, Tiny sat in his room thinking of her. He shed a single tear into an envelope and inserted it into the sound hole of his ukulele. 'Thanks for that great classic moment,' he wrote in his diary, 'when Miss Vicki that beautiful angel who was in John Wanamaker's store today in Philadelphia came, shook my hand, got two books for her sister as well. I was afraid to give her my address. Will I meet her again? I believe I will—Lord willing—when I am back in Philadelphia.'

The local reporter kept his promise, and the next morning the paper carried a headline asking, 'Who Is The Mysterious Miss Vicki?' The article included Tiny's description of Vicki and how he felt about her, and urged the mysterious girl to come forward.

Back in Haddonfield, Vicki's mother saw the article. 'I think that's you!' she told her.

Meanwhile, Tiny left Philadelphia for a television appearance in New York. He returned four days later, on June 7, for another series of book signings. When Vicki's mother read of his return, she urged her daughter to go along to the book signing. 'Go and see if that was you he was talking about,' she said. Vicki and her sister Tracy duly arrived at the signing, and Tiny was ecstatic. She passed along her address and promised to come to his next appearance that day.

Afterward, Tiny hurried back to his hotel room and ordered a trophy over the phone. 'Look, I met this beautiful girl named Miss Vicki,' he said frantically, 'and I've got to have a trophy today!' Normally, Tiny's trophy ritual took place at the end of the year, but Miss Vicki had moved him in such a way that, for the first time, Tiny gave a trophy in the middle of the year. The store had a trophy delivered to Tiny's hotel by 1pm. It was three-and-a-half-feet tall and topped with a golden angel, arms stretched to the heavens. The inscription read:

To the World's Most Beautiful Girl,
Miss Vicki
From Tiny Tim, 1969

Tiny was thrilled by the idea of giving Vicki the trophy. Ron DeBlasio, on the other hand, was furious. 'Why are you wasting money like this?' he yelled. 'You want to go back and live with your mother?'

'Mr. DeBlasio, please, don't do this to me,' Tiny insisted. 'Let me have it.'

DeBlasio begrudgingly handed Tiny the $55 for the trophy. Tiny arrived at the book signing carrying the trophy under his arm. Vicki arrived near the event's end, at which point Tiny picked up the trophy and made an announcement to the crowd. 'Ladies and gentlemen,' he said, 'this is Miss Vicki. I give out a trophy to the most beautiful girl I meet every year, and she is definitely the most beautiful girl of 1969.'

Vicki could barely hear what Tiny was saying. 'He was trying to explain it to me,' she recalls, 'but I can't honestly tell you what he said because I was so overcome by what was going on.'

Tiny went on to explain that this yearly ritual was touched upon in *Beautiful Thoughts*, sparking the spontaneous sale of yet more books.* As he signed more autographs, Miss Vicki shyly answered a few questions from reporters. She accompanied Tiny to a third signing and, at the end of the day, visited him in his hotel room.

When Vicki arrived home, her parents were puzzled by the imposing golden statuette in her arms. When she explained it, they were surprisingly unfazed by the eccentric pop star's advances on their seventeen-year-old daughter. 'Isn't that cute?' Mrs. Budinger remarked. 'Where should we put it? Let's put it on your dresser. Make sure you dust it!'

'I was the second youngest of five girls,' Vicki explains. 'So my parents had been through every generation … my oldest sister was born in 1949, they went through the 50s, and the 60s … so they kind of had to roll with it. They were actually kind of cool, in that, they didn't question me to the degree that I would or some other parents would.'

Whatever Vicki and her family thought of Tiny's bizarre gesture, Tiny viewed the exchange as a declaration of his passion and let himself go entirely into obsession. 'Dear Lord, Thank for this great day and night—no doubt the best of 1969 so far,' he wrote. '[Miss Vicki] is so beautiful. A classic. She moves me [with her] sensuality, sweetness, aggressiveness, feeling, and loveliness. Thanks O Lord for letting me know lots of girls but above all—Miss Vicki Budinger.' The next night, back in New York City, Tiny visited the Cloisters Museum and Gardens after hours. Sitting in the stillness, he thought about Vicki, and wrote in his diary that he 'saw her in the leaves, on the water, in the stars, on the air.'

---

* A page in the book features an illustration of a young girl holding a trophy with the inscription 'Winner.'

Tiny and Vicki began to exchange letters and talk on the phone. 'I think there was a lot of excitement about [the budding relationship],' Vicki's younger sister Tracy Farquhar, who was ten at the time, would later recall. 'It was all very romantic.'

In the meantime, when not writing or talking to Miss Vicki on the phone, Tiny's book tour continued through Cincinnati, Detroit, Milwaukee, St. Louis, Miami, Denver, Atlanta, Mobile, and back to Seattle. The crowds were impressive, and in the wake of his appearance at Wanamaker's in Philadelphia, a spokesman for the store revealed that a 'predominately female crowd ... between 8,000 and 9,000' had been present to see him. Those numbers put Tiny's 'drawing power [at Wanamaker's] on a par with Princess Grace of Monaco, comedian Bob Hope, and Richard Nixon, before he became president.'

Despite the impressive turnouts, Tiny's managers were again frustrated by Tiny's willingness to oblige his fans. 'People lined up around the block wherever we were at these book signings but nobody bought the goddamn thing,' Mark Hammerman recalls. 'They'd give him napkins and pieces of paper, and I remember the Doubleday people standing behind him and saying to me, He's supposed to autograph the book. There was no one in the world who could stop him. If someone came up to him and said, Tiny, will you sign my neck? he would do it.'

Nonetheless, *Beautiful Thoughts* was selling at a rate of 5–10,000 copies a week, at $2.95 per copy. Doubleday had Tiny make an appearance at the American Booksellers Association Convention, where he told reporters how he felt about the political unrest at college campuses across the country. 'These things were taking place in 1868 as well,' he told the *Saturday Review*. 'There will always be strikes, and wars, and rumors of wars. The Devil reigns.'

Tiny went on to discuss his long hair and falsetto voice, explaining that his image was part of a 'cycle' that began in the 50s, but that he was planning a 'new cycle' for 1970. 'He would not reveal its nature,' the *Saturday Review* reported, 'but I predict he will take it all off.'

During an appearance on *The Jack Linkletter Show* at the outset of the book tour, Linkletter had asked him, 'Do you feel inhibited now? You can't change your name anymore?'

'No, in fact, I believe there'll be times I'll be changing my name again,' Tiny replied. 'I have a name coming up called Herbert Braintree.'

Linkletter did not ask Tiny to elaborate as to how Herbert Braintree might differ from Tiny Tim, but Tiny gave additional details when interviewed by

Maclean's in November 1968. 'I don't aim to keep this hair,' he said. 'There will be a change. Just the other day I went for a facial at Aida Grey's salon in the Beverly-Wilshire Hotel … we were there for two hours and the makeup consultant was looking me over. I said I would love to try something else. So she painted half my face white. From here to here it was all white. And from here to here it was all purple. A real purple color. Deep purple. I loved it, but when my manager came to pick me up he told me to take it off. This is another experimentation for the future. I will have a two-tone face. I think it's great and fits my personality.'

* * *

In the event, there was not to be a Herbert Braintree or a two-tone face. That summer, Tiny began to feel the rumblings of a major fault line in his management structure. On June 10, he discovered that Ron DeBlasio and Jeff Wald were splitting from Roy Silver to form their own company in the wake of Bill Cosby's departure from Campbell Silver Cosby. They were taking Biff Rose and The Turtles with them. Tiny detailed the events in his diary in a brief but poignant note:

LATE FLASH—MR. DEBLASIO LEAVES MR. SILVER. TAKES MR WALD AND ARTISTS BIFF ROSE AND THE TURTLES WITH HIM. EXTRA—CHOOSE TO STAY WITH MR. SILVER.

According to Tiny, Cosby had accused Silver of mishandling his money. '[There were] rumors that [Silver] was using Mr. Cosby's money, and Cosby was furious,' Tiny later recalled. '[Cosby] said, How come you didn't use your own money for these investments?'

In fact, the situation had been brewing for some time, as Tiny had noted in his diary as early as April 16 that he was 'worried situation looks bad.' When the news broke, he spent the day praying and speaking to both Silver and DeBlasio. The split sent Silver's reputation and businesses into quick decline, but Tiny decided to stay with him out of loyalty. 'Mr. DeBlasio is young aggressive and smart,' he noted. 'He has less to lose.'

Tiny's arrival in Seattle on June 19 coincided with the release of his new single, 'On The Good Ship Lollipop,' featuring the patriotic B-side for which he had fought so hard, 'America, I Love You.' During a radio interview, a DJ pulled out a copy of the new single. 'I'm dying to hear it!' Tiny exclaimed.

In fact, Tiny had heard nothing of the finished product. When the needle dropped, he was horrified by what he heard. Richard Perry had been against the recording of the song, and Tiny believed he had deliberately sabotaged the single by producing a 'harsh' backing track and mixing the vocals poorly. When the song ended, Tiny 'blasted Reprise and Richard Perry' on air, telling the audience, 'This record is junk! Don't waste a dollar on it!' He then picked up his ukulele and sang the song the way he believed it should have sounded. In the lobby of the radio station, a representative from Reprise Records began frantically searching for a telephone to call Mo Ostin.

When the news reached Ostin, it sounded the death knell for his relationship with Tiny, whose public betrayal of Reprise compounded the commercial shortcomings of the *Second Album* and the disappointing performance of 'Great Balls Of Fire.' The thin ice cracked.

'[Ostin] was so angry that I did this,' Tiny later told David Tibet, 'though he didn't realize that I knew Perry had done a bad job on this, and that I knew Perry hadn't wanted to put that record out.' Ostin resigned himself to letting Tiny's contract expire in 1971 and refrained from answering his calls.[*] Tiny fired off a telegram to Richard Perry after the radio interview, informing Perry that he would never serve as his producer again. Having ensured that his new single would stagnate, Tiny left the country for an appearance in Canada at the Toronto Pop Festival on June 21, on a bill with Sly & The Family Stone, Steppenwolf, Procol Harum, The Band, Johnny Winter, The Velvet Underground, Chuck Berry, and Blood Sweat, & Tears. 'People stood up and screamed, *screeeaamed*,' Mark Hammerman recalls. 'I don't know how many thousands of people, just pouring out love to him.'

From Toronto, it was back to New York for a radio interview with Bob Fass and appearances on *The Dick Cavett Show* and *The Tonight Show*, and then down to Philadelphia to speak to Mike Douglas. On June 27, Tiny returned to New York for a concert for 3,500 people at the Wollman Rink in Central Park, with Stillwater as his opening act. Unfortunately, Tiny did not receive the same type of adulation in his hometown as he had in Toronto.

'Although Tiny Tim used his falsetto with considerable skill, he had surprisingly little stage presence and showed little ability to sustain his songs

---

[*] In subsequent interviews, Ostin did not appear to regret his decision to sign Tiny Tim and never downplayed their initial successes together. 'The Beatles told producer Richard Perry that they loved [*God Bless Tiny Tim*],' he told Fred Goodman of the *New York Times* in 1995. 'You should listen to it. It's wonderfully made.'

even within his own ground rules,' John S. Wilson of the *New York Times* reported. 'Taken one chorus at a time, he had his amusing moments, but a tiny bit of Tim went a long way.'

Tiny returned to California on June 29. During this period, the media reported Tiny and Miss Vicki engaged in a chaste, exclusive, long-distance courtship. Tiny's diary reveals a different story, however. Tiny was running wild. He proposed to a fifteen-year-old Miss Jan while passing through Alabama on his book tour. He was also simultaneously corresponding with Miss Karin, a young Doubleday employee he met on the book tour, to whom he also awarded a trophy. He discussed marrying Miss Karin as well. He also continued to see Miss Tricia in his room.

On June 30, Tiny spent the afternoon with Miss Tricia before picking up a tenacious Miss Carol Chase from the airport and proceeding to engage in 'lots of sin' before she returned to Chicago the following morning. He also reported 'sinning' with a different Miss Vicki and a series of pampering sessions with a Miss Riley. On July 15, the fifteen-year-old Miss Jan from Alabama traveled to see him, intent on marriage. In an effort to nullify the girl—and her enraged father, who was 'coming after him'—Tiny told her that he loved her, promising to marry her after she turned eighteen. Then, at a party hosted by Dick Clark, Tiny was propositioned by Cynthia Plaster Caster to create a plaster mold of his penis. He turned her down politely.

Fears about his mortal soul notwithstanding, Tiny had other problems. An old acquaintance from his days at the Scene, Joe Kaufman—who, along with his brother Ken, was a friend of Tiny's crush Miss Cleo—had caught wind of the changes in Tiny's management and began to put pressure on Tiny to dump Roy Silver and let him take over. Kaufman had no discernible management experience, and had only just recently been released from a yearlong stint in prison. There are no descriptions of Joe, but one source described his brother Ken as 'a gangster wannabe who hung out in Brooklyn.'

On July 31, Kaufman appeared in Los Angeles and informed Tiny that they would be signing a new contract together at his upcoming performance in Atlantic City. The following night, Tiny went out with Kaufman to the Whisky A Go-Go. After a few drinks, Kaufman began making his intentions clear. Of Butros's vocal resistance to the contract, he said, 'Even if your father does not want you to sign, you're gonna!' In his diary, Tiny wrote that Kaufman 'may be connected to some interesting gentlemen,' and that accompanying his words was a 'gesture of threat.'

Before the Atlantic City run, Tiny had a six-night engagement at the Sahara Tahoe Hotel on Lake Tahoe with comedian George Carlin and Jackie Gleason's June Taylor Dancers, which he considered a 'very successful engagement.' But the phone calls from Joe Kaufman, pressuring him about signing a contract, continued. 'Though the situation is rough, with thy Grace O Lord Jesus I'll be OK,' Tiny wrote in his diary. He was joined by Miss Tricia, and one night he downed eight beers and 'sinned' with her. Brimming with angst, Tiny left Nevada on August 11, vowing to never see the girl again.

The following day in Topeka, Kansas, provided a light-hearted reprieve when Tiny was named 'Fan of the Year' at the National Baseball Congress. In a speech to the event's attendees, he recalled watching the Dodgers' unexpected 1965 World Series victory. 'So many fans know more about baseball than I do,' he told the crowd. 'Maybe I'm in the lower one-tenth, but I'm honored.' He also predicted a future World Series in which earth's baseball players would be pitted against players from the moon.

Tiny finally landed in Atlantic City on August 17. He was scheduled to perform four shows a day for a week at the Steel Pier. Vicki Budinger and her mother arrived the next day, checked into a hotel across the street from Tiny's, and attended a show. The next afternoon, Vicki visited Tiny in his hotel room before his show. It was only the second time the two had met in private, and after chatting for awhile, Tiny looked up at Vicki and said, 'You know, I think you'd be the perfect person for me to marry.'

Vicki was dumbfounded. 'You could have knocked me over on the floor with a feather!' she recalls. 'I thought, What, are you crazy? Are you out of your friggin' mind? What!? Here I was, this seventeen-year-old girl … he had told me that he was thirty-seven … that's a pretty huge difference.'

Vicki balked at his casual proposal until she remembered perusing family scrapbooks containing marriage certificates and pictures of several female relatives who had married considerably older men. One of her great-grandmothers had married a twenty-seven-year-old man when she was sixteen, and another married a forty-year-old man at the age of seventeen. Furthermore, in her opinion, Tiny did not act his age. 'He didn't really seem to be old to me. He looked young and he also behaved young.'

Vicki asked for time to think it over, and Tiny obliged her request.* 'Is this

---

* Tiny gave two different accounts of Vicki's reaction. He told *Playboy* in 1970 that 'she jumped up and down and said she'd love to,' but told Harry Stein in 1976 that 'she didn't say yes, and she didn't say no; she said she wanted to think about it.'

really what I want to do with my life?' Vicki wondered. Her mother instantly approved; her husband, however, seemed open to the idea but needed some convincing. 'My parents wanted me to have someone who would take care of me because they were worried about what I was going to do with my life at that point,' she says. 'They said, here's someone who's going to take good care of her, and he'll love her, and he's successful, so why not? They clapped their hands together and were like, OK, there she goes.'

The next day, Vicki accepted Tiny's proposal. Enthralled but suspicious, he collapsed to his knees and prayed. 'If you want fame or glory, you don't have to go down the aisle with me. But if you do, there's a higher source that knows about it.'

Today, Vicki is unable to articulate a clear reason as to why she decided to marry Tiny Tim. While many have suggested that his fame was a big part of the attraction, she remains unsure. 'I wonder sometimes … was that part of it? I don't think so, but I suppose … if I had met him on the street or at school would it have been different? There may have been an element of that.'

In his diary, Tiny mulled over the age difference and Vicki's motivation for marriage. '[I pray] to understand her youth,' he wrote, 'her seventeen years of age, her desire for publicity, fame, fortune, prestige, and all the other things you O Lord have given me and which Satan's will may have already placed in her heart.' He questioned his own desires as well. What did Vicki possess of specific value to Tiny? Just as he had silenced those who had said he would never become famous, he suspected that part of him aimed to silence those who felt he could not land a beautiful woman. He worked through his thoughts in his diary. Admitting that he had always wanted 'a beautiful woman of my own ideals (in looks and stature), which Miss Vicki is,' he wondered, 'Am I really using Miss Vicki as an object for my conquest egotistically?' He was also under no illusions as to the fact that 'the world and enemies as well as friends will be anxiously awaiting for the marriage to quickly dissolve … believe me not only will once again the scoffers be fooled by this marriage being a success but also how happy this marriage will turn out for all people to see and for above all not for me or Miss Vicki but for the glory of Thy name o Blessed Lord Jesus.'

As a sort of emotional preparation for matrimony, Tiny began a cathartic download of his life to Vicki. 'I told her about all the lovely girls like Miss Cleo and Miss Corky,' he told *Playboy*, 'and that I'd kissed a few. I told her that I can get very emotional when the Dodgers are playing baseball or when the

Maple Leafs are playing hockey … I can be very hard to live with during a hot pennant race. If my teams lose, I just want to be alone. I also told her that I'm moody and funny-tempered, and about my cosmetics and toilet habits, and that I often eat meals alone. She thoroughly understood.'

Tiny also insisted on visiting with Vicki's parents in person to receive their blessing, and it seemed they too wanted a face-to-face discussion. On August 20, Alan Budinger and Vicki's youngest sister Tracy joined the group in Atlantic City. To Tracy, who accompanied her parents on the trip, the possibility of a celebrity joining the family was exciting, though she did pick up on the serious tone of the discussions between Tiny and her parents. 'My parents spent quite a few late nights in serious discussion with him about his proposal,' she recalled. 'I think it was all just a lot of fun for me at my age; Tiny was always very sweet to me and we had a good time with him.'

Vicki's older sister, Genie Bramlett, remembered more clearly some apprehension on the part of her parents, in particular her father, and maintains that the family was not seeking to gain from Tiny's fame. 'They didn't say yes on the spot there, absolutely not,' she says, 'because she was so young, and my father balked a bit because of her age and, yet, there was a feeling of being swept away and a feeling of meant-to-be, and there it was in front of us. … My mother was a saint and went with the heart and the love … she wanted to do it, Dad needed a little convincing, so there it happened.'

The Budingers' main concern was that Tiny, as a celebrity, would grow tired of Vicki and move on. Tiny assured them that he did not blame them for thinking that way. 'If I had a daughter, I'd be ten times as tough.' He insisted that he remained fond of every girl he had known. 'I still have a cookie given to me by Miss Corky in 1967, which I keep in an empty Elizabeth Arden Blue Grass Velva Shampoo jar sealed with Scotch tape. I also still have Miss Cleo's gumdrop and many more mementos. I would be just as faithful—if not more—to Miss Vicki.'

Mrs. Budinger suggested that they wait a few years, or at least until after Vicki's eighteenth birthday, but Tiny insisted that an extension would prove superfluous. 'I told your daughter everything low about me,' he said. 'If I wanted your daughter in any other way I wouldn't have to go through with this now—sitting here and being questioned and all of this … if I wanted your daughter in any other way, we could have just gone to B-E-D, and I could have said goodbye to her the next morning. But the only way I want her is right in the grace of the Lord's eyes. That's the way it has to be.'

Somehow, this satisfied the Budingers. But though they had given their consent, Tiny was suspicious that they still harbored doubts about his sincerity, noting in his diary that 'their lips said yes but their eyes did not.' He told them so: 'Now look, your world and my world are different, you see,' he said. 'But my suggestion to you is to just pray the good Lord helps you change your heart in time by whatever good works I do.'

Tiny's parents also joined the couple in Atlantic City. Though they thought Vicki was a 'nice girl,' Tillie insisted she was too young for Tiny. Her words had no effect, and Tiny's predisposition toward the insubordination of his parents remained fully in tact. 'I like young girls,' he replied. Officially betrothed, Tiny Tim and Miss Vicki spent the next few nights at the Steel Pier. Mark Hammerman, in the room next door, listened in amazement as the couple chatted endlessly between Tiny's shows. 'They sat up for days and nights talking!' he recalls.

Despite his recent bout of philandering, Tiny showed restraint and only kissed his fiancé a few times during their visit. He also requested Vicki attend a one-week retreat at Jack Wyrtzen's Word of Life camp. Despite her hesitation, he explained that if she went 400 miles to 'inquire' about Jesus, no matter what happened, she would get an 'F' for effort. She departed on August 22 to attend the retreat in order to 'please him.'

* * *

With his love life sorted, Tiny turned his attention to his management. Joe Kaufman and his assistant, Joe 'Cappy' Cappelluzzo, visited Tiny in Atlantic City and informed him that he would sign the contract by the end of the week—a move that Tiny knew would hit Roy Silver 'like a Pearl Harbor attack.' Kaufman and Cappy, true to their word, arrived the same day Vicki departed and announced to Mark Hammerman that they were taking over.

'The other guys moved in on his management,' Hammerman recalls. 'Roy and I talked about it and decided these were not guys to fool around with, and Tiny kind of let himself be carried along with what these guys could do for him.' Kaufman and Cappy, he says, were able to convince Tiny that he 'wasn't being handled properly or wasn't being treated right or whatever it was, [so] he went with them. When they threatened anybody around not to mess with it, I got onto a plane and flew back to LA. I don't think I saw him after that.'

Upon Hammerman's retreat, Joe Cappy became Tiny's road manager. A Korean War veteran turned roofer, and a cousin of gangster and future actor Tony Sirico Jr., he was later described by his own son as 'just a knock-around Brooklyn guy who fell into that whole thing.' Tiny offered a similar description. 'He was very tough and he came from Brooklyn,' he told Johnny Pineapple in 1994. 'He was very dangerous. He was, you know, he was a wonderful man, he was a wonderful gentleman, but you'd never get in trouble with him. It's not important *who* he knew.'

Despite Cappy's 'knock-around' disposition, Tiny warmed to him quickly, and they began to discuss his wedding plans with Miss Vicki. Cappy—who was kind enough to drive Tiny's parents back to New York City—suggested that he marry Vicki on December 25, because of the date's religious significance. Tiny thought this was a good idea and asked Vicki's parents to send out invitations.

Meanwhile, Vicki called from Wyrtzen's retreat to tell Tiny she loved him. She had been listening to sermons two or three times a day, 'for what seemed like hours,' and found the camp and its followers 'a bit cultish.' Perhaps sensing that Vicki had not taken to the born-again views espoused at his camp, Wyrtzen called Tiny and advised him against marrying her. But Wyrtzen's relationship advice failed to have the same influence on Tiny as his sermons. After all, as Tiny declared in his diary, he loved Vicki more than even his cosmetics or the Dodgers.

CHAPTER TEN
'BEING OF SOUND MIND ...'

I would never use the holy sacrament of marriage for publicity reasons. The good Lord knows what's in the heart, not just the outward appearance. When I gave Miss Vicki her ring on Mr. Carson's show, he asked right out of the blue if we would get married on his show. I thought it was a great idea for several reasons. Mainly, I thought it would save our families a lot of trouble and expense, so I told him yes.

TINY TIM TO *PLAYBOY*, 1970

In late August 1969, Reprise Records released what would be Tiny Tim's last full-length album on the label, *For All My Little Friends*. 'Mr. Tim is headed straight back to the charts with this delightful venture into the world of children's songs,' a promotional advertisement declared, noting that a standout of the record is a version of the 'nearly forgotten' 'Chickery Chick.'

The cover art resembled that of his first album with Reprise: Tiny Tim, ukulele in hand, standing on a hillock, covered in Easter flowers, surrounded by a collection of smiling children of varied ethnicities, with a clever endorsement by *Rolling Stone* rock critic John Mendelsohn on the back cover:

There once was a songbird named Tim,
Who, in singing, went out on a limb,
But the kids didn't care,
Or make fun of his hair,
Cos they all realized the groovy in him.

The album lacked the production values of Tiny's previous Reprise albums, however. Perry had delegated the majority of the production to his engineer, Gene Shiveley. Perry's tracks—'On The Good Ship Lollipop,' 'Mickey The

Monkey,' 'I'm A Lonesome Little Raindrop,' and 'What The World Needs Now Is Love'—feature full orchestration and Perry's signature attention to detail. Shiveley's tracks, on the other hand, are largely of Tiny accompanying himself on ukulele, with sparse additional instrumentation. Despite the availability of other songs recorded during the lengthy demo sessions for the album, a decision was made to include 'The Viper' from *God Bless Tiny Tim* as well as snippets of Tiny's narration from the *Second Album* rather than record new narration, intros, and outros. With a new producer at the helm, a disinterested label, and a distracted Tiny, the result was an inconsistent but tedious cluster of redundant songs about animals and manners.

Ironically, and perhaps to spite Richard Perry, Tiny would later intimate to Harry Stein that he felt the album was 'technically much better than the other two' and add that Gene Shiveley 'did a great job.'* Furthermore, he felt that the single, 'I'm A Lonesome Little Raindrop,' was 'about the best thing [I] ever recorded.' The album earned Tiny his only Grammy nomination, in the category of Best Album for Children. Ultimately, it lost out to Peter, Paul & Mary's *Peter, Paul & Mommy*.

Despite the Grammy nomination, *For All My Little Friends* did not put Tiny Tim back on the charts. Neither did either of its singles, 'Mickey The Monkey' b/w 'Neighborhood Children,' released on September 10, or 'I'm A Lonesome Little Raindrop' b/w 'What The World Needs Now Is Love,' released on October 22. Frustrated, Tiny decided to further alienate his label and Richard Perry. 'I've made three LPs now,' he told the *Montreal Gazette* in April 1970, 'and except for a couple of songs like "Tip-Toe Thru' The Tulips," I don't like the way I sound on records. I want to do the old tunes like they sounded in the 10s and 20s. I don't think I've found the producer who can put me down right, who can capture the sound of the good old songs.'

* * *

On August 26, immediately following his stint at the Steel Pier, Tiny departed with his new road manager, Joe Cappy, for an extensive tour of Australia. The schedule included a myriad of television and radio interviews, concerts, and personal appearances, all of which took its toll on Tiny, who came down with bronchitis. Despite the impact it had on his voice, Tiny continued with

---

* Richard Perry, on the other hand, loathed the release and was reportedly distraught upon hearing that the 2006 Rhino CD boxed set *God Bless Tiny Tim: The Complete Reprise Masters … And More!* was to contain the album.

his engagements at the prestigious Towers of Chevron Renaissance Hotel, even though he thought his voice 'was awful—high voice especially.' While convalescing in his hotel room following the completion of his gig at the Towers on September 10, Tiny dispatched a 'telegram of goodbye' to Miss Vicki, writing in his diary the following day that he missed her. Upon his return to Los Angeles, on September 12, he immediately called her to make amends.

On September 17, after a few days of rest, Tiny and Joe Kaufman traveled to Philadelphia for an appearance with Mike Douglas. Later that day, they drove to New Jersey for two shows at the Trenton State Fair. Tiny was joined by Vicki in New Jersey and the media caught wind of the two's intentions. Upon leaving the fair, Tiny answered a few questions from the press. He described how they had met in Philadelphia at a Wanamaker's Department Store and revealed that they had 'been engaged for some time.' He dismissed any concerns about their age difference, remarking, 'I really do believe I'm nineteen and I try to stay that way.'

The following day—'perhaps the greatest day in my life so far'—news of the engagement broke, and a gaggle of reporters followed the couple to Tiffany's, where they picked out a one-and-a-half-carat diamond engagement ring. The next day, Tiny announced the engagement on *The Tonight Show*. Newspapers and news stations hyped the appearance, announcing Tiny's intention to 'make it official that he will marry a seventeen-year-old New Jersey girl.'

To open his segment on the show, Tiny reprised 'Livin' In The Sunlight, Lovin' In The Moonlight' from his first appearance. 'I see love hasn't affected your singing,' Carson said. 'You sound as happy as ever.'

'Miss Vicki's so nice to me,' Tiny replied. He then went on give Carson the scoop—'in respect of the many great times I've had with you here'—that they were to marry on December 25, in Haddonfield, New Jersey.

'Now, this is your first marriage, isn't it?' Carson asked.

'Yes, Mr. Carson, and last … the fact that she is seventeen, I would like to say that a lot of prayer is involved at the moment and, of course, I've always loved youth, but only in the right way.'

Tiny went on to tell the story of how the two meet, and Carson joked that Tiny was about to marry his 'biggest fan.' Then, after a commercial break, a bashful Vicki joined Tiny on the stage, appeasing the rabidly curious crowd.

'Hello, Vicki,' said Carson. 'This is kind of a new experience for you—just relax, we're all friends here—we're delighted that you're here. Have reporters been after you all day, I suppose? Calling you and talking about the marriage?'

Vicki only giggled in response, allowing Carson to add, 'You're just like a typical bride to be, right? Not too much to say.'

'Well, Miss Vicki is so awed by this now,' Tiny said, answering for her— something he would do throughout their relationship. 'Look at me, I was on TV so long and at all these lovely clubs in the village, and I'm shaken like a leaf because it's like a new experience. So I can't blame Miss Vicki for being so innocently slow in speech.'

'Tiny, you have kind of the old-style Southern manners,' Carson said. 'You say Miss Vicki, that's kind of nice.'

'Well, I always believe in calling women and gentlemen by the name because of respect,' Tiny explained. 'Also, if I may say, I have a little ring here.' From his pocket, Tiny produced the engagement ring he and Vicki had chosen together prior to the taping.

'This I did not know about, either!' Carson exclaimed. 'This is not put up, believe me!' He then took the ring from Tiny and held it up to the camera. 'Really, your bride should show that, not me!' he joked. 'That's a beautiful ring. If you had bought a few more books, you'd have had a bigger stone there, Vicki! You better place it on your intended bride's finger there.'

With that, Tiny slipped the ring onto Vicki's finger, inciting applause from the audience. 'Now you're officially engaged,' Carson remarked.

Immediately following the couple's sentimental display, Carson asked Tiny about his relationship history, hoping to incite some purgative admissions. He was not disappointed. Tiny quickly admitted that he was saving himself for marriage—a fact that made his eccentricities even more pronounced. 'I'm no saint,' he said. 'I have, to my sorrow, slipped in that, and thank-God-to-Christ he's protected me and I never had any relations with a woman.'

'But you've kissed your intended,' Carson asked, after the audience's laughter subsided. Tiny admitted that he had 'slipped twice,' to which Carson assured him that 'a little kissing isn't bad before marriage.'

'You plan to have a family?' Carson asked.

'That's one of the main reasons for marriage,' Tiny replied, to thunderous laughter and applause.

A little later in the interview, after Vicki's exit, Carson leaned in to Tiny and asked if the couple would like to be married on *The Tonight Show*. Tiny accepted immediately, without conferring with his bride-to-be. He later admitted that he had accepted partly so that NBC would foot the bill, and also to spare Vicki's parents' house from becoming a 'center for attraction.'

Miss Vicki watched Tiny accept Carson's invitation from the greenroom. 'I was sitting back there going, What?! Are you out of your mind?' she recalls. 'Well,' she thought, 'I'll talk to him and I'll fix that.'

Tiny and Vicki subsequently held a press conference, flanked by his parents and management. He assured reporters that it was not a problem that Vicki did not yet know how to cook and 'offered to give her top billing.' When asked what she liked about Tiny, Vicki replied simply, 'Everything. I can't pinpoint anything.' Tillie, meanwhile, 'simply shrugged' when asked what she thought of her daughter-in-law-to-be. Tiny's management also confirmed that the ceremony would take place on *The Tonight Show* on either Christmas Eve or Christmas Day. When Vicki was asked what sort of wedding she wanted, she replied, ironically, 'A traditional one.'

Vicki tried in vain to talk Tiny out of holding the wedding on *The Tonight Show*. 'We were going to get married at my parent's house, remember?' she pleaded. She waited patiently for Tiny to see sense and repeal his decision, but the moment never came. 'All the time I kept thinking he was going to say, No, no, no, that's not a good idea. But he didn't.'

'I remember Vicki being mortified,' her older sister Genie recalls. 'By that time, Tiny was coming to dinner … we got to know him and it was a big happy family around the dinner table and I think I might have said, Why did you say yes? and he just laughed and chuckled and chortled and that was that and it was inevitable.'

Tiny and Vicki's unprecedented wedding quickly became world news. Newspapers and magazines—from local papers in New Jersey to *TIME*—were littered with headlines: 'Tiny Tim Loves Miss Vicki,' 'Tiny Tim Finds Love,' 'Teenager Topples Tiny Tim,' 'Tiny Tim Announces Engagement,' 'Tiny Tim Announces Troth To Teen-Age New Jersey Fan,' and, most appropriately, 'Tiptoe To The Altar.' In *TIME*, Tiny and Vicki's photograph was featured prominently next to one of Princess Margaret.

With Tiny's mainstream career under an aggressive media siege, his marriage was not spared. It was hinted that the marriage was a fluke—the next step in an elaborate and somewhat distasteful affectation. 'Forget that [Miss Vicki's] … engaged to marry Tiny Tim,' one snarky reporter wrote in the *St. Petersburg Time*s, 'and you'd think she was any girl in love … honestly.'

'There are those who think this thing's a big gag,' *Motion Picture* magazine noted. 'Is this for real or is Tiny putting us on again?' *Again?*

Tiny, on the other hand, maintained that he was 'shocked' by the media's interest in his engagement. 'I hope I can live up to it,' he wrote, of the media hype following a concert appearance in West Virginia a few days after the news broke. It did not take long for the press to find the Budingers' address and phone number, and not only was their phone line tied up by an incessant press, but their house, too, was infested with reporters toting cameras and microphones.

Vicki's younger sister Tracy remembers it all vividly, describing the press invasion as 'one of the hardest things' the family had to deal with. 'My parents would be very welcoming and cordial with them, and they would appear to be very friendly and kind. Then, the next day, we would read some horrendous account of how weird we all were, or they would pick up on some offhand remark and use it against us. It really was very disturbing and sad. Reporters would call at any hour of the day or night to do a live radio interview with no warning; my parents would answer the phone and hear, You're on the air.'

On another occasion, Vicki's parents were 'so tired of the incessant phone calls and knocks on the door' that they sent Tracy to greet the reporters. 'They sat me on the front steps and asked me a stream of ridiculous questions. I remember rolling my eyes at them. When they wanted me to blow kisses at the end of the interview, as Tiny used to do, I refused, saying that I wasn't doing one of their "cute endings." My mother laughed so hard she cried when she saw the interview on the news that night.'

Upon hearing of the negative kickback at her family's home, Vicki's older sister Genie decided she would not advertise her involvement with Tiny Tim, but a certain infamy still clings to her family today. 'We heard negative [feedback] for forty years,' she says. 'Nobody knew him. We knew him. He sat at the dinner table. Yes, there was a lot of negative feedback, not surprisingly. I lived in a different town ... and was never bothered by reporters, but on a personal level, I can remember a lot of negative feedback, so I didn't talk about it. To this day, I will reveal it to a new friend very rarely.'

Negative feedback or not, it did not take long for Tiny to endear himself to the family. 'We always enjoyed his visits,' says Tracy. 'He would sit for hours playing music ... we had a lot of laughs with him, and I think he enjoyed spending time with us. I remember playing a song for him that I had written on my guitar, and he was extremely gracious. I also remember having a ring stuck on my finger, and he was able to get it off with the moisturizing cream he always carried with him. I also remember him visiting one Halloween; he answered the door to surprise the trick-or-treaters! It was always an adventure when he would visit.'

Mr. and Mrs. Budinger embraced the fact that Tiny Tim would soon be their son-in-law. When contacted for a statement, Mrs. Budinger dismissed any concerns that they were not behind their daughter's decision. 'We're very fond of him,' Emma Budinger told one reporter, while to another she explained, 'He has his eccentricities, but we all have. His are a lot more than others. He has a lot of dimensions. We feel very light-hearted about it.'

Vicki's father, Alan, particularly enjoyed Tiny's presence. He was an art supply salesman and an amateur painter who painted under the name 'Hillary.' Tiny would visit him at the family home and keep him company while he was painting, bringing with him his wind-up gramophone and Rudy Vallee records. The two would discuss baseball, hockey, music, and life.

After spending considerable time with his soon-to-be son-in-law, Alan Budinger described him to the *Philadelphia Daily News* as a 'very sensitive person with a deep appreciation of the finer things in life. I'm going to do a portrait of Tiny, in the next couple months. He's a challenging character. He has many fine features. His eyes are beautiful. They're piercing eyes. Tiny's eyes tell you he's honest.' While there is no record of such a painting, Alan did do a portrait of Tiny and Vicki together in Victorian clothing and setting. His connection to Tiny attracted interest in his work, landing him a string of gallery shows. 'Oh, I'm sure being Tiny's father-in-law has something to do with it,' he told the press.

'I didn't foresee that,' Vicki later said of all the attention, 'but then when it came to be … I was very uncomfortable. If you look at any old photos of us you'll see me looking all cranky and weird because I didn't get it. I was like, Why are these people hassling us? Why are these people following us everywhere? I was a child. I didn't understand or expect what finally did come about.'

An increasingly overwhelmed Vicki joined her parents in defending her fiancé. 'I've met lots of people and thought they were nice,' she told a reporter. 'I liked their looks, but I never thought about them for the future. This time, I knew he was the one. There couldn't be anyone else. He felt the same way … He's no joke, and he's not effeminate. He knows it, I know it and the Good Lord knows it.'

Vicki was further affronted when Joe Kaufman began to give her directions as to what meals she should order at restaurants and how she should act when out with Tiny. Sensing her uneasiness, Tiny comforted her and reminded her that as long as she still wanted him, all was well. Conversely, things with Kaufman were not fine. He had deposited the $14,000 Tiny earned in Australia into his personal bank account. When Tiny was questioned by Butros and his lawyer, Mr. Seidel, as to why he had allowed the thumb-breaker to come on board, Tiny replied only that it had been due to 'spiritual pressure.'

On September 23, Tiny fired Kaufman via Mr. Seidel and his father, who confronted Kaufman over the missing $14,000 at attorney Charles Moerdler's office. Meanwhile, Tiny flew back to Los Angeles to beg Roy Silver to take him back, and Silver did. Tiny noted that Silver greeted him 'fairly,' warning him 'not to call anyone.' Tiny did not heed Silver's advice. Four days later, he received both Kaufman and Cappy in Los Angeles and rehired them.

Ultimately, Tiny's reasoning had much to do with saving his mortal soul. Since arriving back in LA, Tiny had put his impending marriage on the line when he entertained a Miss Iris in his room, applied cold cream to her face, and allowed her to perform oral sex on him. 'I do not know how far career will go with [Kaufman and Cappy],' he wrote in his diary, 'but they do take a personal interest in friendship with me and will be the crutch I need to fight temptation. I do not want to let Miss Vicki down again by sinning with another woman as I did ... last night and this morning.'

The following day, Miss Iris returned home to San Diego, and Tiny, released from the immediate peril to his soul, admitted to himself the truth about Joe Kaufman. 'I do not see much of a future in show business with Mr. Kaufman in the picture as a manager,' he wrote. 'He probably wants to hitch his wagon to a star! But I must go along with him for a while.' When informed that Tiny had, again, decided to split from him, Silver withheld Tiny's sheet music and arrangements and refused to release Tiny from his contract unless he was paid $10,000. He also drew up a release disallowing Tiny from questioning Silver's management of Tiny's earnings. Left with no alternative, Tiny agreed to pay the money, signed the release, and re-hitched his wagon to the disreputable and inexperienced Kaufman and Cappy.

* * *

On October 1, Tiny returned to New York for another appearance on *The Tonight Show*. Because Carson and the crew would be on vacation over the Christmas holiday, it was decided that the wedding would take place on December 18 instead. Tiny agreed, adding, 'As far as Christ is concerned, it was always Christmas with him.' Meanwhile, Miss Iris had followed Tiny to New York, hoping to hold him to a promise that he would organize a party for her 'professional career.' Tiny had already admitted his misstep to Vicki, who had the misfortune of meeting Iris at a photo shoot with Tiny at the Cloisters Museum and Garden. In his diary, Tiny mentioned only 'danger on the horizon' regarding his engagement.

On October 5, Tiny returned to Los Angeles for a taping of *The Andy Williams Show*, which yielded—aside from a humorous performance of 'I'm A Lonesome Little Raindrop,' with Tiny flanked by a chorus line—a wild segment featuring Tiny, Nancy Sinatra, and the Osmond Brothers antagonizing a bewildered Bob Newhart with a frenetic rendition of 'The Thank You Song,' an obscure ditty from the short-lived Broadway musical *Maggie Flynn*.

The following day, Tiny's Maple Leafs fandom was celebrated at Maple Leaf Gardens in Toronto. An unlikely friendship had formed between the singer and the Leafs' players and personnel. Tiny had once worn his Leafs sweater on *The Tonight Show*, and the Leafs' bulletin board carried an autographed photo of Tiny that read 'God Bless Mr. Punch Imlach.' Glen Woodcock, who operated the Maple Leaf Gardens scoreboard, fielded constant calls from Tiny 'to get the up-to-date score.' In fact, for one playoff series, Leafs media director Stan Obodiac attached a transistor radio attached to a phone so that Tiny could listen to the play-by-play in Los Angeles. The owners of the team, Harold Ballard and Stafford Smythe, humorously clashed over whether or not they should cash a $1 check Tiny had sent for the 1968– '69 team calendar. One Toronto reporter joked that they 'didn't cash the [check], but they shortened the players' benches and added more rail seats to offset the lost revenue.' Punch Imlach even asked Tiny to travel with the team toward the end of the season that year as 'good luck.'

That night, flashbulbs popped and the audience cheered as defensemen Jim McKenney and Mike Walton gave Tiny a hockey sweater and a pair of skates and escorted him out to center rink. Because Tiny was unable to stand on the skates, the two supported him amply. 'They had to help me get them on as if I had polio,' Tiny recalled. 'It was a great moment.'

'They put him on a pair of skates, but he couldn't stand up,' McKenny recalls. 'I was one of those guys that held him up … the old guys on the team wouldn't touch him. They said they thought he might have lice or something … but Shakey [Mike Walton] grabbed me. He says, Come on, we'll get some ink here, let's go help him out. There was a photographer there, and we'd do anything to get in the paper … I remember hanging on to [Tiny] … he was like a jellyroll. He had no muscle or anything. But I liked him. He was OK.'

During his promotion of 'I'm A Lonesome Little Raindrop,' Tiny had deluded himself into believing that Vicki did not have feelings for him, which led him on another romantic flight of fancy. He called Miss Iris and convinced her to meet him in California, to run away and elope. Shortly thereafter, he reneged and sent a telegram to Iris telling her not to join him in California, and also tape-recorded a phone call to the girl in which he repeated his instructions.

When Tiny arrived in New York on October 13, he visited the Budingers' house and told Vicki what had happened with Miss Iris. She forgave him, and the two spent the next few days together, with Tiny accompanying Vicki and Genie to a fitting for Vicki's gown.

On October 18, Vicki flew to England with Tiny for an appearance together on *The David Frost Show*. After Tiny performed 'I'm A Lonesome Little Raindrop' and threw on a cowboy hat for a country-style version of 'Skidrow Joe' with a steel-stringed, baritone uke, Frost steered the conversation toward Tiny's recent engagement. Though he admitted none of the details of his ongoing antics, he expressed an uneasiness about the engagement.

'I hope I can make her happy,' he said. 'Marriage is like another adventure and a surreal thing, but through prayer—through Christ and His blessings—I think it'll happen if she says yes. I never take anything for granted until it happens.'

'But she must have said yes,' Frost replied.

'But it's like the last of the ninth: the game is never over until the last man's out. Of course, I'll never change my mind.'

Vicki then joined the pair as the house band played 'Tip-Toe,' and Frost asked her for clarification. 'I was interested that Tiny said *if* you'd say yes, but you've said yes,' he wondered. Tiny, she replied, was worried that 'maybe later I'd change my mind, so right now he won't say that he's sure about it.'

'Will you change your mind?' Frost asked.

'No, I know I won't, but he just says he won't take it for granted.'

'And what made you sure, Vicki, that Tiny was the man for you?'

'It wasn't anything I could say, but I just knew it couldn't be anybody else.'

* * *

The following day, Vicki returned to the States, and Tiny remained in Britain for a six-week tour that he had come to call the Battle of the Bulge. Their time together had reinforced Tiny's resolved to marry Vicki, and he vowed, following the tour, to never be separated from her again.

The tour saw Tiny performing in all corners of Britain and Ireland. It was during this period that he first began to experiment with an electric megaphone—or 'singing bullhorn'—in order to 'bring back the sound before the electrical system in an acoustic-alike way,' and, truly, the megaphone added an element to Tiny's already antiquated style, which gave the impression of a gramophone. One reviewer likened the bit to a 'space-age Rudy Vallee routine.'

On October 30, Tiny, megaphone in hand, entered IBC Sound Recording Studios in London to record a medley of English patriotic songs from World War I and II, consisting of 'There'll Always Be An England,' 'It's A Long Way To Tipperary,' and 'Bless 'Em All.' Backed by bandleader and clarinet player Harry Roy and his band, famous for the scandalous 30s song 'My Girl's Pussy,' the session produced an authentically vintage sounding recording. Reprise Records called itself 'Reprise-o-Phone' for the release, and issued a UK-only ten-inch 78 of the resulting recording, replete with a British flag and illustrations of British soldiers on the label. 'Have You Seen My Little Sue' was featured as the B-side. The inclusion of Tiny's megaphone experimentation on the release delighted him. The following day, he performed the same British patriotic medley live with Harry Roy and his band on *The David Frost Show*. Reprise UK then issued the medley as a UK-only 45, also featuring 'Have You Seen My Little Sue' on the flip side.

On November 1, Tiny closed out an engagement at Luton's Caesar's Palace, after which the crew traveled to Ireland for several more shows. The singer was poorly received in much of Ireland, receiving a negative review in Dublin immediately. 'Thanks for the strength to continue on after a bad review of act and Mr. Joe's wish to get out of Ireland,' he wrote in his diary, after they arrived in Cork on November 4. However, by the time he had arrived in Belfast, Tiny was in a frenzied state, pining for Miss Vicki.

During the tour, alone in his room, Tiny was steadfastly shielding himself from temptation. He spent his time rehearsing possible songs to sing to Vicki following the ceremony on *The Tonight Show*. 'What A Friend We Have In Jesus,' 'Love Divine,' 'To God Be The Glory,' 'No One Ever Cared For Me Like Jesus,' 'Beloved,' 'You Are The Rose Of My Heart,' and 'All That I Want is You' were all considered. By the time the tour reached Newcastle, Tiny's pining for Miss Vicki had reached a fever pitch. On November 12, he threw an 'early-morning explosion,' during which he ran into the hallway outside his hotel room shouting. He threw chairs in his room, damaging the hotel room walls, broke a glass bottle, and smashed two ukuleles. Following the incident, Tiny visited a doctor. The following night, he was called out for four encores at La Dolce Vita, and then for five encores at the Latino Club on November 15.

Finally, it was back to London to perform at the 2,286-seat Palladium, where Tiny was introduced to Princess Margaret.* He also performed a smaller show at the popular music industry hangout the Speakeasy. After one show, Tiny partied with some fans in his hotel room and became inebriated on hard cider. During the course of the party, he held hands with a female and became so excited by the innocent action that he ejaculated in his pants. Always on hand, Joe Cappy intervened. Tiny felt Cappy was doing a 'tremendous job in keeping expenses down and handling things' and was pleased by the fact that all of his checks were being made out to him directly and then forwarded to his accountant in Beverly Hills. Kaufman, meanwhile, was back in the States and becoming increasingly agitated by the fact that Tiny had not signed an official contract designating Kaufman as his manager. Butros was vehemently opposed to his son signing with Kaufman, and Tiny, nervous about making it official, deferred to his father, stating that he would not sign a contract unless his father approved.

Kaufman had other problems. On November 19, the Associated Press carried a story that the 'manager of Tiny Tim' had been arrested by the FBI.

> The FBI yesterday announced the arrest of the manager of singer Tiny Tim on charges of transporting $90,000 in stolen securities to London.
>
> Joseph Kaufman, 40, a theatrical agent who manages the well-known singer, was picked up at his home in Tarrytown and charged with the illegal transportation of stolen property.
>
> John F. Malone, assistant director of the FBI in New York, said that the securities, actually New York City bonds, were taken in a burglary in January 1968, from the offices of Dewey, Ballantine, Bushby, Palmer and Wood, a Manhattan law firm.
>
> Malone's statement contained no information on how Kaufman allegedly came into possession of the bonds, when he made the trip to London, or the current whereabouts of the securities.

Kaufman was released on $25,000 bail. Seizing the moment to oust Kaufman, Mr. Seidel sent Kaufman a letter on November 24, dismissing him as Tiny's

---

* A photo of Tiny with Dusty Springfield and Princess Margaret after the show also shows David Bowie in the crowd that night.

manager. Kaufman angrily sent a message to Tiny in England threatening to call off the wedding if Tiny did not drop Seidel. When Tiny failed to comply, Kaufman conceded that he had no real authority to cancel the wedding. When Tiny finally returned to Los Angeles, on December 1, he was met by Butros, his cousin Harold Stein, and a detective hired to 'safeguard' him from Kaufman, who had apparently also come to California with the intention of meeting with Tiny. Following this last attempt to meet with Tiny and regain control of his career, Kaufman faded from Tiny's life. Cappy, however, sensing a regular paycheck, endeared himself to Tiny, and was retained as Tiny's manager.

Somehow, in the midst of the confusion, Tiny found time to write (or dictate) a lengthy article for *Playboy* about 'The Great Crooners.' The article described Tiny as 'otherworldly' and featured a psychedelic illustration of him listening to a gramophone. Though more reputable publications, like *LIFE*, had termed Tiny a 'loser,' *Playboy* offered him a forum to expound upon his knowledge of turn-of-the-century popular music. He chronicled his experiences collecting records and learning to love music of the past. He profiled the careers of Henry Burr, Arthur Fields, Byron G. Harlan, Irving Kaufman, and Billy Murray, listing their various pseudonyms and most famous songs, how many records they made, which singing groups they were members of, and why they should be credited as the first crooners. He wrote about the creation of the electric microphone, and the crooners' inability to adapt and their slow evaporation from popularity, making way for a new generation of crooners: Gene Austin, Nick Lucas, and Vallee—'the greatest of them all,' to whom he dedicated almost an entire page—and acknowledged Bing Crosby and Russ Columbo as following closely behind. He conceded that Crosby was technically the 'most accomplished' of them, thanking him for the kind treatment he had received on *The Hollywood Palace*, and stated a personal belief that crooning began to 'degenerate' after 1935, as the style became commercialized and then parodied.

* * *

With his wedding just seventeen days away, Tiny began preparing himself by writing a series of detailed, sometimes insightful, often perplexing entries in his diary regarding his rules for marriage and his hopes for himself as a husband, culminating in an epic list containing eighty-four bullet points. The first was a quote from John 3:18: 'To love not in word or tongue but in deed and in truth.' In the second, which would later end up in his wedding vows, Tiny advised himself to be 'not puffed up, not jealous but kind, patient, forgiving, understanding, slow to anger, gentle, long suffering, true.' The third, too, was certainly of noble intent as he vowed 'to come to her at anytime no matter what time of day or night as long as she wants me, no matter what my mood is as long as she (Miss Vicki) wishes me near her I will be there as long as she wants me even for 365 days a year if she wants me close to her just to satisfy her in any emotional state I will be there forever and never leaver her side or bed as long as she (Miss Vicki) wants me.'

Though many of Tiny's entries were biblical or chivalrous, the vast majority concerned 'S-E-X'—a significant preoccupation for the virgin thirty-seven-year-old.

> *Miss Vicki may be startled by my hairy body so I must go slow and keep lights low at the beginning … remember that this wedding (Lord willing) with Miss Vicki is not to an ordinary girl but to a dream … don't try to change her, let her be as she is, give her freedom … No man (Including Mr. Kaufman) will make any decisions concerning her. I will not listen to Mr. Kaufman or anyone when she is concerned … first 3 marriage days of abstinence to be taken very seriously, if necessary Mr. Cappy will move in with me … I must not be afraid to tell her of any weird sex ideas I have …*

A few days later, Tiny went through the list with Vicki, and on December 5 he traveled to New York City, where he remained until the wedding. Despite the media circus, they acted much as any betrothed couple, even stealing away for some kisses and heavy petting. 'Forgive me as body, lips, hands were pressed against Miss Vicki,' Tiny wrote in his diary. According to Vicki, they were oblivious to all that was happening around them. 'We weren't aware of [the hype] at all,' she recalls. 'We thought it was just some little dinky idea, seriously.'

They could not, however, tune out the throng of reporters who descended upon City Hall in New York City on December 9, as Tiny and Vicki, chaperoned by Mrs. Budinger, filed for their marriage license.* While waiting in line, Tiny treated reporters to renditions of 'Goodbye Girls, I'm Through' and 'If I Had My Life To Live Over.' As he and Vicki signed the license, news cameras rolled, flashbulbs popped, and a dozen microphones hovered nebulously around them.

---

* Tiny signed the license as Herbert 'Buckingham' Khaury. Accordingly, this assumed middle name was also later used in the wedding ceremony.

'Vicki, was it love at first sight?' asked one reporter.

'It was really love at first fright,' Tiny interjected with a grin.

'No, don't say that!' Vicki scolded in jest.

'What would you say, Vicki?' the reporter asked, still trying to get an answer from her.

'Oh, I think so,' she replied.

Another reporter jumped in. 'Tiny Tim, would you sing us a song that would express how you feel right now?' Tiny obliged, delivering a rendition of the 1920 Kaufman Brothers tune 'When The Preacher Makes You Mine.'

As the couple left City Hall, one reporter asked if Tiny and Vicki would have children. 'Well,' Tiny replied, 'I don't believe in birth control, so, basically, whatever happens will happen.'

* * *

For the final days before the ceremony, the two were consumed with last-minute details of the wedding and fittings with Jeffrey Martin, who designed handmade, Victorian-era clothing for the wedding: for Vicki, a $2,500 off-white gown of Paduasoy with a lace collar and sleeves, to which Vicki would later add a vintage cameo. For Tiny, a black velvet knee-length frockcoat with satin lapels and a ribbed satin vest, replete with a black cape, top hat, and a cane. One reporter who was present at one such fitting described it as being 'like a Mad Hatter's tea party.'

Reverend Jack Wyrtzen had been Tiny's first choice to officiate the wedding, but after careful consideration and consultation with Cappy and Butros, Tiny decided he could not accept Wyrtzen's condition that he immediately renounce show business and cut his hair following the televised event.[*] Only the day before the wedding, the Reverend William Glenesk, a Presbyterian minister from the Spencer Memorial Church in Brooklyn Heights, famous for incorporating 'rock'n'roll and hippie poetry in his services,' was selected for the job.[†]

---

[*] A draft of a management contract between Tiny and Kaufman, penned by Tiny in his journal at an unspecified date, indicates that Tiny had been considering quitting show business in order to join Wyrtzen at his fellowship. It includes a clause stating that Kaufman 'will permit Tiny to leave at any time during this contract' should he want to 'go to the World of Life or any other religious ministry.'

[†] In 1972, Glenesk sued the producers of *The Tonight Show* for $500 because the appearance paid only $265, only for him then to be forced to pay $275 to join the American Federation of Television and Radio Artists and charged three years' worth of dues.

Members of the press and eager fans jostled for the 350 seats in the *Tonight Show* studio. Tiny's already troubled relationship with Rudy Vallee took another turn for the worse when Vallee, upon receiving his invitation, requested that NBC cover his travel. When NBC refused, Vallee opted out of attendance. He would subsequently criticize the dignity of the ceremony and Tiny's talent as a singer.

On the day of the wedding, a gaggle of reporters tailed Tiny to his final wedding preparations, including a stop at the beauty salon to be groomed by 'top beauty consultant' Mark Traynor. But when Traynor flashed a pair of hair shears, Tiny absolutely freaked out.

'No! No! No!' he exclaimed, his hands fluttering. 'I don't want my hair cut! I didn't know what you were saying!'

'Weren't you serious about getting it cut, Tim?' one reporter, eager to expose some aspect of the wedding as disingenuous, asked. 'Is this just a publicity gimmick? You weren't serious about getting your haircut?'

'I never knew about it until today,' Tiny explained. 'I never knew I was gonna get my haircut. I knew it was gonna be fixed and taking these knots out of it, but I never heard it was gonna be cut. I just heard it today on this show.'

'You aren't even gonna get it trimmed for your wedding?'

'We'll hardly take any off. You won't notice the difference,' Traynor assured him.

'I can't take the scissor on it,' Tiny said with a sigh. 'I get funny.'

Tiny's publicist, Selma Gore, was quick to step in and explain to the reporters why Tiny was at the salon. '[Tiny is] a meticulously clean man—he takes several showers and washes his hair every day,' she explained, 'but he doesn't comb it. Traynor isn't going to cut it but will groom it, and may take off a quarter inch where needed. He'll probably look like Errol Flynn in a swashbuckling period piece.'

The reporters then moved on to more pressing questions. Would being married hurt his image? 'No, I'm not a sex symbol like Tom Jones.' Was he nervous? 'Not as nervous as I'll be tonight. I hope I'm worthy of her. I've got the regular bridegroom nervous feeling.'

The wedding was attended by many of Tiny's extended family and acquaintances from the old neighborhood. As was to be expected, many of those who had been unkind to Tiny before his fame had changed their tune in public, but Tillie's sisters and many others had not curbed their negative remarks behind closed doors. Strangely, Tiny selected Joe Cappy as his best man and Cappy's brother Jimmy and their brother-in-law, Santo Scupelliti, as ushers. Vicki, on the other hand, made less mob-oriented choices for her wedding party, selecting Genie as her maid of honor and her other two sisters, Allene and Tracy, as bridesmaids.

As pages, Tiny reluctantly agreed to have his nephews, cousin Harold's sons. Sometime before the wedding, Harold had suggested it would be 'nice' if the boys were in the wedding, and Vicki had agreed. 'Oh, that'd be so great!' she said. 'They're so cute!' After the meeting, Tiny berated Vicki for agreeing to Harold's suggestion and revealed that he had not forgotten that he had not been invited to Harold's wedding.

'[His family] didn't respect him until he became [famous] and all of the sudden they wanted their kids in the wedding,' she explains today. 'He did not want them in it, but it was too late and they were already trying on their clothes, and he was really not happy with that. That was my first inclination of him being miserable [about] his past and his family and stuff.'

As the taping loomed, six hundred people crowded into the lobby at 30 Rockefeller Plaza. *Brady Bunch* star Florence Henderson, a scheduled guest on the program that night, ran into an old woman in the restroom who begged her for help getting a seat. There were also reportedly eighty members of the international press at the event.

Rita McConnachie and Sharon Fox, the de-facto heads of Tiny's fan club which had issued what would be their last Tiny-Gram in November, found themselves backstage among the gaggle of reporters who, not having access to the studio itself during the ceremony, were looking for any shred of information they could incorporate into their reports.[*] The Chicago press had already had a field day with the two girls. They appeared on local radio and gave interviews to local newspapers about the wedding. Backstage, the press assembly descended upon the two girls, backing them into a corner and asking them questions in rapid-fire succession.

---

[*] Shortly after the wedding, Sharon Fox and Rita McConnachie ceased their efforts for the Tiny Tim Fan Club, which effectively ended all active promotion behind Tiny. Tiny's cousin Roslyn Rabin considered taking over their duties. In an undated letter from Fox to Rabin, Fox made it clear that she could no longer afford to work to promote Tiny without pay, and suggested Vicki should involve herself in her husband's promotion. 'I will be glad to do all I can to help you with the fan club for TINY,' she wrote. 'An organization behind a star is very important, and I know TINY doesn't have one. … I think Vicki should help, if she will be staying home after the baby. I know if I were married to a star, I'd be helping with his promotion. I would be glad to work for any star, if I could get paid for it.'

'We had never had this experience before,' McConnachie recalls, 'and we were against the walls and we were separated and we had the microphones just like you see on TV [in front of our mouths] with all the press just asking all sorts of questions. It was definitely an experience.'

Vicki's sisters still recall the prevailing anxiety of the day. 'The set seemed so bright and surreal, and I was shaking like a leaf,' Tracy notes, while Genie remembers watching the reactions of her family, and the commotion in the studio. 'Here's what I remember about that day: big nerves. Vicki was in some other zone. My father was so nervous, it wasn't funny, and he was not a nervous guy, and I remember the main thing behind the scenes was the tulips being flown in … some outrageous thing that came from Holland.'

Indeed, the thousands of tulips adorning the studio had been brought in from overseas. When news of the wedding broke in September, Jim Harney of Aberdeen's Flowers in Chicago, aware of the fact that there was a very limited supply of tulips during the winter months, made arrangements to purchase the entire supply of tulips during that period. 'It was a gamble, really,' he recalls. 'I knew he needed tulips, because he was famous for "Tip-Toe Thru' The Tulips," so I knew if I bought all the tulips that came in then they had to choose us [for the job], because nobody else had tulips.'

Harney's wager worked. Before long, a *Tonight Show* producer contacted him, nervously asking, 'How much are you gonna charge us to do this?'

'I'm not gonna charge you anything,' Harney replied. 'I just want the publicity.' For three days leading up to the wedding, he and his team worked tirelessly to complete all of the flower arrangements for the set, which incorporated some 10,000 yellow, red, and white tulips, all flown in from Holland. To prevent the tulips' wilting, the studio was kept at a crisp 55 degrees right up until the ceremony.

Shortly before the taping, Tiny and Harney struck up a conversation. After making small talk, Tiny opened up about his anxiety over the marriage.

'Oh Mr. Harney!' he said. 'I wonder if I'm going to be able to please her!'

'Well, do the best that ya can,' Harney replied.

* * *

The taping took place on the afternoon of December 17 1969. After Ed McMahon's obligatory 'Heeeerreeeee's Johnny!' Carson emerged onstage wearing a tuxedo. 'I've never seen our audience so well dressed,' he said, gesturing to the wedding guests. 'You look lovely, all of you.'

'People thought that we have been kidding about Tiny Tim getting married on our show, ' he said, 'but we are not. It happens tonight.'

With that, the show unfolded. Carson first read excerpts from a forthcoming Funk & Wagnall publication, *The Wonderful World Of Weddings*, and then displayed—and tried on—a tiara that had belonged to Napoleon and Josephine, along with a 26.77 carat diamond ring that once belonged to the British Royal Family.

Florence Henderson, who shared a manager, Sandy Gallon, with Tiny at CMA, was Carson's first guest and opened her segment with a lackluster rendition of Petula Clark's 'My Love.' 'I was very serious about choosing that song, because I know Tiny is very serious about this night,' she explained to Carson afterward. 'And I also thought that was the type of song he would sing to Vicki.'

During their conversation, Carson carefully took some credit for Tiny's fame. '*He made the choice* to be married on the show because he, in a way, started here,' he explained. 'I think he mentioned the young lady the first time on this show, then he announced he was engaged, then he announced his wedding plans. So it's kind of a culmination.'

'I saw him upstairs before,' Henderson added. 'He looks great. He looks better than usual. The circulation seems to have improved.'

'I didn't know there was anything wrong with his circulation.'

'Well, he always looks so pale, but he looked really excited.'

'Well, it's his wedding day!' Carson replied.

Next, they were joined on stage by comedienne Phyllis Diller, who at the time was preparing to star in *Hello Dolly* on Broadway but had taken time out from rehearsals because she 'wouldn't want to miss a sexy occasion such as this.' Then Nick Lucas was brought out to perform his signature songs, 'Rose Colored Glasses' and of course 'Tip-Toe,' suggesting that Tiny had been graced with at least one choice in the show's line-up. After a brief interview with Lucas about his life as a performer and married man, and an instrumental version of 'Age Of Aquarius' courtesy of Doc Severinsen and his band, Carson threw the show to one more commercial break before the big event.

'And now here's the moment you've been waiting for,' Carson said, when the show returned, 'which a lot of people did not think would come to pass on this show, but it did: the wedding of Mr. Tiny Tim and Miss Vicki Budinger.'

The curtains parted to reveal an aisle flanked by beds of tulips on an elaborate Victorian set. In the center of the stage, a double door parted, through which the wedding party began to walk toward the audience. The Cappys and Sal wore their suits stiffly, looking almost comical next to Vicki's sweet but anxious looking sisters. A visibly nervous Vicki followed cautiously, escorted by her father, and Tiny met them at the end of the aisle. Reverend Glenesk walked onto the stage and began the ceremony. The two read vows to each other, which smacked of Tiny's syntactical style.

> I, Herbert Khaury, being of sound mind, in the presence of our Lord and savior Jesus Christ, the son of God, and these witnesses, do humbly and happily and most gratefully rely on thy parents' consent, take thee, Miss Victoria May Budinger, as my lawfully wedded wife. I promise with the help of our Lord and savior Jesus Christ to love, honor and obey, work and provide for thee and be with thee in sickness and in health, in happiness and in sorrow, in joy and in tribulation and I further promise thee to be sweet, gentle, kind, patient, not puffed up, charitable, slow to anger and swift to forgive with the strength Christ gives me as long as we both shall live. Amen.

Tiny kissed Vicki, Reverend Glenesk declared them 'husband and wife,' and the audience applauded as Mr. and Mrs. Herbert Khaury approached the guest couch to the strains of Mendelssohn's 'Wedding March.'

'Well congratulations, Tiny,' said Carson, as the couple took their seats. 'And Vicki, you look just as pretty as brides always look … it came off very well. I think it a was a lovely ceremony. How do you feel?'

'I really feel—great,' said Tiny, to laughter and applause from the audience. 'I say this most humbly, I only pray I can make Miss Vicki happy. I really believe I've been blessed with perhaps the most beautiful girl I've ever seen.'

'Well, I know how you feel about her,' Carson replied. 'Vicki, how do you feel? I know these are dumb questions to ask newly married people, I know that, but somebody always does. How is a bride supposed to feel? Was it easy enough for you? Were you comfortable?'

'Mm-hmm.'

When Vicki took a glass of champagne from a tray of glasses carried out by Ed McMahon, Carson noticed that Tiny looked concerned. 'That's champagne, Miss Vicki,' said Carson, prompting Tiny to whisper in his ear. 'Oh, I see. You don't care for champagne. That's all right. I'll take care of this, Vicki, if that's all right. Tiny, I didn't get to kiss the bride. Is that all right?'

Tiny let out a high pitched 'Ohh!' as he grabbed Vicki's hand and awkwardly pulled it within Carson's reach. Carson, however, got up from his desk and kissed Vicki's cheek.

'She's a good kisser,' Carson said as he sat back down, causing Tiny to blush. They were then joined onstage by Henderson, Diller, and Lucas for the champagne toast. Tiny prepared a toast of milk and honey for himself and Vicki on the spot, sparking a humorous exchange between him and Carson as he heaped spoonfuls of honey into the glasses of milk.

'I used to drink alcohol,' Tiny revealed, 'but Miss Vicki got me out of that.'

'She's gonna be a good influence for you, you think?'

'She certainly will be. I pray to make her happy. This is the good Lord's food. He said, eat honey and live.'

After toasting the bride and groom, Carson closed the episode by inviting Tiny to perform a song for his bride. Tiny naturally obliged, accompanying himself on autoharp on 'Song For Valentine's Day,' a song by his friend Max Sofsky, which Tiny retitled 'Wedding Song For Miss Vicki.'

Oh, won't you come and love me,
Oh, pretty Vicki mine,
Oh, won't you come and love me,
And be my valentine.

Florence Henderson, who smiled and quietly watched Tiny's performance, would later admit that she had not taken the ceremony very seriously, and suggested that Carson had not either. 'I remember when they're sitting next to Johnny and … while Tiny is talking, Johnny is kind of looking at me rolling his eyes like, *I don't believe it.*'

Vicki's sister Genie also sensed that the other guests on the show that night had not taken the event that night seriously. 'There should not have been other guests on, in my opinion,' she says. 'They were in the camp of "isn't he a freak?" and "isn't this ridiculous?" and I think they should have been shown the door … I don't know if that was decided upon for balance or what, but I remember [Henderson and Diller] just giving us dirty looks.'

Following one last commercial break, Tiny read off a list of thank-yous to various personnel involved in planning the wedding, and then strummed his ukulele and crooned 'You Were There.' Vicki sat quietly and smiled as Tiny performed for her. Momentarily, they both seemed impervious to the multiple cameras, to the studios lights, to the seats full of strangers, and to the television audience of millions who would soon be gawking at the them.

Sources would later estimate that a whopping 45–50 million people tuned in to watch the prerecorded program. In New York, 84 percent of those watching TV that night tuned into the wedding, and Con Edison had to provide extra power to handle the overload. In Chicago, the police reported reduced crime, while in Los Angeles, there was reportedly less traffic on the roads. The event was the zenith of Tiny's career as a performer. Johnny Carson, meanwhile, would not break that night's ratings until his final appearance on the show in 1992. He received a 44 percent Nielsen rating, knocking competitor Merv Griffin out of the box. In the final hours of the 60s, Tiny Tim's Cinderella story stood front and center as the biggest publicist coup of the decade.

'I thank you for being with us to televise this tonight,' Carson said, at the close of the episode. 'We wish you both much, much happiness. We'll see you tomorrow night. Good night.'

* * *

A photo shoot followed the show, during which reporters trampled Jim Harney's delicately prepared tulip patches. The wedding party then walked to the reception at the Ground Floor Restaurant at CBS headquarters on Sixth Avenue, the waiting limousine having been hijacked by the press. Footage of Tiny and Vicki's wedding reception entrance shows a barrage of reporters, microphones, and flashbulbs popping, and, in the madness, handfuls of rice flying, as if someone had attempted to maintain some semblance of a reception.

'It was just nothing but photographers,' Vicki recalls. 'All my family and friends were supposedly there, but I never saw them … they served food, but we didn't have any. Looking back, to me that's kind of weird. It was a wedding reception and I had no food, no alcohol, no drink.'

The wedding party was seated at a long table lined with microphones. Beyond the sea of reporters and the blinding lights, Vicki could not see any of her friends or family, though she knew that they were there. 'It was a big long table and [Tiny] and I were sitting at it,' she says, 'and, next to us, on either side, were the people that were in the wedding party like his manager, his manager's brother; in front of us, were cameras and microphones and people taking pictures. It was one of those things that wasn't well planned out.'

'There was a massive surge of press and gatecrashers trying to get there,' her sister Tracy recalls. 'Then, when we got there, we were almost not allowed in. There was a tremendous crowd pushing and shoving at the door. A reporter lifted my pregnant cousin up to get her out of his way. We had to push our way to the wedding party's table, and then by the time we got served, there was very little food left … it was pretty frightening and very sad.'

Tiny, however, seemed unruffled. 'There wasn't one time that I was aware I was on TV,' he nonchalantly told the reporters at the reception.

'I can remember just looking at Tiny, because he was so OK with [everything],' Vicki's sister Genie recalls. 'Our nerves were soothed by just looking at him. He was OK with it. He was in his element, truly.'

When pressed as to what marriage meant for his sex life, Tiny repeated with conviction that he was not too concerned with sexual satisfaction. 'We must keep the mind cool,' he said. 'Put the laws of Christian cleanliness first and man last [and] not having any sex or anything [for three days].' Asked about some of the wording in the vows he and Vicki had written, in particular the bit about 'being of sound mind,' he clarified that it had been added so that 'everybody will know I know what I'm doing.' He balked when one reporter suggested that the marriage was in some way less legitimate because the ceremony was held on television. 'It doesn't matter where you're married—on television or on the sea—as long as you keep the marriage laws.'

The London *Times* later reported on the atmosphere. 'Radio and television reporters, thrusting tightly gripped microphones almost in the mouths of the victims asked the same questions over and over again, vainly hoping to break through the thick crust of banality and reveal some eternal truth. It was a hopeless task.' Meanwhile, a curious member of the press approached Tillie and asked if she was proud of her son. 'And why shouldn't I be?' she replied, eyebrow raised in suspicion.

The wedding guests were too crowded even to dance. 'It was a nice reception, but it was a circus,' Rita McConnachie recalls. 'It was just so much. It was crowded.'

Later in the evening, Jim Harney approached Johnny Carson in hopes of getting a picture, as 'a favor for a Chicago florist.'

'What do you want me to do?' Carson replied, a few drinks deep. 'Stick a tulip up my ass?'

In the midst of the pandemonium, Tiny and Vicki's wedding gifts—which had been stacked on a side table until they were ready to be opened, and came from family, friends, Tiny's fans, and even Arab Sheiks—disappeared. 'It was sad more so for the people who gave them to us,' Vicki later noted, 'because I couldn't send thank-yous. People probably thought, How ungrateful.'*

At one point, Tiny and Vicki were led over to their seven-foot wedding cake, which was adorned with figurines in their likenesses. The cake had been prepared by the Three Little Bakers in Delaware, owned by three brothers who previously performed as The Acromaniacs in the 1930s and 40. The cake had been displayed for the press in their bakery before being transported to New York for the wedding. Prior to the cutting of the cake, Tiny, upon request, serenaded Vicki with another song. Like the gifts, the figures on the cake and every piece of structural hardware disappeared shortly after the cutting.

Rita McConnachie had her only interaction with Tiny at the close of the evening, just as he and Vicki were being ushered out of the reception. 'He grabbed my arm and he pulled it, and he pulled it so hard he was dragging me out the door with him, and he says, You have to come with me. I was laughing, like, what is he doing? He was panicking. It was like a panic thing … he was serious and it was like a panic attack or something and it just kind of threw me … She was already out the door. People were there—who they were, I don't know—maybe it was just too much [for him]. I don't know the reason.'

Trying desperately to drag Rita out of the reception with him was not the only thing Tiny had done to buffer himself from the reality of his very real marriage. He had also allowed Miss Jan, a fifteen-year-old admirer, to attend the ceremony. The two had met in June 1969, the same month Tiny had met Miss Vicki, and Jan soon became obsessed with him, hoping that she might marry him one day. However, in September 1969, the young girl's hopes that she would become Mrs. Tiny Tim were dashed by the news of Tiny's engagement to Vicki. The fear of returning to public school following such an embarrassing and heartbreaking shock proved too much for her, and her parents enrolled her in a private school.

In a surprising turn of events, however, Jan's parents, at the urging of her therapist, allowed her to fly to New York City to attend Tiny's marriage to Vicki. As she later told Harry Stein, she visited Tiny at the Waldorf-Astoria on the day of the wedding, at his request, and confessed her feelings. Tiny

---

* The official explanation was that 'thieves' had crashed the wedding and made off with the gifts. Tiny went to his grave believing this explanation. In 2014, Joseph Cappelluzzo Jr., son of Joe Cappy, revealed to Miss Vicki that a closet in his family's house had been stacked with the wedding gifts for years following the wedding but eventually vanished. He belatedly gave Vicki all of the cards that had accompanied the gifts.

was 'understanding,' she recalled, but their conversation was cut short by Joe Cappy's knock on the door. Tiny hid Jan in the bathroom. Later that evening, Jan sat paralyzed in the audience as she watched the taping of Tiny's marriage to Miss Vicki.

After the reception, a limousine took Tiny and Vicki back to the Waldorf-Astoria. As they made their way to the hotel, the couple were free to speak to one another at long last. 'Listen,' Tiny said, turning to Vicki, 'I know we're married and all, but there's always going to be other women. You're never going to be the only one. There will always be other women in my life, and I just want you to know that. I'm always going to give out trophies to women that I like.'

Vicki was crushed. 'After a while it was just kind of like a buzz in my ear, but he was still talking,' she recalls. 'I was completely heartbroken. I was seventeen years old. This is my first … serious love and he's telling me I'm not going to be the only one. Until that moment, I thought that he had chosen me out of everyone: *Oh, here's the woman that I love. Here's the woman who understands me. Here's the woman who's going to always be there for me.* Now he's sitting there and telling me right after we said our wedding vows and he's telling me, No, you're not going to be the only one. That hurt our marriage from that moment on. It was never really right after that … I was devastated. I cried from that moment on and for the next two days.'

The sting of Tiny's words still haunts Vicki to this day. Today, watching a video of the wedding ceremony at the request of the author, she remarks, 'Oh my God, [watching this is] so sad. I looked at this young person—who I almost didn't think was me—and I saw myself so full of hope and expectation and it made me feel sad because none of the expectations that I had or nothing that I thought and hoped for materialized. I remember sitting there and looking at him singing … at that moment I was very happy.

'I thought we [knew each other] but we really did barely know each other, huh? But at the time I thought we knew each other well because we had written lots of letters to each other and we talked on the phone a lot and we spent some time together—not a lot—but some time. Now that I'm older and I'm looking back, we probably didn't know each other very well at all. He just decided, that's the kind of chick I want, and I went along with it. He was from a whole other world than me. They say opposites attract, but it wasn't really ever good or happy … at some point I think we came to the idea that [we were] so different that we didn't understand each other's histories or who we were.'

Of course, on December 17 1969, Vicki was not afforded the benefit of hindsight. She wondered if she simply ought to go home. 'Should I call my parents and go home?' she thought to herself. 'Or should I try to make him love me?' Ultimately, she decided to stick it out, vowing that she would find a way to 'change his mind about stuff.'

Later that night, Vicki helped Tiny pen his diary entry for that day. The entry addressed Miss Jan's presence at the wedding, and included a lamentation for the end of bachelorhood. In a show of solidarity, Vicki added her own comments, initialing them 'V.B.'

> *Thank you for the greatest day ever. For this evening I got married for the first time and the last I pray to the most beautiful girl I know—Miss Victoria May Budinger. I pray I can be worthy of her and make her happy. The wedding was performed for the first time on television on Mr. Carson's Tonight Show. Later the reception followed and all of my friends going years back were there. I also had my first trial of the realness of married life when later at the Waldorf in our suite I thought of days of being single which are now no more. Thank you as Miss Corky, Miss Cleo, and Miss Pam McDonough were among the many girls who came. Also Miss Jan traveled 3,000 [miles] from Aptos, California, to see the wedding. Miss Jan came to my room earlier in the day, and I made sure she got a ticket. I only want Miss Vicki Budinger, but Miss Jan's presence was a security on a foundation in case I lose her (You won't! (V.B.)) Thank you for this great gift of Miss Vicki. I pray I can always walk in Thy Grace more and more. Although I could not resist Miss Vicki—I will try again tomorrow to keep the three-day Tobias situation.*

Just what was the 'three-day Tobias situation?' Much was to be made later about Tiny and Vicki's sex life, and of course Tiny had discussed his views on the subject at length in the months leading up to the marriage. On one pre-wedding appearance on *The Tonight Show* alongside television psychologist Dr. Joyce Brothers—a premeditated pairing no doubt—Tiny revealed that, in addition to having separate bedrooms, there would be a three-day 'waiting period' before he consummated his marriage in honor of the Old Testament story of Tobias's son, who had done the same. 'Today we usually follow examples of political leaders and heroes who are men and idols,' Tiny explained. 'I think the families would be much better off if we took examples from the saints and apostles or the prophets … if I remember correctly, Tobias's son was supposed to marry someone who had seven husbands before. Tobias was very religious and said why should my son do this? But an angel from the Lord came down and said, believe me, the good Lord wants it that way. The only requirement was that they had to pray three days and three nights and stay separate so that the Lord would bless their marriage by putting him first …

'I don't believe that S-E-X is the most important part of marriage,' he added, the audience chuckling at his spelling out of the word. 'I really think that S-E-X is the least important part of marriage.'

'Why are you spelling it, Tiny?' Carson asked.

'Well basically I believe it is a very precious word,' he replied, 'the same with L-O-V-E, and those two are delicate words and sometimes people use it like common day use and it loses its flavor and its power. So that's why I'd rather spell it.' His priority, he explained, were to make Vicki happy, mentally and emotionally, with sex to follow only at her initiation. 'In other words, basically, her wish, if it's right, is my command.'

'Tiny Tim, you're not living with a woman as brother and sister,' Dr. Brothers interjected. 'You're marrying a woman. You can develop an emotional relationship and express it and the finest expression is within the realm of sexual relationship. If you keep separate, and she has to make a very definite point of coming to you or asking you to come to her, then it is much harder to develop, in a natural way, the part of marriage that is a very basic part of that marriage.'

'Well the thing is,' Tiny replied, 'believe me she'll know when, uh . . .'

'When you smash the ukulele, that's it!' Carson added. 'When you hear crunching wood and strings going *BOING*, get in there!'

After a final dissertation from Tiny on his plans to keep hygienically clean within the marriage by stepping up his use of lotions and creams and suchlike, Dr. Brothers, perhaps sensing a serious disconnect in Tiny concerning sexual relations in marriage, warned him, 'I still think that even the Jergen's lotion people think there's more to marriage than keeping your face soft.'

While Vicki would later claim that she and Tiny did not have sex for the first six months of their marriage, Tiny's diary indicates that there was foreplay on the wedding night. The next day, the couple left New York for the honeymoon in the Bahamas. That day too, he reported, he 'could not resist' more foreplay. Finally, shortly after midnight on December 19, Tiny began the three-day abstinence from 'touching or seeing' his wife. 'The pain really took place about 10pm,' he wrote. 'Not that bad, but was enough. However, this is the example of Tobias in the old Catholic Bible test meant to glorify Thy name. I'm wiser to copy it for the same glory of Thy name O Lord.'

For the next two days, Tiny and Vicki endured the 'Tobias situation.' '[The] pain of not seeing Vicki though she is in the next room is heavy,' Tiny lamented in his diary, as he sat alone in the dark of his room, consuming only Melba toast and water and reading Reverend Billy Graham and Dr. Norman Peale literature for fortitude.

'All I did was lie on my bed, and I can tell you I wouldn't want to go through that again,' Tiny later told *Playboy*. 'I was getting very, very depressed. She was next door, and I didn't know what was going on. I thought she might have gone out to see the Bahamas, but she, too, had stayed in her room the entire time. She was so faithful.'

Finally, on December 22, the Tobias situation ended, and Tiny, at the age of thirty-seven, lost his virginity. 'Having blessed intercourse as well as other romantic delights all throughout the day for Thy glory o Blessed Jesus.' These 'romantic escapades' would continue throughout the next several days. Prepared to go where others would not, Harold Reimis, during his interview with Tiny for *Playboy* a few months later, asked Tiny directly how it felt to have 'S-E-X' for the first time.

'It was simply wonderful,' Tiny related. 'Miss Vicki was very understanding and very pleasant. She seemed to be a woman of experience. I can really tell you the honest truth: there was not a single bit of embarrassment on her part or mine. Instead, there was humility and reverence in the act, because whenever Christ is there and whenever things are done in his name, somehow the way is shown.'

Though Tiny and Vicki had enjoyed nearly a week together without much interruption, theirs was a working honeymoon, and on December 24, Tiny opened at the House of Lords, performing two shows nightly at 10pm and 1am. In a week's time, 1969 ended, and the 70s began.

Thank you for a beautiful wife in Miss Vicki.
Dear Lord—Thanks as 1969 came to an end tonight. Thank you for two nice shows at the House of Lords. Thank you also for the greatest, most exciting year ever. For all the health and blessings and good fortune, the marriage of course to Miss Vicki, the hardships, the trials, the escapades—which will be described in better length (Lord willing) in the 1970 diary. We also pray for thy blessings on SEX.

CHAPTER ELEVEN
DON'T BITE THE HAND THAT'S FEEDING YOU

I'd love to see Christ come back to crush the spirit of hate and make men put down their guns. I'd also like just one more hit single.
TINY TIM TO HAROLD RAMIS, *PLAYBOY*, JUNE 1970

Tiny's engagement at the King's Inn in the Bahamas yielded his first consistent supporting act and backing band, The Enchanted Forest, an all-girl rock group comprised of recent graduates of the School of Visual Arts in New York City: Missy Wolcott on bass and vocals, Sandy Klee-Phillips on drums, Peg Porter on lead guitar, and Fran DiCicco on organ. Originally performing under the name Act IV, they changed their name at the request of the prolific songwriter Mort Shuman, writer of the hit song, 'Viva Las Vegas.' Shuman had been managing a completely different band named The Enchanted Forest, who had just recorded 'Never Gonna Get My Love,' which was issued as a single on Amy Records. When the group broke up unexpectedly, Shuman asked Act IV to become the new Enchanted Forest. Banking on the value of the original group's album existing in the absence of their own, Act IV agreed.

'Really, our talent was not equal to the fact that we were a novelty,' says Missy Wolcott. 'Let's face it: we were an all-girl band before The Go-Gos and all that. So we were easily booked. We had no problem. They didn't care what we sounded like. "All girls? Yeah, OK."'

Eventually, The Enchanted Forest were booked to play in the Bahamas through their agent at Creative Management Agency, or CMA. Upon arriving, they were surprised to find themselves opening for Tiny Tim. They were further surprised to learn that the house band, who were supposed back Tiny, had instead elected to go home for the holidays. At the request of their manager, the girls approached Tiny about extending their collaboration from opening act to backing band.

Aside from the fact that, according to Sandy Klee-Phillips, Tiny 'had more makeup than the band,' they instantly found him likable and approachable. 'We didn't know that he was really a real person,' says Missy. 'We thought he was an act until we met him, and we realized that was really what he was. He was a real sweet, innocent man.'

Tiny was instantly enamored with the group. 'He had nicknames for us,' says Sandy. 'I only remember mine: it was The Classic Beauty. Well, I couldn't forget that.'

There was one problem. 'We said, "Tiny, we can't do the 20s and 30s songs. Do you know 50s?"' Sandy continues. 'He said, "I love the 50s!"' With that, they began rehearsing selections from the 50s to work into Tiny's performance, such as … 'Earth Angel' and 'Great Balls Of Fire,' which were already staples of Tiny's live shows.

After some rehearsals, the girls realized that, although Tiny was fun, they had their work cut out for them. 'Tiny was not perfect,' says Sandy. 'He was not on pitch a lot of the time. He was not consistent. Missy would always tune Tiny's uke, and then Tiny would play with the knobs and tune in back to the strange tuning he had had previously which was not the same key as the band.'

'Tiny would just go off,' Missy adds. 'We would have a plan with the set and all of the sudden Tiny would start playing something else, but we'd try to fill in because of the ease of oldies, three-, four-chord things, which were easy to get in the groove of.'

By the time they opened on December 24, Tiny and The Enchanted Forest had fleshed out a show. The band backed Tiny on a number of songs they had rehearsed, and Tiny changed things up by playing guitar or banjo on a few numbers. Audiences and reviewers alike seemed to respond positively to the pairing of Tiny with an all-girl rock group, even if the compliments were backhanded. One reviewer described The Enchanted Forest as being composed of 'young women whose long hair swayed in time with Tim's. But unlike the star, they evidently had not mastered that intricate maneuver in which the hair, with a sharp jerk of the head, is tossed back over the shoulder. It is sheer genius.' Other reviews were more complimentary, with one noting that the 'audience exploded' over Tiny's encore version of 'Earth Angel,' which saw him 'on the floor, completely on his back, screaming like a maniac … completing the song with a flurry of kicks. Could this be the Tiny Tim who until he met Miss Vicki, said he had never kissed a girl? Could this be the Tiny Tim we know and love?' the reviewer asked.

In a backstage interview, Tiny confirmed that he would be incorporating more recent songs into his act, giving Vicki the credit for showing them to him. 'She introduces me to many of these songs, like a Creedence Clearwater number I'm going to do. I'd sure appreciate it if she'd introduce me to all these new tunes.' Joe Cappy, too, confirmed that Tiny would be 'getting into more rock music' and that he would recreate his manic conclusion to 'Earth Angel' on *The Ed Sullivan Show* the following week, and soon be wearing 'bellbottoms, a body shirt, and a scarf.'

Vicki found The Enchanted Forest to be a saving grace. Although Tiny was writing in his diary of 'sweet moments with Miss Vicki,' she felt uneasy in her marriage. 'Thank God [they were] there because we became friends, and I had four girls to be friends with because I was kind of lonely,' she says. 'They were really nice to me and I really liked them … I was really thinking about [running away] because at that point I knew [Tiny] didn't really want to be with me … I don't know what would have happened if they weren't there.'

Impressed with The Enchanted Forest, Tiny soon extended the girls the opportunity to tour with him regularly. But while Vicki had joked with the girls about running away together, to Tiny she objected to the idea of her husband touring with them. During an ensuing argument, Tiny declared that he doubted whether her love for him was sincere. Vicki dropped the issue and, on January 3 1970, Tiny closed out his engagement at the House of Lords.

Back at NBC studios in New York City, Carson took the stage for an episode of *The Tonight Show*, and during his monologue delivered the joke, 'Tiny Tim and Miss Vicki are on their honeymoon. There are already signs of trouble in the marriage. Last night, Miss Vicki hung a sign on their hotel room doorknob that read: Disturb.' The audience erupted with laughter.

Upon returning to New York, the sense of uneasiness in their marriage, described by Vicki and hinted at in Tiny's diaries, continued, despite the emergence of headings scribbled on the top of pages in Tiny's diaries such as 'Thanks for a beautiful wifey in Miss Vicki. (Thanks for a beautiful husband in Mr. Herbert Khaury every day (VB)).' According to his own diary, Tiny accused Vicki of not caring for Christ 'from the heart.' He seemed to have little understanding of how his words affected his young brides's confidence in their marriage. 'I told her I wanted to be single again,' he wrote. 'But I told her I also loved her enough to marry her.' He would then become frustrated by the repercussions of his words. 'Miss Vicki still acts childish,' he wrote later. 'Thinks I don't love her + thinks she's no good for me. I pray + believe she'll get rid of these silly notions. If she only knew how much I love her. She will one day (Lord willing).' Furthermore, Tiny seemed to fancy himself a spiritual adviser and mentor to Vicki, and intended to impart upon her all that he had learned about the world and human nature during his decades performing in the New York underground. He purchased an abundance of pornographic magazines and showed their contents to his young wife in order that she became aware of 'what evil is in the world … She was amazed at these happenings + inquired as to the shock of the world's evil.'

Another incident occurred during a meeting with Tiny's new lawyers, Mr. Levy and Mr. Ferris, who had recently replaced Mr. Seidel, to discuss a plan by which Joe Cappy and Ron DeBlasio would co-manage him. Tiny became incensed by Vicki's giggling as she snacked on pine nuts during the meeting. He took her into the next room and scolded her like a child. Vicki reacted insolently. 'I took Mr. Levy in my room and apologized for Miss Vicki's follies,' Tiny wrote later. 'He said don't stop her from growing up … it's due time.'

Tiny was at least polite enough to reserve his complaints about Vicki for his diary, telling the press when asked about their relationship, 'Oh, we've had our yeses and noses, but really she's very efficient. Miss Vicki is the most perfect creature in the world. I'm so lucky.' He left out the fact that he may have had to force some of those 'yeses,' such as with his impending appearance on *The Ed Sullivan Show*. When Tiny revealed to Vicki that the show's producers had requested that she sing a medley of love songs with him while wearing a wedding dress, flanked by backup singers and dancers dressed up like a wedding party, Vicki was horrified. 'Oh, God no. Are you kidding me?' she protested. 'I would rather shoot myself first!'

'Anybody else in the world would die to be doing this!' Tiny told her. 'You have to! You can't say no! That's an insult! You can't insult Mr. Sullivan!'

'Oh, but I—'

'I don't care if you don't want to do it! Do you know how many people in this world would love to be on this show?! Well, too bad. They're asking you, and you have to do it.'

Vicki caved to Tiny's questionable rationale. 'I couldn't argue with that logic,' she recalls. 'It was like, Oh, a million people out there would love to have this opportunity and I'm going to say no? That's bad. I can't say no because other people would be ashamed of me. Meanwhile, they probably would have been happy if I didn't do it.'

Vicki agreed to do the show but began to waver as soon as she arrived at the first rehearsal. Tiny retaliated by treating her coldly in front of Sullivan's production staff. 'I was very disturbed when we walked into the Sullivan offices for the first day of rehearsals, because I had to tell the man she didn't want to do it. And she sort of cried there,' Tiny later told *Confidential* magazine. 'I was really rough on her. But then when we got back I said, I'm sorry that you felt that way and you cried in public, but supposing [The Enchanted Forest] lost their [spot] because you wouldn't appear? Well, darling?'

When Tiny and Vicki retired that evening, the argument continued. Vicki claimed she 'looked bad and couldn't sing.' Tiny rationalized that talent had nothing to do with it. 'It's just that you're hot now in the headlines, and they want you to appear there,' he said. When she refused, Tiny, nervous that Sullivan would cancel the appearance, tried another tactic: he allowed Sullivan's music director, Bob Arthur, to find a replacement for Vicki. It worked. Another woman was all the motivation Vicki needed to change her mind. She reluctantly agreed.

For the next few days Tiny, Vicki, and The Enchanted Forest rehearsed for their appearance. 'I remember having a choreographer telling me, Do this. Go here. Go there,' Vicki recalls. That night, January 11, both Tiny and Vicki's friends and families, along with Tiny's friend, A&P Grocery Store heir Huntington Hartford, were in the audience. Tiny performed 'Earth Angel' with The Enchanted Forest and then returned to the stage with Vicki to perform a medley of love songs, including 'Strolling Through The Park,' 'You Are The Rose Of My Heart,' 'Where Have You Been Hiding All These Years?,' 'Honey,' 'Positively, Absolutely,' 'When My Sugar Walks Down The Street,' 'Sweet And Lovely,' 'Honeymoon Hotel,' 'You'll Never Know Just How Much I Love You,' 'Because Of You,' and 'Happy Together.'

To her credit, Vicki held her own. 'I never wanted to do the Sullivan show,' she told *Confidential* shortly thereafter. 'I felt like … if I didn't do it I think they might've dropped the whole thing and I didn't want that to happen. But I really didn't want to do it because people get the wrong idea … like I joined the act or something, and I didn't. I couldn't.' She felt vindicated when she accompanied Tiny to his appearance on *The Red Skelton Show* on January 12 and Skelton, who had caught her appearance on *Ed Sullivan*, advised her, 'Don't ever appear in a wedding dress. That was wrong.'

While in Los Angeles, in between a taping for *The Andy Williams Show* and opening at the Troubadour, Tiny saw fit to address his management situation. Without Silver, Cappy had been struggling to fill the void left by the experienced professional, and DeBlasio once again took over a management role in Tiny's career. Tiny noted in his diary before leaving New York that DeBlasio and Cappy were 'still at odds' over managing him. When Cappy and DeBlasio met face-to-face in Los Angeles, things did not seem to improve. 'Tension between Mr. Cappy and Mr. DeBlasio very apparent,' Tiny wrote, 'but—Mr. Cappy, in my opinion, silently understands that Mr. DeBlasio knows his business and is really the leader.' Ultimately, it was determined that Cappy would serve as East Coast Manager and DeBlasio as West Coast Manager. DeBlasio refused to be intimidated by Cappy and his brother Jimmy. 'They were sort of pretenders,' he recalls. 'They wore the clothing, they talked the talk, they walked the walk, but were not [real tough guys].'

Tiny and Vicki's wedding had invigorated popular interest in Tiny, saving him from impending bankruptcy, and both managers remained invested because they saw the opportunity for steady commission in the near future, at least. DeBlasio told the press that Tiny's net worth in January 1970 was 'about three cents.' At the end of '69, his appearance fee for one-nighters had dropped to $2,500, due to management upsets and general oversaturation, but the wedding and ensuing media allowed Tiny to command up to $10,000 for one-nighters and $25,000 for week-long engagements.

Tiny's renewed popularity was evident when he opened at the Troubadour on January 13. As fans lined up around the block, he and Vicki posed for pictures backstage with the actor Jack Wild and other celebrities in attendance, including Peter Fonda, Biff Rose, Nick Lucas, Mama Cass Elliot, and Ricky Nelson. Though Vicki was spared the stage, Tiny did introduce her to the audience, remarking on how he 'can't get over a girl like you marrying a boy like me … the honeymoon is never over.' He performed a medley featuring 'I'm Walkin',' 'Goody, Goody,' 'Blues Suede Shoes,' and 'Bad Moon Rising,' in addition to his usual rock staple, 'Great Balls Of Fire.' Beyond that, the shows consisted of his usual material: 'Peter Pan (I Love You),' 'Just A Gigolo,' 'Buddy, Can You Spare A Dime?,' 'You Are My Sunshine,' 'California, Here I Come,' 'I Love Me,' and 'I Enjoy Being A Girl.' When he returned for an encore, he was showered with flowers from the audience.

The reviews were positive but skeptical. The *Los Angeles-Harold Examiner* remarked simply, 'He can't trill—but what a range.' For Robert Hilburn of the *Los Angeles Times*, 'His musical effectiveness is chiefly a matter of individual attitude. It is part of a total impact that is highlighted by his own eccentric behavior.' The fact that Tiny was enjoying renewed popularity due to his marriage was not lost to the press either. 'Tiny Tim tiptoed into the Troubadour Tuesday riding a wave of national curiosity as well as basking in what is obviously a nice turn upward in his career,' another reviewer wrote. 'Following his marriage on national TV, you would have to be hiding under a rock not to know about Tiny Tim … [he] should be in for a pretty long run, shopping bag and all.'

Vicki found the influx of formerly distant celebrities into her proximity exhilarating. She accompanied Tiny to a *Laugh-In* taping, where she, Tiny, and comedienne Carol Channing were photographed with Ringo and Maureen Starkey. On the same set, Vicki also met the actress Ruth Buzzi, and the two began to correspond regularly and shop together.

On January 19, Tiny opened at the Omni Shoreham Hotel in Washington DC. With television host Art Linkletter and Nielsen Media Research founder Arthur Nielsen in the audience, Tiny became self-conscious of his show and, fearing he was going over poorly, decided to try out something new. Grabbing his megaphone, he adjusted his voice to his Billy Murray style and belted out a medley of George M. Cohen songs. 'I couldn't stand the show I was doing, and I started to sing without stopping to save face and, apparently, it helped,' he later recalled. He documented a standing ovation in his diary that evening. Sensing he was onto something, Tiny continued to experiment with medleys, making them a permanent fixture in his live show from that point onward.

* * *

On the morning of January 24, Vicki threw up. 'Is she expecting?' Tiny wrote in his diary. Ron DeBlasio, too, hinted to the press that there might soon be a tinier Tim. 'I guarantee that Miss Vicki will be pregnant before the year is out,' he told *Parade*'s Lloyd Shearer. 'Beneath his falsetto Tiny is really a tiger.' (Previously, when asked by Shearer whether the marriage had been consummated, Vicki had replied, 'What does that mean?' When reminded of this today, she says that pretending to be naive was her way of saying, 'I am a lady and therefore refuse to answer, and you are not a gentleman for asking me such a thing.')

Tiny and Vicki returned to Los Angeles and, despite their discovery on February 2 that Vicki was, in fact, pregnant—and also anemic—she accompanied him to a series of concerts and publicity appearances that included a stint at the Grand Hotel in Anaheim, California; concerts in St. Paul, Minnesota; television appearances with Red Skelton and comedian Pat

Paulsen; shows in Baltimore, Maryland; and a week-long engagement with The Enchanted Forest at the Beverly Hills Hotel in Toronto.

Her first reprieve came when Tiny departed for a three-week tour of Australia. News of the wedding had of course traveled across the world, and surviving footage shows Tiny mobbed by crowds upon his arrival at the airport. Tiny broke the news that Vicki was expecting to an excited crowd and boasted in interviews that he was considering brand names like V-8 and Crest for the baby. He also appeared at Australia's largest festival, the Moomba Parade, and even taped a one-hour TV special for Channel 7, *A Special Tiny Tim*, which featured a then-unknown Little Nell dancing wildly behind him during 'Rock Around The Clock.'* He also made a return ten-day engagement at the Chevron Towers on the Gold Coast.

While Tiny was away in Australia, he sent Vicki cards and flowers every day, and the two had an emotional reunion at the airport in Pittsburgh, Pennsylvania, on March 22. Later that afternoon, Vicki suffered from shortness of breath and blacked out. A doctor advised rest and food. However, *Movieland* and *TV Star Parade* ran photographs of Tiny and Vicki schmoozing with actress Mia Farrow and composer Andre Previn at a party hosted by Huntington Hartford in New York shortly thereafter.† Vicki also accompanied Tiny to five days of shows with The Enchanted Forest at the Holiday House in Monroeville, Pennsylvania, and then to his engagement at the Fremont Hotel in Las Vegas.

Meanwhile, back east, Vincent Canby of the *New York Times*, in his review of the documentary *Woodstock*, declared that Tiny Tim was revered by members of the anti-war movement and others who rallied against the establishment for no other reason than the fact that his 'very existence is a put-on, and ... the most insidious form of dissent.' It seemed that the press was becoming increasingly ambivalent about Tiny Tim, as shown by one 'rave' review of his performance at the Fremont Hotel, which dubbed him 'the masker, ingénue, soubrette, character actor, vaudeville, grimacer, clown, fool, tragedian, and the great pretender.'

Tiny's engagement at the Fremont was also the American debut of soon-to-be chart-topper Helen Reddy, wife of one of Tiny's managers, Jeff Wald.

---

* *A Special Tiny Tim* survives today as, decades after the special was taped and shelved after airing only once, Martin Sharp's cousin, who was working for Channel 7 at the time, rescued the tape from a pile of tapes selected to be thrown away.
† She and Farrow were friends for a time and even went shopping for baby clothes together.

A different Australian artist had been scheduled to open for Tiny but had canceled at the last minute. When DeBlasio suggested Reddy, Tiny knew it was simply because of Reddy's relationship with Wald. He was agitated when he discovered that DeBlasio and Wald were paying her $7,500 for the week—a hefty sum for a virtually unknown artist.*

Reddy's paycheck not withstanding, Tiny's relationship with both DeBlasio and Wald was deteriorating rapidly. Tiny's lackadaisical attitude toward money was still a source of contention and, as a result, Wald was still asking hotel management to bring all of Tiny's charges to him for approval.

When a pregnant Vicki began to experience cravings, Tiny immediately responded by joining her in a 'food-eating binge' and ordered from room service some thirty-five chocolate malts, sixteen banana splits, twenty-four ice-cream sodas, twenty-seven sundaes, and several dozen pastries. He tipped the room-service waiters $40 and $50 each, and was agitated when Wald responded by instructing the hotel to not fulfill anymore of his lavish requests. What's more, the management at the Fremont Hotel complained that Tiny was so 'sluggish' from all the sweets that 'he was barely able to sing.' They were further annoyed when Tiny was heard instructing his audiences not to 'foolishly gamble away their money at Las Vegas casinos.'

The figurative icing on the cake came as a demand for a new megaphone. Tiny's was malfunctioning, and he demanded a new one. Wald reminded Tiny that $150 for a new megaphone was not an option, as the malfunctioning one could be fixed for less. After one show, Tiny, believing that the show had suffered from a lack of megaphone, flew into a rage. In the heat of the moment, he grabbed an ashtray and hurled it at Wald, stormed back to his room, locked the door, turned off the lights, broke furniture, and refused to come out unless he received a new megaphone.

'He blamed all of us,' DeBlasio recalls. 'It was a real hissy fit, and I didn't like that behavior. As far as the megaphone was concerned, he was always breaking megaphones because he never knew the mechanics of it or would misplace it some place, it was an ongoing situation.'

---

* Aside from Helen Reddy, several other entertainers who would grow to be major acts in the 70s received their start opening for Tiny Tim. Barry Manilow opened for Tiny in the early 70s in the cabaret lounge of Continental Baths in New York City, an establishment that boasted of its aim to bring back 'the glory of ancient Rome.' Open to men twenty-four-hours a day, the Baths had a disco dance floor, swimming pools, and saunas. The facilities also featured machines that dispensed KY Jelly and a warning system that could alert patrons if the police entered the premises. Elsewhere, Billy Joel opened for Tiny.

On Friday, April 10, Tiny was scheduled to leave the Fremont and head to the Southern California Festival of Flowers at Century City in Los Angeles. Ron DeBlasio had convinced the city of Los Angeles to declare it 'Tip-Toe Thru' The Tulips Day,' with the day's events due to culminate in Tiny crowning the festival queen and giving a charity concert for orphans. On the day of the event, DeBlasio learned that Tiny had not left Las Vegas, nor did he have any intention on doing so. The festival organizers announced that *Laugh-In*'s Chelsea Brown would crown the Festival Queen in his place.

Tiny's behavior not only left a crowd of orphans in the lurch but also torpedoed a plan DeBlasio had been formulating to salvage Tiny's career. During one of Tiny's engagements in Las Vegas, it occurred to DeBlasio, as it had to Reprise, that children were naturally drawn to Tiny. He tested the waters by arranging for Tiny to spend time with children and observed the results.

'I would invite the high rollers' kids backstage to talk to Tiny after the show,' he recalls. 'Tiny would sing more songs to the kids and take pictures with them and it would really make a good impression on the kids and the parents. I didn't know how effective that was until I met one of the pit bosses, who told me that the kids felt great and that reflected on the parents.'

DeBlasio, like Roy Silver, contends that Tiny did not net as much money from touring as he claims. 'A lot of the dates we did have, they did not do well because they were tied in with heavy promotion. The owner of the Latin Casino in Philadelphia [where Tiny played in 1969] spent thousands of dollars. He couldn't believe it: he had hired a huge staff that night, and in a venue that could hold 2,500 people, there were less than 400. Tiny wasn't that kind of an attraction—our audience really was very, very young kids, and I knew we couldn't stay there long because we could feel that the business was running out of things for him in the particular area he was in.'

Searching for other outlets for his artist, DeBlasio had pitched the idea to Warner Bros of producing a children's show featuring Tiny Tim. 'He would talk to the kids and then they would animate him, and he would sing songs and they felt it was absolutely [a good idea],' he recalls. 'The promotions on that would have been enormous ... because he was on Warner Bros Records and this was with Warner Bros Animation, we all thought this would be a good move and there would be synergy between both divisions ... Tiny loved the idea, too, and all we had to do was chill him out for a while. He wanted to make a lot of decisions on his own because he had spent most of his life with no management or any other advice, but it was not to his advantage to start behaving on his own because he didn't know the business skills and wasn't getting the proper response as to what he should do. When an artist gets very big, a lot of people around them will tell them what they want to hear, and Tiny was falling into that trap ... before you know it the artist starts losing control, and they don't know it until they're too far gone to retrieve it.'

When Warner Bros hesitated to green-light the project, DeBlasio arranged the 'Tip-Toe Thru' The Tulips Day' so the company's executives could see Tiny interact with children firsthand. 'All he had to do was fall in line, and just use his own story and sort of chill it for a while, because word was getting out that he was unpredictable, and a lot the industry people were beginning to feel it. Industry people have to be convinced before they take a chance on a new area for an artist.'

Tiny's failure to travel to Los Angeles was sure to result in a definitive 'no' for the proposed television show, and DeBlasio decided he could not take it any longer. After meeting with his other partners at DeBlasio Wald & Day, Inc., he departed Los Angeles to talk to Tiny face-to-face. 'Turning it around was the only way to go, and Tiny didn't do it,' he says. 'I went up to Vegas and gave him his megaphone and gave him his season tickets to the Dodgers and said, I'm firing you.'

Tiny took the items in his hands, looked back at DeBlasio, and said, 'Thank you.' It was the last time they ever spoke. In his diary, Tiny gave away little, writing a single headline, just as he had when he split with Silver: 'Mr. DeBlasio and Mr. Wald fired for negligence in Las Vegas.'

Though Ron DeBlasio felt he was left with little choice, the split was painful, and he remains adamant that, had he been able to execute his plans for Tiny's career, things would have turned out differently. In the following weeks, several articles surfaced chronicling Tiny Tim's breakup with his management. On April 21, DeBlasio gave an interview to the *Los Angeles Times*. 'One of the reasons [Tiny] didn't go [to the Festival of Flowers] was spite,' he revealed. 'By not going he was punishing those who wouldn't give in to him about the new megaphone.'

The next month, the *Enquirer* printed a story in which DeBlasio further explained the situation and maintained that ridding himself of Tiny was worth the $100,000-a-year loss in income for DeBlasio Wald & Day, Inc. Following DeBlasio's departure, Tiny's publicist, Gary Strongberg, announced that his agency was going to dump him as a client, too. 'I can only agree with what Mr. DeBlasio says about him,' Strongberg told the *Enquirer*. 'He lets people down, misses engagements, then when you try to talk to him, he locks himself away … he's always been impossible to deal with.'

Tiny Tim offered a weak rebuttal to DeBlasio's claims. 'I didn't mean to miss the Flower Festival and let those nice people down, but I could not help it … I'll get a new manager, one who understands me more.' In his diary, his only comment on these events was that 'DeBlasio and Wald make false statements to the press.'

Shortly thereafter, the papers announced that Joe Cappy would now serve as Tiny Tim's manager. The sycophantic Cappy refuted DeBlasio claims, stating that Tiny Tim had not missed the flower festival for 'capricious reasons' but because he had been 'suffering from sciatica.' He also claimed that DeBlasio had simply 'wanted out.'

Vicki was disappointed to see DeBlasio go, but she understood his reasons for leaving. 'I liked Ron DeBlasio very much,' she later said. 'He was very polished, and he was very nice, and he really seemed to care … he quit because he couldn't take it anymore. Tiny would call him at three o'clock in the morning and say, Room service is closed, and I … really need some tomatoes and lettuce, can you get me some? Ron would say no, then Tiny would ask, Well, what am I paying you for?'

Since Joseph Kaufman's arrest in 1969, Vicki found that the Cappelluzzos made her nervous. 'They looked like mobsters,' she recalls. 'I used to always overhear [Tiny and Joe's] phone conversations and sometimes in-person conversations. Me and Tiny used to have separate rooms … but I could hear him on the phone, saying, You got to get rid of her …'

It also came to Vicki's attention that Joe had advised Tiny not to marry her in the first place. Before the marriage, according to Vicki, Joe had said, 'You know what? Don't marry her. We could make her road manager, and she could travel with you for a while, but don't marry her. It's a bad idea.'

Tiny nonchalantly told Vicki about Joe's accusations, and the resulting conversations often went the same way:

'Joe says you're no good,' Tiny would tell her. 'You just want money.'

'Did you stick up for me?' Vicki would ask. 'Did you tell him that's untrue?'

'Well … no.'

'That was really hurtful to me,' Vicki explains. 'Cappy thought I was up to something or I wanted something. It wasn't helpful because as it was our marriage was already shaky, and now I got this other guy coming along and telling him, Get rid of her, send her home, tell her to leave.'

* * *

Despite the personnel shift, Tiny Tim's tour motored along. On April 18, Tiny and Vicki arrived in Montreal for a two-night engagement at the Casino Royale in the Diplomat Motel. Here Vicki celebrated her eighteenth birthday. *Montreal Gazette* reporter Dan Lanken, who watched Tiny's rehearsal, commented that 'any notion that Tiny Tim is anything less than a serious, committed musician could have been easily dispelled in watching him work out with the band … [running] through a dozen songs, meticulously setting the tempos and ironing out the arrangements.' Being newly married, expecting a child, and incorporating more contemporary pieces into his repertoire had helped humanize Tiny—at least to those who were still paying attention. 'People may laugh at Tiny Tim and say they can't figure him out,' Lanken concluded, 'but that's the people's fault, not his. In an era where everything from governments to our neighbors lie to us right and left, we just can't appreciate an honest man.'

After Montreal, they traveled to New York for the first time since their marriage for a week at the San Su San Club in Mineola, Long Island. Then it was on to a nine-day engagement at the Cork Club in Houston, Texas. There, Tiny was well received, and had the opportunity to meet Gene Austin, one of his idols from the Tin Pan Alley era.

The nearly two months of straight touring took its toll on Vicki. At 1am on Friday, May 15, she was admitted to Houston's Methodist Hospital after experiencing 'severe abdominal pains.' Earlier in the day, a hotel doctor had assured her that she was experiencing indigestion and had given her a few pills. When the pain did not subside, Vicki insisted she be taken to the hospital, and, approximately four hours after checking in, she suffered a miscarriage.

Up to this moment, the press had reported on Vicki's pregnancy sardonically, often tastelessly, with one reporter even cracking jokes about Vicki delivering on *The Tonight Show*. But when the news of the miscarriage broke, a momentary hush fell. As *Movie TV Confidential* put it, 'Reporters kept a respectful distance. They had delegated one of their ranks to ask for a statement, not really knowing what to expect from America's clown prince.'

'Children, to Tiny Tim, mean even more than to the average man,' *Movie TV Mirror* astutely observed. 'Because Mr. Average Joe doesn't have to prove his manliness. But Tiny Tim, who has made a career of falsetto songs and prancing delivery, does. His courtship, marriage, and virility have been the object of a thousand jokes; his paternity would have put an end to all that.'

On May 16, Bud Westman, a spokesman for Tiny Tim in New York, informed the press that Vicki was 'out of danger' and that the deceased child was a boy. 'The son we lost is God's test of our faith,' Tiny said solemnly. 'It's not for us to understand the Lord's ways … it is for us to accept His will and have faith in the goodness and wisdom of God. He doesn't give us burdens more than we can bear.'

The exact cause of Vicki's miscarriage is unknown, but the presumed culprit is physical and mental stress. Public interest was apparently enough that a Dr. Eugene Scheimann published an op-ed on the subject in the *Lodi News-Sentinel*, in which he concluded, 'Goldfish in captivity can't breed. The same, more or less, is often true of human beings. If we are put in a fish bowl with everyone watching us, we often can't do what nature intended.'

Tiny, who elected to finish out his engagement at the Cork Club despite Johnny Carson's offer to come and finish in his stead, blamed himself for the miscarriage. 'Despite the doctor's saying that traveling did not lose the baby,' he wrote in his diary, 'I still believe that if I obeyed my father and Mr. Levey my lawyer and Mr. Cappy my manager and left her home the baby would have been alive.' The following day, as he closed out the Cork Club, he added, 'Baby I pray may he rest in peace.'

When Tiny Tim learned of the hospital's protocol regarding the disposal of his son's body, he opted, instead, for a proper burial in a $250 casket. A small ceremony was held, and the baby was put to rest under the name IT, 'child of Mr. and Mrs. Herbert Khaury.' 'They wanted to throw the body away,' Tiny later told *Oui* magazine reporter Josh Alan Friedman. 'I said, Never mind, I want a casket for him, that's still a life … and they asked, What name you wanna call it? I just said, name it IT … that's actually somewhere in Texas, in a children's grave. I said if I ever get to heaven, maybe IT'll open the door for us.'*

Instructing Vicki to remain in the hospital for another ten days, Tiny went back to New York City to appear on *The Tonight Show*. Breaking his personal vow to 'be there at her side in all emergencies,' he asked one of his agents, Mr. Dima, to remain behind with her. 'I begged him to please stay with me,' Vicki later told Harry Stein. 'I didn't want to be alone for a week in a strange city. But he just said, 'Business is business, and flew off with his entourage.'

'Questions now arise how will she react when we are together again (Lord willing),' Tiny wrote, after arriving in New York. 'Why does she doubt my love for her? Is it her hospital [stay] and the past dilemma of the baby's loss? Is she

---

* 'It' is buried in the 'Babyland' plot of Memorial Oaks Cemetery in Houston, Texas.

tired of me? Does she yearn for freedom, home and mother, the very things she denies with her lips? It is true that I do not have the flavor of June 3 1969 in my heart for her but I know that and have to work and pray for thy help o Lord to renew it.'

* * *

Tiny went into the studio in New York on May 19 to cut a new single, 'Don't Bite The Hand That's Feeding You,' to be coupled with 'What Kind Of An American Are You?' Irving Squires, his agent at CMA, produced the record, with famed Broadway composer and arranger Luther Henderson conducting. Written in 1916 by Vera Vanderlaan, 'Don't Bite The Hand That's Feeding You' was intended to shame Americans—immigrants in particular—who did not support World War I. The B-Side, 'What Kind Of An American Are You?' was of the same ilk. No doubt Tiny aimed to re-appropriate these songs to shame those protesting the conflict in Vietnam.

Meanwhile, with Tiny's permission, Vicki joined him in New York before the ten days elapsed. She was still clearly in a fragile condition, with Tiny noting in his diary several days later that her bleeding was finally slowing. As Vicki recuperated, Tiny enjoyed a three-day stint as guest host of *The David Frost Show*, interviewing the likes of Dr. David Reuben, author of the best-seller *Everything You Always Wanted To Know About Sex (But Were Afraid To Ask)*, psychologist Dr. Joyce Brothers, jazz musician Billy Taylor, and actor-director Orson Welles. After Tiny performed The Beatles' somber 'Yesterday' on autoharp, Welles remarked, 'There's very few performers who can say this, but there can be no competition in the Tiny Tim department.'

At this point, both Tiny and Vicki were physically and emotionally frayed. Their marriage was turbulent, and Vicki was still recuperating, but the loss of Ron DeBlasio's children's show meant there would be no rest from the constant touring. Tiny's new management team did not have the experience, contacts, or clout to explore any ancillary revenue sources to allow him a rest. Furthermore, Tiny owed money to the Cappys, commission to his agent at CMA, and additional sums to lawyers Mr. Levy and Mr. Ferris, accountant Mr. Paige, and his touring musicians—and he needed to provide for his wife. Additionally, a mess of legal battles loomed, signaled by the arrival of a summons from George King of a case in the amount of $1.5 million. Phone calls from Kiki Hall's attorney, and a $50,000 bill from Tiny's previous attorney, Mr. Seidel, for the *Concert In Fairyland* lawsuit, also waited in the wings.

Tiny, unable to curb his irresponsibility with money, splurged $640 on an 8-track player and spent $600 on cosmetics during this time. The Cappys were left with no choice but to accept any and all bookings on offer to keep their collective heads above water, and in May 1970, Tiny, with Vicki in tow, began a virtually never-ending tour of one-nighters, with only a very few weeklong engagements.

The bump in Tiny's appearance fee following his marriage had dwindled as well. Most of the one-nighters paid only $1,500, and his management even accepted $750 in Allentown, Pennsylvania. Weeklong engagements paid around $10,000. Even with his strenuous schedule, Tiny was seeing small profits. 'Am I working for nothing?' he wrote. 'Is it true that lawyers, managers, + bills + my own spending have caused no profit since I've made the grade?'

Then The Enchanted Forest broke up. Tiny was left, once again, at the mercy of house bands sight-reading his unusual repertoire. The split had been pending since Tiny threatened to fire the band in Texas after keyboardist Fran DiCicco told him he had a 'twisted mind.' 'I must learn to have my own band,' he wrote, after a show at the Psychedelic Lounge in Garfield, New Jersey. 'Otherwise I don't give people their moneys worth because I arrive there with strange bands + they don't get the music in time.'

Despite the enthusiastic crowds and fun moments—visits with Sammy Davis Jr. and Frankie Valli, along with an appearance alongside Rudy Vallee on *The Dick Cavett Show*—it did not take long before this grueling schedule began to take its toll on Tiny physically. A show in Kentucky was canceled when Tiny lost his voice. He knew it was not a sustainable way to make a living, writing in his diary, 'I must make it either in records, movies, or television—or not at all. The way I am handled right now by people who just want to grab any engagement they can for me—so they can put a dollar in their pocket, even at the loss of the talent you've given me, O Lord, (the voice) must end … even if it means I go back to 601 [West 163rd St]. I believe (Lord willing) I will blossom out and get rid of all these people.'

Tiny did not allow his exhaustion to negatively impact his performances. Bruce Bissell, who had previously promoted Tiny's show at the Vancouver Coliseum in late 1968, organized a ten-day engagement at Isy's Supper Club in Vancouver, British Columbia. 'I have to tell you, honestly, it gives me goose bumps to think about it now,' he says. 'It was amazing. He was so polished. All these people came to kind of jeer him and kind of go, Oh, God, look at this, and write lousy reviews. He absolutely stoned that crowd. It was amazing. His theatrics, he used mirrors that he would sing into, looking at his face, and do all these things. He was absolutely smooth.'

If touring had taken its toll on Tiny and Vicki as a couple, Tiny's appearance on *The Tonight Show* on July 20 yielded no indication that anything was amiss. 'I saw you sitting in the back with Miss Vicki,' Carson said to Tiny. 'You seemed as passionate as ever, you were actually smooching in the green room. You're one of the first couples I've seen in a long time smooching in the green room before they go on ... if I remember, the first girl you ever really fell in love with was Miss Vicki, right? Is that true? Was that the first girl you were ever attracted to? Or just the first girl you just really wanted to get married to?'

'Well, I would say that I was attracted to so many,' Tiny replied, 'but I believe that Miss Vicki is it: the one I adore most of all.'

* * *

On July 29 1970, Reprise Records released 'Don't Bite The Hand That's Feeding You' b/w 'What Kind Of An American Are You?' 'I believe both sides will be my first million dollar single,' Tiny wrote, 'and will begin a new record career where I will outsell every record output in the past.' By this time, it was no secret that Tiny Tim, despite his flower-child image, was an ardent supporter of President Nixon and the Vietnam War. He appeared in newsreels welcoming home troops returning from Vietnam and sang for injured veterans at a hospital in New Jersey.

While appearing on a television program earlier that year, Tiny was asked by the host to give his opinion on the war. When he failed to regurgitate the usual anti-war rhetoric, and further replied that he was in full support of the war effort, audiences were shocked. 'Those commies,' he told the host, 'need to be taught a lesson.'

'Perhaps the new trend of my success will be the defending of my country and its position with the Vietnam–Cambodian war,' Tiny mused in his diary. However, his political ignorance was revealed when he was asked to explain his support of the war by Harold Ramis during an interview for *Playboy*. 'I believe that the United States has never been wrong in a war,' Tiny said. 'I think we are in Vietnam because we remember Pearl Harbor, and we're trying to see that a thing like that doesn't happen again ... I do believe we have the right to protect what we have.'

When Ramis asked how he could support the war in the face of atrocities at the hands of US soldiers, notably the My Lai Massacre, Tiny—who felt that Nixon's best presidential move had been inviting Reverend Billy Graham to the White House—maintained that this was collateral damage, suggesting that the children who were killed in the process would be raptured into the next world. 'That was terrible, terrible,' he said. 'But in a place like Vietnam, you can't tell who's your friend and who's your enemy. Anyone over there may be carrying a weapon of destruction. It's a shame that children have got to be there, but don't forget that the Israelites in the Bible killed the children of their enemies. You see, the good Lord knows there is another world coming and what will happen to these children when it comes.'

Decades later, Tiny maintained his support for the war. 'I believed we were right [to be] in Vietnam,' he told David Tibet in 1995. 'I felt that we were in Vietnam only as a police action; in fact it wasn't even a war. And that explanation started to turn and confuse more people, and according to my management, put a damper on the hippies that were following me. It wasn't that they didn't still like me, but it seemed to take the edge off things. Frankly, I felt that President Nixon, as far as this country was concerned, made a grave error in stopping the war the way that he did, because it caused a lack of respect for America after that.'

Tiny was more relenting on the counterculture when it came to drugs, stating that he felt hate and prejudice were more dangerous. 'Everybody condemns those who take drugs,' he explained to Harold Ramis, 'who have long hair, who have free love and who go to political demonstrations, but let's look at our so called righteous Christians. They have drunken parties in their homes. They say we should love thy neighbor, but they live in all-white communities and move out when a black man moves in. They say they don't believe in divorce, but they don't seem to mind going out with other women. Of course, it's wrong to take those terrible drugs—they ruin the body and the mind—but it's just as wrong to be filled with prejudice. As far as I'm concerned, the temporary effect of a drug is nothing compared with the venomous normality of hate, which is found in 99 percent of Christian homes today.'*

While Tiny was willing to give his fans a pass for using drugs, they were

* 'This is Tiny at his best,' Miss Sue adds. 'Standing up for the cultural scapegoats and pointing out the hypocrisy of the self-righteous. Tiny grew up being marginalized, and he wasn't going to stand by and see others demonized by people who were guilty themselves. He didn't want to attack anyone, and his mild-mannered way of talking softened his criticism, but he had a compulsion to defend anyone being subjected to shame and blame. He hated that.'

not going to give *him* a pass for provocatively releasing a single that urged those who did not support the war to 'go back to your home or the sea.' A few weeks after its release, Tiny asked a Reprise employee how the record was selling. 'We sold seventeen copies!' the employee replied.

If his message was lost on the general public and record buyers, Tiny decided to mail a copy of the single to one person who might appreciate it: Vice President Spiro T. Agnew. To his delight, he received a thank-you letter by return.

Another ill-performing piece of Tiny-bilia was Parker Bros' *Tiny Tim Game Of Beautiful Things*: a two-to-four-player board game in which, playing as a little shopping bag, the object is to collect small cards featuring various 'beautiful things' worth so many points, such as 'a hot shower,' 'the wonder of a sunrise,' 'a field of tulips,' and 'the star spangled banner.' When all of the cards are removed from the playing board, each player totals up his points, and the player with the most points is the winner. The packaging featured a gloriously oversized outtake from the *God Bless Tiny Tim* cover shoot, psychedelic graphic artwork, and another image of Tiny in the center of the game board, grinning mischievously.

'What's all this about?' a perplexed David Frost asked, upon examining a copy of the game when Tiny appeared with him on August 24.

'It's a lovely game for the nice kiddies,' Tiny replied.

'What about the nasty kiddies?'

'They can play it, too.'

Despite the fact that millions had tuned in to watch Tiny's wedding, the kids did not want to play his *Game Of Beautiful Things*. Parker Bros executives watched as copies of the game collected dust on toy-store shelves. But while his new single and board game were duds, his impending appearance at the 1970 Isle of Wight Festival would turn out to be a surprise hit. 'It's going to be a thrill, going there again,' Tiny told Frost. 'I've always loved England, and this Isle of Wight is going to be interesting because there's gonna be about 250,000 people watching this and TV screens all the way back on the island, I hear.'

'It'll be absolutely great,' Frost replied. It was.

Remembered as the 'British Woodstock,' the 1970 Isle of Wight Festival took place from August 26–31 at the East Afton Farm on England's largest island. The festival had previously taken place in 1968 and 1969, but 1970 is regarded as the 'largest and most famous,' with some estimates putting the attendance as high as 700,000. The line-up included Jimi Hendrix, Chicago,

The Doors, Joni Mitchell, Donovan, Jethro Tull, Emerson Lake & Palmer, The Who, Joan Baez, Free, Miles Davis, and, to the surprise of many, Tiny Tim.*

Sandwiched between Joni Mitchell and Miles Davis, Tiny appeared on the fourth day of the festival, August 29. In the weeks leading up to the festival, many had expressed doubts over whether or not he belonged on such a bill. As Tiny later told Ernie Clark, 'All the rock papers and the trades were saying, What in the world … are they out of their heads? … And I was wondering, maybe they're right?'

It is not clear who exactly was responsible for bringing Tiny Tim to the festival, but if any of the individuals involved in the festival's planning were nervous about it, their concerns appeared to be realized by the spectacle created backstage before Tiny's performance by Tiny's management.

A section of Murray Lerner's documentary, *Message To Love: The Isle Of Wight Festival 1970*, is devoted to the question as to whether or not the festival should have been free to the public. Tiny is asked twice in the film, and replies both times to the affirmative, stating 'Oh, sure' and 'Of course it's a good idea to have it free, but get rid of those terrible marijuana drugs!'

Tiny's statement stood in stark contrast to the actions of his managers, who are shown demanding his appearance fee in full, and in England— not Scottish—pounds, before they would allow their client onstage. Festival employees are then seen counting huge stacks of money; Bert Block, who had booked all of the American acts at the festival, remarks to Lerner, 'Tiny Tim … can't sing and play with his ukulele without the money first. It doesn't tune up without the money, Murray!'

Tiny Tim's backing group consisted of a jazz trio featuring Tiny's then musical director, Leo Stone, a piano player from Queens, New York, and two British musicians: Jack Richards on drums and Cas Caswell on double bass. Caswell later recounted on his website that the trio were offered only £40 apiece—which they never received.†

Once Tiny's management had their $7,500 in hand, Tiny Tim's jazz trio took the stage as planned. The festival's master of ceremonies, Rikki Farr,

* Tiny and Vicki saw Donovan backstage at the festival. Tiny noted in his diary that Vicki had said that she thought Donovan was 'handsome.' Vicki recalled the meeting fondly, noting that Donovan wrote a song for her and mailed her a copy of it on cassette. 'I think he had a crush on me. He was so cute.'

† When Lerner's film of the festival was released in 1996, Caswell and Richards each received $500 for their appearance on the recording. 'It's the longest time I have ever had to wait for gig money,' Caswell later wrote.

addressed the unruly ocean of people who were waiting for the next act. 'A festival, at one time or another, might need some humor, but having listened to his LPs and meeting him in person, I think there's not only humor, there's a lot of warmth, so please, would you extend your warmth to the incredible Tiny Tim!' A visibly nervous Tiny then took the stage, holding his ukulele over his head before opening with 'Waltz Of The Bells.' The crowd remained moderately quiet until Tiny pulled a small bell from his pocket and rang it into the microphone, inciting cheers and whistles.[*]

'Thank you! God bless you,' Tiny said, after finishing his opener. 'And what a thrill it is to be here in England, at the lovely Isle of Wight. My dear friends, most of these numbers you may not know, but the memories linger on of those artists who were just as great as the Presleys and The Beatles and The Rolling Stones in the beginning of our phonograph industry, great English stars like Mister Charles Harrison and Randolph Sutton and all the rest!'

He then launched into 'On The Good Ship Lollipop,' 'Hot And Cold Water,' and 'Love's Ship,' but his performance peaked during a medley of 'He's Got The Whole World In His Hands,' 'Down By The Riverside,' 'When The Saints Go Marching In,' 'Great Balls Of Fire,'—during which he ripped off his tie and threw it into the sea of onlookers—and Creedence Clearwater Revival's 'Proud Mary.' As the medley continued, the audience became increasingly enthralled, swaying in unison, hands extended. Tiny too, seemed to transcend the moment as he plowed through the medley, eyes rolled back, looking up to the sky and jerking his hips around. Finally, he began 'Tip-Toe,' which was met by a tremendous roar of applause. He followed it with a medley of British music-hall tunes, sung through an electric megaphone.

'Thank you so much, my dear friends,' he told the crowd through his megaphone. 'At this time, this is not a megaphone, this is a singing horn, transistorized by six little batteries! You can take it to parties with you and entertain your friends! It also has another use, I don't hear anyone today singing through this horn. It brings back sounds in an acoustic-alike way!'

As Tiny broke into 'There'll Always Be An England,' a hot-air balloon

---

[*] While this is the correct version of events, as they coincide with the actual recording of the show, Tiny remembered the situation differently in his 1993 interview with Ernie Clark, stating, 'My opening number was an old song from 1929, *I'm always high, high, high, up in the hills, watching the clouds roll by*. All of a sudden I heard a faint cheer'—perhaps because they thought the word 'high' was a drug reference.

in the colors of the British flag appeared on the horizon beyond the stage. 'There rose the biggest goddamn hot air balloon you ever saw,' one audience member later wrote of the moment, 'emblazoned with red, white, and blue stripes—Synchronicity! The crowd went ape and everyone was on their feet, applauding the bloody balloon as much as they were applauding Tim.'

Other members of the audience that day have expressed similar points of view regarding Tiny's performance. 'It was very moving for me,' Steve Dunphy recalls. 'Just to get up in front of all those people on your own takes a great deal of courage. To turn around a crowd that is just waiting impatiently for the next big name group to come on, and has started throwing coke cans, etc., takes someone a bit special … I was only about sixteen at the time, and saw him more as a novelty act … [but] his response to the crowd, and their eventual response to him, showed him to have something a little special.'

After a brief reprise of 'There'll Always Be An England,' he shouted out his signature phrase, 'Thank you and God bless you all,' before exiting the stage as the band played 'Baby Face.'

'Thank you, Tiny Tim! Thank you, Tiny Tim!' Rikki Farr yelled into the microphone as the crowd roared.

While Tiny remarked humbly in his diary that he 'did pretty good,' the news of his ecstatic reception at the Isle of Wight broke in London. On his way back to the city, he was handed a copy of the *Sunday Times*, which featured a glowing review that stated, 'Tiny Tim stole the show! … He did it without even an electric instrument!' The *New York Times* also reported on Tiny's success at the festival, with columnist Russel Baker commenting, 'On the Isle of Wight, Tiny Tim led thousands of youngsters at a rock festival in a mass singing of "There'll Always Be An England." Yes, Tiny Tim and thousands of pop-music fans, it looks as if there always will.'

If Tiny hoped that the influx of positive press might mend his tarnished relationship with Mo Ostin of Warner Bros, he was disappointed to learn that Ostin was unmoved. 'I don't usually get good reviews,' he told Tibet. 'This was the best I ever got … [but Ostin] did not want to know of the concert's success, as he was trying to get rid of me anyway … you can do the greatest concert, but if you don't sell records, they don't care. I alienated them, and they didn't forget it.'

Tiny's hunch—that the executives at Warner Bros. were simply waiting for his contract to expire—was reinforced by the fact that no new album was released during a year of media frenzy and positive reviews at high-profile engagements like the Isle of Wight festival. 'Don't Bite The Hand That's Feeding You' was Tiny's only record release in 1970. Upon returning from England, he spent two days in the studio, recording 'Earth Angel,' 'Carnival's Ended,' the Irving Caesar composition 'Hallelujah, Bless The Peace,' and a duet with Miss Vicki on the Dick Haymes classic 'Put Your Arms Around Me, Honey,' also featuring The Enchanted Forest, but the antiquated songs were never released.*

Mo Ostin was not the only party unmoved by Tiny's performance at the Isle of Wight. Hopes that Murray Lerner's film might provide additional exposure for Tiny were dashed after Lerner clashed with Columbia boss Clive Davis. CBS Films had first refusal rights on the picture, but Davis walked out of a screening of Lerner's first cut of the documentary on hearing Tiny's version of 'There'll Always Be An England.' 'If Tiny Tim is in this film,' he told Lerner, 'we're not putting this out.' The film would remain unreleased until 1996.

Even if Mo Ostin and Clive Davis wanted nothing to do with him, Tiny continued, full steam ahead. On October 4, he made his fourth appearance on *The Ed Sullivan Show*. Vicki must have been relieved to discover that he was due to appear alone, performing a medley of songs from *For All My Little Friends* ('On The Good Ship Lollipop,' 'Two Times A Day,' 'Hot And Cold Water') and a frenetic version of 'The Other Side,' with stock footage of a shark swimming behind him appearing courtesy of a primitive blue screen.

After a short tour of Florida, Tiny returned to England in mid-October for a tour scheduled to run until December 14, but things did not go to plan. At the Batley Variety Club, ex-Coldstream Guards Trooper Jim Smith believed Tiny was mocking the audience with his medley of English songs sung through his megaphone. 'I'll shut him up for running down England!' Smith yelled. He jumped onto the stage and, in an attempt to grab the microphone from Tiny, knocked it to the floor. A frightened Tiny retreated hastily, and the ex-trooper was escorted from the premises. Shortly thereafter, Tiny departed England and returned to New York, cutting short the intended six-week tour after only one week and forfeiting around $60,000. 'He was terribly upset about [the incident],' Alan Field, Tiny's British agent, told the press. 'He said although only one person had accused him of insulting Britain, he was surely one of

---

* While Tiny logged in his diary that The Enchanted Forest backed him at the session, band members Missy Martino and Sandy Klee Phillips have no knowledge of it. All of these tracks remain unreleased, with the exception of 'Hallelujah, Bless The Peace,' which was finally issued on *God Bless Tiny Tim: The Complete Reprise Masters … And More* in 2006.

many—in which case Tiny felt he should not be performing in Britain at all … we couldn't persuade him to change his mind.'

Smith was then asked whether he had any regrets about the tour, and it seemed that he did. Tiny had left Britain, Smith said, 'because his conscience was troubling him. I should've shoved that megaphone right down his throat when I had the chance.' The November 1970 issue of *Rolling Stone* carried the headline 'Tiny Tim Departs England in a Snit.' He was also threatened with expulsion from the musician's union, and slammed with several lawsuits presumably from concert promoters who lost money due to his cancellations.

* * *

Although Reprise gave no signal that it intended on renewing Tiny's contract when it expired at the end of 1971, someone gave the go-ahead to give him one more single on his way out of the door. Young producer Joe Wissert, who had previously been a dancer on *American Bandstand* and had produced The Turtles' *Happy Together*, was selected to produce the record. 'I volunteered for everything at that time,' Wissert explains. 'Tiny was a little cold; I had helped the Kinks when the were a little cold and thought I could make Tiny hot again.' Wissert decided to attempt to capitalize upon the Miss Vicki angle, requesting that the couple take a stab at Frankie Avalon's 1959 hit 'Why?'

When Wissert met Tiny, he did not see any of the bad behavior that had been described by the media over previous six months. 'His spirit was intact,' he recalls. 'Whenever I saw him, he was always very positive. I liked him a lot.'

When Tiny and Vicki entered the Western Recorders studio in Los Angeles on November 30, they seemed in good spirits; Wissert recalls the couple were hugging and kissing during breaks in the session. As with her appearance on *Ed Sullivan*, Vicki was not thrilled about the idea of singing on record. Nonetheless, Wissert and engineer Lee Herschberg, who had also worked on *Tiny Tim's Second Album*, looked on enthusiastically as she hesitantly laid down her vocals for the track.*

'We did it and they played it back,' Vicki recalls. 'I said, Oh, that's horrendous, can you just take me out? They said no, no, no, and they tried to doctor it or something and it still was bad. Then they made us do it again a couple of times and they played it back and I said, It's so bad. They said,

---

* Some of the other personnel on the record included former Chess Records session drummer and future Earth Wind & Fire bandleader Maurice White, along with strings arranged by the prolific Nick DeCaro.

We've heard a lot worse. It's not that bad. You should hear Linda McCartney, she's not that good either. We can doctor it. It will be fine.'*

The following day, Tiny returned to the studio to record the B-side, a version of 'The Spaceship Song,' which he had written in 1963 for Miss Snooky, featuring ukulele stylings by Tiny and piano accompaniment by Nick DeCaro. Of the fact that he had written the song for Miss Snooky, Tiny told the press, 'I found it very difficult to tell my wife why I'd written the song for Miss Snooky. But, of course, I tell her everything.' Ultimately, very few heard the A-side, let alone its B-side, as copies of the white label promo, featuring a mono and stereo version of 'Why,' sat unplayed at radio stations across the country. 'I never saw a stock copy of the record,' says Wissert. 'I was always disappointed we didn't get anything for Tiny with that last record. I was enthusiastic about it. It's just that nobody else was.'

Tiny and Vicki spent their first anniversary in Cape Coral, Florida, where Tiny was performing at the Cape Colony Inn & Resort. Despite a full tour schedule, Tiny traveled back to New York to tend to his father, now seventy-nine years old, who, due to complications from diabetes had had both legs amputated earlier and was now in the hospital with more complications. When Tiny arrived in Butros's hospital room, the two men wept when they saw each other. 'He is in suffering condition,' Tiny wrote in his diary. 'I pray his soul is saved + that the end comes quickly.' Having resigned themselves to the fact that the end was near, Tiny returned to see Butros with his accountant and attorneys to draw up the old man's will.

At the same time, Tiny's agent at CMA, Irving Squires, the man responsible for generating the majority of Tiny's income, was threatening to drop Tiny completely if Tiny did not fire Joe Cappy. However, in a transparent display of questionable ethics, Squires, despite threatening to drop him as a client, accepted a $1,000 Christmas bonus from Tiny.

It was to this backdrop that Tiny and Vicki's new single was released, on New Year's Eve 1970, to coincide with another appearance on *The Tonight Show*. The booking had given Tiny the opportunity to end the year on a positive note, despite the tumultuous state of his career. However, his attitude upon arriving at the taping was sour. 'I was in a terrible mood,' he later told Harry Stein. 'I knew my career was going down and I saw it getting worse.'

---

* An additional duet, a version of 'Dance With A Dolly (With A Hole In Her Stocking),' exists in the Warner Bros archives but was not included on *God Bless Tiny Tim: The Complete Reprise Masters … And More.*

Actor and comedian Dick Shawn was filling in for Johnny Carson for this particular episode, and the producers of the show wanted Tiny to sing a comedic number with Shawn. Tiny resisted, instead stating that he wished to sing the patriotic World War I song 'Our Flag.' Ultimately, the producers caved in and allowed Tiny to perform it, but during the taping Tiny became combative. After a member of the audience booed during his performance, Tiny took it upon himself to address the audience during his interview. 'Listen,' he said sternly, 'I don't mind if you boo me, but I'm sick and tired of people booing the flag and booing this country. If you don't like it, get out of here!' Shawn, who was seated at Carson's desk, blushed with embarrassment.

* * *

The incredible exposure Tiny enjoyed in 1970 revealed several aspects of his personality, drastically altering his fan base and the media's focus. In addition to his outspoken support of the Vietnam War, Tiny had penned an article for the Christmas 1970 issue of *Esquire*, titled 'The Perfect Mother,' in which he expounded upon his opinions of female gender roles. 'A mother's place is in the home,' he wrote, 'not outside competing with men. Basically, it's the law of the scriptures and a law of nature. Man came from God, woman came from man. Woman is the second choice. Her duties were to take care of the home and scrub the floor and raise the children. Today she has free will to go against nature—to go out to vote, to compete for a job. … They're free to do it, just like I'm free to drive a car drunk if I want to, but I'll get hurt.'*

The past year had also seen Tiny take a bride, lose a child, and undergo a highly public falling out with his management. He was no longer an enigma of innocence and love, and the media had ceased asking, 'Is he putting us on?' Though Tiny was aware that his career was troubled, he did not consider Ron DeBlasio's advice from the previous April to 'chill' and reevaluate his career path. Now, 'America's clown prince' was wearing out his welcome.

---

* Interestingly, though not surprisingly, Tiny named Calvin Coolidge's mother, not his own, as the mother he admired most as Coolidge 'stood for forthright principles.'

CHAPTER TWELVE
THE BLESSED EVENT

[The 70s] came and opened a whole new era, and most of the stars of the 60s faded out of sight … Hendrix, Joplin, and Morrison were gone, may they rest in peace. I was also gone—with a name, however. I did get the name. However, I went back to working jobs I had worked on my way up.

TINY TIM TO JOHNNY PINEAPPLE, NOVEMBER 11 1994

In January 1971, Tiny Tim and Miss Vicki—several months into her second pregnancy—set out on a brief tour to promote 'Why.' The tour began in Philadelphia and then moved on to Minneapolis, where Tiny signed autographs for several days at an auto show. 'Thanks, O Lord, as I must hold some kind of autograph record,' he wrote in his diary, 'for I signed autographs at the auto show from about 1:45pm to 10:45pm—without stopping.'

When the auto show's president offered to build Tiny a race car decaled with tulips, Tiny boasted to the *Milwaukee Journal*, 'I'll be entering it in drag races. I don't know how to drive, but he said he'll teach me.' While thousands of curious auto-show attendees were willing to take a few moments to get an autograph, the general indifference to Tiny's new album was palpable. The *Journal* joked that the new record was 'perhaps coincidentally' entitled 'Why?'

Despite Tiny's spike in popularity as a result of his marriage, he was still living on the edge financially. He toured almost constantly, but his shows were often poorly attended. 'The place was sparsely filled and mostly empty—a disappointment to the owners financially,' Tiny noted in his diary, after a concert at the Depot in Minneapolis. The following day, Joe Cappy returned to New York after a dispute over his salary, and Tiny commented bitterly in his diary about Cappy's extramarital activities: 'both his wives' had not received any money. Upon Cappy's departure, Tiny's dentist and sometime conductor Marvin Lewis flew out to temporarily replace Cappy as manager.

Though they barely had enough money to continue, Tiny, Vicki, and Lewis pressed on to Milwaukee, Wisconsin, and then to Denver, Colorado. There, Tiny was encouraged by larger crowds, along with the news that CMA had picked up his option for another three years. The group then traveled south to Houston, Texas, for a weeklong return engagement at the Cork Club. 'Thanks as we have new jobs (Lord willing) + as work is still available,' a relieved Tiny wrote in his diary.

In Houston, Tiny made concert, TV, and radio appearances to promote 'Why,' toured the Houston Space Center, and learned a little more about where his money was being spent. In addition to paying management and lawyers and supporting his own wife, who commanded a $200 weekly allowance, which she would sometimes splurge on '$300 and up' dresses, Tiny received news that his agent at CMA, Irving Squires, had requested $3,500 for 'favors.' Aware that he had recently given Squires $2,000 in addition to his usual commission, Tiny, incensed, fired his lawyers, Levy and Ferris, for having paid Squires extra money and reported Squires to his superior at CMA. Squires received a slap on the wrist, and Tiny was assigned a new agent—somebody, as he described it, who was a 'less important booking agent in the company' with considerably less pull and connections than Squires. On January 22, having dismissed Levy and Ferris, Tiny sent a handwritten letter from his hotel in Texas to attorney Jack Rabin, husband of his cousin Roslyn Rabin, granting him power of attorney.

On January 21, an episode of *Love American Style* aired featuring Tiny Tim, *The Brady Bunch*'s Robert Reed, and *Laugh-In*'s Judy Carne. Tiny played an eccentric millionaire whom the stranded couple believes to be a vampire. On January 24, he returned to Los Angeles for appearances on *The Reel Game* and *Hollywood Squares*. Album sales and touring income were not sufficient to support him or his various dependents, and further appearances on the shows *Juvenile Jury* and *Truth Or Consequences* signified a shift in Tiny's career as his music began to take a back seat.

Meanwhile, 'Why' was immobile on the charts. 'We needed a hit record very badly (Lord willing),' Tiny wrote. 'I believe not only will we have so many hit records, it will be unbelievable.' Though there would be no more Tiny Tim records on Reprise, with his contract due to expire later in 1971, Joe Wissert and Tiny recorded a few tracks during one last demo session. The songs from the session include 'The American Pioneer,' 'You Were There' (which Tiny had sung to Miss Vicki during their wedding on *The Tonight Show*), 'Let's Find

Out Tonight,' 'It Took A Good, Good Woman,' and a medley of 'Beloved' and 'Don't You Mind It Honey If The World Goes Wrong.'

A few months later, in a radio interview with the Oakville Culture Corner in Ontario, Tiny discussed his issues with his recordings thus far and made mention of what looked like big plans on the horizon for his recording career. 'Recording is one of the weakest things I'm in and that should be the strongest,' he said. 'I really feel that I haven't been recorded right. This is maybe my fault. Maybe sometimes you might sing better on the microphone than you do in a recording studio. I don't know.'

All was not lost, however, for now Tiny revealed that rock'n'roll songwriting partnership Leiber & Stoller were 'going to be producing me very shortly. They produced all the Coasters hits in the late 50s. Of course, it's a thrill to be with them.' Unfortunately, this intriguing partnership never materialized. Instead, Tiny and Vicki toured upstate New York and Canada before returning to New York City for what would ultimately be his final appearance on *The Ed Sullivan Show*. On this particular episode, Vicki, now seven months pregnant, was to perform a duet of 'Why?' with Tiny. She was about as unenthused about the idea as she had been a year prior, and received another scolding from Tiny for her ungrateful attitude. As ever, Vicki consented, and made her second appearance on the show.

During rehearsals, Vicki became increasingly self-conscious about what she called her 'reedy, off-key voice,' and it was decided that Tiny would sing the majority of the song. Furthermore, Sullivan's staff decided the segment was to have a turn-of-the-century theme. The two were placed in a white gazebo, with other couples strolling arm-in-arm behind them. Vicki was once again mortified when she was outfitted in an oversized, fluffy monster of a dress to cover her pregnant stomach. A massive, wide-brimmed hat, tied in a large bow under her chin, completed her costume. Tiny had not seen Vicki prior to rehearsal and was taken aback by the size of her hat. As the music began, he turned to her, and she watched as his eyes moved from her face to the hat. Suddenly, he burst into laughter, and Vicki, nervous and feeling ridiculous, began cracking up as well. In fact, the two were laughing so hard that, after five tries, they still had not made it all the way through the song.

'I'm sorry,' Tiny told the director, 'just give us a minute.'

'I don't think we ever got through the entire song without laughing,' Vicki later recalled. 'I mean … I looked ridiculous in that get up … I was very skinny and tall, and I have a very small head.'

After three days of rehearsals, Tiny and Vicki went to the Ed Sullivan Theater for the live taping. Backstage, Vicki felt an anxiety attack approaching. 'I can't do it,' she pleaded. 'I want to go home. Please, I just can't!'

If she expected Tiny to become angry, she was surprised when his face softened and he took her hand. 'It's OK,' he said. 'You will be just fine. Just look at me, don't look at the cameras.'

'Just then I believe he got it,' Vicki later wrote. 'I wasn't being ungrateful when I said I didn't want to do [the show] ... I was scared ... I didn't want to make a fool of myself.'

The two went out onstage and took their seats on the set. 'I was shaking with fear,' Vicki recalled, 'but when he started to sing, he looked at me and I saw ... something in his face, in his eyes. ... He was nervous ... nervous for me! He understood how scared I was and he helped me through it ... he really did. It was very generous and kind of him.'

While in New York, Tiny visited with Jack Rabin to make official Rabin's appointment as his lawyer. As Sam Rabin, Eddie Rabin's younger brother, recalls, 'We lived in a very middle class, but leaning toward upper class area in Brooklyn, so nobody really knew that [Tiny] was my cousin. This girl across the street was getting married in her backyard. I guess there must have been anywhere from fifty to seventy-five people there ... [Tiny] pulled up in a long stretch limo, and came into the house to see my father. ... Tiny Tim just rings our doorbell with Joe Cappelluzzo. I felt so sorry for the bride because at least half the wedding party, maybe more, starts leaving the wedding and walking across the street to our house, crowding up the front steps, looking in any window they could to get a glimpse of Tiny Tim. It was a hysterical scene.'

Soon, Tiny Tim and Miss Vicki were back on the road, touring Ohio, Arkansas, Vermont, and Massachusetts. The effects of Tiny's demotion within his booking agency were immediately apparent. In a diary entry, he described the Bronx Lounge in Marlboro, Massachusetts, as 'the worse place I've been in in a long time.'

As Tiny watched his bookings spiral downward, the anxiety of giving birth was beginning to get to Vicki, who was now around eight months pregnant. Tiny felt the brunt of her anxiety and endured several of Vicki's mood swings, during which she told him that she hated him. 'My dear wife felt the pressures of expecting,' he wrote of the incident. One newspaper even relayed, via Tiny, that Vicki had 'wailed about the terrifying aspect of having the baby.'

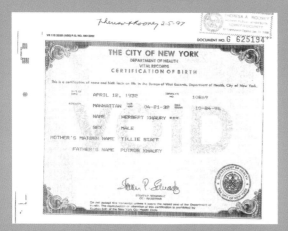

CLOCKWISE FROM TOP LEFT Herbert Khaury's birth certificate, listing his date of birth as April 12 1932; lacking an 8x10, Tiny ran to a photo booth to take this picture for Ronny Elliott at Steve Paul's club the Scene in 1967; a young Herbert as Larry Love in 1952; with his father, Butros Khaury, on Riverside Drive, New York, c. 1939.

CLOCKWISE FROM TOP LEFT Tiny
performs in the Circus Maximus
room at Caesar's Palace, Las
Vegas, August 1968; a set of Tiny
stickers; a local TV appearance
in Houston. OPPOSITE Resting on
a bench during a break in his
Rolling Stone cover shoot.

FROM TOP A portait of Tiny and Miss Vicki; Tiny's *Beautiful Things* board game; the happy couple duet in 1970; Vicki's signed copy of Tiny's book, *Beautiful Thoughts*.

OPPOSITE Tiny (and pigeons) perform at the Santa Monica Civic Auditorium, June 1968.

ABOVE Tiny and Vicki cut their wedding cake at their reception while crooner Nick Lucas looks on, December 17 1969; Tiny's aunt, Bella Stein, and his parents, Tillie and Butros, at the wedding.
LEFT The marriage certificate.

CLOCKWISE FROM LEFT Tiny poses with baseball legend Dizzy Dean and TV host Irv Kupcinet; Tiny's diary entry from his wedding day, as dictated to Miss Vicki; onstage with The Enchanted Forest at the San Su San Club in Mineola, Long Island, 1970; backstage with Vicki and The Enchanted Forest.

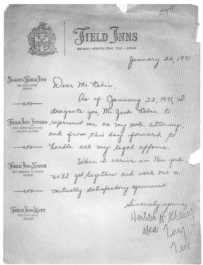

CLOCKWISE FROM TOP Jim Cappy, Tiny, and artist Francisco Poblet in 1973; a hand-written letter from Tiny granting power of attorney to Jack Rabin, 1971; The New Tiny Tim Show, 1974. **OPPOSITE** On the set of the 'Juanita Banana' video, 1973.

THE NEW TINY TIM SHOW

On the set for Serenity Bennama

ABOVE Tiny argues with his manager after being told to keep it down by hotel staff during an all-night concert for Richard Barone and friends in Tampa, 1976. RIGHT Tiny performs for Barone and co. OPPOSITE The Tulips twirl around Tiny at Humpin Hanna's in Milwaukee, 1975.

ABOVE Tiny with his daughter, Tulip,
and his friend Harve Mann in 1981.
OPPOSITE, FROM TOP Tiny and Martin
Sharp chat before a peformance
in 1978; at dinner during a tour
with *Roy Radin's Vaudeville Revue*,
1979; Tiny's business card.

TINY TIM
THE
'ETERNAL TROUBADOUR'

The Neal Hollander Agency, Inc.
9956 Majorca Place, Boca Raton, FL 33434
407/482-1400 Fax: 407/479-0035

TINY TIM

20th CENTURY PROMOTIONS
Personal Management
Area Code: 508-679-5240
Telephone (401) 467-1832

ABOVE On the set of the 'Won't You Dance With Me' video, 1989.
LEFT A promotional shot of Tiny from 1988, from Gil Morse's 20th Century Productions.
OPPOSITE Tiny during his stint as part of Allan C. Hill's Great American Circus in 1985.

CLOCKWISE FROM TOP LEFT Tiny performs in Ogunquit, Maine, August 1996; with Tiny Head Brian Blouin on the evening of his second *Tonight Show* wedding, October 31 1994; with his third wife, Susan Gardner, on their wedding day, August 18 1995; the wedding invitation.

On March 11, a lengthy article in the *Spokesman Review* featured a candid interview with Tiny in which he detailed Vicki's fears. After devoting a few sentences to Tiny's appearance, describing him as 'a whopping 230 pounds of charismatic put-on' and noting that he was becoming 'distressingly overweight' from 'a campy cyclone of Coca-Cola, ginger snaps, grapefruit, animal crackers, and honey,' reporter Christy Marian focused in on Vicki's pregnancy. 'She won't go to no male doctor,' Tiny revealed. 'Miss Vicki sometimes gets hysterical thinking about birth. I let her read the book *Expectant Mothers* so she'd know how it's done.' He went on to say that he had been trying to locate a 'reputable female doctor' in New Orleans, where he was scheduled to perform around her due date in late May. About the baby itself, Tiny did not have much to say. 'If it's a boy again, I won't call it Tiny Tim Jr. … My child has to make it on his own.'

Also on Tiny's mind was his father's rapidly declining health. In January, Butros had been transferred to the Harkness Pavilion at New York-Presbyterian Hospital, and was telling his doctors he was holding out to see the birth of his grandchild. On March 10, Tiny wrote, 'I pray for my father who isn't doing very well.' Vicki recalls visiting Butros in the hospital. 'It was very sad because [Tillie and Butros] were looking forward to having a grandchild. I went to visit him in the hospital and we knew he wasn't going to make it too much longer, and … that was a sad thing. He was a sweet man, very sweet man.'

Less than a month later, on April 2 1971, Butros passed away at the age of eighty, only a little over a month before Vicki's due date, and ten days before Tiny's thirty-ninth birthday. Alan Budinger immediately began working on an oil painting of Butros by which their forthcoming grandchild could remember him. According to Vicki, Tiny's fear of succumbing to a death similar to that of his father seemed to outweigh his grief over the loss. 'Tiny seemed scared not for him but for his own self, like, Oh, I hope that doesn't happen to me. I don't think he was able to empathize very well.'

Vicki's recollection of Tiny's reaction notwithstanding, his diary entries indicate that he was saddened by Butros's death and reminded of the sacrifices his father had made for him.

Thank you O Lord for letting me have such a wonderful earthly father, as well as mother and now wife. My father tried to do everything for me. He gave me all he could to make me happy. He was poor in money but rich in love for me. He was kind, strict, and he put his whole heart and soul in me. Thanks as he lived to see my success and also the wedding, although he failed to live to see the Blessed event (Lord willing).

He went on to list the lessons he had learned from his father:

1. Always hold money with me—at least $25.00.
2. Not spend foolishly.
3. Be wise.
4. Be careful.
5. Not waste.

There was little time to dwell on Butros's passing, however, because Vicki's due date was fast approaching, and accordingly she soon ceased traveling. Tiny's propensity for unconventional opinions and his characteristic transparency revived some curiosity in the media regarding the couple's plans for the labor process. In particular, would they follow the trends of natural childbirth, and would Tiny join Vicki during labor? TV host David Frost posed these questions during Tiny and Vicki's appearance on his show on February 19.

Asked by Frost whether he was in favor of a natural childbirth, Tiny said that he was, 'But since I'm not a woman, I couldn't force my interpretations on her. Women go through so much when they have blessed events and there's so much pain and so much torture, I don't think a lot of men can feel what they go through. … As far as watching, I would love to watch … if I had the nerve to look at it.'

After the stifled laughter from the studio audience had faded, Frost asked Vicki, 'You'd like your husband to be there, wouldn't you?'

'Well, if he could take it, but I don't think he could, he might faint,' Vicki replied, inciting another round of laughter from the audience.

Ultimately, Tiny's presence or lack thereof was moot. Vicki went into labor prematurely at 4:30am on May 10 1971. She was alone at the time and had to hire a cab to take her to Doctors Hospital in Manhattan, where she gave birth to a six pound, ten ounce baby girl. Tiny arrived at the hospital the following day, and the press took what would become widely circulated photographs of Tiny gazing at the baby through the observation window of a nursery.

'She's beautiful, and my, she's got a lot of hair!' Tiny exclaimed, as he saw his daughter for the first time.

'Thanks as Miss Vicki and the blessed event are doing fine,' Tiny wrote in his diary. 'Thanks as it took only twenty-eight minutes for Miss Vicki to deliver. I am sorry my father did not live to see it, but thanks as my mother and all of us did.'

Though Butros had not lived to see his granddaughter, she did have his eyes. 'They're brown,' Emma Budinger told the press. 'Just like Mr. Khaury's eyes. Tiny has eyes like his father, and the baby has eyes like Tiny.'

Before leaving the hospital on May 14, Tiny took questions from reporters and remarked that he was happy the baby was a girl 'because boys get into fights and little girls don't.' Asked if he would like his daughter to have a career in entertainment, he replied, 'As long as she's spiritually happy and healthy, then that's all that matters.'

Tiny and Vicki had not yet decided on a name when she gave birth, and it was cruelly suggested by a comedian that the child be named 'Vic-Tim.' The subject had already come up during the *David Frost Show* interview, when Tiny had said he was considering the names of some 'commercial brands' for his child: 'some soaps I use, some hand creams, or face creams, or aftershave lotions … I always look for originality.'

'That certainly would be fairly original, wouldn't it?' Frost said with a chuckle. 'Do you have any favorite names, Miss Vicki, at all?'

'No,' said Vicki, letting out a long sigh of resignation.

Tiny suggested they name their daughter 'Tulip.' Vicki thought the name sounded like a publicity stunt and told him so, but to no avail. 'He refused to sign the birth certificate, otherwise. So I said, Fine. It didn't really seem like I had a choice, but it turned out OK.'

Though Vicki had no say in the naming of her daughter, she put her foot down with regard to their living situation, and demanded they find a permanent residence. 'We can't live in hotel rooms,' she told Tiny. 'I can't sterilize the bottles when we don't have a kitchen.' In fairness, finding a home was something they had been discussing for some time, and this, too, had come up on their recent appearance with David Frost.

'We have been thinking of getting one in New Jersey near her mother's place,' Tiny revealed.

When Frost asked what sort of house they were looking for, Vicki seemed unsure, but Tiny, of course, had some thoughts on the matter. 'I would like to have two separate bathrooms, one for her and one for myself. Then, after that, I would also love to have nice, strong doors, where no thieves can come in. Bars, inside the windows and outside the windows.' He went on to explain that he would like to find somewhere with 'steel floors, and steel doors, and steel walls. This way, you can't get no rats in there or roaches or those termites or anything like that.'

In the end, there would be no steel house, nor would they move to near Vicki's mother's house in New Jersey. There were, however, separate bathrooms. Tiny consulted with Joe Cappy, who found a double apartment, 7E, in the Premiere House at 1401 Ocean Avenue in Brooklyn, near Brooklyn College. Tiny did not view returning to New York as a positive development, however. 'The hardest part was moving with Miss Vicki to Brooklyn in 1971,' he later said. 'When Miss Tulip was born. We had seven rooms in a nice area [but] three were not furnished and Miss Vicki was already disturbed. She was very unhappy and I could sense the end was near.'

'I made curtains for his bedroom … And he took the master bedroom. Tulip got the little one,' Vicki later recalled. 'I got the living room and slept on the floor … until we got a sofa … Tulip slept next to me most nights.' The house, she added, 'wasn't furnished at all. It had a table and chairs and a bed and a crib.'

Compounding Tiny and Vicki's already fragile relationship was the fact that the Cappys seemed intent on driving a wedge between them. 'They hated me,' Vicki recalls. 'At the time I was so upset and saddened and scared, but, now looking back, of course they hated me. Their job was to protect him … from people taking advantage of him because he was easily, very easily, taken advantage of. Tiny hired [Joe] to be his lookout person and his bodyguard and everything else and I just come along, you know? They didn't know me. Our relationship was quite antagonistic … it was a difficult relationship, because we all traveled together all the time, everywhere. It would be me, Jimmy, Joe, and Tiny, and they just hated me … I just wanted to have babies and cook and stay home and make a house and be happy. It was really stupid of me, but that's what I wanted, and it didn't happen.'

* * *

As the Cappys' intentions crystallized, Vicki was not the only one who felt the sting of alienation. In late 1970, shortly before he moved back to New York, Tiny called his occasional music director to do some arranging. When John Rodby arrived at the Sunset Marquis Hotel for a meeting, he knocked on Tiny's door. From inside the room, Rodby heard Joe Cappy's unmistakable Brooklyn accent demand, 'Who's there?'

'This is John Rodby,' he replied. 'I have an appointment with Tiny Tim. I am supposed to do some orchestrating for him.'

After a minute and a half, Cappelluzzo barked, 'GET LOST!'

Tiny's cousin Sam Rabin says he still fears 'even mentioning [Joe Cappy's] name.' Cappy was 'very cordial' to the Rabins, but then one day the mask slipped. 'He left our house and … I hear somebody screaming in a heavy Brooklyn accent at somebody across the street. I looked out the window and it was Cappy. He must have parked in the neighbor's driveway, and the neighbor opened their window and said something to him, and he just went berserk. … he was a different person until I heard him lose his temper, and then all of the sudden I saw another side of him.'

Robert Fenster, a Brooklyn real estate agent and friend of Tiny and the Rabins, has a similar story to tell. Fenster, a fellow record collector who had an office just around the corner from Tiny's New York apartment, would often visit him to 'sit and bullshit.' He helped Tiny track down a copy of the notorious *Concert In Fairyland* album* and made Tiny weekly tapes of the top ten radio songs to help him stay up to date with current musical trends. Then one day his phone rang. It was Joe Cappy.

'You don't make the tapes for Tiny anymore,' Cappy said.

'Why?' Fenster asked.

'Because we're in charge, and we tell you not to do it anymore,' Cappy barked, before abruptly hanging up the receiver.

Fenster never received an explanation for the brusque treatment. 'If I was charging him, I could see why they'd say don't do it,' he says. 'But, it was a friendly thing. It was nobody's business. At one time, Cappelluzzo had told him he was not to speak to anyone—not just me personally, but to have nobody come over the house, don't call anybody, don't speak to anybody. They had control over him … he had no friends he could talk to.'

Moreover, Tiny's career continued to stagnate under the Cappys' direction. Lacking any real contacts, they had no option but to stay the course with Tiny's lackluster booking agent at CMA. When they explored moving him to a new agency, Tiny's reputation had declined to the extent that no other agencies of note were willing to sign him.

Tiny faced the same problem with recording labels after Warner Bros/ Reprise decided not to renew his contract. Isolated, broke, and with no real prospects on the horizon, he had little choice but to sit back and watch the

---

* Fenster had had a difficult time locating the record, but found a copy at a record store owned by a friend on Bleeker Sreet. The friend wanted $25 for the album, but Fenster was able to snag it for $15. 'I never told him Tiny was in the car,' he recalled. 'If I did, he would've charged $100!'

collapse of his brief empire. 'In those years it was tough to visit my mother, who still lived at 601 163rd Street in the 70s,' he later said. 'Going back to the old neighborhood, there were no autographs asked for. The coolness of the public was already there. I could walk down the street and walk into stores. Here and there people would ask for autographs, but you knew it was over.' Reminiscing about baseball stars of years past who 'died to win,' he told himself, 'You gotta keep moving. You can't lay there and feel sorry for yourself. Millions have never made it. This is the cross you have to bear. You got the roses, you get the thorns.'

Though Tiny was prepared to accept the thorns, he was most distraught by what his situation meant for his parents. 'You know when I really knew that I'd blown it?' he recalled in 1981. 'One day I went to visit my mother, and I looked around that same tenement house that I'd started out from every morning on my way to the messenger service, and I knew that I'd never be able to get her out of there. That hurt.'

* * *

In lieu of well-paid live shows, Tiny continued supplementing his income with celebrity appearances and guest spots. On August 18, he appeared, flanked by several *Playboy* Bunnies, at a tree-planting ceremony in Baltimore hosted by the city's mayor. The event ended with a three-car collision of passing rubberneckers. Then, in early September, he co-hosted the 1971 Miss Teenage America Pageant with actress Gloria DeHaven. In addition to posing questions about everything from drug abuse to women's liberation to the forty-two contestants, Tiny performed Billy Murray's 1915 number 'Long Live The Ladies,' The Peerless Quartet's 1913 cut 'Everybody Loves A Chicken,' and, of course, 'Tip-Toe.'*

Tiny discussed the pageant with Johnny Carson during his latest appearance on *The Tonight Show*. 'It was a thrill for me,' he reported, prompting Carson to ask, 'Did your bride, Miss Vicki, mind you doing this?'

'She trusts me completely,' Tiny replied. 'And she was down to see Tom Jones.' After the audience's laughter had subsided, Carson asked some more about Vicki's appreciation for Jones, with Tiny revealing how she 'collects

---

* Miss Tennessee's response was most likely to Tiny's liking. 'I can't stand anything that will take away a woman's humility,' she replied. 'Of course they are qualified for these jobs and I believe they should get them if they are as qualified as the men, but I don't like the way they are doing it.'

his pictures and puts [them] up on the kitchen cabinet.' He then took the opportunity to talk about his new business venture, Vic-Tim Records. 'I tried to name it Tiny Tim Records,' Tiny explained, 'but, of course, ASCAP and BMI told me that name was taken, so we finally came down to Vic-Tim, like Vic and Tim.'

'How many recording artists do you have on your label?' Carson asked.

'Well, I'm the *only* one,' Tiny explained, sending the audience into hysterics, 'but it's a real thrill because now I can help other artists if I click.'

The inspiration for the record label had come from a column in *Billboard* magazine called 'Brite Star's Pick Hits.' What at first Tiny believed was an official record chart was actually an advert masquerading as a chart. The ads were commissioned by Brite Star Promotions in Nashville, Tennessee, which listed its small releases alongside current hits. Undiscerning readers would be given the impression that these unknown records were competing with major releases. These small releases were part of a 'song poem' scheme by Brite Star. Hopeful songwriters were encouraged to send in lyrics and pay Brite Star to produce a record featuring their lyrics. Tiny himself was hoodwinked into paying $3,000 to handle the pressing and distribution aspects of his records on the Vic-Tim label, which he would record and produce at his own expense. Nevertheless, he was impressed with Brite Star's design work on the album: light blue with tulips around the outer edge, a candid black-and-white photo of Tiny and Vicki at the bottom and the words 'Jesus Saves' at the top.

Tiny and Brite Star hit the ground running, grinding out four Vic-Tim singles in 1971. Because there was no real production budget, Tiny arranged to record direct to acetate at Sander's Recording Studio, the same place he had cut the records for his 'classics' like Miss Snooky and Tuesday Weld.* The Vic-Tim releases usually had a similar theme on both sides. The first, Vic-Tim #777, had a theme of death. It featured as its A-side 'Why Did They Have To Die So Young (Hendrix, Joplin, And Morrison),' a song Tiny penned in honor of the three named performers, and as its B-side the 1897 Hattie Nevada country-folk song 'Letter Edged In Black.' Vic-Tim #778, the follow-up single, had a prison theme, and featured '(Whispering Voices) The Ballad Of Attica Prison,' which Tiny had written and recorded in the early 60s, and

---

* According to Bob Blank, in-house engineer at Sander's Recording Studio at the time, Tiny was still making one-off records for women he met on the street in the early 70s. Blank recalled that Tiny would sometimes run into the studio 'almost breathless' and insist on recording a song right away for a woman he had just met.

a cover of the 1925 Vernon Dalhart hit 'The Prisoner's Song.' Both records featured Tiny on guitar, singing in his country & western style, and in both cases he was clearly attempting to strike a nerve by releasing songs pertaining to current events.

Brite Star put the records at the very top of its fake 'Pick Hits' chart in *Billboard*. 'I think [they] put it number one,' Tiny later said. 'I mean, who knew where to buy it? ... Of course, you couldn't fool nobody, but it got the mention.'

Tiny also had plans to use his label to help out some of the up-and-coming talent he had discovered while touring. Appearing on *The David Frost Show* in September 1971, Tiny boasted of discovering 'Mr. John McCormack, the toothless opera singer,' and Donna Joint, a performer who 'cracks her nose and she also squishes her eyeballs.' Ultimately, Tiny signed only one artist to his label, a country & western singer named Toni Lee. The result was the only Vic-Tim record that does not feature Tiny, Vic-Tim #779, featuring Lee's renditions of 'What I Can't Get At Home' and 'Break It To Me Gently.'

* * *

Recording and developing his own label also put Tiny in touch with a young producer and concert promoter named Roy Radin. Radin was booking acts for the second run of his touring show, *Roy Radin's Vaudeville Revue*. In June 1971, Radin entered Sander's recording studio while Tiny was working on material for Vic-Tim. He had followed Tiny's career and believed Tiny would be a perfect act to include in his show. When the two men spoke, Radin addressed Tiny as 'Herbie.'

'Please call me Tiny Tim, Mr. Radin,' Tiny replied.

'Herbie,' Radin said, 'you could do a lot for me. In turn, I could do a lot for you.'

Roy Radin had show business in his blood. He was the son of Alexander 'Broadway Al' Radin, who had been a successful nightclub owner from the 30s to the 50s. His mother, Renee Radin, had been a showgirl. 'It was a very easy natural step for him, especially with his personality,' says Kate Radin, Roy's younger sister. 'He could sell ice to the Eskimos when he was a kid. He sold the most raffle tickets in his catholic school and stuff like that, so it was kind of a natural thing for him to become a promoter and producer.'

Radin aspired to be as successful and connected as his father, if not more so. In his teens, he booked acts in Long Island nightclubs, and at the age of sixteen, having dropped out of ten different schools, he decided to run away from home. He told his sisters that he planned to join the circus, make as much money as possible, and then come back for them.

During this period, Radin worked as a bellhop, a busboy, and a waiter, sold counterfeit gold coins, sang in Greenwich Village coffeehouses, went to Canada, and finally returned to America to work as a publicist for the Clyde Beatty Circus. 'I saw how they were packing them in,' he later told the told the *New York Times*, 'turning over 6,000 people a day with two dead mules, and I said to myself, that was the way to go.' Shortly thereafter, Radin happened upon the novel idea of putting together a vaudeville revival troupe made up of musical and comedic acts and to embark on a tour of the East Coast, performing in Masonic Temples, high-school auditoriums, and other small venues. It was to be, as Radin put it, 'Real family entertainment.'

'Roy was a genius at giving the audience what they wanted,' says Kate Radin. 'He took [celebrities] into these little towns that would never get a chance to see [multiple] stars ... with a live orchestra, for an affordable price. It was a great show, and it worked well for the 70s, and it was a win-win situation.'

Weighing in at 300 pounds, the baby-faced Radin grew a beard and began to wear expensive three-piece suits to hide his age, as he was barely over twenty. His larger-than-life persona and flashy lifestyle put him at an advantage when negotiating bookings, though he was younger and less experienced than the vast majority of producers and concert promoters in the business.

The 1970 line-up of *Roy Radin's Vaudeville Revue* included Toastmaster General George Jessel (an old friend of Radin's father), J. Fred Muggs The Chimp, and juggler Kenny Sherburne. The shows doubled as benefits for local law-enforcement and fire-department unions like the International Brotherhood of Police Officers. Radin would donate half the proceeds from his ticket sales, which cost $2.50, to whichever police or firefighting union was sponsoring that night's show. He apparently made the majority of his profits from ads purchased by local businesses in the show's program.

As his business grew, Radin was often able to recoup his expenses for the entire tour in a mere three days. He ran tours through the spring and fall, each ranging between thirty-six and forty-two days, with most of them turning into pure profit. 'We heard one night in Cleveland he cleared over one hundred grand, and back then that was a lot of money for a show, especially when you have a $2.50 ticket,' says Tim Fowler, Radin's musical director on several tours. 'Yet he'd fight us for a $25 a week raise for the musicians.'

Looking to raise the profile of his *Vaudeville Revue*, Radin began to seek more recognizable talent. He introduced himself to Tiny, who thought he was like a younger version of Flo Ziegfeld, the Broadway impresario of the 1900s. Tiny agreed to headline the 1971 *Revue*. Not only was he a good match for this sort of program, it provided him with some much needed steady income.

'Tiny Tim was the object of wildly enthusiastic applause, no matter what he did,' the *Schenectady Gazette* reported. 'The audience could hardly bear to allow him to leave the stage.'

Like Tiny, many of Radin's acts had seen better times. Over the years, the line-up would include names like The Drifters, Danny & The Juniors, Dean Martin's Golddiggers, Ronnie Spector & The Ronettes, Eddie Fisher, George Gobel, and The Ink Spots, but Radin rejected the notion that they were has-beens. 'We do nothing but packed houses everywhere we go,' he told reporters. 'We send out people who other people, middle-Americans, middle-aged … will respond to.'

Many of the acts who joined Radin's tours have described him as unpleasant and notorious for cutting corners to save money. It was also blatantly obvious to them that he had a drinking problem and was addicted to cocaine. 'This was the bottom rung of show business,' Eddie Fisher later wrote in his autobiography, *Been There, Done That*. 'The nicest thing I can say about Roy Radin is that he was the sleaziest person I'd ever known. He was guzzling cocaine. Along with producing the show he was making coke deals.'

As the tours became successful and Radin grew richer, he became more and more difficult to work with as his intake of cocaine increased steadily. According to long-time bandleader and conductor Tim Fowler, even George Gobel, who 'loved everybody,' referred to Radin as 'super prick.' When Gobel appeared on *The Tonight Show* after one of Radin's tours, he told Johnny Carson, 'Roy Radin knows as much about show business as a pig knows about church on Sunday.' Another of Radin's acts, George Jessel, once remarked, 'Before he died, Adolf Hitler set up this tour.'

'[Roy] was a very crude guy,' says Joe Terry of Danny & The Juniors. 'He liked me, but I didn't really like him. He would do things to save money like have the bus driver run the sound system and buy microphones from Radio Shack. From what I understand he was generally not nice to women … he was just really not a nice guy.'

Radin's sister Kate, on the other hand, insists that the tours were not always so tumultuous, and that the atmosphere in those early years was pleasant. 'There was no drug abuse allowed whatsoever, anywhere. It was never tolerated.'

In addition to including Tiny on his tours, Radin decided to help produce the fourth Vic-Tim release, #1001, 'White Christmas' b/w 'Rudolph The Red-Nosed Reindeer.' Unlike Tiny's first two singles on his label, this one had much higher production values, thanks to Radin. Artie Butler, who had arranged *God Bless Tiny Tim*, was brought back on board to create the musical arrangements, and it was decided that the single would include a children's choir. An eleven-year-old Kate Radin was one of the children selected.

On the morning of the recording, Roy called his sisters, who were living with him in Hampton Bays, Long Island. 'Get ready, get ready, you're late for school!' he said. 'I'm picking you up right now!' The girls quickly put on their uniforms and waited outside until, unexpectedly, the whirring of helicopter blades was heard above, and Roy landed on the lawn. From Hampton Bays, Roy flew the girls to LaGuardia airport, where a limousine was waiting to take them to the studio. Roy instructed his driver to drive through a ghetto in Lower Manhattan, where he found several boys playing outside. He offered the boys' mothers $50 each if they would allow them to perform on the record, and once they accepted, the boys piled into the limousine.

'We went to the studio in New York and Uncle Herbie came out, and we had our little headphones on,' Kate Radin recalls. 'It was just a wonderful, wonderful day. I'll never forget the last note that Tiny hit on "White Christmas," and how us girls had to take the headphones off because he hit such a high note because it was so ear-piercing.'

The record was pressed, and ads ran in the trade magazines, calling the single a 'GREAT STOCK-ing ITEM!' To promote the record, Tiny was booked to make an appearance on *The Tonight Show* on December 9 1971. After singing 'White Christmas,' he joined Carson on the couch for an interview. It was his fourth appearance of the year, and his twenty-first in total. But as Laurence Leamer notes it his book *King Of The Night: The Life Of Johnny Carson*, 'The magic was gone.'

Out of respect of what they had done for each other's careers, Carson made no mention of Tiny's fading appeal. Instead, they chatted about Tiny's impending two-year anniversary, and how he and Vicki had had only 'about four' arguments since they had been married, mostly about Tiny's tendency to 'keep the floors dirty.' They also discussed Tiny's return to a diet of 'peanuts, molasses, wheat germ … honey, and water,' which he found 'thrilling.' Tiny blushed when Carson asked him, teasingly, whether he had been 'turned on by any of the Bunnies' during a recent performance at the Playboy Club.

It was later revealed that *Tonight Show* talent booker Craig Tennis, who had been responsible for launching Tiny's tenure on the program, had prepared a question that Carson either did not have time to ask or simply opted to skip.

A SERIOUS QUESTION FOR A MINUTE. WHAT IS THE STATUS OF YOUR CAREER? SOME PEOPLE HAVE SUGGESTED THAT IT'S ALL OVER.

Tennis did, however, pose the question to Tiny prior to the taping. 'Mr. Tennis,' Tiny replied, 'frankly, it's going down.'

A year and a half earlier, on May 18 1970, Carson had, at Tennis's suggestion, declared, 'It seems as if Tiny Tim's career will outlast the opinions of his detractors. Tiny first appeared on *The Tonight Show* a little over two years ago, and rather than being merely a flash in the pan, he is still working regularly.' After this latest appearance, however, he would not be invited back to the show for some time, while his Vic-Tim Christmas single quickly faded from view.

'It is a very sad thing,' Tennis later told biographer Harry Stein, 'but it was as if the whole phenomenon dissipated. It was just suddenly gone. And as Tiny faded, no one pushed us to have him on. There was no pressure at all from his people. That would have extended it a little while.'

It was not just *The Tonight Show* that was losing interest. In 1971, Tiny made only one appearance on his other mainstay, *Laugh-In*, appearing alongside the original cast as '*Laugh-In*'s first and favorite guest' for the show's one-hundredth episode special on November 1. The prevailing message was that he was back, but the reality was that he had never gone—rather, he had been passed over. Either way, Tiny played along and delivered the jokes the show's writers had written for him. 'I'd like to thank Mr. Rowan and Mr. Martin,' he said, 'for making a well-known personality out of a plain, ordinary guy like me.'

At the close of 1971, *Playboy* magazine featured a verse about Tiny Tim in a poem about the year gone by.

Tulip-tripping Tiny Tim,
Is the happiest of pappies,
But now he wears galoshes,
As he tiptoes through the nappies.

CHAPTER THIRTEEN
'THIS THING KILLS ME TO THE BONE'

Miss Vicki turned out to be much more spunky and opinionated than Tiny had bargained for. He, in turn, was much more stubborn, inflexible, insensitive, and lost in this world of his own ideas. He had all these romantic notions about everything that [were] shattered by the reality of living with someone.
SUSAN KHAURY, AKA MISS SUE

One morning in early 1972, Miss Vicki took baby Tulip for a walk in their Brooklyn neighborhood. Though almost two years had passed since the televised wedding, she still found herself struggling with the public's unforgiving scrutiny. A woman peered into the baby's carriage and said, 'Oh, thank God, she doesn't look like her father!'

'I hope your kids don't look like you!' Vicki snapped back.

'I was just appalled that someone had the gall to say that,' Vicki recalls today. 'What would make her think that was a good thing to say to me? I had just had a baby. I loved her father. I didn't think it was nice for her to say something like that!'*

At home, Tiny was testing Vicki's patience as well. As their marriage progressed, it was becoming clear that the lifestyle Vicki desired for herself and her daughter would not be a reality. 'I envisioned in my head a home with hardwood floors and matching dishes and sheets and feather beds and children and cooking dinner every night. That never came to be. Our life was on the road in hotels—that's what he wanted and that's what he liked. All he cared about was having fun and going and doing his shows. There was nothing wrong with that—that was his life and I chose to marry him. I'm not saying he was wrong, I'm saying I was stupid for thinking it would be different.'

---

* Tiny later told *Motion Picture* magazine that he was 'relieved' that Tulip looked more like Vicki. 'Being ugly is difficult,' he said.

Despite her frustration, Vicki worked valiantly to save the marriage and protect her naive husband. She knew that Tiny's handlers were syphoning a generous portion of his earnings and, conversely, that Tiny had squandered a solid share of them himself on food binges, excessive tipping, cosmetics, and gambling via his OTB telephone account. By 1972, he was in debt to the tune of $20,000. His last major television appearance had been on *Laugh-In* on January 3, and aside from a smattering of shows in New York and New Jersey, no one else was knocking.

'Tiny was home, and he wasn't on the road,' Vicki recalls. 'He wasn't getting any work, and he wasn't getting any phone calls, and we had rent to pay and other things. I decided I better go do something, I didn't want to be homeless.'

With her tall, thin physique, people had always told Vicki that she should model. Aware of this, Tiny suggested that she contact Ford Modeling Agency. Vicki did so and then visited the agency, where she had some test shots taken. A few days later, an excited Eileen Ford called her back to the agency. 'You need to see the shots!' Ford exclaimed. 'You look like an angel!'

Ford helped Vicki land a few jobs around New York City over the next few months, until Tiny—who had once told David Frost that 'a woman is more romantic when there's a mystique on her'—put a stop to it. A photo in which Vicki had posed with her arms folded across her chest, creating the illusion that she was covering he breasts, had set him off. He called Ford and demanded that she cease encouraging Vicki's modeling ambitions. 'I don't know if we can keep you if he's going to call us up and give us a hard time,' Ford told Vicki.

Eventually, Ford dropped Vicki, and things took a turn for the worst. At the start of their marriage, many of the couple's arguments had been petty. Tiny, for instance, was 'disturbed' by the fact that Vicki would forget to put the cap back on his toothpaste, while Vicki would often chastise her husband for being 'a pig in the house.' Two years on, however, their arguments had reached a fever pitch. Tiny's religious convictions and outdated views on marriage left his wife feeling alienated and insulted.

'A woman's place is behind the stove,' he told her.

'There isn't much room behind the stove,' she replied. 'There's only about an inch and a half.'

The couple's intermittent and peculiar sex life came to a complete halt when Joe Cappy went snooping through Tiny and Vicki's apartment while they were away. When Cappy discovered birth-control pills hidden in Vicki's bathroom behind a light fixture above the medicine cabinet, he thrust them into Tiny's face, sending him into a fury. Feeling betrayed, he demanded Vicki stop using all contraceptives, but she stood her ground and retorted that she did not want Cappy in their home anymore. The result was a bitter stalemate.

'I didn't want any more babies because I knew a drunken monkey with a loaded pistol was a better parent than he'd ever be,' Vicki explains. 'Tiny was angry and I was humiliated.'

'That's fine,' Tiny told Vicki. 'If you don't want any more children, we're not going to do it anymore.'

Tiny also forbade Vicki from having visitors while he was away, including her sister Tracy, which meant she would spend weeks alone with Tulip while Tiny toured. But then, when Tiny returned home, she did not find his presence all that uplifting, either. 'Tiny was settled,' Vicki later told *Journal* magazine. 'He had a wife and a kid. Fine. To him it was like having a piano. He probably thought, Well she's unhappy, she'll get over it. The most important thing to him was his career. I came second, if that.'

Today, Vicki shares many of the same opinions about Tiny's lack of interest in domestic life and his out-of-touch attitudes to gender roles in the home as she did when she was twenty-three, but her perspective has softened with time. 'Even if he were alive today, he would never know how to be a parent, father, husband, or a friend, or anything, and it's not his fault, he just … didn't know. He was really good at performing, and that's when he was most comfortable, but when he was alone with people like friends, relatives, even my family, he was so uncomfortable. He couldn't relate to other people very well. I wanted to have a little house and have children and cook dinners; he just wanted to travel. … I don't think he was [capable of loving anyone]. It's sad, but no. That's not his fault, the poor thing. His mother was really hard on him and his father was a little nansy-pansy, so I don't think he learned the capacity to love or to be loved in return.'

Vicki kept a calendar on the refrigerator to track Tiny's departure and return dates, and before long it got to the point where she would dread his return. 'Just before Christmas [1971], I decided: next month I'll have to tell him that I'm leaving,' she told *Journal*. 'But January went by and I said, Well, next month, next week, tomorrow, later on—until one day I realized I would be seventy-nine years old and still be saying, Tomorrow.'

Finally, on February 22 1972, Vicki wrote Tiny a letter announcing her departure. She collected a few of her possessions, bundled Tulip up, and set out for her parent's house in Haddonfield, New Jersey. She had been waiting for Tiny's next round of tour dates, so she would be able to slip away unceremoniously. 'I was a real coward,' she says, 'and I waited until he went away and I just left.'

Tiny wrote several irate telegrams to Vicki's parents, asking how that could have raised such a 'horrible girl.' 'My mother was so heartbroken, because they loved him,' Vicki recalls. 'They thought he was so wonderful, and those telegrams were so terrible. They were nasty and mean. Looking back, he was mad. He was mad at me. He was mad at them. He was mad at everybody.'

The media, which had been skeptical of the union in the first place, quickly caught wind of the separation. True to form, Tiny had no problem gushing to the press. 'This thing kills me to the bone,' he told the *New York Times*. When reporters suggested Vicki had married Tiny for his fame, he disagreed. 'I can only believe her words,' he replied, 'that she married me because she loved me.'

Initially, the press reported that Vicki's modeling aspirations had caused the split; soon enough, however, word leaked about another man. *Motion Picture* reported that she had 'become enamored with a handsome male model,' adding that 'some rather spicy photographs of her had been taken, which Tiny's trying to locate.' Predictably, the gossip columns made liberal use of 'Tip-Toe' puns, with *Screen Stories* noting, 'One can tiptoe through the tulips for so long without things getting a bit too thorny.'

Then as now, Vicki is aggravated by the suggestion that she pursued modeling in order to springboard a career from Tiny's fame. 'I was just trying to make a living so that we could pay the damn rent!' she says. 'Sadly, it was taken a different way.'

Tiny maintained that he did not want a divorce for 'religious reasons,' but Vicki did not believe him. 'I think it was more of a public-appearance thing,' she says. 'He didn't want it to look bad. The religious thing was part of it, but he could bend that however he wanted. He was afraid people would say he failed at his marriage … his career was everything to him, so I think he was concerned that if I left him that it was going to hurt his career and his image.'

Tiny spoke out against the possible divorce when he arrived in Kansas City, Missouri, for a weeklong engagement at the *Playboy* Club. 'I don't care if it is ten years, twenty years, or never when she returns, this ring stays on my finger until death do us part,' he told the press. He admitted that he had not yet been served divorce papers, but had already filed a preemptive countersuit against Vicki.

At first, correspondence between the two of them was hostile. Vicki told Tiny, 'I don't love you anymore. I changed my mind. I don't believe in what you do. I want to live, I want to live in this world and not the world to come.' Over time, however, both parties began to soften, and Vicki found herself able to appreciate some of Tiny's qualities again. 'He could be fun. He could make me laugh,' she recalls. 'He was very much a gentleman, I must say. He was never rude or unkind. There were too many other things that got in the way. I don't think that so much had to do with him, I think it had to do more with the outside world.'

On May 26 1972, Vicki and Tulip returned to the apartment in Brooklyn. Articles about their separation continued to be printed well into June, and news of their reconciliation did not break until August. It was Vicki's mother who informed the *New York Times* that the couple had 'dropped separation and court proceedings against each other.' The fact that news of reconciliation came from Vicki's camp probably had to do with her conditions for her peaceful return. She asked that Tiny be less candid with the press, and also requested that he be more conscious of his spending, quit gambling, and curb his messiness.

Tiny, too, had demands. 'The door is always open for her to come back,' he told *Modern Screen*, 'if she returns on my terms.' Tiny's stipulations included no further modeling work, a VD test, and a standing order to obey Tiny's will unconditionally. Vicki agreed, with no real intention of obeying Tiny's every demand. 'I accepted [the conditions] without meaning it,' she told Harry Stein. 'I mean, for heaven's sake, I wasn't a fool.'

Another of Vicki's requests had been increased privacy. However, she agreed to appear with Tiny—and Tulip—on *The Mike Douglas Show* on August 23, to discuss the status of their relationship. After discussing the details of his recent diet, through which he lost forty pounds, Tiny confirmed the 'terms' of the couple's reconciliation: 'She must stay at home and travel with me wherever I go, and, also, I just must watch over her and whatever I say goes.'

'Is that true, Miss Vicki?' Douglas asked, turning to Vicki.

'Well, so far, he hasn't made any terrible demands,' Vicki replied with a smirk.

'I'd like to ask you, when you two were separated, did you date other men?' Douglas asked.

'Not really,' Vicki replied, after a long pause.

* * *

Meanwhile, Tiny's career was expiring at the same rate as his marriage. With the exception of a 'Back-To-Back Hits' re-issue of 'Tip-Toe Thru' The Tulips With Me' b/w 'Great Balls Of Fire' by Reprise Records, his record releases were becoming more and more obscure. In 1972, he put out his last two releases on Vic-Tim records. Both featured 'Grandpa Tim' performing in the style of Byron G. Harlan, with piano accompaniment. Vic-Tim #1006 featured a cover of Rod Stewart's 'Maggie May' b/w 'When You and I Were Young, Maggie'; and Vic-Tim #1007 contained a version of the Tom Jones hit 'Delilah' b/w a rendition of the Jonathan Edwards hit 'Sunshine.' According to Tiny's friend and producer Martin Sharp, the latter pair of songs was not selected arbitrarily: 'Delilah' was in honor of Miss Vicki, and 'Sunshine' was for his management.*

While the 'Grandpa Tim' recordings disappeared almost immediately, 1972 did yield a release on the more reputable Scepter Records. The single was the brainchild of Norman Bergen, a Brooklyn-based pianist with an impressive resume who had recently branched out into producing. He first met Tiny at the suggestion of the singer's cousin, Eddie Rabin, and recalls that when he went over to Tiny's apartment in the Premiere House, they had to conduct their meeting on the floor, as Tiny owned so little furniture.

'What do you think, Mr. Bergen?' Tiny asked, after playing him a couple songs. 'I don't know what would work right now. I need another hit. I don't know if I should be singing in the high voice or the low voice.'

Eventually, Bergen pitched a record to Victrix Productions, who in turn presented it to Scepter Records. When Scepter agreed to distribute the record, Victrix gave the single a green light and commissioned Irwin Levine and L. Russell Brown—who shortly thereafter penned the smash hit 'Tie A Yellow Ribbon 'Round The Old Oak Tree' for Tony Orlando & Dawn—to write a song that would suit Tiny's falsetto.

Levine and Brown came back with a song entitled 'Am I Just Another Pretty Face?' The lyrics were catchy and the irony was inescapable. 'Movies,' written by Allan Merrill, was selected as the B-side. The recording session was held at Scepter Studios, located next to Studio 54 in Manhattan, with Don Casale, known for his work with Iron Butterfly and Vanilla Fudge, engineering,

---

* Tiny also recorded a version of 'My Way' in the same style, but the master was lost after Tiny mailed it to a disreputable promoter in Nashville, Tennessee, and never heard from him again.

and Charles Macey, who had played guitar on 'The Lion Sleeps Tonight' by The Tokens, on ukulele.

Just before the tapes began to roll, Tiny quietly approached Bergen. 'Can you come into the booth with me so I know when to come in on the song?' he asked. Bergen obliged and duly conducted Tiny during the takes.

The record was cut and promo copies were distributed to radio stations. Bergen anxiously awaited news about his latest release, but none came. 'I don't remember hearing anything about this record,' he recalls. 'It was like nothing happened. If we had any airplay, anyplace, I would've heard about it. I just never heard a word.' To add to the single's woes, Tiny, in yet another act of self-sabotage, sent a telegram to Victrix to say that he was 'appalled' by the recording, vowing that he would 'never plug that record.'

As 1973 began, Tiny continued producing and releasing his own records, convinced that he was the only person capable of doing so correctly. He dissolved VicTim Records, and created his second record label, Toilet Records, 'because that's where my career went.' Attorney Jack Rabin helped Tiny coin the label's slogan, 'Sit and Listen.' Its first release was a translated version of the Spanish song, 'No Tengo Dinero,' or 'I Ain't Got No Money.' In lieu of cash to pay professional musicians, Tiny located an instrumental track of the song and recorded his soulful rendition over it. The B-side featured Tiny and his ukulele performing a falsetto rendering of the old standard 'Alice Blue Gown.'

Tiny arranged to record the tracks at Sander's and paid for the small studio to handle the pressing of one thousand copies of the single. Though he was the record's producer, he refrained from crediting himself as such due to an outstanding contract with another company (presumably Brite Star). Instead, he used the alias 'Ophelia Pratt'—'prat' being an old English slang term for a woman's genitals.

'He really was afraid he would get in trouble with the record label,' recalls Bob Blank, who engineered the session. 'Of course, the irony was that he insisted that my name go on the label and I thought, Well, he doesn't want to put his name on there [so] why should I put my name on there? Who was I to have an ego at that time? I was just a young, struggling recording engineer, so I thought it might be good publicity. Now, I'm so glad my name is on there.'

Nonetheless, without a single outlet for distribution, the record was little more than a vanity project. Seemingly unconcerned with recouping expenses, however, Tiny forged ahead with plans for a second Toilet Records release, this time, to showcase a new talent, Mr. Isadore Fertel, a thirty-seven-year-old short, bald, Jewish man with thick Coke-bottle glasses whom Blank describes as looking like 'the ultimate accountant.' His personality, however, was far from conventional.

Fertel was born in 1936, to a wealthy family in New Orleans. His parents, by subjecting their son to various rudimentary and unrefined operations on his eyes to remove cataracts, had seriously damaged his vision. As a result, he was forced to wear comically thick lenses, which made his eyeballs appear gigantic. This and his effeminate voice made him a target for ridicule in school. Like Tiny, he had spent hours in his room, listening to pop music on the radio and fantasizing about becoming a famous singer. He had a penchant for cross-dressing (as 'Isabel'), generally disliked men, and kept primarily to the company of women. Though he was often rebuffed, he managed to marry a woman in 1959, and their stormy relationship resulted in marriage, divorce, separation, re-marriage, re-divorce, and one child, a girl. The child was reportedly conceived only with the supervision of Fertel's sister-in-law, who made sure they finished the deed.

By 1973, Fertel was living in a dingy one-room apartment on the Upper West Side and had made a reputation for himself as an active member of the National Organization For Women. He canvassed, distributed flyers, and organized rallies. He also had the distinct honor of serving as the only male member of the New York Radical Feminists. 'I hate men,' he told Harry Stein. 'I only want to be around women. I wish I [was] one.' His dedication to the women's liberation movement inspired him to compose, among other songs, 'Susan B.,' in honor of the feminist reformer Susan B. Anthony.

Much to the dismay of his on/off wife and extended family, Fertel began performing his songs onstage. His big moment came in 1971, when he was invited backstage to sing for Tiny between shows at a beach resort in New Jersey. Tiny was so moved by 'Susan B.' that he put Fertel on the bill with him. For most of the early 70s, Fertel served as Tiny's opening act in New York and New Jersey.

'He had a very strange sounding voice,' Tiny later told Ernie Clark. 'Talking of mine, he had one too!' Indeed, Fertel's singing voice was reminiscent of a lispy Ethel Merman. Regardless, Tiny was a genuine believer in his talent. 'I tell you, I'm impressed with his songwriting,' he later told a radio interviewer.

'Mr. Fertel is a great star of the future. If there's the right type of project for him, he could really be a smash.'

Though there were many parallels between the two men, Tiny's politics were very different to Fertel's. In fact, he found them genuinely perplexing. 'He's the only man I know who is for women's lib,' Tiny later told Richard Barone. 'He doesn't want to be a man, he wants to be a woman, and he just loves women's lib.'

Although the two men would stop speaking for a year when Fertel encouraged Vicki to leave Tiny because of his outdated views on women, they would end up becoming close friends. 'I think it comforted Tiny to be friends with someone who was weirder than him,' Tiny's friend and real estate agent Robert Fenster speculates, while Harry Stein summed up Tiny Tim and Isadore Fertel's relationship very succinctly when he declared, 'Isadore Fertel is Tiny Tim's Tiny Tim.'

Vicki did not enjoy Fertel's visits to the apartment. 'Tiny had that guy in our apartment every friggin' night of the week,' she recalls. 'I know he was a nice fellow, but I just couldn't take it. I had a baby in the other room and they were singing … she would wake up crying because they were noisy and they were loud.'

After one all-night session, Vicki pleaded with Tiny to send Fertel home.

'No,' Tiny snapped. 'We're making music here.'

'Oh, is *that* what that is?'

Tiny and Fertel's collaboration was immortalized on Toilet Records #102. No longer concerned about contractual disputes, Tiny credited himself as the producer of Fertel's single and shelled out the money to make the recording possible. Both tracks—'Susan B.' and a cover of the Helen Reddy hit 'I Am Woman'—feature Fertel accompanied by piano.*

Fertel seemed 'very nervous' to engineer Bob Blank. 'I don't think he had ever been in the studio before. The best I can remember was that they were very unwilling to spend a lot of money on this so it was kind of like, Get it right! and it put everybody under pressure.'

As with Tiny's own Toilet Records single, there were very few resources available to promote the release. Much as he had made rounds with his ukulele and acetates in the 50s and 60s, Tiny had Fertel disseminate copies himself in the hope that the record would find someone who cared. Unfortunately, no

---

* Dubs of Fertel's Toilet Records tracks were later found on a cassette tape that belonged to Marvin Lewis. An actual physical copy of the record has never been seen.

such break came. 'In '73 it got into the hands of [the actress] Arlene Francis,' Tiny told Ernie Clark years later, while chuckling. 'When she saw this record, I tell you, she threw it in the wastebasket!'

Isadore Fertel's Toilet single was his first and last time on record, and it also marked the end of Tiny's foray into record production, but the two men would continue to perform together during the years to come.

Later in 1973, Tiny returned to collaboration with other producers and labels that wished to take a chance on him, one of whom was drummer-turned-songwriter/producer Howard Tashman, or Tash Howard, as he was known professionally. Howard had been a fan of Tiny since 1968. Though he wrote over 100 songs, he is best known for his 'Juanita Banana,' a ridiculous yet entertaining duet, sung between a fictional banana grower and his daughter. The song was recorded by a slew of artists, and was a minor hit for Howard's studio band, The Peels, in 1966.

Somewhere along the line, Howard connected with Tiny Tim, and they began to collaborate. Howard had Tiny record 'My Nose Always Gets In The Way,' which he had obviously written with Tiny in mind:

My ears cannot see,
What my eyes tell my mouth,
'Cause my nose always
Gets in the way!

They also recorded a version of the German folk song 'The Happy Wanderer,' an odd but fun ditty called 'Lie Down With The Dogs,' and, of course, the obligatory version of 'Juanita Banana,' cut as a Tiny duet. The orchestration was elaborate: a mariachi band appeared on 'Juanita Banana,' with a children's choir and kazoo orchestra on 'My Nose Always Gets In The Way.'

Generally, Howard's music was more successful in international markets. The Peels' 'Juanita Banana' was a #13 hit in the Netherlands, while his song 'Sunshine' was also recorded (as 'Soleil') by French pop star Francoise Hardy in 1969. This would also prove the case with his collaborations with Tiny. 'Juanita Banana' b/w 'My Nose Always Gets In The Way' and 'The Happy Wanderer' b/w 'Lie Down With The Dogs' were issued by Belaphon in Germany, while in Belgium and Italy, Polydor licensed 'The Happy Wanderer' b/w 'My Nose Always Gets In The Way.' Each release also received a unique picture sleeve, and it is these that provide the clearest window into Tiny and Howard's collaboration.

Francisco Poblet, an artist who had trained under Salvador Dali and worked as an illustrator for Walt Disney and Warner Bros, had an office in the same building in Manhattan as Tash Howard's studio. They developed a friendship, and Howard commissioned Poblet to paint a portrait of Tiny for each of the two singles. For 'The Happy Wanderer,' Tiny is shown sitting beside an improvised 'banana tree'; for 'Juanita Banana,' Poblet produced an image of Tiny wearing Latin-style dress and a headdress made of fruit. The latter was based on a still from a music video the three men shot together, for which Poblet played the part of mariachi bandleader, with bananas in his holsters instead of pistols.

'We filmed in Central Park [by] the fountain,' Poblet recalls. 'Tiny walked down the stairs with the long dress and the headdress with the bananas, which kept falling off. Then we shot on a bridge. It was hilarious!' According to Poblet, the 'Juanita Banana' video became 'very popular in Europe,' particularly in Germany. They also shot a music video for 'The Happy Wanderer' on a set constructed in Howard's studio. 'They had a whole background, mountains and everything behind Tiny Tim,' says Poblet. 'When you saw it on the camera, you thought he was in the Alps!' Neither video has surfaced in the US.

As is evident from the production values Howard put into his collaboration with Tiny Tim, he had more in mind than just a few singles. According to Poblet, Howard 'idolized' Tiny Tim. 'He thought he was a star. He thought he didn't have the recognition he deserved. He wanted to put Tiny's songs and his personality and his real persona to the public.'

Howard had Poblet storyboard an animated music video of Tiny Tim, as the Happy Wanderer, leading all of the bugs out of a city and to the sea. The character was then to be incorporated into a children's safety campaign called HAPPI, or Health & Accident Prevention People, Inc. Tiny and Howard planned to release toothpaste, music, and films, all aimed at children, and put Poblet to work designing brochures and other artwork. But then Howard was diagnosed with cancer, and the collaboration was suspended.

In the end, Howard did not pass away until 1977, and it seems his collaboration with Tiny may have ended in much the same way as many of Tiny's other enterprises. An undated letter found in the estate of Tiny's then-attorney Jack Rabin suggests a power struggle between Tiny and Howard over material they were to record:

My Dear Mr. Howard,

HERE YE—HERE YE

This is to let you know that any future work with you for records will only be the songs I choose, with my own arrangements and my own ideas, put down the exact same way I choose.
　I will have 100 percent control of all my records, songs and works.
　Take me to court if you wish, and join the line of twenties.

HAPPY NEW YEAR

Sincerely,
Herbert Khaury
AKA Tiny Tim

Tiny would also note in his diary Howard had 'almost' sued him, but he failed to elaborate further.

* * *

Perhaps encouraged by his European success, Tiny began to spend more time working outside of the country. In the summer of 1973, he performed at air force and naval bases in Guam, the Philippines, and Tasmania.* Unwilling to leave Vicki unsupervised, Tiny had her accompany him, so they left Tulip with the Budingers in New Jersey.

As the fall of 1973 approached, the couple's relationship continued to sour. They began arguing with increased intensity until, finally, it became physical. When, one night, Vicki decided abruptly that she was too tired to attend a Randy Newman concert with Tiny at Lincoln Center, his temper flared.

'We have to go!' he announced. 'They're expecting us!'

Vicki refused to reconsider, and Tiny detonated. He swung his arm back and struck Vicki forcefully in the head. 'It wasn't pleasant, I must say,' Vicki recalls. 'He was full of contradictions. He was like "Jesus this" and "Jesus that," and meanwhile he could be so mean. I didn't get it. I tried, but I didn't really get it. He could reinterpret anything so he could do what he wanted to

---

* While performing for the troops, Tiny was given a Green Beret cap. Upon returning, he wore it on *The Mike Douglas Show*, to the bemusement of the audience.

do.' Vicki decided to let the incident go but vowed to call her mother if he raised a hand to her again.

In November 1973, Tiny, accompanied by Vicki, Jim Cappy, and a small backup band, embarked on a month-long tour of England. Almost immediately, the tour erupted into a hotbed of problems when Cappy sensed that Vicki was romantically interested in their Italian guide, Amos Levy. Tiny later told Harry Stein that Vicki's crush was confirmed when Levy told him that Vicki had slipped a note expressing her feelings into his laundry. Today, Vicki denies leaving Levy a note; she did admit to Harry Stein that she liked Levy but said she had no intention of acting on her feelings. Nevertheless, Tiny confronted her, and Vicki threatened to kill herself. In response, Tiny, who once described his heart as 'colder than a Frigidaire,' ordered up a set of steak knives and, calling Vicki's bluff, dared her to use them to do the job. Within days, however, the issue was moot.

One night, fatigued by driving, Levy nearly fell asleep at the wheel. Cappy took over but became disoriented by driving on the left side of the road. He made a sharp turn and rolled the bus. Both Vicki and Cappy suffered broken collarbones and immediately returned to the States.

To everyone's surprise, Vicki recovered from her injuries quickly enough to return to England for the final week of the tour. Joe Cappy, who had flown out to relieve Jim, suspected that she had returned for nefarious purposes. Today, Vicki maintains that she had gone back only in an attempt to 'salvage the marriage … if I was going to cheat, would I have gone to the UK and do it under his nose?' she asks rhetorically, adding that she had also wanted to show Joe Cappy that he was wrong and that she was, in fact, a devoted wife.

Tiny was happy to see her. When he called Joe to tell him Vicki had returned, she overheard Cappy tell Tiny, 'She came back to see that driver, not you.' Vicki grabbed the receiver and screamed at Joe, 'I've had enough of it! This is where it ends. You're trying to drive a wedge between us. How dare you accuse me of coming all the way from America to be with my husband when you have a wife and a girlfriend back home!'

Cappy hung up abruptly. The phone rang again a short while later, and Tiny answered. 'See what she's really like?' Joe exclaimed. 'I told you!' Tiny said nothing in his wife's defense. A huge fight ensued, and Vicki gave her husband an ultimatum: 'It's either him or me, baby.'

'You can do what you want,' Tiny replied, 'but I'm not going to let Joe go.'

A tour of Australia followed, and Vicki was not invited. 'Tiny said, I'm going to Australia, and we can't afford to bring you, so you're not coming,' Vicki recalls. 'He needed [his management] more than he needed me, so I didn't get to go.'

Vicki flew back to New York City. Tiny purposely sent her home without keys to their apartment, noting in his diary that he had done so in order that she might 'avoid the occasions of sin.' When Vicki revealed during a phone call that she had an extra set of keys, Tiny was incensed. 'Her goal is to torment me,' he wrote in his diary. 'I pray that she's handled right.' Per Tiny's orders, Jim Cappy changed the locks on the apartment door, but by then, Vicki had already returned to New Jersey.

For Vicki, the marriage was over, and no amount of religious rhetoric from her increasingly vindictive husband could save it. 'I realized one day that it wasn't really what I wanted to do with myself—be with somebody who didn't want to be with me,' she explains. 'So, I just decided to go home and have a life by myself—with my child, of course, but without somebody who didn't care about us, because he really didn't. I don't mean to be mean and put him down, but he didn't care about me and he really didn't care about her. That's *not* his fault. I don't think he was mean or anything, he just didn't know how to be a parent or a husband, and it's my fault that I chose someone who didn't know how to do that.'

Tiny's subsequent tour of New Zealand was cut short due to poor ticket sales, and he returned to the States earlier than planned. Vicki traveled to Brooklyn and met him at the apartment so that they could speak face to face. 'The last time I left,' she told him, 'you were on the road. This time I'm telling you to your face. I'm tired of this marriage and I'm tired of you.'

'My dear, you know the spiritual consequences of your act,' Tiny replied. 'But if you insist on traveling this wrong path, you cannot be stopped.'

With that, after five years of marriage, television's most famous couple parted ways. From that day forward, the heading on each page of Tiny's diaries changed from '*Thanks for a beautiful wife in Miss Vicki*' to '*Thanks as I had a beautiful wife in Miss Vicki*.'

Meanwhile, Bing Crosby made an appearance on *The Tonight Show*. 'Whatever happened to Tiny Tim?' he asked.

CHAPTER FOURTEEN
FEARS OF FAILURE

And so the year 1973 comes to an end. It was a nice year. Another year of anxiety, however, career-wise, but still I thank you for letting me live through it.
DIARY ENTRY, NEW YEARS DAY 1974

'My next guest has the distinction of being the only person ever married on *The Tonight Show*,' Johnny Carson began. 'We haven't seen him for a while and we thought you might be interested in what he's been up to these days. He opens tonight at the Holiday Inn in Torrance for a week, then he'll be at the Holiday Inn in Ventura for a week, and on November 23, he opens in Phoenix, at the Safari Hotel. Would you welcome back, please, Tiny Tim.'

The curtains parted, revealing a four-piece rock band in flower-patterned purple dress shirts. Tiny entered with a microphone, but instead of his usual wrinkled suit, he was dressed in a sequined tuxedo embellished with two sparkling ukuleles on the jacket. His hair had been dyed a chestnut brown and was neatly trimmed and combed. A brand-new Tiny Tim, financed and produced by Roy Radin with the cooperation of the Cappelluzzos.

After blowing a few kisses, Tiny looked into the camera meaningfully and began a new song, written for him by Tash Howard and Mark Barkan, 'Me And The Man On The Moon.'

Years ago they said I'd never make it,
They tried to stick a pin in my balloon,
They said I was too strange,
That my dreams were all in vain,
But they said the same about,
The man on the moon …

In early 1974, Tiny Tim's life was in shambles. Vicki was gone for good, and with almost no booking for the first four months of the year, Tiny had little to do but sit in his barren apartment and brood. He passed the time watching television, singing, and making daily calls to his mother and the Cappys. He also filled his time raging at Miss Vicki. When she called to ask for Tulip's crib, Tiny sent a telegram via Jack Rabin's office informing her that nothing currently in his possession was hers, as she had 'abandoned the house.' He immediately sent another, under his own name, scolding her for her 'dollar-sign ambitions.' A third was then sent to Emma and Alan Budinger, blaming them for 'the downfall of their daughters.' Alan responded with a telegram to Jack Rabin, advising 'Mr. Khaury' not call their home again.

It did not end there. Vicki wrote Tiny a letter pleading to be 'set free.' Tiny replied with a 'blistering' telegram to Mr. Budinger, whom he addressed only by his professional alias, 'Hilary,' in which he threatened to 'take Miss Tulip.' His misery was compounded when, on February 21, Maple Leafs defenseman Tim Horton died in a car accident. Two months later, on April 12, Tiny's forty-second birthday, the Maple Leafs were eliminated from the Stanley Cup playoffs.

It was against this backdrop that Tiny joined Roy Radin's *Vaudeville Revue* for a few dates during the spring. Afterward, Radin announced his intention to finance a brand-new show for Tiny in which they would update his repertoire and revamp his image. With no other prospects for his career on the horizon, and debts to the tune of $30,000, Tiny had virtually no choice but to oblige. Joe Cappy, too, recognized that the current climate rendered Radin's offer a fait accompli, even if he resented the idea of becoming 'Radin's stooge.'

On June 7, Tiny signed a seven-year management contract with Roy Radin, who was now entitled to 20 percent of his earnings. The Cappelluzzos continued to receive an unknown percentage, and another 10 percent went to CMA. Tiny's financial situation was so dire, in fact, that even his long-time accountant, Jack Paige, washed his hands of the problem. 'This is not the first time we had this intention,' Paige wrote in his resignation letter, dated July 15, 'but because of our long-standing relationship we always changed our minds. … The present circumstances are very objectionable to us, and since we feel absolutely powerless to correct them or even make a constructive contribution we have no alternative but to withdraw.'

Radin's first point of business was a full Tiny Tim makeover. First, his trademark paper shopping bag was replaced with a canvas traveling bag.

Next, he was fitted for two new custom-made suits: one was black with two sequined multi-colored ukuleles on the jacket, the other made of gold lamé with limestone tulips on the front of the jacket and a ukulele on the back. 'The beginning of a comeback,' Tiny wrote optimistically in his diary, after seeing the design for the suits.

Radin hired a young arranger, Tony Monte, who had been part of the Greenwich Village scene in the 60s, to assemble a twenty-minute medley of songs from the 40s to the 50s and 60s and back again. After they had settled on a fee of $6,000—'a decent price,' Monte notes—Tiny suddenly stood up and asked, 'Mr. Radin, how can you take advantage of this boy like that? You're fleecing him—you're making him work for nothing.'

'Roy now starts to go crazy,' Monte recalls, still amused by the scene today. 'I turned around and I'm looking at [Tiny] and I thought [to myself], This is probably worth 60,000! He kept saying it until Roy finally said, Get him out of here! Joe [Cappy] jumped out and took him to another room. Tiny was saying to me, Don't let them do this to you! Tell them to give you more money! All I wanted to do was get out of there.'

Tim Fowler, Radin's musical director and conductor, was tasked with locating a touring band for Tiny. Radin wanted hip, young, talented musicians who would work for next to nothing, so Fowler called his former jazz teacher at Berklee College of Music in Boston. The teacher recommended Larry Klug as a keyboardist and bandleader and Ken Hatfield as a guitar player. Hatfield, in turn, reached out to bass player Ed Sterbenz. On drums, Fowler brought in his friend Tony Tedesco, who also had attended Berklee and had already done of one Radin's tours. The boys came out to Long Island for an audition, and were given the job immediately. In short order, Radin convinced the band to serve not only as Tiny Tim's backing band but also as the rhythm section for the full orchestra, which would ultimately link up with Radin's 1974 *Vaudeville Revue* fall tour. Additionally, Radin would be paying them only $135 a week to perform as many as eight shows per week—a fee made possible by an old vaudeville pay scale, still valid through the musicians' union.

'We didn't care,' Hatfield says, 'because we got out of school.'

Within a few days, the boys had relocated to Radin's compound, which included his house, his mother-in-law's house, and a bungalow in the backyard that served as Tiny's new quarters. Tiny's bungalow had a pair of sliding glass doors that lead out to a concrete patio. The musicians were instructed to set up on the patio and were given a few, cheap T-shirts reading 'THE NEW TINY TIM SHOW' in iron-on, felt letters.

After settling in, Radin gave his guests a tour of the house. He and his wife, freshly inducted members of the nouveau riche, had been busily purchasing antique furniture and what they thought were collectibles. 'The more I looked [around],' Tony Monte recalls, 'I realized they didn't have an estate. It was just a lot of land with a funny-looking house. In his office, Roy had pictures of himself next to sheriffs—plural—from counties in Texas and Georgia with guys in hats and guns. That's who Roy was. He wanted to be next to these guys in power.'

* * *

Tiny Tim & The Timmies began rehearsing for the New Tiny Tim Show on August 5. Monte remembers the day not for the realization of his compositions but because of a small mistake and a big upset.

'We take a break,' Monte recalls. 'It's hot as hell. I have to pee. I used his bathroom. I didn't know I wasn't supposed to do that. I pee. I come back out and Tiny finds out and goes in to look. He sees that a towel was moved or something's not right, and he has a fit.' Roy Radin came running over to Monte. 'You're supposed to use the other one! That's Tiny's bathroom.' As Monte recalls, they had to get Tiny a motel room for the night. 'He wouldn't go back in there.'*

The Timmies, meanwhile, were having difficultly interpreting Tiny's music. Prior to his stardom, he had accompanied himself only on his ukulele, but during the height of his fame he had sung with all kinds of musical ensembles, even full orchestras. In the few years since he had fallen from grace, he had again become accustomed to accompanying himself. 'My issue was his timing,' says Larry Klug. 'He would drop beats and bars at will and just go wherever he wanted to because he was just so used to playing ukulele by himself. We were always trying to figure out, should we follow him? Should we stay where we are? What should we do?'

Tiny, in turn, had been voicing his concerns about the viability of the

---

* A day or two later, Monte had a curious encounter with Joe Cappy. 'Joe brought me to breakfast the next day, or the day after that … he didn't want anymore problems with anything … He said to me, You know, I'll tell you what my given name is: it's Joe Violence. He wrote it down. He pushed it over the table and I thought, Jesus Christ, why is he telling me this? I have no idea why he said that.'

new show since July. 'What good is it if he can get the work and I am his puppet?' he asked rhetorically, in his diary. Radin interpreted Tiny's behavior as ungrateful and berated him. He began to remind Tiny frequently of the money and time he had already invested in the show. By early August, Tiny had mellowed a bit, and to his credit, Radin offered to let Tiny produce the show if it flopped at its New York City opening in September.

'[Mr. Radin] is honest, strong-willed, and a man of his word,' Tiny concluded. But while he had resigned himself to taking part in the new show, Tony Monte and The Timmies could sense his apathy. 'He didn't want to do this from the start,' says Monte. 'He didn't want to come up to the rehearsal. He was always sleepy. He used to wait for us and we'd go look at music … and he'd fall asleep … He had the suit fitted. He said it didn't fit, it was too tight … they were trying to make him like Alice Cooper.'

'I got the feeling that … he didn't like that tuxedo,' Tony Tedesco adds. 'The impression I got was, This is not me. I definitely got that from him and I remember him saying that. That costume was something that he would never wear … [everything] was in somebody else's hands. He wasn't making the decisions.'

On August 9, everyone crowded into Tiny's bungalow to watch the resignation of President Nixon.* Just six years earlier, on an episode of *Laugh-In*, Nixon had famously asked the question, 'Sock it to me?' Later in the same episode, the show's cast dressed up and imitated Tiny while introducing *The Laugh-In News*. The following month, Tiny Tim had headlined the Royal Albert Hall shortly before Richard Nixon became the thirty-seventh President of the United States. Now, he watched a disgraced Nixon resign the presidency from a small TV in a bungalow in Long Island. It did not seem to bode well for Tiny's big comeback.

Before the crew set out on tour, Radin booked an early iteration of the show at a rock club in Hampton Bays. The crowd was full of his associates and other affluent residents of the area whom he hoped might invest in his show-business endeavors. Downstairs, the audience took their seats, and The Timmies warmed up. Meanwhile, upstairs in Tiny's dressing room, all hell broke loose.

Tony Monte attended the show with his friend Dr. Nick Catalano,

---

* Tiny did not express his views while watching Nixon's resignation with the band, but later, when they went on tour, he told the press that he did not believe Nixon had done anything wrong, calling the Watergate scandal 'the biggest farce of all.'

and both were present for the argument that ensued between Tiny and his handlers. For reasons that remain unclear, Tiny had reservations about being the 'new' Tiny Tim. According to Catalano, he ripped off his tuxedo vest and yelled, 'I'm not signing this music!'

Eventually, Radin and the Cappies were able to persuade him to perform. Downstairs, the band had no inkling of what had happened. 'He knew how to manipulate people with an edge and anger,' says Monte. 'He didn't want to do this from the start … and now he goes in and he sees that there's a million people in this place … this is where he's going to get them, because they got a full house … [but ultimately] he did [the show], without the vest.'

'[The band] didn't know about all the sturm und drang it often took just to get Tiny to walk out onstage,' Ed Sterbenz adds. 'Jimmy Cappy always looked unhappy, nervous, and *burnt*. Wow, what a gig Jimmy had!'

On Monday, August 12th, Tiny Tim & The Timmies flew to London, Ontario, for their first four dates. Tiny called it a 'great opening' in his diary, but it was also the night The Timmies got their first taste of Tiny's dark inner conflict. As Sterbenz recalls, the musicians were just getting ready to go to sleep when 'we hear this tremendous argument next door, screaming and yelling. We hear this woman screaming with this man, *screaming*! Boom! Stuff is hitting the wall. Larry says, That's Tiny's room, isn't it? We ran down and knocked on Jimmy's door and said, Something's going on in the there! He said, No, no, don't worry about it. We said, What do you mean? He said, That's Tiny having an argument with himself. The next day, we did the gig, and everything was fine.'

When rehearsals resumed in Long Island, following the engagement in Canada, two beautiful, young female backup singers, dubbed The Tulips, joined the troupe, Mimi 'Miss Violet' Siggia and Susie 'Miss Rose' Chin. As soon as the girls arrived, so did word that Pete Townshend of The Who was considering inviting the New Tiny Tim Show to be The Who's opening act on an upcoming tour of Europe. (It was also rumored that Townshend had expressed interest in having Tiny play the Pinball Wizard in *Tommy*.)

Rehearsals ran daily from 10am to 8pm. While the band was working with Tony Monte, The Tulips worked on choreography. In the evenings, the complete ensemble worked together with Tiny. The Timmies' T-shirts were replaced with polyester dress shirts, and the girls received tights and tailcoats. 'I think they were trying to make us like The Archies … like The Monkees,' says Sterbenz.

Radin's younger sisters were excited by all of the activity at his house. 'I remember the dancing girls and their crazy outfits and Tiny and all his crazy outfits,' Kate Radin recalls. 'It was hysterical … pee your pants laughing … and Roy got all upset with us girls, because we thought it was kind of funny, but we were young!'

By the end of August, an hour-long show had begun to solidify. The Timmies kicked things off with a short jazz set. Tiny Tim would then emerge, in the gold lamé tuxedo, flanked by The Tulips, while the band played the theme from *2001: A Space Odyssey*. As The Tulips danced around him, Tiny launched into Tony Monte's big medley of the 40s, 50s, and 60s, which opened with 'Great Balls Of Fire,' 'At The Hop,' 'The Monster Mash,' 'The Fly,' 'Blue Suede Shoes,' and 'Rock And Roll Is Here To Stay.' From there, the medley moved into a sampling of Beatles songs such as 'A Hard Day's Night,' 'Lady Madonna,' 'Eight Days A Week,' and 'Yellow Submarine,' before concluding in the 40s with 'Drinkin' Wine, Spo-Dee-O-Dee,' 'Beat Me Daddy, Eight To The Bar,' 'Bei Mir Bist Du Schoen,' 'Don't Sit Under The Apple Tree (With Anybody Else But Me),' 'Roll Out The Barrel,' and 'Sing, Sing, Sing (With A Swing).'

'Me And My Shadow' followed, during which The Tulips trailed Tiny and he pretended to trip over them. As he 'recovered' from the fall, Tiny would lament to the audience, 'It's not easy being the new Tiny Tim, it was a lot easier being the old one. Then again, come to think of it, no it wasn't.' With that, the band lit into Howard and Barkan's biographical ballad of Tiny Tim, 'Me And The Man On The Moon.'*

At the mid-point of the show, Tiny changed into the black tuxedo and returned with his ukulele in hand. He would sing a number or two in falsetto with his uke—typically 'Nobody Loves A Fairy When She's Forty' or 'There Are Fairies At The Bottom Of My Garden'—and then treat the audience to an updated version of 'I Got You, Babe,' parodying the newly divorced Sonny & Cher. Uke still in hand, he would then perform his only hit, 'Tip-Toe Thru' The Tulips With Me.'

* With its inspirational lyrics about attaining what most perceived to be unattainable, 'Me And The Man On The Moon,' is in a completely different league to the other songs Tash Howard wrote in Tiny's honor. Perhaps this was down to the influence of Mark Barkan, the man behind Leslie Gore's 'She's Just A Fool' and Manfred Mann's 'Pretty Flamingo.' Ed Sterbenz recalls two men—one of whom was presumably Howard—showing up to go over the song with the band. This suggests a sense of pride from the writers, and perhaps bigger plans for it beyond Tiny's stage act.

After another costume change, Tiny appeared shrouded in a black cape and illuminated by a green spotlight. While he grinned and cackled maniacally, Ed Sterbenz kicked off the bass line to 'The Other Side.'* During the bridge, Tiny encouraged the audience to have 'a swimming time as we sing,' and would occasionally add a dose of religious cynicism. 'My friends, can you picture it? You're going into the sea, you and your filthy sins! You didn't listen to me! Now you're all singing, the world is singing, and I'm gonna have a gay time! Sing for those ice caps, because they're melting and we're gonna have a gay time!'

Tiny's first encore was 'Earth Angel,' for which he would strip down to his pants and a black undershirt and roll around on the floor, kicking. Then, as if to show that underneath the new rock band, the dancing girls, and the swanky tuxedos, the new Tiny Tim was still very much the old Tiny Tim, he would return for a final encore, wearing one of his trademark outfits—sports coat, plaid shirt, gaudy tie, and wrinkled dress pants— and close the show with a rousing rendition of 'I've Got to Be Me.'

The final dress rehearsal for the New Tiny Tim Show was held at Radin's estate on August 29. Tiny noted in his diary that he had prepared by downing three beers beforehand. Radin and the Cappies had invited their friends and associates over to watch the show and meet its star at a reception following the performance. Tony Monte and Dr. Nick Catalano were again in attendance.

'There was a party to show *these people* Tiny Tim,' Catalano recalls. 'Radin throws the party—this is the show, this is what we're working on, folks. People in the neighborhood heard all this bullshit going on. There's a huge fountain, a grotesque fountain spitting out Manhattans. There are people all around … wise-guys and their wives or girlfriends with these bouffant hairdos and fur coats in the middle of the summertime in the Hamptons … these guys all know me as Tony's friend, a producer, but also a professor at a university. So they're all being very deferential and somehow we were talking about hunting: You should go. You should come with us. They take me to the car [and] they open up this trunk with all these guns in it. That was the opening salvo, and it was like, What the hell? … I'm thinking to myself, What the hell has [Tony] gotten himself into? Who are these guys?'

'I don't know everything that was going on, but I do know this: Roy, he was a wannabe tough guy,' Monte adds. 'He wanted to impress the wise-

---

* Referred to as 'Ice Caps' on the band's set lists.

guys … He wanted everybody to think that he was a big shot, so he wanted to get connected to the Cappies and their friends.'

The week before the official sendoff was consumed with more rehearsals, meetings with Enzo Custom Clothiers (who had designed Tiny's tuxedos), and a photo shoot with famed celebrity photographer James Kriegsmann. Finally, on September 12, Tiny, The Timmies, and The Tulips, tailored, practiced, and promoted, set out to the Midwest to reclaim Tiny's stardom.

* * *

The opening salvo of the New Tiny Tim Show was a two-day stint at a bowling alley bar in Carterville, Illinois. The Timmies drove their own vehicles behind Cappy, who carried Tiny and The Tulips. Ed Sterbenz's first impressions of the tour were pleasant. 'Well, in the beginning I think people came to see him as they know him, and it became this big show, and I would think they were a little impressed by what it was,' he recalls. 'Tiny always drew tremendous applause. I don't remember any hecklers. I don't remember any problems.'

From Illinois, the tour pressed on to Dearborn, Michigan, for a two-day engagement at the London Bridge on September 15 and 16. Reviews were again positive, with Jim Schutze of the *Detroit Free Press* declaring Tiny to be 'the same sweet-mad shy-brave monster you had almost learned to love in the final hours of the 1960s.'

Asked if he was enjoying himself in Detroit, Tiny replied bluntly, 'No, I'm not … I'd really like to record instead.' He explained that the purpose of the tour was to build momentum for a new record. A note on Ed Sterbenz's set list from a month later—the words 'New Single' next to 'Me And The Man On The Moon'—ties in with this, but no such single was ever issued.[*]

After Detroit, the tour hit Fort Knox, Kentucky; a naval base in Charleston, South Carolina; a marine base in Jackson, North Carolina; and Babylon, Long Island. Then, on October 2, the New Tiny Tim Show linked up with Roy

---

[*] It was long believed that Tiny had never recorded 'Me And The Man On The Moon' in the studio, until the author of this book discovered an unreleased ODO Studios acetate featuring a studio version of the song in 2008. As none of The Timmies recall playing on the track, it is possible that it was recorded during Tiny's sessions with Tash Howard the previous year. The song's co-writer, Mark Barkan, is unsure why it was never released at the time. 'As I remember there was objection by another party in control to releasing it, not Tash. Tash became ill a year or so or maybe two years after it was recorded. I really think this could have been a major hit for Tiny.' It was finally released officially on *Tiny Tim: Lost & Found Volume 1 (Rare and Unreleased 1963–1974)*.

Radin's *All American Vaudeville Revue* for twenty-three one-nighters at venues in Pennsylvania, Ohio, and New Hampshire. Tiny performed only an abridged version of his set, and The Timmies became the supporting band for every act.

Tiny's tenure with the *Revue* left a strong impression on many of his fellow musicians. According to Tim Fowler, Radin's coordinator, the actor Donald O'Connor dubbed him an 'idio-genius' because 'he couldn't tie his own shoes but he could tell you who recorded a song … who first recorded it … and give you a history of the whole song … his mind was amazing, but he was so child-like in his dealing with humanity.'

Fowler goes on to recall an incident when he and other members of the touring party were eating at a restaurant across from their hotel, watching Tiny's attempts to cross the multiple-lane highway between the two. 'He'd get about halfway across and people would recognize him and honk and start waving at him, and he'd run back the way he came instead of going the rest of the way across the street.' Finally, the laughter in the restaurant gave way to sympathy, and Frankie Maffei from Danny & The Juniors ran outside to escort Tiny across the street. Another of Fowler's favorite memories is of playing baseball with the crew on off days. 'Tiny would come and umpire the game, and he'd come fully dressed. Everyone's in shorts and T-shirts and sneakers, and here's Tiny in his tuxedo.'

Tiny's gentle nature gave the traveling ensemble a fairly one-dimensional understanding of his character, however—until they were surprised one night by his reaction to O'Connor's horsing around backstage. 'Take a bow!' O'Connor would shout, motioning as though he was going to hit the unsuspecting person in the groin. 'He was cracking everybody up,' Fowler recalls. Everybody, that is, except Tiny.

'A star of your stature shouldn't be doing things like that,' Tiny told O'Connor, wagging his finger. 'It's much too beneath you.' Later, when O'Connor pulled the stunt again, Tiny dropped his voice to a deep baritone and barked, 'Cut that shit out!'

'We all just froze and Tiny just walked away,' Fowler recalls. 'I never saw anybody get Tiny riled until then, and of all the people to get him pissed off was sweet Donald O'Connor!'

By the middle of the tour, the low pay and constant travel had begun to take its toll on all of the performers and crew. Tiny felt the brunt of this irritability after he jokingly described the *Roy Radin's Vaudeville Revue* as a 'cavalcade of has-beens.' 'Oh man, did he hit a sore spot with all the acts,' Fowler says. 'They all wanted to kill him for that one. For some time he was given the cold shoulder. It was just something that came to his head, and he thought it was humorous. But at the time he said it we were in the middle of a tour and everybody was exhausted and it just struck everybody the wrong way.'

Those on the tour were privy to many of Tiny's peculiarities, like his tendency to wrap a plate of food from the nightly dinner buffet and eat it in the privacy of his own room. He had evidently not yet curbed his penchant for ordering copious amounts of room service, either. One time, after struggling to decide which pancakes to order, he requested one of each type. He then called Tim Fowler's room. 'Oh, Mr. Fowler, I have a bunch of pancakes here I can't eat. If I put the cart outside would you see if the guys would like to eat them?'

Inevitably, Tiny's conflicted views on sex made themselves known to an unlucky few on tour. Once, when Jackie Vernon and Tim Fowler took a peek at what was in his shopping bag, they pulled out his Bible, opened it, and gasped. 'Inside the Bible he had these grotesque pictures of sexual diseases that have gone berserk,' says Fowler. 'Like a case of gonorrhea that has just run rampant and these horrible disfigurements. This is how he kept himself under control.'

Even so, Tiny remained easily excitable. Every night, the entire ensemble performed 'There's No Business Like Show Business' and then stood hand-in-hand for a company bow. Milton Berle, the headliner, signaled the bow by squeezing the hand of the person next to him, and on it went on down the line. Tiny stood between The Tulips, and on the night in question, Suzie Chin tickled his palm with her middle finger. Tiny let out a squeal and tensed up.

Later, Roy Radin paid a visit to her room. 'Suzie, what did you do to Tiny?' he asked.

'What do you mean?' she replied. 'I just tickled his hand a little.'

'Well, don't do that anymore.'

'Why?'

'Because it costs a lot to clean those lamé pants.'

As the *Vaudeville Revue* tour neared its conclusion, Tiny knew that his act was still in its infancy, and that the response of small audiences in rural areas, however enthusiastic they may be, was not a true gauge of his success. 'This act seems to be breaking well,' he told the press. 'But the real answer will be when we open in New York at Jimmy's.'

Hoping to drum up some additional publicity, Tiny and his new entourage appeared on *The Mike Douglas Show* alongside Paul Williams and Richard

Dreyfus. A few days, later Radin held a pre-engagement press conference. 'People used to come expecting to see some freak,' he told the press. 'His talents have never been fully tapped. He's an entertainer, a helluva entertainer. The falsetto *crap* is only two minutes in his new show. People are gonna go crazy when they hear him and see him. They're gonna say, I can't believe this is Tiny Tim. We're gearing up for Vegas.'

Tiny, however, soon veered from the script, taking a moment to lambaste the women's liberation movement. Pulling out his Bible, he declared, 'It says right here, Man is over Woman.' Elsewhere, asked why Miss Vicki was not part of the new act, he replied, 'I blame women's lib.'

In late October, upon completion of the *Vaudeville* tour, the New Tiny Tim Show began a weeklong engagement at Jimmy's. With most of the show's kinks having been worked out on the road in the Midwest (including the removal of '16 Tons' and an 'audience participation' segment during 'Yellow Submarine'), the act was well-received by the 350 people who attended opening night, and reviews were positive, even if the compliments were somewhat backhanded.

'Attempting a comeback from critical revulsion and his asexual image that insisted—love me, I'm weird—Tiny Tim has resurfaced with a lot more shtick and a lot less sick,' *Newsday* declared. 'Audiences still laugh at him, but not out of embarrassment as before.' For *Variety*, 'Even in this formative process, the guy is getting laughs,' while the *New York Daily News* concluded, 'No getting around it. Tiny Tim is stranger than ever. But strangely likeable.'

* * *

Buoyed by the success of the Jimmy's engagement, Tiny upheld his end of the agreement with Radin and continued west with the new act. They would make two television appearances together, the first of which was on *The Merv Griffin Show* on November 11. Roy Radin was adamant that Tiny should have his own conductor for the appearance, and since Griffin's show refused to pay The Timmies to appear with Tiny in lieu of the house band, Ken Hatfield was chosen to conduct Griffin's star-studded band—a task he found particularly daunting. After Hatfield had struggled through several attempts to run Tiny and the band through 'Me And The Man On The Moon,' Griffin's conductor/pianist Mort Lindsey came to the rescue. 'I got away from the bandstand as fast as possible,' Hatfield says.

After the segment, Merv Griffin approached Hatfield to 'offer encouragement,' only for Tiny to quickly pull him aside and suggest that

Griffin's friendly veneer covered another motive. 'Mr. Hatfield, Mr. Griffin likes boys!' Tiny announced.

'I was so shocked that I was speechless,' Hatfield recalls. 'Then our handlers told us to get in the limo to go back to our hotel. The ride home was very quiet.'

The next day they headed to Burbank, California, for an appearance on *The Tonight Show*. Tiny had been hesitant to approach Carson's people after a three-year break in contact, but Roy Radin was not afraid to try and take advantage of what little pull Tiny Tim's name might still have. Booker Craig Tennis was hesitant—Tiny, he felt, was 'yesterday's headlines'—but Carson overruled him.[*] And so, on November 12, Tiny Tim & The Timmies waited nervously behind the curtain of the *Tonight Show* stage for the taping of their segment.

'I was scared out of my wits,' Larry Klug recalls. 'I was this young dude. First time I'd ever been on national television.' Tiny, too, felt the gravity of the performance. His first appearance on the show in 1968 had triggered a surge in sales of *God Bless Tiny Tim* and 'Tip-Toe Thru' The Tulips With Me,' and the same show had given his career a much-needed shot in the arm when he married Miss Vicki on air. Could it now revive his career or bedazzle Carson into a regular booking?

The new Tiny Tim, however, was a very different sell. He was no longer the unprecedented, androgynous phenomenon of 1968–69. He had set and worn out the precedent in a flash. His separation and career troubles had been widely publicized, and it was no longer enough for Carson to quiz Tiny about his diet or incite shy giggles by asking about 'girls.' Tiny would have to account for the decline in his popularity and the failure of his marriage.

After performing 'Me And The Man On The Moon,' Tiny sat down for the interview. Carson did not bother asking about the New Tiny Tim Show. Instead, he inquired as to the status of Tiny's career, remarking how 'everything was going just great … then all of a sudden things started to go downhill and then you sort of disappeared?'

'Yeah, well, those things happen in life,' Tiny replied. 'You have your streaks and slumps, whether it's in baseball, or hockey, or in life.'

'So what have you been doing all this time?' Carson asked.

Tiny explained that he had spent some time in the 'minor leagues,' before attempting to steer the conversation toward his new show, but Carson was not

---

[*] Asked about the appearance some years later by Harry Stein, Tennis called it a 'charity booking.'

biting. Instead, he wanted to know how the money Tiny had made during the peak of his success had 'evaporated' ('I spent quite a bit on cosmetics,' Tiny replied) and about the collapse of Tiny's marriage.

Unable to restrain himself for the sake of the new act, Tiny came out swinging. 'Unfortunately, Miss Vicki left again this January,' he began. 'I'll be waiting, I don't believe in divorce. If she comes back twenty years from now, fine—under my terms, of course.' Of those terms, he revealed, 'She has to take a blood test … I would put a lock on the telephone so she does not call her parents or her sisters or anybody … I would also put no television, no records, unless I give her permission.'

Tiny was able to briefly plug his new act by introducing The Tulips and The Timmies for a performance of the 40s portion of the Tony Monte medley, but ultimately this latest *Tonight Show* appearance offered little in the way of publicity for the new Tiny Tim. The group continued to tour, but by the end of November, the media's coverage of Tiny's new act ceased abruptly in favor of news about Tiny's former 'sweet angel.'

The last time Tiny had heard from his estranged wife was on October 24, when she called Roy Radin to request that Tiny return her things. 'I told him to tell her I want nothing and I have nothing for her,' Tiny wrote bitterly in his dairy. It came as a shock, then, when many of the major newspapers carried a story first covered by the *Philadelphia Sunday Bulletin* on December 1 and then syndicated by the Associated Press: 'Tiny Tim's Ex-Wife Reported On Welfare.' The article quoted a Camden County welfare office employee, who said that Vicki had been receiving welfare checks for $235 a month since August under her maiden name, and that Tulip, now three years old, was living with her in England. At first, Tiny made no public statement, deferring to Joe Cappy, who voiced only suspicion. 'We don't know anything about Miss Vicki being on welfare,' he told the press. 'I doubt if she is, though. Tiny is sending her money for the baby every month.'

On December 3, another smattering of articles appeared. Now, it seemed, not only was Vicki on welfare but she had been working as a go-go dancer at Minnie's Lounge in Camden, New Jersey, while receiving welfare checks. The manager of the bar said he had 'no doubt' that the girl in his employ was Miss Vicki, and that she had been working for him since June. 'She didn't want anyone to know who she was,' the manager revealed. 'She was a nice, quiet kid who was trying to earn some money to support her daughter.' (The club's $5 an hour had evidently trumped the $1.75 she had been making at a boutique.) Another reporter even caught her act and described it in detail for an article entitled 'Miss Vicki Whatever Happened To That Shy Little Girl' ('She spun, she kicked her long legs, she grabbed a pole at the edge of the small stage and whirled around it.').

After reading the articles, Tiny spent hours on the phone with the Camden County Welfare Board, reporters, and the Camden County Prosecutor Office, before listing his concerns in his diary.

1. Where is she? 2. Is she in England? 3. If so, is she with Amos Levy? 4. How about the baby? … I pray for her, that she's OK. And comes back quick. She charged me for desertion. Also is she on drugs? I pray for her.

On December 5, the papers carried Tiny's thoughts on the matter. 'To tell you the truth,' he said, 'this report took me by surprise and it was a shock.' He went on to mention that he'd confirmed with his attorney, Jack Rabin, that Vicki was receiving $100 a month from him. 'My attorney said she may have misrepresented her case to the welfare board,' Tiny added, 'and that they may charge her with fraud. I'm sorry to see what's going on.'

In response to reports that Vicki had been receiving welfare checks while working at Minnie's Lounge, office director Frank Senatore announced that Vicki's welfare claims were 'being investigated.' In the midst of the media frenzy, everyone connected to the story had weighed in—with the notable exception of the subject of the controversy. Where was Vicki? In an effort to locate her, the press contacted both Vicki's landlord in Cherry Hill, New Jersey, and her mother. Both stated that Vicki and Tulip had departed for England three weeks prior, but neither knew the reason. Her whereabouts were officially confirmed for Tiny when Isadore Fertel received a Christmas card from Vicki on December 12, postmarked in England.

If the controversy surrounding his wife were not embarrassing enough, the December 1974 issue of *People* magazine carried a photograph of Tiny, taken during a break in touring, seated Indian-style on the floor of his apartment on Ocean Avenue, holding up an eviction notice and grinning maniacally. Two large holes can be seen in the wall behind him, and a portion of the carpet is torn from the floor. Apparently, when Tiny returned from the Ontario dates in August, a problem with the building's water system had caused a flood in his apartment, and the maintenance staff had created the holes while Tiny was away. In any case, *People* magazine chalked up the eviction to Tiny's inability to pay the rent. Tiny maintained that he had stopped paying his rent because the problems had not been fixed. When the case went to court, Tiny did not attend the hearing, lost, and was ordered to pay the Premier House three months rent. He then received an eviction notice on November 11. He was now homeless.

* * *

As the months passed, the New Tiny Tim Show began to slump. In Sioux Falls, South Dakota, a blizzard shut down the tour for two more days, during which the band received no additional pay. 'We were stuck in a Holiday Inn for three or four days,' Ed Sterbenz recalls. 'It was just brutally cold. There was snow as far as you could see and there was a state of emergency.' Weary of both the show and its inconsistent yet grueling travel schedule, the entire touring party was on edge.

A series of annoyances and setbacks made things worse—a bomb threat in Illinois, Tiny falling over the drums and smashing his ukulele, the band narrowly colliding with an eighteen-wheeler and crashing into a snow bank. Tiny was frustrated by his lack of control over material, and he was still struggling with the costume changes. The shows were often in small clubs without proper dressing room facilities, so Jim Cappy would have to 'improvise some cover,' as Ken Hatfield put it, for Tiny to get changed behind. On one occasion, the barrier slipped, 'revealing Tiny in an awkwardly comprising position, and only partially clad.' The audience found it hilarious, Hatfield says, but it 'did little to alleviate Tiny's misgivings about the whole venture.'

Tiny continued to battle with Roy Radin over the show's content. 'He said I was not doing what we rehearsed,' he wrote. 'It's true in a sense, but it's hard when you do not believe in what you are doing.' He was even becoming passive about resurrecting his career in interviews. 'When you're hot you're hot, when you're not your not,' he told the *Milwaukee Journal*. 'I had my share on top; now it's somebody else's turn.'

'We kind of started at the top and there was nowhere to go,' Sterbenz recalls. 'We did the Carson show, the Griffin show … that's it. After that, it was another club, another club, another club … we didn't have an itinerary anymore. We had two nights here then five days off. Then we had one night here and four days off. Most of us were going back and forth to Boston on the bus.' Despite the gaps between the shows, however, the musical relationship between singer and band was 'almost telepathic at that point. Tiny would go off on tangents. He would drop the ball and we'd catch him. He really trusted us.'

On December 19, the band traveled on to Chicago for an appearance on *The Phil Donahue Show*, where Tiny began to show his frayed nerves. After performing 'Me And The Man On The Moon' and a version of Scott Fagan's 'Carnival Is Ended,' he sat down for an interview. As he settled into his usual rhetoric about the role of women in society, some of the women in the audience began to heckle him. Instead of taking it in his stride, as he had when Phyllis Newman laughed at him on *The Tonight Show*, he argued with the audience, appearing irrational and unstable. And he was. Scribbled in the margins of Tiny's 1975 diary are a series of dark, disjointed phrases and sentences. 'The way I spend money is a felony.' 'You've reached a point of no return.' 'Miss Vicki was never in love with me, but what I represented. She married me for laffs.' 'I'll pay my bills with the allowance I get for my candy.' 'You wouldn't know responsibility if you fell over one on the street.' 'Be patient with others, God has been patient with me.' 'You don't believe in yourself—at least a horse would try to finish.'

* * *

The New Tiny Tim Show took a month off in January 1975, so Radin put Tiny up in the Golden Gate Motel in Brooklyn. The media's preoccupation with Tiny's legal troubles and the Vicki saga had not yet subsided, and on January 13 it was reported that, despite evidence that she had asked that her name be taken off of the welfare rolls prior to working part-time at Minnie's Lounge, Camden County officials were planning to 'continue' their welfare fraud investigation into Miss Vicki. On January 23, Tiny circled the date in his diary, noting that Vicki had been 'gone for a year.'

The tour resumed in February, but by the end of the month, The Timmies and The Tulips had had enough. 'I think I was the first one to say, I'm leaving,' says Sterbenz. 'Then Ken said, If you're going, I'm going. Then Larry said, Well, maybe it's time.'

The original New Tiny Tim Show played its last show in Lancaster, Pennsylvania, on March 1. Garry Dial, a jazz student at Berklee, had been asked by Tim Fowler to replace Larry Klug on keyboard. He was lured by the promise that the band would have the opportunity to play their own set before Tiny's show, that gigs would be steady, and that he would be paid $200 a week and receive his own hotel room, and could bring his girlfriend along with him.

As soon as Dial arrived in Lancaster, he realized something was not right. 'I remember very distinctly walking into the bedroom and there was Ed Sterbenz and Kenny and Tony and they're all like, Man, we gotta get outta here,' he recalls. 'They were super pissed off because there were no gigs for the next six nights.' Dial soon discovered that the promised rate of $200 a week and his own hotel room was contingent upon the band playing six gigs a week. Then, when he showed up for a rehearsal, Tiny too told him he should leave as soon as possible. 'These are bad men,' Tiny warned him, presumably referring to Radin and co. ('The vibe I got was that it was a mob thing,' Dial recalls.)

'I just got here,' Dial protested, unaware of Tiny's capricious disposition. 'Well, I would get outta here now,' said Tiny. '*I'm* gonna get outta here.'

Indeed, an undated letter discovered in the estate of Tiny's attorney, Jack Rabin, suggests that he really was trying to 'get outta' there.

> *I am through doing the Roy Radin show. I will go back to doing what I've always been doing before I signed the contract on June 17 1974, or thereabouts, which is my own act. I will direct my own shows, I will produce my own shows, I will produce my own records, and I will select my own songs, at all times, every time, and I will fail or succeed on my own merits, not on somebody else's. If this means being out on the street, that's my own hard luck. I can't thank you and your wife enough for your time, patience, kindness, and the most charitable of all efforts that I have received from you.*

Despite this, Tiny did not take off with the Timmies, and as the former members peeled off to enjoy their previous lives, it became clear to Tiny that Radin was his life. Replacements were found, and though the new Timmies threatened to quit after being thrust into live performances with only a week of rehearsals, they resumed touring at the end of March.

Ed Sterbenz made sure to keep in touch with Tiny. He sent him a birthday letter on March 31 and received a reply three says later.

> *I still am sorry you and the other Timmies left, but I pray we will always keep in touch. The new band is rounding into shape. Two new girls have also been added … who knows how long this new group will continue … Lord willing we go by van to Alabama, Sunday, April 6. Poor Mr. Cappy. He must drive.*

Unfortunately, the new New Tiny Tim Show was to continue for only a few more days before it came to an abrupt and disastrous end. On April 7, Jim Cappy was driving Tiny and the new Tulips through Mechanicsburg,

Pennsylvania. When he came to a stop at a red light, he noticed a car driving erratically down an off ramp on the opposite side of the road.

'Boy, look at that guy, he's really speeding,' he said. Everyone in the car turned to watch as the car swerved, jumped the divider, and burst into the oncoming traffic. Before Cappelluzzo could avoid it, the rogue vehicle hit them head on. 'I was sitting in the back, reading the *New York Times*. And the next thing I knew, I was in Holy Spirit Hospital,' Tiny later told the press. 'We could have been under the tulips instead of tiptoeing through them.'

The passengers of both cars were rushed to Holy Spirit Hospital in Camp Hill, Pennsylvania. Tiny Tim suffered a punctured lung, eight broken ribs, and torn ligaments in both ankles. Jim Cappy suffered a collapsed rib cage. The driver of the other car, Paul Croop, was fatally wounded in the accident, and his wife was critically injured. It was later reported that Croop had suffered a heart attack while driving, which had caused him to lose control of his vehicle.

'It was like a disaster,' Joe Cappy recalled, when interviewed for the Tiny Tim episode of *E! True Hollywood Story*. 'We spent months getting this new act together which we had high hopes for. It all looked great … and then it all just went down the drain.'

While in the hospital, Tiny received 300 letters wishing him well. Vicki's mother even called to check on him. After his release, Tiny spent the next three months recovering in a room at Joe Cappy's house. The accident not only cost him his new act, but it also brought about the final blow with his attorney, Jack Rabin. In May, Tiny had called Rabin to ask how much money was owed to him through his insurance. 'I'm your lawyer, not your insurance man,' Rabin replied, to which Tiny said, 'If you cared about me, you would know these things.'

When Tiny assigned Rabin as his new lawyer, there were already several pending lawsuits against him. One had been filed by his former manager, George King, who had reportedly resorted to working as a gigolo for elderly women after show business failed him, even though his contract with Tiny was technically still valid until 1973. When Tiny became famous, King found the contract and sold a portion of it to a friend, who then sold portions to others. King then set about suing his former client for one million dollars, plus interest.

When the case finally made it to court in 1974, the scene was comical. King arrived in court wearing a Beatles wig, while despite Jack Rabin's attempts to silence his client, Tiny confessed that King had given him his stage name, that he signed the contract in question, and that he owed King money. As it turned out, King, enterprising as he was, was not the first to sue Tiny over an outstanding contract. He dropped the suit when he found Tiny had nothing left for him to collect.*

Rabin became increasingly frustrated at Tiny's inability to learn from his mistakes. Despite Rabin's pleas, he still continued to sign anything that was placed in front of him without consultation. The plaintiffs usually had written evidence of contractual obligations, and Tiny had a habit of confessing in court. Before long, two entire filing cabinets were devoted to Tiny Tim. After a couple unfavorable court verdicts, Tiny refused to pay for his legal services, but Rabin continued working for free. He stayed on as Tiny's lawyer even after Joe Cappy paid a visit to his family's house to threaten him. ('You better start doing a better job of representing Tiny.')

Tiny's friend and home insurance agent, Robert Fenster, sums up the situation: 'Tiny was taken over by people who didn't like Jack. It caused animosity between them.' However, when Tiny accused Rabin of not caring, Rabin, who had represented Tiny without pay, endured his freewheeling attitude in regards to signing new contracts, answered late night phone calls about trivial matters, and listened to outlandish courtroom confessions, quit on the spot. Tiny then sent Rabin a note of dismissal, writing in his diary, 'It was quite nasty. He was lethargic in handling my affairs.'

* * *

On August 14, the Associated Press reported that Miss Vicki had returned from her eight-month stay in England and had resumed working at Minnie's Lounge in New Jersey. Wearing only a black bikini, Vicki finally broke her silence and sat down for an interview with a reporter who visited her between shows at Minnie's. She rejected the idea that she was not deserving of welfare and maintained that she had not been working while she was on welfare due to her inability to dance because of a kidney ailment. 'The welfare was not a fraud,' she said. 'When I went back to work I wrote a letter saying I was no longer eligible. Then I went to London.'

Vicki also rejected Tiny's claim that he had been sending her regular payments to help support Tulip, now aged four. To Vicki, however, the issue of whether or not Tiny was paying her child support was irrelevant. 'I don't think he should have to pay for a mistake that I made,' she told the reporter.

---

* After telling this story to Harry Stein, Tiny still referred to King as 'a wonderful man!'

Though she stated she was not actively pursuing a divorce through the court system, she confirmed that she had no plans to reconcile with her estranged husband. 'We're legally married, but it's over,' she said. 'I love him, but we just can't get along. He doesn't want to get a divorce and it doesn't really make any difference … I was seventeen when I was married and still growing up. Now I believe in astrology and think dancing is fun.'

The article did not explain why Vicki had been in England for eight months. Apparently, with Tiny out of the picture, she paid another visit to Eileen Ford. Remembering what had happened a few years earlier, Ford decided not to represent Vicki herself, but recommended her to her affiliate in England. To Vicki's surprise, she received an invitation from the agency, inviting her to England to work there. She sold her engagement ring to cover the expenses of relocating across the Atlantic. While in the UK, Vicki sold a juicy account her marriage to Tiny Tim to the London *Sunday Mirror* for $15,000. It was titled 'My Insufferable Marriage To Tiny Tim,' and different variations of the article appeared in different tabloids across Europe. One of the most startling admissions in the piece concerned Vicki's reasoning for marrying. 'I married Tiny because he was famous,' she wrote. 'We had separate bedrooms … I tried my darndest to stimulate him romantically, but to no avail.'

Amos Levy, the Italian tour guide who had been the source of controversy during Tiny's November, 1973 tour, read in the newspapers that Vicki was in London and tracked her down. They began to spend time together. At first, Vicki was flattered by the attention, but Levy soon became possessive and started to show up unannounced at Vicki's home and at her modeling gigs. He also started to tell people that he was Vicki's manager. It was not long before Vicki's agency became annoyed, and she saw the situation as 'almost a repeat of the Ford episode.' When Levy, whom she learned had a criminal record, would not take the hint, Vicki decided to return home. Before she did, she accepted an offer to pose for nude photographs in exchange for £4,000 pounds—a large sum of money in 1975.

The photos came out in the October 1975 issue of *Oui* magazine, then owned by Playboy Enterprises. Two of the photographs featured a nude Vicki posing with a framed 8x10 picture of Tiny, while in the accompanying article, Vicki claimed that she and Tiny had not had sexual contact for six months during their marriage; that Tiny had been with men and was not interested in women; and that she had been young and foolish when she married him.

Vicki maintains that she had been resistant to posing with Tiny's photo.

'They took a lot of pictures I didn't like, but they told me I could choose which photos they could use,' she explains. 'It's my fault. I shouldn't have let him direct me in that way. I was afraid to be uncooperative because I needed the money.' She went back to America without telling Levy, who later wrote to her from prison. His letters were marked 'Return To Sender.' Back home, Vicki appeared on NBC's *Tomorrow*, on the same episode as Miss America. After the taping, host Tom Snyder remarked, 'I felt that Miss America had something to say and Miss Vicki had precious little to say.'

Tiny, on the other hand, had a lot to say. He had been living in a dingy motel room in Brooklyn since July, and was being interviewed extensively by Harry Stein for his forthcoming biography (ironically due to be published by Playboy Press). Stein was privy to Tiny's reaction to the photographs in *Oui*:

> Look what that girl has done now! … I tell you, this girl has got the mark of Cain upon her … she's got to be taking drugs or drinking or something. … I give her fair warning—She's got to come back to me, through the grace of Christ. Unconditional surrender! As long as I am living, I am the only one for her. Let's see how the world treats her when she goes down the drain … this is a disgrace!

On December 18 1975, Tiny filed for custody of Tulip through the Camden County court system, claiming that Vicki was 'mentally, emotionally, and morally unfit' to continue to take care of their daughter. No follow-up articles appeared in the scandal sheets, however, and Tulip remained in Vicki's care. Neither Vicki or Tulip have ever faulted Tiny publicly for his lack of participation in Tulip's life. 'I never thought [of it as he abandoned us] and I don't think she did either,' Vicki said later. 'Back in those days, fathers did that. They moved on to another life. I raised her by myself, and she was fine.'

Tulip's memories of her father are vague. 'I don't really have that many memories because my mother and he split when I was two,' she told Lowell Tarling in 2002. 'I didn't really spend that much time with him … he would call every once in a while, I really didn't know him so I didn't have any impression of him because basically I just talked to him on the phone.' While he 'seemed like a nice person' to her, she found it hard to reconcile that with the things her mother told her about him. 'As a kid, those things really stick with you, and it made it very difficult for me … I was always almost embarrassed of my father because she made him look so bad in my eyes.'

In any case, had Tiny been awarded custody, he would not have been financially able to care for a child. The tabloids seemed to have all but missed the fact that on September 10, shortly after Harry Stein had witnessed Tiny's meltdown over the nude pictures of Vicki, the Cappelluzzos decided that they could no longer afford to pay for Tiny's hotel room at the Golden Gate Motel. Shortly thereafter, he temporarily moved back into his old bedroom at his family's apartment at 601 West 163rd Street in Washington Heights.

Aside from lying in bed with the blankets pulled over his head for extended periods of time, Tiny spent most of his time in the old apartment brainstorming about a comeback. He would acknowledge September 10 1975 as the day he hit rock bottom. 'I wasn't hot anymore,' he later told John Elder. 'My manager refused to pay the hotel bills and I went home to mother, back to that dingy apartment where I came from, with nothing but loud noises from outside all the time … I didn't dare go [outside] because I was too ashamed.'

It was becoming increasingly difficult to fall back on the militant positivity that had guided him through his pre-fame years. The sharp slide in his career, the failed comeback attempt, the broken marriage, the lawsuits, the financial failure, and the public embarrassment at the hands of the media had systematically ground him down. 'I often felt depressed,' he later told the *National Enquirer*. 'I didn't care if I lived or died—and I felt dying was the better option.'

When Tiny returned home, there was no heroes welcome; no 'Welcome Home Tiny, We Love You' draped on his building.

Dear Lord,

As I predicted at Lake Tahoe to Miss Tricia Porche, I came back to be with my mother at the old tenement house I left to go to Hollywood in November 1967.

As I look out from my room window all my father's words, my mother's words, Mr. Levi's words, for me to not waste my money came to me and really felt what I wasted in the past. In my shame, my mother's shame in my being back I believe I have learnt my lesson—I will save my money.

(Lord Willing) I will soon be back on top again.

This day I was born again.

Tiny Tim
AKA Herbert Khaury

CHAPTER FIFTEEN

CAN'T HELP BUT WONDER WHERE I'M BOUND

It's a long and a dusty road,
It's a hot and a heavy load,
And the folks I meet ain't always kind.

'CAN'T HELP BUT WONDER WHERE I'M BOUND,'
FROM *TINY TIM'S SECOND ALBUM*

Tiny remained at his parents' for thirteen days, before moving to a hotel room on September 23 with money from Tillie. Shortly thereafter, he was served with divorce papers. Rather than utilize his energy and resources for finding a stable place to live, he struck a deal with divorce attorney, Doris Sassower, who agreed that she would be paid for her work when Tiny received his settlement money from the accident. The two spent the latter half of September assembling a plan to block Vicki's divorce. There came a mild reprieve when Tiny received word, through his musical director, Marvin Lewis, that Vicki had left Amos Levy, who was left 'in despair.'

'Thanks for that,' Tiny wrote in his diary. 'She was never his anyway.'

Relations between Tiny, the Cappelluzzos, and Roy Radin had been getting 'stiffer and further apart' since the road accident in April. To make matters worse, Tiny had fired attorney Larry Hirsch, a personal friend of Radin's who was handling the lawsuit relating to the accident, and replaced him with Phillip Damashek. Tiny had Damashek levy a $500,000 lawsuit against Radin, but buckled immediately under pressure from Radin. Joe Cappy, however, intervened, and forbade Tiny from dropping the suit.

In November, when Tiny returned from tours of upstate New York and Hawaii with Marvin Lewis, he began to receive calls from Mario Ricci, Radin's thuggish lawyer. Ricci had one message: drop the lawsuit, or else. In a remarkable show of bravado, Tiny traveled to Radin's house for a private meeting with him and Ricci. They ordered Tiny to drop the lawsuit, lest he be 'blackballed.' Figuring he had nothing to lose, Tiny refused to drop the suit. Radin quit as Tiny's manager on the spot.

Without Radin, the Cappys were once again in complete control of Tiny's career and began to pursue whatever bookings they could find. Tiny took an offer to appear exclusively in Hawaii for an indefinite period, traveling there on December 1. When he arrived, however, he found that the agents who had offered him a $10,000 fee could only produce $5,000. Their promises of steady gigs and new records fell short as well. When one engagement closed after only one night due to poor attendance as the result of an airline strike, the *Honolulu Advertiser* pounced on Tiny's bad fortunes, reporting that only two people attended the show, and that Tiny was stuck in Hawaii with no money to return home.

Defeated, Tiny returned to New York on December 27. He spent the last few days of 1975 brooding in his hotel. On New Years Eve, he considered crashing Vicki's go-go dancing act at Minnie's Lounge in Camden, New Jersey, but he did not have money for a car. Alone in his hotel he wrote, 'I spoke to … both Cappys. They did not invite me to their New Years party. Money friends, I guess.'

* * *

Unlike 1975, 1976 at least yielded a record release, on the unknown label Kama Records: 'Howard Cosell (We Think You're Swell),' a falsetto tribute to sports announcer Howard Cosell. In the latest mark of Tiny's ardent patriotism, the B-side featured 'The Bi-Centennial Song (I Believe In America).' In between the refrain—*You have always come through / You old red, white, and blue / May your stars and your stripes ever wave*—Tiny issued a spoken monologue of his concerns surrounding inflation, taxation, rising prices of goods, corruption in government, Watergate, pollution, social revolution, and other problems facing the country. He was paid $500 for the record, of which a limited number of copies were pressed, and never heard about it again.

Perhaps due to exhaustion, or because their cash cow was drying up, the Cappys had begun to take a step back from actively managing Tiny's career. This gave Tiny the freedom to pursue offers from other booking agents, which he welcomed at first, but things quickly got messy. Over the next few years, he would accumulate a revolving door of small-time managers and agents similar to those he had known prior to his stardom: Mr. Jacoby (who 'knows the big boys'), Mr. Ward, Mr. Rocky, Mr. Connolly, Mr. Zehn, and, of course, the mysterious 'Johnny D.,' whom Tiny described in his diaries as 'the big man' and 'the godfather.' His new lawyer, Mr. Gargano, an associate of 'the big man,' was also on the payroll. Eventually, Joe Cappy retained his oversight, lording over the smaller agents and collecting a commission. Tiny's crowd of courtiers made many promises, delivered little, but always came to collect when Tiny got paid.

Caught up in a web of agents and contracts, Tiny soldiered on in seedy nightclubs and motel lounges. He found solace in collaboration, working with virtually anyone willing to put in the effort. During this time he recorded countless tapes in private homes and ramshackle recording studios across the country. One of these collaborations was with sixteen-year-old aspiring musician and producer Richard Barone.

During a tour of the Southern states with Australian-born small-time agent Peter Ward in February 1976, Tiny performed at a Travel Lodge Motel in Tampa, Florida. Barone, who was well versed in popular music from the 60s, and often attended shows in smaller venues, was nonetheless surprised to learn that Tiny Tim would be performing there. 'The Travel Lodge Motels in Florida were kind of like these road side motels,' he recalls. 'It wasn't really a place where concerts would be held.' Nevertheless, Barone and his friends drove out to see the show, but as minors, they were not allowed inside the motel's lounge. Instead, they listened intently through the door. At the show's end, Tiny burst through the lounge doors and into the lobby, and Barone seized the moment to speak to him. When he explained that he and his friends had not been able to attend, Tiny replied, 'Well why don't you come to my hotel room, and I'll do the show for you there?'

Barone and his friends were ecstatic. 'He was a true star to me, so we were thrilled,' he says. For the rest of the evening, the three teens sat, entranced, watching Tiny Tim perform from the edge of his bed, as if to a stadium of thousands. Tiny's performance piqued Barone's interest in producing, and he suggested the group return the next night with a tape recorder. The next afternoon, Barone borrowed a cassette recorder from a friend, and, that night, Tiny took the three teens on a musical odyssey. In between stories of the Page Three and Miss Snooky, Tiny performed versions of the 1916 Henry Burr song 'Baby Shoes,' falsetto renditions of Neil Sedaka's 'Laughter In The Rain' and Janis Ian's 'At Seventeen,' and several takes of the 1925 song he hoped would be his next single, 'I've Never Seen A Straight Banana.'

Tiny relished the attention, and the adulation the kids bestowed upon him cheered his heavy spirits. By the end of the session, he excitedly thanked them for making his trip to Florida a 'heavenly sunshine,' repeating several times, 'These moments are rare!'

While Barone proved to be a great outlet for Tiny, Tiny's approach to music influenced the young producer and performer as well. 'He helped me see a wider view of pop than my narrow view of the time, which was more just contemporary artists that I liked,' Barone says. 'He would show me something that I still keep with me, which is that pop is this sort of continuum. He would make connections between all the artists … there was a lot of cross-referencing going on. He was truly a musicologist and musician, with an understanding of pop music that was unparalleled … he knew what songs did, what they could do, and he understood the lineage of pop music from the Edison discs and wax cylinders, to the most current records.'

After the Travel Lodge in Tampa, Tiny Tim continued on his tour of Florida, stopping next in St. Petersburg. Richard and his friends visited Tiny there as well. At the time, one of them, Marla, was working at a local four-track recording studio, Recnac Recording, and Richard wanted to try something more serious than the hotel room tapes. 'Why don't we go to the studio and make a real recording?' he suggested to Tiny, who agreed.

When they picked Tiny up at his hotel, Barone found himself momentarily alone with Tiny while the girls freshened up in the bathroom. He watched Tiny applying his makeup in the hotel room vanity mirror. His smile had faded, and his eyes had lost the enthusiasm of a few minutes prior. 'Oh, youth,' Tiny said, in low voice. 'Where have you gone?' When the girls returned, Tiny immediately regained his convivial expression, smiling as he stepped back from the mirror. To Barone, Tiny looked considerably older than his forty-four years.

The trip to the studio was quite a spectacle. 'Tiny was in my front seat, warming up the whole time,' Barone continues, laughing as he recalls the rubberneckers staring in disbelief at the small car containing one of the world's most recognizable faces. 'We're in traffic, and Tiny was singing at the top of his lungs, with the trash bag full of paprika-spiced popcorn, which he said was good for his voice, and his ukulele … you can't miss a true star, so there was a lot of activity on both ways of that drive.'*

---

* Tiny mentioned the benefits of popcorn on his voice again two years later, during an appearance on *The Merv Griffin Show*. 'I always wondered why I talked higher coming out of a movie,' Griffin replied.

Barone wanted to record Tiny Tim just as he had in the hotel room, because he 'liked the chemistry' of Tiny in a relaxed environment, with only his ukulele, singing a variety of his own selections freely. When they entered the studio, Tiny sat Indian-style on the floor of the studio while Barone positioned a few microphones around him. Then he rolled tape and let Tiny 'do his thing.' After a few sessions, they had a considerable amount of material: various songs from the turn of the century, as well as several takes of 'I've Never Seen A Straight Banana' and a version of 'Dear Tuesday,' on which Tiny accompanied himself on a 12-string guitar. This material, combined with the hotel room recordings, would be for a full-length album.

It was at this point that Barone began to register alarm at Tiny's optimism. 'I was still in high school and didn't really have any kind of connections to be making an album,' he recalls, 'and he was treating me as if I was an actual producer … I really did the best I could, but really, I had no connections at any labels.'* Tiny excitedly discussed plans to release 'I've Never Seen A Straight Banana' as a single. 'It has to hit,' he told Barone. 'We could all be in California by Christmas!'

While recording with Tiny, Barone learned another lesson about the music business. While at Recnac, the studio's owners pulled Tiny aside and made a back-door deal to record a disco-themed take on 'Tip-Toe Thru' The Tulips' called 'Tip-Toe Disco.' 'I was appalled,' says Barone. 'This was exactly the type of thing that I was trying to get Tiny away from, but it gave me a sense of the types of shady deals that sometimes go on in show business.'

Aside from offering some humorous one-liners from Tiny—'I put some magic on my ukulele strings, they started jumpin', doin' crazy things!'—'Tip-Toe Disco' did nothing but present Tiny as a novelty act trying to cash in on a popular dance trend by rehashing his own brief celebrity. Copies were pressed in 1977 on the small TCC label, but it went nowhere. Tiny, too, must have held 'Tip-Toe Disco' in no regard, as he remained focused on the material he had recorded with Barone and adamant that they find a label to help wrap up and release it. However, when Barone sent the tapes to a few labels, he received no response. He was also distracted by the overwhelming desire to start a career of his own. 'Tiny was telling us all these stories because he knew that I didn't need

---

* Barone did, however, introduce Tiny Tim to John Lennon associate David Peel. The two got together once they were back in New York and Peel recorded Tiny singing, in addition to other Beatles-related material, a cover of Peel's own hit, 'Bring Back The Beatles.' The tapes remain unreleased.

to be in Tampa—I needed to be in New York City,' he explains. After finishing high school, Barone moved to the city, where he enjoyed success with his group, The Bongos. His recordings with Tiny were shelved until 2009.[*]

* * *

As the year trudged on, there were rumors of Tiny possibly appearing as a scoutmaster in a TV series like *The Brady Bunch* or *The Partridge Family*, but it never came to fruition. Instead, he continued traveling the Deep South with Peter Ward for another series of engagements—some semi-prestigious, the rest on a par with the Travel Lodge Motel. One newspaper article from the period covered an engagement in Miami, mentioning poignantly that the venue was only seven blocks from the Fontainebleau Hotel, where Tiny had earned $65,000 eight years earlier. Another article quotes an interaction between Tiny and a local woman who told him her son thought he was 'a genius.' Tiny replied that her son 'must have been drinking.' He had also begun to describe himself as 'down and out' during interviews.

A portrait of Tiny during this period is provided by Harve Mann, who, along with his then-partner Cheree Cookman, served as Tiny's opening act and backing band during the latter half of 1976 into 1977. 'I had an act called The Harve & Cheree Show,' Mann explains. 'Florida was our home base at the time, and we recorded our first recordings at a studio in Florida, and I wrote all the music, but there was one song that was kind of in Tiny's style. It was kind of a throwback to the 20s. We were talking like, God, if we could get this to Tiny Tim.'

As fate would have it, Cheree met Peter Ward and convinced him to come and see The Harve & Cheree Show at Disney World. Ward liked what he saw and offered the duo the opportunity to serve as Tiny's opening act and backup band for an upcoming tour through Nashville, Florida, and California. Mann's recollections of Ward make him sound much softer than Tiny's usual cohorts. 'He didn't seem like a gangster. He was a nice guy.'

To Mann, the idea that Tiny was a has-been—and what's more, that Tiny seemed to buy into that idea—was ridiculous. 'His career hadn't faded that much. He always worked. I mean … [this] was not his highest period, but we worked big places. There's a lot of celebrities like this: they're not exactly right at the top, so they'll do some jobs where it's, you know, maybe not the pride of

---

[*] They were released on CD in 2009 by Collector's Choice Music as *I've Never Seen A Straight Banana: Rare Moments Volume 1.*

their career, but at the same time, the next day or next week, they'll be doing some big thing.'

Harve & Cheree's tour with Tiny Tim began on August 23, at the Winston County Fair in Double Springs, Alabama. After their opening act, Harve would switch over to an electric keyboard and conduct whatever pickup band had been booked, provided there was one. 'I remember the first show. I thought things had gone wrong,' Mann recalls. 'I went back to see [Tiny] and he [had] loved it. He was very happy if you were energetic, particularly during [the] long medley … it would always end up with people jumping around, dancing and going crazy. I never did any show with him where he got less than a standing ovation. His live performances were always a success, and it felt great to be a part of it.'

The Deep South was a curious setting for Tiny, as it was difficult to predict how audiences would react to his effeminate image. The receptions ranged from enthusiastic to downright hostile. One pianist he worked with, Bill Calloway, recalls playing piano for Tiny at a trailer park bar. The stage was situated inside a steel cage, which was only accessible via a ramp. Once the performers entered the cage, they were locked in, and the ramp was removed. They endured a constant barrage of bottles and cans hurled at the cage.

There were other reminders, too, of Tiny's fringe status in the Bible Belt. One time, Harve Mann overheard Tiny gasp as he watched a popular televangelist proclaim, 'We don't need these false prophets, we don't need these fake Christians, we don't need these fruitcakes like Tiny Tim going around saying they're a Christian!' Another time, a chair was hurled in the direction of the stage, though Mann believed it had been done out of genuine excitement for Tiny's medley. 'I don't think it was vindictive, but it came close enough to where he looked a little unnerved by it. He made a comment: Oh, my God, did you see somebody threw a chair at me?'

On their way out of a show in Alabama, Harve Mann got a taste of Tiny's religious sincerity. A member of a rock band with whom they had shared a bill approached their vehicle as they prepared to leave.

'Hey, Tiny,' said the man as he held up a joint, 'wanna get high?'

'Keep away, Satan!' Tiny exclaimed, as Ward's car pulled out of the parking lot.

As the small tour made its way down through the South, Mann, like Richard Barone before him, was captivated by Tiny's stories of his years in the big time. 'I was fascinated with him,' Mann recalls. 'Late at night, I'd just sit in his room and he was ... just talking about this that and the other, Rudy Vallee and *Laugh-In*, and I was fascinated.' Like Barone, Mann recorded a voluminous amount of material while visiting with Tiny in his hotel room.*

Meanwhile, the Playboy Press published Harry Stein's book, *Tiny Tim: An Unauthorized Biography*, which included numerous interviews with Tiny alongside accounts from Miss Vicki, Richard Perry, Ron DeBlasio, Roy Silver, Craig Tennis, and Jack Rabin. In addition to Tiny's relatively accessible former associates, Stein had also tracked down and included interviews from several obscure figures from Tiny's past, like Kiki Hall and George King.

Harry Stein notes that though Tiny Tim generated some interest from reviewers—it was reviewed in both the daily and Sunday *New York Times*, for instance—it did not sell well. 'The book had some huge fans,' he recalls, 'including Nora Ephron, with whom I was then working at *Esquire*, and who almost served as its unofficial publicist. And over the years it has had a cult following and generated some serious film interest. But at the time, no one really understood why anyone would be interested in Tiny Tim or his fly-by-night career.' To date, *Tiny Tim: An Unauthorized Biography* has not been reissued in any capacity, and it remains largely unavailable.

Before the book was pulled from shelves, however, Tiny was able to get his hands on a copy, and read it, along with the accompanying book reviews, while they were on the road. Mann watched Tiny's reaction to the book and subsequent reviews, which were peppered with base comments like 'a loud, Jewish, yenta mother can really do a kid in.' Many of the reviews addressed Tiny's sexuality, which Stein chronicled but drew no definitive conclusions about. Many also questioned Tiny's sanity. One even suggested that Tiny was schizophrenic, and when Tiny came upon the supposition, Mann saw a half-bewildered, half-amused expression wash across his face. 'I think he liked it in a certain way,' he recalls. 'It's the same look he'd get if we went to a place and there wasn't a big audience or a lot of sales for the show. He was funny like that.'

In October 1976, Tiny—his anger perhaps reignited by Vicki's comments in Harry Stein's book, and still miffed by his failed bid for custody of Tulip—launched a $15 million lawsuit against Hugh Hefner and Playboy Enterprises, Inc., which owned *Oui* magazine. He sought damages for the incorporation of his photograph in Vicki's nude photo spread. According to the *New York Times*,

---

* Mann was also able to get Tiny into the studio, where they laid down recordings of several of Mann's compositions, including, 'Haribee,' 'Perhaps In The Next Life,' and 'Any Rainy Day.' They remain unreleased.

he charged that the photos used his image in a way that was 'erotic, suggestive, and lewd' and that they were 'humiliating, embarrassing, and unnatural.' It seems his desire to extract some form of revenge for the photo spread must have gone unfulfilled, however, as no other information on the lawsuit has been made available, and Tiny never discussed it in interviews.

* * *

In 1977, Tiny appeared on two singles, the first being the aforementioned 'Tip-Toe Disco.' The second, '(I'm Gonna Be A) Country Queen' b/w 'I Ain't No Cowboy (I Just Found This Hat),' was of considerably better quality. Produced by the soon-to-be successful country singer Leon Everette, the single was released on True Records. The A-Side, about a straight-laced country singer who has decided to shake things up by becoming a drag queen, feels almost autobiographical in parts:

> *I've been thinkin',*
> *It ain't my singin',*
> *That's holdin' up the show,*
> *It's the way I look that just ain't hookin',*
> *The folks on Music Row …*

Tiny's foray into country music yielded little more than a few pot shots from critics. 'Hope it's as "successful" as Twiggy's wasn't!' one reviewer sniped. Tiny, too, was less than optimistic, telling the *Palm Beach Post*, 'I'm not becoming a country star. Eddy Arnold has no fears.' But he did become irked when the press insinuated that his country-music recordings were an 'about-face.'

'I'm the same man I always was,' he told the press. 'I'm nothing but a song-plugger. I've always practiced country songs in the mirror … none of these things are new to me.' In any case, the record failed to chart, and no further recordings with Everette followed.*

* * *

In March, Tiny and Miss Vicki saw each other for the first time since their separation in 1974. Vicki paid Tiny's $95 cab fare to that so he could visit her

---

* Tiny had alluded in interviews to the recording of a third country song with Everette, possibly a version of Lanny Grey's 'I Never Harmed An Onion (So Why Do They Make Me Cry?'), but it remains unreleased.

and Tulip in southern New Jersey. Details of the meeting cropped up in a few errant articles around that time, with Tiny telling the *Rome News-Tribune* that Vicki looked 'great' and was 'very kind' to him.

'He came once during those years,' Vicki recalls. 'Tulip was … four or five. He called and said he wanted to see her. He did that several times and I would say, Fine, let me know when, and then he would never call back. One night, he finally got there at 3am. She was asleep. She had to go to school in the morning. He said, Oh, just wake her up. I said, No, she has to go to school in the morning. He sat on the couch and we talked for a little while and he left.'

Though she had been cordial to her estranged husband, after three years of separation, Vicki wanted to finalize the divorce. She had grown increasingly annoyed at Tiny's refusal to cooperate. 'It was very frustrating,' she says. 'I didn't have money to spend on a lawyer … and it's not like he did, either.'

By then, Tiny's divorce attorney was Phillip Paley, who had been assigned to the case by Doris Sassower. Paley remembers Tiny's argument was simple, even if he did needlessly prolong their meetings by reading passages from his diary detailing his desires for other women. 'As I recall it, he had no dispute with the idea that the child should live with Miss Vicki and nothing bad to say about Miss Vicki. He made clear that he had committed no act of matrimonial wrong. He did not believe that courts had any power to dissolve marriages if there was not an act of fault involved … so he wanted me to do whatever I could to try to preserve the marriage and try to reconcile.'

The courts, however, were not in Tiny's favor. In 1971, the state of New Jersey had passed the Uniform Divorce and Marriage Act, which introduced the 'no fault' divorce, whereby the spouse asking for a divorce does not have to prove the other is at fault. 'I explained to him that it was an uphill battle,' says Paley. 'He said that he wasn't going to use the child as a bargaining chip. He was going to be honorable and straightforward. So I thought that he was a sincere guy.'

Adding to Tiny's already low state of mind, he was greatly 'disturbed' when on October 14, just ten days before the divorce trial, his idol, Bing Crosby, died of a massive heart attack. As the days ticked down, Paley made sure that his client was aware of the court date, October 24, and of the argument he planned to present the judge. When the day arrived, Vicki was present with her attorney, and a myriad of reporters swarmed the courtroom, but Tiny was *in absentia*. After a short recess, during which Paley attempted in vain to contact Tiny, Judge Lowengrub reconvened the hearing.

'Mr. Paley,' he said, 'What is your position?'

'I am satisfied that there is an argument to be made that the no fault divorce statute is unconstitutional when it's applied to somebody who believes there is a possibility of reconciliation,' Paley replied.

'I am satisfied that your argument is not sound,' Judge Lowengrub replied. 'I'm going to take the testimony of Vicki Budinger, and she will testify that there is no possibility of reconciliation, that the parties have been living separate and apart and have not had marital relations for a period of eighteen months. We're going to deal with the custody of the child and award it to Vicki Budinger.'

With that, Judge Lowengrub granted Vicki a divorce from Tiny Tim; their marriage, which had been conceived and conducted in a media firestorm eight years earlier, now unraveled in a mere ninety minutes in court. Vicki did not seek alimony or child support for Tulip, now six, and was glad to be rid of the weighty matter. Furthermore, the media's unwillingness to print more than a hundred words on the subject shows that reporters, like Vicki, had lost interest in even the spiciest of Tiny's troubles. Accompanying an article was a photograph of Vicki looking resplendent as she exited the courthouse. Though Paley filed an appeal, it was rejected.*

In subsequent interviews, Tiny explained that he had been in Florida during the divorce hearing and could not afford to fly to New Jersey. He also remained adamant that he felt the divorce was not legitimate. 'I don't believe in divorce,' he told Joan Rivers in a 1989 interview. 'Miss Vicki got her divorce because the state of Jersey gave it to her, but I never signed anything.'

* * *

In January 1978, Tiny performed at the Allied Joint Force Command base in Naples, Italy. From there, he headed back to the States to headline the Comedy Store, where he was one of the first solo acts to appear on their brand-new main room stage. Of course, the high-profile booking was met with the obligatory jabs from the press. 'Fans of Tiny Tim can stop wondering what happened to the camp creation of the 60s,' the *Wilmington Star News* reported. 'He's back on the scene—for the moment, at least. And looking as tacky and seedy as ever.'

When the show opened on January 18, the reception was mixed. The

---

* Both Sassower and Paley later sued Tiny for unpaid legal fees. Paley says he was eventually paid, but it is unclear whether Sassower was.

Los Angeles Times gave a bad review and *Variety* gave a positive one. Tiny was visited by his old friends from the Phantom Cabaret, Wavy Gravy and Severn Darden, and also by crooner Nick Lucas. Even more important, however, was a visit by several former friends who wished to bury the hatchet: Roy Silver, Jeff Wald, Ron DeBlasio, and Richard Perry. Tiny was moved that the four men, about whom he had made inflammatory accusations to Harry Stein just a few years prior, had come to wish him well. He called them all onstage and addressed the elephant in the room, as he later related to Harve Mann. 'I said right over the microphone, I did say those things, but if anyone comes up like they did after this, I really appreciate that, and I won't mention this to the press no more—and I never have since that time. I have told the press, even if [Roy Silver] did take this money, which I'm not sure if he did anyway … he was still the best manager I ever had.' After the show, Tiny accompanied the group to Silver's Chinese food restaurant on Sunset Boulevard. 'I pray to forgive them all,' he wrote in his diary later that night, 'start a new page.'

The next afternoon, Richard Perry took Tiny on a tour of his recording studio, Studio 55. Despite this, Tiny was quick to tell the *Pasadena Star-News* that his public appearance with DeBlasio, Wald, Silver, and Perry was nothing more than a gesture of good will. 'Though they still have their fame, they were yesterday's headlines,' he said. 'I never look back—and now I have to find tomorrow's Richard Perry.' This statement seems absurd when one pauses to look at Richard Perry's successes following Tiny Tim. In the eight years since their split, he had produced hit records for Barbra Streisand, Ringo Starr, Harry Nilsson, Carly Simon, Manhattan Transfer, and Diana Ross, and was about to launch his own label, Planet Records, on which he would score several top five hits with the Pointer Sisters.

On January 23, the same day the *Pasadena Star-News* article ran, Tiny was fired from the Comedy Store engagement due to poor attendance. 'I will be back in Hollywood, Lord willing,' Tiny wrote in his diary. 'This time I will make it again.'

Before leaving Los Angeles, Tiny taped an appearance on *The Merv Griffin Show*. Heavier than ever before, Tiny lumbered out onto the stage and sang a rehashed version of 'Tip-Toe' in cracking falsetto, along with 'Good Morning Mr. Zip Zip Zip' and 'It's A Sin To Tell A Lie,' sung as a duet with frequent audience member Mrs. Miller.

Griffin seemed unaware that Tiny had been performing in town. 'Where have you been?' he asked. 'I haven't seen you for a while.'

'Well, I've been working all the time,' Tiny explained. 'It's just I've been working smaller clubs in Pennsylvania, New Jersey, and New York.' He omitted his recent short-lived booking at the Comedy Store.

Tiny returned to New York for an engagement at the Copacabana, which had begun operating as a discotheque. Now that he was back in the immediate vicinity of his corrupt clique of managers and agents, they all took an increased interest. A dancer was added to his performances, and she would occasionally bear her breasts onstage, depending on the virtues of the venue.

Tiny's diary entries from the time indicate a frustration with the state of things past and present. 'My heart O Lord is hateful,' he wrote, on May 11. 'It hates people who reject me … it is especially hateful of Jews.* It hates people like Florence Henderson, who also they say said nasty things about my wedding in 1969 when she was on the show. But O Lord I pray for the strength to forgive and a heart to change—to love.'

* * *

The late 70s saw a mild resurgence in Tiny's social life. He began to wear trendy, burgundy three-piece velvet suits with wide lapels, flared slacks, and ruffled tuxedo shirts, and he sometimes went out dancing in nightclubs. When the papers ran photos of him dancing with actress-model Victoria Johnson at Studio 54, Tiny made it clear that he had no intention on moving on from Vicki, despite the divorce. 'I'm married till death do us part,' he told the *Washington Post*. 'I believe marriage is a sacred institution. I cannot get married again.'

Some temptations managed to slip past Tiny's moral declarations. Miss Jan, the young girl who had attended Tiny and Vicki's wedding and watched on in abject misery, was now in her early twenties, and had not given up the chase. Tiny had successfully shielded himself from her when she materialized at the New Tiny Tim show in Torrance, California, thanks to Jim Cappy. She succeeded only in watching the show as an audience member, but apparently became so worked up during his rendition of 'Sunshine' that she fainted.

By 1978, Jan had moved to New York City, and Tiny continually vacillated between showing affection for her and attempting to banish her from his life.

---

* According to Miss Sue, 'Tiny never got over his constant sense of rejection by his mother's side of the family. They also disliked his father, and that was just as much of a problem to him. Tiny just didn't identify as being Jewish. He knew it intellectually, but emotionally he had trouble accepting it. To him, his mother had been cruel to him, and the Jews were her people, and he painted them all with the same brush.'

He had his agent, Mr. Jacoby, tell her to leave him alone and 'make a new life for herself,' but when she showed up at one of his shows at the Copacabana in March, he allowed her to visit. Finally on August 19, after forty-six years of relative celibacy outside of marriage, he succumbed to temptation.

After Jan departed, a devastated Tiny phoned Miss Vicki. When Tulip answered the phone, he wept. The next day, however, despite a returned call from Miss Vicki, he had sex with Jan again, but the self-loathing continued. 'Miss Jan is just another glory seeker and publicity freak looking for a big name,' he wrote. 'I pray to get rid of her and start anew.' The next day, Jan visited Tiny on her lunch break, hoping to give him a bag of oranges, but he refused to let her up to his room.

Many years later, Tiny admitted to his third wife, Miss Sue, that he also had sex with an exotic dancer named Miss Popcorn during this period. 'It was a one-night stand that he impulsively gave into it,' Sue recalls, 'and he felt deeply pained and terribly ashamed about it, because it was the only physical relationship that he had that was not accompanied by a close emotional relationship. It was pure sex, and Tiny didn't believe in that. I think it was right after his marriage [to Vicki] was over. He was being sexually active finally, and I'm sure it was very difficult to go back to being celibate after being married.'

The episode with Miss Jan started a sexual avalanche of sorts for Tiny. Once, while walking the city late at night, he was confronted by a prostitute, bent on taking his wallet in exchange for a sexual favor.

'What do you want, Tiny?' she asked suggestively, as she began touching him. Defeated, he asked her for a hand job. Whatever occurred sexually, the prostitute did take his wallet, and afterward Tiny had to find a pay phone to call Harve Mann, who was living in New York City. 'I don't know if he actually got [the hand job],' Mann says. 'He felt so terrible, probably because he gave in to sin. He called me up and I came and got him home. [Later] he sent me a note and thanked me … he really felt guilty about that.'

On another occasion, Tiny called Mann up to invite him to a movie, but gave him only the address of the theater and not the title of the film. 'We get there and it's a porno movie,' Mann recalls. 'Tiny has a hood on, and he had a strategy that I bought the ticket and he slipped in real fast. As it turned out, Tiny had seen a picture—I guess the ad for this film—in the newspaper and he liked the girl. I don't think it was lust as much as this was an *angel*, and he was gonna save her. I don't know. I think the only reason he wanted me there was just for protection, and to buy the tickets. I remember there was this one scene where a priest was doing it with the girl. He reacted real strongly: Oh, my goodness, there's gonna be a lawsuit!'

Tiny began to conflate his newfound interest in pornography with a desire to jumpstart his career. He was, after all, living in New York City during the so-called golden age of porn. In Times Square in 1978, adult theaters vastly outnumbered traditional movie theaters. Tiny had first mentioned the idea of appearing in a smut film to Harry Stein in 1975, outlining his ideas for a project to be called *The Seduction of Mr. T*; Marilyn Chambers, the star of *Behind The Green Door*, would seduce him. Another would be entitled *The Man They Love To Hate*; Tiny would sing Kris Kristofferson's 'Help Me Make It Through The Night' in falsetto while being seduced by a beautiful vixen.

In a taped conversation between Tiny and his mega fan and future producer Martin Sharp, known among Tiny Tim collectors as *The Pickle Method*, Tiny described some of his sexual desires and motivations in detail. He explained that though he had been married and preached family values, he justified his own failed relationships and interest in pornography by conceding that he simply could not function with women in any normal capacity.

'I am no good for women,' he said. 'I can't function with them in the normal world the way the others do. I can't take them out for meals ... I can't be seen with them in public.' He then went into a convoluted explanation of how his sexual desires differed from those of other men. In short, he felt that, because his primary aim was to pleasure and worship women, he occupied a moral high ground. 'I always want to keep these women ... like people collect stamps or coins. I consider that as the greatest gift that the Lord has given to man, to be cherished and framed and adored in God's grace and righteousness.'

Finally, Tiny arrived at the nub of his point. 'These are the ideas that go through my mind, clashing with God's laws, of course,' he said. 'This is why doing a porno movie would not be new to me, because when I'm alone in my room after 12, these [things] go on constantly.' He also believed that a porno film was the perfect vehicle for introducing the public to his 'serious' singing style, and planned to juxtapose his nude scenes against a soundtrack featuring his versions of standards like 'Wonderful World Of Romance' and 'Wrap Your Troubles In Dreams.' His idea was for these songs to be 'brought to a non-clothed entity for the first time in this business with a major name ... we have the world at our feet in this generation today, which is only buying these types of movies ... people would look at this movie and say, Hey, as bad as this movie is, this guy can sing.'

Unlike some of his other, wilder ideas—which included a scheme to 'dehydrate water and put it into bags'—Tiny's adult film concept almost came to fruition. That same year, he received a call from comedian Jackie Vernon, whom he knew from the tours with Roy Radin. Vernon pitched Tiny's movie idea to Bucky Searles, the writer, composer, and performer of 1976's *Alice in Wonderland: An X-Rated Musical Comedy*, and Searles was interested in having Tiny's film produced. All Vernon needed to proceed was a letter of permission, which Tiny's lawyer, Mr. Gargano, provided, and a promise to keep the affair 'confidential: no press, no public.'

Tiny received a call from Searles, and they began to discuss the finer details of the project: the movie was to be produced in California, and Tiny would have complete control over the casting process. Though Searles was concerned as to whether Tiny could maintain an erection throughout the duration of each scene, Tiny was not worried. He felt the focus was to be on the 'fantasies of Tiny Tim,' which meant penetration not by him but by 'artificial ones.'

According to Tiny, Searles was on the verge of buying him a ticket to California, until Jackie Vernon thwarted the deal. There was a 'money problem,' Tiny told Martin Sharp. 'I hear Mr. Vernon got a little greedy.'

Vernon had asked Tiny not to go to Hollywood until he had returned from an engagement in Indiana, and, 'out of respect,' Tiny agreed. When Vernon returned, he informed Tiny that he no longer wanted to do business with Searles, having instead found a producer in San Francisco. Then Tiny fielded a call from the 'San Francisco party,' who offered only net points on the project in exchange for his work on the picture. Mr. Gargano rejected the offer and asked that the new party put $100,000 in escrow in good faith, 'just in case … the movie takes the opposite effect,' as Tiny put it.

Negotiations continued, and Gargano flew to Law Vegas to meet the 'San Francisco party,' who was surprised by Tiny's financial expectations, having evidently been told by Vernon, 'Forget Tiny. He doesn't need too much money.'

'To make a long story short, the whole deal fell through,' Tiny told Sharp. 'In one light, I was happy, because I prayed to the good Lord about this. From the standpoint of career, I was not, but naturally I can understand.'

While all of this—Miss Jan, Miss Popcorn, the porn projects—was going on, Tiny began to communicate with Vicki again on friendly and possibly romantic terms. In June 1978, she attended one of Tiny's performances, and Tiny wrote that she was 'beautiful as ever.' The next day, the two spent the afternoon talking on the telephone, and Tiny also began helping Vicki with her rent payments. 'Possible reconciliation nearer than ever,' he wrote optimistically.

The two had also briefly rekindled their romantic sensibilities in March 1977, curiously just six months before the divorce proceedings. In a 1979 interview with *Soho Weekly*, Tiny claimed that he had visited Vicki at that time and that they had 'made love only once … [but] been talking ever since.' Whatever happened between them, it did not have staying power, and nor did it bring Tiny closer to Tulip. Once, Tiny wrote during this period, when the little girl answered the phone for her mother, he found himself unable to introduce himself as her father.

* * *

In July 1978, Tiny found himself on Roy Radin's *Vaudeville '78* summer tour, for which he was billed as The King Of Nostalgia. The *New York Times* caught up with Tiny at a show for the Patrolmen's Benevolent Association in New London, Connecticut, where Tiny claimed that Radin's tours were his ticket back to the big time.

'Oh, there's nothing to do at home, anyway,' he told reporter Fred Ferretti. 'Miss Vicki's gone. There's no place like Hollywood, and I believe that it will be through this tour that I will come back. The odds are against it, but I have to keep working. I'll never stop fighting to get back. I don't want to go to Asia or Europe. I want to go to Hollywood and climb the mountain again.'

Whether Tiny truly maintained such a hope is difficult to ascertain. In contrast, Donald O'Connor painted a bleaker, and perhaps more honest, picture of the situation to Ferretti. 'Would I like to retire?' he asked. 'Sure, but if I did, I'd have to eat my newspaper clippings … the only thing left is Roy.'

After Radin's summer tour, Tiny returned to New York in late July and found himself 'depressed and down over my career, girls.' He preoccupied himself by producing *The Tiny Tim Variety Show* for Channel C in Fort Lee, New Jersey. His agents were momentarily pacified by the $3 audition cost and talk of 250 eager auditionees. Tiny's mother, Tillie, was his first guest.

On October 19, Tiny Tim and Marvin Lewis departed New York City for an extensive, several-month long tour of Australia at the invitation of artist Martin Sharp. While Tiny's lame duck agents in New York seemed content with the status quo, Sharp was about to risk his own career and fortune in his attempts to revive Tiny Tim's.

CHAPTER SIXTEEN

THE ETERNAL TROUBADOUR

I know Mr. Sharp believes in me so much—and I praise the Lord for that—and maybe he's made a cult movie which at the very least will survive as a museum piece. But Mr. Sharp, I think, is interested more than ever in my thoughts on this world and its cataclysmic times, on my fundamentalist spiritual attitudes.

TINY TIM, SPEAKING AT THE *STREET OF DREAMS* PREMIERE IN BRIGHTON, ENGLAND, 1988

During the course of Tiny's career, many took a passing fancy to his music, shock value, or exhaustive knowledge of song, but they usually did so for their own benefit. His revolving door of managers, producers, and female companions, as well as a fickle fan base, bloodthirsty media cohorts, and largely unsupportive family, frequently left Tiny adrift and lonely. However, there was one who must be distinguished as Tiny's Truest Fan: Martin Sharp.

Considered Australia's most prominent pop artist, Sharp rose to prominence in the world of art and entertainment as the co-founder of the underground magazine *Oz*, for which he also served as both a contributor and art director until 1965. The magazine achieved its notoriety when the Australian authorities charged its three founders, including Sharp, for printing 'obscene' material.

In Sydney, Martin went on to enjoy a string of successful art exhibitions and published a book entitled *Martin Sharp Cartoons*. He then made his way to London, where he quickly integrated himself into the art and music scene and was introduced to a young musician named Eric Clapton. Sharp offered up a poem to Clapton that became 'Tales Of Brave Ulysses,' the B-Side to the Cream single 'Strange Brew.' Over the next few years, Sharp designed a slew of album covers, including Cream's *Disraeli Gears* and *Wheels Of Fire*.

After spending some time living in a tent in Bob Whitaker's studio, Sharp decided to move into a historic Georgian building, the Pheasantry, with Clapton and filmmaker Philippe Mora. At this time, he began exploring big band and depression-era music by the likes of Bing Crosby and Al Jolson. Clapton took note of Sharp's budding interest in music from the 20s and 30s and suggested that they attend Tiny's concert at the Royal Albert Hall. Clapton had caught Tiny's act at the Scene, and had, according to Sharp, 'been very touched by Tiny.'

'I was completely amazed,' Sharp recalled. 'I thought, This man will be—he is the best. He will be always honored.' He published his recollections of the concert two years later, in *Oz*, calling Tiny 'a true minstrel of the age … the wise man playing the fool, ambiguous, moldy-voiced, emerging as a great star at a late age after years of developing his art in obscurity.'

His head still spinning from Tiny's 'truly virtuoso performance,' Sharp went home, grabbed Clapton's copy of *God Bless Tiny Tim*, and cued it up on his turntable. 'It changed my life, that night,' he later recalled. 'I really thought it would be so hard to get to see him, and I never realized we would become great friends. The future was not visible to me at that stage; I just knew I'd seen someone [who] was a totally modern artist. A lot of people thought he was just doing nostalgia, but, to me, he was a totally modern artist and a pioneer of what could be called post-modernism, if you like.'

Over the next few years, Sharp's prediction that Tiny would earn global respect did not quite pan out, but his popular decline did make him more accessible. Sharp became a regular attendee of Tiny's shows and often spoke with him afterward. In 1974, when Tiny performed at the Western Suburbs Leagues Club in Newcastle, Australia, Sharp came prepared with a recorder and recorded the entire show off the soundboard. This, he said, is the moment when 'things started.' That recording marked the beginning of a Tiny Tim audio library that would eventually grow to include over a thousand hours of recorded interviews and performances.

'Tiny was so pleased that there was someone interested in him,' Sharp said. 'People loved him, even though they came to gawk at him as a curiosity, but he swept them away with his medleys. He touched them all with the great old songs and songs that were in everyone's blood stream, somehow or the other.'

In Newcastle, Sharp recorded Tiny in his dressing room as he performed a heart-wrenching rendition of 'To Die Of Love.' He knew that Tiny was singing about Miss Vicki, and said so.

'How do you know these things?' Tiny replied, shocked.

'You stand very naked before me,' said Sharp.

'The good Lord has blessed you with a fantastic inner-sight, my friend, because there's so many who sit around and think I'm out of my mind. It's very rare that people like you understand this.'

Sharp subsequently traveled to London to try to drum up further interest in Tiny there, but to no avail. 'In the end, I realized it was going to be up to me,' he said. 'I couldn't understand why people couldn't see what I could see. It seemed amazing to me that the master of the language of popular song and who was patriotic in his way and understanding of America … should not be the King of New York. That was his rightful position, and I thought a world that is not appreciative of Tiny Tim is not a world I admire.'

For Sharp, the places Tiny was performing were 'where faded stars went to grind their days,' and he told him so. 'I felt it was necessary to try to break him out of that sort of regime. When he came to Australia and we worked together … it was like these were his years of exile.' Over the course of the next year, Sharp continued to correspond with Tiny, as well as visiting him in Brooklyn at his apartment at the Premiere House. With each visit, his collection of tapes grew, and in June 1976 he brought Tiny out to Australia to fulfill a series of engagements, including several shows, recording, and filming. He would go on to visit Australia eleven times in total.

Surprisingly, the Cappelluzzos cooperated fully with Sharp's plans. 'They were very protective of him,' said Sharp. 'I don't think they saw him as an artist, but they were loyal to him.' He did however receive several nasty phone calls from Regency Entertainment, Tiny's official talent representatives in Australia, who 'got very cross with me for not having their permission. I just couldn't help myself, I just had to work with Tiny.'

While Tiny was in Australia, Sharp arranged to record some tracks with proper accompaniment. He was nervous about assuming the role of record producer, but his desire to work not only *with* Tiny but *for* Tiny, along with Tiny's encouragement, helped Sharp overcome the hesitation.

'I know nothing of recording,' Sharp had said.

'But you understand my songs, Mr. Sharp,' Tiny replied. 'That's the main thing, and desire is the greatest talent.'

Sharp had his work cut out for him. Not only did he receive 'pretty constant' discouragement from his own friends and acquaintances, Tiny's handlers were not motivated to free Tiny from what Sharp, quoting William Blake, called the 'Satanic Mills of Show Business.' 'It was very hard to … get

Tiny away from obligations and get him out of that context and to a place where he could get creative,' he said. 'I think the desire Tiny had to work moved it along, and it was really like he was working in exile. … He should have had a huge entourage and many people looking out for him but, here he was, pretty much a single person.'

Although the first recording session was to take place in his living room, Sharp invited along his friend and sound engineer Geoff Dorian, pianist Sharon Carlcast, and Nathan Waks, a classically trained cellist and arranger. Because Sharp was a well-known Australian artist and Waks a well-known Australian musician, the two traveled in the same social circles. Unaware of Sharp's fascination with Tiny Tim, however, Waks was surprised when Sharp called him and said, 'I've got Tiny Tim here. He's coming over.' Waks, who was seventeen years old in 1968, and had been studying classical music in Paris and England at the height of Tiny's fame, had not put much stock in Tiny Tim. He thought of Tiny as a 'freak-show [who] was enormously popular for a short period of time.'

Eight years later, Waks's opinion of Tiny Tim had not changed, but he still decided to help out with Sharp's session. 'I went out of respect, because Martin was a great artist and a friend,' he recalls. 'I wouldn't have said no, and I was intrigued.'

Martin Sharp would describe the collaboration between Nathan Waks and Tiny Tim as 'profound … like the music meeting the singer,' but Waks remembers it differently. 'At first, I thought it was a bit of a freak-show, and then the more I got to know Tiny and the more I talked to Martin, I realized that both of them were intensely serious about what they were doing … Martin had this vision of Tiny as a twentieth-century philosopher … the way he kind of wove in through the parables and some of the monologues and stuff where it's sort of religious, but humanist at the same time.'

The group recorded only a few songs during their first meeting, leaving Waks to echo the same frustrations as other musicians who attempted to play with Tiny. 'First of all, I didn't know any of the songs, and he was not musically accurate. He would leave beats out sometimes or put extra ones in to basically go with the word flow. It would *sound* coherent, but it was difficult to follow musically sometimes, because … that's just the way he was and once you got used to it and the band got used to skipping beats or adding them. There are passages of those performances which are remarkably together, considering rehearsal was never really something that was meaningful, other than getting to know roughly what was going to happen. There was no way to rehearse what was actually going to happen.'

Whatever the band and engineer felt about the session, Sharp and Tiny were pleased with the outcome, and the living room session served as the framework for plans on the horizon.* Though Tiny did not return to Australia in 1977, Sharp took any opportunity to heap praise upon him, in January 1977, in the Australian magazine *Quadrant*.

> It's hard to describe an artist without precedent; it's difficult to define in prose a musical experience which explodes all existing frontiers of popular song; no one like Tiny Tim has ever happened before and no one like Tiny Tim will ever happen again. …
>
> The closest analogy is the lyrebird, not only the most beautiful song bird in its own right, but composing concert collages of all other birds' songs woven together. I see Tiny Tim as a human lyrebird, The Man Of A Thousand Voices, The Eternal Troubadour, a Tin Pan Alley Orpheus singing for his lost Eurydice.

The Eternal Troubadour and The Human Lyrebird were just two among many nicknames Sharp bestowed upon Tiny; Eternal Troubadour in particular is perhaps the most apt nomenclatures for Tiny Tim. Historically, the medieval troubadour served as a library of music, and through travel and performance, he connected Europe in popular song for hundreds of years. Like Tiny Tim, troubadours carried in their minds extensive collections of music and were responsible for keeping alive that which would have otherwise been forgotten. Romantic and humanistic, troubadours focused on themes of chivalry, love, humor, and the metaphysical. Eternal themes, to which Tiny gave his life.

* * *

After a lull in 1977, Tiny and Sharp's partnership gained momentum. Martin Sharp was willing to throw some financial resources behind Tiny Tim projects,

---

* The vast majority of the session, which included renditions of 'After The Ball,' 'Laugh Clown Laugh,' 'My Daddy Long Legs,' 'With My Guitar,' 'Because I Love You,' 'I'll Take Care Of Your Cares,' 'Baby Shoes,' 'When They're Old Enough To Know Better,' and 'Believe Me If All Those Endearing Young Charms,' remains unreleased. The only track to be released thus far is 'Stardust,' which appeared on the 2008 compilation of the same title featuring unreleased Martin Sharp–produced Tiny Tim recordings.

and serious discussions began about bringing Tiny from Sharp's living room to the masses. Sharp wanted to assist Tiny in whatever path he decided to take, believing that Tiny's use of popular song was not unlike his own artwork. 'Tim's appropriation of song is very much like my appropriation of images,' he later said. 'We are both collagists taking the elements of different epochs and mixing them to discover new relationships.'

Tiny also respected Sharp as an artist, explaining to fan club president Bucks Burnett that Sharp 'speaks to me a fan *and* an artist.' Yet as was the case with any professional or personal relationship with Tiny, all was not roses. Tiny considered throwing an early wrench in their collaboration. On October 27 1978, Tiny wrote in his diary of how Sharp 'got a bit wicked with his tongue … making a remark about me being a godfather to Miss Tulip. It will be more difficult for him now.'

Eventually, the two men happened upon the idea of a medley concert, in which Tiny would try to set a world record by singing the longest medley of songs ever attempted. Wanting to frame the show like an athletic event, Sharp called it The World Professional Non-Stop Singing Record, drawing on the legendary 1975 boxing match between Muhammad Ali and Antonio Inoki. His aim, he said, was to 'bring a Barnum & Bailey element to it … to give a context to Tiny's great gifts, and make it a challenge against time.'

Tiny decided that his goal would be to sing for two hours nonstop. For the venue, Sharp chose the Palais de Dance at Luna Park in Sydney, Australia, a floating pontoon ballroom and theater where, in 1973, he had been hired to reconstruct the massive clown face that served as the park's entrance. The concert was scheduled for January 12 1979.

In addition to the marathon medley at Luna Park, Sharp began generating money for three more Tiny Tim projects: two full-length albums and a film documenting their work together and centered around the Marathon Medley. Sharp named the business created to produce the projects after the 1932 Bing Crosby number Tiny planned to record, 'Street Of Dreams.'

The two albums, *Chameleon* and *Wonderful World Of Romance*, were intended to offer very different approaches in terms of production and curation. Sessions for the first were held at 301 Studios in Sydney on January 9, January 16, and May 10.* The title, *Chameleon*, spoke to Tiny's musical versatility. The album was approached as a conventional album and utilized a full band, under the

---

* The latter session also included 'Tiny Tim's EMI Medley,' a thirty-minute recreation of the World Professional Non-Stop Singing Record concert.

direction of Nathan Waks. Tiny chose the majority of the material, and the album, which was later released in a limited quantity of 400 copies in 1980, contained a total of twelve songs: 'Brother, Can You Spare A Dime,' 'It's A Long Way To Tipperary,' 'Deep Night,' 'The Song Without A Name,' 'The Hukilau,' 'The Great Pretender,' 'My Song,' 'Street Of Dreams,' 'Country Queen,' 'Mickey Mouse Club March,' 'Staying Alive,' and 'My Way.'* Outtakes from the sessions include versions of 'Summertime,' 'St. Louis Blues,' 'Courage My Friend,' 'Dietetic Baby,' and 'Dancing In The Street.'

In the liner notes, Sharp wrote of how Tiny 'sings with passion for those who gave their best in faith for a better world, only to discover that the system that had welcomed their courage and strength of their youth cast them aside like rubbish, when the war was over, the work done. ... Tiny, too, helped build a dream and found himself among the forgotten ones.'

For Nathan Waks, who had been promoted from living room cellist to Tiny Tim's musical director in Australia, the projects were satisfying, but he did not share Sharp's philosophical outlook on the work. 'I saw my role as being quite specific: to get the best musical result,' he explains. 'There were some times when it was quite breathtaking to listen to and quite virtuosic—the switching he would do live was quite amazing to hear.' For Waks, the highlights included 'Street Of Dreams,' 'Brother, Can You Spare A Dime,' 'Stayin' Alive,' and 'My Way.' 'I remember [those] as being the most musically satisfying because they were doing something that I felt was good enough to stand on its own.'

Waks also sought to steer Tiny away from using his falsetto, which by 1979 was beginning to become raspy. 'As he got older, he had greater difficulty hitting the high notes. His voice was in good shape, and I encouraged, as much as possible, the deep, full, rich sound that he could make, because that was, to me, the most musically satisfying.'

It had always been a goal of Tiny's to replicate the sound, acoustics, and style of the recordings made during the early years of the recording industry. In the past, he had experimented with the bullhorn and manipulation of his voice, but still he felt that the modern engineering of his records did not do him justice, so he began exploring other means of achieving that authentic sound. It intrigued him that virtually all of his favorite recording artists had not enjoyed the luxury of multi-track recording, but instead had recorded live to a master disc.

---

* The version of 'Country Queen' is the same version that was released on True Records in 1977. Sharp acquired the rights to the song in order to include it on the album.

Prior to recording in Australia, Tiny had enjoyed the opportunity to record to an Edison cylinder record, the first medium for music distribution, which was most popular between 1896 and 1915. Employees at the Edison Museum in Illinois had devised a way to record new music onto old Edison cylinders by shaving off the existing grooves and using restored acoustic-era recording equipment to record new grooves. Tiny, with the piano accompaniment of Marvin Lewis, cut two cylinders: a version of 'School Days,' performed, as always, in the style of Byron G. Harlan, and a version of 'Goodbye Boys,' sung in the style of Billy Murray. 'I actually recorded through a horn to the other end of the room,' Tiny later told Ernie Clark, 'and I now know how singers like Billy Murray, Byron G. Harlan, and Henry Burr felt. Once you made a mistake you had to go on or do the whole thing over again. We don't realize what we have, we can erase our voices.'

The experience at the Edison Museum had been electrifying for Tiny, and he expressed interest in recording an entire album using this direct-to-disc method. Given his resolve to help Tiny realize his vision as an artist, Sharp instructed his team, headed by Waks and engineer Jeff Doring, to devise a way to record an entire album using this technique, once again at 301 Studios.

'Tiny loved that because he was always wanting to record on Edison discs,' Sharp explained. 'The master was cut at the instant. There was no tape involved. It went straight to the mother mold.'

In addition to the need for special equipment to record directly to a master disc, special attention needed to be paid to the manner in which Tiny was recorded. Jeff Doring had Tiny lie comfortably on his back in the studio and sing into the wide end of an old-fashioned, Rudy Vallee–style megaphone. The megaphone was suspended by a microphone stand above Tiny's face, and a vocal mic was positioned just above the megaphone.

Due to the live nature of the recording, it was imperative that the studio and control booth work in synchronicity. Any mistake would mean scrapping an entire side of the record, creating additional expenses for Martin Sharp, who was already over-extending himself financially. Much of this responsibility fell to Waks, who found himself quietly opening doors for personnel who needed to enter and exit the studio, as well as lying on the floor underneath the piano, giving reassuring hand signals to Tiny. 'The idea at the time was both about quality of sound [and] more importantly about recreating the whole ambiance of the early recordings which of course were live, albeit much shorter takes than the direct to disc!' Waks recalls.

Given Tiny's unpredictability, Waks decided that stripping down the album's accompaniment would help to ensure fewer mistakes. He accompanied Tiny on cello for only one song; for the rest, either Tiny accompanied himself on ukulele or Marvin Lewis played the piano. Although many artists had worked with Tiny and adapted to his peculiarities, Waks knew Lewis was the best choice, given the delicate nature of the gig. 'He could follow Tiny better than anyone else, so he was very helpful.'

Wonderful World Of Romance was recorded on January 11 1979 in two takes. The first take went unissued and contained the songs 'Wonderful World Of Romance,' 'A New Kind Of Old Fashioned Girl,' 'Love, You Funny Thing,' 'Million Dollar Baby,' 'Prisoner Of Love,' 'Goodnight, Sweetheart,' 'Stand Up And Sing For Your Father,' 'Memories Of France,' 'When You Look In The Heart Of A Rose,' 'That Wonderful Mother Of Mine,' and 'For The Sake Of Auld Lang Syne/Wandering Down Memory Lane With You.' Predictably, Tiny drifted into a dream-like state, threading a series of romantic songs together. On the second take, he substituted, 'Million Dollar Baby' for 'As You Desire Me' and 'Prisoner Of Love' for 'Auf Wiedersehen, My Dear.' In 1980, 200 copies were pressed from the master and released without cover art. There was just a simple, black-and-white label, reading '*Wonderful World Of Romance* For TINY TIM Fans Only DIRECT TO DISC.'

* * *

Tiny, Sharp, and their loyal collaborators had no chance to rest following the *Wonderful World* recording session. The next day, January 12, was the day of the World Professional Non-Stop Singing Record.

At a press conference prior to the concert, Tiny, wearing a navy-blue suit jacket with shiny, pink lapels and a gigantic bowtie, sat in front of a wall plastered with posters for the impending concert and fielded questions from reporters.

'Have you been training this morning?' a reporter asked.

'No,' Tiny replied. 'I've been training for the last eight years.'

After recapping the creation of the medley in the presence of Art Linkletter, and his subsequent success with the medley at the 1970 Isle of Wight Festival, Tiny explained the significance of the Marathon Medley. 'The goal will be at least to go straight for two hours without a stop … but, this marathon, the purpose of it, really, is maybe for some athletic justification,' he said, with a chuckle. 'I can't play tennis, I certainly can't run—unless I saw a mouse.'

Though they understood the catalyst was primarily curiosity, Tiny, Sharp, and the others involved were satisfied by the response from the Australian media. 'There was quite a lot of interest in it,' Sharp recalled, 'and I think it was a good angle to get publicity and there were quite a bit of television people there and reporters and articles written at the time.'

The choice of venue, Luna Park, was appropriate, not only because of Sharp's relationship with the place, but also for the historical implications and general absurdity of the affair. Inspired by the original Luna Park in Coney Island, New York, Sydney's park opened in 1935, and had been a fixture of fun for decades. Additionally, the park's owner, since 1969, was Leon Fink, a cousin of Nathan Waks.

Since Tiny's arrival in Australia, a camera crew, also managed by Sharp, had been filming the events leading up to and including the Marathon Medley for a documentary. 'It was really supposed to be a concert film interspersed with interviews, like he was training,' Sharp explained. All of the events described here were captured by Sharp's crew.

On the night of the show, Luna Park personnel wore 'TINY TIM WORLD RECORD' T-shirts, while Sharp and company opted to deliver Tiny Tim to the floating venue via boat. As they approached the dock at Luna Park, Tiny surveyed the crowd.

'There's a lot of people linin' up out there already,' one person in the boat exclaimed.

'For the games!' Tiny replied, turning around with a grin. 'Unless they changed it, free admission, and then if I didn't get anybody, you know it's a sad thing.'

A few cameras flashed as a member of Sharp's entourage helped Tiny off the boat and up into a reception area within the Palais de Dance. Tiny went immediately to his dressing room to meditate and prepare. In his dressing room, Tiny changed into a custom-made tuxedo patterned with classic comic strip characters made by tailor Tony Vannici in Sydney, at the behest of Sharp. He tucked a sheet of tissue into his collar to protect his shirt and bowtie and began to apply his make up.

As Tiny prepared, Marvin Lewis sat on a couch directly behind him. Though Lewis was an agnostic and Tiny a Christian, the two would often engage in deep, metaphysical discussions, sometimes arguing over their spiritual views. At this moment, however, Tiny made it clear to Lewis how much he appreciated all of his help and loyalty over the last decade.

'I sit here in my mirror, and a mirror is a reflection of the past,' Tiny said to Lewis. 'I think of how wonderful you've been for nine years—a man who didn't have to do all this, backing me up when I didn't have a cent, and, even though I owe you a lot, still, you've been faithful to me.'

'Why, thank you, Tiny,' Lewis replied.

'Tonight is the night of the big show and, just before I go on, another puff from Elizabeth Arden,' Tiny continued. 'With all the great cosmeticians in the world, remember, if you haven't got a face, they can all give you one.'

If Tiny was nervous, he did not show it. As he waited in the wings for the show to begin, he told Sharp, 'I'll want to bail at one hour, I'll want to bail at two hours, and the rest is gravy!'

Though the record was Tiny's to set, his musicians, too, were in for a marathon. Marvin Lewis, the band's lead man, might have been well versed in Tiny's repertoire, but even he was not infallible when it came to the singer's sudden shifts and substitutions. 'Marvin led the marathon in a way,' Sharp recalled. Though they had rehearsed prior to the show, none of the songs Tiny sang then made it into the marathon. 'Tiny would sing blocks of songs and try to shake up the musicians and try to sing a song that they didn't know. You'd occasionally find them all lost with what to play, and Marvin once or twice was lost. Like the fox being pursued by the hounds—the musicians being the hounds—he'd always try to shake them off if he could.'

Nathan Waks, who took advantage of the fact that the cello, in those years, was not well suited for live performances, focused entirely on coordinating the orchestra. He found it difficult to approach Tiny and suggest a more suitable approach to rehearsing. 'You never quite knew what he really thought,' Waks says, 'because having a normal conversation with him wasn't easy. He was not a normal human being … you couldn't do normal activities with him.'

Tiny was seemingly receptive to the idea of rehearsing, but Waks' suggestions were largely futile. Sometimes, he says, when Tiny performed a song like 'Stayin' Alive,' the performances would be 'coherent, in the sense that he would do them pretty much … within a structure every time. But the medleys were, by their very nature, streams of consciousness.' Although he was consistently frustrated by the medley's lack of musical coherence, Waks was impressed by the brilliance of Tiny's performance. 'Tiny knew the words [to the songs] but he would sometimes interpolate his own monologues into those songs. That's where the genius of it was; that somehow he had a thought process that he was following and that lead him to drop a verse or skip a beat without thinking about it.'

The resulting performance, says Waks, was 'a continuous stream, like a James Joyce style of writing in a novel. You either got into the words or music or both. Some people were just following the words … I obviously had to follow the music more than anything else. Some people followed both, and, obviously Tiny prepared in some way, but I don't think he knew what he was actually going to do. No two gigs were the same, ever. There were certain standard songs that would appear, but he would just go off down a pathway that would lead him down five or ten songs and then, depending on what was happening, he would go down somewhere else.'

Waks ultimately realized that conventional efforts to prepare for the medley would prove impractical. Accordingly, he began to explore other methods that might be better suited to Tiny's approach and could also prevent the orchestra from getting lost. Sometimes, Waks explains, they would start in the key of C, only for Tiny to announce, mid-song, 'Maestro, the key of G.' This, Waks says, was 'a warning that we were turning a corner or shifting gears. So we rehearsed that kind of thing a couple times, to try to get a sense for what style we might be moving into.' He and Tiny also assembled a list of songs suggesting which ones might work best in each key. 'So there was a process of some sort, but it was not at all normal.'

When the time of the concert came, Waks was content that he had prepared the orchestra to the best of his ability. The success or failure of the World Professional Non-Stop Singing Record was now in the hands of fate. As the orchestra played 'The Old Lamplighter,' Tiny Tim, with his hair teased out like tumbleweed, wearing his custom suit and bowtie, stepped into the spotlight. After struggling for a moment to make his way through the crowded stage, he found his mark and blew his signature kisses to the cheering crowd.

Tiny picked up the microphone, Marvin Lewis played a few notes on the piano, and a large digital timer on the side of the stage was activated. Beginning with the 1878 song 'Mr. Phonograph'—one of the first songs ever recorded onto a phonograph cylinder—Tiny went into a medley that would ultimately last approximately two hours, twenty minutes, and forty seconds. The audience cheered as the timer hit two hours, and when Tiny did not stop singing, they, too, continued to dance and sing along. Without pausing once to even take a drink of water, Tiny remained the centerpiece of the entire event, unfaded and undiminished in the frenetic flurry of bright lights, fog machines, bubble machines, strobe lights, and cheering crowd. By the show's conclusion, Tiny Tim held the world record for continuous, nonstop singing.

'It was a great night,' says Waks, 'because the people that came mostly knew someone who was connected in some way. Not a lot of people came in off the street, so most of the people knew that it was something special. So they danced and they smoked joints and they got into what Tiny was doing. He was encouraged and just kept going further.'

Sharp used four 16mm cameras to film the concert and synchronized the film's audio by instructing the cameramen to shoot the concert's large clock timer every time they changed reels. 'It was quite an achievement at the time, to film such a long concert,' Sharp recalled. 'A couple of times all the cameras almost ran out, but it was quite an adventure.'

In Nathan Waks's opinion, the film of the event is not entirely representative of its extraordinary nature. The medley itself, he notes, 'is much harder to listen to objectively, because there's all sorts of strange noises and it's not accurate, and there's thumping and crashing, but if you were there and into the groove, you got into some kind of a scene that had merit simply by the fact of its vocality, rather than the individual segments of it. You could take any one song and say, Well that wasn't accurate, that was out of tune, that didn't have right beats, or whatever, but, when you put it all together and were there, listening to it, it was impressive.'

As Tiny approached the end of the medley, he began to throw modern songs into the mix, illustrating the progression of song through the decades. In the final stretch, he sent the orchestra scrambling for a moment when he shouted 'Key of A!' and began to belt out the lyrics to 'Joy To The World.' From there, he jumped from 'When The Saints Go Marching In' to 'We All Shine On' and back. Approaching the final bars of 'When The Saints,' the audience went wild when Tiny reached into his shopping bag, pulled out his uke, and delved into 'Tip-Toe.' Finally, to signify the end of his musical journey, he performed a cover of The Bee Gees' 'Stayin' Alive.' The Palais De Dance erupted with cheers at the song's epic conclusion. Tiny had performed a whopping 139 songs.

'Thank you so much, my dear friends!' Tiny exclaimed, speaking to the audience for the first time. 'Thank you, God bless you!' In the midst of the cheers, Nathan Waks hopped up onto the stage and spoke quietly to Tiny for a moment, while Martin Sharp triumphantly announced, 'I think we've witnessed an historic event!'

'My dear friends,' Tiny told the audience, 'you're so nice tonight, and I thank you so much for everything. How about a great hand for the following people tonight on this wonderful, wonderful night that you've made it so.' He ran down the list of names, thanking MC Adrian Rawlins, opening act Jeannie Lewis, and the band, heaping particular praise upon Marvin Lewis ('After tonight, his fingers will be insured by Lloyd's of London!').

After hailing Waks, 'the wonderful producer of my records,' Tiny called 'the one and only Mr Martin Sharp' to the stage. The audience cheered wildly as Sharp, smiling shyly, made his way up. 'You know, I wanna tell you something,' Tiny said, as he stood next to Sharp. 'I wanna tell you something about this night. Now, I've met many people who try to do things, and I met Mr. Sharp about ten years ago without knowing it. Later on, I met him in Tasmania in '73, in '74, here, in Australia, in '76 again. He went through more, and I'm not kidding you, than any person I know to fill a dream. If the impossible dream song is made for anybody, it's for Mr. Martin Sharp, because he succeeded where everyone else failed. Mr. Sharp, I thank you, personally. I mean that … a great hand once more.'

Finally, to bring the evening to a close, Tiny introduced 'a rare rendition' of Kris Kristofferson's 'Help Me Make It Through The Night,' complete with classic saxophone introduction, followed by an Elvis-style encore (complete with the usual 'this is not an imitation' disclaimer) of 'Pledging My Love.' Ripping off his jacket and bowtie and unbuttoning his shirt, Tiny sank to his knees and finally collapsed to the floor, thrashing about wildly as the band played the song's final notes and the crowd cheered. Then, as the music faded, Tiny hopped back to his feet. 'Thank you and God bless you all!' he said as he blew kisses, collected his things, and exited the stage to the tune of 'The Old Lamplighter.' The concert timer now read two hours and thirty-five minutes. A beaming announcer hopped onto the stage and grabbed the microphone. 'The new world heavy weight singing champion!' he announced. 'The one and only Mr. Tiny Tim!' As the lights faded, audience members were heard calling for more and shouting, 'We love you, Tiny Tim!'

* * *

Following the concert, several positive pieces ran in papers and publications across the country. One article, by reporter Anne Stone, echoed Martin Sharp's reverence for Tiny Tim. 'Each time you thought he might stop,' wrote Stone, 'that the natural crescendo of a song would trick him into it out of sheer force of habit, he was right in there with the next one, before you could even finish the thought … he did not sing to us, but somehow Tiny made us feel he sang for us, and that he needed us there.' She also praised the collaboration between Sharp and Tiny. 'Martin Sharp is the master artist of the comic strip, the primary colors, the bold outline in black,' she wrote. 'Tiny Tim has to be his perfect subject—the only livin', breathin', singin' comic strip fantasy.'

Elsewhere, in *The Age*, Alan Attwood called the show 'mad and marvelous, and Luna Park was the perfect place for him. Tiny Tim was a much better performer, and singer, than most people ever realized.'

Shortly after the concert, Tiny returned to the States, and Martin Sharp set to work cutting together the film of the Marathon Medley. However, six months later, on June 9 1979, a further unexpected event at Luna Park drastically altered the course of Sharp's documentary. That night, the Ghost Train ride, a staple of the park since it opened in 1935, erupted into a fiery inferno, claiming the lives of seven passengers. As one writer later put it, the park's slogan, 'Just for Fun,' had lost its meaning. The park was closed immediately; a police investigation followed but provided few answers.

In the immediate aftermath of the fire, the New South Wales government became involved in the operational affairs of the park. When it became clear that the existence and historical integrity of the park were in danger, Sharp flew into action. Together with fellow artist Peter Kingston, he launched the Friends Of Luna Park organization to draw attention to the issues surrounding the park. Sharp believed that the fire had been the result of an arson attack by someone who wanted to repurpose the valuable waterfront property. When asked, just prior to his passing, if he felt that an act of sabotage had caused the Ghost Train fire, he replied, 'I'm sure of it.'

The fire at Luna Park became a new point of focus in Sharp's film, transforming the narrative into a loose association between the Marathon Medley and the tragic fire. In Sharp's mind, the two events were linked. Tiny's concert had taken place on a full moon, and the fire occurred exactly six full moons after. 'To a certain degree,' he said, 'the concert was prophetic of the fire.' Nathan Waks was not convinced, however. 'It got all mystical and difficult for me to follow,' he says.

As the scope of the film ballooned, Sharp found the project increasingly difficult to manage. He lost potential backing from interested financiers, because the fire was too controversial a subject. He eventually took out a second mortgage, and later put his mansion on Sydney Harbor, which he had inherited from his parents, up for sale in order to continue the work. Thankfully, he was saved at the eleventh hour by a substantial royalty check for 'Tales Of Brave Ulysses,' which allowed him to keep his home and continue with his Tiny Tim/Luna Park cinematic opus.

There was talk of taking the marathon medley on tour, but it did not come to fruition.* *Street Of Dreams* took Sharp's undivided focus, and though he and Tiny would continue to collaborate on a number of projects, none were as grand as those of 1979 and 1980. 'At one time there was some thought that they might really resurrect his career in a big way,' Waks recalls. 'Tiny wanted to do that—the idea of fame again was something he had always lusted for … but it never really happened.' For Waks, Sharp and his work were simply 'not commercial at all,' while Tiny was not 'reliable enough in a musical sense' to mount a full comeback.

Meanwhile, in America, the 1979 oil crisis was driving up gasoline prices and creating long lines at the pumps. Few could have guessed that the overthrowing of the Shah of Iran and the decrease in Iranian oil production under the government of Ayatollah Khomeni could have possibly served as a comeback vehicle for Tiny Tim. But if anyone thought otherwise, they were in for a surprise.

---

* Tiny would later express interest in breaking his nonstop singing record at the 1984 Olympic Games in Los Angeles. 'Imagine seeing me for three hours on the Olympics?' he told *Oui* magazine's John Alan Friedman. 'I think it's the best thing for the career right now.'

CHAPTER SEVENTEEN
DO YOU THINK I'M SEXY?

After '79, [Johnny Carson] never used me again because I rolled on the floor when I did 'Do You Think I'm Sexy' and a belly button showed and that was the end of that.

TINY TIM TO HOWARD STERN, MAY 6 1994

In 1979, Tiny released a new single, 'Tip-Toe To The Gas Pumps,' written by a young songwriter named David Heavener from Louisville, Kentucky. The two had met back in 1977 and recorded some auxiliary material together in 1978: 'old standards' and 'vaudeville material,' which they recorded with an unnamed piano player, as well as a Heavener original, 'The Hickey On Your Neck,' which he adapted for Tiny, adding a lyric about a 'tiptoeing turkey … kissing your tulip … and makin' you a nervous wreck.'

When Tiny returned from Australia in January 1979, Heavener called him up and pitched his newest song, 'Tip-Toe To The Gas Pumps.' Always game to cash in on a current event or fad, Tiny did not need convincing.

'Oh! Brilliant, Mr. Heavener! Brilliant!' Tiny exclaimed, when he heard the song title and lyrics.

Let's tiptoe to the gas pumps,
Fill 'er up, give me all you've got,
Till I scream, 'I've had enough,'
Everybody clap your hands,
And sing in harmony,
Come tiptoe to the gas pumps with me!

Tiny returned to Kentucky and recorded the single over a few late-night sessions at Fultz Recording Studio. Because his voice was hoarse due to a cold,

Heavener, a singer and talented imitator, rerecorded almost a quarter of the song in Tiny's voice. Shortly after Tiny returned to New York City, however, Heavener's phone rang. It was Roy Radin, who had a bone to pick.

Heavener still uses caution, only somewhat jokingly, when describing the encounter. 'I want to make sure I don't get myself exterminated,' he begins. 'Roy Radin, at that time, somehow came into the picture. He wasn't in the picture until I recorded the song—that I know of. Then I started getting calls from Roy, wanting to know what me and Tiny were doing.'

A self-described 'Kentucky boy,' Heavener did not back down. 'What the hell do you want?' he asked.

'Listen,' Radin replied coldly, 'I don't think you know who you're dealing with. I could snap my fingers and you'd be gone.'

Later, Heavener's phone rang again. This time it was Tiny, who warned Heavener to watch his tongue when speaking to Radin. 'You can't talk to Mr. Radin like that.'

* * *

By 1979, Roy Radin had reached the apex of his wealth, braggadocio, and addiction to cocaine. According to his sister Kate, his behavior and personality had shifted darkly since his divorce in 1978. 'It was almost as if he was starting to live his young life he never got to live at eighteen, nineteen, twenty,' she recalled. 'He was very broken-hearted after his divorce, and he got into the crowd of the Studio 54. He just got completely addicted to the cocaine and the people that were around him—we used to call them coke whores—he used to get really, really mad at us when we confronted him about it. He said he would be able to kick it.'

At the same time, *Roy Radin's Vaudeville Revue* was in decline. According to Tim Fowler, 'It really started to collapse in '79. He was under investigation in five states for illegal distribution of funds because he was taking too much money and not giving enough to the charities.'

In the meantime, at Tiny's request, David Heavener visited New York City for a few weeks. While he was there, he got a closer look at some of the gentlemen in Tiny's entourage. '[We] hung out at this Brooklyn restaurant,' he recalls. 'The guy that ran the show there, from what I remember, they called him Johnny D. He was probably, around that time, maybe sixty-five, seventy—a big guy—and he had all his cronies, and you could tell this guy was packing. Anyway, [after] about three days hanging out there, he finally came up to me and started talking to me, and I remember him looking at one of his guys and says, I like this kid. I want you to take care of him. The guy comes up and gives me a wad of $100 bills, like, $2,000 in $100 bills. I got back to my hotel room that night and I looked it, and it was a lot of money.'

Heavener rang Tiny and told him what had happened.

'Mr. Heavener,' Tiny replied, 'when Mr. D. likes someone, he takes care of them and makes sure everything is OK. Is everything OK?'

'Yeah.'

'Good. That means he's doing his job.'

'Tiny,' Heavener continues, 'I assume [he] was connected with … some of *those* guys, you know what I'm saying? I was a kid so I didn't ask any questions.'

Although Tiny did not shy from introducing Heavener to mobsters, he did worry a great deal about the boy's mortal soul. 'When we traveled,' Heavener recalls, 'I would get my own hotel room, and I'd always find this good looking girl, and if Tiny knew I took her back to the room, he would stand outside my door preaching—beating on the door and preaching the gospel—to the point where the girl would get mad or freaked out and leave.'

In the meantime, Heavener was shopping Tiny's single around. He managed to get it into the hands of Steve Alaimo, the vice president of disco label TK Records, home of KC & The Sunshine Band. When they showed interest, Heavener sold it to them—and Roy Radin blew a gasket. 'He went crazy,' Heavener says. 'I heard that Radin was after me and I heard that Johnny D. was after him!' In any case, Radin did not did not enact revenge, and when Heavener left Kentucky for Nashville to pursue a songwriting career, he lost contact with Tiny Tim.

Radin did, however, manage to bully TK Records into giving him a piece of the action. 'Tip-Toe To The Gas Pumps' was released by TK Records' subsidiary label, Clouds, with a label reading, 'Produced by: David Heavener for Roy Radin Prod. Ltd.'

Steve Alaimo and TK Records President Henry Stone were willing to take a gamble on anything they thought might be a hit. 'It was the time of the gas shortage, obviously, and we were putting out records by everybody,' Alaimo explains. 'We were a hot record company. What we did at this company was if there was something that was hot at the time—some dance thing, some groove thing—we'd go after it.' For Alaimo, 'Tip-Toe To The Gas Pumps' was 'a pretty timely record … we got some airplay on it [and] it rejuvenated Tiny's career a little bit.'

'Tip-Toe To The Gas Pumps' peaked at number 80 on the *Billboard* charts and landed Tiny guest appearances on *The Merv Griffin Show*, where he had not appeared since 1977; *The Mike Douglas Show*, where he had not appeared since 1974; and, most significantly, *The Tonight Show*. For all three appearances, Tiny opened with 'Gas Pumps' and closed with a cover of Rod Stewart's 'Do You Think I'm Sexy.'

Radin had approached *The Tonight Show* about having Tiny on the program against Tiny's wishes, and Carson extended an invitation. Unlike Tiny's previous appearance, where the conversation centered around the dissolution of Tiny's career and marriage, this time Carson approached the interview with the friendly rapport the two had enjoyed before Tiny's life and career had become so publicly complicated.

After Tiny performed 'Gas Pumps,' which seemed to amuse Carson, he sat down for the interview. 'It's been a long time,' Carson said, drumming his fingers on the desk, aware of the awkwardness surrounding Tiny's extended absence from the program, but Tiny seemed not to bear a grudge.

'You've been so wonderful,' he told Carson.

'You are one of the people who make life interesting, Tiny,' Carson replied. Then, after briefly discussing the Marathon Medley and Martin Sharp's forthcoming documentary, he addressed Tiny's physical state, since he had ballooned since his last appearance on the show in 1974.

'I'm always afraid I might pass away and miss all those great pizzas and great spaghettis,' Tiny replied.*

The conversation then turned to Tiny's tours with Roy Radin—'The Ziegfeld of the 80s'—and Miss Vicki's recent remarriage. Tiny, of course, felt that he remained 'legally married to her until death do us part,' and as such continued to try to 'strengthen myself against the temptations of the world.'

After a commercial break, Tiny returned to the stage, and *The Tonight Show* band began to play 'Do You Think I'm Sexy.' The performance was initially much the same as his other television appearances, until, inexplicably, Tiny decided to take it to the next level. As the song reached its climax, he ripped off his jacket and threw it to the floor. Then he awkwardly grabbed

---

* 'Food is like a narcotic, the taste is great, but you have to pay for it,' he told interviewer Lynda Guydon a few months later. He went on reveal that his typical breakfast consisted of 'six eggs, six strips of bacon, four bowls of cereal, two glasses of juice and a pitcher of milk.' Around the same time, *Newsweek* reported that Tiny had gone on a diet of 'unsweetened spaghetti sauce and melba toast.'

his snug red polyester dress shirt and ripped it open, pulled it out from under his suspenders, and tossed it to the cheering audience. Sinking to his knees, he grabbed his last layer, a Luna Park Marathon Medley T-shirt that read 'THE TIME MACHINE,' and lifted it violently, exposing his entire stomach and chest. Then, bouncing wildly on his knees, his belly bulging between his tuxedo pants and raised T-shirt, he finished the song by belting partial phrases and lyrics into the microphone. Upon the final pants-tightening note, he fell to the ground, kicking and squirming, to the audience's wild applause.

Carson looked shell-shocked. 'I don't believe it,' he mouthed. As Tiny collected his clothes, while blowing kisses to the cheering audience, Carson sent the show back to commercials. 'There's just nothing that can be said,' he said, clearly in disbelief. 'We'll be right back!'

Tiny's performance was the talk of the *Tonight Show* staff. Jeff Sotzing, Carson's nephew and a staff member at that time, watched a tape of the segment after it had aired and called it 'the deal-breaker.' It would be Tiny's final appearance on the show while Carson remained as host.

Reviews of the appearance were predictably harsh. 'If ever there was a creature of television,' Peter J. Boyer of the Associated Press wrote, 'it is this man Herbert Khaury. Found by television, made by television, dumped by television. It was kind of sad seeing Tiny Tim on *Tonight*, thick-bellied and sprawling onstage. He's an oddball that people quit laughing with and began laughing at; then finally, worst of all, they quit noticing altogether.'

While the reception was harsh, the visibility caused a slight surge of attention. Two days later, the *Washington Post* carried a blurb about Tiny in its 'Suspicions' section. The short piece answered rumors that Tiny was seeking to perform for Ronald Reagan on the campaign trail. Tiny denied the rumors and endorsed the current president, Jimmy Carter, 'a wonderful, religious, very fair man doing a fine job.'

Tiny also filmed a bit part in the Warner Bros motion picture *One Trick Pony*, starring Paul Simon. 'Life hasn't exactly been a bed of tulips for falsetto singer Tiny Tim,' *Newsweek* reported in February 1980. 'But his career appears to be on the rise. Says Tim: I believe in Miracles. ... The turnabout began last summer, when he recorded a novelty song about the gas crisis. That led to a return appearance on Johnny Carson, which Tim considers "the very heart of show business."'

The most intriguing nugget of information in the *Newsweek* article was that Vicki and Tiny has reunited for a business venture, opening a nightclub in Glendale, New York, where 'she dances and he sings.' The estranged former couple announced their forthcoming performances together to Tom Snyder, the host of *Tomorrow*. Miss Vicki confirms that the reunion was 'strictly business'. 'They offered me to do it, and it paid, and I needed money because I was still raising my daughter,' she explains. 'He sang and I came out and danced but we didn't really talk or have anything together … I got paid and he got paid and we all went home and that was that.'

* * *

In September 1980, Tiny returned to Australia for further concert appearances and to shoot additional footage with Martin Sharp for *Street Of Dreams*. Consumed with trying to save Luna Park from destruction, Sharp shot Tiny singing the 1930 Rudy Vallee song, 'Wind In The Willows' in front of the park's clown-face entrance.

'My dear friends,' Tiny said, as he looked into the lens, 'I hope you'll listen well as you listen to the words of this song … ironically, in a sense, they apply to the great Luna Park, to which I had such great experiences in 1979.'

Sharp isolated the audio and released 'Wind in the Willows' as a single, coupled with an original song by Australian composer and Sharp associate Alistair Jones, 'The Luna Park Song.' The single was pressed and issued in a limited quantity in Australia with corresponding Martin Sharp artwork. According to Jones, it was intended to serve as a 'rallying call for the Friends of Luna Park.' It was also the only Tiny Tim single released in 1980.

By the end of the year, whatever optimism had been generated by 'Tip-Toe To The Gas Pumps' had worn off. 'I'm still hoping to be a major star,' Tiny told the *Washington Post* on December 8, 'maybe not what I was back then, but something more than I am today … maybe it might be time to get out of the business, but I hope not. I love this and if the people want me, I'll be ready.'

He echoed these same sentiments in an interview with the *National Enquirer*, which took place before a show at a restaurant called the Wagon Wheel in Queens. 'I've gone from rags to riches, then riches to rags,' he told the hungry tabloid. 'This sure is a long way from getting married on the Johnny Carson show. But then, who knows from here? You come up, you go down, you come up again. It's just like an elevator … right down to the basement, then back up to the top floor again … Something always comes along. I do get depressed many times, sitting in my room and wondering what's going to happen next. But I still count my blessings.'

CHAPTER EIGHTEEN

FOREVER MISS DIXIE

I looked like this before Boy George was born!
TINY TIM TO THE *GETTYSBURG TIMES*, JUNE 1985

The year 1981 was Tiny's thirtieth in show business, his career having begun, according to his calculations, with his bombed performance at the Loew's Christmas party in 1951. In April, he was joined by friends and business associates for a thirtieth anniversary party at the Bloomin' Pub in Manhattan, attended by both Vicki and Tulip, who was nearing her tenth birthday.

The same year also marked the tenth anniversary of *Roy Radin's Vaudeville Revue*. Though the *Revue* had a revolving door of performers and a tumultuous atmosphere, Tiny made it clear that he had no intention of finding work elsewhere. When the *Day* caught up with Tiny at a rehearsal before a show at New London High School in Connecticut, the reporter, Steve Fagin, pointed out to him that he was sitting in the same exact spot as he had during last year's rehearsal. 'Yes, and I'll be sitting in the same spot the next year,' he replied, 'and the year after that, and twenty years after that. I love being with the show, even if I'm just a spec now. They even have me after Zippy The Chimp!'

* * *

In 1981, Staten Island performer and producer Michael Nerlino sought to reinvent Tiny Tim as a disco act. After meeting Tiny and his latest manager, Mr. Rocky, at a nightclub, Nerlino decided to write a single with Tiny in mind, 'Comic Strip Man (Biff, Bam, Slam),' and have Tiny perform a few other disco songs he had written: 'Tell Me That You Love Me (My Sweetheart),' 'Honest, Dear, Honest,' and '(I'm The) Soul Twister.'

When they began to discuss the style of the recordings, Nerlino was adamant that Tiny steer away from using his falsetto. 'I talked him out of it,'

Nerlino recalls. 'I wanted him to have a different sound. He said, You know, Mr. Mike, you're right.' Nerlino also added a couple female R&B backup singers to the mix. 'Honest Dear Honest' and '(I'm The) Soul Twister' were recorded in May 1978, with the others following some time later.

'They are commercial tunes and could bring me back,' Tiny wrote in his diary after hearing the mixes. 'However, I don't think they are strong enough.'

Nerlino promoted the album heavily and optimistically. *Cashbox* carried advertisements informing promoters to 'WATCH THEIR MAIL [for] THE NEW SINGLE FROM THE NEW TINY TIM.' The record's picture sleeve featured different illustrations of Tiny on either side, and advertised 'Comic Strip Man (Biff, Bam, Slam)' as the 'hit single' from the new Solid Brass album *Tiny Tim: I Won't Dance*, and 'Tell Me That You Love Me (My Sweetheart)' as the 'title single' from the forthcoming *Tiny Tim: Tell Me That You Love Me*. The records also came with a printed note from Tiny Tim containing a telephone number for ordering 'Tell Me That You Love Me' bumper stickers and straw hats. 'Tell Me That You Love Me (My Sweetheart)' and 'Honest, Dear, Honest' were also issued together as a single. The record is scarce; this author has never seen a copy. Nerlino also issued a 33rpm twelve-inch promotional single featuring extended mixes of 'Comic Strip Man (Biff, Bam, Slam)' and '(I'm The) Soul Twister.'

Armed with promotional records, straw hats, stickers, female backup singers, and a Superman outfit made for Tiny by Mrs. Nerlino, the two men set forth to promote the brand-new single from the 'new' Tiny Tim. Disc jockey Dale Reeves at New York's Disco 92 WKTU played 'Comic Strip Man (Biff, Bam, Slam)' ad nauseam, and Tiny and the backup singers made several concert appearances to promote the single. According to Nerlino, they were well received, and Tiny was 'swarmed' by teenagers wherever they went. After one show, a group of teenagers challenged Tiny to a few games of pinball, which he won.

Nerlino's take on Tiny Tim also generated a good deal of interest in Asia, so Nerlino took Tiny, Bobby Rydell, and The Four Aces on a tour of South Korea. 'The Koreans were crazy for Tiny the same way American teenagers did with The Beatles,' he recalled. 'Korea was airing Tiny Tim music the whole time he was there. He was washed up in America, yes, but if you went to Korea or Japan, forget it! We ended up at the Shilla Hotel [in Seoul], swarmed by kids and photographers.'

According to Nerlino, Mr. Rocky attempted to get 'Comic Strip Man' onto the soundtrack of an installment of the *Superman* film series starring Christopher Reeve. Unfortunately, but not surprisingly, the deal fell through, and the momentum of the single seemed to flag, despite the strong airplay and concert appearances. Nerlino blamed Tiny's management for the ultimate failure of 'Comic Strip Man' and the eventual scrapping of their plans to release the two full-length albums. 'His managers messed everything up,' he said.

Tiny released two other singles in 1981. 'Zoot Zoot Zoot Here Comes Santa In His New Space Suit,' a modern Christmas song about Santa Claus ditching his sleigh for a robotic, space suit, was issued as a single and appeared as the title track on an LP featuring other children's Christmas songs, the rest of which were performed by songwriter Bruce Haack. The album and single were released on the RAJO label, with the back cover of the LP featuring a black-and-white drawing of Tiny in profile, reminiscent of the back cover of *God Bless Tiny Tim*. Though the *New York Daily News* endorsed 'Zoot Zoot Zoot' as a 'rather hip song,' the album disappeared from sight and Tiny later described it to Harve Mann as 'a terrible bomb.'

Tiny's other release this year was 'Yummy Yummy Pizza' b/w 'Oh, Oh, Oh, Those Landlords!' It was issued by the unknown Top Billing Records and reportedly given out at a New York City pizza chain.

* * *

During this period, Tiny spent more time in and around New York than he had in previous years. He moved his mother out of the old family apartment at 601 West 163rd Street, where she had lived since 1942, into a one-bedroom apartment in the Olcott Hotel. He and his mother shared room 1512. It was Tiny's first official residence since his eviction in 1974.

The Olcott had offered rent stabilized one-bedroom apartments with kitchenettes since 1930. By the time Tiny moved in, the building had seen better days. 'I never slept with the lights out because roaches don't like the light,' he told *The Birdman Show* in 1996. Though he was scared of the roaches, he was kind enough to issue a warning ahead of the exterminator's visit. 'Get out here now,' he would shout. 'They're going to spray you!'*

---

* The hotel was close to the Dakota, where John Lennon and Yoko Ono had lived. In November 1980, Tiny Tim passed Lennon on the street. 'I know he wanted to say something, but it was the heat of the day, and I understood he wanted his privacy, so I just kept walking,' Tiny told Geoffrey Giuliano in 1984. About a month later, Lennon was assassinated. Tiny later wrote a song in tribute to John Lennon titled, 'Here Lies John Lennon.'

During this period, Tiny often appeared on the popular New York City public access program *Beyond Vaudeville*. Host Rich Brown was one of the few who was impressed by Tiny's disastrous 1979 appearance on *The Tonight Show*, and had also seen Tiny in *Roy Radin's Vaudeville Revue*, which served as inspiration for the structure of *Beyond Vaudeville*. Tiny's 1979 *Tonight Show* appearance 'fit right into what I was looking for in entertainment,' says Brown. 'That, combined with the Radin show, just gave me this whole different perspective on what an entertainer could be. The Radin show ... was a throwback to an earlier time ... [and] Tiny was just an interesting package, because I had an affinity for music from the early part of the century, and Tiny clearly cared about that music and introduced it in a successful way to a new generation.'

Through Tiny, Brown met his old protégé, Isadore Fertel. Though they still sometimes fought over Tiny's views on women's rights, Fertel began once again to serve as Tiny's opening act in the New York area. 'I was just blown away,' Brown says of seeing Fertel for the first time. 'He did his "Rock Around The Clock" in Yiddish and [an original called] the "Regan Begin Song." He just came out and sang a cappella. I hadn't seen anything like him before. He was such a unique personality, and his songs were so original.'

Brown recalled that despite their sometimes-strained relationship, Tiny and Fertel had a genuine appreciation for each other. 'When Tiny was in a room with Izzy, he would just light up. Tiny clearly loved him [and] took some pride in presenting him. I remember they [once] sang "Easter Parade" together. I think Tiny felt a certain kinship with him, because Izzy was not a regular person. He was definitely an eccentric and an original, as was Tiny. So it was natural that they would gravitate toward each other.'

* * *

On March 13, Tiny joined the crew of the cruise ship the *SS Norway*. He was to perform for five weeks as the ship sailed from Miami to the Virgin Islands and back again. One night following his show, Tiny visited the disco club on the boat's top level to mingle. During a conversation with a fan, he felt a hand grasp his arm. He turned around to see Miss Dixie.

'Whadda ya say, sweetheart?'

'There she was, twenty-five years old, ohhhh, ha ha!' Tiny later recalled. 'She was divine.'

For the next three nights, Miss Dixie attended Tiny's shows, and afterward they would go dancing at the disco club. On the last night of the cruise, she and Tiny followed their usual routine and headed up to the disco club for drinks and dancing after his concert. While up there, another girl approached Tiny and asked if he wanted to dance.

Tiny deferred to Dixie, who scowled. 'Go and dance with her,' she said.

'My heart was in my mouth,' Tiny recalled. 'I didn't wanna dance. I wanted to be with [Dixie] ... how could she dare tell me to go and dance with her when I wanted to dance with Miss Dixie?'

Tiny danced with the other girl, and when he approached Dixie afterward, an argument ensued. 'I don't wanna see you no more!' she yelled.

'Well,' Tiny replied, 'I don't wanna see you no more!'

Tiny left and stumbled back to his room; an hour later, Dixie called.

'I'm sorry we got excited like that,' she said.

'Don't even worry about that,' Tiny replied. 'It's all over.'

At sunrise, Tiny was woken by the ship's intercom, announcing a fire on the ship and instructing passengers to proceed to the deck. Tiny set off in search of Miss Dixie. 'I had to get to her room to make sure she was alright,' he recalled. 'I didn't want to be the coward I was in the past. At least, not with this one.' When Tiny reached her door, panting from the exertion and smoke inhalation, there was no answer. He turned and ran to the upper deck, where he discovered Dixie waiting for him. The two embraced and reconciled.

Back on US soil, the courtship continued. Tiny visited Miss Dixie at her home in West Virginia, where he met her daughter and her motorcycle enthusiast father. Though the details are scarce, an intense relationship followed. 'He loved her very much,' Martin Sharp recalled. 'She was his muse in a big way. She was quite a beautiful woman. We had to listen to lots of stories about Miss Dixie.'

There were, however, limits to the relationship. Tiny would not engage in sexual activity with Dixie until marriage, and Dixie could not get married. She had been widowed in 1978, after her late husband had been one of thirty persons killed when a construction tower collapsed, and was allegedly dependent upon her status as a widow to receive settlement payments. Because Tiny was not able to furnish the financial assistance needed to support her daughter, marriage was out of the question.

Nevertheless, Tiny showed his affection the best way he knew: with a trophy. 'The all-time trophy winner was ... [the] only woman I've ever loved more than any other woman in the world,' he later told *Oui* magazine, 'now, yesterday or tomorrow. Forever Miss Dixie.' Eventually, Tiny gave in to temptation and, in an attempt to protect his soul, performed one of his 'spiritual' marriage ceremonies—as he had with Barbara Williams—before going to bed with her.

When Tiny traveled to Australia in September 1982 to prepare for a series of engagements organized by Martin Sharp, he debuted a new song he had written, 'Forever Miss Dixie':

> *Skies may be cloudy,*
> *And skies may be blue,*
> *But, my darlin',*
> *I'll always love you.*

During an interview on the Australian radio show *Fast Forward*, Tiny was asked by the host, 'What do you think you'll be doing when you're eighty years old?'

'Good question,' he replied. 'If I live and I'm healthy, if I'm married to Miss Dixie, I would be so happy, I wouldn't want anything else.' (If not, he continued, he would 'go to where young girls hang out … look for that one angel I dream of … [and] send them flowers and cards and bouquets and presents.')

'Forever Miss Dixie' was among the many songs Tiny performed on September 5 1982, during perhaps the most prestigious concert of his post-mainstream career, at the Sydney Opera House. 'Before we get underway,' Adrian Rawlins, reprising his role as MC, told the audience, 'our artist has asked me to let you know that he dedicates this evening to you, his friends all over Australia. We're going down a tunnel of tunes, a tunnel of times, many styles, many varieties of song, but through them all our artist will show us his sincerity, his love, his life, and his deep commitment to romantic beauty. So would you, please, put your hands together, open your hearts, and give a warm Sydney welcome to the one and only Eternal Troubadour, Mister Tiny Tim!'

Tiny crossed to the microphone, wearing a custom-made suit resembling a Jackson Pollock painting, and opened the concert with 'Street Of Dreams.' In addition to the ensemble specifically assembled for the concert, including Nathan Waks on cello, he was joined by Australian musicians Billy Belcher and his large brass band and the Wright Brothers. As the concert drew to a close, Tiny performed 'Tip-Toe' with Belcher's band; then, after a quick medley featuring 'When The Saints Go Marching In,' 'Waltzing Matilda,' 'Take Me Out To Luna Park,' he called Alistair Jones to the stage to accompany him on piano for an inspired rendition of Charles Aznavour's 'To Die Of Love.' As he left the stage, the crowd leapt to their feet and began clapping and stomping, shouting, 'More! More!' True to form, Tiny returned to the stage and, after again thanking those who helped put the concert together, closed with an encore performance of 'Heartbreak Hotel.'

As Martin Sharp recalled, there had been no skepticism about putting on a Tiny Tim show at the Sydney Opera House, and the reception to the show was positive. 'It could have been bigger. It wasn't such a big crowd,' he said. 'It was a good crowd, an enthusiastic crowd, but it wasn't packed … [there was a] very good reaction … Tiny was very pleased with it. He did a great show. He was flying by the seat of his pants but he was very creative.'

* * *

That same year, Tiny appeared for the first time on *The Howard Stern Show*, at a time when the 'shock jock' was still at W-NBC. Specifically, he participated in a segment called 'mystery guest,' in which a guest would disguise his or her voice and Stern would give clues as to the person's identity. In Tiny's case, Stern gave several clever clues, including, 'He's known for being small, but actually is quite tall,' 'A friend of Dick [Martin] and Dan [Rowan],' and 'He's a singer, a very fine one.'

After various guesses of Paul Williams, Barry Manilow, and Randy Newman, a caller correctly identified Tiny.

'What's the deal, Tiny?' Stern asked. 'You haven't been around. I don't see you on TV or anything anymore. What's going on?'

'Oh, I've been traveling constantly; Australia, I just came back from there,' Tiny replied. 'I've been to Florida.'

'Florida! What are you doing down there?'

'A place called Hemingway's. I'll be there until New Years.'

'All them old people down there. You gotta be with the young people, Tiny. I'm telling you right now. You don't want to hang out with all the old-timers.'

After discussing Vicki's remarriage and current events, Stern jumped on an opportunity to insult his programming director Kevin Metheny, whom he had famously dubbed 'pig virus.' 'I don't know why the radio stations aren't playing your records,' Stern said. 'You wanna tell our boss to go get lost, go right ahead, man.'

'I know a lot of people that aren't playing my records,' Tiny replied, before launching into a playful rendition of the Rudy Vallee tune 'Good Evening.'

'Tiny, you can sing some music, can't you?' Stern exclaimed as Tiny completed the last bars of the song. 'I love it! … you were the best mystery guest yet!' Though Tiny was not to return to Stern's show for another six years, this appearance was the beginning of a long and mutually beneficial relationship.

In the meantime, Tiny fulfilled his engagement at Hemingway's, a popular Florida restaurant. The gig appears to be one of the last arranged by Tiny's old manager, Joe Cappy, who had by then relocated to Florida. It was at Hemingway's that Tiny met Gary Lawrence, a twenty-nine-year-old arranger, pianist, and graduate of Brooklyn College. Lawrence had been performing with his roaring 20s–style big band, Gary Lawrence & His Sizzling Syncopators. In 1978, he relocated to Florida and, among many other projects, continued performing and recording with different variations of the Sizzling Syncopators. Aside from covering classics like 'Puttin' On The Ritz,' he and his band specialized in 'de-modernizing' current hits, making them sound as if they were recorded in the 20s or 30s.

Lawrence had never been a particular fan of Tiny Tim's, however. 'I always knew him as a pop singer,' he explains. 'I wasn't particularly impressed, I didn't particularly dislike him, I just wasn't into the popular music of the day. But I knew of him.' By 1981, having recorded several 20s-style albums with his band, Lawrence had reexamined Tiny's work and found a new appreciation for him. So when a friend invited him to see Tiny perform at Hemingway's, Gary was thrilled. When he arrived, he discovered that Tiny had been hired not as a singer, but as a greeter. 'He would walk to the tables, say hello, and sing occasionally,' Lawrence recalls. Eventually, Tiny came over to Lawrence's table and, seizing the moment, Lawrence engaged Tiny about turn-of-the-century music. Looking to impress Tiny as a fellow connoisseur of obscure, forgotten songs, Lawrence threw out the title of a rarely heard song called, 'Florida, The Moon, And You.' Naturally, Tiny knew the song, but their conversation was cut short when Tiny was called over to the piano to perform a few songs.

The house piano player, whom Lawrence knew to be an excellent jazz pianist, was not handling Tiny or the old repertoire very well. Lawrence cringed as he butchered 'It's A Long Way To Tipperary.' 'He was destroying Tiny with his accompaniment,' Lawrence says. 'It was awful.' After Tiny's botched set, Lawrence approached him with a proposition. 'If you're gonna sing again, I'd really like to play for you,' he said. 'I think I could do a much better job.'

Aware that his accompaniment needed improvement, Tiny approached the owner of Hemingway's with the idea. 'Nobody plays piano in my club,' the owner grumbled. 'No amateurs.' At that, Lawrence's girlfriend produced a recent newspaper, which had an article about Gary Lawrence & His Sizzling Syncopators on the front page.

'Do you know who this man is?' she asked the club owner. 'You should be honored that he is consenting to play in your club.'

Seeing this, the club owner changed his tune, and Lawrence sat down behind the piano. Tiny approached the microphone and went into a medley featuring his usual material, and then broke into a rendition of 'Florida, The Moon, And You.' Lawrence followed him easily.

After the performance, Lawrence spoke with Tiny more candidly. 'Tiny was so impressed, because it's a very obscure song,' Lawrence explains. 'I told him that my specialty was taking a new song and doing it an old style, and he liked the idea … I wanted to present him as the honest to goodness musical historian that he was, which nobody had any respect for. My whole thing with my band was we did not [change] the music at all. We presented it exactly the way it would have sounded in the 20s, and I wanted Tiny to be part of that.'

Though they did not record together immediately, the two spent time together in Florida, and Lawrence also visited Tiny in New York, where he was appalled by Tiny's treatment at the hands of his management. Once, he accompanied Tiny and Neil Hollander of Banner Talent—another one of Tiny's many 'agents'—to a taping of *The Uncle Floyd Show*. On the way there, Tiny turned to Hollander and innocently asked, 'Wouldn't it be nice if Mr. Lawrence and his band could play for me?'

'Yeah? Just be glad that you're working,' Hollander snapped back.

In 1982, Tiny and Lawrence finally scheduled a session at Inroads recording studio in Miami, where they recorded 20s-style versions of Morris Albert's 1975 hit 'Feelings' and Rod Stewart's 'Do You Think I'm Sexy.' Tiny opted to perform the songs in two unique styles: 'Feelings' in the style of the early Bing Crosby, and 'Do You Think I'm Sexy' in the style of Al Jolson. The session was a successful one, and Lawrence, at his own expense, pressed a limited number of copies of the results on his Vo-Do-De-O-Do label.

A local filmmaker also produced a ridiculous music video of 'Do You Think I'm Sexy' for a Florida cable-access show that showcased videos by local artists. Shot on VHS, the video features Tiny, flanked by three dancing girls in different outfits—including purple tights—parading about in a variety of different locations: a Holiday Inn, a tennis court, and a golf course. The fact that this is Tiny Tim imitating Al Jolson while performing Rod Stewart makes the video one of the most peculiar artifacts from Tiny's career.

Tiny, unsurprisingly, was critical of the video. 'I thought I was moving,' he told the *Lakeland Ledger*. 'But in the video, I'm just putting my hands on my hips. I wasn't moving at all. And it doesn't look like I'm singing the song because my mouth isn't in sync with the record.'

In addition to the video, the Florida-based Musigram Company experimented with the idea of issuing Tiny Tim 'Do You Think I'm Sexy' greeting cards. The company made four different mockups featuring a six-inch flexi-disc of the song. Sadly, the cards did not make it past the test marketing stages.

What happened next is another chapter in Tiny's book of self-sabotage. Shortly after pressing the record, an article ran in the *Chicago Tribune*: 'Tiny Tim's Not Back.' The article recapped Lawrence's background and the fact that he and Tiny had recorded together. 'Those who heard the recordings were impressed,' the *Tribune* alleged. 'There were offers for concerts, TV appearances, talk-show spots, and a record-company deal. But Tiny failed to show up for the first few TV appearances and talked about everything but the new record during an interview with a newspaper.'

The article also stated that Lawrence was 'dissolving the partnership and withdrawing the record.' It then quoted him as saying, 'That's three strikes … he's hindering me. I own the record and I can withdraw it the same way I released it. Tiny is a very, very nice guy, but he's absolutely no help at all.'

The article also carried a short quote from a seemingly bewildered Tiny. 'That's news to me,' he said. 'I can't understand why [Lawrence] would want to [pull the record].'

Lawrence would later claim to have no knowledge of the *Chicago Tribune* article, and denies that there had been any ill will on his part. 'The truth of the matter was basically Neil Hollander and Banner Talent were supposed to market the record and get me a deal with a label that would put it out and they actually dropped the ball on the whole thing,' he says. 'It had nothing to do with Tiny, because once the thing was recorded it was a matter of getting a label to put it out and then we would have probably promoted it, the two of us, but we didn't get to first base on it.'

Eventually, Tiny and Gary Lawrence fell out of touch. 'Tiny changed his phone number like people changed their underwear,' Lawrence adds. 'He was a funny guy; he did not want to deal with people from the past. If you had done something with him a long time ago, then that relationship was over and done with. He never really bothered with me after '83 or '84.'

* * *

Tiny continued traveling through 1983, performing where work presented itself and seeing Miss Dixie as often as he could. He included 'Forever Miss Dixie' on a four song, twelve-inch, country-themed EP he recorded in Australia that year, *Keeping My Troubles To Myself*, produced—or rather 'Instigated'—by Martin Sharp. Aside from the usual suspects, Tiny was accompanied by two of Australia's finest and most popular guitar players, Tommy and Phil Emmanuel, aka The Emmanuel brothers.

Aside from 'Forever Miss Dixie' and the title track, the EP also included 'The Bible My Mother Left For Me' and 'The Last Mile Of The Way.' The cover featured Tiny's profile at a microphone in black-and-white, and 2,000 copies were pressed for release through Martin Sharp's Street Of Dreams, Pty.

It was a well executed but perplexing release: the tracks all clock in at over four minutes, and a few feature improvisational, religious monologues. 'You know, this generation we live in gets harder to understand every day,' Tiny preaches, on 'The Bible My Mother Left For Me.'

> I see kids popping pills, smoking pot, getting stoned; they think it's the way. Others go for liquor like their parents did before; it's Alcoholic's Anonymous, that's where they're headed for. Then there's the wayward ones who couldn't stay at home; lost and forsaken, don't know where they're going. Others find their kicks in pornography, in selling their bodies for pleasure and profit, while their souls cry, 'Stop it! Stop it!' Then there's the gambler who doesn't win; his family in despair while he rolls the dice again. The rich man who had all he needs, say the headlines, just committed suicide. Yes, he had everything; wealth, possessions, fame, but no peace inside. You know, I cry for each and every one with love and charity and wonder if their lives would different be if their mothers left them a bible like the bible my mother left for me.

The title song, 'Keep My Troubles To Myself,' was a Harve Mann composition, which Mann had no idea was being recorded until Tiny gave him the EP some time later. Mann was evidently not pleased with Tiny for taking the liberty of adding a religious diatribe. 'That whole rap was Tiny, he just made that up,' he says. 'I don't know if it was off the cuff or he thought about it … it doesn't shed a light on the song, at least the way I feel. I mean, I don't hate it. I love that he was inspired to start talking. He says something like, I think it's good to lie. I'm not crazy about that.'

Though the details are scarce, Tiny's relationship with Miss Dixie appears to have come to a tumultuous end at some point in 1983. She may have solved her settlement issue in regards to her widow status, but Tiny remained apprehensive about marriage. 'Tiny loved Miss Dixie very much,' Martin Sharp recalled, 'but was concerned she had had her tubes tied and was concerned if he should marry her.'

When Australian television host Don Lane extended an invitation for the two to exchange wedding vows on his show, however, Tiny's hesitation momentarily faded. Dixie, on the other hand, was not interested in having a televised wedding. 'She thought Tiny was trying to make her another Miss Vicki,' Sharp explained. 'Tiny was thrilled because he couldn't afford it. They had a few arguments.'

According to some, these arguments grew violent. Years later, when speaking of Miss Dixie, Tiny told his friend and fan Jim Foley—who will become important to this story later—about a fight with Miss Dixie in which she pulled a kitchen knife on him and chased him from the house. As the story goes, Tiny hid in the bushes and found himself mesmerized, watching Dixie searching for him ferociously in a pair of daisy dukes.

Tiny's widow, Miss Sue, later summed the couple's union as 'this kind of fake marriage where they promised they were going to be together, but then things didn't work out, so I guess they had a fake divorce. I don't know.' Despite the 'fake divorce,' Tiny continued to discuss his love for Miss Dixie. When asked by *Oui* magazine the following year what Dixie might do if Tiny showed up on her doorstep tomorrow, Tiny replied, 'She'd slam the door in my face and say get the heck outta here. Oh, bitter, she's bitterly angry at me. Oh, Miss Dixie. You can take them all. If I could have bought gold, she'd have an all-gold trophy. The only woman to slap me in the face. In death, if I get to heaven, that's the only one I want.'[*]

* * *

Dixie's mental state was not the only thing upon which Tiny had a polarizing effect. A decision to have him headline Ottawa's 1983 Canadian Tulip Festival

* It is possible that Tiny and Dixie reconciled. Years later, while recording *Songs Of an Impotent Troubadour*, Tiny revealed that he 'met the beautiful Miss Dixie again with her daughter when I played Alan C. Hill's Great American Circus for the second time in '85 and '87.'

also raised a few tempers. The appearance was Tiny's first in Ottawa since a 1976 engagement at the Talisman Motor Hotel. Intending to create some excitement around the festival, then in its ninth year, the local newspaper could not resist putting a negative spin on Tiny's upcoming appearance under the headline 'Spring Festival Organizers Hope Faded Falsetto Will Pull Crowds.' Referring to Tiny as a 'paunchy' and an 'aging falsetto singer,' reporter Janice Middleton noted that several aldermen 'roared with laughter' when they heard Tiny had been chosen to headline. The organizers were stuck with defending their decision. 'So what if Tiny Tim's forty pounds heavier,' general manger Paul Akehurst stated. 'Apparently he's a perfect gentleman and a superb performer.'

The misinformed notion that Tiny Tim had been contracted to perform at a government-sponsored—and taxpayer-subsidized—event was simply too much for some upstanding citizens, and several of them submitted editorials. 'Tiny Tim's only talent has proven to be an ability to gain publicity and notoriety,' wrote one Gwen Krokar. 'The tulips, the tourists, and Ottawa tax payers deserve more respect.'

In truth, Tiny's performance fees were underwritten by a local sponsor. Additionally, he had paid for his own airfare, hotel, and incidentals after learning that the festival was a nonprofit, community event. The negativity surrounding Tiny's appearance compelled Paul Akehurst to issue a detailed account of just how much respect Tiny had actually shown 'the tulips, tourists, and Ottawa taxpayers': 'He offered to arrive two days early, stay one day later than contracted for … [and was] contracted to give two concerts and two public appearances, a total of four musical performances. In fact, he gave us eight musical performances, eighteen separate and individual private interviews and radio/TV appearances, and attended four private parties for volunteer organizers at which he sang for periods ranging up to three hours … all on his own time and at his own expense.'

That was not all. Tiny also joined the Ottawa Police Force Choral Group at an event commemorating the opening of a new police station, purchased sheet music for and quickly memorized fifteen French-Canadian chansons, had sheet music for twenty Canadian popular songs delivered to him from Fort Worth, Texas, purchased a new ukulele and paid to have it outfitted to accommodate the festival's equipment, and even offered to pay the National Capital Commission the cost of any tulips he might have accidentally trampled while tip-toeing through a tulip bed for the benefit of photographers. When he left Ottawa, he remarked to Akehurst, 'Please thank the people of Ottawa, including the skeptics, for at least giving me another chance.'

Ottawa's skepticism and/or disdain at Tiny's inclusion on the festival bill was testament to the fact that audiences had by no means grown indifferent to Tiny Tim.

* * *

Since 1971, *Roy Radin's Vaudeville Review* had continued to provide the steadiest source of employment for Tiny, but Radin's cocaine addiction and personality transformation during the late 70s and early 80s had caused many of his performers and associates to regard him negatively. Jackie Vernon had apparently nicknamed Radin 'the most hated man in show business' and proclaimed that Radin's funeral would 'be the most attended funeral in the world, because when you give the audience what they want, they will show up.'

Little did Vernon know how quickly Radin's funeral would become a reality. On May 13 1983, Roy Radin went missing. His body was discovered by a beekeeper and a US Forest Service Officer a month later in a canyon sixty-five miles north of Los Angeles; according to a report in the *Los Angeles Times*, he had been shot almost two dozen times and, for good measure, dynamite had been inserted into his mouth and lit.

Roy's sister Kate Radin's observation that 'people loved him like their king' seemed true only in regards to Radin's increasingly extravagant lifestyle and his dictatorial treatment of those around him. He had long since sold his Long Island estate, and subsequently purchased a sprawling mansion in the Hamptons called, appropriately, Ocean Castle. He became notorious for throwing decadent, cocaine-fueled parties. It was not long before his life began spiraling out of control.

In 1980, actress-model Melonie Haller was found strung-out and injured on a Long Island Railroad train. When questioned, she claimed Radin had drugged and raped her at gunpoint. The allegations were never officially substantiated, but the incident made public Radin's decadent lifestyle and cast a shadow over the *Vaudeville Revue*. Although some artists jumped ship, Tiny Tiny stuck it out until the 'cavalcade of has-beens' came to its abrupt end with Radin's violent one.

The full details of Radin's murder are a messy, complicated, drug-and-sex-filled drama involving everyone from Hollywood producers to the head of the National Bank of Puerto Rico, and have already been the subject of dozens of articles and books. When his remains were discovered in early June 1983, the once 300-pound man had been reduced to a 98-pound skeleton. As the authorities began their investigation, the former members of the *Vaudeville Revue* remained largely detached, and when a final *Revue* was put together in 1984, few of Radin's former acts chose to participate, many of them speaking ill of their former employer. 'At the time that he died it was like rats jumping off of a sinking ship,' Radin's sister, Kate, recalls. 'I was disgusted with the way that people behaved afterward.'

Tiny Tim, on the other hand, reacted differently. 'Tiny always supported me when I defended Roy,' Kate Radin adds. 'Tiny remembered the good years. People remember the bad times, but five years of addiction does not wipe way twenty-five years of hard work and sobriety. He was a good friend to Roy through his addiction where other people were not. ... There were not a lot of true friends in the businesses, but Tiny was one of them.'

Not only did Tiny stand up for Roy, he also comforted Kate throughout the investigation, which lasted nearly a decade. 'Tiny was an angel to me,' she says. 'He was a wonderful support to me over the phone and in person. Tiny had such grounded beliefs; he was so strong in his beliefs that it didn't matter what other people thought. He knew who he was. That's the type of thing that you can carry with you, and it gets you through any situation. When we used to hug each other, we used to cry because we could feel the power of Roy between us. That was always hard.'

Though it was undeniable that Roy Radin had met his end in the California desert, Tiny and Kate briefly entertained the notion that he had somehow dodged the assassination and changed his identity. Tiny told Kate that he thought he had seen Roy in the audience at one of his shows in Australia after his murder. 'We really thought that he got away and he was OK because it was too hard to imagine anything else,' Kate recalls. 'The reality of the grief was completely overwhelming.'

According to Kate, Tiny was deeply affected by Roy's death. 'Roy helped [Tiny] through his divorce ... [when Tiny] was heart broken and shattered ... reminding him of his talent and reminding him that he could not control what other people do. He was more than just a producer; he was a good friend. Tiny loved him. That's what I loved about him. He genuinely loved Roy. It wasn't about making the rent and getting a show, because Roy would always help him. He always found an outlet for Tiny to pay his rent. Roy had a great respect for talent.'

CHAPTER NINETEEN
MISS JAN

She had a vibe that was very much like a wall. You couldn't break through it.
TINY'S FRIEND AND SOMETIME CONDUCTOR HARVE MANN

In May 1984, Dennis Hunt, a reporter for the *Los Angeles Times Syndicate*, visited Tiny Tim at his hotel room in Los Angeles, just before Tiny was to depart for a performance at a high school in Ontario. His account of the subsequent events appeared in an articled entitled 'Tiny Tim Knocks: Will Opportunity Follow?' When Hunt entered Tiny's hotel room, he observed that it was several degrees warmer than the balmy temperature outdoors. Tiny explained that the air conditioner was not working properly, but soon discovered that he had accidentally turned on the heat instead of the air conditioning. 'It may be my fault,' Tiny, who was decked out in a blue tuxedo jacket, purple shirt, polka dot tie, and tennis shoes, told Hunt. 'I do silly things sometimes.'

The two engaged in a routine discussion about Tiny's illustrious past and stagnation since the late 60s, and Tiny gave his traditional responses. He referred to the two albums with Martin Sharp and recent singles like 'Yummy Yummy Pizza' as 'flops,' and called the Gary Lawrence–produced 'Do You Think I'm Sexy' and Sharp sanctioned version of 'Highway To Hell' as 'potential hits.' He also plugged his latest single, 'I'm Just A Lonesome Clone' b/w 'I'm The One (That They're Crazy About),' produced by the relatively unknown Long Island based singer-songwriter Lou Stevens and due to be released on Stevens's private label, Clone Records, the following month.

'I'm going to keep trying and trying until I make it again,' Tiny told Hunt, pounding the table with his fist. 'I'm going to try and try until it finally happens.' Then, in a surprising deviation from his typical, platitudinous interview responses, Tiny professed his love for a new woman. 'I am in love with this lovely woman, Miss Jan,' he said. 'Her parents say I am a has-been, and I want to prove them wrong.'

Though some aspects of their relationship over the following years are fairly well documented, Tiny's initial courtship with Miss Jan is mysterious. Some sources, including the *National Enquirer*, indicate that Jan Alweiss, a native of Valley Stream, New York, was working in New York City as a graphic artist when she met Tiny at a Christmas party on December 14 1983. Wherever this meeting was, Tiny remembered paying her for her photograph. 'I remember, I paid sixty-five bucks to get her picture when I first met her in '83,' he later told Howard Stern.

True to Tiny's tendency to cram the outset of his relationships with romantic promises and flights of fancy, things took off very quickly. 'My heart was taken away,' he later told *Newsweek*'s David Gates, of the moment he first laid eyes on her. Jan, too, recalled that both of them were smitten with each other. 'He promised me the best night of my life,' she told the same publication. 'We went out to dinner and a disco and I got flowers the next day—twice, in the morning and in the evening.'

Ten years later, in 1994, Miss Jan and Tiny appeared together on *The Howard Stern Show* and briefly discussed when they had met.

'When you met Tiny, was it love at first sight?' asked Stern.

'Oh, there definitely was chemistry,' Miss Jan replied. 'Our eyes met. It was very classic.'

'And then, of course, Tiny would not touch you until you were married?'

'Oh, he was the perfect gentleman. It was a real find at the time … he is very, very romantic. In fact, when I met him I don't believe he had my home telephone number, he only knew where I worked and his chauffeur did drop me off that evening, but he did send flowers to my office the next day and nobody would believe that it was really Tiny Tim. He signed the card Tiny Tim. Then when I got home at night, I had flowers at home, too.'

Neither Jan's father's disapproval of their romance nor their age difference hindered the intense courtship. Tiny was fifty-two and Jan thirty-four years old. Her parents, Tiny told the *Enquirer*, 'wanted her to marry a well established man, but she overruled them. She kept telling me, 'You're my happiness … you're the only one I want.'

Despite Jan's willingness to defy her parents, and society in general, Tiny had doubts about her sincerity. Harve Mann, Tiny's friend and sometimes-conductor, remembers an attempt by Tiny to pawn her off on him. 'Tiny had this idea that I was a stud with women, which was not necessarily true, but he had that idea that I would just show up and the girl would flip for me,' Mann recalls. 'So I went there and … meet Miss Jan and my observation was that she didn't have the slightest interest in anybody but Tiny. I mean, I could have been invisible. I told Tiny. I said, That girl is totally enamored by you. It was obvious.'

Technically, Tiny believed that it was against God's laws to get married more than once, but in this case he felt that he had been given no other choice. Years later, when asked about this issue by Robin Quivers on *The Howard Stern Show*, he paused to order another Bud Ice and replied, 'First of all, you're right there … I only believe in one marriage. I didn't divorce Miss Vicki. She did it to me. I tried to fight it … so the state of Jersey gave her the divorce. I still didn't marry. She got married again. So what should I do? She got married. Should I sit around and like women and let them touch me?'*

Tiny finally voiced his concerns to Miss Jan. 'Why do you want me?' he asked. 'You can have a million men.'

'You have what many men don't have—sincerity,' she replied. And so, on June 26 1984, at the Imperial Palace in Las Vegas, Tiny Tim and Jan Alweiss tied the knot. 'I would have married her quicker if I had the cash. I didn't want to waste time,' Tiny later told Howard Stern.

At first, things appeared to be going well. Jan joined Tiny in his one-bedroom apartment at the Olcott Hotel, which he still shared with his mother. In July, the newlywed couple was photographed licking the same ice cream cone by the *National Enquirer*—an uncharacteristic action on Tiny's part. 'I've never felt like this with any man before,' Jan told the *Enquirer*. 'I feel that this is right. This is the man I love—and he loves me.'

Despite Tiny and Jan's 'natural attraction,' the newly created trio of Tiny, Jan, and Tillie quickly grew volatile. As Miss Sue explains, 'Both Jan and Tiny's mother were both known to be difficult, so that was no surprise.' She also theorizes that Jan's similarity to Tillie played a crucial part in Tiny's decision to marry her. 'He seemed to have plunged into the terrifying but exhilarating situation of being with someone who was very much like his mother. So he could re-create all the turmoil and arguing that he had with his mom, which would've been very familiar.'

---

* In the same interview, Tiny also detailed that he had not missed a shower since December 20 1989, when he was sidetracked while preparing to take a shower at the twenty-second hour of him having not bathed, and Miss Jan seductively asked, 'What do you want? Me or the shower?'

Unlike Miss Vicki, who had suffered Tiny's bleak living situations rather passively for years, Jan found it unbearable to live with Tillie while Tiny was touring and expressed her dissatisfaction emphatically. Within weeks of their wedding, Tiny questioned the durability of their marriage.*

On July 17, Tiny appeared on *People Are Talking* and reminisced about his marriage to Miss Vicki. He also spoke unabashedly of problems with Jan. 'I hope it lasts another week, because right now I'm having some problems,' he said. 'I'm very insecure, I'm very jealous, and she'd better not be looking at too many men.'

To Tiny's dismay, Jan left the Olcott Hotel just one month into their marriage. A seldom-referenced article in the *National Enquirer* sheds some light on their hasty separation, detailing an incident at Grossinger's Hotel in the Catskill Mountains. Jan, who had joined Tiny for the show, annoyed him by inviting eight people to their dinner table. An argument ensued, and Tiny pulled the table cloth off the table, sending everything on it crashing to the ground. 'I must have blacked out because I wouldn't step on a roach,' he told the *Enquirer*. 'But I got up, grabbed her by the arm, and dragged her across the floor and up the stairs. ... Then I hit her—in full view of everyone. I don't remember what I did.'

The incident caused Jan to seek an annulment, and Tiny did not contest her decision. 'We've consented to allow her to be the plaintiff,' he said, 'and it will be for annulment … I have not yet received the papers. I don't know what it's going to be based on. It will be uncontested … I love her immensely—I still do.'

There was no follow-up article, so it is assumed that Jan abandoned the annulment. She found an apartment two blocks from the Olcott Hotel, and she and Tiny continued to see each other sporadically. The logistics of the relationship baffled many of Tiny's associates and members of his family. 'They had kept separate residences, and she was like a mystery woman,' Tiny's cousin Hal Stein later said, when interviewed for the Tiny Tim *E! True Hollywood Story*.

Tiny discussed his domestic struggles with anyone who would listen. He detailed the drama to his longtime fan and friend Kathy King, who witnessed

---

* Around this time, Tiny informed the press that he planned on trying to annul the marriage on the grounds that there had been no witnesses present, despite witnesses being listed on the marriage license. He then did an about-face and revealed that he wished to renew his vows to Jan and perhaps be married in outer space. Neither the annulment nor cosmic wedding ever happened.

every chapter of Tiny's mainstream and post-mainstream career and had been among the dozens of girls with whom Tiny corresponded in 1968. Over the course of decades, she had made him a custom Maple Leafs/Dodgers pillow, visited Tiny at the Sherman House in Chicago in 1969, kicked a kid in the shin for making fun of Tiny's red socks at a *Beautiful Thoughts* book signing, made him a red vinyl shopping bag with tulips that he took on *The Jackie Gleason Show*, cried when he married Vicki, and, when they divorced, took calls from Tiny, who asked 'What do I do now?'

'He didn't trust Jan,' King explains. 'He was pretty much afraid of her. He said she was like the Devil at times. Then he had to pray a lot, too, about it because he was always afraid that the Lord was going to hurt him or something … They had these little games that they played with each other where they would flirt with somebody else and then blame each other for flirting with these other people. So it was a constant thing like that. It was like they would get off on it or something.'

Not surprisingly, living separately did not put an end to the dramatic nature of Tiny and Jan's marriage. Tiny suspected that Miss Jan was cheating on him. In an interview with John Elder of the Melbourne *Sunday Age*, he admitted that things were 'better' when he and Jan and lived apart, but acknowledged that it did nothing to quell his paranoia. 'It fuels my jealousy, of course,' he said. 'I've had to watch her every minute … the day after I gave her a going-steady ring, an ex-boyfriend, an Australian man, came into town and they went out together. Well, at two o'clock in the morning I sneaked over to her house, two blocks from mine. I put my ear close to the door to see if he was in there. I couldn't hear anything. But guess what I saw outside her door? … She'd left garbage in there. And I saw the packaging from a Hungry Man's TV dinner. It's a big dinner for hungry men.'

Was it possible that Miss Jan had simply been very hungry? 'Maybe she was,' Tiny conceded. 'I'll give her the benefit of the doubt. But it got me thinking. I have to watch her everywhere I go. But I stay married to her because I know I'll be rewarded in heaven.'

Toward the end of 1984, Tiny discovered a contraceptive foam sponge in Jan's bathroom, hidden at the bottom of a laundry basket, which further exasperated him. Tiny was vehemently opposed to birth control in all forms due to his belief that couples must 'be fruitful and multiply,' and he was incensed that she had been using it secretly. 'I don't believe in rhythm or birth control or anything that stops production of blessed events,' he later told television host Joan Rivers. When he found the foam, he continued, 'I almost collapsed!'

Tiny's 1989 appearance on Rivers' show provided a better view not only of Tiny's marriage with Jan but also of his opinions about relationships in general. Asked whether he was glad to have divorced Miss Vicki, given that he then 'had the chance to meet a second person,' Tiny replied, 'I'm glad in one way, because I do love both of these women. I mean, they're both wonderful. It's like finding a thousand dollar bill in the street twice, but the fact is … I'm sorry for the situation with Miss Vicki and now I'm sorry for the situation with Miss Jan.'

Asked whether or not he paid alimony to Miss Jan during their separation, Tiny expounded on the strange nature of their relationship. 'She works herself. Where she works, I don't know. She won't tell me, and that's one of the reasons why I've separated from her … I said, Well, if you don't tell me where you're working, I'm not gonna tell you where I'm working.'*

Rivers reminded Tiny that the young women he courted might have ambitions of fame and fortune. 'They're using you!'

'Well, perhaps, but if you find the right one—'

'Do you think you'll find the right one?'

'Well, Miss Jan told me something very interesting. She said to me, Why are you marrying me? … I said, Well, because you have the kind of looks I want. She said, Then why shouldn't I marry you for your money? And she's right.'

'Tiny told me that the night he met Miss Jan she had just received a modest inheritance and was bragging about it to all who would listen,' Miss Sue adds. 'He took her aside and said, You should never tell people what you have. She immediately said, Oh, then you must have something that you are not telling people about. He insisted, of course, that he did not, but she would never believe him.'

---

* Jan would later tell Howard Stern that she was 'involved in promoting clubs and special events for charity.'

CHAPTER TWENTY

THE GREAT AMERICAN CIRCUS

These little kids, they pick on clowns. They step on clowns' feet and the clown keeps on smiling, saying, You little brat! The thing is, people don't know. These kids, sometimes they kick the clowns in the shin. Sometimes the clowns get angry.

TINY TIM TO JOHNNY PINEAPPLE, NOVEMBER 11 1994

'And now, the moment you've all been waiting for!' ringmaster Billy Martin announced. 'The great American circus proudly rolls out its red carpet for our very special guest star, surely, one of the entertainment's world's most colorful and unique personalities, America's very own Eternal Troubadour, here he is, the one and only, Tiny Tim!'

Tiny Tim shuffled out to the center of the ring wearing a garish, green suit covered in multicolored balloons with 'Allan C. Hill's Great American Circus' sewn into the back. His hair was dyed bright red.* He carried a triangle-balalaika shaped ukulele under one arm, and the other was linked with the arm of a young stage girl. Grabbing the microphone, Tiny huffed, 'Ladies and Gentlemen, boys and girls, what a thrill it is to be here today in beautiful, wonderful, fabulous, enchanting Niagara Falls! Niagara Falls, New York! A big hand for this great place!' After introducing the band and thanking the circus hands for 'rolling out the carpet,' Tiny began his ten-minute set.†

Meanwhile, a man who would become another of Tiny's friends and

---

* Tiny used Loving Care, Shade 81 (Redwood Brown) every two weeks. 'The feeling when you cover those grays, it's like forty years have gone back,' he later told Howard Stern. 'I'm really grateful for Loving Care.'

† His sets around this period would include renditions of current hits, such as, 'Beat It,' 'Sexual Healing,' and 'Super Freak.' 'My show is up-to-the-minute,' he told the *Hamilton Spectator*.

documentarians, Bruce Button, sat in the audience, clutching his video camera. Button, like many of Tiny Tim's most devoted fans, had adored Tiny since the late 60s and continued to follow his career. Although his fandom now brought him to a modest circus in Niagara Falls, Button and Tiny had crossed paths once before, at a very different point in Tiny Tim's career.

In May 1970, Tiny Tim and Miss Vicki, still entrenched in Tiny's stardom, flew in to Toronto International Airport, en route to Hamilton, Ontario, for a three day, $4,500 engagement at Diamond Jim's Tavern. They were met by two Cadillac limousines described by Stewart Brown of the *Hamilton Spectator* as being replete with 'TV, white plush seat covers, and embroidered doilies.'

In Hamilton, Tiny was showered with gifts and adulation, while over one hundred members of the community awaited Tiny's arrival at Diamond Jim's under a banner strung over the entrance that read 'God Bless Tiny Tim and Miss Vicki!' As the couple exited their limousine, the onlookers cheered with excitement. Fifteen year-old Bruce Button was in attendance, and when the owner of Diamond Jim's asked if any children in the audience wished to meet Tiny before the show, he spoke up.

Bruce and the other kids were brought backstage to meet Tiny Tim, who, Button recalls, was wearing orange socks, a peach-colored tie, a double-breasted gold sports jacket, and beige shoes. He was applying his customary white makeup. 'Of course, I was only fifteen, so I was star-struck and tongue-tied. Here I was, face-to-face, meeting the great one,' Button recalls. Tiny signed an autograph for Button, who managed to say only 'Gee, thanks, Mr. Tim' before returning to his seat.

After a few minutes, the lights dimmed, and Tiny appeared onstage. 'What a thrill it is to be here tonight in beautiful Hamilton, right near the home of the Toronto Maple Leaf Hockey Club!' he said, pulling his ukulele from his shopping bag and starting into a falsetto rendition of 'On The Good Ship Lollipop.'

Tiny had just begun to develop his infamous medleys, which he incorporated into the show that night in Hamilton. In addition to turn-of-the-century songs, he included modern rock hits like 'Bad Moon Rising' and 'Rock Around the Clock.' 'You got the feeling Tiny could go on forever,' the *Hamilton Spectator* wrote. Then, pulling out his electric megaphone, Tiny sang a brief medley of wartime songs before closing with 'Tip-Toe.'

'Thank you so much!' he shouted into the microphone as he exited the stage, blowing kisses to the audience. 'How wonderful you are! God Bless you all!'*

Within two years, Tiny had completely faded from the limelight, but Button remained a loyal fan. He watched Tiny's occasional television appearances, clipped newspaper and magazine articles when they popped up, and tracked down as many of his records as he could find. And now, having caught wind of Tiny's 1987 circus tour, they traveled to Tonawanda, New York, to see the show. This time, however, Tiny did not arrive with his beautiful young bride in a limousine. Local politicians and famous athletes were not waiting to meet him. Nor had the citizens of the town hung up a banner in his honor or cheered upon his arrival. Instead, the Buttons were greeted by a circus tent squatting in a muddy field.

* * *

Tiny first performed with the circus in 1984, and shortly after his first stint, Allan C. Hill changed the circus's name from the Hoxie-Brothers Great American Circus to the Great American Circus, and, ultimately, to Allan C. Hill's Great American Circus. After his first few weeks, Hill offered Tiny a full contract for 1985, and the siren song of steady work called to him. He signed the contract. Jeffrey Zaslow of the *Wall Street Journal* broke the story with an article entitled 'The Bloom Is Off The Tulips: Tiny Tim At The Circus':

> Tiny Tim knows that … he's an oddball draw. 'I have to look at myself the way the world looks at me,' he says. 'Naturally, they see me as a curiosity, a freak.' … He knows he brings ridicule on himself. But his eccentricity took him to the top, he says, and it's part of him, 'like an arm.' Sure, he's swallowing his pride at intermission by signing autographs alongside two clowns. Swarming children collect all three signatures in their circus coloring books; Tiny Tim is just another clown.

The move garnered a great deal of media attention for Tiny. Joe Butkiewicz,

---

* Tiny Tim made a different impression on the management of Diamond Jim's Tavern. Years later, co-owner Max Mintz mentioned Tiny in an article for the *Spectator* about the history of the tavern and some of the eccentricities of the performers who were booked there. 'With Tiny Tim it was Chinese food,' Mintz said. 'He'd get twenty dishes and eat them all himself. He ate and ate until just before the show [and] said, I'm sick, I can't do it. I said, Get him an aspirin, put him in the shower, get him out there. The place is packed!'

a reporter for the Pennsylvania *Times Leader*, asked, 'Did Tim join the circus? Has the circus joined him? Or has Tim's life always been something of a sideshow?' Dan Hogan of the *New Chief* chimed in, too, asking Tiny about his steadily expanding body. 'I love to eat,' Tiny replied, before listing his favorite foods as pizza, Chinese food, and popcorn. Truly, the lanky man from the clubs of Greenwich Village had changed. He now weighed 240 pounds.

Despite the discouraging press, Tiny retained a positive outlook. 'I'm very grateful I have this job,' he told Hogan. 'Producer Allan C. Hill has innovated something new here. I'm the very first singer who's been up there and down to ever come back and work this long for the circus. Presley worked for the circus before he became a name. Joe Lewis and Tom Mix were down and worked for the circus … If I have another hit record, I'm back on top for another twenty years.'

In truth, Tiny's name carried more weight than any other performer Hill had featured in his show. Accordingly, Hill made certain that every piece of promotional material he produced boasted Tiny Tim's inclusion in the show. He even released a special press kit exclusively about the new addition, which stated that the engagement was Tiny's 'childhood dream.' It also featured Tiny's biography wedged incongruously between circus-related FAQs about what camels eat and 'What happens if an elephant gets sick?'

'If you can do this, you can do anything,' Cheryl Martin, wife of Ringmaster Billy Martin and 'Ballerina of the Air,' told Tiny when he signed on. She was right, Tiny later said. 'It was a great adventure, because it was a different dimension of show business. They live in their own world.' In addition to Billy and Cheryl Martin, Tiny's fellow performers included the Suarez-Loyal-Repensky riding troupe; an elephant act under the direction of Tim and Antoinette Frisco; the Steeple Family's bear and chimp act; the 'high wire thrills and chills' of the Great Wallenda Duo; and, last but not least, a pair of clowns, Omar-Gosh and Cheeko.

The circus tour started in Fort Myers, Florida, made its way up the East Coast and back down through the South, and ended in Sarasota, Florida, visiting 200 cities between March and November. The circus arrived in a different town each morning, performed the first show at 4pm and another 7pm, retired for the evening at 11pm, and was back on the road at 5am. Easter Sunday was the only scheduled holiday. Tiny made a point of not complaining about the grueling schedule, which must have taken its toll on the now fifty-four-year-old man. As the circus' resident celebrity, he was given the royal treatment: 'I had a broken-down Airstream trailer,' he later said. 'The air conditioner didn't work. It looked nice from the outside.'

On August 7 1985, while passing through Genesee, New York, the driver of the truck in which Tiny Tim was a passenger fell asleep at the wheel. Shortly after 7am, the truck drifted across the highway and struck another vehicle before slamming into a restaurant. Both Tiny and his driver sustained shoulder injuries but were not seriously injured. After the accident, the circus began to provide Tiny hotel rooms in an effort to ease the strain of traveling.

He was compensated a cool $100,000 for the arduous 1985 tour and $108,000 in 1987. As in his heyday, much of the money was routed everywhere except Tiny's bank account: each week, 20 percent went to a series of agents, another $500 to his agent Mr. Rocky, and $200 to yet another manager.* He also continued to pay rent on his apartment at the Olcott Hotel, and for a nurse to care for his mother, who was now in her mid-nineties. After his own spending, which still included a plethora of beauty products and more-than-generous tips, he noted that if he 'cleared $3,000 when the circus ended, that was a miracle.'

One person to whom he did not give too much of his paycheck was Miss Jan. 'She gave me a hard time and she didn't stay with me,' he explained. 'She was very independent, who knows where she went in the eight months or who she went with, and the fact is I wasn't even a year married to her.' Considering that Jan had filed a suit demanding $1,000 in monthly alimony payments—and had lost—Tiny's atypical stinginess seemed personal, and perhaps justified.

Jan was quick to bury the hatchet when she discovered how much Tiny was earning at the circus, and she joined him on the road in March 1985. Her newfound positivity vanished, however, when she caught sight of Tiny's trailer.

'Darling, I know it's a little broken, but there's nothing wrong,' Tiny said, trying to reason with her. 'I'm gonna be with you here.'

'Look … I can only be here a week,' she replied.

According to Tiny, they fought 'day and night' for the next week. When one argument dragged on until two in the morning, one of the circus' managers pounded on the door and yelled, 'This is not a night club! Have

---

* Though it is unclear just how much 'managing' Mr. Rocky actually did, he had been waiting for some time to cash in on their association. 'He got $500 a week from me [when I traveled with the circus], and he deserved it,' Tiny told Johnny Pineapple, 'because since '78 he got nothing, he laid off me. He was told by *some nice gentlemen*, When he makes money, that's when you start taking it.'

a clown take her to the airport!' The clown, however, was unwilling to drive, and ultimately the fight was settled at the local police station.

When Mr. Rocky caught wind that Miss Jan was causing a stir on the road, he issued her a warning. 'I called [Mr. Rocky] up and he said, You tell her, if you get fired from this circus, she'll hear from me,' Tiny recalled. 'So, of course, I did tell her. So it was rough from that angle.' Soon after Rocky's phone call, Miss Jan returned to New York.

Despite the issues with Jan, 1985 did see a positive development in Tiny's personal life in the form of a reconnection with his daughter, Tulip. Though she had not seen her father since she and Vicki had attended his 'thirty years in show business' party in 1981, the fourteen-year-old now expressed a sudden desire not only to communicate with her father but to stay with him as well.

With Vicki's blessing, Tulip visited Tiny in New York City before Tiny left for the circus. According to Vicki, Tulip described the visit as 'awkward and unusual.' 'He didn't know what to say to her,' Vicki adds. 'I totally understand … it was like meeting a stranger. She went back a few more times after that and would call him and write letters.'

* * *

In terms of recording, Tiny's only release of 1985 was a single—his first self-release since 1973, and also his last. The record features Tiny on Suzuki's Omnichord, a bizarre electric musical instrument with chord buttons and a digital strumming censor, performing two of his own compositions: 'She Left Me With The Herpes,' and a song that would later become a favorite of Howard Stern's, 'Santa Claus Has Got The AIDS This Year.' Given Tiny's disapproval of premarital sex and his intense fear of sexually transmitted diseases, the songs seem, on one level, like natural subjects for Tiny, but their lyrics stand in stark contrast to his characteristically innocent subject matter.

A slow digital beat from the diminutive Omnichord backs 'She Left Me With The Herpes,' and the audacious lyrics leave no room for misinterpretation. After a spoken intro of 'Ouch! Ouch! Ohh!' the song is startling in its childlike perversity:

She let me with the herpes,
Oh, why did she do that?
Last night I sat upon my chair,
And gave it to the cat.

The ridiculous lyrics continue with the herpes spreading to his face, a place he 'can't repeat,' his guitar, and his chambermaid, turning his life into a 'social wreck.' Toward the song's conclusion, Tiny goes into a small rant that offers his solution for the growing problem of STDs: 'Listen everyone, let's all get married and stop fooling around! Be true to your wives and husbands! Be true and the herpes will go away!'

The single's B-side has become even more notorious. Set to a slightly faster beat, again, courtesy of the Omnichord, 'Santa Claus Has Got The AIDS This Year' is truly one of the most bizarre and offensive songs ever committed to tape. Employing his Grandpa Tim voice, Tiny begins the song with another spoken intro, announcing, as Santa Claus, 'I won't be around this year … I'm a bit sick!' He then launches into another set of outrageously ill-informed lyrics:

> *Santa Claus has got the AIDS this year,*
> *And he won't be 'round to spread his Christmas cheer,*
> *The reindeer all look blue,*
> *They know what he's going through,*
> *Santa Claus has got the AIDS this year.*

Tiny's spoken oration exposed his misconceptions about the AIDS epidemic but also speaks to America's prevailing ignorance of the disease during the early 80s. 'I'll be back next year!' he says. 'Don't cry for me, a doctor will cure me!' He even once told Howard Stern, 'I do drink beer from the straw instead of from the glasses, because of AIDS going around.'

Later, Tiny would vaguely acknowledge the sensitive nature of the song by giving several jumbled explanations as to why he wrote it. Given his personal variety of religion and condemnation of sinful behavior, it is probable that Tiny viewed AIDS as a punishment for philandering and/or homosexuality. However, in his back-pedaling, he seemed unable to make up his mind as to whether he was referring to AIDS, the disease, or Ayds, a short-lived weight-loss candy bar.

When re-recording the tune for *Songs Of An Impotent Troubadour* almost ten years later, Tiny gave an answer that seemed to combine both explanations. 'The AIDS, in my opinion, is from sins because of disobedience to God's laws and fornication, sex before marriage, whatever. This song was written when Ayds was still a reducing candy bar—way before Rock Hudson, way before

Liberace … no one's trying to make fun of anyone, we are sorry for those who have it. When I wrote this song, it was just a word.'

Though Tiny would repeat on several occasions that AIDS was born out of 'disobedience to God's laws,' David Tibet, a Tiny Tim fan and collaborator, wrote a forgiving comment in the album's liner notes, reaffirming Tiny's fantastical explanations for his song lyrics. 'Tiny asked me to point out that the "Aids" referred to in his classic composition "Santa Claus Has Got The Aids This Year" refers to the well-known weight-reducing candy bar, not the terrible disease, which came into the headlines some years after he wrote his song.'

In 1995, when Howard Stern played the song during one of Tiny's appearances on his show and praised the songwriting, Tiny again repeated his dubious claim that the candy bar was the inspiration for the song. 'I should say Mr. Stern, that when that song was written in 1980,' he said, 'before the Rock Hudson scandal, it was not written to make fun of AIDS, it was written because Ayds was, at that time, a diet candy bar, A-Y-D-S, and AIDS was just a small little word.'

'Yeah, and AIDS was just like—if we even knew what it was,' Stern replied, purportedly accepting the explanation. 'You should put it in context, that's true, but it's still a good song. The tune was what was good, too. You wrote that yourself, too, right?'

'That's why I don't write too many songs.'

Like the songs, the 45 itself is also an odd item. Pressed by the non-existent Generic Records, the sleeve boasts that 'She Left Me With The Herpes' is Tiny's 'greatest song yet,' and that 'Santa Claus Has Got The Aids This Year'—'A SERIOUS SONG'—is the 'song of the century.' The credits confirm that the songs were 'produced by Tiny Tim in his living room' and that they represent the 'first recording ever played entirely on the Suzuki Omnichord.' They also list a management company, 'Steve Goodman Associates,' alongside a phone number that to this day still connects to the switchboard at the Olcott Hotel.

Predictably, this strange little record went nowhere. Even Dr. Demento, who had included 'Tip-Toe' on his 1985 compilation album *Dr. Demento Volume Three: The 60s*, did not acknowledge receipt of the record when Tiny mailed him a copy. In fact, many of the records never even left Tiny's hotel room.

'I made about a thousand copies,' Tiny confessed to Harve Mann, 'and I have about a thousand copies.'

* * *

Tiny's contract with Allan C. Hill's circus was not renewed in 1986, but the year did see the release of *The Eternal Troubadour*, his first feature-length album since *Chameleon* and *Wonderful World Of Romance.** Radio veteran Jack Gale produced the album. Gale had worked in radio since 1944 and had been Johnny Cymbal's manager in 1963 when the smash hit 'Mr. Bass Man' blew up. He had also been awarded the first Disc Jockey Of The Year award by *Billboard* magazine. By the 80s, he was also releasing albums on his own Nashville-based label, Playback Records, and selling them via television infomercials. He teamed up with former Grand Ole Opry pianist Jim Pierce to produce a slew of 'greatest hits' albums for country acts like Johnny Cash, Del Reeves, Johnny Paycheck, Roy Drusky, Billie Jo Spears, and even a few original albums such as *Tina Turner Goes Country* and *Country Laine* by Frankie Laine.

Eventually, they happened on the idea to release a Tiny Tim record. Given that Tiny had no other notable hits beyond 'Tip-Toe Thru' The Tulips,' Gale insisted that a reworked version of the song be included on the new album. 'I thought people would be disappointed if they got an album with twenty songs and they didn't get "Tip-Toe" in there,' says Gale. The additional tracks included songs from the turn of the century, like 'Till We Meet Again' and 'Baby Face'; reworkings of 60s material like Don Ho's 'Tiny Bubbles'; and a new version of Tiny's 1977 non-hit '(I'm Gonna Be A) Country Queen.'

Tiny traveled to Tennessee to record the album, and Gale immediately took a liking to him. 'He was a delightful guy,' Gale says. 'He really was.' Shortly after Tiny's arrival, Gale, Jim Pierce and Gale's wife, Lovey, brought Tiny to a local supermarket. 'Tiny said he wanted to get some groceries or something. He did not like eating in restaurants. He did not want to catch herpes from their silverware and dishes and their food.' As they prepared to enter the supermarket, Gale knew they were in for an experience. 'Johnny Cash and Eddie Arnold and everybody shops here,' Pierce cautioned. 'It's no big deal.' Within minutes of their arrival, the store's manager came running out of his office, yelling, 'Is Tiny Tim here!?'

'Pretty soon, there were about 300 people in that supermarket looking for Tiny Tim!' Gale recalls. 'He caused a crowd. And what did he buy? He bought about fifteen [rolls of] paper towel, and he bought a bunch of mustard pickles and olives … that's what he was eating. He didn't want to use the

---

* The same year also yielded a CD single featuring three different versions of Tiny performing the Billy Bland hit 'Let The Little Girl Dance,' all recorded in 1983, but the scarcity of existing copies suggests that it was never widely distributed.

hotel's towels, so he bought all those towels. He had his own eccentricities. Whatever floats your boat, you know?'

The group returned to the hotel and, before they retired to their respective rooms, Gale reminded Tiny to be punctual the next morning. 'Eight o'clock in the morning, you have to be out here in my car.'

'Yes, Mr. Gale,' Tiny replied. 'No problem. I'll be right there.'

With that, they retired to their rooms. Gale's sleep was disturbed, however, when the phone in his room rang at 5am the following morning. It was Tiny.

'What's the matter? What's the problem?'

'Well, I just wanted to let you know, I'll be there at eight o'clock. I'm taking my first shower.'

A half hour later, Gale awoke with a jolt when the phone rang again. 'The phone rang again … and again, again,' Gale recalls. 'He was taking his second and third shower, and he wanted to let me know.'

By 8:00am they were on their way to Swanee Recording Studio, where *Tiny Tim: The Eternal Troubadour* was recorded over the next few days. When Tiny realized that some of the old standards were not to be recorded in their entirety, however, the entire production halted. He had brought with him original lyric sheets—including verses and introductions from songs like 'It's A Long Way To Tipperary' that had long since dropped from the sheet music—and was upset that the musicians were unable to play all the verses. Ultimately, the majority of the songs had to be recorded without the original verses and introductions. 'Tiny was very upset about that,' Gale recalls. 'He wanted the music to be authentic, but there was no music for the verses, and we had no idea.'

Once Tiny compromised, the mood lightened, and the rest of the recording went smoothly. The sessions yielded the following tracks: 'Tip-Toe Thru' The Tulips With Me,' 'Sweet Rosie O'Grady,' 'Shine On Harvest Moon,' 'Baby Face,' 'Till We Meet Again,' 'It's A Long Way To Tipperary,' 'Prisoner Of Love,' 'Those Were The Days,' 'When You Wore A Tulip,' 'Pennies From Heaven,' 'Tiny Bubbles,' 'When The Saints Go Marching In,' 'Just A Gigolo,' 'Happy Days Are Here Again,' 'Bill Bailey, Won't You Please Come Home?' 'Country Queen,' and 'Beautiful Dreamer.'

Gale also arranged a video shoot, featuring Tiny Tim, in a tuxedo, lip-syncing to some of the songs on the album. The footage was later cut into an infomercial to promote the Playback Records release. The LP features a humorous cover photo of Tiny Tim attempting to 'tiptoe' through—but looking as if he is about to trample—a small bed of red tulips. The liner notes boast about Tiny's unmatched knowledge of turn-of-the-century music, his unchallenged possession of the world's 'nonstop singing record,' and, of course, his wedding on *The Tonight Show*. Furthermore, they mention Tiny's favorite color (white) and food (spaghetti), and note that Henry Kissinger attended the same high school as Tiny. 'Do you think Henry went there because Tiny did???'*

Around the time of the album's release, Gale returned home one day to find several phone messages from Tiny, lamenting the fact that 'Beautiful Dreamer' had not made the album. 'It was advertised and we did it,' he said, 'but it's not on the album.' Gale confirms that they had rehearsed the song, 'and it was wonderful … [but] for some reason it never made the master.'

Gale also booked Tiny an appearance on *Nashville Now*. Before the taping was underway, he placed a dozen tulips underneath Tiny's guest chair. 'You give everyone on the show a tulip,' he instructed Tiny. During the taping, Tiny sat down in his chair and handed host Charlie Chase a tulip from under his seat.

'This is for you, Mr. Chase,' said Tiny.

'Oh, this is your trademark,' Chase replied, taking the tulip. 'You give these out everywhere you go?'

'No,' Tiny replied. 'My producer, Mr. Jack Gale, told me to give it to you.'

Ultimately, *Tiny Tim: The Eternal Troubadour* was not a big seller for Playback Records. 'I always go for the thing that people say is not gonna happen and you can't do it and so on and so forth and, to me, I just thought Tiny Tim [could work],' Gale explains. 'It did not turn out that way. It was not a *Billboard* success, so to speak. We sold a few to collectors and things like that, but it never really did anything.'

* * *

Lousy record sales aside, 1986 carried with it more heartache for Tiny Tim. On July 3, his beloved idol, Rudy Vallee, passed away at his home at the age of eighty-four. Even Vallee's passing was quickly overshadowed, though, by the death of Tiny's ninety-five-year-old mother, Tillie, just six days later. By that time, Tillie was no longer living with Tiny at the Olcott Hotel. After difficult

* In 1987, Bear Family Records issued the album on CD under the title *Tiptoe Through The Tulips/Resurrection*, with modified cover art and different liner notes, making Tiny the only living singer whose recordings were available concurrently on cylinder record, flat record, cassette, and compact disc.

deliberation, he had agreed to place her in a nursing home when she began to require constant care.

Even in the final years of her life, however, Tillie's demeanor did not soften. Miss Sue recalls Tiny telling her of a time toward the end when he sang 'I'll Always Be Mother's Boy' to Tillie. 'She looked for a moment as if she might betray some sign of positive emotion, but in the end she couldn't manage it. She turned away with a noncommittal remark. He told her he was going to be on TV that evening, and she pretended not to care. Later, he opened the door a crack and saw her tune in to watch.'

Nevertheless, Tiny took his mother's death hard. A few years later, in his interview with Joan Rivers, he called her 'a saint of a mother.'

Aware of Tiny's tumultuous personal life, Rivers pressed him further. 'Who do you confide in? Who do you trust?'

'I know it sounds crazy,' Tiny replied, 'but, you know, my mother was Jewish, my father was Catholic; I just talk to Jesus Christ and the sweet blessed mother. I tell them all my problems and I can not tell you the answers I get, because if not for them, I would be who knows where right now.'

Tillie was buried next to Butros at Woodlawn cemetery in the Bronx. The modest tombstone features images of both Tillie and Butros, with a third image of Jesus Christ positioned between. Underneath a caption reading 'JESUS BE,' the inscriptions, clearly written by Tiny, read 'BELOVED MOTHER' and 'BELOVED FATHER,' lauding them as 'A SAINT OF A MOTHER' and 'A SAINT OF A FATHER.'*

Though Tiny was more than willing to discuss various and unconventional issues weighing on his mind, he failed to make mention of his mother in an interview he gave shortly after her death, suggesting it was an ache too personal for even the famously candid Tiny Tim to discuss publicly. Instead, he spoke positively of an upturn in his career: 'I'm getting a lot more fan mail now than I was ten years ago. And I have a lot of new things I wish to accomplish. I'm always looking for the next hit record ... I never stop trying.'

Though Tillie's nursing-home stay and death rendered moot Miss Jan's refusal to cohabitate with Tiny, they continued to live separately. Miss Jan had allegedly been fired from her job as a commercial artist, and she blamed Tiny

---

* Tiny also sought to have a memorial created for Rudy Vallee. 'I wrote a letter to President Reagan when [Vallee] died,' Tiny told *Goldmine*'s Tom Kidd in 1990. '[He] referred me to this one or that governor, but no one has responded. I still think we should have a street in Hollywood named after this great and innovative singer.'

for this as it occurred after he sent her a singing telegram, performed by a large man portraying a Buddha, covered in gold paint and wearing only a loin cloth. Afterward, she refused to give him any details about her employment status.

Surprisingly, Tiny inherited $250,000 from Tillie. It's unclear how Tillie had come to possess that amount of money, but Tiny supposed that she had saved it during her years working in the garment industry, while others believed that Tiny's managers had given his parents some of his money 'for safekeeping' during his 60s peak. Regardless, once the money was in the hands of Tiny and Jan, it soon dried up.

* * *

After blowing his inheritance, Tiny signed on for another run with Allan C. Hill's Great American Circus in 1987. 'This is probably the last time I'll do this,' he told his friend Harve Mann shortly before leaving for the tour. He had developed a standard answer to questions about the state of his career. 'It's not a comedown to switch to Vegas shows to the circus,' he told the *St Petersburg Times*. 'I'm the first and only living name that has sung with a circus this long. It's the only living vaudeville around. And it's a thrill to work with circus performers. They really are the best in the business.'

While Tiny may have been exaggerating about his enthusiasm to be touring with the circus, he was not bluffing about his respect for the circus staff, nor their respect for him. 'We're making every effort to treat him like a star,' ticket-seller Jim Ridenour told *The Wall Street Journal*. 'The man's gotta live,' circus hand Roberto Hernandez added. 'We respect him for being here.'

Allan C. Hill also utilized Tiny in other capacities during their collaboration. In June, Hill was one of twenty-seven wealthy bachelors auctioned off in a fundraising event for the American Cancer Society. Two women, who paid a grand total of $23,000 to go on a date with Hill, were flown out to Chicago. While there, Hill took them on a late night elephant ride as Tiny Tim serenaded them.

By the time Bruce Button and his father went to see Tiny Tim perform with the circus in August 1987, it felt old hat for Tiny. When the circus took an intermission, Button queued up for an autograph. 'So here I am waiting in line with all the seven- and eight-year-old kids, I looked ridiculous,' says Button, who had brought a copy of *Chameleon*. 'I thought it would be a good thing to get signed … Tiny probably hadn't seen too many of these floating around because it was an Australian release.'

When Button handed Tiny the obscure album, Tiny looked puzzled. 'Do you *like* this?' he asked. Tiny signed the record and handed it back to Button, who then asked if they could meet for a chat after the show. Tiny agreed. Button was excited, but nervous. 'The first time I met him all I could say was Thank you, Mr. Tim, and now he was going to come out and talk to me.' Since Button's father was a musician and had been interested in a lot of older, big-band music, he and Tiny did most of the talking. During their conversation it began to rain. Tiny Tim told the Buttons to go with him 'to his car.'

'This was the car that he'd been basically living in, going around from town to town, doing the circus,' Button recalls. 'I got into the passenger side, my dad was in the back, and I let Tiny get into the driver's side—it never really hit me that he didn't know how to drive. It seemed odd watching him trying to maneuver himself into that front driver's seat with the steering wheel with all that stuff.'

The 1984 Ford Mustang LX was not quite the Cadillac limousine from Hamilton in 1970, but Tiny did not seem to mind. They spoke about Tiny's career, past recordings, love affairs, and the affinity for big-band music that Tiny shared with Button Sr. When Tiny returned to the tent for his encore, everyone shook hands and went their separate ways. 'I thought, Oh this is great, I've met Tiny Tim, I'm pretty satisfied with that,' Button says.

Two weeks later, Button's father called his son to tell him the circus was going to be in Niagara Falls on September 3. This time, Button brought a video camera along and taped Tiny's performance. During the set, Tiny stopped and thanked Bruce Button for recording the show. Afterward, they met up behind the circus tent and let the camera roll on their lengthy discussion. In the footage, Tiny is seated in his passenger seat, and Button is kneeling outside at the window. The taped conversation serves as an intimate look into one of the oddest points in Tiny's career. The two discuss Tiny's second single for Reprise Records, 'Bring Back Those Rockabye Baby Days,' and Tiny expresses his disappointment with the way the record had been produced. Then, in between swigs from a two-liter bottle of 7 Up, he treats Button to three different versions of the song, in three different vocal styles.

'How long is the reel?' Tiny asks, pointing to the camera.

'About two hours,' Button replies.

With that Tiny straightens up to deliver an official message: 'I'd like to say Mr. Bruce Button … it's nice talking to you here from the Great American Circus in Niagara Falls, New York … and I can tell you that it's so nice having a friend and fan like you … coming down all this way to see this take it or leave it show!' He then croons a version of 'Love Thy Neighbor,' picking up a copy of Vanna White's autobiography midway through and pointing to her photograph on the cover. 'I hope I don't get sued! Sued and divorced!'

'You're still married to Miss Jan?' Button asks. 'I'd read in the papers a while back that you two had split up.'

'We have split up, two times. Three times, at least.'

'But you're back together again then?'

'At this point right now, yes.'

* * *

In September 1987, Tiny and Jan were only recently back on speaking terms. She had been persuaded to join Tiny on his second circus tour, but had reneged on her promise after a blowout the previous December. Instead, she planned to meet him when the circus stopped in Monroeville, Pennsylvania. The details of their constant fighting, separations, and reconciliations remained something of a mystery to the press, and Tiny's commentary—sometimes blatantly chauvinistic—only confused the issue. Asked by the *St. Petersburg Times* whether the idea of an eight-month circus tour might be too much for Miss Jan, Tiny replied, 'I expect a lot of the woman I marry. She must be spiritually and morally dedicated to me, be willing to *serve* me, to meet *my* needs.'

In a January 1987 phone conversation with Harve Mann, Tiny showed that he was perhaps more shaken up by his separation from Miss Jan than he let on to the press.

'I'll tell you, I haven't seen my wife since December 19,' Tiny revealed.

'You're kidding!' Mann exclaimed.

'I wish I was,' Tiny replied. 'She lives in her apartment and I live in mine,' he explained, adding that she would come to 'stay two or three nights' when she knew he'd been paid. 'I may not be a good lover, but I can pay her!' Admitting that he did not know what she got up to when she wasn't with him, he noted his belief that she 'must be sleeping with someone—or many … I want her to get a blood test to see that she's got no AIDS.'

'This is an unusual situation to say the least,' Mann concluded. 'I hope you work out those problems with her.'

'I will, in the divorce court!' Tiny replied. He then turned his thoughts to relationships in general. 'Basically, no matter how good you are in bed, the fact is that you can be good in bed for five hours and you have twenty-four hours in a day. Then the other 19 hours, you want to go out, you don't want the woman around, you have no interest in her, you have your own work to do, you get tired of her, she gets tired of you; you have a sexual moment and then you hate each other afterward … you're gonna get tired of everyone eventually.'

* * *

Despite the occasional threat of divorce, Tiny seemed content to allow Jan to decide the fate of their marriage. 'The fact is,' he told Button, 'if the marriage lasts, it's because she kept it.'

'I think we've taken up quite a bit of tape time here,' Button concluded. 'How about a song before we sign off?'

'All right,' Tiny said, grabbing his ukulele. 'I have a great song here—to all, wherever you might be!' Staring into Button's camera lens, he began a proud rendition of Gene Autry's 1938 hit 'There's A Goldmine In The Sky,' seemingly impervious to the ignoble surroundings of circus equipment and tractors scattered in a sodden field.

There's a goldmine in the sky far away,
We will find it, you and I,
One sweet day,
And we'll settle back and watch the world go by,
Once we find that long-lost goldmine in the sky!

CHAPTER TWENTY-ONE

MARVELOUS MERVO

Marvelous Mervo, at your service,
Marvelous Mervo, 'cause that's my name,
And I'll do my best to entertain you,
With magic and laughter,
'cause that's my game.

THEME SONG TO BILL REBANE'S *BLOOD HARVEST*, AS SUNG BY TINY TIM

In 1987, cult film director Bill Rebane prepared the release of *Blood Harvest*, a horror film starring Tiny Tim. Rebane was born in Riga, Latvia, in 1937 and moved to America in 1952. By 1961, he had settled in rural Wisconsin and began shooting and producing films at his home: the Shooting Ranch. He supported himself as a commercial director, but churned out low-budget horror, science fiction, and exploitation films on the side, including *The Giant Spider Invasion* and *The Capture Of Bigfoot*.

Two years prior to the inception of *Blood Harvest* however, Rebane was engaged in a very different project: organizing a music festival on his ranch. He had booked Forest Tucker, Jaye P. Morgan, and Bill Haley's Comets, but needed another act. He contacted David Jackson, a small-time booking agent in Kansas City, to help fill the slots. 'You really should add Tiny Tim,' Jackson suggested. 'I'll make a deal with you: I'll get Tiny Tim for you for only $1,000, if you give him a screen test while he's out there.'

Jackson had booked Tiny on many occasions, beginning in the late 70s, but in recent years Tiny had expressed a desire to break into movies—specifically 'horror roles, maybe Hunchback of Notre Dame types, maybe freak roles, maybe cripples or whatever,' as he explained in a 1979 interview with the *Soho Weekly*.

'[Tiny] thought he was Lon Chaney!' Jackson recalled.

Initially, Rebane was hesitant to book Tiny. 'I thought he was an enigmatic character,' Rebane recalls, '[but] I wasn't at all sure whether that was the right pick ... I wasn't sure where to place him.' Jackson persisted, and Rebane acquiesced. Almost immediately, Rebane questioned his decision, 'Everyone kept saying to me You've got to be kidding!'

Jackson, too, ran into difficulties. When he contacted Tiny about the festival, Tiny put him in touch with one of his managers, whom Jackson described as a 'real cigar-chomper.' The cigar-chomper was upset that Tiny had been 'discussing business' on his own, and would hear nothing until he received a deposit from Rebane. The conversation became heated, and when Tiny attempted to step in, he was soundly silenced. 'You shut the fuck up!' the cigar-chomper screamed. 'You're not supposed to think! You are the talent! I am the manager! I make the decisions! You keep your mouth shut!'

As the conversation continued, Jackson became aware of a faint mumbling in the background and realized it was Tiny praying the Rosary. 'Instead of involving himself in the conflict any further, he really believed that praying would solve the problem,' said Jackson says. Eventually Jackson calmed the 'cigar chomper' enough to negotiate, and Rebane ended up booking Tiny as the festival's headliner, which drew some 'strange looks' from locals, 'but they all came out of curiosity, and that's when the strange phenomena hit. The moment he performed, it was like magic.'

According to Rebane, the locals took a liking to Tiny Tim's genteel personality and were thrilled when he humored their requests for autographs, pictures, and interviews. 'They absolutely began to love him as both an entertainer and an individual,' Rebane says. 'Oddly enough, the women were absolutely nuts about him.'

Rebane himself came to regard Tiny as a 'fantastic human being' and found his idiosyncrasies intriguing. He remembers Tiny eschewing home-cooked meals in the Rebane household in favor of canned vegetables and fruit, and found it curious that Tiny refused to use bath towels, and instead dried himself with Job Squad paper towels. '[Paper towels are] more sanitary,' Tiny later explained in an appearance on *The Howard Stern Show*. 'They're not cleansed with other germs from other towels.'*

Rebane kept his promise and gave him a screen test after the festival.

---

* After Tiny revealed in an interview that he preferred Job Squad to Bounty, the company offered to send him a large supply of paper towels, but he refused, 'because it would be unfair to [take] advantage of this.'

The results were unconvincing; Tiny seemed awkward and unsure of himself while reading the few lines he was given, and Rebane came to understand that if he were to utilize Tiny in a film, it would have to be a role in which Tiny essentially played himself. Shortly thereafter, such a role presented itself when Rebane purchased the screenplay for a slasher film, which he rewrote as *Nightmare*. The plot centers on Jill Robinson, who after a few rebellious years away from home returns to find her childhood home vandalized and her parents missing. Because her father was a banker who oversaw the foreclosure of many homes in the area, Jill has difficultly extracting information from her neighbors. The only two helpful townspeople are Gary, an old flame, and his mentally handicapped brother, Merv. Things progress, a mysterious serial killer terrorizes the town, and bodies begin to pile up.

As he developed the Merv character, Rebane recalled Tiny's screen test. 'Out of the clear, blue sky, Tiny popped into my head. I immediately called Dave Jackson on the phone and asked, Would Tiny consider doing a lead role in a low-budget feature film?'

Rebane began to restructure the film around Tiny, and his character metamorphosed from Merv, a mentally handicapped adult, to Marvelous Mervo, a demented former clown who had sustained brain damage, and, though no longer working for the circus, still dressed the part. Tiny read the script and loved it.

Rebane faced some opposition in regards to his decision to cast Tiny, but he refused to budge. 'It took a lot of selling to the other people involved that Tiny Tim should be in the lead role in this picture.'

Because of Tiny's renowned ability to recall lyrics, composers, and general information about thousands of songs, Rebane did not anticipate Tiny having an issue memorizing lines. When Tiny arrived at The Shooting Ranch, however, Rebane discovered otherwise. When Tiny turned up in his Great American Circus suit—which he wears in the movie, much to the frustration of Allan C. Hill—he appeared nervous and struggled with the script. 'I worked endless hours with him on techniques on how to work out the part and get into the part for his character,' Rebane recalls. 'He would ask, Mr. Rebane, what do you think of this? Or, Just how should I do this, Mr. Rebane? It was almost like working with a child.'

As the production progressed, Rebane continued to modify Marvelous Mervo to more closely mirror Tiny's personality. At the film's climax, Marvelous Mervo is shot in the stomach. The effect called for the use of a squib: a small explosive attached to a packet of blood hidden underneath the clothing of the actor. Tiny—always hyper-cautious about his physical well-being—grew increasingly nervous about the stunt as the scene approached, but was eventually reassured by Rebane's explanation of what was about to occur. 'Tiny had an incredible trust in me,' Rebane says. 'If he didn't, he probably would've buckled. Once we rehearsed it and got into the character, he had no problem.'

Tiny Tim's lack of coordination proved to be another challenge while navigating the unsteady terrain of the Shooting Ranch. He found it so difficult to steady himself on the uneven floor of the barn in which they were shooting that it became a part of his character's identity. 'When you see him stumble in the film, that was not acting. That was real,' Rebane says. 'It was actually perfect for the role. Once I recognized what his weaknesses were, it was easy to overcome … the whole shoot was a pleasure.' He also had Tiny perform the film's catchy theme song.

Before shooting was completed, *Nightmare* was pre-sold for distribution in the US and UK. Though Rebane had initially envisioned a softer film, he added more nudity and gore to appease his distributors. The film was released on VHS in both the US and UK in 1987, under the title *Blood Harvest*. In the UK, the censors cut out three minutes of footage. Many critics concluded that while the film was little more than an attempt to cash in on the popularity of slasher movies, Tiny's character, a makeup smeared, lumbering, and unnerving version of himself, was the most successful aspect of the film. He did not see the finished film until 1994.[*]

Tiny and Rebane developed a friendship during the production, and both expressed interest in working together on another project. The brainstorming commenced, and Rebane hit upon the idea of a children's television show with musical numbers and Tiny as host, to be called *Tiny Tim & Friends*. Funding was established, sets were built, and a crew was hired. However, as the production began to take form, it became apparent that Tiny had failed to inform Rebane that he had, quite suddenly, developed a fear of children. In fact, Tiny's fear was not addressed in any capacity until he stepped on set, caught sight of the children, and froze. Rebane tried to move the production along, but Tiny remained stiff and unsettled.

Finally, Rebane pulled Tiny aside and asked him what was wrong.

---

[*] Rebane's 'director's cut' of the movie was issued on DVD in 2003 with most of the gore and nudity removed. It has been rumored that Rebane was apprehensive about releasing the uncut version as he was preparing to run for governor of Wisconsin.

Discussing the incident on *E! True Hollywood Story*, he remembered Tiny saying that children are 'smarter than you think.' Interviewed for this book, he recalls Tiny telling him, 'Children can be very mean, Mr. Rebane.' He decided against asking Tiny to elaborate. 'I didn't touch it with a ten-foot pole!'*

Rebane tried to resurrect the shoot. 'Could you just be yourself?' he pleaded. 'Can you just be the jovial Tiny Tim that sings to the kids?' But Tiny clammed up. 'He had to be coaxed through doing it, and it was very awkward and not in character.' Tiny was completely unable to interact with the children, or ad lib conversations, which perplexed even the kids, who were fond of him. Rebane shot enough material for three episodes, but the footage was virtually unusable. The project was scrapped, and it remains unreleased.

* * *

Though they did not work together on another film project, Tiny did attempt to involve Rebane in Martin Sharp's *Street Of Dreams*, the first cut of which premiered on May 27 1988, almost ten years after Sharp started work on it. During that time, the scope of the film had changed dramatically. After the tragic Luna Park fire, Sharp arranged for a film crew to make several trips to New York to capture additional footage with Tiny. Sharp himself remained in Australia, preoccupied with saving Luna Park from destruction, and his absence left Tiny in an ambiguous role as both director and subject.

'I wasn't a director, really,' Sharp explained. 'My ability was to make sure there was a film crew there, and Tiny created everything, really.' Tiny proceeded to aggravate the crew by insisting they film his drunken escapades with a burlesque dancer named Pleasure Aims. He also oversaw some positively unique scenes, one of which shows him in clown makeup and a Pierrot-like costume, swathed in blue light, lip-syncing to his own version of 'The Great Pretender.' The New York skyline twinkles behind him, and a moon dangles above his head. The scene is reminiscent of Kenneth Anger's *Rabbit's Moon*.

Tiny also arranged for the crew to visit his mother at 601 West 163rd Street, before their move to the Olcott Hotel. Tillie, baffled that a crew should want to film her, looked into the lens and asked, 'You want to film *this*?'

By 1988, those who knew Martin Sharp had come to believe that the

---

* This is not the only time Tiny expressed a fear of children. On another occasion, he told his friend Johnny Pineapple, 'These little kids, you just can't trust 'em! ... They're smarter than you think they are. They're smarter than I am! Just too smart.' Pineapple was surprised by Tiny's awkwardness around kids, 'because Tiny, in a way, was kind of childlike.'

film might never be finished. 'Martin Sharp's film has itself achieved a status of myth, mainly because it seemed forever to be a work in progress,' the *Sydney Morning Herald* noted. The same paper then ran another article on the film's release: 'Although the tulips that Tiny Tim tiptoed through to a strange stardom have long ago wilted, Martin Sharp has finally completed his obsessive cinematic tribute to the lovable falsetto freak.'

In the weeks prior to the premiere screening, Tiny called Martin Sharp a 'new Andy Warhol' and said that he believed the film would give people 'some insight into my talent, but the audience isn't ready yet to accept me as more than a freak. People love something new, but they hate it at the same time because it looks so weird. They've been running way from me in the subways since 1956.'

Miss Jan warned Tiny that the film would not depict him 'as anything but a freak.' Tiny, on the other hand, seemed happy to have an outlet to expound upon his unconventional worldview and doomsday prophesies. 'I know Mr. Sharp believes in me so much—and I praise the Lord for that—and maybe he's made a cult movie which at the very least will survive as a museum piece,' Tiny told the press. 'But Mr. Sharp, I think, is interested more than ever in my thoughts on this world and its cataclysmic times, on my fundamentalist spiritual attitudes. Today, all the prophecies are coming true—the murders, deaths, assassinations, children being thrown off the roof …'

Street Of Dreams premiered at the Brighton Festival in England. A self-described 'musical mirror maze,' the film is bizarre yet engrossing. Tiny's Marathon Medley performance at Luna Park serves as the centerpiece; weaved throughout is footage from his years of fame and from the late 70s and early 80s. In its disjointed manner, the film illustrates Tiny's rise to fame and fall from grace, with songs from the Marathon Medley used as transitional material. 'Just One More Chance' is used to segue into scenes dealing with Tiny's relationship with Miss Vicki, while 'Bad Moon Rising' is used to introduce a segment dealing with the film's primary sub-plot: the suspicious fire that killed seven and doomed Luna Park.

At the premiere, Tiny offered Sharp few a few suggestions for future cuts to the film. 'I came to the conclusion last night … that the film should focus more on Luna Park,' Tiny Tim told the *Sydney Morning Herald*. 'More concentration should be held on the nude scenes … the viewers of the movie house—the public—seem to be more interested in more of that instead of having it flash away too quick, so the nude scenes should last longer and be heavier.'

Martin Sharp acknowledged the need for additional changes as well, but was less specific than Tiny. 'I think I've got the form there now … it's just a matter of making what's between the beginning and the end flow a bit better,' he said. He also made clear his plans to screen a new cut of the film in Australia, to coincide with a scheduled visit by Tiny the following June.

Tiny emphasized to reporters that Sharp had not sensationalized his religious views in the film, which, through the use of editing, make Tiny seem like a crazed televangelist. Then, perhaps in an effort to drive home his extremism, he likened the use of birth control to 'stuffing a Brillo pad up the faucet to stop the water flowing.'

In his review for the *Sydney Morning Herald*, Michael Visontay concluded that the film, 'jumping from song to song, roughly edited and without any real narrative thread … is not easy to watch. Half the time it feels quite unreal, almost child-like…' Despite this, Visontay predicted that *Street Of Dreams* was 'destined for success.' Sharp received further encouragement from Nicolas Roeg, the director of *Bad Timing* and *Insignificance*. 'You must keep making this film,' Roeg told Sharp after a London screening, 'until one of you drops.'

The *Street Of Dreams* premiere was actually a two-pronged event. After the screening, Tiny performed a concert, and broke his own non-stop singing record, putting his previous effort to shame with a performance lasting three hours, ten minutes, eleven seconds. This despite the fact that all of the microphones, with the exception of Tiny's, lost power during 'Life Is Just A Bowl Of Cherries,' leaving Tiny to soldier on alone until power was restored to the other musicians' mics.

A recording of the event was released in January 1990, as a three-cassette set entitled *Tiny Tim & The Time Machine: The World Professional Non-Stop Singing Record*. In the liner notes, Tiny explained his vision for the project: 'These great singers and their songs linked the hearts and souls of men, women and children in past times, and I hope that my versions of these melodies can continue that remembrance and send a message to the youth of today (despite its times) as it did for the youth of yesterday. This is more than a cassette, more than a history; this is actually popular music for the soul.'

Upon the album's release, the *Sydney Morning Herald* called it 'perhaps the strangest performance to be committed to tape since the last effort of Molly The Singing Dog. … While some may marvel at Tiny Tim's vocal endurance, others may suggest that anyone who listens to the performance in one sitting should also be awarded a gold medal.'

Street Of Dreams fared well at festivals, but its unconventional content and approach made it unattractive to distributors. Tiny put Martin Sharp in touch with Bill Rebane to help procure a distribution deal in the United States, but though he tried, Rebane could not get anyone to bite. 'It was a tough sell,' he says. 'What killed it for the general market was the scenes of Tiny sitting in bed, drinking a beer, with the naked chick next to him. I've still wondered why he did that.'*

Sharp cut several versions of *Street Of Dreams* in an attempt to increase its commercial viability, but the film was never officially released. Today, bootleg copies circulate among fans of independent and/or obscure cinema. In 1999, *Shock Cinema Magazine* hailed it as 'so unique and inspired that I couldn't stop smiling ... it's not difficult to imagine that Tiny Tim was an offstage weirdo, but it's gratifying to see it chronicled for posterity, while realizing he actually exceeded expectations.'

Despite the film's tepid reception and failure to secure a distribution deal, Martin Sharp stood by his decision to include controversial material in the film. Of the scene featuring the partially dressed burlesque dancer, he said flatly, 'I thought that was a *great* scene.' Regarding a scene in which a transsexual named Miss Natasha dances for Tiny to his own blaring version of 'Stayin' Alive,' Sharp provided a bit more elaboration: 'Tiny preaches to her. He uses her to make the point of illusion and reality ... she was one of those mysterious figures from the twilight world.' Sharp included these scenes in the film out of a respect for Tiny as an artist, given that Tiny had insisted on shooting them in the first place.

Though the film became known among his associates as 'Sharp's Folly,' Sharp did not regret the time or resources he put into it. 'It did feel like there was only a few of us [who cared],' he said, 'but [Tiny] was such a great artist, and as an artist myself, I tried to respect that position. It was always very exciting to work with him. It was a great adventure. I felt that the world that ignored Tiny was not a world I was particularly happy in. I thought it was a real shortcoming. I knew what wonderful material I was getting, and maybe one day it'll become of use.'

---

* Miss Sue says that Martin Sharp 'was obsessed with the question of whether or not Tiny was gay' and that Tiny was adamant that the scenes featuring him drunkenly canoodling with a topless woman would prove he was not a homosexual. 'No one understood why he did this,' she adds, '[but] it seems obvious to me that this was Tiny's hysterical, drama queen way of *demonstrating* his heterosexuality. He apparently felt that nothing else would suffice, because Martin had insinuated so many times that Tiny was gay.'

CHAPTER TWENTY-TWO

TINY SAW ELVIS!

I felt that Mr. Presley's real reason for committing suicide was … the split up from his wife. He didn't know how to keep her, and he was fooling around with many women. The lust of the flesh can bring, also, the destruction of the spirit. … I believe that he committed spiritual suicide because his soul went haywire because of not walking with Jesus Christ completely.

TINY TIM IN MARTIN SHARP'S *STREET OF DREAMS*

By late 1988, Elvis sightings and conspiracy theories had reached their apex. One morning in Westchester, New York, Stuart Hersh awoke with an idea for a song.

I saw Mr. Presley,
Tip-toeing through the tulips,
In my backyard garden late last night.

Hersh was eight years old in 1968 and one of the scores of children who were fascinated by Tiny Tim. When Tiny and Miss Vicki announced their plans to get married on *The Tonight Show*, Hersh collected newspaper clippings about the upcoming ceremony and was allowed to stay up to watch it. He first met Tiny in 1971, at a theater in Brooklyn, and again in 1974, when Tiny opened at Jimmy's with the New Tiny Tim Show. At Jimmy's, Hersh interviewed Tiny backstage for his school newspaper, and Tiny was impressed by the boy's knowledge of his career. In the years that followed, the two became friends. Hersh occasionally phoned Tiny at the Olcott Hotel to chat, and on one occasion presented Tiny with a novelty song penned by his friend Billy Florio, entitled 'Snow White Never Had It So Good.' Tiny rejected it, explaining that he was looking for something closer to 'I Will Survive.'

Shortly thereafter, Hersh became promotions director at WZFM in Westchester, from where he continued to monitor Tiny's career. He was paying especially close attention when, in 1988, NLT Records in Nashville almost succeeded in turning Tiny into a country & western singer.

* * *

Tiny met NLT Records president Gordon Stinson in 1987, while traveling with the Great American Circus. Stinson was impressed by Tiny Tim's versatility and expressed interest in cutting a record with him. 'Tiny can sing anything, any type of music, regardless of the genre,' he told the press.

Produced by Dan Mitchell, who had penned Alabama's hit 'If You're Gonna Play In Texas, You Gotta Have A Fiddle In The Band,' Tiny's album, *Leave Me Satisfied*, included: 'Leave Me Satisfied,' 'Anytime You Need Some Lovin',' 'I've Got A Tiger By The Tail,' 'Everytime I Get To Dreamin',' 'Business Of Her Own,' 'I Wanna Get Crazy With You,' 'That Old Country Waltz,' 'Put Me On Your List Of Easy Lovers,' Eddie Rabin's 'Atlanta,' and 'When You Leave Don't Slam The Door.' It was recorded in early 1988, with the title track released as a single in early March. As the single hovered just inside *Billboard*'s Country Singles chart, executives at NLT Records made a valiant effort to boost its success. A press release appeared in *Cash Box*, boasting of Tiny's seamless transition to country music: 'When the needle is dropped on the disc, many mouths drop open, too. You will hear a baritone vocal which still has the natural vibrato and a unique sound, and you will hear Tiny Tim doing a tight country song his way. But, then … Tiny has become a legend by doing things his way. Tiny Tim is a pleasant surprise for country music!'

Tiny plugged the record on various Nashville-based television and radio shows. He donned a pair of snakeskin boots, a silver belt buckle with a gold *T* in the center, and a western bow tie, and was met with mixed reviews. He was invited to the Kentucky Derby, where the state governor bestowed upon him the honorary title of Kentucky Colonel. During an appearance on *Nashville Now*, however, he proved too extreme even for Southern audiences when he offered his solution to rising divorce rates: 'I really believe it was right in the days of King David … that men should have a concubine of wives.' The remark was met with stifled laughter, scattered applause from a few men, and a chorus of boos from the audience's female contingent.

In the final week of April 1988, following a promotional onslaught by Tiny and NLT records, 'Leave Me Satisfied' peaked at number 70 on the

Billboard Country Singles chart. It disappeared from the charts soon after, however, and plans to release the full-length album were abandoned.

In 1991, Tiny's friend Lowell Tarling visited Gordon Stinson at his studio in Burn, Tennessee. Stinson explained that the single had been pulled from circulation in 1988 and added that he felt Tiny had been 'unreasonable' in not promoting the planned full-length album, while admitting that he still owed Tiny $1,500. With Tarling as arbitrator, Stinson offered to sell Martin Sharp a 50 percent share in the *Leave Me Satisfied* project for $75,000. Sharp, who by now had spent nearly two million dollars in Tiny-related endeavors, declined; Tiny refused to cooperate until he received his $1,500. No one was paid, no deal was made, and *Leave Me Satisfied* remains unreleased to this day.

* * *

Meanwhile, in New York, Stuart Hersh was hatching a plan not to reinvent but to restore Tiny's image. His aim, with 'I Saw Mr. Presley Tiptoeing Through The Tulips,' was to combine Tiny's early image with 'something current and new.' With the help of his friend, songwriter Billy Florio, he wrote and recorded a demo of the 'Elvis' song, featuring Hersh singing in falsetto and Florio accompanying him on piano. Hersh then phoned Tiny at his apartment to say he had 'a great new song for you.'

'Oh! That sounds great, Mr. Hersh!' Tiny exclaimed. Unsurprisingly, he was well versed in Elvis theories, and had in fact been pontificating about Elvis's death for some time. When rumors of Elvis sightings began to circulate, Tiny quickly jumped on board, and he would maintain his suspicions long after the hysteria of the alleged sightings abated. 'I still think he may be alive,' Tiny told David Tibet in 1995.

Demo in hand, Hersh visited Tiny at the Olcott Hotel, where Tiny had been living on his own ever since Tillie's death three years earlier. Hersh observed that Tiny slept on a foldout couch in the living room; his Bible was centered on the bed, and the room was very tidy. The kitchen contained a sampling of the items that Tiny was prone to mention in interviews, like Aunt Millie's Sweet Peppers Tomato Sauce. Tillie's old bedroom, however, had been converted into a chaotic storage closet, containing a giant pile of suitcases, clothing, and other miscellaneous items. The bathroom, needless to say, was spotless. 'It was immaculately clean,' Hersh recalls. 'He had all these little notes on everything saying things like, if you use this type of tissue for this, put it in this waste paper basket here. He also had a speaker phone in his shower because Tiny's motto was, My phone never sleeps … [sometimes] he would answer the phone and I would hear the shower running and he would be conducting the conversation.'

Hersh played Tiny the demo.

'That's really great Mr. Hersh,' Tiny told him, 'but I can't really do the falsetto anymore. Why don't you do it?'

'Nobody wants to hear me doing it,' Hersh chuckled. 'Who the hell am I? You're Tiny Tim! You do the falsetto thing.'

After some coaxing, Tiny agreed to try performing the song in falsetto, and Hersh booked a session at Reeves Audio Recording, located in the basement of engineer Jim Reeves's home in Yonkers, New York. Reeves had worked for twenty-five years at CBS and Columbia Records and had engineered sessions for Bob Dylan, George Harrison, and Lou Reed. Like Tiny, he had been a regular at the Scene during the mid 60s.

Even though Tiny Tim had technically agreed to sing the song in falsetto, he remained wary of the idea. Hersh and Reeves had several discussions about how to approach Tiny's vocals. 'We're going to take the vocal track in pieces, maybe even line by line if we have to, to get that falsetto to sound the best that it can,' Hersh told Reeves.

Tiny's vocals took several days to record. Each day, he only managed a few minutes of solid falsetto before losing it, whereupon they would stop recording vocals and resume the next day. He believed that cold air helped keep his falsetto intact, and ate copious amounts of white Tic Tacs and drank Slurpees during the sessions, which Hersh had to leave the studio to replenish on numerous occasions.

In order to get Tiny 'psychologically psyched up to do the falsetto,' Hersh began to play selections from his Reprise albums on the drive to the studio. He would crank the volume, turn to Tiny, and say, 'Gosh, Tiny, you sounded so great on that!' Before Tiny could respond, Hersh would change the track. 'Listen to how you sound on this one!'

Hersh and co were shocked to discover that Tiny had not played ukulele on the original 'Tip-Toe,' and that he was not as skilled a player as they had assumed he would be. According to Billy Florio, 'Tiny was not able to hear exactly when he was supposed to switch chords, which was very startling to me and [Jim].' The session's participants also noticed some of Tiny's classic eccentricities: he wore the same clothes to every session, carried a toothbrush in his back pocket, and drank beer through a straw. Furthermore, he was convinced of the possibility that Elvis Presley might show up to the sessions and steal his thunder.

'What do we do if Mr. Presley shows up?' he asked.

'Tiny, it's not going to happen,' Hersh assured him. 'If it does, he'll endorse the song, OK?'

Ultimately, Hersh and Reeves had no choice but to assemble the song line-by-line from dozens of takes, while Reeves was able to remove a lot of the edge from Tiny's vocals by slowing parts of the tape and employing a few filters. When Tiny heard the finished track, he turned to Hersh and said, 'You kept your promise to me.' Hersh beamed. During subsequent interviews, Tiny told radio hosts, 'Mr. Hersh got me to do it in the voice I used twenty years ago.'

With a brand-new Tiny Tim track in the can, Hersh set about publicizing the record and drawing attention to Tiny generally. When Tiny decided to walk the New York Marathon, Hersh called the *New York Post* and asked the newspaper to cover Tiny Tim's participation. The next day, a half-page picture of Tiny duly appeared in the *Post*, alongside a quote: 'I do believe Elvis is still around. It certainly makes a lot of sense, unless all these people who have claimed to see him are hallucinating. Maybe he'll come out to buy my new record!' In response to the article, an *Entertainment Tonight* anchor commented, 'If Elvis bought Tiny Tim's new record, it may make him go back into hiding after he plays it!' Tiny, though, was pleasantly surprised that the *Post* had devoted so much space to him. 'How did you do that, Mr. Hersh?' he wondered.

Tiny walked a total of twelve (of twenty-six) miles of the marathon before hanging it up. His sneakers gave him blisters, and one of his toenails had turned blue. But taking part at all was a bold move for a man who had not walked more than a few blocks at a time for the past twenty years. When Tiny took off his shoe to show Hersh his black-and-blue toenail, Hersh noticed several brown blotches under the skin on Tiny's leg and suggested they go to the emergency room.

'No! Mr. Hersh!' Tiny replied. 'They cut my father's leg off!'

Hersh dropped the matter.

* * *

Hersh's next move was to arrange an appearance for Tiny on *The Howard Stern Show*. Since Tiny's original appearance on the controversial show, Howard Stern had gone into national syndication, and the show offered considerable exposure. Tiny had attended Stern's birthday in early '88, and

Stern had then had him on the show in March. The subsequent interview was centered on Tiny's unconventional relationship with Miss Jan, which according to Tiny had ended in a fight after Stern's party. It was the first time Stern had spoken to Tiny in depth, and he became fascinated with the details of Tiny's personal life.

After having Tiny describe the particulars of his and Jan's separate residences, and exploring Tiny's suspicion that Jan was using birth control, Stern could not but help make a few lewd jokes, suggesting that perhaps the real reason for the breakup was because 'you were tiny in your shorts.'

'Well, uh, that could be true, too,' Tiny replied.

'Oh, really? That's hard to believe, Tiny.'

'King David was really small, Mr. Stern, and look what he did to Goliath.'

Now, when Hersh organized the follow-up appearance for Tiny to promote his new song, he knew that Stern was more interested in Tiny's thoughts on women and consumer products than his music. 'He's promoting my song,' he told Stern's producer, Gary Dell'Abate, 'and I really don't want Stern knocking the song.' Dell'Abate gave Hersh his word that the song would be treated with respect.

By the time of Tiny's appearance on the show, on November 23, no record label had picked up the single, so Tiny brought a copy on a reel-to-reel tape. Stern spent a good portion of the interview discussing Tiny's affinity for going to 'topless places, bottomless places … just to look at their faces' and probing him about Miss Jan and masturbation before finally playing the song.

'I think this is going to be a smash!' Stern announced. 'To incorporate the tulip theme again, which brings it back to all those years ago, and into the Elvis, which is a current topic, I think was a stroke of genius.' He then turned to Tiny's theory that Elvis was still alive. 'You know he's dead, right?'

'No, I don't believe that.' Tiny countered. 'I always read the *Enquirer*, the *Globe*, the *Star*, the *Examiner*, *Weekly World News*, and the *Sun* every week … until proven differently, it makes sense. No one saw his body.'

All antics aside, Stern and his people had kept their promise: they played the track and treated it with as much dignity as Stern's program could offer. Novelty DJ Dr. Demento also played the song on his radio show, with Tiny present, and when it finished, turned to him and said, 'This is probably your best song ever.' He later booked Tiny for his twentieth-anniversary television special, which aired on Comedy Central.

Next, Hersh arranged for Tiny to appear as part of MTV's Turkey Day Bash at the Palladium in New York City, hosted by MTV VJ Kevin Seal. Tiny performed 'I Saw Mr. Presley Tiptoeing Through The Tulips' live to a backing track, with an Elvis impersonator positioned behind him onstage, striking classic Elvis poses to cues in the music. Seal and the teenage audience cheered excitedly for a singer, of whom few had probably heard.

The attention excited Tiny but made him anxious, too. 'What are we doing?' he asked Hersh. 'The new song is not on a label, Mr. Hersh. Everybody's hearing it! What are we going to do?'

Hersh had been shopping the song to various labels, and the response, while varied, was largely enthusiastic. 'It appeared to me that anyone else who was handling Tiny around this time pretty much just answered phone calls from people,' he recalls. 'It didn't look like anyone was pushing for him or anyone was trying to build anything for him.'

When Tiny and Hersh first talked about possible labels, top of their wish list was RCA, home not only to Elvis but also to many of Tiny's favorite turn-of-the-century artists. But then Tiny suddenly began pushing to release the song on 20th Century Promotions, a private label run by his latest manager, Gil More, a smalltime talent-booker from Cranston, Rhode Island. Morse, a former associate of Roy Radin's, had been booking Tiny on and off since 1986, and as the one of the only managers to keep him working and help him manage his money (rationing it over time and holding some back for his rent at the Olcott Hotel), Tiny felt indebted to him. 'If it's all right with Mr. Morse,' he would say, 'it's all right with me.'*

While Hersh understood and respected Tiny's loyalty to Morse, he knew that if the track was released on a tiny independent label, all of their hard work would amount to nothing. He suggested a compromise: 20th Century Promotions would press up a few hundred promotional copies of the single—featuring mono and stereo mixes of the song and a paper sleeve showing a photo of Tiny with the caption 'TINY SAW ELVIS!'—while Hersh continued to look for a deal. Tiny agreed, but when Hersh came back to him with the exciting news that RCA had expressed interest in putting out the record, Tiny became combative.

'What about Mr. Morse?' he asked. 'We already have it on his label.'

---

* Tiny appeared to be the biggest act on Morse's roster. His other acts, he says, included Bobby 'Boris' Pickett, a guy from The Platters, and Robin Lynn, a country & western singer who opened for Tiny over a hundred times.

Hersh tried to persuade Tiny that this is what they had wanted all along, even suggesting that they could share the profits from the RCA release with Morse, but Tiny continued to insist that it would be 'unfair' to give the record to another label. Though he could in fact sell the track to whomever he pleased, Hersh knew that, without Tiny's blessing and involvement, it would be pointless. 'The record would come out and make some noise and then people would ask, Where the hell is Tiny?'*

Tiny dealt Hersh another blow after Hersh attempted to arrange a reunion between Tiny and Bob Dylan following a concert in New York City. When Tiny arrived at the box office, he was given two tickets and two backstage passes, but when Hersh called the Olcott Hotel the next day, anxious to hear about Tiny's meeting with Dylan, he was disappointed once again.

'Oh, no, no, Mr. Hersh. Nobody came out and got me.'

'Tiny! They gave you backstage passes! You could've walked straight in!'

'Oh, I would never do that.'

Hersh hung up the phone and his heart sank. 'Tiny … thought he was overstepping his bounds … but it wasn't!' Hersh says today. 'Dylan truly wanted to see him, and God knows what would've taken place—God knows what kind of photos would've ended up in *Rolling Stone!*'

Hersh watched on, incredulously, as Tiny Tim continued to sabotage his career and the track they had recorded together, this time with a heated on-air argument with Howard Stern. Having already been caught off guard when Stern brought up his undefined relationship with Bobby Gonzalez, an increasingly edgy Tiny flew into a rage when Stern took Jesus's name in vain. Stern's insincere apology and attempts to blame co-host Robin Quivers for the slip-up only agitated Tiny further.

'The name of Jesus Christ is being used in vain on this show,' he railed, 'and the FCC allows it!'

After an awkward silence, Quivers asked Tiny to calm down. 'You're very angry,' she told him, 'and I don't like it.'

'It doesn't become you,' Stern added.

After this, Tiny refused all further interview requests from *The Howard*

---

* Since 'I Saw Mr. Presley Tiptoeing Through The Tulips' was never issued commercially, the planned B-side, a ragtime version of Elvis's 'Don't Be Cruel,' also went unreleased, as did an impromptu version of 'It's A Long Way To Tipperary,' captured during the sessions when Tiny seized on the opportunity to break into the old number when the session drummer played a march on his snare while warming up.

Stern Show, effectively killing his one significant tie to mainstream audiences. He then proceeded to sever ties with Stuart Hersh, who since then has had many years to reflect upon what transpired.

'When you put all of these pieces together, I honestly believe that my disconnection with Tiny Tim was because Tiny got scared,' Hersh says. 'Tiny always said to people, Oh, I wish I could make it again and have just one more hit record, but I truly believe that he never thought that that would ever, ever come close to happening again, and I started to make him scared because I was making it happen again for him.' He likens the situation to a TV interview with Charles Manson. 'Every time [interviewer] Tom Snyder talks to Manson about having his freedom and coming out of jail, Manson sincerely looks scared, like he doesn't know the world out there any more, he likes it in jail, he spent most of his life in jail. I think that it was the same scenario: Tiny, at [that] point, had been playing for [almost] twenty years at small, two-bit nightclubs, [and] when it looked like it was finally going to happen, he got nervous, and he changed his phone number on me. That was it … I could not reach him.'

Tiny gave his take on the situation to Tom Kidd of *Goldmine*. 'We recorded ['I Saw Mr. Presley Tiptoeing Through The Tulips'] and Dr. Demento said he thought it was the greatest novelty record he had ever heard. Apparently it went to the kid's head. RCA wanted to call him down and talk about that record, but he didn't know how to handle it and the whole thing blew up.'

Initially, Hersh was crushed by the split. Tiny was one of his childhood idols, and they had become close. Tiny was one of the first people to hold Hersh's daughter when she had been born, and Hersh was the first (and perhaps only) person to play a round of the *Game Of Beautiful Things* with Tiny himself. Tiny had also confided in Hersh some of his darkest fears—including that Miss Vicki and Tulip harbored such a deep grudge against him that they might one day murder him—and in time it seemed that he too joined Vicki and Tulip in Tiny's terrible delusion. When Tiny donated one of his ukuleles to the Hard Rock Cafe in New York City, an event Hersh had booked prior to their falling out, Tiny told another of his agents, George Magdaleno, that he believed Hersh was coming to kill him.

Today, Hersh has come to appreciate having had the experience of working with Tiny, even if it did not turn out as he had hoped. 'It really was, for me, a labor of love. I loved Tiny Tim as a child and got a chance to grow up and write and record and produce a record for him. It was like going full circle.'

CHAPTER TWENTY-THREE
HIDE AWAY IN
I-O-WAY

This record, 'Won't You Dance With Me?'—doggone it, like so many others today, you know, if you're not a record star today, forget it. And I don't have a good track record. I haven't had a hit since 'Tiptoe Through The Tulips,' which was in 1968, and so basically, in plain language, it was a fifty-thousand dollar video: no company wants to touch it right now.

TINY TIM TO DEREK BOSTROM, *BREAKFAST WITHOUT MEAT*, JUNE 30 1989

It opens in a bunker. Two smug-faced lab techs thaw a cryogenic freezing chamber marked 'Tiny' with their flamethrowers. Tiny emerges stiffly and marches from the room and onto the stage of a nightclub. The band is waiting. Meanwhile, a woman, played by Judy Carne, is bullied by her brutish boyfriend. She's had enough, and abandons the apartment with her daughter. They make their way through the city. Back at the club, Tiny, wearing a Martin Sharp suit covered with the sheet music to 'Camptown Races,' sings the words 'dance with me,' imploringly and repetitively. The video staggers through a slew of late-80s stereotypes before Carne arrives at her destination: a 'New Start' shelter. But it is not your regular shelter. The door bursts open to reveal the popping nightclub. Tiny welcomes her with a spooky, 'Ohhh, I think you're beautiful.' They both dance awkwardly as the music fades.

In March 1989, it was announced that Tiny would be reunited with his *Laugh-In* co-star Judy Carne in a music video for his new dance track, 'Won't You Dance With Me?' According to United Press International, they were 'tiptoeing along the comeback trail together,' shooting a video in Baltimore with a $25,000 budget, 'even though the song hasn't been sold to a record company yet.' Half of any proceeds from the release, UPI added, 'will go to the National Coalition Against Domestic Violence.'

The song and video were produced by the relatively unknown Baltimore-based dance duo of Jeff Order and Max Maximum, who jumped at their management's suggestion that they record a song with Tiny Tim. They duly recorded 'Won't You Dance With Me,' a dance track drenched in synthesizer and drum machine, and, afterward, began work on the music video. When that was completed, Order decided to release the track as a music video only. 'Every record company in America wanted to see it,' he explains, 'but nobody wanted to take the chance on it in this country. It did get played a lot in Japan and Australia. We actually received royalties. Also, the video won an … international award. We did a big thing down at the Kennedy Center in Washington.'

The video made its US television debut on *The Arsenio Hall Show* on November 10 1989. Tiny appeared on the show in another Martin Sharp suit, this one patterned in Australian beer labels, and, when asked to perform a song, unveiled one he had written in tribute to the model and actress Jessica Hahn, whom he had met at Howard Stern's birthday party the year before.

> *Jessica Hahn, Jessica Hahn,*
> *I bless the day you were born,*
> *I'd love to get caught in a storm,*
> *With Jessica, Jessica Hahn.* *

After a commercial break, Hall showed a fifteen-second clip from 'Won't You Dance With Me.' Asked if that was Judy Carne with him in the video, Tiny confirmed that it was indeed the 'sock-it-to-me girl' from *Laugh-In*, adding that he was 'so thrilled to have Miss Carne in there.' He also revealed that he and his new collaborators—'two great, young writers'—had attracted the interest of numerous labels, and that he was about to sign his 'first major-label [deal] in twenty years,' but in the end no such deal was forthcoming. Jeff Order confirms that 'Tommy Boy almost took a shot at [releasing the record] … there were a number of people that were interested in it [but] nobody ultimately ended up stepping up and buying it.'

* * *

In March, 1989, CNN reported that Tiny Tim would be running for mayor of New York City as a candidate from the New Age Party—a party he created, and of which he was the sole member. The short-lived campaign produced

---

* Two months later, Hahn appeared on *The Arsenio Hall Show*. She smiled as Hall played the clip of Tiny singing his tribute to her, but did not comment further.

buttons reading 'Tiny Tim for Mayor: As Unique as the City Itself.' His campaign promises included:

- Doggie doo-doos are don't on the streets of New York City. ('It's unfair for the average man or woman to buy a new pair of shoes and step in some dog mess.')
- Bicyclists should be banned from the streets. ('They're a nuisance.')
- Prisons are getting overcrowded, so prisoners should be shipped out. ('Make them work in places like Bangladesh and help the victims. They can even meet women there. They're not confined.')
- Men and women should wash their genitals before going to the doctor. ('It's not adequate for doctors to suffer unless you have an accident in the street.')

After five weeks in the race, Tiny dropped out and endorsed former US Attorney Rudolph Giuliani, whom he said 'appears to be a very honest man with good intentions.' Over a few beers with an Associated Press reporter, Tiny admitted that the campaign had been the idea of one of his managers, Jeff Norman. 'I just went along with it,' he said. 'My campaign fizzled as flat as this beer ... it never seemed to catch fire.'

* * *

During the late 80s and early 90s, Tiny toured with Donnie Brooks' *30 Years of Rock and Roll* tour. The tours were very much in the same style as *Roy Radin's Vaudeville Revue*: Tiny performed at county fairs and high-school auditoriums with acts like Micky Dolenz, Herman's Hermits, Mitch Ryder, and Bobby Day. Mike Pinera, previously of Iron Butterfly and Blues Image, became close friends with Tiny during the tours, and could barely contain his enthusiasm when asked about him. 'I'm glad we finally get to talk about one of my favorite people, Tiny Tim! I think people need to know what a great human being he was, and what a nice guy he was, too!'

Variety gave the show a mediocre review, noting that while the line-up boasted numerous gold records, Grammy awards, and Rock and Roll Hall of Fame members, 'quality hardly measured up to quantity.' The magazine was even less generous about Tiny, who 'chanted tunes far removed from rock in his baritone range and "Tip-Toe Thru The Tulips" in falsetto before writhing on the floor for a send-up of "Heartbreak Hotel." It was not a pretty sight.'

Despite this, Mike Pinera recalls that Tiny's performances 'were always given standing ovations and requests for encores from the people.'

For fans all over the country, the show was an opportunity to meet celebrities, and the performers were happy to oblige. The long autograph lines were full of baby-boomers who wanted to share their memories of Tiny with Tiny. Tiny's one-time songwriter Norman Bergen, who was also on the tour, recalls that if the main acts did not get back on the bus quickly during rest stops in small towns, they would soon find themselves mired in autograph-seeking locals—and that Tiny and Micky Dolenz were the most popular of them all.

The *30 Years of Rock and Roll* tour generally traveled in three buses: one for those who wanted to party, and two for those who didn't. Mike Pinera and Tiny bunked next to one another at the back of one of the quiet buses, and spent a lot of time together. Tiny would sometimes ask Pinera to stand guard so that he was not disturbed while praying the rosary. 'I never had to prevent anybody from going back there, but I did look out for him,' Pinera says.

According to Pinera, Tiny was cooperative when Donnie Brooks and Ron Kurtz hatched upon the idea of a promotional video for the tour called *The 30th Anniversary Of Rock and Roll in 3-D*, for which they hired 'a director and producer that had a new, innovative, and cheap way to do a 3-D compilation video involving everyone on the tour.' Tiny's segment was originally to feature blue-screen graphics of him tiptoeing through a field of tulips, until he expressed dissatisfaction with the idea to Pinera, and the two of them worked up a new storyboard idea. 'It was really out there, very innovative, psychedelic,' Pinera says. 'As he approached the camera, his nose would kind of jump out of the TV screen, and his ukulele and stuff. It was just really, really great.'

After working together on the video, Tiny pitched a 'big creative revelation' to Pinera: why didn't he rework his song 'Ride Captain Ride' as 'Ride Batman Ride' for the new *Batman* movie? Pinera suggested they go one better and record a brand new song, 'Batman Rides Again,' but unfortunately, by the time the final mix was complete, the soundtrack to Tim Burton's *Batman* had been locked-in.*

'Next time we'll have to start a lot earlier,' Pinera told Tiny, and so they did, working quickly to complete 'Dick Tracy Rides Again' shortly after Warren Beatty's *Dick Tracy* was announced. When Touchtone Pictures said it would not accept 'unsolicited' material, the song was eventually released on

---

* It's unlikely, in any case, that the film's producers would have been receptive to lyrics such as 'It may be a little tricky, getting by Miss Vicki' anyway.

the unknown Fresh Squeezed label, with 'Ready For Love' (another Pinera composition recorded by Tiny) as the B-side.

In 1991, Pinera and Tiny embarked on what would be their last tour together. Tiny was now fifty-nine years old, and the years of constant traveling were taking their toll on his health. At the outset of the tour, Tiny shared a startling prediction.

'I probably don't have much longer on the planet,' he told Pinera. 'The Good Lord above us is calling me home.' He knew how it was going to happen, too: 'I will be onstage, singing "Tip-Toe Thru' The Tulips" with my shoes on, and my ukulele in hand; I will be performing when it happens.'

During the tour, Donnie Brooks noticed the blotches underneath the skin on Tiny's legs and, like Stuart Hersh, demanded that Tiny see a doctor. This time, Brooks, who was even taller than Tiny, insisted; a doctor promptly prescribed Tiny medication to improve his circulation. Whether Tiny took the medication regularly is not known, but one longtime fan and friend, Kathy King, recalls him being 'really groggy-looking' and 'out of it' when she saw him before a shown in Minnesota around this time. Initially, she says, she was told he was too 'exhausted' to see her; when he eventually came crawling out of the bus, he barely knew who she was. 'He was just like, Just another show, I don't even know what city this is. That's what he said! He was … bus-lagged.'

* * *

Despite these signs of his failing health, the self-described 'soldier of show business' continued to work nonstop. He featured in a Diet Pepsi Super Bowl commercial in which he, Jerry Lee Lewis, Charo, Vic Damone, a dog, an accordion player, and Bo Jackson audition to sing the new Diet Pepsi theme, and appeared on *The Heart Album* by Mike Cassone, a largely unknown eccentric from New York City. Although his business card boasted that he was a 'Producer of Stars,' precious little else of Cassone is known. Among the other 'stars' on *The Heart Album* are 'Andy Warhol Superstar' Ultra Violet and 'club sensations' Jimmie & Debbie Devita, while Cassone himself is billed as bandleader, producer, arranger, mixer, mastering technician, chief engineer, and 'the all-around music man.'

Of the sixteen tracks on the album, Tiny appears on six. He is the sole vocalist on one, and performs duets with 'European sensation' Ella Ray and 'Australian superstar' Tess Winters on the rest. Tiny's solo track, 'Deep Freeze Mama,' seemed positioned to be the album's single. In the liner notes, Cassone claims responsibility for 'making Tiny sing with a new sound à la Presley, with Mike's "magic" and styling.'

Cassone operated a low-rent music school with his partner, Mr. Jakobi, and was known to boast that he was known as 'The Ear' for his skills behind the mixing board, which are woefully absent on *The Heart Album*. Even Tiny seemed dubious, however, mockingly referring to Cassone as '*The Ear*' in a phone conversation with Harve Mann around the time of the session. Mann subsequently attended one of Tiny's studio sessions with Cassone and Jakobi, whereupon the 'New York hucksters,' as he calls them, listened to his demos and suggested they'd like to sign him, too. 'Tiny looks at me—and I'll never forget this, this is my favorite Tiny story—and he goes, Let me put it to you this way, Mr. Mann, if Mr. Jakobi and Mr. Cassone both discovered gold in California, it would be only a question of which one pulled the gun first.'

The press release that accompanied *The Heart Album* called it a 'collector's item' and mentioned two follow-up albums. It also included a ballot in which radio stations could vote whether or not Tiny Tim should be in a 'Hall of Fame,' though it did not specify which one. The fiftieth station to respond to the question would receive a free copy of the album and a possible lunch or dinner with Mike Cassone and his 'artists.' Tiny never promoted *The Heart Album* in any subsequent interviews, and the album remains one of the most perplexing and poorly mixed albums in his discography.

* * *

In 1992, Tiny appeared on a compilation released by K-Tel Distribution called *Silly Songs*. The album offered a brand-new recording of 'Tip-Toe' alongside other novelty tunes such as 'They're Coming to Take Me Away, Ha-Haa' by Napoleon XIV and 'Itsy Bitsy Teenie Weenie Yellow Polka Dot Bikini' by Brian Hyland.

In late March, Tiny made another quasi-annual pilgrimage to Australia, this time to appear at the Age Comedy Festival. Martin Sharp had also arranged a few more concerts and public appearances, and had booked a recording session to expand Tiny's 1983 version of 'Highway To Hell' into a feature-length album, to be titled *Tiny Tim: Rock*. Sharp had already secured distribution through Regular Records, which released the 'Highway To Hell' / 'Last Mile Of The Way' single in 1983. ('You're a brave man,' Tiny told label head Martin Fabinyi. 'I think this is the first time a heavy metal song has ever been recorded by someone over fifty-five.')

To accompany Tiny, Sharp recruited Her Majesty, a band comprised of aging rockers. The sessions produced a six-and-a-half-minute version of Bon Jovi's 'You Give Love A Bad Name' a sixteen-minute 'I Love Rock And Roll Medley' containing versions of 'Great Balls Of Fire,' 'Whole Lotta Shakin' Goin' On,' 'Shake, Rattle, And Roll,' 'Rock And Roll Is Here To Stay,' 'At The Hop,' 'Hound Dog,' 'Don't Be Cruel,' '(Let Me Be) Your Teddy Bear,' and mind-numbing versions of Billy Idol's 'Rebel Yell' and Barry McGuire's 'Eve Of Destruction,' each clocking in at just under twenty-four minutes.*

On May 22, Johnny Carson taped his 4,531st and final episode as host of *The Tonight Show*. Four days later, the *Wall Street Journal* reported that Carson's final appearance had drawn higher ratings than the episode featuring Tiny Tim's wedding, estimating a viewership of 55 million. When contacted by *People* magazine—which named Tiny and Vicki's wedding as *The Tonight Show's* 'Weirdest, Wildest Moment'—Tiny expressed regrets about the marriage for the first time. 'I wish I had never married Miss Vicki. From the control booth, when I saw her coming down the aisle, it was like a soap opera. I was more elated by being at the height of glamour than by getting married.'

Some of Tiny's fans were surprised that Tiny had not been invited to appear on Carson's final episode. Tiny, however, was not. 'Of course he didn't invite me back to the show!' he later told Mike Carano, in the short documentary *God Bless Tiny Tim*. 'He did not want the competition with that one-two punch! He wanted to go out without a Tiny Tim! ... If I was as big as him, do you think I would want him back and say a goodbye thing? He was afraid to. I don't care if he don't like me no more. He was afraid to bring me back because it would have been a competition with him ... that's human nature!'

* * *

In June 1992, Tiny tried his hand at politics once again, signing on as comedian Pat Paulsen's running mate for the upcoming presidential election. Paulsen's campaign had become something of a tradition: he had run in every election beginning in 1968. Tiny had appeared on Paulsen's show, *Pat Paulsen's Half A Comedy Hour*, and the two had known one another since the 60s.

Again, Tiny detailed a few policies he would seek to implement if elected.

---

* Martin Sharp instigated another session on April 16 for *I'll Never Get Married Again*, a country album that went unreleased. The album was to contain 'I Know God Still Loves Me,' 'The Banjo Picker's Wife,' 'I'll Never Get Married Again,' 'Me And Bobby McGee,' 'In The Middle Of The Night,' and 'Geraldine.'

He proposed banning credit cards, which saw as the 'demise of the citizen,' and had a unique plan in invigorate the economy. 'If I were president I'd abolish spending,' he told the *Des Moines Register*. 'I'd put a fifteen-year moratorium on every purchase. Folks would have to fix and make do with what they have and save up for fifteen years and only buy new items at the end of the moratorium.' He also proposed a plan to send children who were not performing well in school to work. 'You can tell at eight or nine if school's doing any good. If it isn't, don't let them linger there.'

Tiny first discussed the campaign during a radio interview in Denver, Colorado. After admitting that the campaign was light-hearted, he expressed his support for sitting vice president Dan Quayle's dedication to 'family values,' adding, 'I think a lot of people underestimate the wisdom he has. There's extreme liberality … to permissiveness … [and] I think somebody needs to take a stand.' He went on, after that, to assert that the real cause of AIDS was 'the disobeying of God's laws and fornicating,' and criticized Elizabeth Taylor and HIV-positive basketball player Magic Johnson for raising money for AIDs research.

Although Tiny's ultra conservative views were a regular aspect of his personality, the issues over which he obsessed changed with time. His support for the Nixon administration had centered on his staunch approval of the Vietnam War, but by the 90s his main issue had become abortion. Tiny's widow, Miss Sue, believes that it touched a personal nerve with him. 'He never said so, but he must have wondered if [his mother] regretted having him at all,' she says. 'I believe this led to his obsession with the evils of abortion, his idealization of motherhood, his loyalty to the pro-life Catholic church, and his one-issue, pro-life conservative political leanings. Tiny found much to admire in certain Democrat politicians, but he could never vote for them because of his preoccupation with abortion and the right to life.'

Though it had been launched in jest, the Pat Paulsen/Tiny Tim campaign ticket performed remarkably better than expected. In the North Dakota Republican Primary, they beat Ross Perot and came in second to George Bush. In total, they received 10,984 votes in the states where they were on the ballot, coming in fifth place in the final primary results, beating out Maurice Horton, Gov. Harold Stassen, and Jack Fellure.

Tiny voted for George H.W. Bush in the 1992 election, explaining to Steve Oswalt of Des Moines' KCCI-TV 8 that Bush's stance on abortion was the main reason. 'I know that the world has a big depression conflict, but it means more not to kill a life. We can always overcome depressions with new ideas, but to kill a life is depriving a person of tasting pizza, of having hamburgers or chili, ice cream, and even staying at the Hotel Savory and enjoying their wonderful things. So, the fact that he had the nerve to stand out against abortion means a lot to me, while the other two hemmed and hawed.'*

* * *

As Tiny pontificated about solving the country's problems, he had his own trouble brewing back home in New York City. By 1992, his handling had been taken over by a Mr. Connolly, a former police officer for the New Jersey Transit Authority. But although Connolly was just one in a line of many managerial ruffians, Tiny's age and deteriorating health made him increasingly fearful of his 'protection.'

In late October, Tiny's contempt for and fear of Connolly reached a head when Connolly failed to replace a stolen ukulele that Tiny required for a show. When Tiny expressed frustration, Connolly's assistant, Mr. Leifer, asked if he 'had a problem with that' while punching the palm of his hand threateningly. Tiny was terrified. As it happened, he had recently received a management offer from Stephen Plym, another small-time talent manager, from Des Moines, Iowa. Plym had booked Tiny on and off since 1971, and the two had remained in touch. Plym proposed that Tiny sign a three-year contract with his company, Entertainment America of Iowa, and relocate to Des Moines. Then, Plym and his partners—Curtis Dixon, owner of Premier and Glamour Studios, Mike Debonis, and Mike Lister, owner of Quick Tax and Magnum Industries—would pay for Tiny's room at the nicest hotel in the city, the Savory. Plym also guaranteed a $1,000 weekly salary against future earnings. Essentially, all Tiny had to do was leave New York, and Plym would handle the rest.

As a solo artist, Tiny had last performed in Des Moines in February 1991. The gig, booked by Plym, was not so much a gig but rather a guest appearance at a basketball game held in the gymnasium at Graceland College between former Iowa State players against former members of the Minnesota Vikings football team. When asked how much money Tiny

---

* While Tiny supported conservative candidates and the Republican Party, he was never tapped to campaign for or endorse the GOP in any official capacity. In fact, the GOP rebuked an offer he made to perform at the 1984 Republican National Convention, with party spokesman Gary Holtsma quoted as saying, 'I really don't know what to say, honestly.'

received for his gymnasium performance by the *Des Moines Register*, Plym jokingly replied, 'Not $50,000.'

In any case, Tiny accepted Plym's proposition. No doubt his desire to escape New York had as much if not more to do with the decision than the belief in new career opportunities. Since he knew his actions would be highly scrutinized by Connolly, and that Miss Jan would most certainly object to his leaving New York City for the Midwest, Tiny told almost no one of his escape plans. He quietly slipped out of the Olcott Hotel at 6am on September 26, resurfacing on a park bench in downtown Des Moines for an interview with Steve Oswalt of KCCI-TV 8 on October 28.

'How long do you see yourself living here, staying at the Savory [Hotel]?' Oswalt asked.

'Well, if things go well, Lord willing, at least a year,' Tiny replied. 'I mean, it's a beautiful hotel. This is not a plug: it's a beautiful hotel. The showers are so powerful—the most greatest showers I've ever seen, number one. Number two, it is a small room, but even the metal faucets are so well built. The tile is excellent. There's no room for roaches or rats or mice.' Some—including his wife—had questioned Tiny's desire to move to the Midwest, but 'that's where they make their mistakes; this is a God-fearing city, people are very honest here … everything is clean and nice … I think it's perfect the way it is. … New York needs plenty [of changes], Chicago may need plenty, LA may need plenty, but Des Moines is perfect the way it is.'

When asked why he had wanted to leave New York, Tiny dodged the question and instead began to reminisce about the old New York of his childhood. He then performed the Sam Lewis and Joe Young hit from 1916, 'Way Down In Iowa (I'm Gonna Hide Away),' its lyrics suggesting that he had come to Des Moines for some much needed solace:

I'm gonna hide away, on a little farm in I-o-way;
I'm gonna ride away, on the road that leads to yesterday.

CHAPTER TWENTY-FOUR
SWEET SUE, JUST YOU

No one else it seems ever shares my dreams,
And without you dear I don't know what I'd do.

'SWEET SUE (JUST YOU),' WRITTEN IN 1928 BY VICTOR YOUNG AND WILL J.
HARRIS, AND RECORDED BY TINY TIM IN HONOR OF MISS SUE

In early 1993, Tiny Tim and Stephen Plym were riding high. Tiny had landed a high-profile appearance on NBCs *Laugh-In 25th Anniversary Special*, and since NBC was footing the bill for the first time since Tiny's televised wedding, he and Plym were staying at the Loew's Santa Monica Beach Hotel, where Tiny was seen most often in the hotel bar. (The *Hamilton Spectator* later quoted an 'NBC insider' who remarked that he 'sure knows how to take advantage of a network expense account.')

Tiny, wearing a brand-new suit, spattered with the faces of the *Laugh-In* cast, and accompanied by Miss Jan, who sported a form-fitting gold dress and red cape, attended a panel discussion moderated by the show's producer George Schlatter alongside Goldie Hawn, Dick Martin, Henry Gibson, Alan Sues, Arte Johnson, Judy Carne, Ruth Buzzi, Lily Tomlin, Chelsea Brown, and fielded questions. When Schlatter asked the group who they would 'sock it to,' Tiny raised his hand and shouted out, 'I'd like to sock it to my first wife, Miss Vicki!'

'I think you've already done that, Tiny,' Schlatter replied.

All joking aside, Tiny was there to pay tribute to the show that had launched his career. '*Laugh-In* was important to every one of us,' he said during the press conference. 'It brought us here today. No one here can really pass it by lightly. It was our step to success.'

Tiny and Plym's string of successes continued. When Plym heard about Larry King's final broadcast on late-night radio, he called NBC and offered

Tiny Tim. To his surprise, they accepted, and on January 28, Tiny and Plym traveled to Washington DC for the star-studded event. Miss Jan came down from New York City and met them.

'This is my new wife,' Tiny told reporters, pointing to Jan.

'Actually, we've been married for eight years,' Jan chimed in, setting the record straight. 'I live in New York, he lives in Iowa.'

Tiny had not been a guest of Larry King's before, and he was excited at the prospect. 'Mr. King is so wonderful,' he told the press. When a reporter mentioned the toothbrush sticking out of Tiny's shirt pocket, Tiny explained that it was 'not just any toothbrush' but a 'Dr. Butler toothbrush, with a gum massager.'

'I've got something stuck right here,' Jan joked, pointing to her teeth. 'Will you get it?'

In the interview, the veteran talk-show host asked Tiny where he thought his career was headed. 'I want to get a hit record,' Tiny replied, reiterating a tried-and-true platitude, 'and I know I can be good in horror movies.'

Tiny and Jan's brief reunions in California and Washington DC were also brief in their civility. In an effort to woo Tiny back to New York, Jan asked Tiny to fill out an application for a luxury condo. He obliged her, but they were denied on the grounds that Tiny had 'no assets and no liabilities.'

'You really don't have anything do you?' Jan asked with disdain.

* * *

Back in Des Moines, local residents were intrigued by their new neighbor. One in particular was so intrigued that he swiped Tiny's ukulele at one of his first gigs since relocating, at a 'Juke Box Saturday Night' on Court Avenue. 'It was a heinous crime, even though some of the customers thought the miscreant had done society a favor,' Marc Hansen of the *Des Moines Register* later wrote. The ukulele was discovered in a trashcan on the south side of the city the next morning. 'I've been telling people about finding Tiny Tim's ukulele bag,' the finder, Kim Roberts, told the press, 'but the people who live here are younger and they have no idea who I'm talking about.' She did least receive a $100 finder's fee, and Tiny called to personally thank her.

A reporter for the Sydney *Sun Herald*, Elisabeth Wynhausen, once observed, aptly, that Tiny was a 'soul with the same literal-minded belief in the Bible as in the National Enquirer.' In this, she was not wrong. Soon after the ukulele incident, Tiny began to share his fantastical beliefs and opinions with the people of Iowa through his own radio spot, *Tiny Tim's Tabloid Radio*, which debuted locally on July 25. 'He's your neighbor, Des Moines,' host Richard Lee announced, 'and probably the most internationally famous and well known resident of our city … Tiny Tim!'

In addition to making impassioned proclamations that natural disasters such as recent flooding in Iowa were the result of an angry and vengeful God, Tiny spent his airtime analyzing celebrity gossip and alternative medicines featured in popular tabloids. 'I promise as much as possible, to always tell the truth,' he told listeners. 'If I am wrong and if I slip sometimes, I will correct myself. I have a higher source to answer to.'

Tiny acknowledged that his sources contained sensational and untrue stories, but he felt they contained more fact than fiction. 'I'm sure the mass media of people are wise enough to decipher the fantasy from the fact,' he said. Of course, Tiny was often a subject of the gossip rags he endorsed. Just six months after he moved to Iowa, the *National Enquirer* ran an article entitled 'Tiny Tim's Desperate Pleas to Daughter: Please Forgive Me!' It chronicled Tiny's 'failed relationship with his poverty-stricken daughter,' who it transpired had been placed in foster care after a falling out with her mother at the age of thirteen, given birth to a daughter, Charisse, at sixteen, and was now five months pregnant with her second child and living with her unemployed husband in a tenement apartment in a rough part of Burlington, New Jersey.

'I'm heartbroken to find out that Tulip is living hand-to-mouth in a bad neighborhood—but it's my fault,' Tiny told the *Enquirer*. 'I wasn't a very good father and I wasn't there when she needed me. I'd give anything to fix things up, if she'd just say the word.' He explained that he had not heard from Tulip in a long time, and suggested that the situation was so dire that perhaps she and her husband could not afford a telephone. He confirmed that the last he had seen of Tulip was in 1991, when he went to visit her and his granddaughter. 'We hugged a little bit,' he said. 'But to Tulip I'm a stranger. I haven't earned the right to be called Dad.'

Asked why he had not been there for his daughter, Tiny explained that their relationship had been a victim of circumstance and his own failings. 'I was bankrupt and trying to patch up my failing career. I could hardly support myself, much less Tulip and Miss Vicki. … I wanted a better life for Tulip, and I feel really badly for her. No child should have to go through what Tulip went through—the foster homes, her parents' breakup, being a teenage mother … I want to be allowed to be Tulip's dad and Charisse's granddad. I know I threw away my chance years ago. But I hope she reads this article in the *Enquirer* and gives me another chance.'

Whether or not Tulip read the *Enquirer*'s torrid and highly personal account of her life is not clear; in any case, it did not bring about a tearful reunion between father and daughter.

* * *

The release of the Martin Sharp–produced album *Rock* in late 1993 was met with little fanfare. Nonetheless, Sharp jovially announced that 'success is coming now' for Tiny following initial sales of 1,000 copies, and Tiny flew to Australia to promote the release. The press there enthusiastically declared that he had 'been transformed from a timid-voiced mouse ... to a growling rock'n'roll rebel,' while Tiny himself declared that he felt like 'I've been reborn.'*

Not everyone was impressed by Tiny's heavy metal act. Richard Walsh, the managing director of Australian Consolidated Press, was so disturbed by Tiny's act when they appeared on *The Ray Martin Show* together that he later mentioned the experience in a lecture on the strength of ACP's 'brands' at the Securities Institute. 'I encountered Tiny Tim,' he told the audience. 'That was really sad. He is a global brand in a state of advanced decay, reduced to belting out what purports to be heavy metal music. He doesn't sing, he shouts into the microphone in a total travesty of himself and the music he's trying to imitate.'

Rock ultimately failed to make any significant impact outside of Australia, with Sharp blaming Regular Records for the album's shortcomings. 'They didn't seem to get behind it at all,' he said. 'I received one [royalty] check for $75. It was such a rarity I didn't want to cash it. These records weren't very profitable, and it was hard to get anything back from them to put into the next one. ... It's been a huge job trying to get Tiny's stuff out,' Sharp added. 'I'm good at getting it down, but not so good at getting it out.'

Though Sharp's Tiny Tim projects had not been popular or financial successes, he still brought Tiny into the studio during his 1993 tour. Over the course of several sessions, on November 10, 14, 15, and 25, they recorded a collection of Christmas songs and covers of 60s material. It was to be the last time they saw each other.

---

* He would soon have to revert to his previous image, however, when a taxi dispatcher asked a driver to prove that Tiny Tim was really in the vehicle, prompting Tiny to quiver through 'Tip-Toe' over the radio.

* * *

The following year, 1994, started with a bang. Tiny appeared on *The Miss Howard Stern New Year's Eve Pageant*, a pay-per-view special that aired in the final hours of 1993. Although he had avoided Stern and his radio show since their broadcast argument in 1989, yet another agent, Wayne Knight, persuaded him to capitalize on the exposure.

Stern hosted the special, which featured forty women in highly sexualized competition for $50,000 and the title of Miss Howard Stern. Tiny judged the event, along with an eclectic group of celebrities, has-beens, and infamous personalities including: 'At Seventeen' singer Janis Ian, Ku Klux Klansman Daniel Carver, penis severer John Bobbitt, *All In The Family* star Sherman Hemsley, *Star Wars'* Mark Hamill, and boxer Smokin' Joe Frazier.

During the program, Tiny sang a song in Stern's honor, his original plan to sing the 1916 Billy Murray ditty 'Long Live The Ladies' having been nixed when ASCAP demanded $5,000 in royalties for the privilege. Instead, Tiny composed a new song just before going live:

The girls all love him,
They're crazy about him,
That man named Howard Stern.
They can't resist him,
They long to kiss him,
But he's true to his wife,
You bet your life,
That man named Howard Stern!

Though the *New York Post* called it 'the most disgusting two hours in the history of television,' the program was purchased by 400,000 households and broke a subscriber record for a non-sporting event. Tiny was not paid for his appearance, but was instead compensated with first class travel, a hotel room, and a $500 food *per diem*, of which he spent $370. The exposure proved invaluable, however, with Tiny receiving over thirty booking requests following the program.

A few days later, in a conversation that was recorded for distribution to the Tiny Tim Fan Club, Tiny fielded questions from his fans posed to him by club president Bucks Burnett. Asked about his long hiatus from *The Howard Stern Show*, he claimed that he was 'never mad at Mr. Stern,' adding that while

'Stern 'goes overboard … that's his job.' Of the 1989 interview, he said that Stern had 'kept on ranting and asking more questions' after Tiny had tried to give an honest answer to the question of whether or not he had had a homosexual experience with Bobby Gonzalez, which eventually caused Tiny to react 'very angrily.' After noting that he had refused numerous invitations to appear on Stern's show since then ('I did not want to give him a second chance'), he admitted that he had done the *New Year's Eve Pageant* at Wayne Knight's insistence. 'I thought five years was enough, and it was important to the career, so I went on.'

In the recording, Tiny also gave his thoughts on the events of the pageant, in particular Stern's attempts to bribe John Wayne Bobbit to expose his surgically reattached penis for $15,000, and offered the shock jock a piece of career advice: 'Retire right now, while [you're] ahead.'

Four months later, however, on May 6, Tiny made his return to Stern's radio program after a gap of five years and three months. Stern briefly explained Tiny's absence from the show.

'Thanks for having me again,' Tiny said.

'What do you mean?' Stern exclaimed. 'We've wanted to have you for a long time.'

'Yeah, it was you who wasn't coming,' Robin Quivers added.

Tiny admitted that he had decided to blow up over Stern's 'mocking' of Jesus Christ to cover up his embarrassment about having to discuss the homosexual affair. 'Let me tell you something,' Stern interjected. 'Tiny's all man. Tiny's married a bunch of women. This guy's had sex with some of the most beautiful—if anyone is no homo, it's Tiny Tim!'

The silly interview veered from the subject and hit upon a few intriguing, albeit trivial details. Tiny confessed that he had not had an 'affair' (meaning sexual intercourse) with Miss Jan since 1989. He also explained that he never turned off the lights in his bedroom due to an incident in 1985 and saw 'beetle bugs' on the ceiling of a Florida hotel.* Finally, Howard asked Tiny to detail all of the products he was currently using: Pazo (for hemorrhoids), Charmin toilet paper, Dickenson's Witch hazel (for his 'rear end'), Jergen's Body Shampoo (three times a day), and an Oil Of Olay renewal cream, which he would use to cleanse his face up to eight times a day.

After the show, Tiny returned to Des Moines, where he moved from the

---

* 'Because of this experience,' Miss Sue says, 'I never saw Tiny in a darkened room the entire time I knew him. He said, I never turn out the lights because that is when *they* come.'

Savory Hotel to the Hotel Fort Des Moines. His room, which staff referred to as the 'Tiny Tim suite,' had a window that opened to a view of a brick wall, and when Tiny squirreled up to unlock his door it was only just wide enough to allow visitors to slip in. Reporter David Richards gave a detailed account of the scene in an article for the *Washington Post*:

> Tiny Tim compares the Fort Des Moines Hotel to the plaza in New York, but Suite 527 … is closer to a vintage Holiday Inn. The shag carpet is rust colored, and the sofa, covered in a brown floral fabric, looks like a pile of dead leaves. A Christmas stocking hangs from the knob of an opened desk drawer. … In one corner is a kitchenette, stocked with tins of Green Giant garbanzo beans, five-pound sacks of potatoes, red and white, and a dozen quart bottles of Old Milwaukee beer.* His meals, these days, consist mostly of raw potatoes and beer.

In the same interview, Tiny also admitted that he was a diabetic, and his failure to adequately manage it led to other complications. (Careful readers might take note of his exceptionally poor diet of 'potatoes and beer' in light of this.) He was having serious problems with the circulation in his legs and barely had any feeling in his feet, which meant simple tasks like using stairs and stepping off of curbs had become increasingly difficult. He had apparently resigned himself to the fact that if he developed gangrene, his legs would be amputated, as his father's had. 'I've got to watch the diabetes,' he said, 'but praise the Lord, they can take off my leg. I'd rather have the beer.' Further problems ensued. 'I must say that I'm impotent,' he revealed to Alexander Laurence. 'I discovered this in July 1994. It happened like that maybe because blood diabetes or age.' 'If I can go on another ten years,' he told another reporter at the time, 'I'll be a sight to see.'

Tiny's arrangement with Stephen Plym landed a few more high-profile engagements, including an appearance on WWF television with Jerry 'The King' Lawler, and a guest-spot on *Late Night With Conan O'Brien*, for which he sang 'Easter Parade' with comedienne Victoria Jackson. He was also considered for the role of 'old woman' in *The Naked Gun III: The Final Insult*, but after placing a bonnet on his head and filming himself reading lines from the script, the filmmakers opted to cast a female instead.

---

* His other favorite beer during this period was Molson Ice. 'It gets me there quickest,' he told a reporter for the *Fort Lauderdale Sun-Sentinel*.

* * *

Ultimately, Tiny's relocation to Iowa did not yield enough work for Plym to keep their enterprise afloat. When Plym could no longer pay for Tiny Tim's hotel room, the responsibility fell to Tiny. As a result, their contract soured, and the two began to drift apart. A lonely Tiny began spending hours watching CNN and Televangelist Robert Schuller's *The Hour Of Power*, racking up phone bills in excess of $3,000, and sleeping only five hours a night. Aside from an occasional dinner with Mr. and Mrs. Plym, his social life consisted almost entirely of passing conversations with hotel staff. He left the hotel only for gigs, and to stock up on Depends, paper towels, fistfuls of lottery tickets, and tabloids at a nearby Dahl's Foods. 'Ah, bless his heart,' *Kansas City Star* reporter Shril Kasper heard a bystander say as she watched Tiny scratch a lottery ticket at Dahl's. 'Some people make fun of him. I don't think they should do that.'*

It appeared that this was the end of the road for Tiny Tim: an obscure has-been, sick, far-removed from friends, and estranged from his wife and daughter. But the 'old war horse of show business' held on to a shred of optimism. 'As long as I can sing, I will keep trying, trying to make it one more time,' he told the *Washington Post*. And then he met thirty-nine-year-old Sue Gardener.

Sue had grown up in Minneapolis, Minnesota, the daughter of a wealthy business tycoon, George Gardner. She first saw Tiny on television when she was twelve, and she soon got hooked. Even at that age, she had already developed reservations about societal norms. In particular, she felt very uncomfortable with traditional gender roles and found that her sense of being different from others often left her feeling alienated and misunderstood, but when she saw Tiny on television, she was deeply moved by his transparent honesty, quirky humor, and complete disregard for conventional behavior. 'This is the ideal human being,' she thought to herself, 'the first person I've seen from my home world.'

Although many considered Tiny to be shockingly unattractive, Sue was one of many young girls who found him entrancing. He was tall, dark, and exotically different. He also seemed approachable and likely to treat everyone, even children, with consideration. As his career took off, Sue collected his recordings and created a kind of shrine to him in a corner of her bedroom. Friends and associates of her parents paused to read the small, typed note she

---

* Elsewhere, Tiny explained, 'I love the numbers. Something about matching the unknown with the unknown.' Asked what he would do with the money if he were to win, he cryptically replied that he 'would disappear.'

posted by the front door of her home, 'TINY TIM IS ALWAYS WELCOME HERE.' She even kept a log of how many hours she had spent listening to *God Bless Tiny Tim*, which she describes as 'the soundtrack to the Indian summer of my childhood years.' When Tiny Tim married Miss Vicki on *The Tonight Show*, she did not watch; she was too grief stricken.

'Many women found to their surprise that he was very attractive in an off-beat kind of way,' Sue explains. 'They responded to his romantic sensibilities and seductive demeanor, which was much more apparent in person than on TV. People got it so wrong when they described him as being asexual, probably because of his childlike mannerisms at times. That might have seemed innocent and oddly prudish to some people, because they didn't understand it, but in fact everything about Tiny was a come-on. He simply found child-like mannerisms to be sexy. He was attracted to young teenage girls, and his imitation of the personalities of the young girls he loved was reassuring to them, as he well knew.'

As Tiny's star faded, so did the crushes of scores of adolescents. But Sue's feelings for him did not. While her celebrity crush took a back seat to practical love affairs and adult life, the eccentric crooner always lingered in the back of her mind. She continued to take note of sporadic Tiny Tim updates in newspapers and magazines, and met several people who knew him. While in college, she contacted his management and asked to be informed of shows in her area so she could write an article about him, but no one followed up. 'I would often read about his concert appearances after the fact,' she says.

Come the early 90s, Sue, a Harvard graduate and part owner of her family's industrial supply business, still found Tiny intriguing. She even once sang *God Bless Tiny Tim* in its entirety to her friend Bea Flaming. In 1994, she read an unflattering article about Tiny in a Minnesota newspaper, which reported that he was 'down-and-out' and living in Des Moines. She picked up the phone and dialed the Hotel Fort Des Moines, which had been named in the article. Tiny did not answer, so she left a message.[*]

A few weeks passed, but then, just as she had begun to resign herself to the fact that Tiny would not be calling, she received a mysterious phone call

---

[*] Tiny was sometimes uncharacteristically secretive. He used the alias 'Dorian Grey' while staying at the Olcott Hotel in New York City, at Howard Johnson's in Rhode Island he used the names 'Lester Lush' and 'Tony Russo,' and in Des Moines he used the name 'Fred Farmer.' He also attempted to make his answering machine recording in Des Moines inconspicuous. When a caller reached the machine and the recording clicked on, he or she would hear a loud gong followed by Tiny Tim, in a deep baritone, announcing: 'PLEASE LEAVE A MESSAGE AFTER THE BELLTONE.'

from a man whose voice she did not recognize. 'Tiny was a person of many accents,' she explains. 'He would sort of put on these various accents that he could imitate, including most of the New York ones and some of the New Jersey ones. So this was one of his tough-guy New York [accents] he decided to pull out of the hat that day. At first I thought it was a joke … but then I started to think, Well, who would think that he would have a low, raspy voice?'

After detailing the depths of her admiration for him since her childhood, Sue asked if she could visit him in Des Moines. Tiny paused for a second and then asked, 'What do you look like?' Sue found the question rude but answered to the best of her ability.

'I'm reasonably attractive,' she said.

'Are you slim?'

'Oh, yes.'

'Well … OK.'

Though Sue was 'quite shocked' at Tiny's bluntness, it did not deter her desire to meet him. They planned a meet at the Hotel Fort Des Moines on the afternoon of July 28. All was fine until Sue revealed that she planned to bring her boyfriend along with her. 'Oh, honey, this is a terrible time of year to travel,' Tiny told her, his tone changing. 'If something should happen to you, I wouldn't want to be responsible.'

Sue would hear nothing of canceling—'I've wanted to meet you for twenty-six years!' she told him—so, on July 28, she and Dennis—actually her fiancé—headed down to Des Moines. During the drive they discussed the possibility of having Tiny sing at their wedding. As they neared their destination, Dennis looked over to Sue, singing along to a cassette of *God Bless Tiny Tim*, and joked, 'You're still in love with Tiny!'

'The guy's like seventy or something,' Sue said. 'It won't be the same.'

'Yes it is,' Dennis replied. 'You're still in love with him.'

They arrived at the Hotel Fort Des Moines and waited in the lobby for Tiny Tim, per his instructions. While Sue stood in rapt anticipation, doing her best to remain calm, Dennis wandered off. Finally, the elevator doors opened and out stepped Tiny Tim.

'I was shocked at how big he was,' Sue later wrote. 'He was six-foot-one, broad shouldered, barrel-chested, and overweight. He still had the long hair. He looked very much how I remembered him … [but] he was huge, unbelievably huge, and he was wearing this light blue suit that was very unbecoming and made him look even larger.'

'Are you Miss Sue?' he asked.

'Yes,' she said.

'I'm Tiny Tim.'

At first, Sue thought the Hotel Fort Des Moines an odd place for Tiny Tim, but she soon came to realize that the surroundings were fitting. 'It's a formerly opulent hotel that had become run down. It was a strangely suitable environment for him, as he was also aged and in reduced circumstances, but presented himself with the dignity of better days gone by.'

Tiny, Sue, and Dennis went to eat in the hotel dining room. As they were shown to their table, the room began to buzz. At first, Sue recalls, 'he looked at me with slight disdain ... and then I'd look at him and think, You are so old.' But that would soon change. 'You're basically the way you've always been,' Sue realized. 'Within five minutes we were just kind of staring at each other like, Oh, wow!'

Tiny dominated the conversation, and his stories grew increasingly blue, with Dennis 'egging Tiny on to be more and more ridiculous.' Sue shifted uncomfortably in her chair as Tiny recounted his adventure with Miss Candy and a jar of honey at Caesar's Palace in 1968. After dinner, they all went upstairs to Tiny's room so Sue could record his stories of his childhood and experiences in show business. Tiny had a few beers and proceeded to talk for several hours. 'At one point he just closed his eyes and it was like we weren't there, and it didn't matter. He was just talking to the world, the universe; he was recording his voice for posterity, and we were just the people who happened to be there, and if we had walked out he wouldn't have noticed. Nixon, Elvis, every crazy thing in the world ... he just went on and on and on.'

At 11:30, Sue lightly tugged on Tiny Tim's sleeve. He snapped out of the past and into the present, opened his eyes, and looked at her indignantly as if to say, 'What is it?'

'It's very late,' she told him. 'I need to rest.'

'Miss Gardner, if you're tired, the couch is there,' Tiny replied, 'but I must go on!'

Trying desperately not to laugh, Sue laid down on the couch for another forty-five minutes. She would later hypothesize of Tiny's tendency to deliver lengthy, rambling monologues that his 'imaginary life was much preferable to the difficult realities from which he escaped into fantasy about days gone by, in which he could imagine that life was more simple, gentle, and full of love and romance. That was the dream, and the vibe, to which he could transport his listeners. … In person, and in private, this sense of time travel, almost of mind meld, was so intense that leaving his presence did feel like an unwelcome awakening from a beautiful dream.'*

When Tiny felt satisfied that enough information was committed to tape, he allowed Sue and Dennis to pack up their belongings and say goodnight. They made plans to see each other again the following afternoon. As they took the elevator back down from Tiny's floor, they finally allowed themselves to laugh, and by the time they got to the lobby, they were howling like maniacs.

'So that's your dream boy?' Dennis asked.

'You bet,' Sue replied, suddenly sobering.

The following day, they drove around for a while, with Tiny squashed into the middle seat of Sue's pickup truck (and 'pull[ing] out all the stops … to make us realize that we could laugh because it was so uncomfortable'), before returning to the hotel, where Dennis and Sue recorded Tiny singing old love songs in the style of Rudy Vallee. Like the previous night, Tiny continued to give Sue 'appraising looks,' which she returned. Her prediction that age would have changed her feelings about Tiny Tim was wrong. And she definitely had not anticipated that he might reciprocate her feelings.

'It never occurred to me that Tiny Tim would be interested in me,' she said. 'Even when I met him … I was dumbfounded by the fact that he was interested in me, and he was being very obviously flirtatious, too. I kept saying to myself, No way, this isn't happening. … You just had no idea how to take him, what to feel, what to do, or what to think. It was almost hallucinogenic.'

On the way home, Dennis and Sue discussed their experience with Tiny. 'I feel like we have left the Land of Oz,' Dennis told her, 'and everything is black and white. I miss him.' When Sue admitted that she, too, missed Tiny, Dennis quipped, 'I think *you'll* marry Tiny and *I'll* sing at the wedding.'

Not knowing what to say, Sue remained silent. Shortly after returning to Minnesota, however, the couple called off their engagement. 'The romantic attraction had faded years ago,' Sue recalls, 'and I had been getting ready to settle; to marry for friendship and companionship. I felt something for Tiny that I never thought I'd feel again, something I hadn't felt in a long time, maybe ever. I thought that as crazy as it was, and impractical, and a total set-up for heartbreak, I knew that I wanted to be with Tiny. Even though I didn't

---

* This talkativeness stood in marked contrast to the old Tiny, about whom a woman Sue met who had become acquainted with him back in Greenwich Village recalled, 'He didn't say a word.'

think it was possible, I had to give it a try. Dennis liked Tiny tremendously, and when the attraction became very apparent, right away, he was happy to stand aside and let me live out my childhood dream of marrying Tiny Tim.'

Upon reflection, Sue realized that Dennis knew something that she did not. 'He knew that it was not going to be an easy or simple thing being with Tiny. He knew it wouldn't last forever. He knew it wouldn't even last a long time.'

* * *

Tiny and Sue began spending hours on the phone, and when they were not in direct communication, Sue played the tapes she had recorded in Des Moines. Though their mutual attraction was clear, there was one obstacle: Miss Jan. When Sue broached the subject, Tiny unleashed his usual commentary: that Jan had not been faithful to him and had deceived him by using birth control. Jan, on the other hand, vehemently denied all accusations that she had cheated, even turning up unannounced midway through Tiny's May 1994 appearance on *The Howard Stern Show* to defend herself on air.

'Tiny loves me so very much,' she told Stern. 'He exaggerates his paranoia and fear of losing me and he has been excessively jealous … to the point of almost losing his mind or making everyone around him lose their mind.' But while she denied that anyone else was involved, she admitted that 'I'm not really in love with Tiny now … at this point it seems like I should get a life, I think he's in agreement of that, also. It's been a long time.'

Tiny remained largely silent, unconvinced. What was not discussed was Tiny's vow to Jan that he would never under any circumstances seek a divorce. As far as Sue was concerned, the unhappy marriage endured out of convenience. Jan didn't want to give up her rent-controlled apartment, while Tiny seemed to think 'Well, I can see other people, because we're separated, but then on the other hand I can still make love with Miss Jan because, after all, we're still married.'

The marriage was truly over, at least as far as Tiny was concerned, but Sue wanted to hear it herself, from Jan. Sue's health had been delicate for several years and she was planning to visit a specialist in New York, so she asked Tiny to call Miss Jan and ask her if she would be willing to meet Sue for lunch to discuss an article she was writing about Tiny. In fact, the real reason was so that she could find out the current status of their marriage. The two women made plans to meet, but when Sue called Jan from New York to confirm, Jan answered groggily and said she didn't want to get together after all.

At this point, Sue felt she had done all she could to verify Tiny's story, and Jan's behavior seemed consistent with what she had heard from others. She therefore decided to forge ahead with her budding relationship with Tiny. They had been spending several hours each night on the phone, and she had gained a better understanding of his repertoire. She considered several different projects for him, but then settled on a simple, informal interview about his knowledge of early American popular music.

In late August, she flew Tiny up to Minnesota for a pre-production meeting. Upon arrival, Tiny asked that she take him to the grocery store. He shuffled up and down the aisles for at least an hour, stopping to inspect dozens of items. After a long time in the store, Tiny sighed deeply. 'I'm sorry for taking so long,' he said. Emboldened, Sue put her arm around him. 'There is nowhere in the world that I'd rather be, than with you, here, in Cub Foods.' Tiny's eyes widened. He looked at Sue, looked at her arm around him, and looked at her again. Slowly, he put his arm around her, and the two embraced in the middle of the aisle. Later, at the checkout, he whispered, 'Oh, two friends meet.'

'He was shocked, too,' Sue recalls. 'We were both shocked, each of us thinking, Are you really interested in me? Really? Really?'

On September 14, the fifth day of Tiny's visit, he asked Sue to marry him. 'I remember when he asked me to marry him I thought, This is an odd question … of course! Then I thought, Well, I guess we have to say this even though it is completely obvious, yet it was not to him.'

Later that night, Tiny asked Sue repeatedly to reassure him that she really intended to marry him. 'Every time he asked me I was hurt almost. It was sad that he had to keep asking me that. He just couldn't quite believe it. What he didn't realize was that it was equally unbelievable to me that he had asked.'

The two spent the next several days 'in a whirlwind of endearments.' After that, Tiny left Minnesota for Tampa, Florida, where he was to record a brand-new album. After leaving Minnesota, he called his manager, Gil Morse, in Rhode Island.

'Mr. Morse,' he said. 'We've got a problem.'

'What's that Tiny?' Gil replied cautiously.

'I'm in love.'

'Oh, brother! That is a problem! Are you really in love, Tiny?'

'Yes, Mr. Morse. I'm in love with Miss Sue.'

CHAPTER TWENTY-FIVE

SOME SORT OF BAD ALICE COOPER VIDEO

This whole thing looks like some sort of bad Alice Cooper video!
JAY LENO TO TINY TIM, OCTOBER 31 1994

On a Friday night in early 1994, a telephone rang in Quincy, Massachusetts, just as it did every Friday at 10pm.

'Oh, hello, Mr. Foley?' said Tiny Tim, calling from Des Moines.

'Hey, Tiny,' Foley replied. 'How are you?'

'I'm good, but I'll tell you what,' he said. 'I just got a letter from Mr. Charles Manson.'

'Yeah?' Foley asked. 'What'd it say?'

'It said something about how the 60s need to be kept alive, and I'm one of the only people doing anything to keep the 60s alive, but I need to do more!' Tiny told him.

'What else did it say?'

'I don't know, I tore it up!'

Manson and Tiny had met previously. In the 60s, Tiny performed at the Hog Farm commune, and Manson had introduced himself as a fan. Tiny later remembered him as a 'sweet man' and said that he 'seemed like a nice guy.' He also told the *Toronto Sun* that he believed Manson had been framed.

'Tiny, you know you're going to be on a list, right?'

'What do you mean, Mr. Foley?'

'Well a high-profile serial killer writes you a letter—that's probably something that the FBI takes interest in. Nothing is going to happen to you, but you're probably on a list somewhere.'

'Oh, gosh! I'll tell you, what a week it's been!' Tiny said, shuffling his mail. 'What's this here? Oh, this phone bill. I gotta cut this short.' The line went dead.

Since the early 90s, Jim Foley had operated as the unofficial ringleader of a group of die-hard Tiny Tim fans in the New England area who identified themselves as Tiny Heads, a play on the Grateful Dead's Deadheads. Most had been children or teenagers during Tiny's heyday, and had remained loyal fans for decades.

In addition to Foley, the core of the group included Elizabeth Hoffman, a writer from Vermont; Mark Mitchell, a graphic artist from Massachusetts; Pat Barreatt, who had witnessed Tiny's meeting Miss Vicki in 1969 but was now living in Cambridge, Massachusetts; Mark Frizzell, a local filmmaker; Renee Bowan, an enthusiastic fan from Kennebunkport, Maine; and the youngest members of the group: Ben Roth, a twenty-four-year-old from Providence, Rhode Island; and seventeen-year-old Brian Blouin from Methuen, Massachusetts.

The Tiny Heads would help Tiny tremendously during the 90s by generating promotional materials and assisting with the distribution of his music. On December 12 1994, several of them appeared on NPR's *All Things Considered* to discuss their enduring love for all things Tiny. 'Everyone that sees Tiny becomes obsessed,' Foley told the show's Dan Gaddiman. 'I built my life around seeing his live shows. It's nearly caused problems in my marriage over this thing … whenever Tiny's around, I have to see him. If he's not around, I have to call him on the phone. If he's not available on the phone, I have to write him a letter. I can't stay away from him.'

Tiny's had a simple explanation as to why he had such devoted fans. 'We live in a dangerous, cold, hateful, godforsaken society,' he told a reporter after an event at Providence City Hall around Christmas 1993. 'And I'm against that.' The Tiny Heads were more than just a fan club—they were Tiny's friends. When he had a negative experience at a gig, the Tiny Heads were there, watching out for him, or providing reassurance. They also sometimes acted as a buffer between Tiny and his manager, Gil Morse. And, of course, given their close proximity to Tiny, they ended up in some colorful predicaments.

In 1995, Tiny was booked to perform at a New Year's Eve show at a fetish club in Cambridge, Massachusetts. Morse had recently broken his pelvis and could not leave the house, so it was left to Foley, Ben Roth, and Mark Mitchell to transport Tiny from the airport to the show, collect the money, run the merchandise table, and then drive Tiny back to Rhode Island. According to Roth, Tiny had seemed troubled from the moment he got into the car, and his mood darkened when he learned that the club had not hired a band to back him for his planned tribute to Dean Martin. He would have to play a solo set instead. Foley and Roth knew that Tiny could perform for hours with or without a band, but they also understood that he could suddenly lose that ability if things were not going his way. This was one of those times. The set started out fine, but then, a few songs in, Tiny looked over at Foley and Roth and grinned.

'I just want to make this clear,' he said, turning back to the audience, 'this is not meant to offend anyone.' Then, ignoring the Tiny Heads' panicked, frantic waves, he started into 'Santa Claus Has Got The AIDS This Year.' When he finished the song, the audience was silent. 'You could hear a pin drop,' says Roth.

Tiny finished his set after only forty minutes to a sad smattering of applause. He then sat at the merchandise table for half an hour, without a single autograph request. After Foley managed to wrangle some cash out of the club's owners for Tiny's shortened set, they packed up hurriedly and ushered Tiny toward the door. As they left, a club employee handed Tiny a 'Safe Sex Kit.'

'Disgraceful! How dare they!' Tiny exclaimed, scattering the colorful contents on the sidewalk. The drive back to Warwick, Rhode Island, was silent.

* * *

Jim Foley also helped facilitate the recording of what would become Tiny's favorite of his own albums, *Prisoner Of Love: A Tribute To Russ Columbo.* In the summer of 1994, Tiny had complained that he was 'sick of making crappy novelty records' and wanted to try 'something different.' Through his friendship with transgressive punk singer G.G. Allin (who was also a Tiny Tim fan), Foley had been introduced to Mark Robinson of Ponk Media, who in 1991 had recorded Allin's country album *Carnival Of Excess.*

Robinson felt similarly equipped to help Tiny depart from his usual repertoire, but Tiny was resistant to the idea. 'He's an amateur!' he protested. Foley subsequently learned that Tiny had asked Robinson if he could assemble a seventy-six-piece marching band for a twenty-minute version of Notre Dame's fight song. 'Tiny would have you chase your tail to see how far you'd go,' Foley notes. 'He would throw a wrench into the machinery for his own amusement.' He encouraged Robinson to be patient, explaining that Tiny often tested people by judging their reactions to his outlandish requests, and eventually the two resumed a dialogue.

'What is it that the studios and big labels won't let you do?' Robinson asked Tiny. 'Because that's what I want you to do.'

At first, Tiny suggested putting out some acoustic ukulele tracks as Edison Cylinders ('not practical!'), before they eventually settled on the idea of a tribute to Columbo, a rival to Bing Crosby and Rudy Vallee whose life and career was cut short by a tragic shooting accident at the home of photographer Lansing Brown. Columbo left behind an impressive body of work, in which Tiny was well versed. A full album in Columbo's style was a natural choice for Tiny, and certainly a departure from material like 'I Saw Mr. Presley Tip-Toeing Through The Tulips.' It was also an idea he had been considering for some time, having first mentioned it to *Oui* magazine in 1984.

Robinson recruited Paul Reller to produce the sessions. Reller, a professor at the University of South Florida, had experience composing everything from contemporary classical to experimental rock music, and was, according to Robinson, 'an absolute genius.'

After much persuasion, Tiny arrived in Tampa, Florida, on September 20 1994 to start work on the album. Robinson and Reller were well prepared. Reller had assembled a small orchestra, comprised of his band, Clang, and twelve additional musicians, several of who volunteered to perform without compensation. The plan was to record two songs each night over five closed sessions in the auditorium at the University of South Florida. Each song would be recorded live, to more closely resemble recording practices of the 30s. Tiny had previously furnished Robinson and Reller with a list of ten Russ Columbo songs he wanted to record, and Reller had painstakingly transcribed sheet music for the orchestra from the original recordings.

The session began at 8pm. When Tiny entered the auditorium and was greeted by the small orchestra outfitted with meticulously accurate sheet music, he was pleased. As he and Robinson were leaving the first session, the sound engineer handed Robinson a tape of the songs from that night.

On the way to Tiny's hotel, Robinson pulled over in a small parking lot to listen to the tape. As the first notes of 'Paradise' came through the speakers, Tiny beamed. 'Oh, *ohh*, Mr. Robinson,' he gushed.

'He just had that look,' Robinson recalls. 'He didn't even have words … he was absolutely, freaking knocked out by the way these tapes sounded and that kicked him into overdrive. I think that's when he realized it was the record he'd always wanted to do.' From that point forward, the sessions continued flawlessly. 'I think he was honored to be paying tribute to someone he really looked up to as an artist, and it's my contention that he didn't want to have anything compromising that.'*

Robinson remembers a few humorous anecdotes from his tenure with Tiny in Florida. On one occasion, while shooting some video footage in a nearby park, he noticed Tiny was walking on tiptoes. 'I'm just making sure I don't step on any spiders or ants,' he explained. 'It takes a long time for them to build their houses, and I don't want to disturb them.' Later that night, Tiny made them late to the recording session when he became immersed in checking the expiration dates on loaves of bread at a 7-Eleven.

On another occasion, Robinson took Tiny to the post office so that he could send money orders to everyone from hotel staff to his daughter. 'He'd spend twenty dollars to overnight ten dollars... he was sending all the people money he didn't have.' He even saw Tiny tip the bagger in a grocery store. 'He didn't have much money, but he was generous,' Robinson says. 'It was everybody else before him.'

The last session for *Prisoner Of Love* was held on September 25. By the end of the night, all ten songs Tiny had selected from Russ Columbo's repertoire were in the can: 'You Try Somebody Else,' 'Time On My Hands,' 'All Of Me,' 'Sweet And Lovely,' 'More Than You Know,' 'Paradise,' 'Just Friends,' 'Save The Last Dance For Me,' 'Prisoner Of Love,' and 'Auf Wiedersehn, My Dear.'

'I think the biggest thing is the fact that we put him in front of an orchestra, again, letting him do what he wanted to do,' Robinson concludes. 'The big thing was letting Tiny have the freedom to do what he wanted to do in his heart, and Russ Columbo was such a huge influence on him. I think, in general, the overall sound that we had is the big thing.'

Tiny left Robinson to handle the album's release and flew back to Rhode Island. There he linked up with Gil Morse and the Tiny Heads, who were to accompany him to his one-month engagement at Spooky World, the world's largest Halloween theme park.

* * *

Spooky World, formerly located in Berlin, Massachusetts, was one of the most popular tourist attractions in New England during the 90s. It had expanded

---

* Sometimes, if they finished early enough, everyone would gather around while Tiny took out his ukulele, sang songs, and reminisced about the past. Several of these recordings—'Hollywood Cowboys,' 'Medley For England,' and a pre-*Girl* version of 'I Believe In Tomorrow'—were released on a split EP with G.G. Allin in 2009.

from a humble hayride to include six haunted houses, three museums, rides, games, and rotating celebrity residencies. In 1994, the celebrities in attendance included Bobby 'Boris' Pickett, Kane Hodder from the *Friday The 13th* film series, and Tiny Tim.

Spooky World owner and CEO Dave Bertolino had already considered hiring Tiny for a stint at Spooky World before he caught wind of a Tiny Tim show at a Holiday Inn in Peabody, Massachusetts. There he met Gil Morse and Tiny, whom he describes as 'quite a gentleman' and 'such a kind soul.'* His business partners did not share his enthusiasm, however, querying whether Tiny Tim had anything to do with Halloween. 'I said, You know what? He's very entertaining, and that's what Spooky World is—a Fellini Circus—and who better than Tiny Tim to help put it together?'

Per Gil Morse, Bertolino updated Tiny's rider to include the stipulation that his dressing room remain stocked with fresh apples, birch beer, and sarsaparilla soda, and with that, Tiny was booked for the 'Scareaoke' stage at Spooky World 1994. 'He was just wonderful,' Bertolino recalls. 'One of the things about Spooky World is you could sometimes be [in line] an hour, maybe even two hours, and you were anxious to be entertained. So, we'd bring various acts out and… when we brought in Tiny, it just clicked.' Although he was contracted to do two shows a night, 'it was rare that he did less than four or five shows in a night. And he was happy to do it.'

Not only was Tiny a hit onstage but many wanted to meet him as well. 'He had just a constant flow of people in front of him that he would sign autographs for,' Bertolino recalls. Tiny refused to charge for autographs, so Bertolino came up with the idea of having photographs printed for him to sign. 'He would sell the photograph, and the autograph was free.'

The Tiny Heads were thrilled to have Tiny in the area for a whole month. Tiny obliged them by fulfilling interview requests, posing for pictures, and, at seventeen-year-old Brian Blouin's insistence, performing the first and only live version of the *Blood Harvest* theme song, 'Marvelous Mervo.' For Miss Sue, however, the month-long residency was nothing but filled with heartache. Although, many readers of the *Ellsworth Journal* would probably have guffawed at Tiny's earnest insistence that 'I can be a lot sexier than people perceive me to be,' there were still plenty of young women interested in him.

---

* He also felt that Tiny's relationship with Morse was one that was fulfilling to them both. 'I don't think it was just money. I think it was also a labor of love and they really liked each other.'

Shortly after arriving at Spooky World, Tiny began a flirtation with a Miss Karen, a red-haired, fair skinned eighteen-year-old who worked as a witch at the park. Though the dalliance was harmless at first, Tiny pushed the envelope. A video taken by Ben Roth's girlfriend, Krista, shows Miss Karen waiting in line for Tiny's autograph. When she reaches him, they giggle and whisper for a moment, before Tiny abruptly pulls her close and kisses her on the lips, in full view of several dozen onlookers. 'I'm in *looove!*' Karen exclaims to the camera as she walks way. 'That was such a phenomenal kiss. I'm never washing my mouth again!'

Tiny began to call Miss Karen onstage during his performances, serenading her with songs like 'Which Witch Is The Witch For Me.' They also enjoyed romantic outings in the afternoons before work. Sue was 'crushed' when Tiny called and confessed that he and Karen had carved their initials into a tree. Why was he seeing Karen, she asked, when they were engaged? Tiny's perplexing justification was that he was unsure that Sue actually intended to marry him, as no ring had yet been given, and because Tiny was strapped for cash, the ring buying responsibility fell back on Miss Sue. 'You better send a ring or else I don't know what's going to happen here with Miss Karen,' he told her.

The next day, a determined Miss Sue purchased a diamond-studded gold ring and had it shipped overnight to Spooky World. Upon its arrival, Tiny declared that he could no long have contact with Miss Karen. The next day, Ben Roth received a call from Tiny. 'I had to say goodbye to Miss Karen,' Tiny said, 'but I think she'd make a good girlfriend for you. You should give her a call.' To his girlfriend's relief, Roth did not take Tiny up on his suggestion.

* * *

By mid October, the park's staff had learned of Tiny's plans to marry Miss Sue, and given that the twenty-fifth anniversary of Tiny's wedding to Miss Vicki was looming in December, it was suggested that Tiny wed Miss Sue on *The Tonight Show* in a live broadcast from Spooky World, but Tiny's current wife, Miss Jan, made it an impossibility. Besides, Tiny wanted to marry Miss Sue in a Catholic church. Those involved in the idea's conception knew that the publicity would be invaluable, however, so instead Tiny proposed renewing his wedding vows to Miss Jan.

'I thought it was in very bad taste in many ways,' says Miss Sue. 'It wasn't an appropriate venue for any kind of wedding; he and Miss Jan were in the process of getting divorced, and Tiny and I were about to announce our wedding.'

Bertolino contacted *The Tonight Show*, where initially the idea was not well received. 'It wasn't something they were interested in, and then they changed their mind and within a day or two later we heard back and they were all over us. So, the next thing we know … they put it on their calendar. Shortly after, we heard that Bill Maher was assigned to narrate the piece, so he was coming out.'

Tiny's fans were excited about Tiny's return to *The Tonight Show*, but Tiny sensed that the new host, Jay Leno, was not thrilled by the prospect. 'Nobody was speaking about it,' he later told Bucks Burnett. 'No questions were asked. … Then Mr. Leno came out in *TV Guide* just a week and a half before this thing was going on, and he said he was his "own man" … so it is my opinion that Mr. Leno did not want this at all.'

Tiny attempted to back out of the appearance, telling Bertolino that he could no longer go through with it because it would 'steal the specialness' from *The Tonight Show*'s previous host, Johnny Carson. Bertolino reluctantly contacted the show's producers to cancel, only for Tiny to have a change of heart after speaking to Carson, who he said told him, 'This is good for your career. I'm not bothered by it.'

Miss Jan arrived and assumed, for one final time, the role she had been playing for nearly ten years: devoted wife. Gil Morse also made good use of the publicity, assigning his clients, Bobby Pickett and country singer Robin Lynn, the roles of best man and maid of honor. Lynn, who had performed with Tiny countless times, disliked Jan immediately. She felt that Jan was drawing an undue amount of attention to herself, and that she was not handling the ceremony in a dignified manner. 'She just tried to make the whole thing a total joke,' Lynn later said, when interviewed for *Tiny Tim: The Last Hurrah*. 'We didn't get along because she didn't love Tiny for the good person that he was.'

Halloween rolled around, and the *Tonight Show* crew arrived to prepare for the broadcast. While several of the Tiny Heads attended the taping, their de facto leader, Jim Foley, refused. 'Tiny and I had a big argument that day because I didn't want him to do it,' he recalls. 'I basically told him he was going to look like a horse's ass … because I knew that Bill Maher was involved, and he hated everyone, and Jay Leno hated Tiny, and Tiny knew it—double disaster.'

For Miss Sue, the whole situation was so distressing and insulting that she threatened to call off the engagement. After a heated conversation with her, Tiny called Foley and told him that he felt he owed it to Miss Jan to go through with the show, 'because she never had a chance in the limelight like Miss Vicki … I've already committed and I have to stick to my guns no matter what the repercussions are.'

When the time neared, Tiny put on his tuxedo and top hat—a toned-down homage to his 1969 wedding suit—while Jan abandoned plans to wear a $450 white-and-gold dress in favor of a short, black off-the-shoulder number complete with braided headband and black veil. According to Dave Bertolino, she also demanded compensation for a trumped-up list of expenses, 'and I think we paid into most of it.'

As night fell on Spooky World, the *Tonight Show* crew prepared for the live broadcast, and the audience assembled around the Scare-aoke stage. In New York, Leno went live. The segment opened on Tiny backstage with Maher, who introduced 'the man of the hour' and likened Tiny's original televised wedding to 'the Kennedy assassination—except, of course, a little sadder.' Dismissing any suggestion that he might be nervous, Tiny revealed that the ceremony 'will be wonderful for Miss Jan, because she needs a lot of help in the limelight.'

'Well, he's seventy-two [sic], he's got a high-pitched voice, and his name is Tiny … it sounds like a dream wedding night for any girl!' Maher concluded, inciting laughter from Leno and his studio audience. After a commercial break, Leno gave a brief and dismissive recap of the 'very strange event' that had taken place on *The Tonight Show* twenty-five years earlier, before cutting back to Maher at Spooky World, where the wedding party was lined up in front of a crudely painted dungeon backdrop. On the left stood Bobby Pickett, Kane Hodder, and Tiny Tim; on the right stood Jan, holding a plastic pumpkin on a stick in place of a bouquet, a flower girl, and the other female members of the wedding party. Right in the thick of things stood Maher, who announced that the guests included 'friends of the bride, and friends of the groom, and, of course, friends of Satan,' adding with a smirk that Tiny had told him 'marriage is sacrifice.'

After the bride and groom shared a perfunctory kiss, Leno likened proceedings to 'some kind of bad Alice Cooper video. Bill, I'm afraid we've got to run here, you've certainly earned your money tonight!'

When the show ended, Jim Foley knew he had been proven correct. 'It was painfully bad,' he recalls. 'I couldn't have planned for this to go any worse.' Miss Sue watched the show from a neighbor's house, and 'smiled wryly' when they wondered allowed what it could be like to watch your fiancé renew his vows with his wife on TV. Actor Kane Hodder found the event even more ludicrous than *Friday The 13th*. 'I've seen a lot of bizarre shit in my career,' he said in 2013, 'but that might be at the top of the list.'

Following the broadcast, Tiny gave interviews to various media outlets. In one, he announced that he and Jan were on the rocks, and that he was 'in love with Sue Gardner from Minneapolis, Minnesota.' Ben Roth watched the broadcast with the now-forgotten Miss Karen, who had since quit her job at Spooky World, and who broke into hysterical sobs and locked herself in the bathroom when Tiny mentioned Miss Sue. The next day, the Associated Press concluded, 'Halloween doesn't get much scarier than this.'

Though Bertolino feels that the segment could have been handled with more respect, he considered it a success. 'I don't think it was handled right by NBC, but … it's a positive to have any kind of coverage on a celebrity. It keeps the flame going, especially when it's network coverage. He was seen live on *The Tonight Show*, coast to coast, and that hadn't happened in a lot of years.'

Unfortunately for Bertolino, the end of the broadcast did not mean the end of his dealings with Miss Jan, who demanded more money following the appearance. 'She was kind of brushing up against me, and I asked for our team of security to come into the office, because I wanted a witness there … the two of them stood there with arms crossed, watching this whole encounter. I remember her saying to me, I'm a woman; you're a man. It's like, OK, is there anything else you want, Jan? Those actual words stayed with me all those years.'

Miss Sue was completely appalled by the entire spectacle. 'I thought the whole thing was very exploitative and dishonest,' she recalls. 'I was disappointed with Tiny for carrying out that whole farce. I thought it was very insensitive to Miss Jan, and I don't know how she was persuaded to participate, either. I was also infuriated by the way he was treated by [Bill Maher]. I found the whole episode distasteful and ludicrous, as I am sure most people did, but there was nothing I could do about it.' While many would have called it a day at this point, Sue persevered. 'I was very much in love with Tiny. I also realized that his relationship with reality was not as strong as it is for most people, which was part of the package, and I had to accept that if I was going to be with him, which at the time I wanted more than anything.'

Tiny, the protagonist of the whole affair, never expressed regret, and insisted he had done right by Miss Jan. He did, however, maintain his suspicions that Leno had not wanted to do the segment. 'I don't bear any resentment,' he told Bucks Burnett, 'because as much as he didn't want it, I didn't want it ten times more.'

* * *

Fortunately for Tiny, Miss Sue's anger soon subsided, and a few days after the broadcast, he visited her in Minneapolis to shoot the interview series she was producing. His arrival drew the attention of her neighbors—perhaps even more so than the massive, bright blue house she had constructed in the middle of her neighborhood.

On November 11, Tiny sat down with Johnny Pineapple, Sue's neighbor and contracted cameraman, for the interview. Coincidentally, Pineapple played the ukulele, and he and his son Paul shared Tiny's affinity for vintage music. Sue had been keeping Pineapple up to date as to the developments between she and Tiny, describing him as 'wonderful' and 'a great guy.'

Prior to meeting Tiny, Pineapple had made many of the same one-dimensional assumptions as had so many others—and, like many others, his opinion was radically modified when they met. 'Before I met him, I kind of figured, oh, this was a marketed ... quirky little one-of-a-kind, unique novelty act that we are just gonna milk until we can milk it no more. Then you meet him and, *woah*, you're transported to a different stratosphere.'

Pineapple's knowledge of turn-of-the-century music, combined with his recent investigation into Tiny's career, precipitated by his neighbor's romantic interest in the singer, made for a compelling, six hour interview. The unreleased footage, which eventually circulated among Tiny fans and collectors, opens on Tiny taking a drink of beer from an oversized can. Perhaps as a courtesy to Miss Sue, who was averse to drinking, he begins by explaining why the beer is essential for the interview, calling it 'a musical pleasure to bring back in my head, at least, the great years of the 1890s, 1910s, 20s, and even the 30s ... I call it the golden brew of music.'

With that disclaimer out of the way, Tiny is off, relating story after story and song after song of what he calls 'the white man's soul ... these are the songs that thrilled the nation, thrilled the world ... thrilled as many white people in their communities as the blacks were thrilled with the soul and song of their sufferings ... these melodies were fantastic melodies.'

For six hours, Pineapple listened intently to Tiny and found himself overcome with the same reverence that Martin Sharp, the Tiny Heads, and many other friends and fans had developed. 'I don't think [Tiny] ever had an

IQ test, but I believe it had to be off the charts,' he says. 'He was the kind of person that could not get dressed and walk down the street by himself. It's that dichotomy of what I believe was Asperger's [syndrome] … he was obsessive-compulsive [about] music … once I got to know him, woah, I realized I was dealing with a living biographer to a bygone era … [and] that once this guy is gone, the knowledge is gone. … I realized I was sitting at the throne of greatness.'

Tiny's habit of rattling off names, dates, matrix numbers, and other details about the music he performed was often noted during his life, but he was rarely fact checked. Pineapple and his son tested it out, and to their amazement they found that he was correct. 'Tiny had a kind of deal with numbers. We were sitting in my house one time, and he would say stuff like, Well, I remember the day I met Frank Sinatra … he had just finished singing the fabulous "Blue Hawaii" on the old Bluebird label … why, I believe the matrix number was—and he clicks off a nine digit number. What Tiny didn't realize is that my son had a tape recorder going. Sometime later on, we rewound it, jotted down the matrix number, and my son looked it up in the Library of Congress. I swear to God, the number was right.'

* * *

Before Tiny's trip to Minneapolis, he officially filed for a divorce from Miss Jan. He did so on November 1, the day after the renewal of his wedding vows. According to Sue, when Jan realized that divorce was an imminent reality, she started to bargain. 'Jan began talking again about looking for a larger apartment in New York, but he really didn't want to live there anymore,' Sue explains. 'It was not only too expensive and too dangerous, but there were people there he really didn't want to be around. She even talked about moving to Des Moines if that was what it took to save the marriage, but he scoffed at the idea, knowing it would never last.'

When her tactics failed, Jan became furious. According to Sue, Tiny was 'obviously shaken' by Jan's 'violent objection' to the divorce. Some of that anger was directed at Sue, too. She accused Sue of not understanding her side of the story, when in fact, Sue says, she had tried to visit Jan in New York, only for Jan to cancel the appointment. When Sue indicated that she was still willing to hear what Jan had to say, Tiny forbade the conversation, explaining that he had done so at the behest of his divorce attorney.

'I already knew how she felt by then anyway,' Sue says. 'It was kind of late for her to speak up. She knew that he saw other women, just as she also dated other guys, but that had gone on so long without either of them developing any other serious relationship that she probably underestimated what was going on until things had gone too far with me and Tiny to end it easily.'

* * *

In December 1994, Tiny and Jan made an appearance as husband and wife on *The Geraldo Rivera Show*.

'So what's happening?' Rivera asked Tiny. 'I understand there's something going on with you on the marital front? How many marriages have you had?'

Tiny explained that he had had 'two legal marriages,' and one other that he 'shouldn't have done,' to Miss Dixie. When he then revealed that Miss Jan was in the audience, Rivera invited her up onstage. There, after denying Rivera's suggestion that she and Tiny had an open marriage, Jan made clear that they had 'been married for ten years, and I am his second wife, I am Miss Jan, I'm not the third wife.'

At Rivera's urging, Tiny then confirmed that he had 'fallen in love with Miss Sue Gardner in Minneapolis,' adding that he wanted to marry her 'if circumstances permit it.'

'Are you going to give him a divorce?' Rivera asked Jan.

'I have been alerted that divorce papers are on their way to me for Christmas,' she replied.

'Well, Tiny, you got married before a live studio audience. I guess it's only appropriate that you get divorced before one also!'

* * *

On December 22, CNN ran an update on Tiny's martial status in a segment entitled 'Tiny Tim To Spend Holidays, Life With Miss Sue.' The excited bride-to-be disclosed her nearly life-long adulation of Tiny as he smiled at her affectionately. 'I had fifty-five pictures of him on my wall when I was a kid,' she admitted.

Outwardly, Tiny seemed comfortable with the finalization of his divorce from Miss Jan and marriage to Miss Sue, but she could tell he was conflicted.

He told me that he felt that God 'understood' about our relationship, and the impossibility of reviving what he had years ago with Miss Jan. However ... Tiny was very, very guilt-stricken and deeply upset by the divorce. From the day it became official, he never again wrote in his prayer diary, which he had kept for decades.

I never understood this crazy relationship for the longest time. I really didn't understand how emotionally compelling it was to him and to her and how even though they gave every appearance of being a separated couple that had really gone their own separate ways they really hadn't. When they finally did officially divorce, it was extremely wrenching to them both, and I wish I hadn't been any part of that especially because he made that stupid vow that he would never divorce her for any reason. You should never encourage anybody to go back on a vow …

Tiny said they had not seen each other for two years when he and I met, and they spoke on the phone about twice a year. … As she had increasingly made a new life for herself with other boyfriends, he had come to regret that promise [to never divorce] but still felt bound by it.

Despite Tiny's scruples about his divorce and impending third marriage, the publicity from the second *Tonight Show* wedding and his continued appearances on *The Howard Stern Show* had incited more interest in Tiny than he had received in decades. As 1994 drew to a close, NPR host Dan Gaddiman closed his segment on the Tiny Heads with a rundown of everything Tiny had on the horizon, which included 'six albums, two documentary films, a proposed TV Christmas special, an interactive CD-ROM project, and lots of touring.'

Most important of all, Gaddiman continued, was *Prisoner Of Love*. 'It's the first time Tiny has ever been given complete artistic control in the studio, and the results, say veteran Tiny Heads, may be the best thing he's ever done.'

CHAPTER TWENTY-SIX

I KNOW GOD
STILL LOVES ME

You cheer me up when I am down,
You make me laugh just like a clown,
I know God still loves me,
Because he gave me you.

'I KNOW GOD STILL LOVES ME (BECAUSE HE GAVE ME YOU),'
AS PERFORMED BY TINY TIM AT HIS WEDDING TO MISS SUSAN GARDNER

As Tiny began to spend a greater amount of time in Minneapolis, the residents and local media began to take notice. Particularly titillating was the fact that he was dating the daughter of an affluent local businessman. As a result, newspapers took to reporting on Tiny and Sue as if covering a juicy Hollywood scandal, covering 'where we went, what we ordered, everything that we said, everything that was said about us.'

Sue learned the extent of the public's diligence the hard way. At a bagel shop, Tiny began to speak emphatically about 'making love' and what it was going to be like to do so after their marriage. Though Sue was perturbed that those within earshot might hear his audibly erotic proclamations, Tiny carried on. Finally, a woman sitting nearby stood up and stormed out. As she passed their table, she hissed, 'Why don't you go find a bedroom!' Undeterred, Tiny moved close to Sue and kissed her passionately. The next morning, a column appeared in the gossip section of a local paper. The author quoted a bagel shop employee who, as he watched Tiny and Sue kissing, had called his company's headquarters. 'Tiny Tim in is in here with some young girl, and they're kissing,' the employee said. 'Do I really have to look at this?'

'No,' said the voice at corporate. 'You can close your eyes.'

Johnny Pineapple, on the other hand, remembers the locals receiving Tiny with more enthusiastic decorum. 'It was like the entire of city of Minneapolis welcomed him like the newest big deal celebrity in the city,' he says. 'He and Sue were hobnobbing with all sorts of people, the movers and shakers. He was involved in the political circles and the spiritual and religious circles and the clubs and the bars. Everybody was excited that he was here and the neighborhood was just buzzing.'

When tickets went on sale for Tiny's show at the popular venue Lee's Liquor Lounge, they sold out in eight hours. 'You couldn't beg, borrow, or steal a ticket,' says Pineapple, who accompanied Tiny to the show and introduced him onstage as 'the next president of the United States.' Pineapple was thrilled by the eclectic audience, which even included members of the Minneapolis chapter of the Hell's Angels and stars of the Minnesota Vikings football team. 'At one point, everyone had their lighters up in the air, and you saw everything from outlaw bikers to grandmothers and in between in that audience,' he recalls. 'It was just amazing … you would wind him up [for] song after song after song, and the crowd basically just went crazy.'

* * *

In early 1995, Tiny insisted that Sue visit a doctor for additional testing with regard to her severe allergies that often left her feeling fatigued. She promised to undergo two weeks of testing at the Mayo clinic in Rochester, Minnesota, but only if Tiny would submit to a physical evaluation as well. He agreed.

Shortly before their respective appointments, however, they traveled down to Des Moines for a short stay in Tiny's hotel room. It was during this trip that Sue began to understand a few of the more incongruous aspects of Tiny's private personality. On the drive, they began to run dangerously low on gasoline. Sue found a gas station and pulled up to the pump. As soon as she put the car in park, she and Tiny noticed a group of skateboarding teenagers nearby; as they approached, Tiny tensed.

'Honey,' he said, struggling to maintain his composure, 'get me out of here … get me out of here NOW!'

Sue obediently pulled out onto the road, leaving the inquisitive teens behind, and found a different gas station. The same thing happened on other occasions with different groups of young guys. 'I think it had to do with times in New York,' Sue says, 'where he had been taunted and followed around and intimidated.'

A similar incident took place in a sunglasses store, when three elderly ladies caught sight of Tiny and began singing 'Tip-Toe' as they tiptoed toward him. 'He turned away from them and they were very hurt and upset, and they didn't know what to do … he kept creeping down the counter, trying to get away from them, until he literally walked into the corner and stood there with his face in the corner and his hands up around his face, like a little kid that was being bullied.'

Eventually, Tiny and Sue arrived in Des Moines, where they had arranged to meet a few guests during their stay. 'Do you want to watch me put on my makeup?' Tiny asked. No sooner had he begun then she found herself transfixed by the grandeur of the routine as he applied various cold creams and moisturizers and then removed them all, while muttering to himself, 'I cleanse, and then moisturize, and then tissue off, tissue off, tissue off …'

He would go through 'eight different kinds of moisturizers and tissue them off,' before applying foundation 'like finger-paint' and drawing circles of red on his cheeks with lipstick, rather than blush, 'because he said it would last longer.' Finally he would take out a giant powder puff and go 'Bang! Bang!' The powder went everywhere—'all over his hair and all over his clothes.'

Sue learned that while Tiny was fastidious with his makeup and lotion, he refused to groom his hair. 'Look at sheep,' he would tell her. 'They don't brush their hair, and look how much they have.'

It was also during this trip that Sue began to comprehend some of Tiny's curious tendencies regarding the way he dressed—in bright, colorful outfits that were often assembled like the layers of an onion. 'He had this thing of wanting to be more refined, and more correct, and more proper, and more virtuous than the chaotic situation he grew up in,' she explains. 'One his things was always wearing a tie, even in bed, with his pajamas. Sometimes if he was going to go out he would just put on his clothes over his pajamas so he wouldn't have to bother to change when he got home.'

Sue made several futile attempts to address Tiny's disheveled appearance during the course of their life together. 'When I met him all of his clothes were just terrible,' she says. 'I took him to a high-class men's store in Wayzata and bought him some nice suits … and when we got home he completely mixed up the outfits and always wore the wrong stuff together. … If he put on brand new, beautiful clothing, within five minutes, he looked like he had been sleeping in it for a week. I don't know why, he was just always disheveled, and there was nothing you could do about it.'

* * *

On a weekend trip to Des Moines, Tiny and Sue were besieged by a crew from the celebrity gossip program *A Current Affair.* Though Sue had felt the power of the local media in Minnesota, nothing had prepared her for this. 'They came on like gangbusters … all these people with cameras, lights, microphones … there was like a herd of them.'

Tiny kissed Sue in front of the cameras, and talked about their marriage plans, but *A Current Affair* was more interested in dredging up the twenty-five-year-old saga of Tiny Tim and Miss Vicki. Vicki had recently been uncharacteristically talkative to the press, ostensibly in an effort to generate new business for Aqua Luna, a New Age shop she had opened in Maple Hill, New Jersey. Her remarks culminated in a front-page story in *STAR*, published on February 28 1995, that took considerable liberties with many aspects of Vicki's relationship with Tiny, which she declared to be the biggest mistake of her life. She also claimed that she and Tiny had spent the first three days of their honeymoon completely separate; that Tiny had not had sex with a woman prior to their marriage but had admitted to sleeping with men; that Tiny wished he had been born a woman; that he often had male visitors late at night; that he wore women's underwear; that their marriage had been a last ditch effort to save his floundering career; and that they did not have sex for the first six months of the marriage. Some of Vicki's statements are true, others intentionally misleading, the rest entirely false.

Vicki expounded on the topic of Tiny's supposed wish to be a woman during an appearance on *The Howard Stern Show* following the release of the inflammatory article. 'Robin, you can understand, so let me address this to you,' she said. 'Do you ever look at a magazine or picture or see a woman and go, Wow, she's really attractive? That's how he looks at women, because he would like to be one.'

Vicki's mention of 'male visitors,' meanwhile, is a distortion. When interviewed for this book, she explained that the male in question was Isadore Fertel, with whom Tiny was rehearsing music. The supposition that Fertel was visiting for other reasons is very likely false. Furthermore, Tiny clarified the issue of his wearing women's underwear during his own, shockingly candid interview with Stern: 'I wanted to find out how silk felt, so I did buy these bloomers to see how it felt. It felt nice and soft and smooth, but it didn't have any openings so I quickly discarded it.'

Perhaps, the most farfetched of Vicki's declarations was that she and Tiny did not have sexual intercourse for the first six months of their marriage. Her miscarriage at six-and-a-half months pregnant, on May 15, 1970, indicates that the child would have been conceived within weeks of their wedding.

Finally, the claim that Tiny married Vicki for publicity reasons also stretches credulity. The couple's original plan was to hold a small ceremony at her parents' house in Haddonfield, New Jersey, on Christmas Day 1969; the idea of holding the wedding on live television came from a third party.

A Current Affair aired its 'Tiny vs. Vicki' segment shortly thereafter. This time, Tiny too began making dubious accusations, suggesting, as narrator George Cicerone put it, that his daughter, Miss Tulip, 'didn't spring from his flower bed.' Now, Tiny added, 'I want to have a DNA test to see if she's my daughter or not.' In a subsequent appearance on *The Howard Stern Show*, Tiny explained that it was Miss Jan who first raised his suspicions, asking him, 'How do you know this is your daughter? How do you know that Miss Vicki didn't fool around?'

For Miss Sue, of all the mudslinging between Tiny and Vicki, it was Tiny's public demand for a DNA test on his daughter that was the most disturbing. 'I just hated that,' she says. 'I *hated* that.' She had actually visited Tulip at her apartment in New Jersey in August 1994, before she and Tiny officially started dating, to try to clear up the issue, and she knew instantly that this was Tiny's daughter. 'She had his bone structure, not just in her face, but in her whole body … it *was* Tiny!' After returning to her hotel, she called Tiny to tell him. 'That girl is your child … I'm sure of it.' In the end, there was no paternity test. The dust-up amounted only to a flurry of scandal-sheet articles and a schlocky *Current Affair* segment.

After their short stay in Des Moines, Tiny and Sue traveled back to the Mayo Clinic in Rochester, Minnesota, where a phlebotomist explained that Tiny was in the beginning stages of congestive heart failure as the result of years of untreated diabetes. 'He had already lived ten years with diabetes before I met him without taking care of it,' she recalls. 'He was in the last stages of starting get the type of complications that you get from diabetes. His heart was enlarged.'

When Tiny left the room, Sue spoke candidly with the doctor.

'What can you do when a heart is enlarged?' she asked.

'Not much,' the doctor replied. 'It's like an old tire, where the tread is worn down.'

'Is there a way to retread it?'

'No. There is not.'

Since Tiny was ineligible for a heart transplant due to his extremely poor overall health, Sue began the tiresome and frustrating process of attempting to extend his life. Every step was a major battle, given Tiny's reluctance to even try to control his blood sugar, take his medicine, or adjust his diet. 'He had this annoying logic about it,' she says. 'You just wanted to clonk him over the head. I think that once he took the pill he had to acknowledge that he really couldn't drink unlimited amounts of beer and eat unlimited amounts of sugary foods … he had to acknowledge that he was diabetic and do something about it. It was something that he just did not want to address.'

Before Tiny and Sue got married, Tiny, naturally, had a few conditions: first, that Miss Jan would be 'taken care of' financially; second, that the Catholic Church approve of their marriage; third, and most important, that Sue's father had to approve of the marriage.

Tiny's first condition was met when he learned that Miss Jan was eligible to receive social-security benefits by virtue of their having been married ten years.* The second was eventually worked out following consultation with Bishop Lawrence H. Welsh of the Archdiocese of Saint Paul and Minneapolis, who determined that, since neither of Tiny's previous weddings had taken place in or been sanctioned by the Catholic Church, they were not recognized by the church. As such, he and Sue were within their rights to have a Catholic wedding—as long as they attend a yearlong premarital counseling course. They contested this point, Sue arguing that 'Tiny's very old and very ill—we don't know how much longer he's going to be alive,' and the bishop relented.†

Tiny's third condition proved the most difficult to meet. George Gardner was an affluent, upper-class businessman who saw Tiny as 'something from outer space.' On the way to their official introduction, Sue's car broke down. George came to the rescue, and when his gold Mercedes appeared in the rearview mirror, Tiny grew visibly nervous.

'Hellooo Tiiiny,' George said, in an elaborate, sing-song voice, 'Howww arrre youuu?'

'He talked to Tiny as if he were a dog trainer addressing a nervous dog,' Sue recalls. 'He didn't know how to interact with him at all.'

---

* After Tiny's passing, Miss Sue gave Jan 'financial reparations,' in part because she felt guilty for 'taking away Jan's right to be Tiny's widow,' but also because she felt Tiny would have wanted her to do so.

† 'The poor bishop,' Sue says, 'kept looking at Tiny and just didn't get it. He kept looking at me like, Why in the world would you want to marry this man?'

Once they arrived at Sue's parents' luxury home, Tiny spoke very little, until the conversation turning to a dying uncle, and Sue's stepmother said, 'Death is very scary. What could be more scary than death?'

Suddenly Tiny became animated. 'I know something that's scarier than that,' he said. 'Did you ever think about where we were before we were born? We didn't have to be born as human beings. We could've been anything … '

'Like what?' Sue's stepmother asked.

'We could've been this,' he replied, picking up a handful of nuts from a bowl next to him.*

Sue took private delight watching her parents' attempt to politely navigate Tiny's bewildering statements. 'Tiny believes that inanimate objects have feelings,' she explained.

'Tiny!' Sue's stepmother replied, cracking up. 'I think you're a Buddhist!'

Though her father had relaxed, Sue always sensed that there was something about Tiny that unnerved him. 'Even though they felt that they could laugh, my dad was never comfortable around Tiny—not ever,' she said. In any case, she accepted that her father's perpetual discomfort in Tiny's presence was better than his disapproval. As the product of a wealthy family, she had always felt pressure to marry someone as successful as her father.

> Marrying Tiny was kind of like: top this. He's the only guy that I ever dated who was more successful than my dad—even financially. … Even though he didn't have the money he had that incredible fame, and charisma, and he was good looking, and everyone liked him, and he was the center of attention and he just eclipsed my family completely. My dad and my stepmother were used to being important people when they went places, but when they went anywhere with Tiny, it was like they weren't there. But that's what it was to be with Tiny anywhere, nobody existed when he was in a place all eyes were on him, everybody else faded away.

Tiny and Sue set their wedding date for August 18 1995. As Sue and her stepmother began making preparations, Tiny headed back out on the road. Although Tiny told the *Toronto Sun* that he wanted to 'be married on a rocket

---

* Tiny had been pontificating on this subject for decades. While promoting *Beautiful Thoughts* in June 1969 he told the *Milwaukee Journal*, 'The good lord could have created me as a lamp, foot or white cloth bag … I am not an ashtray, and an ashtray is not me.'

ship at NASA,' Sue selected the Immaculate Heart of Saint Mary, the church she had attended as a child in Minnetonka, Minnesota.

When the time came to discuss the legal aspects of their union, Tiny insisted they sign a prenuptial agreement stating that, in the unlikely event that Sue passed away before him, he would not be entitled to any of her money. 'I do not want anything,' Tiny told reporters. 'Not one red cent from Miss Sue or her father's fortune. I came into this marriage with nothing. I'm coming out with nothing.'

In May 1995, Tiny made yet another appearance on *The Howard Stern Show*, where he publicly acknowledged his diabetes for the first time. He also confessed that he was now 'very impotent,' although fortunately it appeared not to be a problem with his new 'attendant,' Miss Sue: 'She doesn't need much she says she loves me immensely, she doesn't care.' Later, when asked about Vicki's claim that he wore women's underwear, he denied the accusation, explaining instead that he wore Depends adult diapers 'instead of underwear … I throw it away every day; it's nice and sanitary.'

'Are you embarrassed in front of your fiancé, that she would see you in your Depends?'

'Absolutely not,' Tiny replied. 'Oh, she hasn't seen me yet in my Depends.'

While Tiny was spewing intimate details to Howard Stern, Sue was sitting on her hands in Minneapolis, where her stepmother had taken over all the wedding preparations. 'My stepmother is a very strong-willed person who is used to getting her way,' Sue says. 'I had never been through a formal wedding like that. I did get to choose my dress, but everything else was kind of chosen for me; the flowers, the bridesmaid's dresses, and everything.'

* * *

On August 18 1995, about 800 people (not including press) crowded into the Immaculate Heart of Saint Mary Church for the wedding of Tiny Tim and Susan Gardner. 'I would have been happy with a backyard barbeque,' Sue recalled. 'I never wanted [a big wedding], but I knew that Tiny would like it, and I knew that the family would like it.' The church swelled with people, including hundreds of Sue's stepmother's friends and all of her father's employees. Guests filled every row in the center and spilled into one wing of the sanctuary, with the other wing designated for press and television crews. A tent was set up in the parking lot so that everyone could be seated for the meal, and a congratulatory telegram arrived from Johnny Carson.

Several Tiny Heads convened in the parking lot outside, waiting for the service to begin. *Tiny Tim Times* editor Gregor Brune had returned from a mysterious hiatus and carried with him the fourteenth and final issue of his fanzine, which he distributed among the Tiny Tim Fan Club. He had abruptly quit writing his newsletter after a tumultuous experience at Tiny-Palooza in Dallas the previous summer, and now warned Jim Foley, 'Beware of Tiny Tim. He surrounds himself in a vortex of madness.'

As the vortex spiraled upstairs, Tiny was hidden in the basement with Johnny Pineapple and a reporter from the *National Enquirer*, not realizing the service had already begun. 'All of the sudden I'm backstage and the entire bridal party is lined up and the organ is blasting [the wedding march],' Pineapple recalls. 'Everyone is going, Johnny, where's Tiny? The wedding's starting! The wedding was half an hour earlier than Tiny thought. He just about didn't make his own wedding!'

Pineapple made a mad dash for the basement, pulled Tiny to his feet, and ushered him upstairs. The ceremony included a full Catholic mass, complete with choir. Sue and Gil Morse, who served as best man, cracked smiles when Tiny, asked by the priest if he will 'accept children lovingly from God and bring them up according to the law of Christ,' replied, 'If we can have them, yes.'*

'That's the right answer, Tiny,' said the priest with a grin.

Before the exchanging of rings, Sue and Tiny both recited the vows they had written for one another.

'Oh, great Yahweh god of Israel, through Jesus Christ, your son, and his blessed Jewish mother Mary, most holy, give me the strength to give my dear wife, Miss Sue,' Tiny said. 'The greatest gift one can give his wife, next to obeying you, and that gift is faithfulness. For if I praise her with poems, give her diamonds and pearls, silver and gold, fame and notoriety, take her all over the world, have her adored by kings and queens, and give her all that money can buy, and am not faithful to her, this marriage is a failure. I must have only one woman, Miss Sue. See only one woman, Miss Sue. Give all I have to one woman, Miss Sue. And to all others, say adieu. Being faithful to my wife, sweet Sue, is being faithful, oh, God, and pleasing to you.'

---

* According to Pineapple, Morse had designated himself as the best man: 'We were all sitting around Tiny's house one day when … Gil Morse kind of shouted out, I got dibs on best man! There was never an invitation formally from Tiny or so or a request formally made. Tiny looks at Sue, and Sue looks at Tiny, and they just kind of shrugged their shoulders and said, Yeah, OK, that's fine.'

'Dear Lord, please give me the grace to be a loving wife to my husband, even when I don't feel like it,' Sue said, in her statement. 'Please help us to grow spiritually together. Please help us to find new ways to serve you. Let our love each other strengthen us to love and serve others. Please show us your will for our lives and help us to fulfill it. Please give us many long, happy, and healthy years together. Please bless everyone who has come here to celebrate this day with us. In Jesus's name, amen.'

After the blessing, lighting of the unity candle, prayer of the faithful, sign of peace, Lord's Prayer, and a final blessing, the priest announced, 'I'd like to present to you, Mr. And Mrs. Khaury.' The congregation applauded as the newly married couple turned and started down the aisle. When asked how they were feeling, they remarked that they were surprised that the ceremony had not included a kiss and obliged, several times over, when asked to kiss for the cameras. Sue had not been crazy about allowing the press at their wedding, but she acknowledged Tiny's desire to cooperate with them.

'Do you have plans for a honeymoon?' a reporter asked.

'Well, right now the honeymoon is right here, in Minnesota,' Tiny replied. 'Right now there isn't anything planned at this point.'

'He has to be out of town in three days for more jobs,' Sue interjected, 'and we just got the furniture back in our new home, so I'm going to unpack boxes, and he's going to go one the road.'

The wedding reception took place in a gymnasium attached to the church. It was an impressive event: several hundred people were present, as well as a full band, hundreds of gifts, and seven wedding cakes. It was, however, a 'dry' reception, a policy put in place by Miss Sue to curb Tiny's tendency to overdrink.

For Tiny and Sue, the whole reception was a whirlwind of pictures and handshakes. They barely had a chance to eat before Tiny's performance with the band. His set consisted of songs from the *Sweet Sue: Album Sampler*, an abridged version of a forthcoming full-length album, *Sweet Sue*, that was given to guests at the wedding: 'Sweet Sue, Just You,' 'I Know God Till Loves Me (Because He Gave Me You),' and 'Only Forever.' Pausing between each song to kiss Sue, Tiny seemed a bit shaky, but gave a well-received performance. He closed with 'Roll Out The Barrell' and, another selection from the wedding album, 'The Minnesota Polka.'*

---

* The full-length album, never released in it's entirety, was to feature nine additional tracks: 'My Melody Of Love,' 'Always,' 'Just A Little Bit More,' 'The Minnesota Polka,' 'Near You,' 'I Do,' 'It's Only A Paper Moon,' 'Onesy, Twosy, I Love Yousy,' and 'The Laughing Policeman.'

That night, Sue and Tiny retired to separate rooms at the Marriott in Eden Prairie, Minnesota. Sue's shared faith with Tiny meant that she was open to a religious meditation period following the wedding: twenty-four hours dedicated, as Tiny told the press, 'to the God of Israel.' He also vowed to fast and drink nothing but 'spring water' to 'atone for his sins.' When the meditation period was complete, Sue and Tiny returned to Sue's house, where, after some time, Sue undressed and entered Tiny's room. 'It was the first time he'd seen me naked,' she said. 'He just looked at me up and down disdainfully, like, I've seen better. I was kind of shocked ... he was a connoisseur of women the way people are a connoisseur of wine or cars.'

Within three days, Tiny was back on the road. The marriage publicity had boosted his visibility, and Tiny began fielding calls for radio interviews, gigs, sitcom walk-ons, and recording offers. Several record labels with Tiny Tim projects in the can released them.

Tiny continued to keep his hotel room in Des Moines, 'just in case,' at a cost of $750 a month. Meanwhile, Miss Sue worked on getting used to being Mrs. Tiny Tim. 'Even when after we were married,' she later wrote, 'sometimes I'd be driving along and I'd look over and he'd be sitting there in the car and I'd be shocked all over again,' she said. 'I'd think, Tiny Tim is in my car and I'm married to him. You'd think I'd get used to it, but I don't think I ever did.'

Tiny gave a command performance—via telephone—on *The Howard Stern Show* the month after the wedding. Robin Quivers addressed Tiny's 'impotence problem,' which Tiny revealed had abated briefly, during which time 'Miss Sue [gave] me more love in a week and a half than two wives in thirteen years,' but had since returned, and was now 'worse than ever.' Sue, he added, didn't mind. 'She's happy with me the way I am.'

'I've never heard him this happy,' Stern interjected.

In October of 1995, Tiny traveled to Laughlin, Nevada, for a series of shows. While he was there, Sue got a call she had been dreading: 'Tiny was in congestive heart failure. He refused to be admitted to the hospital, and the hospital refused to treat him as an outpatient. He couldn't walk thirty feet without stopping to catch his breath, and coughed constantly. He could not lie down flat because his lungs filled up with fluid, and he hadn't slept in three or four days.'

Ironically, Tiny had just been discussing his own mortality with *CUPS Magazine* reporter Alexander Laurence, who asked, 'Will you get to heaven?'

'It's up to Him to judge,' Tiny replied. 'I can never make that judgment. I have to work harder all the time.'*

Sue hopped on a plane for Las Vegas. Throughout the flight she stayed glued to the phone, demanding that Tiny's hotel do not to let him onstage. Upon her arrival in Laughlin, she located a doctor who would treat Tiny as an outpatient, and who was able to quickly stabilize Tiny with medication. Upon their return to Minnesota, Tiny endured another series of tests on his heart and overall condition. The prognosis was not positive: he had three-to-five years to life at most.

While many people, faced with a prognosis that dire, might consider retirement, Tiny would not cancel a single engagement. In December, he was back in the studio with Howard Stern for an interview that began, unusually, with a discussion of Tiny's new Christmas song, 'Susie Snowflake.'† It was to be released on a cassette EP entitled *Tiny Tim Christmas Magic*, which would offer two versions of 'Susie Snowflake' (one delivered in Tiny's bombastic baritone, the other with a relaxed narration style) and two versions of Tiny reciting 'Twas The Night Before Christmas' over an R&B backing track.

Elsewhere in the interview, Tiny explained that he was 'fuming mad' at Del Monte for falsely labeling their product 'Golden Raisins,' when in fact the box contained black raisins. He also detailed his current diet (water, bananas, apples, and 'sometimes Domino's pizza'); his lack of sex life ('I still haven't consummated the marriage'); and Sue's 'environmental disease': 'She can't stand the smell of Sharpie pens, she can't stand the shampoos I use, I have to clear out all my cosmetics, and now … she's afraid I have bad teeth in the back, and she'll get infected.'‡

On December 16 1995, Tiny made his last appearance in England when he played a concert in London, at the Union Chapel. The event was organized and produced by British fan and Current 93 founder David Tibet. But though Tiny delivered a solid performance, Tibet took note of his health problems, which he detailed in his liner notes to *Tiny Tim Live In London*.

---

* He also explained that one perk of dying was that 'I think there will be s-e-x in heaven.'
† He also recorded a duet with Elissa Montanti, 'Don't Walk Away.' It remains unreleased.
‡ Sue's environmental illness also made it impossible for Tiny to watch television in her home. According to Johnny Pineapple, 'The entire house was insulated and wrapped in tin foil, because, according to Miss Sue, this would keep out of all the formaldehyde and [other chemicals] that Sue believed she was allergic to. [It] formed a perfect dead zone for any kind of TV [signal]. Tiny was absolutely livid. He threw down the remote control in utter disgust. He was sitting there just fuming. It was great irony.'

'He seemed tired. He had problems walking but showed enthusiasm for everything, endlessly accommodating to interviews, requests for autographs, singing songs from his infinite repertory. His Heart was Vast. He rushed headlong through what he termed "A Century Of Song," leaving us all stunned with his energy and conviction.'

Tiny returned to Minneapolis to spend Christmas with Sue and her family and friends. He received an alarm clock from Sue's brother: a wolf playing a saxophone that said, 'Hey, hey, it's time to get up, so you can get down. whooooooooo!' Sue smiled as she watched Tiny push the button over and over like a child. From Sue, he received a nickel-plated brass Dobro ukulele with an electric pick up—his 'dream instrument.'

Around this time, the Gardeners had a dinner party, and at one point, everyone gathered around to listen to an audio recording of Tiny's appearance on *The Hollywood Palace* with Bing Crosby. Afterward, Sue's friends and parents—who, being Tiny's age, were also fans of Crosby—listened intently as he regaled them with stories from the taping.

Aside from the strain of Tiny's constant touring schedule, everything seemed stable between Tiny and Sue. However, the impending high-profile release of his new album, *Girl*, was about to bring to the surface an issue that would disrupt the foundation of their new marriage.

CHAPTER TWENTY-SEVEN
THIS IS NOT MADNESS OR ACTING

> *[Tiny Tim] is truly one of God's greatest hits. If they put out a cassette or*
> *a movie called* God's Greatest Hits, *with only ten people out of all the*
> *humans that have ever lived on this earth, Tiny Tim, I guarantee it, would*
> *be in the top five, and the other four would all be beautiful women, and Miss*
> *Stephanie Bohn would probably be one of them.*
>
> **JAMES 'BIG BUCKS' BURNETT**

During the first year of Tiny Tim and Miss Sue's marriage, Tiny was on
the road for 300 days. The media buzz generated by the wedding motivated
producers to bring Tiny into the studio to record new material and inspired
the release of four albums he had recorded previously: *I Love Me, Tiny Tim:
Live In Chicago, Tiny Tim's Christmas Album,* and *Songs Of An Impotent Troubadour.*[*]

   I Love Me was released by Ponk/Seeland Records. Produced by Pink
Bob and Steve Rubin, the album consisted of a handful of new Tiny Tim
recordings and several of the old regulars.[†] After the album's release, Tiny
told Pink Bob that he felt *I Love Me* represented 'the breadth of his musical

---

[*] In addition to these albums, snippets of interviews with Tiny Tim were included on three
Beatles-related releases: *Things We Said Today: Talking With the Beatles, John Lennon Forever,*
and *Dark Horse—The Secret Life Of George Harrison.* Meanwhile, David Tibet, with the help
of Martin Sharp, released a single containing, on one side, Tiny's rendition of 'Tip-Toe
Thru' The Tulips' from his 1968 concert at the Royal Albert Hall, and on the other side,
a Martin Sharp–produced track entitled 'Devil May Care.' The single was included as a
flex-disc with issue #18 of *Ptolemaic Terrascope,* which also featured one of Tibet's interviews
with Tiny.
[†] 'I Love Me,' 'If I Had You,' 'Take Me Out To The Ball Game,' 'Another Brick In The
Wall Pt. 2,' 'She Left Me With The Herpes,' 'I Woke Up With A Cold,' 'The Star Spangled
Banner,' 'Depression Medley,' 'Religious Medley', 'I Saw Mr. Presley Tip-Toeing Thru The
Tulips,' 'Comic Strip Man,' 'Tell Me That You Love Me (My Sweetheart)'),' 'The Laughing
Policeman,' 'True Love,' 'Sweet Sue, Just You, and 'What A Friend We Have In Jesus.'

interests.' When asked about the unique 'Depression Medley,' on the album, Pink Bob called it Tiny's 'personal avant-garde "Revolution #9" statement.' ('Mr. Pink Bob,' Tiny added, 'you've thought of everything for this one!')

Bughouse/Pravda Records released *Tiny Tim: Live In Chicago.* Consisting entirely of live recording made in the city on December 9 1993, the album captures Tiny's final performance with Illinois-based group The New Duncan Imperials. *Tiny Tim's Christmas Album*, produced by Martin Sharp and recorded during Tiny's final visit to Australia, in November 1993, was released on David Tibet's label, Durtro Records, and features Tiny's treatment of nine Christmas classics.* Five months prior to Tiny Tim and Miss Sue's wedding, Tibet had also released *Songs Of An Impotent Troubadour*, a freeform album comprised entirely of Tiny's original compositions.

The album's producer—James 'Big Bucks' Burnett, then president of the Tiny Tim Fan Club—got in ahead of the curve in anticipating the impending publicity for Tiny and Sue's wedding. Burnett and Tiny had known one another, and worked together intermittently, since 1982. Their collaboration would, however, introduce one of the most profound threats to Tiny and Sue's marital bliss.

Burnett's introduction to Tiny Tim followed the pattern of many others. 'My dad was kind of a Tiny Tim fan, and we always watched *Laugh-In*,' he says. With the passage of years, Burnett all but forgot about Tiny Tim, but was reminded of him when he heard a radio advertisement for Tiny's upcoming concert at Confetti, a small nightclub in Dallas, Texas. 'I thought it might be kind of strange to go see what Tiny Tim might be like in the 80s,' he recalls. 'So I went, and we did an interview at his hotel room that evening at about 3am … he was absolutely one of the most interesting and fascinating people I've ever met … I was always curious as to what he would say or do next.'

Two years later, in 1984, a fan club Burnett created for the TV show *Mr.*

---

* 'White Christmas,' 'The Christmas Song,' 'Silent Night,' 'Rudolph The Red Nosed Reindeer,' 'I Saw Mommy Kissing Santa Claus,' 'That's What I Want For Christmas,' 'All I Want For Christmas Is My Two Front Teeth,' 'O Holy Night,' 'Rainbow On The River,' and Donnie Brooks' 'Mission Bell.' The latter two songs were recorded for *Tiny Tim's Pop Album*, which has never been released in its entirety. It too was recorded during Tiny's final Australian sessions in 1993, and was to feature a curious selection of mostly 60s covers: 'Satisfaction/Yellow Submarine Medley,' 'St. Louis Blues,' 'Caravan,' 'My Girl,' 'House Of The Rising Sun,' 'People Are Strange,' 'Those Were The Days,' 'I Am I Said,' 'Without You,' and 'Ego Testicle.' A few of these tracks are on the 2007 Japanese compilation of Martin Sharp–produced Tiny Tim material, *Stardust: I'll Never Get Married Again.*

Ed received some national press. In an effort to capitalize on the club's new notoriety, and with the fifteenth anniversary of the Woodstock Music Festival looming, he decided to create the Edstock Music Festival. He booked Tiny as a headliner, along with T Bone Burnett and Joe Ely.

In June, Burnett flew Tiny to Texas to record a version of 'The Mr. Ed Theme Song.' Three thousand copies of the single were pressed on pink vinyl, backed with 'Memory' from the Broadway musical *Cats*, as Edstock souvenirs. The following month, Tiny returned to Texas for the festival itself, which was held at the Bronco Bowl in Dallas. Despite receiving a fair amount of local and national coverage, only 200 tickets had been sold prior to the event. The festival began as planned on July 7, but with only 300 people in attendance. When news of the dismal ticket sales reached Burnett's crew, they demanded immediate payment. In order to keep the show running, he got on the phone and borrowed money from anyone he knew who could spare it.

The Edstock Music Festival left Big Bucks $25,000 in debt, and for a few years he decided to forgo any creative financial endeavors. He surfaced again in 1988, with the idea of recording Tiny Tim singing 'Stairway To Heaven.' He first called Jimmy Page, with whom he was friendly, and asked if he would object; Page loved the idea. Burnett then called Tiny and played him a jazz arrangement of the song. 'Right on the spot he sang for me an a cappella version of a passage from the song and said he would do it,' he recalls.

Burnett wanted to bring in a group capable of contributing real originality to the cover, and his first choice was the Denton-based rock/polka group Brave Combo. To his delight, they said yes. Formed in 1979, Brave Combo had garnered a following for going against the grain by playing rock renditions of polkas and polka renditions of rock songs. The idea of working with Tiny Tim intrigued them. 'We were open to challenges, hence the name Brave Combo,' bandleader Carl Finch explains.

On May 18 1988, Tiny Tim and Brave Combo rehearsed at Fourteen Records, Big Bucks Burnett's record shop. The next day they went into the studio to record 'Stairway To Heaven,' along with the Hoagy Carmichael standard 'Stardust.' Brave Combo transformed the classic rock arrangement into a jazz epic evocative of The Lounge Lizards. That night, Tiny performed at Club Dada in Dallas as part of an event organized by Burnett called Ed-a-Go-Go. With Tiny acting as master of ceremonies for the Miss World Peace Beauty Pageant and performing with a pick-up band call The Potatoes, the gig sat well within his bizarre repertoire. However, the evening took a turn for the dramatic when Burnett introduced Tiny to a twenty-year-old, blonde-haired, blue-eyed Miss Stephanie Bohn.

Bohn, who played guitar in her own band, Wayward Girl, asked Tiny to sign an ancient Kent ukulele of her grandfather's that she had brought for the purpose. Tiny was very interested in the instrument, and went on to describe its history to Stephanie. 'It was strange,' Stephanie later told Burnett, 'because I instantly felt, I guess, a kinship with him.'

For Stephanie, that 'kinship' was platonic. Tiny, on the other hand, was completely staggered by the young girl, declaring her to be the 'Eternal Princess' for whom he had searched the New Jersey woods as a young boy. 'He basically flipped his lid,' Burnett recalled. 'That was the girl he had been looking for his entire life, he said. So it kind of freaked him out.'

'That was an unbelievable day!' Tiny later told Burnett. 'Wow, I tell you, what … a … dream!'

As Burnett later put it, during what he called *The Endless Discussion*, 'Meeting Stephanie Bonn was perhaps the most significant thing to occur in the life of Tiny Tim … [but] had I know at the time what I was doing, I might not have done it … it unleashed an entire chain of unpredictable events.'

Tiny and Stephanie began a regular correspondence. Initially, Tiny's letters were friendly, and he encouraged Stephanie in her various endeavors. As their correspondence continued, however, Tiny suddenly became concerned that Bohn and Burnett might have feelings for one another. They both reassured him that they were only friends, and Tiny dropped the issue—for a while.

* * *

After Tiny's first recording session with Brave Combo in 1988, it was suggested that the group record a full-length album. Tiny proposed a tribute to either Michael Jackson for The Beatles. 'I didn't really like the idea at all because Brave Combo was already walking a pretty fine line between serious and novelty, and we never wanted to be viewed as a novelty band,' Carl Finch recalls. 'We wanted to push things away from novelty … we did record a bunch of The Beatles stuff, but we totally blew off the Michael Jackson thing pretty quick.'

Tiny duly returned to Denton in 1990 to record several Beatles covers, including a cha-cha rendition of 'Hey Jude' and perhaps the most sinister version of 'Girl' ever committed to tape.* After recording 'Girl,' which became

---

* Also recorded but not included on the album are a polka rendition of 'Ob-La-Di Ob-La-Da' and an acoustic version of 'Across The Universe.'

the album's title track, Big Bucks Burnett and Brave Combo decided that the overall theme of the album was bigger than just a tribute album. '[Tiny] was such a fucking romantic, he really was,' Finch says. 'So, the whole idea of this being based on love was the obvious thing after a while. The recording of "Girl" just blew our minds—we just couldn't believe how wonderfully it turned out.'

Finch asked Tiny to allow them to pick a few songs from the Tin Pan Alley songbook he carried with him. 'That was a real turning point,' he says. 'It went from an interesting, borderline novelty project to something that I felt had some artistic weight.' Finch and Burnett soon learned that no Tiny Tim recording session could be completed quickly, however, as each song would require numerous takes. 'The first vocals tracks of ["Bye Bye Blackbird"] are really shy, unimpressive, no power, no commitment, not even as good as calling it in—just kind of there,' Finch says. 'By the twentieth or twenty-fifth time it was full-on Tiny, and he was doing what you hear on the record.'

Tiny had grown accustomed to the freeform nature of his shows, and since Martin Sharp had often allowed him to record in the same manner in Australia, he proposed the same ad hoc method to Finch. 'Tiny wanted this to be Brave Combo and Tiny Tim playing live and to not do the music first and let him sing, but he wasn't really prepared ... he wanted us all playing at once, and we were doing fine, and he would ... would screw something up, and he'd go, Oh, no, no. We gotta start over.'

Tiny's recording methods were not the only thing halting production. He also delivered a religious sermon, which included the observation, 'I believe the Lord is a moody guy.' According to Finch, the sessions would be repeatedly held up by either 'story time' or 'sleepy time.' In between takes, Tiny would 'prop himself up in a chair and snooze.'*

While Tiny was working on the album in Texas, a full-page ad for Kenwood Stereo Systems appeared in a number of magazines. It featured a large photograph of Tiny with the caption, 'True Kenwood can make anything sound good.' When Finch asked if he was bothered by the ad, Tiny seemed unfazed. 'My job is to entertain,' he explained, 'and if they want to put my head on cockroaches and shoot me with Raid, so be it!' Unbeknown to those

---

* Tiny's religious routines would often keep him awake for hours at night, and sometimes all night long. Among his many self-imposed and self-conceived rituals was that he offer God the 'first fruits' of his voice every morning, which generally meant praying between 2am and 4am. According to Miss Sue, he would insist that his success was a miracle from God.

working on the album, Tiny had been paid $5,000 for the use of his image.

Before returning to New York, Tiny performed at Club Dada again, and went to see Stephanie Bohn. He taught her a few songs on the ukulele, and they sang together. Afterward, he pulled Burnett aside and asked him to discourage Stephanie from contacting him. 'He was having trouble believing that she was acting of her own free will,' Burnett later explained. 'I kind of found it surprising that he was he was still holding on to these types of ideas after two and half years but nevertheless agreed.'

Shortly after Tiny left Denton, he began to send Stephanie letters again. At first, the letters were not overtly romantic, but when Tiny mailed her a stuffed kitten and high-quality ukulele, his inclinations became clear. When she did not reciprocate his advances, Tiny grew frustrated. He repeated the charge that Bohn and Burnett were romantically involved. His suspicions grew into a paranoid belief that Burnett was using Bohn to manipulate him into continuing their business relationship—something they came to call 'The Great Conspiracy Theory.'

Tiny stopped answering their letters, changed his telephone number, and forbade his managers in New York to relay his contact information to Burnett. 'I was just really surprised that he had these types of ideas,' Burnett later said. 'But … trying to change Tiny Tim's mind can be more difficult than trying to change all eighteen wheels on a big semi-trailer … so I finally just sort of accepted everything as it was and decided that if I would ever be friends with Tiny Tim again it would be because he had a change of heart, or there was an act of God or something.'

Two years later, in December 1992, the *National Enquirer* ran an article portraying Tiny Tim's infatuation with Stephanie Bohn as the obsession of a lecherous old man. 'The article basically made him seem like a creepy old man,' Jim Foley recalls. 'Tiny didn't care, though. When I mentioned that the article did not make him look good he just said, Yes, but did you see the picture they printed of Miss Stephanie? He sat there kissing the page the photo was printed on.'

In the meantime, Burnett, like a government in exile, remained president of the Tiny Tim Fan Club. The club had grown exponentially and gone international. It even included a few famous names like the Sex Pistols' Johnny Rotten and Partridge Family star David Cassidy. The fan club's newsletter, *The Tiny Tim Times*, written by fan Gregor Brune, offered updates on all the latest Tiny Tim records, concerts, and appearances. Through the fan club, Burnett corresponded and traded 'Timorabilia' and recordings with other Tiny Tim fans all over the world. He also began speaking with Martin Sharp.

Many of the club's members were puzzled by Tiny's refusal to speak with the group's president and inquired as to why that was. In 1993, Burnett answered their questions on a cassette tape he called *This Is Not Madness Or Acting*. The tape consisted of three parts. The first is a recording made by fan-club member Jerry Wilke on April 10 1993, in which Tiny addresses Burnett directly:

> Dear Mr. Big Bucks Burnett, this is Tiny Tim … speaking via the Alexander Graham Bell telephone … I know you're not to blame. You've done wonderful things … and through you … I met the most beautiful woman in eternity, Miss Stephanie Bohn … I can't help it that fate has made me oblivious to your callings and writings and I can't help it if Miss Stephanie … will always be in between us. I'm sorry that you have to be, by fate, the sacrificial lamb. … Now, this is not madness or acting, heaven knows the way I feel … no ticky, no shirty. No Miss Bohn, no Mr. Burnett.

Tiny also revealed his plans to have his gravestone inscribed with the words, 'Oh, God, my I have, in death, the love I lost in life: Miss Stephanie Bohn.' Relieved that Tiny had seemingly dropped the 'Great Conspiracy Theory,' Burnett played the tape to Bohn. Their subsequent conversation, from May 20 1993, formed the second segment of *This Is Not Madness Or Acting*. After Bohn explains that a romantic relationship with Tiny 'could never happen'—'I'm twenty-five, I'm still in college, I have so much ahead of me in life'—Burnett makes an appeal directly to Tiny, asking to be let back into the fold.

> Tiny, if you're listening, I say this in front of anybody else who's listening, you'll always be my friend, I'll always like you, love you, I'll always wish that we could be friends again—active friends—not communicating through third parties. Get over it, big guy! Give me a call!

The third segment in the series is a recorded phone conversation between Tiny Tim and Martin Sharp, which Sharp forwarded to Burnett. After unveiling a new song, 'I Used To Love Jessica Hahn (But Now I Love Stephanie Bohn),'

Tiny delivers a lengthy, meandering dissertation on the pain of rejection by Miss Stephanie, eventually concluding, 'I have this woman so much in my soul that it sticks to me like … crazy glue.'

* * *

A few months after issuing *This Is Not Madness Or Acting*, Burnett's phone rang. It was eight in the morning. He rolled over with a groan, put the receiver up to his ear, and heard Tiny's voice at the other end. Tiny proceeded to propose something that, if Burnett and Bohn agreed to take part in it, would allow him and Burnett to resume contact. The details, however, were to remain secret, and those involved could never speak of it—and still will not comment on it today. Miss Sue, on the other hand, is more than willing to discuss the covert event, as it had a deeply negative impact on her marriage to Tiny.

In August 1993, Tiny traveled to Dallas for his 'spiritual marriage' to Stephanie Bohn. The event was staged like an actual marriage, and included bridesmaids, candelabra, cake, and tuxedos. Burnett even secured a minister's license in order to preside over the ceremony. Upon completion of the ceremony, Tiny's suspicions about Burnett were mollified, and work resumed on Tiny's album with Brave Combo. Plans were even made for Tiny and Stephanie to duet on a version of the Steve & Eydie hit 'I Want To Stay Here.' Burnett began to explore other creative ideas he had for Tiny, and in July 1994 flew him to Texas to record a video he called *Tiny Tim July 4, 1994*. He had Tiny sit in front of an American flag and sing dozens of patriotic songs.

Two days later, Tiny attended the official dedication of the Tiny Tim Museum, which took up a large section of Burnett's record store. 'He was sort of unimpressed with the idea,' Burnett later recalled. 'I think he was a little offended that it was not an actual museum, [but when] he saw the actual display with photos, records, posters, he was really impressed. It made me feel really good.' The next night, in honor of the tenth anniversary of EdStock, Tiny, backed by The Hasbeens, performed a 'Tiny-Palooza' concert at Club Dada. The *Tiny Tim Times* advertised the show as the 'Tiny Tim gig of the decade (perhaps century).'

Burnett also instigated a three-hour solo recording session with Tiny. Despite a clash over his fee, during which Tiny threatened to place a 'hex' on Burnett and his family, he managed to record Tiny giving a lengthy monologue about his love life and singing every song—all thirty-four—he had ever written for or associated with a girl/woman. The resulting recording became *Songs Of An Impotent Troubadour.**

'*Troubadour* was actually done live, all in one take,' Burnett says. Tiny played 'every song he had ever associated with a girl' in chronological order, 'and he would tell the story of when and how he met the girl and why he associates that song with her, and probably about half of the songs were songs he had written. So we just extracted the dialogue and songs pertaining to the original numbers, because the concept for that album was to record an album of just Tiny Tim originals. No one really knew he was a songwriter, and no one would ever give him a chance to make an album of his own songs. I just thought it would be tragic if that never happened, so I'm really glad I got to do that.'

'I don't know if I am a songwriter,' Tiny later told Burnett while discussing the album. 'These were songs that I dabbled in … Irving Berlin won't roll around in his grave, but, the thing is, these are songs that I try to write in my heart and soul to these woman that I loved and to these, you know, who played a great part in a … pure way.'

By now, Burnett had grown friendly with David Tibet and proposed that he release the album on his label Dutro. In order to make the release more marketable to his fans, Tibet isolated a segment from a telephone conversation he had had with Tiny and overdubbed music by his band, Current 93. This, says Burnett, made it 'ten times less risky' for Tibet. The resulting track was called 'Just What Do You Mean By Antichrist?' and features Tiny pontificating that the Antichrist would be an extraterrestrial, and that his emergence would come in the form of an alien invasion of Earth by his forces.

It will come as no surprise to learn that Tiny believed that contact with another world was imminent. 'The Columbuses of the space years, to the moon, Saturn, Venus, are coming nearer and nearer,' he told Jeff Wilkins of the Schenectady *Daily Gazette* in November 1994. 'I believe … contact will be made. All these sightings of flying saucers can't all be wrong.'

As for the album's title, Tiny had recently announced his impotency

* As for the hex, Burnett says that Tiny 'issued it as an eternal, binding curse, on me and my family. I forget what brought it on, but it was recorded. After the session I confronted him about it. I told him I didn't mind being cursed, but that he had no right to involve my family. He then told me that that part was a test—to see if I would defend my family—and that I had passed the test. I told him that that was bullshit, that he was back peddling. Tiny took back the curse on my family. as I understand it, I remain eternally cursed by the great Yahweh God of Israel.'

on *The Howard Stern Show*, and suggested it as a fitting name for the record. Burnett later told Tiny he was 'quite fascinated' by the title. 'At first I was sort of shocked and repelled, but the more I thought about it, it had a kind of a appealing, profane quality—almost poetic.' He summed it up as 'a shocking name for a Tiny Tim album' but also one that 'implies a triumph of spirituality over any physical limitations.'

'This is really an encouraging slogan for those who are impotent,' Tiny confirmed. 'I use the *Impotent Troubadour* as an encouragement to those who still have love in their hearts but [are] not to complete it, down there, for children.'

Songs Of An Impotent Troubadour sold 1,500 copies upon its release—an impressive number considering its niche status even by Tiny Tim standards. Meanwhile, Tiny's album with Brave Combo had been pre-sold to Rounder Records, which already had several Brave Combo albums in its catalogue and gave the band complete creative control. The final product contained a blend of Tiny's signature material ('Sly Cigarette,' 'That Old Feeling,' 'Springtime In The Rockies,' 'Stardust,' 'Bye Bye Blackbird,' 'All That I Want Is You'), a few classic pop cuts ('New York, New York,' 'Stairway To Heaven,' 'Hey Jude,' 'Over The Rainbow,' 'Girl,' 'I Just Want To Stay Here'), and some new material penned by Tiny's friends (Burnett's 'Fourteen,' and 'I Believe In Tomorrow' by Lou Robino and Bob Pontes). The result blends quirkiness and sincerity and rivals *God Bless Tiny Tim* in its modernization of Tiny as a performer rather than reliance on gimmick and nostalgia, like so many other releases. The extra push from Rounder's publicity machine helped as well.

'We were all very happy with the way it,' Burnett concluded. '[We] wanted to help him make something that would stand as a real album.' At first, the album was to be called *Back To Normality* after a line taken from Tiny's ad-libbed monologue during 'Sly Cigarette.' This was scrapped, however, after a debate over whether or not 'normality' was a word. Finally, reflecting on the pervasive essence of Tiny's infatuation with Stephanie Bohn and its impact on the album's completion, they decided to name the record after its title track, *Girl*.

Girl was released in early 1996 and received unusually positive reviews. ('The law of averages will sometimes catch up,' Tiny told Jeff Wilkins of the *Daily Gazette*.) *Musical* magazine called the album 'a bravura performance' and one that 'revives Tiny … as a serious, quirky, and seriously quirky artist.' For

Buzz, Tiny's 'brilliant' renditions of songs like 'Stairway To Heaven' 'prove he is not lame after all.'* *Entertainment Weekly* called the album 'silly and seriously moving,' the *Denver Post* described it as 'downright touching,' and the *New York Press* hailed it as 'one of the best pop albums of the past year.' Finally, in an article for *Detour* magazine, Burnett wondered aloud whether Tiny's finding his 'eternal princess' and the album's successful release might be proof that 'this is an age of strange, pleasant miracles.'

Despite the good press, Rounder Records soon tired of Tiny, who preferred to promote *Prisoner Of Love,* his tribute to Russ Columbo, which Ponk Media released around the same time. In July 1996, he appeared on *Howard Stern* and called *Prisoner* 'my greatest album ever … but [Ponk owner] Mr. Robinson hasn't got the money Rounder has.'†

Prisoner Of Love vs. *Girl* was not the only controversy. In interviews around this time, Tiny began elaborating about his love for Miss Stephanie, and Miss Sue was furious. Though the issue had been out of sight and mind for some time, the release of *Girl* brought Tiny's obsession with Miss Stephanie back to the forefront of his consciousness. 'I can't love you the same way that you love me,' he had told her cruelly. 'I can't offer you the total love. I have to be honest with you about that. I wouldn't marry someone I didn't love, but Stephanie Bohn will always be the ultimate woman to me. She is the Eternal Princess.'

In retrospect, Sue says, 'I should've said, It's been nice. Goodbye. At the time it was like… he'll get over it. Our love will grow, and he'll forget his infatuation with Stephanie.' Instead, Tiny continued to 'nurse this fantasy about Stephanie Bohn, which ultimately became rather disenchanting for me.' For Sue, the worst part was when he continued to talk about Bohn in interviews. 'It was really just very inappropriate, and hurtful, and dumb, and rude, and mean. It just kind of ruined things for me.'

---

* Pat Boone released a cover of 'Stairway To Heaven' around the same time. When asked about Tiny's version, he dismissed it as 'sickening,' adding, 'I hope that people don't lump him in with me.' Led Zeppelin's Jimmy Page shot back. 'No one will compare the two, because Tiny Tim [is] someone of considerable talent and stature, unlike Pat Boone.'

† There were, Robinson confirms, 'a lot of problems with that. Rounder had hired a firm to market *Girl* a little bit. They had lined up appearances for Tiny, but he didn't want to talk about *Girl* too much because he was so into the *Prisoner Of Love* album, and they finally had to tell him, Look, no more talk about the other record.' After *Prisoner Of Love,* Tiny and Robinson discussed doing a tribute to The Ink Spots. 'Maybe I should paint my face black, get some white gloves, and be munching on a big piece of watermelon,' Tiny suggested.

Sue told Tiny that there was 'no marriage in heaven' but Tiny insisted there was. Frightened by his declining health, she often told him that she looked forward to reuniting with him there, only to be told, 'In heaven because I'm going to be with Miss Stephanie … God can make you a replica of me to be with you.'

'I don't want the replica,' Sue pleaded, 'I want to be with you.'

Frustrated, Sue decided to discuss the matter with Stephanie. 'Why did you go through that ridiculous charade with him?' she demanded. 'You have no idea how difficult that has made it for him to move on to a real relationship.'

'Oh,' Stephanie sighed dismissively, 'what is *real*?'

Sue was stunned to silence, and even now, close to twenty years after Tiny's passing, the issue still evokes strong feelings in her. 'She could have said, I'm sorry, I didn't realized that this was going to hurt him in this way. She may think to this day that was doing him some kind of favor, but she was not, and neither was Bucks.'

Even more irritating to Sue was the way Tiny continued to mention Miss Stephanie in interviews. Around this time, he was asked by John Elder of the Melbourne *Sunday Age*, 'How can you talk this way about a woman who is not your wife?' Tiny replied that he believe he was entitled to have Miss Stephanie—or a heavenly version of Miss Stephanie—as a reward for 'resisting temptation' during his many years of celibacy.

Tiny's infatuation with Miss Stephanie was particularly difficult for Sue to understand because of Tiny's often-impenetrable cognitive processes. In time, however, she came to feel that there was deeper, sadder reality behind the barriers created by his stubbornly illogical actions and words.

'He prided himself in being able to keep people in perpetual confusion, always trying to figure him out,' Sue recalls. 'The more I knew him, the more I became aware of his inherent loneliness behind all that presentation of himself. No matter how much I knew him, I never felt that I knew all there was to know. Even though we were very close, I knew there was part of him that he held back from me, and I have no idea what it was, or why he did not share it with me.'

By the summer of 1996, Sue had become so frustrated and heartsick that she insisted she and Tiny attend marital counseling. Tiny objected to the idea initially, but eventually, reluctantly agreed.

Prior to the counseling session, Tiny discussed his intention to hold steadfastly to his infatuation during his latest appearance on *The Howard Stern*

Show. Stern wished him luck, adding, 'When you come back, please share with us how the counseling session goes.'*

The next day, Tiny and Sue attended their first and final counseling session. Sue described for the counselor Tiny's unwillingness to stop discussing Miss Stephanie publicly, the fact that he carried photographs of her, and how he 'vacillated between being angry with [Stephanie] and continuing to fantasy about her and talk about her.' The response stupefied her.

'The counselor told me if I didn't want to divorce him, I better get used to it,' she recalls. 'That was outrageous. He was supposed to be a Christian counselor, and he's encouraging my husband… to carry around pictures of some other woman in his Bible and to fantasize romantically, perhaps even sexually, about her, and to continue to carry on correspondence and communication with her and to talk about her publicly. What's Christian about that? I just got up and left. I screamed at the guy and just went into a complete rage.'

Later on, when they returned home, Tiny said something to Sue about figuring the marriage was now over, or would be soon. Sue looked at him in disbelief. 'You aren't getting rid of me that easily,' she told him. 'I love you and I'm here to stay.'

After a long kiss, Tiny looked at her and replied in amazement. 'You are some kind of woman,' he said.

Shortly thereafter, Tiny finally decided to get rid of his hotel suite in Des Moines. When he and Sue made the trip to Iowa to collect his belongings, she insisted he keep every last note, every last lottery ticket. 'Someday, people will want all of these things,' she told him.

---

* Tiny's July 1996 appearance on the show occurred just after he had shot a cameo in the $30 million screen adaptation of Stern's best-selling book *Private Parts*. 'Mr. Stern, thanks for having me on your show again and that beautiful movie *Private Parts*,' he said, upon arriving in the studio. There had been some speculation by the media as to what Tiny's cameo in the film would consist of. When Miss Sue was asked to comment, she replied that she was did not know, but she was sure 'it won't be private.' Stern later related the direction he had given Tiny on set: 'Give me a look like you're disgusted with me. Imagine I'm one of your ex-wives.'

CHAPTER TWENTY-EIGHT

'TINY TIM IS SIGNING OFF!'

To my deathbed, I'll try to make it one more time. When I look at these great entertainers—Kenny Rogers, Liza Minnelli, Sammy Davis Jr.—they may think nothing of me. But at one time, even if it was for a scratch, I shared the stage with these great artists. I was a success. It will be in the history books.

TINY TIM TO *ENTERTAINMENT WEEKLY*, NOVEMBER 1996

It was the summer of 1996, and Tiny's health was worsening. 'He would lay in bed all day, and then Gil Morse would call, and he would leave again,' Sue recalls. 'He would be gone for months at a time. He barely made any money, so when he was home, he didn't have any, and he didn't want to spend my money, so he didn't want to go out and do anything. When he did have money he just wanted to go shopping, which meant an exhausting afternoon of being in Walgreen's for three or four hours.'

Eventually, Sue began to loathe the sound of Gil Morse's voice on the telephone. 'It always meant that Tiny was leaving,' she says. 'I could never plan anything without another penny-ante gig interfering. Tiny would disappoint me by canceling any plans we had and getting on the plane once again to go back east to perform at some little fair or to be in a parade.'

'Me and Sue were always fighting,' Morse recalls. 'She was mad because I kept Tiny busy working so much. Tiny wanted to work, and she wanted him home.'

In hindsight, Sue is grateful to Morse for the way he treated Tiny. 'Other people would book him, but they wouldn't give him the kind of support that Gil Morse would give him. When Gil would fly him to the East Coast, he'd meet him at the airport and take him to the hotel and stop at the grocery store so he could pick up some stuff to munch on in his room. When it was time to go to the gig, Gil Morse would, once again, pick him up and take him there and stay the whole time and make sure that Tiny got something to eat and drink and take his arm and lead him around … every now and then [Tiny] would suddenly and unexpectedly fall, so without someone there to take his arm, just in case, it was way too dangerous. Gil made it possible for Tiny to do what he loved right up to the end of his life, and Tiny was grateful for that. In retrospect, so am I.'

Whenever Tiny returned home from traveling, he always brought a gift for Sue and her family as a kind of apology for this absence. The gifts were often as unconventional as the giver: a large pillow decorated with a colorful image of a Native American Brave; a giant stuffed penguin; a two-foot doll that was 'the image of Miss Vicki!' Tiny doted on Sue in other small ways as well. Whenever they went out, Tiny insisted on stopping at a gas station to place a lotto bet, and every time he returned to the car with an artificial flower from inside.

She had also felt much more secure in the relationship since Tiny's relinquishment of his room at the Hotel Fort Des Moines. 'He had lived in hotels much of his life, and came to depend on the staff, the presence of people all around. He finally began to trust that I would be there for him, but he didn't really like it when I left him alone in the house. That felt too isolated for him.'

In addition to *Girl*, 1996 saw the limited release of another feature-length album, *Tiny Tim: Unplugged*, comprising a solo set of Tiny with his ukulele recorded in Birmingham, Alabama, on May 12 1995. The album's dignified cover shows Tiny in a white suit, sitting next to a wind-up gramophone.[*]

In June 1996, Tiny made his final trip to New York City for a collaboration with the punk band Ism. The group had recently enjoyed success with a hardcore-punk cover of David Cassidy's 'I Think I Love You' and were now working on an album with Warner Bros. 'Tip-Toe' seemed like a logical follow-up.

In the studio, Jism, Ism's front man, encouraged Tiny to muster his most 'hardcore-falsetto' voice for his melodic contribution at the end of every chorus, 'Tiptoe through the tulips with meeeee.' Tiny warmed up for the task

---

[*] The year also saw a flurry of compilations featuring Tiny Tim tracks: *Down In The Basement* included four tracks Tiny recorded with The Band in 1967; *Message to Love: The Isle of Wight Festival 1970* included Tiny's show-stopping rendition of 'There'll Always Be An England'; an untitled release on David Tibet's Dutro label featured Tiny singing 'My Inspiration Is You'; and *Mood Swing Music*, a Rounder Records compilation, featured a previously unreleased outtake of 'Girl' from the *Girl* sessions. Rounder Records also rereleased *Tiny Tim's Christmas Album* with new artwork.

with warm beer and popcorn. Jism had also hoped Tiny would contribute a ukulele solo, but when he proved unequal to the task, guitarist Mark Reres took over.

Once Tiny's vocals were committed to tape, Jism moved on to the next item on the agenda: a music video. Shot on 16mm color film, the video is a frenetic collage of 90s punk culture: fast cuts, Dutch angles, and images of graffiti, bondage, and New York streets.

'It was great,' Jism recalls. 'We had a great day. I said, Tiny, I'm gonna do for you what the Red Hot Chili Peppers did for Tony Bennett.'   The day after the session, Tiny was off to New England for engagements with Gil Morse. The album was released later that year by No Label Recordings.

* * *

On June 27 1996, en route from Texas to Pennsylvania to perform between games at a Reading Phillies doubleheader, Tiny landed at the Philadelphia International Airport. Airport employee Nick Cirillo, noting that Tiny looked 'out of breath,' offered him a ride to baggage claim on his electric cart. Tiny climbed in and waited for Cirillo, who had stepped out of the cart momentarily. Suddenly, the cart began moving forward down the terminal. It hit seventy-six-year-old Esther Arthur, fracturing her hip, and cut the arm of a fifty-six-year-old businessman. Tiny grabbed at the wheel frantically, and after about sixty feet of driverless mayhem, managed to crash the cart into the terminal wall. The story of the mishap was covered by the local Pennsylvania media, as well as by the *National Enquirer*, the Associated Press, and even the Sydney *Daily Telegraph*.

Aspersions were cast when Anne Sarr, a witness of the incident, offered an account to law enforcement that differed from Tiny's, insisting that Tiny had been sitting in the driver's seat. 'The driver was helping put luggage in the back and [Tiny] just pulled away,' she told the press. 'He left his guitar [sic] on the front seat right next to him.' Tiny's credibility as a witness did not improve when he admitted to police that he had consumed two beers prior to the accident. By the time he came to discuss the incident with Howard Stern in July, this had increased to four beers, although he insisted they were not to blame. 'They were great beers!'

In Tiny's version of events, after he disembarked from the blame, Nick Cirillo had said, 'Why don't you take the cart outside?' Tiny climbed into the passenger seat and put his shopping bag between his legs. 'I don't know if I was shifting in the seat or not, but it started to roll. I certainly didn't put my foot on the pedal. I know nothing about cars … I got scared. It kept rolling and rolling without a stop.' He admitted that he might have put his foot on a pedal in an effort to stop the cart, and 'might've touched the wheel as it was rolling … I was aiming for the wall.'

After a commercial break, Cirillo called in to the show to offer a different version of events. 'We have witnesses stating that they actually seen him get on the cart. They actually heard him say that when he was a kid his father never let him drive a car … and he said it was rollin' and then he said he didn't know the difference between the brake pedal and the accelerator pedal. We don't know who's at fault right at this point.'

Lowering his voice menacingly, Tiny insisted that he had subsequently been told that the brakes were faulty. 'I would take a lie detector test right away,' he added. 'If you bring those people on, I wish they would take it.'

* * *

In September, Tiny went into the studio with Johnny Pineapple for what would be his final recording session. They recorded yet another version of Max Sofsky's 'Yum, Yum,' aka 'The Pizza Song,' or, as this version was dubbed, 'The Pizza Polka Rap.' According to Miss Sue, 'Like most recording sessions, it was deadly boring, and went on forever.'

'The Pizza Polka Rap,' Tiny's last recording, is an interesting take on a song that had been in Tiny's repertoire for decades. The impetus for the recording occurred one afternoon as Tiny, Sue, and Johnny were watching TV and saw a 'lame pizza ad [that] showed this dorky little guy in this stupid little car driving along a normal looking street, delivering a normal-looking pizza to a normal-looking guy who opened the door of a normal-looking house.'

The commercial lit a light bulb in Pineapple's coconut. He proposed a Tiny Tim commercial where the customer orders a pizza and Tiny Tim, in an outlandish suit jacket, oversized boutineer, and top hat, prepares the pizza in a futuristic kitchen and delivers it in a cartoonish vehicle, all while singing a revamped version of 'The Pizza Song.' They agreed that Pineapple would arrange for the recording of the song, and that Sue would have thirty days to sell the idea to a major pizza chain. If she could not, Pineapple was to take over the effort.

Tiny had recorded a copy of his version with piano accompaniment, but Pineapple wanted to put a different twist on it. 'I want to make it real old-time,' he said, 'something a polka band would do.' He hired a drummer from a Wisconsin based polka band, a bass player, a clarinet/piccolo player, and an accordion player. The improvised rap, recorded in one take over a hip-hop beat, was Tiny's idea. One of the musicians present at the session subsequently told Pineapple that it was 'like Tiny was in the grips of possession'; all of a sudden, he announced, 'I feel a rap coming on!' Sadly, as the forces of nature ultimately nixed any Tiny Tim pizza commercials, 'The Pizza Polka Rap' was never released.*

Later that month, Tiny Tim made his final trip to the East Coast. On September 27, he played a show aboard the Bay Queen, a cruise ship out of Warren Rhode Island. After the show, he had a few drinks with Jim Foley. As they left the boat, with their arms around each other's' shoulders, Tiny asked, 'We're pals, right, Mr. Foley?'

'Of course, Tiny,' said Foley answered.

'Yes, we're the best of pals,' Tiny said, as they approached Gil Morse's station wagon. Before getting into the vehicle, Tiny turned to Foley and sang a few bars of 'We'll Meet Again.'

The next day, Tiny appeared as the headlining act at the Ukulele Expo held in an old barn in Montague, Massachusetts. In attendance were Gil Morse and Tiny Heads Brian Blouin, Renee Bowan, and Mark Frizzel. Prior to his performance, Tiny sat down with representatives from the Ukulele Hall of Fame and made a sixty-minute video entitled *Songs And Stories Of The Crooners*. He made it through the interview without incident, although Blouin noticed that he seemed congested and was coughing more than usual.

As Tiny waited to take the stage, he started getting jittery. 'He was so nervous to go out that night because it was the Ukulele Expo and they had all these big name people singing,' Blouin recalls. He tried to reassure Tiny. 'You're the guy who brought the ukulele back in the 60s. You could go up there without the ukulele and just sing. You're the main attraction so don't worry about it.'

When Tiny's name was announced, Blouin took his arm, helped him onto the stage and adjusted his microphone, and then retreated to the back of the room to record the performance. When he looked back, he could tell something was wrong. Tiny was swaying back and forth. 'Sometimes I have a little trouble with my voice,' he mumbled. Blouin looked down for a moment and suddenly heard a tremendous thud followed by screams from the

---

* Around the same time, Tiny recorded a bizarre but somewhat entrancing techno/dance song entitled 'We Love You, Billy Budd' with Minneapolis musician and DJ Brett Edgar.

audience. His eyes shot back up, and Tiny was no longer on the stage. He had fallen into the seats below and hit his head on the floor.

Blouin rushed to the stage. 'He looked like he cracked his head open above the eyebrow. He wasn't talking or anything.' There were no phones in the barn, so Blouin sprinted down the street and pounded on the door of the first house he saw. A woman rushed to the door, and Blouin blurted, 'We need an ambulance! Tiny Tim just fell of the stage!' By the time the EMTs arrived, Tiny had regained consciousness. A hush settled over the crowd as the they asked Tiny a series of routine questions.

'Sir, how old are you?'

Tiny hesitated as the room its breath. 'Nearing sixty-five,' he said softly.

'When he said that, we knew he was all right,' Blouin recalled. 'That was Tiny talking.'

Someone shouted, 'Hold on, Tiny Tim!' When he managed a feeble wave, the room cheered.

Meanwhile, the concert promoter and Gil Morse were about to brawl. In the midst of the commotion, the promoter had approached Morse and asked, 'Do we get our money back? We didn't count on that.' Morse, who had not wanted Tiny to perform in the first place, flew into such a rage that his wife had to stop him from punching the promoter.

Tiny was loaded into an ambulance and taken to Franklin Medical Center in Greenfield, Massachusetts, where it was determined he had suffered a heart attack.* Morse, Blouin, and Bowan all traveled to the hospital, only to be told that they could not see Tiny. 'That was the worst night ever,' Blouin recalls. 'No one was allowed to see him. I had no way to contact him or anything, so I went out and got a shopping bag and filled it up with Viva [paper] towels and *National Enquirer* magazines and things that he was used to having around. I drove all the way out to the hospital and dropped it off at the front desk.'

On the morning of September 30, major newspapers and gossip magazines reported that Tiny was in 'serious but stable condition.' 'He is in intensive care,' a Franklin Medical Center spokeswoman said. 'But he was sitting up today and [doctors] are guessing he will be here for about a week.'

'I had a slight heart attack and am resting comfortably,' Tiny told the press reassuringly. Two days later, however, Miss Sue told the *Boston Herald* that

---

* Gil Morse later informed Sue that he did not think it the heart attack was the first Tiny had had. 'They thought that Tiny had had a heart attack or a stroke before because they were at a gig one night and Tiny all of the sudden didn't know where he was,' she recalls.

Tiny's heart was 'very weak' and that doctors were unsure whether he would be able to work again.

In Minneapolis, Sue was in a panicked state. Her first impulse had been to fly to Massachusetts, but Tiny dissuaded her, explaining that there was much to be done in Minnesota to prepare for his return. 'He was right,' she later said. 'There were so many things that had to be taken care of. First of all, I had to arrange his transportation, I had to have a hospital bed ready for him, I needed to have oxygen there.'

On October 7, after an eight-day stay at the Franklin Medical Center, Tiny was flown to another hospital in Minneapolis via a $20,000 air ambulance, at Sue's insistence. She did not feel that it was safe to put Tiny on a plane, even accompanied by a nurse. On October 10, as Tiny prepared to return home, Tiny and George Gardiner shared a moment in the hospital room. 'They had kind of a heart to heart, and Tiny was saying that he had a good life and that he fulfilled all his dreams and been blessed,' Sue recalls. 'He [said he] had success with show business, had a child, and felt blessed that he and I had found happiness, and that he prayed he would have courage when the time came. After that, my father said to me, Your husband was truly a man of substance.'

While Sue's father went to fetch the car, Tiny gave a press conference, disclosing publicly that, with congestive heart failure, an enlarged heart, an irregular heartbeat, and diabetes, his prognosis did not look promising. 'When you think of people like Michael Landon dying way before his time, Elvis Presley, so many others who haven't seen a full life, it's a blessing to live this long without pain,' he told the press. 'If I live ten years, it's a miracle. Five years, it's even more of a miracle ... I am ready for anything. Death is never polite, even when we expect it. The only thing I pray for is the strength to go out without complaining.' He also announced that he would no longer perform, 'except for a brief song here or there,' and that he was planning on applying for Social Security.

A *National Enquirer* article painted an even grimmer picture of the situation. 'There's a tragic secret behind Tiny Tim's recent retirement announcement,' the magazine revealed. 'Doctors told him he has only a year to live.'

'Now I just have to make sure I'm good in the time I have left—because the most important thing is that I get to heaven,' Tiny told the *Enquirer*. 'They say my heart is functioning at about 40 percent—and they give me a year.' He also confirmed that heart surgery was out of the question. 'I'd rather go out with the same heart that I came in with—with no scars on it.' Asked if he had any regrets, he mentioned only a desire to have 'managed a little more S-E-X with Miss Sue.'

After a month of rest at home, Tiny began to grow restless. He took to wandering around their home and belting out his favorite songs. Sue could tell he was longing to perform but insisted that he continue to rest. Meanwhile, a schism was forming among Tiny's friends and fans. Some felt that he should be discouraged from performing at all costs for the sake of his life; others insisted that he be allowed to continue performing, because to stop him was to deprive him his reason for living. 'The doctors said if I perform again I could be a goner,' Tiny told the *National Enquirer*. 'But if I can't sing I might as well be dead.'

Privately, Tiny joked to Miss Sue that he planned to have a picture taken of himself in a casket as his Christmas card. Inside the card there would another picture, only this time Tiny would be sitting up in the casket, smiling. The caption would read, 'I'm not dead yet!' Sue dismissed the idea.

After many years of separation, Richard Perry contacted Tiny, and two spent a considerable amount of time on the phone together. When Tiny told Jim Foley of Perry's suggestion that they work together again, Foley replied, 'Well there's incentive to get better.'

Finally, Tiny tested the waters by performing briefly at two small venues. Though he seemed to struggle a little, both shows were devoid of major incident. Nevertheless, Sue noticed a song Tiny had begun singing more frequently, one that she could not identify. It contained the lyrics, 'In the story of Sorento, will they remember me at all?'

Next, Tiny performed at the League of Catholic Women's Ball at the Metropolitan in Golden Valley, just outside of Minneapolis. Jerry Mayeron, the leader of the band who backed Tiny that night, later told the press, 'He kills 'em wherever he goes. That name's magic. He had an amazing career based on a minute-and-a-half song.' Asked about Tiny's health, Mayeron added, 'He just did a couple, three songs, what he's sort of famous for. He appeared a little shaky, but he made it through the show.'

* * *

On the morning of November 27, Miss Vicki received a call from Tulip. She had talked with her father and relayed to Vicki that he was stable but very unwell. 'Oh, he'll be all right,' Vicki replied dismissively, remembering that her own father had lived for several more years after suffering multiple heart attacks. 'You should call him,' Tulip told her.

Vicki thought about it for a moment, remembering the many times they had spoken and ended up yelling and cursing at other, but in the end she decided to call him. 'I heard you were really sick,' she said, when Tiny answered the phone.

'No, I'm fine,' Tiny replied. 'I'm gonna be fine.'

They went on to apologize to each other for all the times they had spoken unkindly to one another. 'I didn't mean it,' Tiny told her. 'We were just being mean to each other.'

They hung up the phone, perhaps intuitively aware that it was the last time they would speak. 'We were nice to each other for the first time in a very long time,' Vicki recalls.

Later that day, Tiny confided in Miss Sue that although he and Vicki had had their share of scrapes, he 'gave her credit' for giving him Tulip, one of the 'biggest thrills and greatest blessings in life.'

* * *

Thanksgiving fell on November 28. According to Gil Morse, Tiny was in 'severe pain' and spent the day in the hospital. By now, he had stopped taking his medication. 'What difference does it make?' he asked Sue when she questioned him about it. 'One day it won't matter.'

Tiny had been booked by Sue's stepmother to perform at a benefit dinner hosted by the Women's Club of Minneapolis called An Evening Under The Stars on November 38. Miss Sue and her stepmother had also purchased several hundred copies of *Prisoner Of Love* to give as gifts to those who had purchased a plate for the evening. That morning, Gil spoke with Tiny on the phone and begged him not to perform.

'I have to do this,' Tiny insisted. 'If I was getting paid I could refuse to do it. But I'm not getting paid, and I don't want them to think I am not doing it because I am not getting paid. I have to do it.'

That afternoon, as Sue and Tiny prepared to leave for the concert, Tiny left his last known recording on Jim Foley's answering machine. Foley's wife had just given birth to their first child, a daughter.

'Congratulations,' he said, sounding tired. 'Good afternoon, Mr. Foley, Mrs. Foley, this is Tiny Tim. I just got your call—your call came earlier, but I was either asleep or I had the phone shut—but I just got the message right now. Congratulations on the birth of your wonderful baby girl. May the Lord bless it real well and thank Jesus Christ, and I just pray that you both have the best, and I thank you for keeping me in touch, and we will keep in touch. Thanks again for letting me know, and congratulations to Mr. And Mrs. Foley, once more. *Tiny Tim is signing off.'*

As Sue and Tiny were getting into the limousine to take them to the event, Tiny became disoriented and fell to his knees as he got into the car. His legs were visibly swollen, and Miss Sue had to hold onto his arm and help him up the front steps of the venue. Although she had reservations about Tiny playing the show, she did not feel it was her place to tell her husband what to do. Even if she had, she says, it may not have made a difference. 'I don't think there's anything more I could have done to stop him.'

A full band had been hired for the event, and Tiny Tim was slotted as a guest vocalist. Bandleader Bob Elledge had been not been informed that his band was supposed to accompany Tiny, however, and refused to do so, claiming that they were not familiar with Tiny's material. Perplexed, Tiny Tim looked at him and said, 'You don't know "I'm Looking Over A Four Leaf Clover"?'

It was agreed that Tiny would accompany himself on the ukulele, and that his set would begin at nine o'clock. By ten, the band had not yet taken a break to allow Tiny to perform his set. Tiny was tired, and Miss Sue told her stepmother that she was taking him home. Her stepmother consulted with the event coordinator, who in turn asked the band to take a break to allow Tiny Tim to perform. Without ceremony or introduction of Tiny Tim, the bandleader abruptly stopped his band. Many of the event's attendees, believing the night over, began to file out.

The event coordinator hurried to the microphone and, in an attempt to retain an audience, gave Tiny a rushed introduction. Tiny Tim took the stage to an almost empty room and began his set, performing with the same spirit as he had always done, playing five songs instead of the 'two or three' he had promised to do. In an article Miss Sue later wrote about her relationship with Tiny Tim, she remembered him looking at her intently as he sang 'When I Grow Too Old To Dream.'

So kiss me, my sweet,
And so let us part,
And when I grow too old to dream,
That kiss will live in my heart.

After four songs, Tiny mustered up 'the high voice' for the last time. He began his most famous song, 'Tip-Toe Thru' The Tulips With Me.' After a few bars, he suddenly cut the song short. The audience applauded as Tiny mumbled 'God bless' and stumbled away from the microphone.

Sue rushed to his side and grabbed his arm. 'Are you all right?' she asked.

'No,' he replied quietly. 'I'm not.'

With that, Tiny collapsed into Sue's arms and then slumped to the floor.

A shockwave went through the crowd. Three doctors in the audience began attempts to resuscitate him while Sue sat a few feet away. 'When they weren't able to bring him around by the first couple of tries, I knew he wasn't going to make it,' she later recalled. Many in the audience were familiar, either through friendship or publicity, of Sue's profound love for her husband, and they watched her with alarm.

An ambulance arrived and Tiny was rushed to Hennepin County Medical Center. 'He isn't going to make it, is he?' Sue said to the driver.

At the hospital, doctors tried for forty-five minutes to resuscitate Tiny. Twice they succeeded in reestablishing a heartbeat, only for it to give out again immediately. Eventually, they allowed Sue into the room, following her request to 'be there when they gave up.'

'I had read that when a person dies, his spirit looks down at the body for awhile,' she later wrote. 'I wanted him to see me there. They let me in and pulled a sheet up to his chin to hide the big needle in his chest, as if I hadn't seen it. I silently hoped he had never regained consciousness, but I didn't ask for details.'

The doctors stood back as Sue kissed Tiny on the forehead.

'I love you,' she whispered.

Tiny Tim was pronounced dead at 11:20pm on November 30 1996. He was sixty-four years old.

Shortly after Tiny died, Sue's father joined her at the hospital.

'How is he?' he asked.

'He's gone,' Sue replied.

A nurse delivered Tiny's wedding ring and a Celtic cross necklace Sue had given him very recently. Then she and her father said a prayer in the hospital chapel and left. The same limousine that had ferried Tiny and Sue to the benefit now took her home. As she stepped out of the limo, she was greeted by the 'most unbearable sight of the evening': the footprints she and Tiny had left in the snow on their way out of the house.

CHAPTER TWENTY-NINE

TIPTOE TO ETERNITY

The memory and aftermath of that huge success also enabled him to endure through all the years after his career had faded, as most entertainers' careers do. Even in old age he could pack a nightclub and get the people up out of their chairs, dancing, or laughing and applauding, like waves of hysteria sometimes. I never heard an audience react like that, to anyone else. And no matter how old, sick and exhausted he was, he loved every second of it. That is what he lived and died for.

MISS SUE

Sue's first call, at 2am, was to Gil Morse. Then she continued down the long list of relatives and business associates, delivering the sorrowful news on into the night. Meanwhile, her stepsister had an odd dream: she was in space, in a place that resembled both a church and nightclub. She saw Tiny, looking as he had in the 60s. He told her not to worry.

The next morning, when Sue opened her front door, she discovered a piece of artwork that had been tucked between the front and screen door. It was a painting of two tulips, captioned 'Tiny Tim: 1932–1996.' Inscribed in the bottom left were the words 'We'll Miss You' as well as the indecipherable name of the artist. News of Tiny Tim's death swept across the world. The Associated Press broke the story, and by the morning of December 1, virtually all media outlets were reporting that the ukulele-strumming crooner who shocked and amused audiences in the 60s had passed away.

Miss Sue offered several statements to the press:

I don't think he had time to feel pain. He died singing 'Tip-Toe Thru' The Tulips' and the last thing he heard was the applause, and the last thing he saw was me.

I believe his spirit left his body with the applause still in his ears.
If he could have chosen a way to go, this is the way to go with big
dramatic flair. That wasn't his style to die in bed. He went out with
a bang. Very theatrical. That was his way, to collapse in front of
hundreds of people.

Miss Sue spent her forty-first birthday, December 2 1996, selecting caskets and
making other funeral arrangements. Her friend Bea Flaming, who had been
in Sue's wedding party, accompanied her to the funeral home and was with
her when she saw Tiny's body for the first time since the hospital. Sue decided
to bury Tiny in a black satin suit, one of Martin Sharp's more conservative
designs. She found a coffin she thought appropriate but began to fret over
an ornate design carved inside the lid. 'With Tiny laying in the casket,' the
funeral director told her, 'no one is going to be looking at those carvings.'

By now, every major news source and publication carried a retrospective
on Tiny Tim. Headlines like 'Tiny Phenom,' 'Tiny Tim Is Stricken During
Tulips, Dies,' and 'Tiny Tim Tip-Toes To Eternity' graced the covers of
newspapers around the world. The coverage ranged from respectful profiles
of his career to brief footnotes announcing the death of a long-forgotten
'novelty' relic from the 60s. Local, national, and international journalists
grappled for witty puns.

'The cultural turbulences of the late 1960s produced many strange
phenomena, but none stranger than Tiny Tim,' the *New York Times* concluded.
'Internally, journalists and critics debated wither Tiny Tim was a put-on or
the real thing. It quickly became clear that he was genuine, a lonely outcast
intoxicated by fame, a romantic in pursuit of the beautiful dream.'

Newsweek called Tiny 'pop's no. 1 super-freak,' while the *New York Daily
News* decided that, 'in the Fellini-esque world of popular entertainment,
where odd is often the norm, Tiny Tim may have been the oddest of all.' For
Russ Mitchell of the CBS *Sunday Night News*, Tiny had enjoyed 'fifteen minutes
of fame that lasted a lifetime,' while the London *Times* summed up his career
as 'a piece of extraordinary schmaltz which, with touching courage, set itself
against the mores of that progressive decade, the 60s.'

In New York City, Howard Stern reminisced with his co-hosts and aired
clips of Tiny's more memorable moments on the show. Gil Morse called in to
tell Stern that Tiny 'thought the world of you,' and it seemed that Stern felt
the same way. 'Let me tell you something: Tiny, I loved him. He was the best

guest I ever had. I loved him, but I'm happy for him that he's finally released from the tortures of life.'

Later, during a filmed retrospective of his years at WNBC, Stern said, 'Tiny Tim was not putting anything on. He was the real deal. This was not an orchestrated "I'm a freaky guy" kind of thing. He was the real deal and there wasn't a false bone in his body. He was phenomenal. I lost a tremendous radio guest, but the world lost the greatest person. ... You know what I'm proud of? Tiny, of course, had great fame in the 60s or early 70s, whenever *Laugh-In* was on and Johnny Carson, but I was able to bring him back in a genuine way and sort of help reinvent him. He was great on the radio. So Tiny Tim, I greatly miss him.'

Numerous other famous personalities who had known and worked with Tiny were asked to comment on his passing.

Ed McMahon: 'He was like a one-ring circus ... everybody thought he was bigger than life, that his act was just a total gimmick or something he could just turn on. What I liked about him is what you saw with him is what you got ... he was the same sincere person you saw on television.'

Dr. Demento: 'He was certainly a prince of a man. He was so gracious and polite that that kind of became part of his cartoon image, calling everyone Sir and Miss.'

Dick Martin: 'He was beautiful. You had to watch him carefully to see if he was putting you on, but he wasn't.'

George Schlatter: 'Everybody who met him was fascinated by him.'
Last, but certainly not least, Johnny Carson: 'He was one of the most ingenuous persons I have ever known.'

On December 3, the *Toronto Star* paid tribute to Tiny and his dogged support for the Maple Leafs, with sportswriter Garth Woolsey concluding that the Leafs could 'use some of Tiny's good luck.' Tiny had come to believe that his fate was linked with the Maple Leafs. In January 1992, he told *MacLean's* magazine, 'No one has pointed out that [the Leafs] started to go downhill about the same time my career collapsed ... they'll win another Stanley Cup when I have another hit.' Now that he was gone, his chances at another hit had become highly improbable. At the time of writing, the Maple Leafs have not won the Stanley Cup since 1967.

On December 4 1996, the Rite of Christian Burial for Tiny Tim was held at the Basilica of Saint Mary in Minneapolis, Minnesota. Hundreds of Tiny's friends, fans, and family packed the massive cathedral. A two-hour visitation preceded the funeral, and hundreds shuffled through, stopping to pay respects at the casket. A ukulele had been placed across Tiny's chest, and many of the guests added their own items to the casket: a stuffed rabbit, prayer books, flowers, and baseball cars. A multicolored rosary was wrapped around his hands. In a show of poor taste, several of the funeral's attendees snapped pictures of Tiny as they passed.

Attendees included Tiny's cousins, Hal and Bernie Stein; his childhood friend Artie Wachter; and a number of the Tiny Heads from New England. Tulip and her family had traveled to Minnesota but could not attend the ceremony as practicing Jehovah's Witnesses. Harold Stein took a second to give a quick interview to the press, which had descended upon the church with a dozen TV and radio broadcast trucks. 'Tiny Tim was a great performer,' he said. 'That's who Tiny Tim was.'

Several fans weighed in as well. 'He was a medium from another place and time,' said Michelle King, who had taken time off from work and flown from San Francisco to attend the funeral. 'He was the truest inspiration and most inspiring person I have ever met.'

Though Gil Morse opted not to attend the funeral, he gave a statement to the *National Enquirer*: 'No one could talk him out [of performing] ... but he left this earth the way he wanted to go—with a song on his lips, and his beloved ukulele in his hand.'

According to Miss Sue, a few celebrities were in attendance, most notably Elton John, who 'kept himself scarce.' Bolstering herself as best she could, Sue graciously greeted the hundreds of funeral attendees offering their condolences and granted an interview with the press.

'There are so many things to say about him, I don't know where to begin,' Sue told the press. 'He really tried to be a good person.' At this, the interview was interrupted by a horrible wail from the visitation line near the casket. There, weeping dramatically, was Miss Jan, her lawyer at her side and a locket containing a bit of Tiny's hair dangling from her neck.

'I heard her screaming in the distance as she saw Tiny's body in the casket,' Sue recalls. 'I instantly knew who that was, as I had heard rumors that she was showing up. I was surprised at how small she was. Even in stiletto heels she was shorter than me, and I am only five-foot-four. She was just as stunning as the pictures, though.'

Sue's friend Bea Flaming had been sitting with Miss Sue when Jan detonated. 'The funeral was very trying,' she recalls. 'We wondered what on earth that noise was. Finally, somebody told [Jan] to knock it off. I don't remember who it was, but I remember somebody telling me they had told her to be quiet and stop it. I believe that she was a good actress. I don't think [she was sincere].'

Shortly after that, the press retreated, and left Sue to continue to greet attendees in the line. Flaming eyed Jan as she made her way in the line toward Sue, all the while weeping uncontrollably. When she arrived, Sue was relieved to find that Jan was 'surprising cordial.' When she continued to sob, however, Sue turned to Bea and said, 'Why don't you take Miss Jan for a while. I think she needs you more than [I do] right now.' Taking her arm, Bea led the stricken vixen to the front of the church to find a seat and handed her off to another friend of Sue's, Sunny Keller.

The service, a ninety-minute Roman Catholic mass, went smoothly, in part thanks to Keller. 'She kind of took Miss Jan ... and kept her quiet for the rest of the ceremony and in place,' Sue recalls. 'Otherwise, things might have been worse. Sunny was a tall, imposing, and stunningly beautiful Scandinavian woman, and there was absolutely no getting past her or acting up in her presence.'*

Sue did not speak during the service but prepared a message that was printed in the liturgy booklet. 'Tiny never wanted to do just enough to get by,' she wrote. 'He always wanted to exceed the expectations. If he was supposed to do one song, he did three. If he was supposed to do two or three, he did five. No matter how he felt, the show must go on. He always stayed until the last autograph was signed and the last question answered. He never wanted to disappoint anyone, especially the Lord.'

Nick Coleman, a reporter for the *Saint Paul Pioneer Press*, later summarized the remarks made by Reverend Dale Korogi, vicar of the Basilica, during his homily. Tiny was a kind man, Korogi said, 'courtly in his manners and lavish in his courtesies,' with 'a heart that saw and acknowledged the dignity of the person before him, particularly the least brother or sister.'

* * *

As the guests filed out of the church, 'Sunshine Cake' from *For All My Little Friends* began to play over the church's PA system. It was Sue's favorite

---

* During the service, Sunny overheard Jan say that she planned to throw herself on the casket. In response, Sunny kept her body turned to block Jan's escape, should she decide to make a mad dash. She also observed Jan's on-again, off-again anguish in relation to the proximity of the camera.

recording of Tiny's, and she had arranged for its broadcast. For some, this was the hardest moment of the funeral.

So why not bake a sunshine cake,
Of course it may keep your dreams awake,
Friends say there's nothing like the flavor,
Don't wait to do your friends a favor,
And for goodness sake, let's bake a sunshine cake.

After the funeral, a private dinner was held for close family and friends. Tiny's friends and family took turns sharing their memories from a behind a podium. Tulip was clearly taken aback when she saw just how much of an impact her father had made on the lives of everyone there. 'I wish I would've known my dad better,' she told those present. 'It was really special to hear how much he meant to all these people.'

Despite the fact that Tiny had told the Associated Press that he did not want to be buried 'with anyone old,' Tiny Tim was interred in a mausoleum in Lakewood Cemetery in Minneapolis. Before the casket closed, Miss Sue stood at Tiny's side and took one last look at him. For reasons she still does not understand, she reached in and removed a single artificial flower and the ukulele. Looking at him again, she realized that it was the only time she had seen her husband's hair combed.

'Wow, that really looks nice,' she thought to herself.

Then Miss Jan too took a last look at the body. 'Before they closed the coffin, she snipped off another chunk of [hair], after commenting that the funeral home had dyed it the wrong color,' Sue recalls. 'She had convinced him to dye it red for many years, but he had dyed it brown again, because that is what I preferred. Suddenly she yelled out, to no one in particular, Does anyone else want a piece of hair? I guess that is how they do things in New York. For a Minnesotan, it was a bit shocking, but I just had to smile weakly. It was another Tiny Tim moment.'

The air remained thick for the duration of Jan's stay in Minneapolis. 'I just felt sort of concerned for Sue until Miss Jan left town,' Bea Fleming recalls. 'I just didn't know if she was going to try to take advantage of Sue or what ... I think she was after her share. I don't know all the ins and outs of it, though.'

After the interment, Tiny's friends and family returned to their various homes. In the months that followed Tiny's passing, Miss Sue returned often to

Lakewood Cemetery to pay her respects. At his grave, she sometimes crossed paths with fans who had made the pilgrimage to see Tiny's resting place. 'That was an odd experience,' she says. 'But nothing about being with Tiny was "normal" from beginning to end—if there ever really will be an end to it.'

There likely will not. Though Tiny Tim has been gone from this earth for nearly twenty years, his influence and legacy have carried on in pop culture and various subcultures. His music has been featured in such disparate productions as *SpongeBob SquarePants* and the 2011 horror film *Insidious*. He pioneered androgyny on prime-time television, paving the way for artists and performers to blur the lines of gender in a public way: David Bowie, Boy George, Patti Smith, Klaus Nomi, Prince, Queen, Lady Gaga, Annie Lennox, kd lang, The New York Dolls, Marilyn Manson, Rob Zombie, Antony & The Johnsons, Steven Tyler—the list goes on. He took the heat as the original freak.

Whether Tiny Tim's story is a tragedy, comedy, romance, or epic, at its root it is the story of a man with a pure obsession. Through his lens there is insight into the depths of exploitation and cruelty inherent in the media, the exhausting and cutthroat world of entertainment, the pressures of fame, the struggles of marriage, and how lonely it can be to be different. If Tiny can be said to have had one love, it was the sublime: in faith, in romance, and in song. He is the Eternal Troubadour.

ACKNOWLEDGMENTS

The author would like to thank the following people for their invaluable assistance with this project: Susan Khaury and Victoria Benson, who both took a chance by opening up to me even though I had no credentials beyond being a Tiny Tim super-fan. Alanna Wray McDonald, without whom I would have never finished this book. My family who always encouraged me, and also politely listened to hours of Tiny Tim's music as well as humored my frequent anecdotes about his life and career: Michelle Audette O'Donnell, William Martell, Timothy O'Donnell, Ginger Martell, Dr. Kathleen Audette, Pierre Audette, Helen Martell, Kenneth Martell, Ginny O'Donnell, Ray O'Donnell, Kylie O'Donnell, Aidan O'Donnell, Gavin Martell, Jason Wallace, Jonathan DeSimone, Martina Martell, Angela Wallace, William Wallace, Gregory Martell, Christina Martell, Mary Whitworth, Scott Audette, Nicole Richards, John and Kathy Coult, Terry and Stan Majeski, Ginger and Tom Sierra, Janis O'Donnell, Christopher Hamman, Michael Hamman, Cassie Whitworth.

The Politburo: Mike Jackman, Eric Jackman, David Elliott, Vito Trigo, Evan Miller, Brad Thomas, Aaron Hamel, Matt Manjourides, Jeff Cornell, Derek Gorman, Seager Dixon, Nicholas Lombardo.

Those who went above and beyond: Richard Barone, Ernie Clark, Martin Sharp, Ed Sterbenz, Eddie Rabin, Jane Cole, Bruce Button, Ben Roth, Brian Blouin, Patricia Barreat, Sherrye Weinstein, Stuart Hersh, Lowell Tarling, David Rowe, Greg Gardner, Bucks Burnett, Harve Mann, Harry Stein.

Peter Sulinski, without whom I would have never become a fan of Tiny Tim.

The many others who have inspired, encouraged, supported, and been friends to me throughout my life, or who in some way helped encourage my Tiny Tim obsession, in no particular order: Nicki Ley, Danielle White, Kevin Christopher, Anna Kelma, Mateusz Radziszewski, Ryan and Lindsay

Moroch, Chris Charbonnier, Chad Cook, Dean Schimetschek, Tony Jackman, Paul Jackman, Annie Jackman, John Jackman, Jon Ficara, Janissa Ramirez, Brian Reed, Caitlin Soha, David Swift, Garrett Goodspeed, Ashley Vanicek, Austin Jennings, Marcus Bones, Eric Sanders, Dylan Avery, Jacqueline Lamontagne, David Pottie, Bartek Ponikwicki, Michelle Hancock, Phil Painchaud, Joe Tyman, Laura Jackman, Greg King, Lloyd Kaufman, Michael Herz, Lisa Carlson, Tom Erb, Michelle Duga, Stephanie Duga, Ava Biffer, Bonnie Butsch, Leeann Gomes, Curt Simmons, Carol Jackman, Terry Reardon, Roger and Maryann Zotti, Megan Klein, Candy John Carr, Dr. Phyllis Zrzavy, Scott Belmo, Phil X. Milstein, Roger Trevino, Anne Shaw, Kathy and Fred Miller, Susan McKinley, Gary and Bev Christopher, Kim Gowac, Samantha Peloquin, Adam Perry, Beau Meyer, Dan Bowen, Laurie Seamans, Kim Ruth, Gwen Rosewater, Erin Elizabeth Seaton, Elizabeth Pursell, Laurie Seamans, Zac Amico, Mark Finch, Britton Blackall, Tyler Bradberry, Ron Mackay, John Brennan, Andy Deemer, Chuck Rinaldi, Mike Pietrasiewicz, Angie Pietrasiewicz, Kelsie Cooper, Doug Sakmann, Jon Gold, Pat Klouman, Jill Barry, John M. Landis, Matt Fedorka, Monster Matt Patterson, Kelley Stieh, Dan Mason, Cassie Baralis, John Foster, Patrick Farrell, Alex Gordon, Jacob Windstein, Katherine Rose, Shannon Jezek, Bob Weiner, Catherine Corcoran, the late Robin Barton, Adam Betts, Katie Miller, Dr. Dianna Wentzell, Holly Donovan, Stuart Kiczek, Shirley Einhorn, Joachim Teverbring, Johan Von Sydow, Derek Wakeham, Sam Wilson, Tracey McDermott, Jeff Szalkiewicz, Conrad Cotterman, Liam Regan, Jay Selevka, Steve Addabbo, Harry Levine, Matthew Billy, Dr. James Fetzer, Cady Knoll, Natalya Waye, Dr. Kristen Nevious, Doug Snyder, Tristan Smith, Cameron Crawford, Tim Dax.

In memoriam: Martin Sharp, Joe Franklin, Barry Feinstein, Gil Morse. The author would like to add a special dedication, written by Eddie and Sam Rabin, for their mother Roslyn Rabin, 'who left us all this year, just a little too soon to see this book released. Tiny was perhaps unaware of his cousin Ros's acclaim as a poet, writing and teaching poetry well into her nineties, but he knew her other contribution: namely her son (and his second cousin), Eddie, who played and wrote music for Tiny.'

A NOTE ON SOURCES

The primary sources for this book are nineteen of Tiny Tim's personal diaries from the years 1952–78 (excluding the years 1960–64, '72, '73, '76, and '77). I also conducted more than one hundred original interviews with participants in Tiny's life and career, including two of Tiny's three wives, Miss Vicki and Miss Sue, and relatives, friends, and collaborators. Tiny's second wife, Miss Jan, had the opportunity to contribute but did not return phone calls on the grounds that she did not 'want any books written about Tiny Tim' (as was relayed to me by radio/television personality Joe Franklin).

Of these interviewees, Susan Khaury, Tiny's widow, is the only one quoted throughout the entire text. Though she and Tiny were married briefly, they were together at a time when Tiny was aware that he was nearing the end of his life, and was looking back retrospectively. Accordingly, he shared with her a great deal of information about his upbringing and career that he had not shared with others.

Author Harry Stein published a biography of Tiny, *Tiny Tim: The Unauthorized Biography* in 1976; Tiny gave an extensive interview to *Playboy* in 1970 and another to his friend Johnny Pineapple in 1994; and Susan Khaury published on tinytim.org a memoir of her marriage to Tiny in 1998. All of these I used as a starting point for research and telling this story, cross-checking dates and facts against Tiny's diaries, hundreds of additional print, television, and radio interviews Tiny gave during his nearly forty-five years in show business, and thousands of newspaper articles directly or indirectly pertaining to Tiny Tim dating from 1963 to present day. It should be noted also that some interview transcripts, such as those with Johnny Carson and Howard Stern, are abridged to include relevant discussion, and do not appear verbatim.

In addition to officially available interviews and recordings, I also sourced a large amount of unreleased material which has been circulated among Tiny

Tim collectors and fans, or made available to me for the first time specifically for this book. Author Lowell Tarling also granted me access to many original interviews he conducted with Tiny and those who knew him whom I was not able to reach, namely Tiny's daughter Tulip and producer Richard Perry. The voluminous amount of material referenced for this project could fill its own book and, so as to be able to list every single one of my sources, we have decided to make them available online at **tinytim.jawbonepress.com**

Author's interviews

Steve Alaimo (phone, December 18 2010), Peter Anders (email, June 30 2011), Mark Barkan (phone, October 19 2013), Richard Barone (phone, December 13 2008), Patricia Barreat (phone, January 18 2009), David Bartelino (phone, March 22 2010), Cindy Bellamy (phone, October 22 2013), Henry Benavides (Facebook message, July 13 2009), Victoria Benson (phone, September 4/24 2009), Norman Bergen (phone, July 8 2009), Bruce Bissell (phone, October 21 2009), Bob Blank (phone, August 5 2010), Brian Blouin (in person, April 18 2009), Genie Bramlet (phone, May 5 2011), Rich Brown (phone, August 21 2011), Gregor Brune (phone, December 5 2014), Bucks Burnett (phone, December 10 2008), Artie Butler (phone, March 19 2015), Bruce Button (phone, March 31 2009), Ruth Buzzi (phone, January 25 2011), Bill Calloway (phone, June 2012), Jim Cappelluzo (phone, December 2006), Joseph Cappelluzzo Jr. (phone, December 8 2013), Dr. Nick Catalano (in person, January 31 2012), Mike Clement (email, December 11 2010), Miss Jane Cole (in person, June 2009), Ron DeBlasio (phone, February 11 2008 and April 14 2009), Gary Dial (phone, May 17 2014), Bill Dorsey (phone, December 4 2014), Steve Dunphy (email, June 10 2009), Tracy Farquhar (email, December 14, 2010), Bob Fass (phone, January 29 2013), Barry Feinstein (phone, August 8 2011), Robert Fenster (in person, October 2009), Carl Finch (phone, March 19 2009), Bea Flaming (phone, June 8 2009), Billy Florio (phone, March 25 2009), Jim Foley (phone, December 2008), Tim Fowler (phone, September 5 2009), Joe Franklin (in person, September 16 2009), Mark Frizzell (phone, January 22 2008), Jack Gale (phone, March 3 2011), Joe Gannon (phone, January 31 2010), Ken Goodman (phone, February 27 2010), Wavy Gravy (phone, September 22 2009), Mark Hammerman (phone, December 22 2008), Jim Harney (phone, September 25 2013), Ken Hatfield (in person, September 28 2011), David Heavener (phone, July 27 2009), Stuart Hersh (phone, March 4, September 9 2009), Kane Hodder (in person, November 2013), Garth

Hudson (email, April 2009; in person, May 2012), Dave Jackson (phone, April 27 2009), Tommy James (phone, March 2 2010), Jism (in person, September 16 2009), Susan Khaury (May 27, July 13/17, August 3/4, October 15 2009), Glen King (email, December 1 2010), Sandy Klee Phillips (in person, August 11 2011), Larry Klug (phone, September 21 2009), Gary Lawrence (phone, January 17 2010), Murray Lerner (in person, December 2009), Ronnie Lyons (phone, August 9 2015), Robin Lynn (in person, April 18 2009), Harve Mann (July 21/22/25 and August 9 2011), Missy Martino (in person, August 11 2011), Rita McConnachie (phone, February 19 2009), Kathy McKinley King (phone, November 18/19, 2013), Jonas Mekas (in person, fall 2009), Charles Moerdler (phone, December 5 2014), Tony Monte (in person, January 31 2012), Barbara Morillo (phone, June 15 2012), Gil Morse (in person, April 18 2009), Jeff and Joyce Order (phone, May 8 2009), Judge Phillip Paley (phone, June 5 2014), David M. Pepperell (email, October 5 2011), Johnny Pineapple (phone, September 13 /15 2011), Mike Pinera (phone, February 25 2009), Francisco Poblet (in person, June 18 2012), Vinnie Poncia (email, June 30 2011), Steve Priest (email, June 5 2012), Eddie Rabin (phone, July 1 2009), Roslyn Rabin (in person, October 2009), Sam Rabin (phone, August 10 2014), Kate Radin (phone, March 7 2010), Bill Rebane (phone, December 17 2008), Jim Reeves (phone, June 26 2009), Mark Robinson (phone, April 29 2009), John Rodby (phone, May 24 2010), David Rowe (phone, December 3 2011), Martin Sharp (phone, July 15/24 2010), Jeff Sotzing (phone, January 2011), Ed Sterbenz (in person, October 4, November 10 2011), Tony Tedesco (in person, November 10 2011), Joe Terry (phone, September 25 2009), Pat Upton (in person, July 2009), Uncle Floyd Vivino (phone, April 21 2009), Artie Wachter (phone, September 21 2009), Nathan Waks (in person June 30 2010), Sherrye Weinstein (phone, January 30 2009), Ian Whitcomb (email, March 23 2009), Paul Williams (email, February 2009), Joe Wissert (phone, spring 2009), Peter Yarrow (phone, February 19 2009).

Select bibliography

Barone, Richard *Frontman: Surviving The Rock Star Myth* (Backbeat, 2007)

Bockris, Victor and Malanga, Gerard *Up Tight: The Velvet Underground Story* (Cooper Square Press, 2003)

Dylan, Bob *Chronicles: Volume One* (Simon & Schuster, 2004)

Fisher, Eddie *Been There, Done That* (St. Martin's, 2000)

Giuliano, Geoffrey *Glass Onion: The Beatles In Their Own Words* (Da Capo, 1999)

Heylin, Clinton *Bootleg: The Secret History Of The Other Recoding Industry* (St. Martin's Griffin, 1996)

Hoskyns, Barney *Across The Great Divide: The Band & America* (Hal Leonard, 2006)

Johnson, Kim 'Howard' *The Funniest One In The Room: The Lives & Legends Of Del Close* (Chicago Review Press, 2008)

Kooper, Vivien, and Plym, Stephen M., *Tiny Tim & Mr. Plym: Life As We Knew It* (Edee Rose, 2004)

Leamer, Laurence King *Of The Night: The Life Of Johnny Carson* (Avon, 2005)

Ruth, Marianne *Bill Cosby: Entertainer* (Melrose Square, 1993)

Spitz, Bob *Dylan: A Biography* (W.W. Norton & Co., 1991)

Stein, Harry *Tiny Tim: An Unauthorized Biography* (Playboy Press, 1976)

Tarling, Lowell *Tip-Toe Through A Lifetime* (Generation Books, 2013)

Tim, Tiny *Beautiful Thoughts* (Doudbleday Publishing Group, 1969)

Wick, Steve *Bad Company: Drugs, Hollywood, And The Cotton Club Murder* (Harcourt Publishing, 1990)

Wojahn, Ellen *The General Mills/Parker Bros. Merger: Playing By Different Rules* (Beard Books, 1988)

Photo credits

The photographs used in this book came from the following sources, and we are grateful for their help. If you feel there has been a mistaken attribution, please contact the publisher. **Jacket front** Kirklees Museums & Galleries **spine** Pierre Dury **2** Archive Photos / Getty Images **233** *photo booth* Ronny Elliott **234** Baron Wolman **235** *Houston* Bruce Kessler **236** *portrait, book* Victoria Benson; *duet* The Enchanted Forest **237** *both images* Henry Diltz **238** *wedding reception* Jim Harney; *marriage certificate* Brian Blouin **239** *Second Album* Rita McConnachie and Sharon Fox; *live, backstage* The Enchanted Forest **240** *Jim Cappy* Francisco Poblet; *letter* Eddie Rabin **241** Francisco Poblet **242** *all images* Richard Barone **243** Rich Zimmerman Photography **244** Harve Mann **245** *Martin Sharp* David Pepperell **246** *video shoot* Carol Fry c/o Jeff and Joyce Order; *promo shot* Gil Morse **247** Heather Hill **248** *live* Bruce Button; *Spooky World* Brian Blouin; *wedding, invitation* Susan Khaury.